D1413529

Introduction to Research in Education

SEVENTH EDITION

DONALD ARY
Northern Illinois University

LUCY CHESER JACOBS
Indiana University

ASHGAR RAZAVIEH
Shiraz University, Shiraz, Iran

CHRIS SORENSEN
Northern Illinois University

Australia • Brazil • Canada • Mexico • Singapore • Spain • United Kingdom • United States

Introduction to Research in Education,
Seventh Edition
Donald Ary, Lucy Cheser Jacobs, Ashgar Razavieh, Chris Sorensen

Publisher: Vicki Knight
Acquisitions Editor: Dan Alpert
Development Editor: Tangelique Williams
Assistant Editor: Jennifer Wilkinson
Editorial Assistant: Larkin Page-Jacobs
Technology Project Manager: Barry Connolly
Marketing Manager: Terra Schulz
Marketing Assistant: Rebecca Weisman
Marketing Communications Manager: Tami Strang
Project Manager, Editorial Production: Paul Wells
Creative Director: Rob Hugel
Art Director: Maria Epes
Print Buyer: Karen Hunt
Permissions Editor: Sarah Harkrader
Production Service: G&S Book Services
Text Designer: Kathleen Cunningham
Copy Editor: Ernestine Ruberto Franco
Illustrator: G&S Book Services
Cover Designer: Kathleen Cunningham
Cover Image: Paul Taylor/Getty Images; ImageFarm/Wonderfile Corp.
Compositor: G&S Book Services
Printer: Transcontinental Printing/Louiseville

Printed in Canada
1 2 3 4 5 6 7 09 08 07 06 05

Library of Congress Control Number: 2005924808

ISBN 0-534-55537-3

Thomson Higher Education
10 Davis Drive
Belmont, CA 94002-3098
USA

For more information about our products, contact us at:
Thomson Learning Academic Resource Center
1-800-423-0563

For permission to use material from this text or product, submit a request online at **http://www.thomsonrights.com.**

Any additional questions about permissions can be submitted by e-mail to **thomsonrights@thomson.com.**

To Sheila, Marion, Nasrin, and Steve

CONTENTS

Part Two
Research Background

PREFACE

We are optimistic about the future of educational research. It is amazing how different research in education has become since we published our first edition in 1972. Now in Chapter 1, in addition to a general overview of the nature and language of science, particularly as it relates to education, we also report on recent federal legislation. Our government is now telling educators that it is important to make evidence-based decisions before taking action, which sounds much like what we have been advocating all along.

Our goal while preparing the first edition of this book was to enable our readers to master the basic competencies necessary to (1) understand and evaluate the research of others and (2) plan and conduct original research with minimal assistance. Although we have remained true to this goal through six editions of our book, the landscape of American education has undergone many changes. As research in education has matured, we have adapted each new edition to provide our readers with the knowledge required to keep abreast of these changes.

THE SEVENTH EDITION

When our first edition was published, the phrase "qualitative research" had not been coined. Now those who maintain that hypothesis testing is not the only way to seek knowledge have developed methods and procedures for use when data come as words rather than numbers, and hypotheses are the result of, rather than the beginning of, the research process. We explain the differences between this approach and what is now termed "quantitative research" in Chapter 2. In Chapter 3 we delve into choosing and clarifying a research problem in either kind of research. We now have two full chapters on qualitative research and one on action research.

Advances in technology have made research in education easier, less tedious, and more rewarding. Today computers have taken much of the grind out of the calculation of statistics, so our statistics chapters concentrate on the rationale of statistical procedures and their uses, with only simple examples to illustrate statistical calculations. We include extensive discussion of useful statistical procedures, such as meta-analysis and effect size, which had not been developed in 1972. In those days the process of locating, organizing, and synthesizing literature related to the researcher's problem was tedious and time-consuming. Now we explain how the Internet, electronic indexes and abstracts, and other aids make these tasks much easier and more thorough.

In this edition we have more graphics and flow charts to illustrate concepts, together with some cartoons. We have included "Think about it" questions at various points to facilitate immediate recall and application and have added more examples from published research. We continue to stress the importance of planning in research, describe designs that have proven useful to researchers, and provide the necessary information to enable you to make the best use of the designs.

We hope that this latest edition will help our readers become more informed consumers of educational research, or be among those who perform rigorous, meaningful research to advance our profession.

ACKNOWLEDGEMENTS

We welcome Chris Sorensen as our new coauthor. We thank Dan McCollum for his excellent work in expanding and updating Chapter 4 (Related Literature) and Georgianna Henry for tracking down obscure material we needed.

We are grateful to Pearson Education Ltd. on behalf of the literary executor of the late Sir Ronald A. Fisher, F.R.S., and the late Dr. Frank Yates, F.R.S., for permissions to reprint tables III, IV, and VII from *Statistical Tables for Biological, Agricultural and Medical Research* (6th Ed., 1974). We gratefully acknowledge the contributions of the following reviewers:

David L. Breithaupt, Boise State University

Reagan Curtis, California State University, Northridge

Cody Ding, University of Missouri, St. Louis

Mary Dereshiwsky, Northern Arizona University

William Holmes, Lamar University

John Huss, Northern Kentucky University

Marie Kraska, Auburn University

Ghazwan A. Lufti, Florida A&M University

Alan P. Moore, University of Wyoming

Alina Reznitskaya, Montclair State University

Brenda Seevers, New Mexico State University

Marsha Zenanko, Jacksonville State University

Chapter 1

The Nature of Scientific Inquiry

KNOWLEDGE IS POWER.

INSTRUCTIONAL OBJECTIVES

After studying this chapter, the student will be able to:

1 List five major sources of knowledge and comment on the strengths and weaknesses of each source.

2 Describe the characteristics of the scientific approach.

3 State the assumptions underlying science and the attitudes expected of scientists.

4 Specify the purpose and characteristics of scientific theory in the behavioral sciences.

5 Indicate the limitations involved in the application of the scientific approach in the social sciences.

6 Define educational research and give examples.

Educators are, by necessity, decision makers. Daily they face the task of deciding how to plan learning experiences, teach and guide students, organize a school system, and myriad other matters. Unlike unskilled workers, who are told what to do and how to do it, professionals must plan for themselves. People assume that professionals have the knowledge and skills necessary to make valid decisions about what to do and how. We generally define knowledge as justified true belief. We "know" something when it is accepted as true or valid. How are educators to know what is true? How do they acquire reliable information? Although there are other sources of knowledge, such as experience, authority, and tradition, scientific knowledge about the educational process makes the most valuable contribution to decision making in education. Educators can turn to this source for reliable information and suggestions to be used in decision making. This fund of knowledge has been made available to educators by scientific inquiry into educational problems. However, education has not always been influenced by the results of such careful and systematic investigations. In fact, the development of an educational science is at a comparatively early stage.

SOURCES OF KNOWLEDGE

Before we further pursue the role of scientific inquiry in education, let us review some of the ways in which human beings throughout history have sought knowledge. The major sources of knowledge can be categorized under five headings: (1) experience, (2) authority, (3) deductive reasoning, (4) inductive reasoning, and (5) the scientific approach.

EXPERIENCE

Experience is a familiar and well-used source of knowledge. After trying several routes from home to work, you learn which route takes the least time or is the most free of traffic or is the most scenic. By personal experience, you can find the answers to many of the questions you face. Much wisdom passed from generation to generation is the result of experience. If people were not able to profit from experience, progress would be severely retarded. In fact, this ability to learn from experience is a prime characteristic of intelligent behavior.

Yet for all its usefulness, experience has limitations as a source of knowledge. How you are affected by an event depends on who you are. Two people will have very different experiences in the same situation. The same forest that is a delightful sanctuary to one person may be a menacing wilderness to another. Two supervisors observing the same classroom at the same time could truthfully compile very different reports if one focused on and reported the things that went right and the other focused on and reported the things that went wrong. Perhaps the reason so many say do not change answers on a multiple-choice test is that they noticed cases where they changed answers from right to wrong and not those they changed from wrong to right.

Another shortcoming of experience is that you so frequently need to know things that you as an individual cannot learn by experience. A child turned loose to discover arithmetic alone might figure out how to add but would be unlikely to find an efficient way to compute square roots. A teacher could learn through experience the population of a classroom on a particular day but could not personally count the population of the United States.

AUTHORITY

For things difficult or impossible to know by personal experience, people frequently turn to an *authority*; that is, they seek knowledge from someone who has had experience with the problem or has some other source of expertise. People accept as truth the word of recognized authorities. We go to a physician with health questions or to a stockbroker with questions about investments. To learn the size of the U.S. population, we can turn to reports by the U.S. Bureau of the Census. A student can look up the accepted pronunciation of a word in a dictionary. A superintendent can consult a lawyer about a legal problem at school. A beginning teacher asks an experienced one for suggestions and may try a certain technique for teaching reading because the supervisor suggests that it is effective.

Throughout history you can find examples of reliance on authority for knowledge, particularly during the Middle Ages when people preferred ancient scholars, such as Plato and Aristotle, and the early Fathers of the church as sources of

PICTURE THIS

Education has its myths.

Joe Rocco

information—even over direct observation or experience. Although authority is a very useful source of knowledge, you must always ask, How does authority know? In earlier days people assumed an authority was right simply because of the position he or she held, such as king, chief, or high priest. Today people are reluctant to rely on an individual as an authority merely because of position or rank. They are inclined to accept the assertions of an authority only when that authority is indeed a recognized expert in the area.

Closely related to authority are *custom* and *tradition*, on which people depend for answers to many questions related to professional as well as everyday problems. In other words, people often ask, "How has this been done in the past?" and then use the answer as a guide for action. Custom and tradition have been prominent influences in the school setting, where educators often rely on past practices as a dependable guide. However, an examination of the history of education reveals that many traditions that prevailed for years were later found to be erroneous and had to be rejected. For generations, it was considered good practice to humiliate students who made mistakes with dunce caps and the like. It is wise to appraise custom and tradition carefully before you accept them as reliable sources.

Authority is a quick and easy source of knowledge. But, as a source of knowledge, authority has shortcomings that you must consider. In the first place, authorities can be wrong. People often claim to be experts in a field when they do not really have the knowledge to back up the claim. Also, you may find that authorities disagree among themselves on issues, indicating that their authoritative statements are often more personal opinion than fact.

DEDUCTIVE REASONING

Ancient Greek philosophers made perhaps the first significant contribution to the development of a systematic approach for gaining knowledge. Aristotle and his followers introduced the use of **deductive reasoning**, which can be described as a thinking process in which one proceeds from general to specific knowledge through logical argument. An argument consists of a number of statements standing in relation to one another. The final statement is the conclusion, and the rest, called *premises*, offer supporting evidence. A major kind of deductive reasoning is the syllogism. A syllogism consists of a major premise and a minor premise followed by a conclusion. For example, "All men are mortal" (major premise); "The king is a man" (minor premise); "Therefore, the king is mortal" (conclusion). In deductive reasoning, if the premises are true, the conclusion is necessarily true. Deductive reasoning lets you organize premises into patterns that provide conclusive evidence for a conclusion's validity. Mystery fans will recall that Sherlock Holmes frequently would say, "I deduce . . ." as he combined previously unconnected facts in such a way as to imply a previously unsuspected conclusion.

Deductive reasoning can answer the question "How likely is it that a student could pass a 20-item multiple choice test with five options per item by chance alone?" Given the premise that there is a 20 percent chance of getting a single item right and an 80 percent chance of getting it wrong and the premise that these same chances are true for every item, Figure 1.1 shows the probability of getting the following outcomes with three items.

The probability of getting three right is .008. There are three ways to get two right and one wrong, so the probability of two right is (.032)(3) = .096. The probability of getting one right and two wrong is (.128)(3) = .384. There is only one way to get three wrong; the probability of that is .512.

If we extended Figure 1.1 to determine the likelihood of getting a passing 60 percent (12 correct items in a 20-item test), we would find there is approximately one chance in 10,000 of passing. The probability of passing two 20-item tests is $(1/10{,}000)^2$ or one chance in a million. The notion that one has a reasonable chance of passing a test through sheer guessing is a myth.

Deductive reasoning has its limitations. To arrive at true conclusions, you must begin with true premises. The conclusion of a syllogism can never exceed the

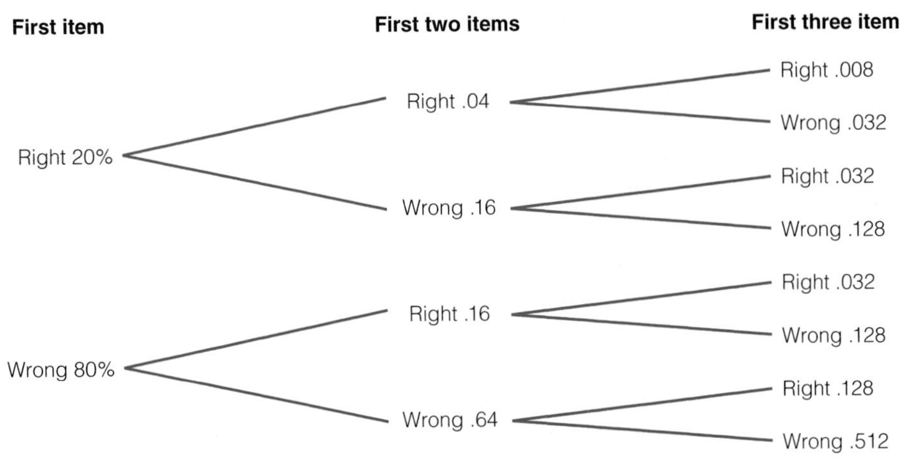

Figure 1.1 Probabilities of Getting Various Outcomes with Three Items

content of the premises. Because deductive conclusions are necessarily elaborations on previously existing knowledge, you cannot conduct scientific inquiry through deductive reasoning alone because it is difficult to establish the universal truth of many statements dealing with scientific phenomena. Deductive reasoning can organize what people already know and can point out new relationships as you proceed from the general to the specific, but it is not sufficient as a source of new knowledge.

Despite its limitations, deductive reasoning is useful in research because it provides a way to link theory and observation. It lets researchers deduce from existing theory what phenomena they should observe. Deductions from theory can help build hypotheses, which are a vital part of scientific inquiry.

INDUCTIVE REASONING

As noted, the conclusions of deductive reasoning are true only if the premises on which they are based are true. But how are you to know if the premises are true? In the Middle Ages people often substituted dogma for true premises, so they reached invalid conclusions. It was Francis Bacon (1561–1626) who first called for a new approach to knowing. He held that thinkers should not enslave themselves by accepting premises handed down by authority as absolute truth. He believed that an investigator should establish general conclusions on the basis of facts gathered through direct observation. Bacon advised the seeker of truth to observe nature directly and to rid his or her mind of prejudice and preconceived ideas, which Bacon called "idols." For him, obtaining knowledge required that the thinker observe nature itself, gather particular facts, and formulate generalizations from these findings. You can see the importance of observation in the following anecdote, attributed to Bacon:

> In the year of our Lord 1432, there arose a grievous quarrel among the brethren over the number of teeth in the mouth of a horse. For 13 days the disputation raged without ceasing. All the ancient books and chronicles were fetched out, and wonderful and ponderous erudition, such as was never before heard of in this region,

> was made manifest. At the beginning of the 14th day, a youthful friar of goodly bearing asked his learned superiors for permission to add a word, and straightway, to the wonderment of the disputants, whose deep wisdom he sore vexed, he beseeched them to unbend in a manner coarse and unheard-of, and to look in the open mouth of a horse and find an answer to their questionings. At this, their dignity being grievously hurt, they waxed exceedingly wroth; and, joining in a mighty uproar, they flew upon him and smote him hip and thigh, and cast him out forthwith. For, said they, surely Satan hath tempted this bold neophyte to declare unholy and unheard-of ways of finding truth contrary to all the teachings of the fathers. After many days more of grievous strife the dove of peace sat on the assembly, and they as one man, declaring the problem to be an everlasting mystery because of a grievous dearth of historical and theological evidence thereof, so ordered the same writ down. (Mees, 1934, p. 115)

The youth in this story was calling for a new way of seeking truth: namely, seeking the facts rather than depending on authority or on sheer speculation. This became the fundamental principle of all science.

In Bacon's system, the investigator made observations on particular events in a class (or category) and then, on the basis of the observed events, made inferences about the whole class. This approach, known as **inductive reasoning**, is the reverse of the deductive method. You can see the difference between deductive and inductive reasoning in the following examples:

Deductive: Every mammal has lungs.
All rabbits are mammals.
Therefore, every rabbit has lungs.

Inductive: Every rabbit that has ever been observed has lungs.
Therefore, every rabbit has lungs.

Note that in deductive reasoning you must know the premises before you can reach a conclusion, but in inductive reasoning you reach a conclusion by observing examples and generalizing from the examples to the whole class or category. To be absolutely certain of an inductive conclusion, the investigator must observe all examples. This is known as **perfect induction** under the Baconian system; it requires that the investigator examine every example of a phenomenon. In the preceding example, to be absolutely sure that every rabbit has lungs, the investigator would have to have observations on all rabbits currently alive, as well as all past and future rabbits. Clearly this is not feasible; you generally must rely on imperfect induction based on incomplete observation.

Imperfect induction is a system in which you observe a sample of a group and infer from the sample what is characteristic of the entire group. An example of a conclusion based on imperfect induction is the present thinking concerning the physical characteristics of very intelligent children. For many years people generally believed that exceptionally bright children tended to be poor physical specimens. Even today cartoonists usually portray the bright child as a scrawny creature with thick spectacles. Terman, a pioneer in the field of mental testing, was interested in the characteristics of exceptionally bright youngsters (Terman, 1926). In a landmark investigation, Terman intensively studied more than 1000

California children who scored above 140 on the Stanford–Binet intelligence test. He found the average height, weight, and general physical health of these children to be slightly above average for children of their age. From this and subsequent studies of the phenomenon, researchers have concluded that bright children, far from being scrawny, are a little more likely to be above average in physical development than children with average IQ scores. Note that this conclusion has not been positively proved. It is simply highly probable. To be positively sure about this conclusion, you would need physical measures for *all* children with IQ scores of 140 or more on the Stanford–Binet. Even then you could only be positive about the characteristics of such children today and could not be 100 percent sure that the same would be true of such children in the future. Although imperfect induction does not lead to infallible conclusions, it can provide reliable information about what is likely to be true and on which you can make reasonable decisions.

An inductive way to investigate the question, "Should you stick with your original answers on a multiple-choice test, or should you change your answers when, upon reconsideration, you think you have a better answer?" would be to go over scored exams and identify items with erasures or crossouts. Then count the changes that go from right to wrong, wrong to right, or wrong to wrong.

Dozens of researchers have published the results of such studies, beginning with Crawford (1928). These studies have all found that more changes are from wrong to right than from right to wrong. Waddell and Blankenship (1994), through a thorough search of the literature for the years 1988–1992 found 61 studies whose results could be combined through meta-analysis (see Chapter 6). The combined results were: 57 percent of changes were from wrong to right, 21 percent were from right to wrong, and 22 percent were from wrong to wrong. Therefore, the best advice is to encourage students to make changes whenever, after rethinking, they find an answer that they prefer over their original one. It is interesting to note that those studies that also asked students and professors their advice found the majority advised sticking with your original answer. The myth that you should stick with your original answer has persisted for generations, despite overwhelming evidence to the contrary.

> It's not so much what folks don't know that causes problems
> It's what they know that ain't so.
>
> Artemus Ward

THE SCIENTIFIC APPROACH

Exclusive use of induction often resulted in the accumulation of isolated knowledge and information that made little contribution to the advancement of knowledge. Furthermore, people found that many problems could not be solved by induction alone. In the 19th century scholars began to integrate the most important aspects of the inductive and deductive methods into a new technique, namely the inductive–deductive method, or the **scientific approach**. This approach differs from inductive reasoning in that it uses hypotheses. A **hypothesis** is a statement describing relationships among variables that is tentatively assumed to be true. It identifies observations to be made to investigate a question.

For example, a researcher interested in increasing student on-task behavior might hypothesize that positive teacher feedback increases on-task behavior. All hypotheses indicate specific phenomena to be observed (the variables), in this case positive teacher feedback and on-task behavior.

Charles Darwin, in developing his theory of evolution, is generally recognized as the first to apply this method in the pursuit of knowledge. Darwin reported that he spent a long time making biological observations, hoping to establish some generalizations concerning evolution. In the following passage, he describes how he arrived at a new approach:

> My first note-book (on evolution) was opened in July 1837. I worked on true Baconian principles, and without any theory collected facts on a wholesale scale, more especially with respect to domesticated productions, by printed enquiries, by conversation with skillful breeders and gardeners, and by extensive reading. When I see the list of books of all kinds which I read and abstracted, including whole series of Journals and Transactions, I am surprised at my industry. I soon perceived that selection was the keystone of man's success in making useful races of animals and plants. But how selection would be applied to organisms living in a state of nature remained for some time a mystery to me. In October 1838, that is, fifteen months after I had begun my systematic enquiry, I happened to read for amusement "Malthus on Population," and being well prepared to appreciate the struggle for existence which everywhere goes on from long-continued observation of the habits of animals and plants, it at once struck me that under these circumstances favourable variations would tend to be preserved, and unfavourable ones to be destroyed. The result of this would be the formation of new species. Here then I had at last got a theory by which to work. (Darwin, 1899, p. 68)

Darwin's procedure, involving only observation, was unproductive until reading and further thought led him to formulate a tentative hypothesis to explain the facts that he had gathered through observation. He then proceeded to test this hypothesis by making deductions from it and gathering additional data to determine whether these data would support the hypothesis. From this method of inquiry, Darwin was able to develop his theory of evolution. This use of both inductive and deductive reasoning is characteristic of modern scientific inquiry.

The scientific approach is generally described as a method of acquiring knowledge in which investigators move inductively from their observations to hypotheses and then deductively from the hypotheses to the logical implications of the hypotheses. They deduce the consequences that would follow if a hypothesized relationship were valid. If the deduced implications are compatible with the organized body of accepted knowledge, researchers then further test them by gathering empirical data. On the basis of the evidence, they accept or reject the hypotheses.

The use of hypotheses is the principal difference between the scientific approach and inductive reasoning. In inductive reasoning, you make observations first and then organize the information gained. In the scientific approach you reason what you would find if a hypothesis were true and then you make systematic observations to confirm (or fail to confirm) the hypothesis.

AN EXAMPLE OF THE SCIENTIFIC APPROACH

In a classic example, award-winning author Robert Pirsig provides a vivid and succinct description of the scientific approach by comparing it to the process of maintaining a motorcycle in good working order:

> Two kinds of logic are used, inductive and deductive. Inductive inferences start with observations of the machine and arrive at general conclusions. For example, if the cycle goes over a bump and the engine misfires, and then goes over another bump and the engine misfires, and then goes over another bump and the engine misfires, and then goes over a long smooth stretch of road and there is no misfiring, and then goes over a fourth bump and the engine misfires again, one can logically conclude that the misfiring is caused by the bumps. That is induction: reasoning from particular experiences to general truths.
>
> Deductive inferences do the reverse. They start with general knowledge and predict a specific observation. For example, if, from reading the hierarchy of facts about the machine, the mechanic knows the horn of the cycle is powered exclusively by electricity from the battery, then he can logically infer that if the battery is dead the horn will not work. That is deduction.
>
> Solution of problems too complicated for common sense to solve is achieved by long strings of mixed inductive and deductive inferences that weave back and forth between the observed machine and the mental hierarchy of the machine found in the manuals. The correct program for this interweaving is formalized as scientific method.
>
> Actually I've never seen a cycle-maintenance problem complex enough really to require full-scale formal scientific method. Repair problems are not that hard. When I think of formal scientific method an image sometimes comes to mind of an enormous juggernaut, a huge bulldozer—slow, tedious, lumbering, laborious, but invincible. It takes twice as long, five times as long, maybe a dozen times as long as informal mechanic's techniques, but you know in the end you're going to *get* it. There's no fault isolation problem in motorcycle maintenance that can stand up to it. When you've hit a really tough one, tried everything, racked your brain and nothing works, and you know that this time Nature has really decided to be difficult, you say, "Okay, Nature, that's the end of the *nice* guy," and you crank up the formal scientific method.
>
> For this you keep a lab notebook. Everything gets written down, formally, so that you know at all times where you are, where you've been, where you're going, and where you want to get. In scientific work and electronics technology this is necessary because otherwise the problems get so complex you get lost in them and confused and forget what you know and what you don't know and have to give up. In cycle maintenance things are not that involved, but when confusion starts it's a good idea to hold it down by making everything formal and exact. Sometimes just the act of writing down the problems straightens out your head as to what they really are.
>
> The logical statements entered into the notebook are broken down into six categories: (1) statement of the problem, (2) hypotheses as to the cause of the problem, (3) experiments designed to test each hypothesis, (4) predicted results of the experiments, (5) observed results of the experiments, and (6) conclusions from the results of the experiments. This is not different from the formal arrangement of

many college and high-school lab notebooks but the purpose here is no longer just busywork. The purpose now is precise guidance of thoughts that will fail if they are not accurate.

The real purpose of scientific method is to make sure Nature hasn't misled you into thinking you know something you don't actually know. There's not a mechanic or scientist or technician alive who hasn't suffered from that one so much that he's not instinctively on guard. That's the main reason why so much scientific and mechanical information sounds so dull and so cautious. If you get careless or go romanticizing scientific information, giving it a flourish here and there, Nature will soon make a complete fool out of you. It does it often enough anyway even when you don't give it opportunities. One must be extremely careful and rigidly logical when dealing with Nature: one logical slip and an entire scientific edifice comes tumbling down. One false deduction about the machine and you can get hung up indefinitely.

In Part One of formal scientific method, which is the statement of the problem, the main skill is in stating absolutely no more than you are positive you know. It is much better to enter a statement "Solve Problem: Why doesn't cycle work?" which sounds dumb but is correct, than it is to enter a statement "Solve Problem: What is wrong with the electrical system?" when you don't absolutely *know* the trouble is *in* the electrical system. What you should state is "Solve Problem: What is wrong with cycle?" and *then* state as the first entry of Part Two: "Hypothesis Number One: The trouble is in the electrical system." You think of as many hypotheses as you can, then you design experiments to test them to see which are true and which are false.

This careful approach to the beginning questions keeps you from taking a major wrong turn which might cause you weeks of extra work or can even hang you up completely. Scientific questions often have a surface appearance of dumbness for this reason. They are asked in order to prevent dumb mistakes later on.

Part Three, that part of formal scientific method called experimentation, is sometimes thought of by romantics as all of science itself because that's the only part with much visual surface. They see lots of test tubes and bizarre equipment and people running around making discoveries. They do not see the experiment as part of a larger intellectual process and so they often confuse experiments with demonstrations, which look the same. A man conducting a gee-whiz science show with fifty thousand dollars' worth of Frankenstein equipment is not doing anything scientific if he knows beforehand what the results of his efforts are going to be. A motorcycle mechanic, on the other hand, who honks the horn to see if the battery works is informally conducting a true scientific experiment. He is testing a hypothesis by putting the question to Nature. The TV scientist who mutters sadly, "The experiment is a failure; we have failed to achieve what we had hoped for," is suffering mainly from a bad scriptwriter. An experiment is never a failure solely because it fails to achieve predicted results. An experiment is a failure only when it also fails adequately to test the hypothesis in question, when the data it produces don't prove anything one way or another.

Skill at this point consists of using experiments that test only the hypothesis in question, nothing less, nothing more. If the horn honks, and the mechanic concludes that the whole electrical system is working, he is in deep trouble. He has reached an illogical conclusion. The honking horn only tells him that the battery and horn are working. To design an experiment properly he has to think very rigidly in terms of what directly causes what. This you know from the hierarchy. The horn doesn't make the cycle go. Neither does the battery, except in a very indirect way. The point at which the electrical system *directly* causes the engine to fire is at the spark plugs, and if you don't test here, at the output of the electrical system, you will never really know whether the failure is electrical or not.

To test properly, the mechanic removes the plug and lays it against the engine so that the base around the plug is electrically grounded, kicks the starter lever, and watches the spark-plug gap for a blue spark. If there isn't any he can conclude one of two things: (a) there is an electrical failure or (b) his experiment is sloppy. If he is experienced he will try it a few more times, checking connections, trying every way he can think of to get that plug to fire. Then, if he can't get it to fire, he finally concludes that *a* is correct, there's an electrical failure, and the experiment is over. He has proved that his hypothesis is correct.

In the final category, conclusions, skill comes in stating no more than the experiment has proved. It hasn't proved that when he fixes the electrical system the motorcycle will start. There may be other things wrong. But he does know that the motorcycle isn't going to run until the electrical system is working and he sets up the next formal question: "Solve Problem: What is wrong with the electrical system?" He then sets up hypotheses for these and tests them. By asking the right questions and choosing the right tests and drawing the right conclusions the mechanic works his way down the echelons of the motorcycle hierarchy until he has found the exact specific cause or causes of the engine failure, and then he changes them so that they no longer cause the failure.

An untrained observer will see only physical labor and often get the idea that physical labor is mainly what the mechanic does. Actually the physical labor is the smallest and easiest part of what the mechanic does. By far the greatest part of his work is careful observation and precise thinking. That is why mechanics sometimes seem so taciturn and withdrawn when performing tests. They don't like it when you talk to them because they are concentrating on mental images, hierarchies, and not really looking at you or the physical motorcycle at all. They are using the experiment as part of a program to expand their hierarchy of knowledge of the faulty motorcycle and compare it to the correct hierarchy in their mind. They are looking at underlying form. From *Zen and the Art of Motorcycle Maintenance* by Robert M. Pirsig, pp. 107–111.

In Pirsig's narrative, we see five steps that are typical in scientific inquiry:

1. *Identification of the problem.* The first step is the realization that a problem exists. The problem may involve a question about something, a discrepancy in findings, or a gap in knowledge. In Pirsig's example, the fact that the motorcycle did not start constituted the problem.
2. *Statement of the problem.* The next step is the clarification of the problem. The investigator states more precisely the nature and scope of the problem that has been identified.
3. *Formulation of hypotheses.* The investigator formulates hypotheses about possible solutions of the problem. In the example, the first hypothesis was

that the motorcycle did not start because of trouble in the electrical system.

4. *Prediction of consequences.* The investigator next predicts the consequences of each hypothesis; that is, what should result if the data support the hypothesis.

5. *Testing of hypotheses.* The researcher gathers objective data to evaluate the adequacy of each hypothesis formulated. If the data support the hypothesis, it is accepted as a reasonable explanation. If the data do not support the hypothesis, it is rejected.

Gribbin (1999) summed up the scientific process with the following quote from Richard Feynman, one of the great physicists of the 20th century:

> In general we look for a new law by the following process. First we guess it. Then we compute the consequences of the guess to see what would be implied if this law that we guessed is right. Then we compare the result of the computation to nature, with experiment or experience, compare it directly with observation, to see if it works. If it disagrees with experiment it is wrong. In that simple statement is the key to science. It does not make any difference how beautiful your guess is. It does not make any difference how smart you are, who made the guess, or what his name is—if it disagrees with experiment it is wrong (p. 4).

THE NATURE OF SCIENCE

The scientific approach is a method of inquiry that is applied in different fields of study. All sciences, although they may differ from one another in subject matter or in specialized techniques, have in common this general method for arriving at reliable knowledge. This method of inquiry determines whether a discipline is a science. Perhaps science is best described as a *method of inquiry* that permits investigators to examine the phenomena of interest to them. In addition to the method scientists follow as they seek reliable knowledge, there are certain other aspects of the scientific approach, which we will examine briefly. These are (1) assumptions made by scientists, (2) attitudes expected of scientists, and (3) formulation of scientific theory.

ASSUMPTIONS MADE BY SCIENTISTS

A fundamental assumption scientists make is that the events they investigate are lawful or ordered—no event is capricious. Science is based on the belief that all natural phenomena have antecedent factors. This assumption is sometimes referred to as **universal determinism**. Primitive people proposed supernatural causes for most of the events they observed. Modern science did not develop until people began to look beyond supernatural explanations and to depend on the observation of nature itself to provide answers.

This assumption underlies any statement that declares that under specified conditions certain events will occur. For example, the chemist can state that when a mixture of potassium chlorate and manganese dioxide is heated, the process will produce oxygen. Behavioral scientists likewise assume that the behavior of organisms is lawful and predictable. Related to this first assumption is the belief that the events in nature are, at least to a degree, orderly and regular and that people can discover this order and regularity of nature through the scientific method.

A second assumption is that reliable knowledge can ultimately derive only from direct and objective observation. Reliance on empirical observation differentiates science from nonscience. The scientist does not depend on authority or tradition as sources of knowledge but insists on studying empirical evidence. In the history of science we find many examples of scientists who rejected the prevailing notions of their day and proceeded with their observations and experimentation. Galileo's early experiments with falling bodies, which may mark the beginning of modern scientific inquiry, resulted in new knowledge that contradicted notions held by the authorities of his day. A corollary of this assumption is the belief that only phenomena that are subject to observation lie within the realm of scientific investigation.

ATTITUDES EXPECTED OF SCIENTISTS

Scientists recognize certain characteristic attitudes that they acquire as they pursue their work:

1. *Scientists are essentially doubters, who maintain a highly skeptical attitude toward the data of science.* Scientists investigate questions concerning the relationships among natural phenomena. Their findings are regarded as tentative, however, and are not accepted by themselves or other scientists unless further investigations can verify them. Verification occurs when repeated observations yield the same or similar results. Verification thus requires scientists to make their research measurements and procedures known so that others may replicate the study and verify, or fail to verify, the findings.
2. *Scientists are objective and impartial.* In conducting observations and interpreting data, scientists seek knowledge and are not trying to prove a point. They take particular care to collect data in such a way that any personal biases they may have will not influence their observations. They look for observable evidence and accept the findings even when those results are contrary to their own opinions. If the accumulated evidence upsets a favorite theory, then they either discard that theory or modify it to agree with the findings.

   In reality scientists are human like the rest of us. Some scientists have been known to report only findings that agreed with their preconceived ideas, or have even made up data to support their contentions. A notorious example occurred when Stalin ruled the Soviet Union. His secretary of agriculture, Lysenko, asserted that environment changed heredity. Those scientists who reported results supporting this contention got published, got to keep their jobs, and got promoted. Those who reported research results contrary to Lysenko's belief often lost their jobs or were sent to Siberia.

   Scientists in other countries tried to replicate these studies, but none of them got results that supported Lysenko's contention. They concluded that the phenomenon did not exist. Soon after Stalin's death, Lysenko's contentions were repudiated, and Soviet scientists admitted that they had reported what was wanted, not what they had observed.

3. *Scientists deal with facts not values.* Scientists do not indicate any potential moral implications of their findings; they do not make decisions for other people about what is good or what is bad. Scientists provide data concerning the relationships among events, but you must go beyond scientific data if you want a decision about whether a certain consequence is desirable. Thus, although the findings of science may be of key importance in solving a problem about a value decision, the data themselves do not furnish that value judgment.
4. *Scientists are not satisfied with isolated facts but seek to integrate and systematize their findings.* They want to put the things known into an orderly system. Thus scientists aim for theories that seek to bring together empirical findings into a meaningful pattern. However, they regard these theories as tentative or provisional, subject to revision as new evidence appears.

SCIENTIFIC THEORY

The last aspect of the scientific approach we consider here is the construction of theory. The ultimate goal of science is theory formation. Scientists, through empirical investigation, gather many facts; but facts by themselves are of limited usefulness. As facts accumulate, scientists must integrate, organize, and classify to make the isolated findings meaningful. They must identify and explain significant relationships in the data. That is where theory comes into play. Scientists formulate theories to summarize and order the existing knowledge in a particular area. A **theory** may be defined as a set of interrelated constructs and propositions that presents an explanation of phenomena and makes predictions about relationships among variables relevant to the phenomena.

Theories knit together the results of observations, enabling scientists to make general statements about variables and the relationships among variables. Theories range from a few simple generalizations to complex formulations of laws. For example, you can observe that if you hold pressure constant, hydrogen gas expands when its temperature increases from 20°C to 40°C. You can observe that if you hold pressure constant, oxygen gas contracts when its temperature decreases from 60°C to 50°C. A familiar theory, Charles's law, summarizes the observed effects of temperature changes on the volumes of all gases: When pressure is held constant, as the temperature of a gas increases, its volume increases; and as the temperature of a gas decreases, its volume decreases. The theory not only summarizes previous information but predicts other phenomena by telling you what to expect of any gas under any temperature change.

Purposes of Theories

Theories serve useful functions in the development of science. They (1) organize empirical findings and explain phenomena, (2) predict phenomena, and (3) stimulate new research. A theory organizes the findings from many separate observations and investigations into a framework that provides explanations of phenomena. We would not have progress if science were comprised only of multiple separate facts. A single theory accounts for many facts and explains by showing what variables are related and how they are related. A theory of learning, for example, might explain the relationships among the speed and efficiency of learning and such variables as motivation, reinforcement, practice, and so on. Researchers have developed useful theories to explain motivation, intellectual and cognitive development, moral development, social development, and so on. From the explanatory framework of a theory, scientists can proceed to make predictions about what will happen in novel situations. If these predictions are supported by scientific investigation, then science proceeds finally to control. As soon as a statement (theory) was made about the relationship between the *Anopheles* mosquito and malaria in humans, scientists could (1) *explain* why malaria was endemic in some areas and not in others, (2) *predict* how changes in the environment would entail changes in the incidence of malaria, and (3) *control* malaria by changing the environment.

Researchers state and test hypotheses deduced from theories, which results in the development of new knowledge. Deductions from a theory permit predictions of phenomena, some as yet unobserved. For example, from theory astronomers predicted the existence of the outermost planets long before they were actually observed. Testing the deductions from a theory serves to confirm and elaborate the theory. If, however, research findings do not support the theory, scientists revise it and then collect more data to test the revised theory.

Criteria for Theories

To serve its purpose in science, a theory should satisfy certain criteria. The following are some of the characteristics of a sound theory:

1. *A theory should be able to explain the observed facts relating to a particular problem.* It should be able to propose the "how" and "why" concerning the phenomena under consideration. This explanation of the events should take the simplest form possible. Scientists favor a theory that has fewer complexities and assumptions over a more complicated one. This rule is called the **principle of parsimony**.
2. *A theory should be consistent with observed facts and with the already established body of knowledge.* Scientists build on what has already been found. They look for the theory that provides the most probable or the most efficient way of accounting for the accumulated facts.
3. *A theory should provide means for its verification.* Scientists achieve this for most theories by making deductions in the form of hypotheses stating the consequences that you can expect to observe if the theory is valid. Scientists can then investigate or test these hypotheses empirically to determine whether the data support the theory. We must emphasize that it is inappropriate to speak of the "truth" or "falsity" of a theory. The acceptance or rejection of a theory depends primarily on its *utility*, or usefulness. A theory is useful or not useful depending on how efficiently it leads to predictions concerning observable consequences, which are then confirmed when the empirical data are collected. Even then, any theory is tentative and subject to revision as new evidence accumulates.

You may recall the old theory of formal discipline, which stated that the mind is like a muscle that can be strengthened through exercise. Certain subjects such as logic, Latin, and Greek were once included in the curriculum because educators believed them to be best for strengthening the mind. This theory of formal discipline prevailed until the early 20th century, when E. L. Thorndike, William James, and Charles Judd challenged it. When their studies independently refuted this theory, educators abandoned it.

4. *A theory should stimulate new discoveries and indicate further areas in need of investigation.*

The goal of theory formation has been achieved to a far greater extent in the physical sciences than in the social sciences, which is not surprising because they are older sciences. In the early days of a science, the emphasis typically is on empiricism; scientists are concerned with collecting facts in particular areas. Only with maturity does a science begin to integrate the isolated knowledge into a theoretical framework.

Although there are marked differences in the number and power of the theories that have been established in the physical and social sciences, theory has the same role to play in the progress of any science. Regardless of the subject matter, theory works in essentially the same way. It serves to summarize existing knowledge, to explain observed events and relationships, and to predict the occurrence of unobserved events and relationships. Theories represent the best efforts to understand the basic structure of the world in which we all live.

LIMITATIONS OF THE SCIENTIFIC APPROACH IN THE SOCIAL SCIENCES

Despite their use of the scientific approach and accumulation of a large quantity of reliable knowledge, education and the other social sciences have not attained the scientific status typical of the natural sciences. The social sciences have not established generalizations equivalent to the theories of the natural sciences in scope of explanatory power or in capacity to yield precise predictions. Frequently researchers in the social sciences disagree on what the established facts are or what explanations are satisfactory for the assumed facts. Perhaps the social sciences will never realize the objectives of science as completely as the natural sciences. Certainly we must stress that using the scientific approach is not in itself a sufficient condition for scientific achievement. Several limitations hinder the application of the scientific approach in education and the other social sciences.

Complexity of Subject Matter

A major obstacle is the inherent complexity of subject matter in the social sciences. Natural scientists deal with physical and biological phenomena. A limited number of variables that can be measured precisely are involved in explaining many of these phenomena, and it is possible to establish universal laws. For example, Boyle's law, summarizing the influence of pressure on gas volume, a law that deals with relatively uncomplicated variables, formulates relations among phenomena that are apparently unvarying throughout the universe.

In contrast, social scientists deal with the human subject. They are concerned with the subject's behavior and development, both as an individual and as a member of a group. They must consider many variables, acting independently and in interaction, in any attempt to understand complex human behavior. Each individual is unique in the way he or she develops, in mental ability, in social and emotional behavior, and in total personality. The behavior of humans in groups and the influence of the behavior of group members on an individual must also be dealt with by social scientists. A group of first-graders in one situation will not behave like first-graders in another situation. There are learners, teachers, and environments, each with variations that contribute to the behavioral phenomena observed in a setting. Thus researchers must be extremely cautious about making generalizations because the data from one group or in one situation may have limited validity for other groups and other settings.

Difficulties in Observation

Observation, the sine qua non of science, is more difficult in the social sciences than in the natural sciences. Observation in the social sciences is often less objective because it more frequently involves interpretation on the part of the observers. For example, the subject matter for investigation is often a person's responses to the behavior of others. Motives, values, and attitudes are not open to inspection. Observers must make subjective interpretations when they decide that behaviors observed indicate the presence of any particular motive, value, or attitude. The problem is that the personal values and attitudes of social scientists may influence both what they choose to observe and their assessment of the findings on which they base their conclusions. Natural scientists study phenomena that require less subjective interpretation.

Difficulties in Replication

The chemist can objectively observe the reaction between two chemicals in a test tube. The findings can be reported and the observations can be easily replicated by others. Replication is much more difficult to achieve in the social sciences. An American educator cannot reproduce the conditions of a Russian educator's experimental teaching method with the same precision as that with which an American chemist can replicate a Russian chemist's experiment. Even within a single school building one cannot reproduce a given situation in its entirety and with precision. Social phenomena are singular events and cannot be totally repeated for purposes of observations.

Interaction of Observer and Subjects

An additional problem is that mere observation of social phenomena may produce changes that might not have occurred otherwise. Researchers may think that *X* is causing *Y*, when in fact their own observation of *X* may cause *Y*. For example, in the well-known Hawthorne experiments changes in worker productivity stemmed not from the varying working conditions but from the mere fact that the workers knew they had been singled out for investigation. Investigators are human beings, and their presence as observers in a situation may change the behavior of their human subjects. The use of hidden video cameras and audiocassettes may help minimize this interaction in some cases, but much social science research includes the responses of human subjects to human observers.

Difficulties in Control

The range of possibilities for controlled experiments on human subjects is much more limited than in the natural sciences. The complexities involved in research on human subjects present control problems that have no parallels in the natural sciences. In the latter, rigid control of experimental conditions is possible in the laboratory. Such control is not possible with human subjects; the social scientists must deal with many variables simultaneously and must work under conditions that are much less precise. They try to identify and control as many of these variables as possible, but the task is sometimes very difficult.

Problems of Measurement

Systematic research must provide for measurement of the variables involved. The tools for measurement in the social sciences are much less perfect and precise than the tools of the natural sciences. Social science has nothing that can compare with the precision of the ruler, the thermometer, or the numerous laboratory instruments. We have already pointed out that an understanding of human behavior is complicated by the large number of determining variables acting independently and in interaction. The multivariate statistical devices available for analyzing data in the social sciences take care of relatively few of the factors that obviously are interacting. Furthermore, these devices permit you to attribute the variance only to factors operating at the time of measurement. Factors that have influenced development in the past are not measurable in the present, even though they may have significantly influenced the course of development. Because the complexity and difficulty of observation, replication, and measurement complicate social science research, researchers must exercise great caution in generalizing from their studies. It is often necessary to conduct several studies in an area before attempting to formulate generalizations. If they consistently confirm initial findings, then researchers can be more confident in making broad generalizations.

Despite the handicaps, education and the social sciences have made great progress, and their scientific status can be expected to increase as scientific investigation and methodology become more systematic and rigorous.

THE NATURE OF RESEARCH

Scientific research is the application of the scientific approach to studying a problem. It is a way to acquire dependable and useful information. Its purpose is to discover answers to meaningful questions by applying scientific procedures. To be classified as scientific research, an investigation must involve the approach we described in the previous section. Although it may take place in different settings and may use different methods, scientific research is universally a systematic and objective search for reliable knowledge.

EDUCATIONAL RESEARCH

Educational research is the application of the scientific approach to the study of educational problems. Educational research is the way in which people acquire dependable and useful information about the educative process. Educators usually conduct research to find a solution to some problem or to gain insight into an issue they do not understand. The ultimate goal is to discover general principles or interpretations of behavior that people can use to explain, predict, and control events in educational situations—in other words, to formulate scientific theory.

The acceptance of the scientific approach in education and the other social sciences has lagged far behind its acceptance in the physical sciences. In 1897 J. M. Rice, a pioneer in educational research, found himself in a situation similar to that described by the quotation attributed to Bacon earlier in this chapter. Rice asked the educators at the annual meeting of the National Education Association's Department of Superintendence if it would be possible to determine whether students who are given 40 minutes of spelling each day learn more than students given 10 minutes each day. He reported,

> to my great surprise, the question threw consternation into the camp. The first to respond was a very popular professor of psychology engaged in training teachers in the West. He said, in effect, that the question was one which could never be answered; and he gave me a rather severe drubbing for taking up the time of such an important body of educators in asking them silly questions. (Rice, 1912, pp. 17–18)

Rice did, in fact, collect empirical evidence on his question and found that the differences in achievement between those spending 10 minutes a day and those spending 40 minutes a day were negligible. He also pointed out that many words children were required to learn how to spell had little practical value. His work led other investigators, such as Edward L. Thorndike, to use documentary analysis to determine the frequency of use of words in the English language. Their work in turn led to improvements in language arts texts and curricula.

Federal Legislation Influencing Education Research

Although educational research is a young science, it has continued to progress since its beginnings in the late 19th century. In the last decade, there has been increased attention to research in education, with two pieces of federal legislation putting education research in the spotlight of national attention: (1) the Elementary and Secondary Education Act reauthorization in 2001—known as the No Child Left Behind Act, and (2) the Education Sciences Reform Act of 2002. Both focus on the need for education policy and practices to be based on scientific evidence. Both also pointed with some skepticism to the existing state of education research.

The No Child Left Behind Act demanded implementation of standards-based reform and annual testing of students in grades 3 to 8 to determine performance levels. In addition, it called for implementation of curriculum and professional development in schools based on scientific evidence. The law mandates that federal dollars may be spent only on instructional methods and materials that have scientifically based evidence of their effectiveness. Peer review was identified as a key concept in the definition of scientifically based research in No Child Left Behind.

The Education Sciences Reform Act authorized the creation of the Institute for Education Sciences (IES) to function as a separate office under a 15-member National Board for Education Sciences. Under the act, research done by the institute was to encompass early childhood through adult education. The passage of the Individuals with Disabilities in Education Act (IDEA) in 2004 also moved research in special education to the IES. Three centers are included in IES: The National Center on Education Research, the National Center for Education Statistics, and the National Center for Evaluation and Regional Assistance.

The Education Sciences Reform Act defined basic and applied research in education. Basic research is targeted to gaining fundamental knowledge of phenomena for the advancement of knowledge in the field but without specific application. Applied research is targeted to gaining knowledge about or understanding of means to meet a specified need and is specifically directed to the advancement of educational practice. The act also defines "scientifically based research standards" in education as those that:

1. Apply rigorous and objective methodology (see Chapters 10 to 17 of this text).
2. Present findings appropriate to and supported by the methods (see Chapter 19).
3. Draw on observation or experiment (see Chapters 10, 11, and 16).
4. Involve data analyses adequate to support the findings (see Chapters 6, 7, and 17).
5. Rely on measurements that provide reliable data (see Chapters 8 and 9).
6. Make claims of causal relationships only in random assignment experiments (see Chapters 7, 10, and 11).
7. Ensure there is sufficient detail to allow replication (see Chapter 19).
8. Are accepted through peer review or independent experts through a rigorous, objective, and scientific review (see Chapter 19).
9. Use research designs and methods appropriate to the research question posed (see Chapters 10 to 17).

National Reports Influencing Education Research

A 2002 report called *Scientific Research in Education* may have influenced the definitions in the Education Sciences Reform Act. The report was published through the autonomous National Academy of Sciences (chartered by Congress in 1863 to advise the federal government on scientific and technical matters). The report provided recommendations for what constitutes rigorous scientific evidence in education, setting forth six principles believed to underlie all scientific inquiry, including education research. These principles for inquiry are:

1. Posing significant questions that can be investigated empirically.
2. Linking research to relevant theory.
3. Using methods that permit direct investigation of the question.
4. Providing a coherent and explicit chain of reasoning.
5. Replicating and generalizing across studies.
6. Disclosing research to encourage professional scrutiny and critique.

The report noted that the choice of method for investigation must be driven by the question posed, that inferences are strengthened through testing using multiple methods, and that both quantitative and qualitative methods are needed to fully explore questions related to educational phenomena. The report concluded that integrating quantitative and qualitative approaches would be likely to accelerate scientific progress.

The National Academies followed up their 2002 report with a 2003 report, *Implementing Randomized Field Trials in Education*, and a 2004 report, *Advancing Scientific Research in Education*. The 2003 report emphasized randomized field trials to establish cause-and-effect relationships. The 2004 report offered recommendations for improving scientific research in education organized around three strategic objectives: promoting quality, building the knowledge base, and enhancing the professional development of researchers. This report also recognized the importance of building strong partnerships between education researchers and practitioners and the need for time and money to support building these relationships. The report concluded that "The field of education research and the related goals of evidence-based education will not be served if the underlying science lacks rigor" (p. 33).

One final report worthy of mention is the December 2003 *Identifying and Implementing Educational Practices Supported by Rigorous Evidence: A User Friendly Guide*. The report, from the Coalition for Evidence-Based Policy, was prepared for IES. The report refers to randomized controlled trials as research's "gold standard" for establishing what works in education and lists the following as practices that have been found effective through such rigorous study:

- One-on-one tutoring for at-risk readers in grades 1 to 3
- Life skills training for junior high students
- Reduced class size in grades K to 3
- Instruction for early readers in phonemic awareness and phonics

The report provides criteria by which to evaluate whether an intervention is supported by rigorous evidence, including key items to look for in the study's description of the intervention and the assignment process, key items in the collection of outcome data, and key items in the reporting of results. The document also lists important factors to consider when implementing evidence-based interventions in schools and classrooms.

Finally, a website has been established by the U.S. Department of Education's Institute for Education Sciences to assist with reviewing education research and determining which practices are supported by rigorous scientific evidence. The What Works Clearinghouse can be found at http://www.w-w-c.org.

SUMMARY

Human beings have sought to acquire knowledge through experience, authority, deductive reasoning, inductive reasoning, and the scientific approach. The scientific approach is widely regarded as the single most reliable source of new knowledge.

The scientific approach rests on two basic assumptions: (1) People can derive truth from observation, and (2) phenomena conform to lawful relationships.

Scientific inquirers seek not absolute truth but rather theories that explain and predict phenomena in a reliable manner. They seek theories that are parsimonious, testable, and consistent, as well as theories that are themselves stimuli for further research. The scientific approach incorporates self-correction, inasmuch as every theory is tentative and may be set aside if a new theory better fits the criteria.

Investigators have used the scientific approach to explain, predict, and control physical phenomena for centuries. As a science, educational research uses investigative methods consistent with the basic procedures and operating conceptions of scientific inquiry. The complexity of educational variables and difficulties in making reliable observations impeded scientific inquiry in education. However, since the beginning of the movement early in the 20th century, scientific inquiry in education has enjoyed increasing acceptance and increasing success both in theoretical and practical research. Recent federal legislation has focused on the need for education policy and practices to be based on scientific research.

KEY CONCEPTS

deductive reasoning
hypothesis
imperfect induction
inductive reasoning
perfect induction
principle of parsimony
scientific approach
theory
universal determinism

EXERCISES

1. Identify the source of knowledge—*deductive reasoning*, *inductive reasoning*, or the *scientific approach*—most prominently used in the following examples:
   a. After extensive observation of reactions, Lavoisier concluded that combustion is a process in which a burning substance combines with oxygen. His work was the death blow to the old phlogiston theory of burning.
   b. Dalton, after much reflection, concluded that matter must consist of small particles called *atoms*. His early assumptions became the basis for the atomic theory.
   c. Later scientists took Dalton's assumptions, made deductions from them, and proceeded to gather data that confirmed these assumptions. They found support for the atomic theory.
   d. Knowing that radioactive substances constantly give off particles of energy without apparently reducing their mass, Einstein developed the formula $E = mc^2$ for converting matter into energy.
   e. Accepting Einstein's theory, Fermi carried on experimentation that resulted in splitting the atom.
   f. After studying reinforcement theory, a teacher hypothesizes that using a tutorial computer program will lead to superior achievement in arithmetic. She devises a study in which the tutorial is used with two sixth-grade classes, while conventional materials are used with two other sixth-grade classes.
2. What is the role of theory in scientific inquiry?
3. What is the difference between an inductive theory and a deductive theory?

4. Give examples of the use of authority and experience as sources of knowledge.
5. Evaluate the following deductive arguments:
   a. All graduating seniors with high GPAs study Latin. John is a senior with a high GPA. Therefore, John studies Latin.
   b. All vertebrates have backbones. This animal has a backbone. Therefore, this animal is a vertebrate.
6. Evaluate the following inductive arguments:
   a. This animal has a backbone. Animals with backbones are vertebrates. I am reasonably certain that this animal is a vertebrate.
   b. This is a student who studies very hard. Students who make good grades tend to study hard. This student probably makes good grades.
7. Which characteristic attitudes expected of scientists are violated in the following statements?
   a. This study was undertaken to prove that the use of marijuana is detrimental to academic achievement.
   b. It proved conclusively that this is the case.
   c. The results show that marijuana is evil.
8. What are the characteristics of a useful theory?
9. Which of the following would contribute to theory development in education?
   a. Evidence that supports the hypothesis of a study.
   b. Evidence that refutes the hypothesis of a study.
   c. (a) only
   d. (a) and (b)

ANSWERS

1. a. Inductive reasoning
   b. Deductive reasoning
   c. Scientific approach
   d. Deductive reasoning
   e. Scientific approach
   f. Scientific approach
2. Theory integrates findings, summarizes information, provides leads for new research, and enables people to explain and predict phenomena.
3. An inductive theory serves to explain previous observations, whereas a deductive theory is developed before extensive observations have been made.
4. Answers will vary.
5. a. The argument is flawed; the major premise is not valid.
   b. The argument is correct.
6. a. The argument is correct.
   b. The argument is flawed; cannot say that because the student studies hard, he or she makes good grades.
7. a. The scientist is objective and impartial.
   b. The scientist is skeptical and regards findings as tentative.
   c. The scientist deals with facts, not values.
8. A useful theory explains the phenomena in the simplest form possible, is consistent with observation and the established body of knowledge, provides means for its verification, and stimulates new investigation.
9. d

INFOTRAC COLLEGE EDITION

Use the keywords *theory* and *educational research* to find an article that discusses the role of theory in educational research. Cite an example of a well-known theory in education.

Chapter 2

The Scientific Approach in Education

REAL SCIENCE IS NOT ABOUT CERTAINTY BUT ABOUT UNCERTAINTY.

INSTRUCTIONAL OBJECTIVES

After studying this chapter, the student will be able to:

1. Describe the major research methodologies used in educational investigations.
2. Distinguish between the philosophical approaches underlying quantitative and qualitative research.
3. List the specific types of research that fall into the broad categories of quantitative and qualitative research.
4. Give an example of a research problem that would be investigated by quantitative methodology and one for which qualitative methodology would be most appropriate.
5. Identify the research methodology used in given examples of both quantitative and qualitative research.
6. List the steps involved in the research process.
7. Distinguish between the characteristics of basic and applied research.
8. Explain the terms *concept*, *construct*, and *variable*.
9. Distinguish among types of variables: categorical versus continuous and independent versus dependent.
10. Distinguish between constitutive and operational definitions and explain the importance of the latter in research.

Educational research is typically divided into two broad categories: quantitative and qualitative research. Each approach has its own terminology, methods, and techniques. **Quantitative research** uses objective measurement and statistical analysis of numeric data to understand and explain phenomena. It generally requires a well-controlled setting. **Qualitative research**, in contrast, focuses on understanding social phenomena from the perspective of the human participants in the study. The data are collected in natural settings, and the research aims at generating theory rather than testing theory.

Historically, quantitative methodology has dominated education research, but in relatively recent years qualitative research has become more popular. As indicated in Chapter 1, however, most recent federal initiatives seem to be swinging the pendulum in the quantitative direction once more. Qualitative research emerged because researchers sometimes found quantitative methods inadequate for investigating many problems in education. For example, if you wished to study children's aggressive behavior in the school setting, it would not be enough to merely record the nature and number of incidents as the quantitative researcher might do. You would also want to use qualitative methods such as observation and interviews to better understand the reasons for the aggressive behavior. Finding answers to the following questions might be helpful: How do such children perceive the teacher and other children at school? How do other children react to the aggressive child? How does the teacher handle aggressive behavior? Such questions would be investigated simultaneously in qualitative research, providing insight and a more comprehensive picture of the behavior.

Quantitative and qualitative research stem from different philosophical assumptions that shape the ways researchers approach problems and collect and analyze data. Quantitative research originated in **positivism**, a philosophic view formulated in the 19th century. Positivists believe that general principles or laws govern the social world as they do the physical world. Researchers can discover these general principles and then apply them to predict human behavior. Positivists thus emphasize measurement and gathering data with objective techniques as the best way to answer questions and to explain and predict behavior. Positivism is often considered the traditional scientific approach, first used in the natural sciences and later extended to education and the social sciences. It typically involves testing theories and hypotheses and generalizing findings to a larger population. The result is research that is systematic and open to replication by other investigators.

Qualitative research is rooted in **phenomenology**, which sees social reality as unique. The phenomenologic approach sees the individual and his or her world as so interconnected that essentially the one has no existence without the other. Thus the researcher can only understand human behavior by focusing on the meanings that events have for the people involved. You must look not only at what people do but also at how they think and feel, and you must experience what happens to them. The intended result of a phenomenologic study is a narrative report so rich and comprehensive that you can understand the social reality experienced by the participants. Furthermore, because researchers do not know in advance how naturally occurring events will unfold or what variables may be important, they do not begin a study with hypotheses.

There has been considerable debate over the merits of qualitative research as compared with quantitative. Some scientists see the qualitative approach as less rigorous and thus less acceptable as a way of doing research. Other scholars deny the relevance of experimental and other quantitative methodology for education. Still others believe that there really is not much difference in the merits of quantitative and qualitative research, both needing to meet high standards of value

PICTURE THIS

Different philosophical bases

and validity. Our position is that both methodologies are valuable in educational research. Which method researchers choose depends not on their preference for methods but on the suitability of the particular method to what they are studying and what they want to find out. If you want to find out what the students in a middle school think about a newly proposed dress code, you would use survey research, which is quantitative. If you want to know how students learn and interact in a bilingual urban elementary school, you would use qualitative methodology. As King (2004) wrote, "There are times when qualitative data are the only appropriate means to answer the scientist's questions" (p. 173). Other times quantitative data are what we need.

We should note that some researchers no longer view the quantitative–qualitative distinction as useful. There has been a trend toward rapprochement, which manifests itself in research where the same study uses both approaches. A caveat, however, is in order. Bogdan and Biklen (2003) state:

> While it is possible, and in some cases desirable, to use the two approaches together, attempting to carry out a sophisticated quantitative study while doing an in-depth qualitative study simultaneously is very difficult. Researchers, especially novices, trying to combine good quantitative design and good qualitative design have a difficult time pulling it off, and rather than producing a superior hybrid, usually produce a piece of research that does not meet the criteria for good work in either approach. (p. 37)

Maxwell (2004) says that mutual understanding of the logic and practice of the other's approach and a greater respect for the value of the other perspective is a prerequisite for the optimal integration of qualitative and quantitative approaches in educational research. The reader is referred to Creswell (2003), Thomas (2003), and Tashakkori and Teddlie (2003) for further discussion of the mixed-methods approach in research.

Reichert and Kuriloff (2004) used both quantitative and qualitative approaches in studying how boys develop their self-concepts within the school setting. The sample included 499 boys attending a college preparatory boys' day school. The quantitative data consisted of measures of the boys' academic performance, self-concepts, anxiety level, gender role conflicts, and various demographic data. In the qualitative part, they conducted in-depth interviews with the boys and asked them to describe themselves, their parents' attitudes toward schooling, and their views of their own place in the school. The quantitative findings showed a strong, negative relationship between self-concept and social anxiety and a positive relationship between self-concept and academic achievement. The qualitative findings amplified these results, suggesting that, all else being equal, boys developed their self-concepts based in part on how they saw themselves reflected in the mirror of the school's social relations. They concluded that schools should help boys reduce their social anxiety and thus enhance their senses of self. Table 2.1 summarizes the major characteristics of the quantitative and qualitative research approaches.

Table 2.1 Comparison of Quantitative and Qualitative Research

	Quantitative	Qualitative
Purpose	To study relationships, cause and effect	To examine a phenomenon in rich detail
Design	Developed prior to study	Evolves during study
Approach	Deductive; tests theory	Inductive; generates theory
Tools	Uses standardized instruments	Uses face-to-face interaction
Sample	Uses large samples	Uses small samples
Analysis	Statistical analysis of numeric data	Narrative description and interpretation

THINK ABOUT IT 2.1

A study was conducted to determine the effect on student performance of implementing a block schedule in high schools. Two high schools in a district were selected to implement block scheduling, and two other high schools continued with traditional scheduling. At the conclusion of the 2-year study, student performance on state tests (adjusted for prechange performance) was compared across the high schools. The results puzzled the researchers. One high school with block scheduling had much higher scores than the control schools, but the other high school with block scheduling had notably lower scores than the control schools. The researchers felt no valid conclusions about the benefits of block scheduling could be drawn and that further research was necessary. How would quantitative and qualitative researchers differ in their approach?

Answer:
The quantitative researcher would suggest an experimental study to try to determine the impact of block scheduling and other demographic variables on student performance. The qualitative researcher would suggest in-depth case studies of the two block scheduling schools to determine what differences in the social context of the schools could account for the different results. Data could be collected through observation and focus groups.

We will now look at some specific types of research included in the broad categories of quantitative and qualitative research.

QUANTITATIVE RESEARCH

Quantitative research may be further classified as either experimental or nonexperimental.

EXPERIMENTAL RESEARCH

Researchers study variables, which are characteristics that take on different values across people or things. Experimental research involves a study of the effect of the systematic manipulation of one variable(s) on another variable. The manipulated variable is called the experimental treatment or the **independent variable**. The observed and measured variable is called the **dependent variable**. For example, assume a university researcher wanted to investigate the effect of providing online feedback to students immediately following course examinations. Using two sections of economics taught by the same professor, the researcher using a random procedure would select one section to receive immediate online feedback about their performance on test questions; the other section would receive feedback during their next class session (independent variables). The researcher would compare the two sections' exam scores and their final grades in the course (dependent variables). If test scores and final grades were higher than could be accounted for by chance in the section receiving online feedback, the researcher could tentatively conclude that there is evidence the online feedback (treatment or independent variable) contributed to greater learning than the in-class feedback.

In experiments, you seek to control all other variables that might influence the dependent variable. In the foregoing example, the researcher would attempt to make sure that both groups had the same instructor; that both sections met at the same time of day but on different days; that lecture notes, readings, and exams were the same; and so forth. The researcher might also check on the ability level and background of the students in the two sections to make sure one section was not superior or better prepared than the other.

To have a "true" experiment, researchers must use a random process such as a coin toss to assign available subjects to the experimental treatments. With random assignment, each subject has an equal and independent chance of being assigned to any group; thus the assignment is independent of the researcher's personal judgment or the characteristics of the subjects themselves. Sometimes, however, researchers cannot randomly assign subjects to experimental treatments for a study. Instead, as in the preceding example, the experimenter must use already assembled groups such as classes. In this case, the research is called *quasi-experimental.* We discuss experimental research more thoroughly in Chapters 10 and 11.

NONEXPERIMENTAL RESEARCH

In nonexperimental quantitative research, the researcher identifies variables and may look for relationships among them but does not manipulate the variables. Major forms of nonexperimental research are ex post facto, correlational, and survey research.

Ex post facto research (also called *causal-comparative research*) is similar to an experiment, except the researcher does not manipulate the independent variable, which has already occurred in the natural course of events. The researcher compares groups differing on the preexisting independent variable to determine its effect on the dependent variable. For example, to answer the question "Do first-grade children from single-parent homes have more difficulty in school than children from two-parent homes?" would require the ex post facto method. The experimenter could not manipulate the backgrounds of children by making some one-parent families and others two-parent families, but instead he or she would identify the children from one-parent homes and compare their achievement with that of children from two-parent homes. Because researchers lack control over many factors, they must be especially careful in interpreting the results of ex post facto investigations. Despite its name, causal-comparative research does not establish a simple causal relationship among the variables of a study. We look at ex post facto research in Chapter 12.

Correlational research seeks to examine the strength and direction of rela-

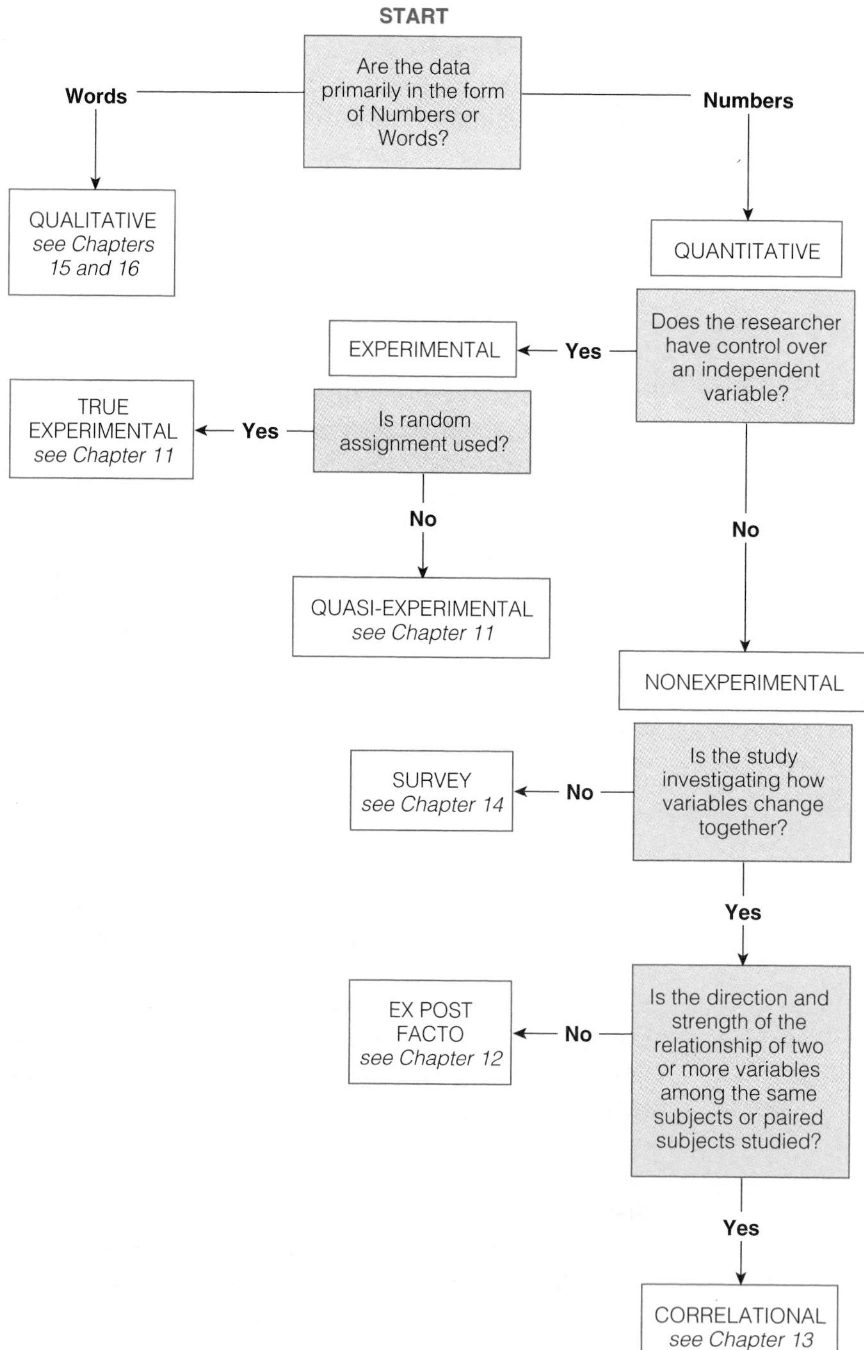

Figure 2.1 Major Types of Quantitative Educational Research

tionships among two or more variables. The extent of relationship is expressed as a numeric index. Some examples of correlational research questions follow: Is there a relationship between the quality of writing samples produced by incoming college freshmen and their performance during the freshman year? What are the relationships among certain noncognitive variables such as academic self-

THINK ABOUT IT 2.2

A study investigated the difference in Spanish grammar performance between high school freshmen taught by two different methods.

1. **(a)** What is the independent variable in this study? **(b)** What is the dependent variable? **(c)** What is not a variable?
2. What would the researcher have to do to make the study a true experiment?
3. How would the study be classified if intact classes were assigned to receive teaching method A or B?
4. How would the study be classified if it compared the Spanish grammar performance of students who had already been taught using method A with the performance of those who had already been taught using method B?

Answers

1. **(a)** teaching method, **(b)** Spanish grammar performance, **(c)** grade level of participants
2. Randomly assign students to teaching methods A or B.
3. Quasi-experimental research.
4. Ex post facto or causal-comparative research.

concept and motivation and college freshmen's academic achievement? We discuss correlational research in Chapter 13.

Survey research (also called **descriptive research**) uses instruments such as questionnaires and interviews to gather information from groups of subjects. Surveys permit the researcher to summarize the characteristics of different groups or to measure their attitudes and opinions toward some issue. Researchers in education and the social sciences use surveys widely. For example, an educational researcher might ask a group of parents about what kind of sex education program, if any, they believe schools should provide for middle school students. A survey of teachers could reveal their attitudes toward the inclusion of disabled children in the regular classroom. Opinion polls are surveys that researchers conduct to determine whom people are likely to vote for or what positions they take on certain issues. We discuss surveys in Chapter 14. Figure 2.1 summarizes the major types of quantitative research.

QUALITATIVE RESEARCH

Qualitative researchers seek to understand a phenomenon by focusing on the total picture rather than breaking it down into variables. The goal is a holistic picture and depth of understanding, rather than a numeric analysis of data. For example, social scientists have long observed that differences in educational background alone do not seem to account for the difficulties black students encounter in a predominantly white university. Researchers could explore the question "How do black students perceive their academic experience in a white university?" using qualitative methodology. The researcher would focus on a few black students and study them in great detail through observation and in-depth interviews. There are many different types of qualitative research; we will consider briefly just seven of the most widely used approaches: ethnography, case studies, document analysis, naturalistic observation, phenomenologic studies, grounded theory, and historical studies. We discuss qualitative research more extensively in Chapters 15 and 16.

ETHNOGRAPHY

Ethnography is an in-depth study of naturally occurring behavior within a culture or social group. Social scientists sometimes call ethnography **field research** because it is conducted in a natural setting or "field." The researcher observes behavior as it occurs naturally, without any simulation or imposed structure. Ethnography requires a variety of data-gathering procedures, such as prolonged observation of the setting, interviewing members of the culture, and studying documents and artifacts. Researchers interpret the data in the context of the situation in which they gathered the data.

Ethnography is rooted in anthropology. Educational researchers use ethnography, for example, to learn how the educational experience in suburban schools differs from that in inner-city schools.

CASE STUDIES

A **case study** is an in-depth study of a single unit, such as one individual, one group, one organization, one program, and so on. The goal is to arrive at a detailed description and understanding of the entity. In addition, a case study can result in data from which generalizations to theory are possible. Freud, for example, used the case study extensively in building theory. Case studies use multiple methods such as interviews, observation, and archives to gather data. Education and psychology researchers have used the case study widely. For example, you might conduct a case study of an inner-city school where the students have achieved at a high level on standardized tests.

DOCUMENT OR CONTENT ANALYSIS

Content analysis focuses on analyzing and interpreting recorded material within its own context. The material may be public records, textbooks, letters, films, tapes, diaries, themes, reports, and so on. When using such documentary sources, the researcher must establish the authenticity of the document itself, as well as the validity of its contents. Education researchers, for example, have used content analysis to study textbooks for their readability or to determine the coverage given to certain topics.

NATURALISTIC OBSERVATION

In **naturalistic observation**, the investigator seeks to make entirely unobtrusive observations of a setting without altering the situation in any way. The goal is to observe and study behavior as it normally occurs. Researchers sometimes use hidden cameras, one-way mirrors, and other unobtrusive techniques so that people being observed are unaware of the investigation. Piaget used naturalistic observation in his research on cognitive development in children.

Phenomenologic studies begin with the assumption that multiple realities are rooted in subjects' perspectives. Thus an experience has different meanings for each person. Through unstructured interviews, the investigator explores the subject's thoughts and feelings to elicit the essence of an individual's experience. A phenomenologic study might be conducted to answer the questions "What is the relationship like between a beginning teacher and his or her mentor? What does the experience mean to the beginning teacher?"

The **grounded theory** type of study is designed to develop a theory of social phenomena based on the field data collected in a study. Experience with the data generates insights, hypotheses, and questions, which researchers pursue with further data collection.

From an inductive analysis of the data, the researcher constructs concepts. He or she then forms a theory by proposing plausible relationships among the concepts. The theory is thus said to be grounded in the data. For example, a researcher interested in mainstreaming in elementary school could observe a number of classrooms and conduct interviews with teachers and students. Analysis of the data could lead to a theory about mainstreaming in the elementary school.

Historical research analyzes documents and artifacts to gain insight into what has happened in the past. Its success depends on the accuracy and completeness of these records. An educational researcher might want to investigate the trends in kindergarten education in a particular school district from its beginnings to the present.

Table 2.2 summarizes the major types of qualitative research.

Table 2.2 Types of Qualitative Research

Type	Major Question
Ethnography	What are the culture and perspectives of this group of people in its natural setting?
Case study	What are the characteristics of this individual, organization, or group?
Document analysis	What can be learned about this phenomenon by studying these documents?
Naturalistic observation	What can be learned by unobtrusively observing behavior as it naturally occurs?
Phenomenologic study	What does this experience mean for the participants in the experience?
Grounded theory	What theory can be derived inductively about a phenomenon from the data collected in this particular setting?
Historical	What insights or conclusions can be reached about this past event?

TYPICAL STAGES IN RESEARCH

All researchers engage in a number of activities regardless of the particular methodology chosen for the research. We focus on these activities in greater detail in later chapters; here, we briefly summarize the steps involved.

1. *Selecting a problem.* The first step is to select the problem to investigate. The problem should be consequential enough to warrant investigation. Also, the answer to the problem is not already available, but the means for finding answers are available. Quantitative researchers typically state the problem in the form of a specific question about the relationship between variables. For example, "Do children who are taught reading through the whole-language approach score higher on reading achievement than children who are taught reading through phonics?" or " What do teachers know about attention deficit/hyperactivity disorder?" Qualitative researchers begin with a general topic of interest. The problem statement may ask the "why" or "how" of certain phenomena. For example, "How do elementary classroom teachers deal with aggressive children?" or "How do high school students become alienated from their peers?"
2. *Reviewing the literature on the problem.* Researchers should thoroughly review the relevant literature to gain more understanding and insight into the problem and to determine what research may already have been done. The beginning researcher will likely turn to the literature for help in locating and formulating a researchable problem.
3. *Designing the research.* The investigator next plans how to conduct research to answer the question. The design is the researcher's plan for the study, which includes the method to be used, what data will be gathered, where, how, and from whom. Quantitative researchers maintain that once this research plan is set forth, it must be followed. Unhypothesized observed relationships among variables may be reported and proposed as topics for future research, but they should not replace the original intent of the study. In qualitative research the design is flexible and may change during the investigation if appropriate. The design of qualitative research is thus often described as "emergent."
4. *Collecting the data.* The next step involves executing the research plan. Quantitative researchers use a wide variety of instruments to gather data, including tests, questionnaires, ratings, attitude scales, and so on. Qualitative researchers also have a toolbox of data-gathering techniques, including in-depth interviewing, participant observation, and document analysis.
5. *Analyzing the data.* The data collected in research must be analyzed. Quantitative data are usually in the form of numbers that researchers analyze using various statistical procedures. Even verbal data, such as compositions written by high school students, would be converted through the scoring process to a numerical form. The analysis of the numerical data in quantitative research provides evidence that supports or fails to support the hypothesis of the study. Qualitative data generally take the form of words

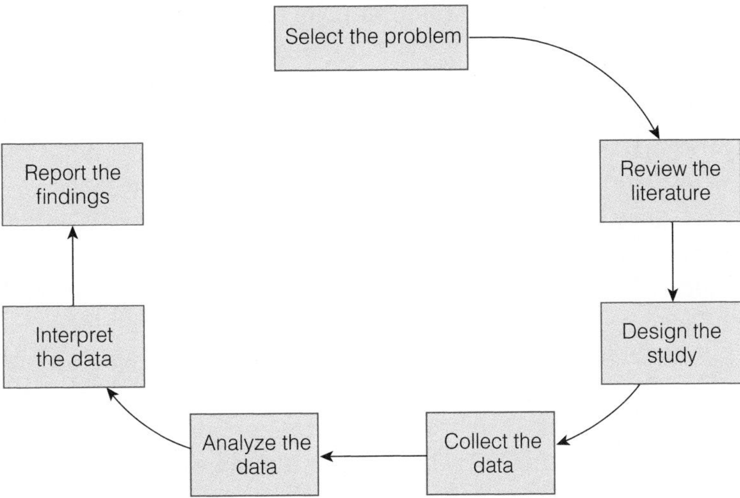

Figure 2.2 Stages in the Research Process

(descriptions, observations, impressions, recordings, and the like). The researcher must organize and categorize or code the large mass of data so that they can be described and interpreted. Although the qualitative researcher does not deal with statistics, analyzing qualitative data is not easy. It is a time-consuming and painstaking process.

6. *Interpreting the findings and stating conclusions.* The researcher next tries to interpret the findings in terms of the research problem. The quantitative researcher typically makes statements about the probability that such a finding is due to chance and reaches a conclusion about the hypothesis. Qualitative researchers present their interpretations and explanations in narrative form. They do not talk about probability but try to emphasize the *trustworthiness* and *credibility* of the findings (see Chapter 16).
7. *Reporting results.* Researchers must make their procedures, findings, and conclusions available in a form intelligible to others who may be interested. This involves clearly and concisely presenting the steps in the study in sufficient detail so that another person can replicate it.

We discuss in detail each of the foregoing stages of a research study in later chapters. It is probably rare for researchers to follow precisely the sequence as we have described in the preceding discussion. These activities often overlap, and researchers may move back and forth from one stage to another. These steps are shown in Figure 2.2.

QUESTIONS THAT EDUCATIONAL RESEARCHERS ASK

The specific question chosen for research, of course, depends on the area that interests the researchers, their background, and the particular problem they confront. However, we may classify questions in educational research as theoretical (having to do with fundamental principles) or as practical (designed to solve immediate problems of the everyday situation).

THEORETICAL QUESTIONS

Questions of a theoretical nature are those asking, "What is it?" or "How does it occur?" or "Why does it occur?" Educational researchers formulate "what" questions more specifically as "What is intelligence?" or "What is creativity?" Typical "how" questions are "How does the child learn?" or "How does personality develop?" "Why" questions might ask, "Why does one forget?" or "Why are some children more achievement-oriented than other children?"

Research with a theoretical orientation may focus on either developing new theories or testing existing theories. The former involves a type of study in which researchers seek to discover generalizations about behavior, with the goal of clarifying the nature of relationships among variables. They may believe that certain variables are related and thus conduct research to describe the nature of the relationship. From the findings they may begin to formulate a theory about the phenomenon. Theories of learning have thus been developed because investigators have shown the relationships among certain methods, individual and environmental variables, and the efficiency of the learning process.

Probably more common in quantitative educational research are studies that aim to test already existing theories. It may be overly ambitious, especially for beginning researchers in education, to take as a goal the development of a theory. It is usually more realistic to seek to deduce hypotheses from existing theories of learning, personality, motivation, and so forth, and to test these hypotheses. If the hypotheses are logical deductions from the theory, and the empirical tests provide evidence that supports the hypotheses, then this evidence also provides support for the theory itself.

PRACTICAL QUESTIONS

Many questions in educational research are direct and practical, aimed at solving specific problems that educators may encounter in everyday activities. These questions are relevant for educational research because they deal with actual problems at the level of practice and lead to an improvement in the teaching–learning process. Slavin (2004) writes that "Enlightened educators look to education research for well-founded evidence to help them do a better job with the children they serve" (p. 37). Some academic researchers, however, criticize practitioner research as not being sufficiently rigorous. But Anderson (2002) also argues for a research continuum for doctoral students in education that includes practitioner research. Such practical questions are, for example, "How effective is peer tutoring in the elementary school classroom?" or "How does teaching children cognitive strategies affect their reading comprehension?" or "What is the relative effectiveness of the problem discussion method as compared with the lecture method in teaching high school social studies?" or "What are the most effective means of providing remediation to children who are falling behind" The answers to such questions may be quite valuable in helping teachers make practical decisions in the classroom. Slavin (2004) says that the ultimate beneficiaries of education research must be children.

These practical questions can be investigated just as scientifically as the theoretical problems. The two types of questions differ primarily on the basis of the goals they hope to achieve rather than on the study's level of sophistication.

BASIC AND APPLIED RESEARCH

Another system of classification concerns whether research is basic or applied. **Basic research** is research aimed at obtaining empirical data used to formulate and expand theory. Basic research is not oriented in design or purpose toward the solution of practical problems. Its essential aim is to expand the frontiers of knowledge without regard to practical application. Much early psychological investigation of reinforcement was basic research. Later, social scientists found that the reinforcement theory resulting from that research had educational applications.

Applied research aims to solve an immediate practical problem. It is research performed in relation to actual problems and under the conditions in which they appear in practice. Through applied research, educators can often solve their problems at the appropriate level of complexity; that is, in the classroom teaching–learning situation. Although applied research may solve some specific question, it may not provide the general knowledge to solve other problems. For example, an elementary school teacher may study the effect of a new method of teaching fractions. She or he conducts the research to answer a practical question, not necessarily to make broad generalizations or to help develop a theory.

This classification of research is not always distinct, however, because there are varying degrees on the basic–applied continuum. Research along this basic–applied dimension is usually classified on the degree to which the findings are directly applicable to solving a practical problem. Basic research often has practical benefits in the long run. For example, advances in the practice of medicine depend on basic research in biochemistry, microbiology, and genetics. Likewise, progress in educational practice is related to progress in discovering general laws through basic psychological, educational, and sociological research.

Actually, in recent years basic and applied research has tended to merge in education and psychology. The trend has been for basic research to move more toward classroom studies because the findings of applied research may help basic researchers complete theoretical formulations. Researchers developing general theories of learning, for example, often go into classrooms because to understand how children learn investigators must consider variables such as context and social structure that are not present in the artificial environments of the laboratory. Once the theories are formulated, they can be tested through further research in the classroom.

LANGUAGE OF RESEARCH

Any scientific discipline needs a specific language for describing and summarizing observations in that area. Scientists need terms at the empirical level to describe particular observations; they also need terms at the theoretical level for referring to hypothetical processes that may not be subject to direct observation. Scientists may use words taken from everyday language, but they often ascribe to them new and specific meanings not commonly found in ordinary usage. Or perhaps they introduce new terms that are not a part of everyday language but are created to meet special needs. One of these terms is *construct*.

CONSTRUCTS

To summarize their observations and to provide explanations of behavior, scientists create constructs. **Constructs** are abstractions that cannot be observed directly but are useful in interpreting empirical data and in theory building. For example, people can observe that individuals differ in what they can learn and how quickly they can learn it. To account for this observation, scientists invented the construct called *intelligence*. They hypothesized that intelligence influences learning and that individuals differ in the extent to which they possess this trait. Other examples of constructs in educational research are motivation, reading readiness, anxiety, underachievement, creativity, and self-concept.

Defining constructs is a major concern for researchers. The further removed constructs are from the empirical facts or phenomena they are intended to represent, the greater the possibility for misunderstanding and the greater the need for precise definitions. Constructs may be defined in a way that gives their general meaning, or they may be defined in terms of the operations by which they will be measured or manipulated in a particular study. The former type of definition is called a *constitutive definition*; the latter is known as an *operational definition*.

Constitutive Definition

A **constitutive definition** is a formal definition in which a term is defined by using other terms. It is the dictionary type of definition. For example, intelligence may be defined as the ability to think abstractly or the capacity to acquire knowledge. This type of definition helps convey the general meaning of a construct, but it is not precise enough for research purposes. The researcher needs to define constructs so that readers know exactly what is meant by the term and so that other investigators can replicate the research. An operational definition serves this purpose.

Operational Definition

An **operational definition** ascribes meaning to a construct by specifying operations that researchers must perform to measure or manipulate the construct. Operational definitions may not be as rich as constitutive definitions but are essential in research because investigators must collect data in terms of observable events. Scientists may deal on a theoretical level with such constructs as learning, motivation, anxiety, or achievement, but before studying them empirically scientists must specify observable events to represent those constructs and the operations that will supply relevant data. Operational definitions help the researcher bridge the gap between the theoretical and the observable.

Although investigators are guided by their own experience and knowledge and the reports of other investigators, the operational definition of a concept is to some extent arbitrary. Often investigators choose from a variety of possible operational definitions those that best represent their own approach to the problem. Certainly an operational definition does not exhaust the full scientific meaning of any concept. It is very specific in meaning; its purpose is to delimit a term, to ensure that everyone concerned understands the particular way a term is being used. For example, a researcher might state "For this study, intelligence is defined as the subjects' scores on the Wechsler Intelligence Scale for Children." Operational definitions are considered adequate if their procedures gather data that constitute acceptable indicators of the constructs they are intended to represent. Often it is a matter of opinion whether they have achieved this result.

Operational definitions are essential to research because they permit investigators to measure abstract constructs and permit scientists to move from the level of constructs and theory to the level of observation, on which science is based. By using operational definitions, researchers can proceed with investigations that might not otherwise be possible. It is important to remember that, although researchers report their findings in terms of abstract constructs and relate these to other research and to theory, what they have actually found is a relationship between two sets of observable and measurable data that they selected to represent the constructs. In practice, an investigation of the relation between the construct creativity and the construct intelligence relates scores on an intelligence test to scores on a measure of creativity.

VARIABLES

Researchers, especially quantitative researchers, find it useful to think in terms of variables. A **variable** is a construct or a characteristic that can take on different values or scores. Researchers study variables and the relationships existing among variables. Height is one example of a variable; it can vary in an individual from one time to another, among individuals at the same time, among the averages for groups, and so on. Social class, gender, vocabulary level, intelligence, and spelling test scores are other examples of variables. In a study concerned with the relation of vocabulary level to science achievement among eighth-graders, the variables of interest are the measures of vocabulary and the measures of science achievement. There are different ways to measure science achievement. The researcher could use a standardized achievement test, a teacher-made test, grades in science class, or evaluations of completed science projects. Any of these measures could represent the variable "science achievement."

Types of Variables

There are several ways to classify variables. Variables can be categorical, or they can be continuous. When researchers classify subjects by sorting them into mutually exclusive groups, the attribute on which they base the classification is termed a **categorical variable**. Home language, county of residence, father's principal occupation, and school in which enrolled are examples of categorical variables. The simplest type of categorical variable has only two mutually exclusive classes and is called a **dichotomous variable**. Male–female, citizen–alien, and pass–fail are dichotomous variables. Some categorical variables have more than two classes; some examples are educational level, religious affiliation, and state of birth.

When an attribute has an infinite number of values within a range, it is a **continuous variable**. As a child grows from 40 to 41 inches, he or she passes through an infinite number of heights. Height, weight, age, and achievement test scores are examples of continuous variables.

The most important classification of variables is on the basis of their *use* within the research under consideration, when they are classified as independent variables or dependent variables. **Independent variables** are antecedent to dependent variables and are known or are hypothesized to influence the **dependent variable**, which is the outcome. In experimental studies the treatment is the independent variable and the outcome is the dependent variable. In an experiment in which freshmen are randomly assigned to a "hands-on" unit on weather forecasting or to a textbook-centered unit and are then given a common exam at the end of the study, the method of instruction (hands-on versus textbook) antecedes the exam scores and is the independent variable in this study. The exam scores follow and are the dependent variable. The experimenter is hypothesizing that the exam scores will partially depend on how the students were taught weather forecasting. In this case, freshman status is a constant.

In nonexperimental studies, a variable that inevitably precedes another variable in time is an independent variable. For example, Bleeker and Jacobs (2004) were interested in investigating the reasons for the gender gap in science careers. While gender differences in performance on math and science indicators such as achievement test scores and grades have declined in recent years, the gender differences in math–science career choices have increased. The underrepresentation of women is especially evident in the physical sciences, where women comprise only 9 percent of employed engineers and 10 percent of employed physicists (National Science Foundation, 2000). As they had hypothesized, mothers' earlier perceptions of their adolescents' abilities were related to adolescents' math–science self-efficacy 2 years after high school; also mothers' earlier predictions of their children's abilities to succeed in math careers were significantly related to later career choices. In this study, childrens' math–science self-efficacy and career choices could partly depend on mothers' early beliefs, but mothers' early beliefs could not depend on their children's later self-perceptions and career choices. Thus mothers' beliefs is the independent variable and children's math–science self-efficacy is the dependent variable.

In some other cases it is not possible to tell which variable is antecedent and which follows. In a study of the relationship between self-confidence and popularity in high school students, either variable could be considered independent or dependent. It is possible for a variable to be an independent variable in one study and a dependent variable in another. Whether a variable is independent or dependent depends on the purpose of the study. If you investigate the effect of motivation on achievement, then motivation is the independent variable. However, if you wish to determine the effect of testing procedures, classroom grouping arrangements, or grading procedures on students' motivation, then motivation becomes the dependent variable. Intelligence is generally treated as an indepen-

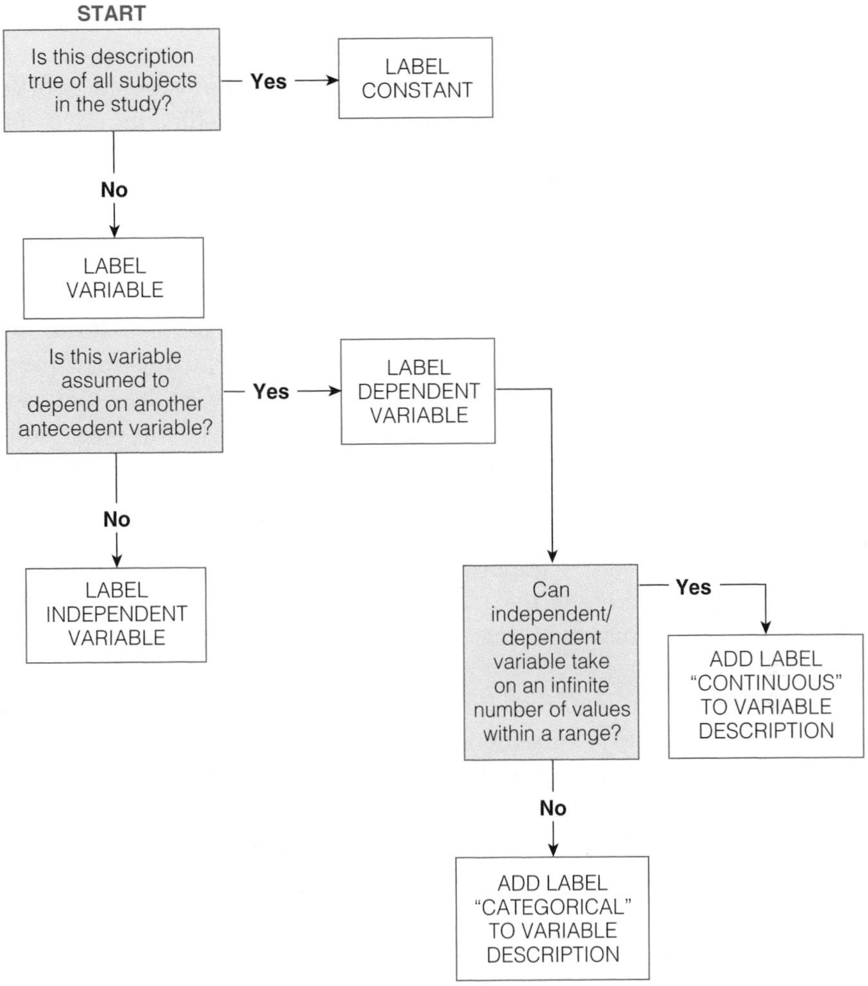

Figure 2.3 Flow Chart for Classifying Variables and Constants

dent variable because educators are interested in its effect on learning, the dependent variable. However, in studies investigating the effect of nursery school experience on the intellectual development of children, intelligence is the dependent variable.

CONSTANTS

The opposite of variable is constant. A **constant** is a fixed value within a study. If all subjects in a study are eighth-graders, then grade level is a constant. In a study comparing the attitudes toward school of high school girls who plan professional careers with those who do not plan professional careers, high school girls constitute a constant; whether they plan professional careers is the independent variable, and their attitudes constitute the dependent variable. Figure 2.3 illustrates a process for classifying variables and constants.

SUMMARY

The two broad research methodologies in education are quantitative and qualitative. Quantitative research deals with questions of relationship, cause and effect, or current status that researchers can answer by gathering and statistically analyzing numeric data. It can be further classified as experimental and nonexperimental. Qualitative research focuses on understanding social phenomena and providing rich verbal descriptions of settings, situations, and participants. The qualitative approach includes a number of different methods, such as ethnography, case study, naturalistic observation, focused interviews, and historical studies. Both qualitative and quantitative methodologies are important in educational research. One chooses the method that will provide the data to answer the research question.

The typical steps in educational research are (1) selecting a problem, (2) reviewing the literature, (3) selecting a research strategy and developing instruments, (4) collecting, analyzing, and interpreting data, and (5) communicating the findings by reporting the results of the study.

Based on the objective, educational research can be classified into two major categories: basic and applied. The primary concern of basic research is to expand the frontiers of knowledge and to discover general laws. The main goal of applied research is to solve immediate practical problems.

At a theoretical level, educational scientists use terms such as *intelligence*, *creativity*, *problem-solving ability*, and *motivation*, which are abstractions from observation of certain behaviors. These are referred to as *constructs*. In quantitative research, constructs are quantified and take on different values. Thus they are referred to as *variables*. There are two major types of variables: independent and dependent. If a variable is antecedent to another variable, it is called an *independent variable*; but if it is the consequence of another variable, it is the *dependent variable*.

In quantitative research, operational definitions are used to specify how variables will be measured in the study.

KEY CONCEPTS

applied research
basic research
categorical variable
constant
constitutive definition
constructs
continuous variable
dependent variable
dichotomous variable
independent variable
operational definition
phenomenology
positivism
qualitative research
quantitative research
variable

EXERCISES

1. Based on the title of each study, classify the following research as *basic* or *applied*:
   a. The Effect of RNA (Ribonucleic Acid) Injections on the Transfer of Skills from Trained Animals to Untrained Animals
   b. Outcomes of a Remedial Arithmetic Program
   c. Conditioning as a Function of the Interval between the Conditioned and Original Stimulus
   d. Teaching Geometry to Cultivate Reflective Thinking: An Experimental Study
2. In a study designed to determine the effect of varying amounts of sleep deprivation on the learning of nonsense syllables, identify the following:
   a. What is the independent variable?
   b. What is the dependent variable?
3. Classify the following variables as *categorical* or *continuous*:

a. Achievement
b. Phonics method of reading versus look–say method of reading
c. Spanish speaking, English speaking, French speaking
d. Muscle prowess
e. Music aptitude

4. What are the characteristics of operational definitions?
5. You are a teacher who has been concerned about the amount of aggressive behavior you observe among the children. You have interviewed parents about their child-rearing practices (use of punishment, rewards, and the like) and the amount of TV viewing and video games the children engage in. You have collected a great deal of data, but you feel that there is no unifying theme. According to the scientific approach, what would your next step most likely be?
6. Which research method (*experimental*, *ex post facto*, or *survey*) would most effectively give you answers to each of the following questions?
   a. Do children who eat breakfast make better grades in school?
   b. Does a unit on proper nutrition change children's breakfast-eating habits?
   c. How many children in school report that they do not have breakfast at home?
   d. Does the institution of a free breakfast program at school make a difference in the achievement of students?
7. Based on the titles, classify each of the following studies according to the research methodology most likely used:
   a. Gender-Based Differential Item Performance in Mathematics
   b. Effects of "On-Line" Test Feedback on the Seriousness of Subsequent Errors
   c. College Students' Views and Ratings of an Ideal Professor
   d. Effect of Early Absence of Father on Scholastic Aptitude
   e. An Alternative High School: An In-Depth Study
8. Give an example of how basic research in the biological sciences has improved the practice of medicine.
9. Give an example of how basic research in learning has improved the practice of teaching.
10. Give an example of applied research completed in your field of interest. List other areas where additional research needs to be done in your field. What variables might be investigated in such studies?
11. What research methodology do you believe would be the most appropriate for investigating each of the following research questions?
    a. How do parents conduct home schooling?
    b. Does collaborative learning promote achievement in the college classroom?
    c. What is the relationship between vocabulary and reading achievement in the primary grades?
    d. Do parents support character education in the middle school curriculum?
    e. What is the relationship between teachers' undergraduate background (education versus liberal arts) and certain measures of competence in the classroom?
    f. How did educational reforms of the junior high school lead to development of the middle school?
    g. What is the influence of family composition on children's conformity to the student role?
    h. What kind of education do students receive in a church-sponsored Christian high school?
12. How would you operationally define science achievement?
13. The following is an abstract from a research journal (Paulson et al, 2004)
    Abstract. This study examined the effectiveness of the Montana Early Literacy Project (MELP) curriculum on literacy and language skills of preschool-age children in Head Start. The MELP model utilizes everyday events and existing routines of classroom and home environments to build literacy and language directly into children's daily experiences. Using a control group design, the researchers analyzed skill development in preschool children participating in a classroom, using the MELP model as a supplement to the traditional Head Start curriculum (n = *14). Results were compared to children who participated in the traditional Head Start*

curriculum (n = *15). Assessments used were the Emerging Literacy Screening from* Building Early Literacy and Language Skills *(Paulson, Noble, Jepson, & van den Pol, 2001) and language sampling. Analyses indicated an important difference in the literacy and language skills gained by children in the MELP classroom, particularly in the areas of narrative discourse, vocabulary, phonological awareness, and print development. Due to the limited sample size, generalization of the data should be interpreted with caution. Nevertheless, findings support the use of the Montana Early Literacy Project curriculum in developing the early literacy and language skills in children who may be at risk of experiencing challenges in learning to read and write.*

a. What research methodology was used in this investigation?
b. What was the independent variable?
c. What was the dependent variable?
d. What was the operational definition of literacy?

ANSWERS

1. **a.** Basic
   b. Applied
   c. Basic
   d. Applied
2. **a.** Amount of sleep deprivation
   b. Number of nonsense syllables learned
3. **a.** Continuous
   b. Categorical
   c. Categorical
   d. Continuous
   e. Continuous
4. Acceptable definitions state a clear-cut procedure for creating or for determining the existence of the phenomenon and its extent.
5. Formulate a theory of aggression in children.
6. **a.** Ex post facto (causal comparative)
   b. Experimental
   c. Survey
   d. Experimental
7. **a.** Ex post facto
   b. Experimental
   c. Survey
   d. Ex post facto
   e. Qualitative
8. Answers will vary.
9. Answers will vary.
10. Answers will vary.
11. **a.** Qualitative
    b. Experimental
    c. Correlational
    d. Survey
    e. Ex post facto
    f. Historical
    g. Ex post facto
    h. Qualitative
12. Answers may vary; an example: "Science achievement is the score on the science subtest of the Iowa Test of Basic Skills."
13. **a.** Quantitative-experimental
    b. The type of curriculum used (MELP and traditional Head Start curriculum versus Head Start curriculum only)
    c. Literacy and language skills
    d. Scores on the emerging literacy screening and language sampling

INFOTRAC COLLEGE EDITION

Use the keyword *independent variable* to locate an article that discusses the use of variables in quantitative research in general or in a particular research study.

Chapter 3

The Research Problem

A RESEARCH PROBLEM IS NOT A NUISANCE; IT IS A STEP TOWARD NEW KNOWLEDGE.

INSTRUCTIONAL OBJECTIVES

After studying this chapter, the student will be able to:

1. Define a research problem.
2. Identify potential sources of problems for educational research.
3. State the criteria to use for evaluating a research problem.
4. Evaluate a given problem for research using the accepted criteria.
5. Take a general problem in an area of interest in education and formulate it in a specific form ready for empirical investigation.
6. Distinguish between the types of problem statements used in quantitative research and qualitative research.
7. Define terms such as *population* and *variables* as used in a quantitative research study.
8. Identify the population and the variables in a given study.

Systematic research begins with a **research problem**. In a classic work, John Dewey (1933) spoke of the first step in the scientific method as the recognition of a felt difficulty, an obstacle, or problem that puzzles the researcher. Your first step in the research process is thus to select a problem for investigation. Selecting and formulating a problem is one of the most important aspects of doing research in any field. Beginning researchers are often surprised to find that this initial stage can take up a large part of the total time invested in a research project. There is no way to do research until a problem is recognized, thought through, and articulated in a useful way.

A researcher must first decide on the general problem area. This step is often difficult for beginning researchers. The difficulty is not due to a shortage of problems but rather to the fact that beginners must select a problem very early, when their understanding of how to do research is most limited. They are uncertain about the nature of research problems and how to go about solving them. Skill in doing research is to a large extent a matter of making wise choices about what to investigate. This skill takes time and repeated effort to develop but the willing beginner can do it.

In order to ask questions that research can answer, one should have knowledge or experience in an area. We often hear students in difficult courses say, "I don't know enough to ask questions." Similarly, unless a researcher has knowledge or experience in an area, he or she does not know what additional knowledge is needed or how to obtain it through empirical investigation.

Furthermore, the problem area chosen for investigation should hold deep interest or be one about which the researcher is really curious. The choice must necessarily be very personal or else the researcher may find it difficult to muster the motivation to carry the research through to its end. Find a problem that intrigues you and you will enjoy the search for a solution. For example, an elementary school teacher may be interested in finding a more effective way to teach reading. A high school biology teacher may want to know if using computer simulations would improve students' problem-solving skills. An elementary school principal may want to know if a mentoring program would improve the effectiveness of beginning teachers.

Once having chosen the general area of investigation, the researcher then narrows it down to a specific statement of the research question. What specifically do you want to know or what do you want to predict? Unlikely as it may seem, once the researcher has selected a problem area and clearly articulated a question or statement, he or she has accomplished one of the most difficult phases of the research process.

SOURCES OF PROBLEMS

The first question most students ask is "How do I find a research problem?" Although there are no set rules for locating a problem, certain suggestions can help. Three important **sources for research problems** are experience, deductions from theory, and related literature. Noneducation sources may also be useful. These sources are appropriate in both quantitative and qualitative research.

EXPERIENCE

Among the most fruitful sources for beginning researchers are their own experiences as educational practitioners. Teachers often have intuition or hunches about new relationships or about alternative ways of accomplishing certain objectives. A geometry teacher may notice that certain teaching methods seem to get better results than others and may plan a quantitative research study systematically comparing the methods. An elementary school teacher may want to investigate the influence of parents' involvement on the academic achievement and adjustment of children. A high school social studies teacher may want to determine what high school seniors know about the process through which political parties select candidates for U.S. president. A high school English teacher might want to investigate strategies for improving the achievement of at-risk students. Some qualitative research problems that may arise from experience are "How do new faculty members become socialized into the total faculty group?" "How does 'pecking order' among high school students evolve over time?" or "What does education mean in the families of my minority students?"

Observations of certain relationships for which no satisfactory explanations exist are yet another source of problems for investigation. A teacher may notice an increase in overt signs of anxiety in students at certain times. To investigate this, the teacher can structure various tentative explanations of the origin of the anxiety and then proceed to test them empirically. This investigation may not only solve the immediate problem but also may contribute to understanding the causes of classroom anxiety. Similarly, educators must make decisions about practices that have become routine in the school situation and are in some instances based mainly on tradition or authority, with little or no support from scientific research. Why not evaluate the effectiveness of some of these practices? Would alternative procedures be more effective? We recommend that you make a list of ideas, noting things that you question. By studying your notes, you will soon identify a research problem.

Educators' everyday experiences can yield worthwhile problems for investigation, and, in fact, most research ideas that beginning educational researchers develop tend to come from their personal experiences. Practitioner research is appropriate for doctoral students in education because most of them have been in the classroom or are currently working full or part time in schools. These studies will be mainly of a type leading to solution of an immediate problem, but sometimes such problems are more appropriate and meaningful for beginning researchers than those logically deduced from theory. In addition, studies derived from teachers' classroom experiences can significantly contribute to the generation of new knowledge leading to the improvement of educational practice. Slavin (2004) writes that "Research in education has an obligation to answer the 'what works' questions that educators, parents, and policymakers ask" and "to produce answers that are well justified" (p. 27).

There is always a need for research that focuses on how to improve educational practice. American schools face a number of critical problems, such as incorporating increasing numbers of educationally disadvantaged students into the educational mainstream and preparing students for an increasingly competitive and technologically advanced workplace. Findings from practitioners' research studies often referred to as action research (see Chapter 17) can play an important role in solving these problems and improving U.S. schools. Young (2001) writes, "Let us return to the ultimate purpose of preparing future researchers in the field: the improvement of education" (p. 5).

DEDUCTIONS FROM THEORY

Theory is an excellent basis for research. Often beginning researchers are fearful of theory, but theory has a direct relevance to research designed to improve educational practice. Theories attempt to explain phenomena in a particular area by formulating explicit principles that account for what happens. The applicability of these general principles to specific educational problems is only hypothetical, however, until research empirically confirms them. Only through research can you determine whether the generalizations embodied in theories translate into specific recommendations for improving educational practice.

From a theory, researchers can generate hypotheses stating the expected findings in a particular practical situation; that is, they ask, "What relationships between variables will appear if the theory correctly summarizes the state of affairs?" They then conduct systematic inquiry to ascertain whether the empirical data support the hypothesis and hence the theory. A theory is thus subject to empirical verification and to revision or even abandonment on the basis of counter evidence. The benefit of theory-based research is that it is tied into a body of existing knowledge.

There may be an educational, psychological, or sociological theory that you have encountered in your course work that you find especially interesting. A beginning researcher can find summaries of theories in journals and textbooks, or you can read primary sources. You might also talk with your professors to see what they are working on or to get their suggestions. Once you choose a theory, you make deductions or predictions based on the theory: If "this" is true, then you should expect to make "this" observation. The researcher might also try to see if the theory holds or can be applied in situations different from the one in which it was developed.

The validity, scope, and practicality of social-cognitive theory, motivational theory, developmental theory, attribution theory, attachment theory, and many others can be profitably tested in educational situations. Reinforcement theory may be a particularly useful starting point for classroom research. Consider the implications for classroom testing that could be deduced from just one postulate of reinforcement theory—namely, that reinforcing responses increases response rate and strength. This theory has stimulated a great deal of research already, but there are still many deductions to be made and tested under classroom conditions. For instance, not enough research has been done on the effect of *lack* of overt reinforcement or of nonreinforcement on correct student responses in classroom situations. Scientists know from experimental laboratory studies with animals that each withholding of reinforcement decreases the probability of that response and eventually extinguishes it. Can research extrapolate this finding to the classroom? In other words, can the teacher assume that correct student responses that are not overtly reinforced will weaken and become extinct? At the present time educators do not have sufficient classroom research testing the applicability of this principle.

Many researchers are trying to understand the roots of youth violence that has occurred in recent years in U.S. high schools. Erik Erikson's classic theory (1959) of personality development may be relevant to understanding this problem. Erikson describes psychosocial development in terms of stages throughout the life span, each of which involves a critical issue or conflict that the person must resolve. Adolescence, one of these stages, has as its major task the development of a positive self-concept or, to use Erikson's term, a strong sense of identity. Forming a strong personal identity is difficult because competing roles and values face the young person. Research shows that adolescents who have achieved a sense of identity are more independent, more socially competent, better able to cope with stress, and have a higher self-esteem. But if the adolescent does not resolve the identity crisis, a sense of inferiority and personal alienation may result. It is interesting that students who have committed violent acts often report feelings of alienation. Erikson's theory could become the foundation for research into school violence. For example, what school practices may contribute to feelings of inferiority, mistrust, and isolation among some students? What are some positive things the school can do to help young people solve the identity crisis? You might want to look at the relationship of gender or ethnicity to the adolescent task of forming a sense of identity, for example. Making and testing deductions from Erikson's theory and reformulating new ones can result in a greater understanding of this phenomenon.

Teachers have long observed that many students when they make the transition to middle school experience a decrease in interest in academic tasks. Of greatest concern, however, is when students no longer believe they possess the ability to learn a particular academic task, a belief called a lack of self-efficacy. Poor self-efficacy beliefs often undermine students' motivation and hence their academic achievement. They develop self-defeating cycles of self-motivational beliefs. Paradoxically, middle school teachers expect greater student independence and self-sufficiency. To meet these expectations, students need to have a repertoire of study and self-regulation strategies that they can access and use. When they do not have effective strategies, many middle school students quit paying attention in class, doing homework, studying for tests, or even attending school. Cleary and Zimmerman (2004) conducted research on a school program called Self-Regulation Empowerment Program (SREP) that was developed from social-cognitive theory. This program was designed to empower adolescent students to engage in more positive, self-motivating cycles of learning. Cleary and Zimmerman hypothesized that as students exert greater control over their learning, they become more motivated learners and will experience a significant increase in achievement in the classroom. The findings supported the hypothesis. These researchers state, however, that there is a need for more formal testing of this theory using experimental designs.

A theory-based approach to research problems results in studies that are easily integrated because they all stem from a common theory. Such interrelated research is especially productive as a means for expanding knowledge in a particular area.

RELATED LITERATURE

Another valuable source of problems is the literature in your own area of interest. In reading published research, you encounter examples of research problems and the way in which research is conducted. There are several ways in which the review of previous research can help in formulating new research problems.

1. *Review of previous research may suggest the desirability of replication to confirm previous findings*. The easiest way to utilize the literature in finding a problem is to repeat someone else's study. An essential characteristic of a scientific research study is that it should be replicable, so that other re-

searchers can verify the findings. Perhaps you find the results surprising or hard to believe, or notice that the results conflict with other studies. Perhaps the study omits important aspects of the phenomena or reaches conclusions not supported by the data. Replication of a study with or without variation can be a worthwhile project for a beginning researcher.

Repeating a study increases the extent to which the research findings can be generalized and provides additional evidence of the validity of the findings. In many educational experiments it is not possible to select subjects at random; rather, you must use classroom groups as they are already organized. Of course, this limits the extent to which the findings can be generalized. However, as experiments are repeated at different times and in different places with the expected relations supported in each study, educators can place increasing confidence in the scientific validity of the findings.

Mere repetition of other studies is not the most challenging research activity, but in most cases replications are not exact. Variation is introduced to clarify some aspect of the findings, to test how far the findings can be generalized, or to investigate factors not included in the original study. For example, in other countries researchers have conducted numerous replications of Piaget's famous studies (1932) of the development of moral judgment in children. These studies have used Piaget's basic approach but have investigated the development of moral judgment in children of different socioeconomic classes, in children of the same chronological age but differing in intelligence level, in children differing in the extent of their participation in their own age groups, in children differing in the nature of parental discipline, and in both boys and girls. Recently, other investigators have used techniques that differed from Piaget's in their attempts to confirm his findings and conclusions. In general, the large body of research stemming from Piaget's investigations has supported his original conclusions. Thus, a single research study, if it deals with a significant problem and if its findings are exciting, can inspire many other studies.

2. *Reviewing published research helps people formulate research questions that are the next logical step from a previous investigation.* The outcomes of one piece of research very often lead to new questions. In the concluding sections of their research reports, researchers often describe new questions that have arisen and will suggest additional studies that should be done. A productive way to extend studies is to introduce new variables into a research design for further control and for determining interaction effects among variables. Many multivariate studies are extensions of earlier single-variable investigations.

3. *Reviewing previous research may stimulate a researcher to ask whether the procedures employed could be adapted to solving other problems, or whether a similar study could be conducted in a different field or subject area or with different groups of subjects.* For example, you may read a study investigating the effectiveness of a multimedia approach in teaching chemistry. Perhaps you could conduct a similar study in biology or in another subject. A study using high school students might serve as a guide to the elementary teacher who is interested in determining whether the same

relationships between variables prevail at the elementary level. Or you might investigate whether the results of a study showing the effectiveness of computers in teaching reading to a regular first-grade class would also apply to a class of learning disabled students.

4. *Reviewing research studies previously undertaken may raise the question of the applicability of their findings to other cultures.* Conclusions from research done in a given culture do not automatically apply to other cultures. This is one reason why in recent decades investigators have placed considerable emphasis on cross-cultural research. In such areas as child and adolescent psychology, social learning, cognitive and language development, achievement motivation, personality development, and educational practices, numerous examples of cross-cultural research appear. The growing number of international students in American universities has both increased interest in this kind of research and facilitated the collection of cross-cultural data. A number of theses and dissertations by students are of this type and provide basis for further cross-cultural studies.
5. *Reviewing previous research may result in detecting inconsistencies and contradictions or in dissatisfaction with the conceptualization, methodology, measuring instruments, and statistical analysis used.* Researchers can often find something to improve on in previous research. For example, in one of psychology's most famous studies, Hartshorne and May (1928) challenged the existing theory and research that concluded that honesty was a unified character trait. They investigated the behavior of several thousand schoolchildren in various temptation situations. They concluded from the low correlations among the temptation measures that honesty was not a general inner trait; rather, it was specific and influenced by the situation in which individuals were placed. Hartshorne and May's research has been replicated many times using different methodologies, populations, tasks, and statistical analyses. Most studies have supported their original conclusion that honesty is not a general personality trait but rather is specific to the situation.

Many other old theories and issues in education can be revived and viewed through new lenses. An example is the effect of ability grouping on student achievement. Since the early years of the last century, hundreds of studies have been done on this problem, yet it is still a topic for research today. Adams-Byers, Whitsell, and Moon (2004) investigated student perceptions of differences in academic and social effects that occur when gifted and talented youth are grouped homogeneously as contrasted with heterogeneously. On the whole, the students perceived homogeneous grouping more positively with respect to academic outcomes; they said they learned more in the more challenging environment provided by homogeneous classes. However, they had mixed feelings about which setting better met their social needs; they valued the social diversity of heterogeneous classes.

In summary, published research can be a great source of ideas for research. With some critical analysis of the research in your field and a bit of creativity, you should be able to find several potentially researchable problems. Reading research will also help you by showing how previous researchers measured variables, selected samples, analyzed data, and so on.

NONEDUCATION SOURCES

Experiences and observations in the world at large, as well as professional activities, can be fruitful sources of research problems. You can adapt theories or procedures you encounter in other fields to apply to education. Often movements that originate outside a profession lead people to new paths of research. The women's movement has led researchers to study gender stereotyping in educational materials, the influence of schools on the learning of sex roles, gender differences in achievement and personality, and so forth. The civil rights movement led to many studies about the education of minority children. The prevalence of the AIDS (acquired immunodeficiency syndrome) epidemic in this country has stimulated a great deal of research on the best procedures and materials to use to acquaint young people in school with the danger of the disease and how best to protect themselves from it. The inspiration for much valuable research in education has come from such noneducation sources.

QUALITATIVE RESEARCH PROBLEMS

Just as is true for quantitative researchers, beginning qualitative researchers can look to their personal experiences and interests, to theory, to the professional literature, or to current social issues and real-world concerns to find a potential problem. You need to identify an area or a topic about which you have a real interest. For example, a beginning researcher might be interested in how learning-disabled students are integrated into regular high school classrooms.

Once researchers have selected the initial focus of inquiry, they need to identify exactly what they want to know about that topic. The focus of inquiry is thus narrowed to the aspect of the phenomenon that will be explored in the research study. The focus of inquiry mentioned above can be stated as follows: "How do other students treat learning-disabled students? How do the learning-disabled respond? Although the qualitative researcher intuitively arrives at hunches about the phenomenon, he or she does not formulate an initial hypothesis that the study tests.

Suppose you are interested in the general topic of violence in the schools. You may have a theory that school violence results when students become alienated over a long period of time. Could this alienation begin in the early years of elementary school? Elementary teachers have long observed that some students are bullies and others become their victims. A qualitative researcher might use naturalistic observation to investigate this behavior in an elementary classroom over a period of time. The investigator could use videocameras and remote microphones to record instances of children being exposed repeatedly to negative verbal or physical actions on the part of one or more classmates. The researcher would want to interview the bullies to find out what they are thinking and what their motives and goals are. The victims would also be interviewed to learn about their feelings. The researcher might also look at gender differences in bullying behavior and the reaction of peers to this behavior.

EVALUATING THE PROBLEM

After you have tentatively selected a problem, you must evaluate it. A researcher must be confident that the problem area is of sufficient importance to warrant investigation, although this is not always easy to determine. Judging the worth of a problem is often a matter of individual values and subjective opinion. However, there are certain criteria you can use to evaluate the significance of a problem.

1. *The problem should be stated clearly, using terms whose meanings are generally agreed upon*. Vague general terms such as "democratic atmosphere" and "compassionate demeanor" must be avoided. Value-laden terms such as "good teaching" or "bad behavior" should also be avoided.
2. *Ideally, the problem should be one whose solution will contribute to the body of organized knowledge in education*. The researcher should show that the study is likely to fill in gaps in present knowledge or help resolve some of the inconsistencies in previous research. Perhaps the study can improve on earlier studies in such a way that it makes more reliable knowledge available. The problem should be one that will lead to new problems and so to further research. Researchers should begin by linking their problem to organized knowledge and consider the type of study that might logically follow their own. A good study, while arriving at an answer to one question, usually generates a number of other questions that need investigation. Most scholars agree that problems rooted in theory have greater potential for satisfying this criterion. The investigator might ask whether the study will yield knowledge about new relationships or will replicate previously established findings.

   Experienced researchers are more likely to focus on theory, but beginners should probably pick a problem that would have an impact on educational practice. You should be able to answer the question "So what?" with respect to your proposed study. Would the solution of the problem make any difference to educational practice? Would other educators be interested in the findings? Would the findings be useful in an educational decision-making situation?

   We suggest that the beginning student in research consider selecting a problem that could possibly be expanded or followed up later in a master's thesis or even a doctoral dissertation. It is helpful if students familiarize themselves with the research efforts of their professors, who not only can suggest related problems needing investigation but may also later serve as a mentor or a doctoral committee member.

   In your effort to locate a problem, however, do not select a question involving trivial relationships. For example, "What is the relationship between popularity with peers and reading speed?" would be considered a trivial problem because it has little or no significance for educational practice, has little relationship to other studies, and has no consequences for theory. The answers to some questions are obvious. A question such as "What is the correlation between verbal aptitude and reading achievement?" would also be considered trivial because educators already have sufficient data on this relationship and additional research is probably unnecessary. There is no need to "reinvent the wheel."

3. *The problem should be one that will lead to new problems and so to further research.*

4. *The problem must be researchable.* Although this criterion would seem self-evident, in practice many problems do involve questions that cannot be subjected to scientific investigation. To be researchable, a problem must be one that can be attacked empirically; that is, it should be possible to gather data that answer the question. Avoid problems that seek to determine what should be done. Many interesting questions in education cannot be subjected to empirical research but must be investigated through philosophic inquiry. Such questions as "Is it good to have sex education in the elementary schools?" or "Should we offer more vocational training in the high school?" or "Should schools give more attention to character education?" are philosophic issues and cannot be answered by scientific investigation. Although these questions as worded cannot be attacked empirically, they might be reformulated into workable research questions. For instance, you might restate the first question above as "What is the effect of sex education in the elementary schools on the attitudes of junior high school students toward premarital sex?" Researchers could design a study to obtain information on this type of question. Although philosophical questions as such are not appropriate for scientific research, people can use the information provided by research to develop solutions to philosophical and ethical questions; that is, the data compiled through scientific research on a problem can be useful to educators as they make decisions involving rights and values. The researcher must also give some attention to the definition and measurement of the variables involved in the question. A problem such as "What is the effect of changes in national priorities on the future of American education?" would not be appropriate for research. It would be difficult to define the terms "changes in national priorities" and "the future of American education" in such a way that they could be measured.

5. *The problem should be suitable for the particular researcher.* The problem may be excellent from the point of view of the criteria mentioned but inappropriate for the individual. First, the problem should be one in which you, the researcher, have a genuine interest and about which you can be enthusiastic. It should be a problem whose solution is personally important because of what it could contribute to your own knowledge or to improving your performance as an educational practitioner. Unless the problem

is meaningful and interesting, it is doubtful whether you would be willing to expend the time and energy to do a thorough job.

Furthermore, the problem should be in an area in which you have both knowledge and some experience. To identify a worthwhile problem, you need to be familiar with the existing theories, concepts, and established facts. Also, you should consider whether you have the necessary skills that you may need to carry the study through to completion. You may have to develop and validate instruments or do complex statistical analyses.

Another consideration is whether researching the problem is actually feasible in your situation. Are the data necessary to answer the question available or will they be? You must make sure that the necessary subjects will be available or that the appropriate school records will be accessible. School administrators are quite often opposed to having research conducted in their schools. So unless you are employed in a school situation at the time, you are quite likely to be left without the means to solve the research problem. One of the authors of this book found it necessary to visit four school systems before getting permission to conduct an educational experiment.

Also, is the problem one that you can investigate and complete in the allotted time? Do not select a problem that is too big or too involved, and be sure to allow adequate time for constructing the instruments, administering the instruments, analyzing the data, and writing the report.

6. *The problem should be ethically appropriate.* That is, the problem should be one that you can investigate without violating ethical principles. Unlike researchers in the physical sciences, educational researchers are dealing with human subjects with feelings, sensitivities, and rights who must be treated ethically. We will discuss ethics in greater detail in Chapters 15 and 19. At this point, we will just mention briefly three issues the researcher should consider:

   a. *Consent.* Researchers need to obtain consent from the intended subjects. Subjects should be able to choose whether they wish to participate in the study. Obtain consent from subjects after taking steps to ensure that they have a complete understanding of the procedures to be used, any risks involved, and any demands that will be placed on them. Obtain parental consent if minor children are to be involved in the study.

   b. *Protection from harm.* Do not plan research that may bring physical harm or psychological harm such as stress, discomfort, or embarrassment that could have lasting adverse effects. Fortunately, most educational research does not involve great risk of harm to subjects.

   c. *Privacy.* A researcher should invade the privacy of subjects as minimally as possible. For example, a researcher may plan to use an inventory that asks adolescents questions about sexual experiences, religious beliefs, attitudes toward parents, or other sensitive topics. In this case, the researcher should not attach names or even identifying numbers to the inventories. Subjects have the right to expect that their anonymity will be preserved. Most educational researchers are interested in group data rather than individual responses; the scores or responses of individuals are generally pooled and reported as group averages, which tends to minimize the risk of invading privacy. Table 3.1 summarizes the criteria of a good research problem.

Table 3.1 Characteristics of a Good Research Problem

1. The problem is clearly stated.
2. The problem is significant (it will contribute to the body of knowledge in education).
3. The problem is one that will lead to further research.
4. The problem is researchable (it can be investigated through the collection of data).
5. The problem is suitable (it is interesting and suits the researcher's skills, time, and available resources).
6. The problem is ethical (it will not cause harm to subjects).

PICTURE THIS

Joe Rocco

THINK ABOUT IT 3.1

How do the questions in the cartoon rate on the criteria for evaluating research problems?

Answers:

1. Carlos: Research cannot answer questions of "should." The question could be rewritten as "Do students who have had a unit on environmental awareness demonstrate greater knowledge of and more positive attitudes toward environmental issues than students who have had a control unit?" Then one could randomly assign some students to have a unit on environmental awareness, while others have a unit not related to the environment. At the completion of the units, one could measure the students on their knowledge of the environment, their attitudes toward environmental legislation, and environmentally appropriate behaviors, such as not littering.
2. Anita: As stated, the question is not researchable. There are so many possible ways to teach fractions that one could never investigate the outcomes of them all. One could operationally define two or three methods and compare the success of students taught by the different methods, using the same test of knowledge of fractions for all groups.
3. Marie: There is no way in this world to determine whose soul has been saved. A feasible question might be "Is the proportion of Baptists who say their souls have been saved different from the proportion of Episcopalians who say their souls have been saved?"
4. David: The question is trivial, because it has been investigated sufficiently in past research.

After the problem has been selected and evaluated, the next task is to state the problem in a form amenable to investigation.

THE PROBLEM STATEMENT IN QUANTITATIVE RESEARCH

The following are **criteria for research problem statements**:

1. *The problem statement clarifies exactly what is to be investigated.* You do this by specifying the variables involved in the problem, stating those variables typically in question form, and operationally defining the variables. We cannot overemphasize the importance of a clear, concise statement of the problem. Beginning researchers often have a general idea of what they want to do but have trouble articulating it as a workable research problem. They find that their initial general ideas, although adequate for communication and understanding, are not specific enough to permit an empirical attack on the problem. They cannot make progress until they can state unambiguously what they are going to do.

To illustrate, suppose a beginning researcher states that he or she is interested in studying the effectiveness of the new science curriculum in the secondary schools. As the problem is stated, you could understand in a broad sense what he or she wants to do and could communicate about it in a general way. But the researcher must specify the problem with much greater clarity if a method for investigating it is to be found.

An essential step involves a definition of the terms involved. What is meant by effectiveness, science curriculum, and secondary schools? The definitions required for research are not usually supplied by a dictionary. For example, *Webster's New World College Dictionary* (2002) defines effectiveness as "producing the intended or expected result." This definition describes the general construct effectiveness but is not sufficiently precise for research purposes. You need to specify exactly what indicator of effectiveness you will use or what you will do to assess the presence or absence of the phenomenon denoted by the concept effectiveness. The same is true for the other terms. In other words, you must operationally define the variables of the problem. As mentioned earlier, an operational definition defines a concept in terms of the operation or processes that will be used to measure or to manipulate the concept.

In this study the researcher might choose to define effectiveness as the improvement made in scores on a test of critical thinking or on a standardized science test. The term curriculum would be defined as the computer-assisted biology course offered to high school sophomores. Secondary schools might refer to those high schools that have certain specified characteristics such as size, type, and so on. The problem in the example given now might become "What is the effect of the computer-assisted biology course on the comprehension of biological concepts in beginning biology students at the sophomore level?" The operational definitions serve to focus the scope of a general question to specific observable variables.

Now that the work is indicated with some clarity and focus, the researcher can proceed to design an experimental study that compares the scores made on pretests and posttests of comprehension of biological concepts by students having the computer-assisted biology course with those of similar students having an alternative biology curriculum. The researcher can now begin to gather some objective evidence concerning a particular curriculum in a particular situation that will shed light on the more general original question.

2. *The problem statement asks about a relationship between two (or more) variables stated in the form of a question or implied question.* Although quantitative research problems generally focus on the relationship among two or more variables, this does not mean that the *exact* words "What is the relationship between . . . *and* . . . ?" have to appear in the statement. The statement *may* appear in that form, or the relationship may only be implied. Neither must you state the problem in the form of a question. Students are often confused on this point. For instance, compare the declarative statement "This study examines the relative effectiveness of reading methods A

and B in teaching slow learners" with the question "What is the relative effectiveness of reading method A as compared with method B in teaching slow learners?" Both focus on the "relationship between variables" but without using those precise words, and both are acceptable ways to present the research problem. Some researchers prefer the question form simply because it is straightforward and psychologically seems to orient the researcher to the task at hand—namely, to plan a method of finding the answer to the question. In some cases both a declarative statement and a question are presented; a more general declarative statement may be followed by one or more very specific questions.

3. *The problem statement should be presented in such a way that research into the question is possible.* One must be able to collect data to answer the question. For this reason, avoid philosophical issues, as well as value or judgmental questions that empirical investigation cannot answer.

   The development of a workable problem is an evolutionary process involving many attempts to sharpen concepts, define operations, and consider ways of collecting data.

THE PROBLEM STATEMENT IN QUALITATIVE RESEARCH

Qualitative researchers also begin with a problem, but they state it much more broadly than in quantitative research. A qualitative problem statement or question indicates the *general* purpose of the study. Formulation of a qualitative problem begins with the identification of a general topic or an area you want to know more about. This general topic of interest is sometimes referred to by qualitative researchers as the **focus of inquiry**. This initial broad focus provides the framework but allows for changes as the study proceeds. As the researcher gathers data and discovers new meanings, the general problem narrows to more specific topics and new questions may arise. For example, Villaume (2000) wanted to know more about the part that teachers play in the success of a school district's language arts reform effort. She felt that successful reform is more than just training teachers to use the new instructional programs, but rather success is linked to the abilities and the willingness of teachers to accept and act on the uncertainty that accompanies change. From this general problem, she stated the specific problem: "The primary purpose of this study was to describe how teachers responded to the uncertainty inherent in language arts reform" (p. 18). She investigated the problem in a case study of one school system.

Whereas the quantitative researcher always states the problem before collecting data, the qualitative researcher may formulate problems after beginning to collect data. In fact, the researcher often does not present the final statement of the problem—which typically specifies the setting, subjects, context, and aim of the study—until he or she has collected at least some data.

In qualitative research, the statement may be somewhat general in the beginning, but it will become more focused as the study proceeds. After exploring the sites, the people, and the situations, the researcher narrows the options and states the research problem more specifically.

IDENTIFYING POPULATION AND VARIABLES

A good strategy for shaping a felt problem—or a vague notion of what you want to investigate—into a researchable problem is to think in terms of population and variables.

For example, let us consider Ms. Burke, an elementary school principal whose question is "Does individual tutoring by upper-grade students have a positive effect on the reading achievement of younger below-average readers?" It is usually easiest to identify the **population**, those people about whom you wish to learn something. The population here is below-average readers. Reading ability is not a variable in this question because all the children being considered have been diagnosed as below-average readers. Having identified below-average readers as the population in the original statement, Ms. Burke should now ask herself if that is really the population she wants. She will probably decide that below-average readers is too broad a category and she should confine herself to a particular age. So she selects below-average second-grade readers.

Now she is ready to look for variables in the remainder of her original statement. "Individual tutoring" can be made into a variable either by varying the type of tutoring used or by varying the amount of tutoring time or by having some children receive the tutoring while others do not. Ms. Burke decides that the last alternative concerns what she really wants to know, so she rewrites the relevant part of the question to "Does receiving a specified amount of individual tutoring versus no tutoring . . . ?" Thus tutoring is the **independent variable** because it is antecedent to reading achievement, and the principal is predicting that the tutoring will have an effect on reading achievement, the **dependent variable**. Recall that the dependent variable is the outcome of interest, and the independent variable is hypothesized to influence the dependent variable. Now it becomes obvious that the word *tutoring* is too general. Unless all subjects receive the same type and amount of tutoring, the results of the study will be meaningless. Ms. Burke decides to use word flash drill as the specific type of tutoring and to specify 15 minutes per day as the amount of time.

The phrase "have a positive effect on" is quite vague until she looks at it in terms of her independent variable. Does word flash drill have an effect on . . . what? She knows it has an effect on word flash recall, but she wants to study its effects on other aspects of reading behavior that might be observed: expressive oral reading, silent reading, positive feelings toward reading, number of books read, comprehension, and so forth. But she is afraid that teachers might rate good word callers as comprehending more and being more positive toward reading, whereas they view the poorer word callers as more inferior on these variables than they really are. She wants a dependent variable that is independent of teacher judgment and decides to use reading scores from the California Achievement Test (CAT) as the dependent variable.

Ms. Burke's revised statement of the problem now reads "Among below-average second-grade readers, is there a difference in CAT reading scores between those who have received 15 minutes per day of individual word flash drill by upper-grade students and those who have received no word drill?" This question tells whom she is studying, what will be done differently for some students, and what she expects differential treatment to influence. Note also that the value judgment “positive effect” has dropped out of the question.

It is often useful to follow this procedure in a formal manner similar to that used for diagramming a sentence. You can begin by drawing a vertical line and writing *Population* to the left and *Variables* to the right. Then list these elements in the study below the horizontal line. For the preceding example, the diagram would be as follows:

Population	Variables
Below-average second grade readers	Word flash drill for 15 minutes daily by upper-grade students versus no word flash drill (independent) Reading scores on CAT (dependent)

Let us take another question: “What is the effect of having experienced versus not having experienced a preschool program on the reading achievement of first-graders?”

Population	Variables
First-graders	Having experienced versus not having experienced a preschool program (independent) Reading achievement (dependent)

This question is complete in that it has an identified population and both the independent and dependent variables. Because “preschool program” precedes “reading achievement of first-graders,” the former can be identified as the independent variable and the latter as the dependent variable.

Let us look at another example: “Does high school driver education do any good?” As it stands, the question has neither a population nor variables. An investigator starting with this question might first decide to compare 19-year-old drivers who have had high school driver education with those who have not. You now have a population statement and an independent variable. Now you can turn your attention to selecting a dependent variable. What effect might having versus not having driver education have on 19-year-old drivers? Let us say you decide that “accident rate” would be a suitable dependent variable. Putting these elements into a diagram, you now have the following:

Population	Variables
19-year-old drivers	Have had versus have not had high school driver education (independent) Accident rate (dependent)

You can now state a complete question: "Do 19-year-old drivers who have had high school driver education have a lower accident rate than 19-year-old drivers who have not had high school driver education?"

The question "What is the relationship of dogmatism to political attitudes among college freshmen?" illustrates another point. Consider this diagram:

Population	Variables
College freshmen	Dogmatism Political attitudes

This question is complete with a population and two variables. But you cannot label the variables as independent and dependent because it cannot be determined which is antecedent to the other.

If you conduct a study to investigate status quo rather than a relationship between variables, it may be complete with only one variable. For example, you might study the opinions of college seniors concerning legalization of marijuana. In this case the population is college seniors and the single variable is their opinions on the subject.

THINK ABOUT IT 3.2

For the revised problems of Carlos, Anita, and Marie, identify and/or add the independent variable(s), dependent variable, and population that they will need to identify in order to begin research on their questions.

Answers:

1. Carlos

Population	*Independent Variable*	*Dependent Variables*
High school students	Unit on environmental awareness vs. control unit	Knowledge of environment Attitude toward environmental issues

2. Anita

Population	*Independent Variable*	*Dependent Variable*
Fourth-graders	Method of teaching fractions	Student success with fractions

3. Marie

Population	*Independent Variable*	*Dependent Variable*
Church members (Baptists and Episcopalians)	Religious affiliation	Whether they report their souls saved or not

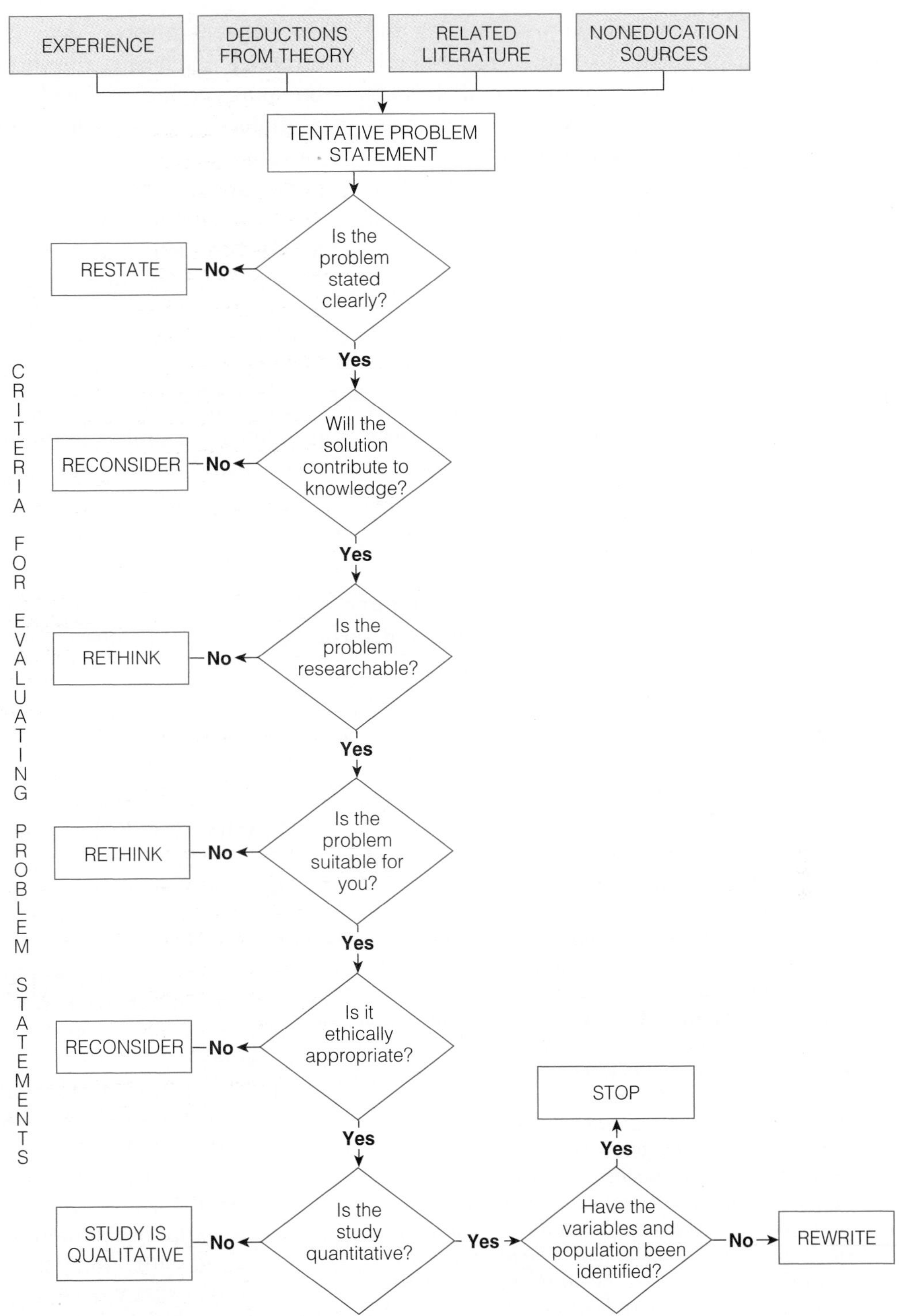

Figure 3.1 Developing a Research Problem

SUMMARY

The first task facing researchers is selecting and formulating a problem. To find a researchable problem, investigators may look to their personal experiences, to theories from which questions may be deduced, to the current literature in their area of interest, or to noneducation sources. They must evaluate the significance of the proposed problem in terms of specific criteria, asking questions such as "Will the problem contribute to the present body of knowledge? Does it have potential for leading to further research? Is it testable—that is, can the variables be observed and measured? How appropriate is the problem with respect to my interests, experience, and knowledge in the area? Do I have access to the data required by the problem, and are instruments available, or could they be constructed, to measure the variables? Can the data be analyzed and interpreted within the time available?" The question should not directly involve philosophical issues, nor should it be so general that a research undertaking is impossible. A quantitative research question asks about the relationship between certain variables. The statement of the question should identify the population of interest and the variables to be investigated. A qualitative research question indicates the general purpose of the study. The criteria for evaluating qualitative problems are similar to those used for quantitative research problems.

KEY CONCEPTS

criteria for research problem statements
dependent variable
focus of inquiry
independent variable
population
research problem
sources for research problems

EXERCISES

1. The following is taken from an abstract of a journal article (Starkey, Klein, & Wakeley, 2004):

   There is growing evidence that socioeconomic (SES)-related differences in mathematical knowledge begin in early childhood, because young children from economically disadvantaged families receive less support for mathematical development than their middle-class peers receive. A pre-kindergarten math intervention, including a pre-kindergarten mathematics curriculum, was developed and implemented in public and private preschools serving low- and middle-income families. Mathematical knowledge of the intervention and comparison children was comprehensively assessed. A significant SES-related gap in mathematical knowledge was found at the beginning of the pre-kindergarten year. The intervention significantly enhanced the mathematical knowledge of children at both levels of SES. Low-income children acquired more knowledge, relative to their starting point, than middle-income children. The extent of mathematical knowledge was similar in low-income intervention children and middle-income comparison children.

   a. What was the independent variable in this study?
   b. What was the dependent variable?
   c. What was the population?
2. Find a quantitative research report published in a journal, and answer the following questions based on your reading:
   a. What problem is investigated in the study?
   b. What is (are) the hypothesis(es)?
   c. What are the independent and dependent variables?
   d. Where did you find the problem and hypothesis(es) stated in the report?
   e. Were the problem and hypothesis(es) stated with sufficient clarity so that you knew exactly what was being investigated in the study?
   f. Did the author suggest further research on this question?

3. Find a qualitative research report published in a journal and identify the
   a. Problem
   b. Methodology
   c. Findings
   d. Conclusions
4. Select a broad area in which you might be interested in doing research and then identify a research problem that you would be interested in pursuing. State this problem in a form for research. What was the source of this problem?
5. The following examples are inadequate statements of research problems. Restate each so that it becomes a specific question suitable for research.
   a. Coaching and performance on the Scholastic Assessment Test (SAT)
   b. Academic self-concept of learning-disabled adolescents
   c. Adolescents with diabetes
   d. Predicting achievement in the first year of law school
   e. Effectiveness of method *X* in the teaching of mathematical concepts
   f. Gender differences and mathematical reasoning abilities of talented preadolescents
   g. High school principals and the expulsion of students
6. Evaluate the following research problems:
   a. Have permissive child-rearing philosophies had an adverse effect on American education?
   b. What is the relationship between the preferred method of leg crossing and the intelligence of American college women?
   c. Should sex education classes be included in the middle school curriculum?
   d. How do students perceive the role of the principal at Central Middle School?
   e. Should we allow prayer in the public schools?
   f. Do after-school programs do any good?
7. State the most likely independent and dependent variables in the following studies:
   a. What is the effect of multiage classrooms on achievement in grades 1 to 3?
   b. What is the relative effectiveness of the whole-language and phonics approaches on reading comprehension of second-graders?
   c. What are the correlates of racial prejudice?
   d. Does taking Latin in high school have an effect on students' SAT verbal scores?
8. List sources of research problems used by researchers and give an example of each.
9. What is the effect of children's reading of good books on their reading skills? Is this question researchable? If not, how would you suggest changing it so that it could be investigated empirically?
10 Classify the following studies as most likely being quantitative or qualitative.
   a. Adolescent Life and Ethos in a U.S. High School
   b. University Professors' Perspectives on Teaching
   c. Gender Differences in Performance on Standardized Mathematics Tests
   d. The Effect of Listening Skills Training on Reading Comprehension of Third-Graders
   e. Attitudes of Voters in Community X toward the Use of Vouchers for School Tuition
11. A principal is interested in knowing if it does any good to keep class sizes small in kindergarten to grade 2. Write an appropriate question for research designed to answer this question.

ANSWERS

1. a. Mathematics intervention program
   b. Gain in mathematical knowledge
   c. Prekindergarten children
2. Answers will vary.
3. Answers will vary.
4. Answers will vary.
5. a. What is the effect of a specific coaching procedure for the SAT versus no coaching on students' performance on the SAT?
   b. How can the academic self-concepts of a group of learning-disabled adolescents be described?

- **c.** How is life for an adolescent with diabetes different than life for other adolescents?
- **d.** What is the relationship of certain specified variables [such as undergraduate GPA (grade point average) or LSAT (Law School Aptitude Test) scores] and grades in the first year of law school?
- **e.** What is the effect of teaching method *X* compared to an alternative method on the learning of mathematical concepts among first-graders?
- **f.** What is the relationship between gender and mathematical reasoning in talented preadolescents?
- **g.** How do high school principals reach decisions about expelling students?

6. a. This question involves a value judgment that is impossible to investigate empirically.
- **b.** This question is trivial, and answering it would make little contribution to knowledge.
- **c.** Research cannot answer questions of value; it can only provide information on which decisions can be based.
- **d.** Although the question could be researched, it is local in scope. Generalization to other situations would be problematic.
- **e.** This question involves a value judgment and as stated cannot be investigated empirically.
- **f.** The question is not researchable because the variables have not been sufficiently defined. What after-school programs and how would one define "doing any good"?

7. a. *Independent*: use or nonuse of multiage classroom; *dependent*: measures of achievement in different areas
- **b.** *Independent*: whole-language and phonics approaches to teaching reading; *dependent*: measures of reading comprehension
- **c.** *Independent*: certain specified variables such as intelligence, age, education, and socioeconomic background; *dependent*: racial prejudice
- **d.** *Independent*: having taken Latin or not; *dependent*: students' SAT verbal scores

8. Educators' everyday experience, deductions from theory, related literature, and noneducation sources

9. The terms *good books* and *reading skills* need to be defined. Restate as "What is the effect of children's reading of four designated classics on their vocabulary growth?"

10. a. Qualitative
- **b.** Qualitative
- **c.** Quantitative
- **d.** Quantitative
- **e.** Quantitative

11. What is the effect of a reduction in class size on the achievement, attitudes toward school, and self-esteem of children in kindergarten through second grade?

INFOTRAC COLLEGE EDITION

Use the keywords *math achievement* + *research* to locate a journal article reporting research on factors that influence math achievement.

Chapter 4

Reviewing the Literature

IF I HAVE SEEN FURTHER IT IS BY STANDING ON THE SHOULDERS OF GIANTS.
SIR ISAAC NEWTON (1642–1727)

INSTRUCTIONAL OBJECTIVES

After studying this chapter, the student will be able to:

1. Discuss the main functions that the review of the literature serves in research.
2. Differentiate among major reference sources in education.
3. Describe ERIC and other education-related indexes, explaining their similarities and differences.
4. Explain how to use *SSCI* (*Social Sciences Citation Index*) in a review of the literature.
5. Describe how to use the Buros Institute of Mental Measurements website as a source of information on tests and measuring devices.
6. Detail a systematic progression of steps in organizing the literature, explaining the purpose of each step.
7. Understand the criteria to use in judging the merit of information on the World Wide Web.
8. Use Boolean operators to execute a search for research articles in ERIC or another online index.

Once having defined a problem, the investigator is naturally eager for action. However, it is a mistake to rush headlong into planning and carrying out research in an area of interest. The topic must first be related to relevant knowledge in the field. It is important for educators and others engaged in research to know how to locate, organize, and use the literature in their field. This chapter discusses (1) the role of related literature in a research project, (2) reference sources in education, and (3) the task of organizing the related literature for presentation in the report.

This chapter was revised and written with the assistance of Daniel L. McCollum, Ph.D., School of Education, University of Houston—Clear Lake.

THE ROLE OF RELATED LITERATURE IN A RESEARCH PROJECT

In quantitative research, the search for related literature should be completed before the actual conduct of the study begins, because the purpose of the literature review is to provide a context and background that support the conduct of the study. In qualitative research a literature search is also necessary but may not occur to the same extent before the study begins, as it does in quantitative research. The literature search in a qualitative study may occur during any phase of the research project. For example, the qualitative researcher may collect data or observe phenomena in order to develop a question or perspective that may then lead to a literature review. In the qualitative study, the literature review may be presented at the end of the study, when the past literature is evaluated against the results of the current research. However, the researcher must always review the literature. This literature review stage serves several important functions:

1. *A knowledge of related research enables investigators to define the frontiers of their field.* To use an analogy, an explorer might say, "We know that beyond this river there are plains for 2000 miles west, and beyond those plains a range of mountains, but we do not know what lies beyond the mountains. I propose to cross the plains, go over the mountains, and proceed from there in a westerly direction." Likewise, the researcher in a sense says, "The work of A, B, and C has discovered this much about my question; the investigations of D have added this much to our knowledge. I propose to go beyond D's work in the following manner."
2. *A thorough review of related theory and research enables researchers to place their questions in perspective.* You should determine whether your endeavors are likely to add to knowledge in a meaningful way. Knowledge in any given area consists of the accumulated outcomes of numerous studies that generations of researchers have conducted and of the theories designed to integrate this knowledge and to explain the observed phenomena. You should review the literature to find links between your study and the accumulated knowledge in your field of interest. Studies with no link to the existing knowledge seldom make significant contributions to the field. Such studies tend to produce isolated bits of information that are of limited usefulness.
3. *Reviewing related literature helps researchers to limit their research question and to clarify and define the concepts of the study.* A research question may be too broad to be carried out or too vague to be put into concrete operation; for example, "What do parenting practices have to do with mental health?" A careful review of the literature can help researchers revise their initial questions so that the final questions can be investigated. The literature review also helps in clarifying the constructs involved in the study and in translating these constructs into operational definitions. Many educational and behavioral constructs—such as stress, creativity, frustration, aggression, achievement, motivation, and adjustment—need to be clarified

and operationally defined. These, as well as many other educational and behavioral constructs, do not lend themselves to scientific research until they can be quantified. In reviewing literature, you become familiar with previous efforts to clarify these constructs and to define them operationally. Successful reviews often result in the formation of hypotheses regarding the relationships among variables in a study. These hypotheses can provide direction and focus for the study.

4. *A critical review of related literature often leads to insight into the reasons for contradictory results in an area.* Contradictory results are not uncommon. You may find the causes of inconsistencies in the kinds of approaches adopted for solving the problem or in the kinds of instruments employed, methodologies used, or analyses made. Comparing the procedures of these studies may explain the inconsistent findings. To resolve such contradictions is a challenge, but it can also provide a significant contribution to the knowledge in your field of interest.

   For example, in researching previous studies on goal orientations (motivation) Elliot and Church (1997) found some literature to support the claim that mastery-approach goal-oriented students (e.g., students whose achievement is primarily due to the intrinsic value of learning) outperform performance-approach goal-oriented students (e.g., students whose achievement is primarily due to seeking a good grade). This frequently led to the conclusion that mastery learning was good and performance orientations were bad. Yet, other literature suggested that both of the goal orientations (mastery and performance) could lead to high achievement. They believed that adding another dimension to the mastery-performance dichotomy would clear up this conflicting evidence. They hypothesized a third goal orientation called performance avoidance (students whose achievement is primarily based on avoiding a poor grade). They designed a study to test the hypothesis that there were three goal orientations, rather than two. They further hypothesized that mastery-approach and performance-approach orientations would both perform well academically, while the performance-avoidance-oriented students would perform more poorly on academic indicators. Using factor analytic techniques (see Chapter 18), Elliot and Church (1997) first supported the hypothesis of the existence of three separate goal orientations. Then, using correlations, they also supported the hypothesis concerning the academic achievement of performance-avoidance students. The addition of this new dimension of motivational goal orientations made clear that mastery- and performance-approach-oriented students tend to do well in school, while those who are trying to avoid failure (performance avoidance) tend to be the students having academic difficulties.

5. *Through studying related research, investigators learn which methodologies have proven useful and which seem less promising.* The investigator develops increasing sophistication after digging through the layers of research that the related literature represents. As you delve into your topic, you soon see that the quality of research varies greatly. Eventually, you should begin to notice that not all studies in any one field are necessarily

equal. You will soon be critiquing studies and noticing ways in which they could be improved. For example, early studies in any one particular field may seem crude and ineffective because research methodology and design are constantly being refined with each new study. Even so, many research projects fail because they use inappropriate procedures, instruments, research designs, or statistical analyses. Becoming proficient at evaluating research to determine its worth helps the investigator discover the most useful research path.

6. *A thorough search through related research avoids unintentional replication of previous studies.* Frequently a researcher develops a worthwhile idea only to discover that a very similar study has already been made. In such a case the researcher must decide whether deliberately to replicate the previous work or to change the proposed plans and investigate a different aspect of the problem.
7. *The study of related literature places researchers in a better position to interpret the significance of their own results.* Becoming familiar with theory in the field and with previous research prepares researchers for fitting the findings of their research into the body of knowledge in the field.

REFERENCE SOURCES IN EDUCATION

It is clearly essential for scholars and researchers to know how to find previous work in their areas. To do this, you should know (1) sources for finding previous work, (2) what agencies collect and organize such information, (3) what forms the resulting databases take, and (4) efficient ways of finding the information you need. To use these sources, you must become familiar with available library facilities and services. Typically academic and larger public libraries have online or printed guides describing their services and regulations and can schedule orientation tours. It is especially important to learn how your library catalog, whether a card or an online catalog, is organized. Most research libraries have converted the traditional card catalog to an online catalog. Most libraries offer instruction in using various library resources, either in a formal class or in a one-on-one meeting with a librarian. Also, you should find out the library's policies and procedures for obtaining books and other materials, such as dissertations and periodical articles, from other institutions through interlibrary loan. Although most academic, public, and school libraries do have some method to obtain materials from other libraries, you will find that libraries vary on which materials may be ordered, who may order them, and whether a charge is involved. Full-text articles (i.e., entire articles) are frequently available through many university libraries' websites and online databases. Therefore, photocopying journal articles, printing from microfilm or microfiche, and using interlibrary loan may not be necessary. Check your library for online access to full-text articles.

BASIC GUIDES

To begin a search of research studies, it is useful to consult basic guides to the research literature to gain a sense of the breadth of resources available. This is particularly true if you are engaged in research that may pull in the literature of more than one field or school, such as psychology, sociology, and women's studies. A very concise and useful guide, *A Bibliographic Guide to Educational Research* (Berry, 1990), is intended to assist students to make effective use of the resources of their college or university library. It provides an annotated listing of more than 700 major research sources arranged by types of materials, such as periodicals, research studies, government publications, reference materials, and tests. The reference materials include yearbooks, directories, bibliographical sources, and handbooks on the methodology of educational research and on form and style for writing research papers. O'Brien and Fabiano's *Core List of Books and Journals in Education* (1991) helps readers find authoritative information about education in the traditional formats of monographs and journals. Arranged by topic, it selects, describes, and in many cases evaluates sources for educational research. Though currently out of print, Balay, Carrington, and Martin's *Guide to Reference Books* (1996) briefly describes and evaluates several thousand reference sources from various subject fields, including education. This work can be ordered from the publisher. Dillon and Hysell's (2004) *American Reference Books Annual* (*ARBA*), published since 1970, covers the reference book output (including reprints) of the previous year in all subjects and provides descriptive and evaluative notes.

REVIEWS OF EDUCATION-RELATED LITERATURE

Reviews that integrate and summarize research studies on specific topics can help get you started on a literature search. They serve as very densely cited overviews of selected subjects in depth and can provide an excellent way to extend your search by locating the sources the authors used to prepare their entries. There are several basic reviews that you can consult.

The American Educational Research Association's *Encyclopedia of Educational Research* (2001), designed to present "a critical synthesis and interpretation of reported educational research," contains signed articles with bibliographies providing well-documented discussions of recent trends and developments, as well as traditional topics. This four-volume encyclopedia includes approximately 200 topics. It is a good basic source for preliminary overviews of research in various areas.

Walberg and Haertel's *International Encyclopedia of Educational Evaluation* (1990) has become one of the definitive works in the field of educational evaluation. The volume is divided into eight broad sections that cover evaluation studies, curriculum evaluation, measurement theory, measurement applications, types of tests and examinations, research methodology, and educational policy and planning. This is an essential work in locating scholarly discussions on fundamental concepts in all areas of educational evaluation.

Dejnozka and Kapel's *American Educators' Encyclopedia* (1991) consists of about 2000 short entries for names and terms frequently found in the literature of professional education. Husen and Postlethwaite's *International Encyclopedia of Education: Research and Studies* (1994) presents "an up-to-date overview of scholarship brought to bear on educational problems, practices, and institutions all over the world" (p. xi). It covers scholarly and professional work in education in the broad sense, surveying current developments in the various branches of education, the availability of scientifically sound and valid information relating to these developments, and the types of further research needed.

An impressive anthology dealing with international higher education, Altbach's *International Higher Education: An Encyclopedia* (1991) consists of 67 essays about major issues, themes, nations, and regions. Another similar source, Clark and Neave's *Encyclopedia of Higher Education* (1992), contains more than 300 articles and essays contributed by scholars from many countries and attempts "a far-reaching, extensive integration" of "the current international knowledge about higher education" (p. xxv).

The influential *International Encyclopedia of Education* and the *Encyclopedia of Higher Education* have been made available together on a CD-ROM the publishers have titled *Education: The Complete Encyclopedia*. The CD version is searchable across both titles, searching both works by subject, title, theme, contributor name, and authors cited within encyclopedia entries. It can be searched full text as well. An added feature that researchers may find useful is the linkage of references to full-text ERIC documents, where they are available.

Another useful review source is the *Handbook of Research on Teaching* (Gage, 1963; Travers, 1973; Wittrock, 1985; Richardson, 2001). Four different editions, published about 10 years apart, list, summarize, and critically analyze research in the field of teaching. Each edition contains authoritative articles by specialists on selected topics in the field. The fourth edition is comprised of 51 chapters from 81 authors, all of whom are experts in their respective fields. Comprehensive bibliographies are included, by selected topics. Among the topics in the fourth edition are: policies for licensing and assessment of teachers, special education, middle school teaching, teaching as a moral activity, and the teaching of physical education. A work similar in scope and authority, the *Handbook of Research on Educational Psychology* (Berliner & Calfee, 1996), is an influential one-volume work summarizing the theory, methods, practice, and research in educational psychology.

Reynolds and Fletcher-Janzen's new *Encyclopedia of Special Education* (second edition, 2000) provides basic information for many disciplines and professions concerned with the education of exceptional children and with their special characteristics, needs, and problems. This three-volume encyclopedia contains more than 2000 topics. The second edition is arranged alphabetically, the various subjects grouped conceptually into 7 major areas: biographies, educational and psychological tests, interventions and service delivery, handicapping conditions, related services, legal issues, and miscellaneous. Current handbooks similar in scope include the *Handbook of Research on Multicultural Education*, second edition (Banks & McGee-Banks, 2003) and the *Handbook of Research on Educational Administration* (Murphy & Louis, 1999). The former consists of 47 chapters critically discussing major theory and research in the relatively new area of multicultural education. The authors discuss history, issues involved, and research problems in such areas as education of ethnic groups, immigration, and academic achievement. In the latter book, sponsored by the American Educational Research Association, eminent scholars discuss, in a cross-disciplinary approach, the last decade of research in the field of leadership and administration. Keogh's *Advances in Special Education*, published annually since 1980, presents comprehensive examinations of major fields and brief, more restricted evaluations of special areas in special education.

The *Review of Educational Research*, a quarterly publication of the American Educational Research Association (AERA) since 1931, reviews and integrates education research literature on both substantive and methodological issues. Seeking to provide summaries of research within broad subject areas in the profession, AERA launched the series *Review of Research in Education*, published annually since 1973. This series aims to identify what research has been done, is being done, and needs to be done in the field. For instance, Volume 27 (2003) is organized around the central theme: policy tools for improving education. Articles focus on the "standards-based" approach to education, which deals with setting standards and the use of assessments, including the professional development of school personnel and of technology. The *Annual Review of Psychology*, published since 1950, employs subject specialists to report on and evaluate research literature, identify trends and new developments in all aspects of psychology for each year, and indicate neglected areas. The now standard *Encyclopedia of Psychology* (Corsini, 2000), a four-volume set, contains 2500 entries, including biographies, and examines 10 areas of psychology, including cognitive, developmental, and educational psychology. Its 500 expert contributors, 350-page bibliography, and extensive indexing make it a valuable source for researchers.

PERIODICAL INDEXES AND ABSTRACTING SOURCES

Having established a broad base of relevant research, theory, and opinion on a particular topic of interest, you can begin to locate additional material not cited in the encyclopedic review sources just discussed, moving instead to the primary literature. You can efficiently access primary literature through **periodical indexes** and **abstracting sources**. These index and abstract sources enable you to locate more specific and usually more recently published literature on your topic of interest. Issued in successive parts at regular intervals, they serve as guides for finding information that is widely dispersed in journals and other sources. The publishers of these periodicals employ professional reviewers who survey and classify papers in published and unpublished sources. These papers are assigned several subject headings, from the thesaurus of descriptors used by the publishing agency, presenting researchers with a fairly comprehensive, reasonably up-to-date, and easily searched listing of work in their areas. The abstracting periodicals publish abstracts of the works they include, also including descriptors that allow for searching of the collections.

History of the ERIC Database

The U.S. Department of Education (USDE) established the Educational Resources Information Center (ERIC) in 1966 to collect, store, and disseminate information on education. Before the ERIC system was established, reports submitted to the Department of Education by its contractors and grantees received an initial scattered distribution and then disappeared, as did reports from other sources. Such materials, as reports from nongovernmental organizations, documents emanating from a school district, or papers presented at professional conferences, are examples of literature that tended to disappear. Not published in books or journals, they were thus infrequently indexed. ERIC was intended to correct this chaotic situation, to collect and preserve unpublished so-called fugitive material of interest to educators, and to make this store of information available to the public.

The **ERIC system**—funded by the National Library of Education and the U.S. Department of Education's Office of Educational Research and Improvement (OERI)—gathered, indexed, and abstracted information for inclusion in the ERIC system through a central processing facility and a network of 16 subject-oriented clearinghouses and 12 adjunct clearinghouses located at various universities and professional organizations across the country. Each clearinghouse was responsible for a specific educational area.

When ERIC began, the ERIC abstracts were made available as paper periodicals, similar to the paper versions of, for example, *Reader's Guide to Periodical Literature*, in two sets, the *Current Index to Journals in Education* (*CIJE*) index, which indexed articles in education-related journals, and the *Resources in Education* (*RIE*) index, which indexed fugitive documents. Articles from more than 800 journals were classified and indexed.

Current ERIC Database

As a result of the Educational Sciences Reform Act of 2002, enacted by the U.S. Congress in part to restructure the U.S. Department of Education, on December 19, 2003, the U.S. Department of Education shut down the ERIC clearinghouse. The CIJE and RIE indexes were no longer. A private contractor, Computer Sciences Corporation (CSC), created and maintains a new ERIC system. A new website was created to search the ERIC database and links to purchase full-text documents became available. The new ERIC is available at http://www.eric.ed.gov. Search terms can be entered into the search engine directly on the new ERIC website. In addition, a thesaurus of search terms is also available on the website.

A new search field is included in the database that allows the searcher to evaluate the quality of the materials (e.g., the peer review status of the journal). Submissions to ERIC are now evaluated on four criteria:

1. Relevance of the submission to education
2. Quality of the submission (completeness, integrity, objectivity, substantive merit, utility/importance)
3. Sponsorship by professional societies, organizations, and government agencies
4. Editorial and peer review criteria

A committee advises CSC on technical recommendations for the new ERIC. Content experts advise CSC on what materials to include in ERIC and implement the system for evaluating submissions to ERIC. The indexing of ERIC is now the responsibility of the Research Triangle Institute, and a CSC subcontractor called Nstein maintains the ERIC search engine. The new ERIC database was fully updated with materials that were created and accepted while the ERIC system was shut down (December 19, 2003, through the end of 2004). With the new system up and running over 107,000 ERIC documents issued from 1993 through July 2004 became available at no cost.

As a general rule, the following steps are components of a successful ERIC search.

1. Determine the keywords under which articles relevant to your study might be listed. These keywords will typically include the population and the variables you have identified in your problem statement.
2. Check the *ERIC Thesaurus* to find which of your keywords are used as descriptors. You may need to find synonyms for the keywords you have listed.
3. Perform the search and copy or print out the entire reference given for any title that may be useful. This procedure simplifies the task of finding the original articles.
4. Search out the articles in their journals at your own institution or through interlibrary loan, or ask a librarian about the possibility of obtaining the articles on-line, either through your library or through other commercial sources.
5. Read the abstract first—if one accompanies the journal article—to determine whether it will be useful to read the entire article. If there is no abstract, start with the summary and conclusion sections.

A search of the ERIC system is an important step in the quest for related literature, but the researcher cannot assume that when this step is finished the quest is completed. Material relevant to your question may not have been included in the ERIC indexes.

Education Abstracts Full Text

Education Abstracts Full Text contains abstracting and indexing coverage for over 475 periodicals included in *Education Index*, as well as the full text of over 150 periodicals. The journals indexed in Education Abstracts Full Text are primarily related to education and psychology. The database is maintained and available through the H.W. Wilson Company (Available: http://hwwilsonweb.com).

ProQuest Research Library

The ProQuest Research Library is a database that covers arts, business, education, health, psychology, social sciences, women's interests, and other areas of scholarly pursuit. The database provides abstracts of material from 2300 journals and offers full text from 1400 journals. Available through many university libraries, ProQuest information can be found at http://www.il.proquest.com/proquest/.

ADDITIONAL DATABASES WITH EDUCATION LITERATURE

Academic Search Premier

Academic Search Premier is a database that provides full-text articles of 4700 peer-reviewed scholarly publications and indexes 8172 peer-reviewed publications. The publications available through Academic Search Premier cover academic areas such as the social sciences, education, the humanities, language and linguistics, computer sciences, arts and literature, and engineering. The database is maintained and made available through EBSCO information services (Available: http://www.epnet.com/academic/acasearchprem.asp).

Professional Development Collection

The Professional Development Collection is maintained by EBSCO information services (Available: http://www.ebsco.com/home). This database provides a collection of 550 full-text journals, including more than 350 peer-reviewed titles. In addition, indexing and abstracts for nearly 900 journals is provided. The titles maintained in the database are primarily related to topics in education.

PsycINFO and PsycArticles

PsycINFO is a database with nearly 2,000,000 records covering 2000 journals, in addition to books and book chapters. The material covered in this database is related to psychology, education, business, economics, linguistics, social work, health care, and many other fields. PsycArticles is a subset of PsycINFO that offers full text for some of the journals referenced through PsycINFO. Information about these databases is available at http://www.psycinfo.com/. In addition, many university libraries subscribe to the PsycINFO service.

InfoTrac College Edition

Supplied by the Gale Group of the Thomson Learning company, InfoTrac College Edition is an online resource for finding educationally relevant literature. The InfoTrac College Edition database provides 15 million full-text articles from more than 5000 periodicals. InfoTrac College Edition is available through Thomson at www.infotrac-college.com.

Web of Science

Created by Thomson Learning, Web of Science is an additional web resource to find literature related to the sciences and the social sciences, as well as education. Information on Web of Science is available at http://www.isinet.com/products/citation/wos/.

Google Scholar

Available at http://scholar.google.com/ as of November 2004, Google Scholar is an online search engine that targets scholarly materials, such as peer-reviewed publications, book chapters, and conference proceedings. Search results in Google Scholar are ordered by relevance, so when a search is conducted, those links listed first should be most relevant to your search. The relevance ranking is determined by the text in the article, the article's author, the publication, and the frequency of the citation of the article in the scholarly literature.

Table 4.1 is a summary of various databases with their respective web addresses.

Table 4.1 Summary of Education Databases

Source	Information Available At
ERIC	http://www.eric.ed.gov/
Education Abstracts Full Text	http://hwwilsonweb.com
ProQuest Research Library	http://www.il.proquest.com/proquest
Academic Search Premier	http://www.epnet.com/academic/acasearchprem.asp
Professional Development Collection	http://www.ebsco.com/home
PsycINFO and PsycArticles	http://www.psycinfo.com/
InfoTrac College Edition	http://www.infotrac-college.com
Web of Science	http://www.isinet.com/products/citation/wos
Google Scholar	http://scholar.google.com

INDEXES OF DISSERTATIONS AND THESES

Master's theses and doctoral dissertations are very useful sources of information for researchers. They provide extensive bibliographies of possible sources, possible study procedures, instruments, or hypotheses that may serve as examples to either emulate or avoid. In addition to the periodical indexes and abstract journals that list some dissertations and theses, such as ERIC and *Psychological Abstracts*, several specialized guides and **indexes of dissertations and theses** can be very useful. *Dissertation Abstracts International* (*DAI*), published monthly since 1938, contains abstracts of more than one million doctoral dissertations submitted to University Microfilms International by cooperating universities (about 795 in 1999), going back to 1861. *DAI* is divided into three sections: humanities and social sciences, the sciences and engineering, and European universities. Electronic searches of *DAI* are available through several major online database vendors. A similar publication is *American Doctoral Dissertations*. Published annually, it consolidates into one list the dissertations for which doctoral degrees were granted in the United States during the academic year covered, as well as those available on microfilm from University Microfilms. It includes a number of dissertations that are not included in *DAI*. *American Doctoral Dissertations* is arranged by subject and institution and has an author index, but no abstracts are provided. *Masters Abstracts International* (1986–) contains abstracts on microfilm of a selected list of master's theses from various U.S. universities and colleges. For a listing of master's theses from U.S. colleges and universities specific to the field of education, a good source is Silvey's *Master's Theses Directories*, which list theses written in participating U.S. and Canadian institutions in the previous year. Issued annually, it does not include abstracts but does provide bibliographical information for each thesis listed.

CITATION INDEXES

Having access to the *Social Science Citation Index* (*SSCI*) (published since 1973), the *Science Citation Index* (*SCI*) (published since 1955), and the *Arts and Humanities Citation Index* (*A&HCI*) (published since 1976) is somewhat akin to having access to a time machine, except you can only go forward in time from the past to the present. If you have read a particularly useful article, published in 1996, through subsequent indexes you can identify more recent articles that cite this article and list it in their references. The Institute for Scientific Information (ISI) published SSCI, SCI, and A&HCI quarterly, yearly, and in 5-year compilations, using the same format for each. ISI subscribes to all the important journals and somewhat important journals in each of its three general areas. For example, SSCI presently receives over 2,000 journals to produce its annual serial. We will use SSCI in our description because most education literature is referenced in that index.

Social Sciences Citation Index (*SSCI*), published in three volumes a year, identifies which authors have been cited during the year in all areas of social science, including education, and what has been written in various areas. It also includes the necessary bibliographic information for both cited and citing authors. This information is made available by way of four indexes:

1. The *Source Index* is an alphabetical list of all authors published in the journals covered by *SSCI* during the year. Complete bibliographic information is provided for the articles published by these authors, followed by an alphabetical list of the first authors of each of the sources cited in each article. The *Source Index* is cross-referenced to secondary authors.

   Some authors will have several articles in the same year. If you are interested in the work of a particular author, the *Source Index* is the place to go.
2. The *Citation Index* presents an alphabetic list of the first authors of all works cited in the articles included in the *Source Index*, followed by the year, journal, volume, and first page for each of that author's cited articles. For each article, the *Citation Index* lists the names of other authors who cited that article, followed by the journal, volume, first page, and year of the article in which the citation occurred. Thus the *Citation Index* lets you follow the work of a particular author forward in time. For example, Huessy and Cohen's 1976 article, "Hyperkinetic Behaviors and Learning Disabilities Followed over Seven Years," an early longitudinal study, found a significant positive relationship between hyperactivity and learning disabilities. Its citation pattern illustrates both a common trend and the article's influence. It was cited frequently (eight times) in 1979 and 1980, with one or two citations a year after that. However, in the 1985 *SSCI*, we find this article was cited most frequently—nine times—in 1984–1985, nine years after its publication. This dramatic increase in citation apparently corresponded with increasing interest in and research examining the phenomenon of hyperkinetic behaviors. The article has been cited once or twice a year since 1985. Figure 4.1 shows the 1985 *SSCI* citation index entry for author H. R. Huessy (only the first author is included in *SSCI*). One of the article's most recent citations is in "Arithmetic Disabilities and ADD Subtypes" (Marshall, Schafer, & O'Donnell) in the May 1999 issue of *Journal of Learning Disabilities*. They found that hyperactive children who also had attention-deficit disorder (ADD) did less well on calculation and letter–word identification tests than did hyperactive children without ADD. Most articles are most

First author — **HUESSY HR**

Work being cited with year, journal, volume, and page — **76 PEDIATRICS 57 4**

Citing authors with journal, volume, page, and year — GUALTIER CT … WALLANDE.JL (under 76 PEDIATRICS 57 4)

Entry	Journal		Vol.	Page	Year
HUESSY HR					
****UNPUB ATTENTION DEFI**					
BLOOMING.LM	PSYCHIAT J		9	175	84
66 MENTAL HLTH LIMITED					
WELLS MH	PSYCH CL N		8	597	85
67 ACTA PAEDOPSYCHIATR 34 130					
BERRY CA	PEDIATRICS		76	801	85
HOLBOROW PL	J LEARN DI		17	411	84
SATIN MS	J AM A CHIL		24	756	85
WALLANDE JL	ADV CL CH P	R	8	113	85
69 J AM MED ASSOC 208 1613					
GOODMAN WK	J CLIN PSY	R	46	6	85
70 ACTA PAEDOPSYCHIATR 37 194					
RANCUREL MD	PSYCHIAT AN		15	88	85
70 ACTA PAEDOPSYCHIATR 37 243					
HOLBOROW PL	J LEARN DI		17	411	84
SHEKIM WO	J AM A CHIL		24	765	85
72 PROGR COMMUNITY MENT 206					
POOLE DL	SOCIAL WORK		30	338	85
73 DRUG THERAPY SEP 52					
EICHLSED W	PEDIATRICS		76	176	85
74 ACTA PAEDOPSYCHIATRY 40 230					
GUALTIER CT	CLIN NEUROP		8	343	85
76 PEDIATRICS 57 4					
GUALTIER CT	CLIN NEUROP		8	343	85
HOWELL DC	PEDIATRICS		76	185	85
HUESSY HR	PSYCHIAT J		10	114	85
LERNER JA	J AM A CHIL		24	42	85
WALLANDE.JL	ADV CL CH P	R	8	113	85
79 CLIN EXPLORATIONS AD 19					
GUALTIER CT	CLIN NEUROP		8	343	85
79 PSYCHIATRIC ASPECTS					
BROWN RT	PSYCHOPH B		21	192	85
HOWELL DC	PEDIATRICS		76	185	85
80 THERAPEUTIC COMMUNIT					
WELLS MH	PSYCH CL N		8	597	85
81 HOSP COMMUN PSYCHIAT 32 351					
REATIG N	PSYCHOPH B	R	21	329	85
84 ATTENTION DEFICIT DI 1					
BLOOMING LM	PSYCHIAT J		9	175	84
84 PSYCHIAT J U OTTAWA 9 56					
REATIG N	PSYCHOPH B	R	21	329	85
85 J THER COMMUNITIES					
WELLS MH	PSYCH CL N		8	597	85

Figure 4.1 *SSCI* Citation Entry (from 1985)

heavily cited in the first couple of years after publication, becoming less frequently cited as time goes by.

3. The *Permuterm Subject Index* takes every significant word and pairs it with every other significant word in each title. Each word in a title is then listed as a primary term combined with each of the other terms as co-terms. An alphabetical listing of the names of authors whose titles contain the words is provided for each paired primary term and co-term. You can then find bibliographic information for each author in the *Source Index*.
4. Bound in with the *Permuterm Subject Index*, the *Corporate Address Index* is an alphabetical listing of organizations with which authors publishing dur-

ing the year are affiliated. Under each corporate entry is a list of authors with complete bibliographic information.

5. *Social Sciences Citation Index* (*SSCI*) is available in both paper and online formats. Neither is entirely efficient for the researcher. The conventional paper version is cumbersome and difficult to search, and the online or CD-ROM versions are expensive enough that relatively few academic libraries provide access to them. (That is the classic problem of using online information sources; you get what you—or your library—pays for!)

GOVERNMENT PUBLICATIONS

The federal government, a major source of education information, sponsors more research, conducts more surveys, and collects more statistics of all kinds than any other organization in the United States. The U.S. Department of Education (USDE) disseminates a vast number of publications, including research reports, surveys, administrative actions, and program descriptions.

For locating specific U.S. government publications, the U.S. Superintendent of Documents's *Monthly Catalog of U.S. Government Publications* (or its online counterpart *GPO Monthly Catalog*, published by the U.S. Government Printing Office, or GPO) is the prime index to consult. Its main section lists documents published by each agency, and it also includes title, author, subject, and title–keyword indexes. Annual compilations by title and subject were included in each December issue until 1975; since 1976 there are 6-month compilations. There are also 5-year cumulative indexes for faster searching back through the years. The online GPO catalog has become very prevalent in academic libraries because it is easy to search. It goes back to 1976.

You can locate publications of state departments of education and other state agencies through the home pages of each state's department of education. As is true of nearly all indexes useful to scholars, most government indexes are now available on the World Wide Web or on CD-ROM. The gateways for government information and publications on education are the U.S. Department of Education website at http://www.ed.gov, and the National Center for Educational Statistics at http://nces.ed.gov. From these sites, you can find links to reports on current research, policy papers, and the searchable text of past and current popular paper resources, such as the *Digest of Education Statistics*, *Projections of Education Statistics*, and the *Condition of Education*. The purpose of the *Digest* is to provide a compilation of statistical information covering the broad field of American education from kindergarten through graduate school. The 1998 *Digest* includes 428 tables from many different data sources. *Projections of Education Statistics to 2009* provides projections for key education statistics. It includes statistics on enrollment, graduates, classroom teachers, and expenditures in elementary and secondary schools, and institutions of higher education. The tables, figures, and text contain data on enrollment, teachers, graduates, and expenditures for the past 14 years and projections to the year 2009. The *Condition of Education* describes the current status and recent progress of education in the United States. The 1999 compendium features an overview essay and 60 indicators in five major substantive areas of education.

TEST SOURCES

A test or measuring device is often required for conducting research, but few researchers have such extensive knowledge of the tests and instruments available to them that they can choose one without consulting expert **test sources**. *Mental Measurements Yearbooks* (*MMY*) (e.g., Plake, Impara, & Spies, 2002) are important reference sources that list tests and provide critical reviews of some length. Published since 1938, these books are specifically designed to help professionals in education, psychology, and industry use standardized tests more intelligently. Each yearbook is arranged in the same pattern and is meant to supplement rather than supersede the earlier volumes. Tests are grouped by subject, and descriptions of each test are followed by critical reviews and references to studies in which the tests have been used. Each volume has cross references to reviews, excerpts, and bibliographic references in earlier volumes. The volumes include aptitude and achievement tests in various subject areas, personality and vocational tests, and intelligence tests. Complete information is provided for each test, including cost and ordering information. *Tests in Print VI* (Murphy, Plake, Impara, & Spies, 2002) serves as an index and supplement to the first 14 *Mental Measurements Yearbooks*. Future editions of *Tests in Print* will appear only through the World Wide Web via The Buros Institute of Mental Measurements (Available: http://www.unl.edu/buros/index.html). The website offers a searchable database of tests and test reviews, which can be purchased online.

Maddox's *Tests: A Comprehensive Reference for Assessments in Psychology, Education and Business* (2003), along with its supplements, is a standard reference work that includes more than 3000 tests available in English. Each test has been given a primary classification and is described in detail in one of the sections and may be cross-referenced in a second category.

Since 1984, Keyser and Sweetland's *Test Critiques* has provided general descriptions and critiques of measurement instruments and also has included a useful cumulative subject index of tests by type of variables. Specialized guides to tests include Compton's *Guide to 75 Diagnostic Tests for Special Education* (1984), Ostrow's *Directory of Psychological Tests in the Sport and Exercise Sciences* (1996), *Tests in Microfiche: Annotated Index* (1975–1994), and the *Educational Testing Service Test Collection Catalog* (1986–1993).

Information about tests may also be found in periodical indexes, ERIC, *Education Index*, *Exceptional Child Education Resources* (*ECER*), and *Psychological Abstracts*, where tests are listed under their specific name in the subject index. You can also search under such subject headings as "Tests" and "Test Reviews." A *Consumer's Guide to Tests in Print* (Hammill, 1992) fills a gap in the literature of test criticism in that it is the only source in which all tests covered are reviewed by means of a standardized evaluation form. You can use this book to select an appropriate test, to teach the process of test evaluation, and to improve the quality of tests.

DICTIONARIES

Almost every academic discipline has its own specialized vocabulary. It is the function of a subject dictionary to briefly explain the words—whether terms or names—that make up a particular discipline's jargon. There are several basic

specialized dictionaries in the field of education. Good's *Dictionary of Education* (1973) is a scholarly dictionary of more than 33,000 words and terms that have special meaning in the educational field. Educational terms used in Canada, England, and Wales are defined in separate sections at the end of the dictionary. Although Good's dictionary is dated, it is still considered a classic in the field. A somewhat more recent work, *The International Dictionary of Education* (Page, Thomas, & Marshall, 1980), includes more than 10,000 entries covering expressions and terms, international organizations, major national institutions and associations, educators, and the like.

The first volume of Husen and Postlethwaite's *International Encyclopedia of Higher Education* (1985) also includes brief definitions of acronyms and a glossary of terms. More recent general education dictionaries are *The Cyclopedic Education Dictionary* (Spafford, Pesce, & Groser, 1998), providing over 10,000 definitions, including World Wide Web and legal terminology, and the *Dictionary of Multicultural Education* (Grant & Ladson-Billings, 1997), which provides more in-depth coverage of 150 terms and contextual examples. In the area of special education, the *Special Education Dictionary* (Gorn, 1997) is a high-quality, short-entry comprehensive work.

STATISTICAL SOURCES

For educational statistics, the federal government, followed by states and local governments, accounts for the greatest number of statistical documents. *Statistics Sources* (Wasserman-O'Brien, 2001), a basic **statistical sources** reference work, is an alphabetic guide to sources of information on over 20,000 subjects, with 10,000 citations from over 2000 sources, print and nonprint, in print and out of print, and domestic and international. It is a subject guide to data on various topics, including education, for the United States and other nations. The 2000 edition of this work also includes listings of the Federal Statistical Databases and Federal Statistical Telephone contacts. Several other commonly known reference works—such as *World Almanac and Book of Facts*, *Information Please Almanac*, and *Statistical Abstract of the United States*—contain statistics from educational fields and other subjects. In general, the data are reliable and sources for many of the statistics are also given.

Three indexes to statistics published by the Washington-based Congressional Information Service are the *American Statistics Index* (*ASI*), *Statistical Reference Index* (*SRI*), and *Index to International Statistics* (*IIS*). The *ASI* indexes and abstracts almost every statistical source issued by the federal government, and the *SRI* indexes and abstracts state documents. The latter also includes many nongovernmental statistics, ranging from those issued by private concerns and businesses to nonprofit organizations and associations. The *IIS* includes major governmental statistics from around the world. It is an excellent source of UN statistical data. These three indexes are also available in CD-ROM and online.

Since 1962, the *Digest of Education Statistics* has covered the broad field of American education from kindergarten through graduate school. This publication includes a selection of data from many sources, both government and private, and draws especially on the results of surveys and activities carried out by the National Center for Education Statistics (NCES). As noted previously, the full text of the digest and other important statistical publications are searchable through the NCES website (http://nces.ed.gov).

OTHER PERIODICAL INDEXES

There are many other periodical indexes in the field of education that are useful for locating up-to-date information on research, as well as contemporary opinion. As already mentioned, *Exceptional Child Education Resources* (*ECER*) is a quarterly publication that contains abstracts of resources in special and gifted education. It uses the same thesaurus, indexing, and abstracting rules that ERIC does, and there is considerable overlap in resources indexed by ERIC and ECER.

One of the standard indexes for the field is the *Education Index*, which has been published regularly since 1929. This index lists articles in 478 periodicals, yearbooks, bulletins, proceedings, and monographic series. ERIC does not index 92 of these 478 periodicals. *Education Index* is the best source for locating journal articles published prior to the establishment of ERIC, as well as for very recent articles, as it typically lists articles about 6 months before ERIC does. A disadvantage of the *Education Index* is that it has few annotations. *Education Abstracts*, an electronic version of the *Index*, contains abstracting and indexing coverage for all 478 periodicals included in *Education Index*, as well as 133 additional periodicals.

In addition to these general indexes, a number of useful specialized indexes are available to the researcher. *Psychological Abstracts* lists the world's literature in psychology and related disciplines. Published since 1927 (indexing materials back to the 1890s), this index includes books, doctoral dissertations, and periodical articles, with a summary of each, enabling the reader to determine the relevance of the material. *Child Development Abstracts and Bibliography*, also published since 1927, provides an author and subject approach to the areas of infancy, clinical medicine and public health, counseling, and developmental, comparative, and experimental psychology. *Educational Administration Abstracts* provides an author and subject approach to specialized journals in the field of educational administration. *Higher Education Abstracts* is a compilation of abstracts from journals, conference proceedings, and research reports relating to college students and student services. Topics covered include counseling and housing, financial aid, and testing and measurement.

There are specialized indexes for every discipline, including business education, industrial arts, and medicine, to name only a few. Some are available electronically and some in print format; many are available through both. The availability of either format depends on the library and its users' needs, the quality of the electronic version of the index, cost, and other factors. Consulting the basic guides to the literature or consulting a librarian will give researchers the names of the specialized indexes in other fields that they may need.

USING ELECTRONIC INDEXES AND ABSTRACTS

Nearly all medium and large academic libraries, and most smaller institutions, provide online access to indexes and catalogs. Many offer brief training sessions to teach users how to do their own searches or provide FAQs (lists of frequently asked questions) or training materials on the library's web page. Most of the sources cited in this chapter have been incorporated into online databases, including *Education Index*, the *ERIC Indexes*, *Exceptional Child Education Resources*, *Psychological Abstracts*, *Social Sciences Citation Index*, *Dissertation Abstracts International*, and Plake, Impara, and Spies's *Mental Measurements Yearbooks* (*MMY*). In addition, there are many other useful online databases, such as the *AIDSLINE* database, *Educational Testing Service Test Collection Catalog* (*ETS*), and *Sociological Abstracts*. One extraordinary database that is invaluable to researchers in nearly any field is *WorldCat*, an online database of nearly 32 million books, journals, music scores, video recordings, films, newspapers, maps, dissertations, manuscripts, and more, in 400 languages. The index includes all the holdings of most academic libraries of size, larger public libraries and specialized collections, and the national libraries of France, Great Britain, Canada, and the U.S. Library of Congress, to name a few. Although no abstracts are given, the libraries that hold each item are listed as part of the item records; this can be helpful information for either the researcher or the interlibrary loan staff to use in obtaining an item.

Advantages of Online Searching

A large, complex index such as *WorldCat* would not be possible without online searching and indexing capabilities. No book or multivolume set could ever be that large! In fact, online searching affords several advantages, no matter the size of the index. First of all, it saves time. When there are several synonymous or analogous terms for the concept(s) involved (such as *attention-deficit disorder*, *ADD*, *ADHD*, *hyperactivity*, *attention deficit*), in only seconds the computer can retrieve and print information, thus eliminating hours or even days for a manual search. Second, it is current. Online databases are frequently updated weekly or biweekly and thus are usually more up-to-date than printed indexes. Third, it allows combined searching. When the research topic combines two or more subjects, the database software can search more than one topic at the same time. Fourth, computer searching allows greater precision than human searching. When a subject cannot be easily identified in printed indexes, the computer provides access by searching titles, words in the abstract, journal title, keywords, subject codes, or additional subject headings that print indexes do not offer. Online computer searching can also bypass superfluous information by specifying parameters such as date and type of publication, publication type, or language of publication. A fifth benefit is uniqueness. Some databases provide information that is not available in printed sources. Sorting functions are another important advantage. Online searches can sort retrieved information according to publication date (descending or ascending order), alphabetically by author, or by title.

For most contemporary researchers, using electronic sources is the research method of choice. In a manual search you must examine numerous periodical indexes for a particular topic, follow the topic through the indexes, and find a few relevant entries that combine the selected term with another of interest. Computer searching, however, can search for many topics at the same time and combine them, using logical concepts known as **Boolean logic** (from the logic system developed by the 19th-century English mathematician George Boole). Figure 4.2 illustrates this concept. Using Boolean operators, "A AND B" asks for those items

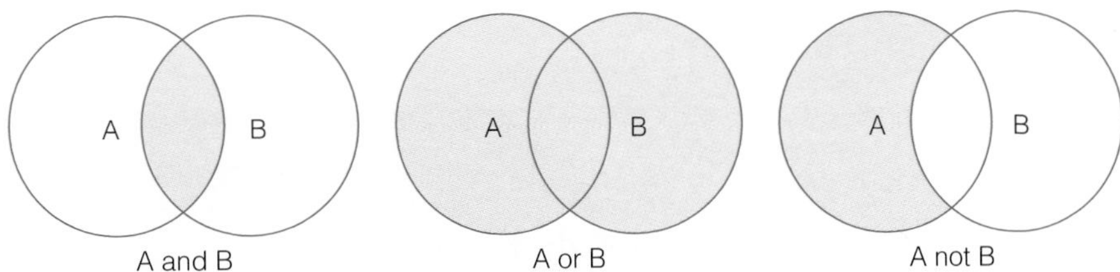

Figure 4.2 Shaded Areas Represent What Is Retrieved by Each Logical Statement

that have both key terms. For example, in August 1999 a search of the ERIC database using the Firstsearch interface found 8407 items with the major descriptor "adult students" and 6219 items with the major descriptor "mathematics education." Twenty-one item records that contain both descriptors were identified. If the researcher requests "A OR B," the computer searches for items that have either or both of the key terms. For example, a request for mathematics education or mathematics achievement would yield items that contain either or both of these terms. A typical search will use both these strategies. For instance, an adult educator interested in mathematics education would use OR statements to include various key terms that might cover the domain of adult education and OR statements to include various items that might cover the domain of mathematics education, together with an AND statement to link the two domains (factors). Another possibility in Boolean searching is using the NOT operator. If the researcher searches "A NOT B," the computer searches for the A term, but excludes anything with the B term. For example, a request for mathematics education NOT calculus will return items that contain the mathematics education term but not those related to calculus.

More important than the mere existence of Boolean searching is the fact that searching online or CD-ROM indexes requires the use of a kind of logic that many students and researchers do not use frequently or really think about elsewhere in their research. It can be difficult to think of terms, possible synonyms for those terms, or how best to construct a search without first gaining experience or seeking the help of an expert, be it a collection of FAQs or a librarian. As well, the searching software used by these sources evolves, so that one mode of searching a database, such as ERIC, may provide a very different way of combining terms than another mode of accessing it, such as using pull-down menus, typing the Boolean operators manually, or using a mapping function to enter the online thesaurus directly. There should always be a librarian or other expert who can help researchers learn to get the most out of any database they may need to use.

THE INTERNET

The statistics on the magnitude of Internet usage are both astonishing and conflicting, ranging from 606 to 785 million users worldwide as of March, 2004, which is approximately 10 percent of the global population (Crumlish, 2004). Nearly 85 percent of incoming freshmen in a 1998 University of California study reported using the Internet for research (Honan, 1999), and in 1996 the American Library Association reported that 87 percent of doctorate-granting university libraries had web pages from which to access resources or get library informa-

PICTURE THIS

The World Wide Web has been a blessing for those seeking related literature.

Joe Rocco

tion (Lynch, 1996). The **Internet**, originally developed in the 1960s by the U.S. Department of Defense and further developed by the science community for use as a communication medium, is a network of networks. Prior to the development of the **World Wide Web**, which uses hyperlinking and graphical interfaces (enabling searchers to click rather than remember the addresses of every site they want to access), few people aside from scientists used the Internet, which was used primarily for file transfer, archiving, and e-mail. Since the web has been available to consumers, the growth in Internet use, and in the variety of uses, both legitimate and suspect, has been unprecedented. As reviewed in this chapter, there are a wide range of Internet sources for scholarly literature and test sources, as well as a magnitude of other types of information. The Internet can help researchers access different databases of various types of materials and subjects around the world.

The strength of the Internet, however, namely its size and comprehensiveness, can work against the beginning researcher and may confound even the most experienced researcher. The old problem of not finding enough information has now been replaced by the equally vexing problem of finding far too much information, and needing to be able to determine the relative quality of the information.

Many new researchers are surprised to find out that search engines such as Yahoo!, Northern Light, or Google do not search for information in the same way a periodical index or online library catalog does—even though the resulting list of "hits" you get searching the former looks very much like the result of a search of the latter. Whereas searching ERIC, for example, usually includes searching by ERIC subject descriptors—created by ERIC and assigned by ERIC to each record—few search engines use what is called a "controlled vocabulary." Instead, the search engine may search the entire document for the term or terms typed in, may search the titles, web addresses, internal metadata tags (labels within html code that identify information on web pages), page headings, or may search them all and employ a kind of weighting system to construct a list of results. According to Danny Sullivan (2000), Internet consultant and editor of *Search Engine Watch* (http://www.searchenginewatch.com), search engines may also check to see if the search term appears near the top of a web document, the frequency of a particular keyword, even the number of sites with links to the page to determine relevancy and assign a weighted score, putting a given web page higher in the list of results the search engine provides. Although you nearly always find *something* when searching the World Wide Web using a search engine, the likelihood that what you find is useful is considerably lower than if an unsuspecting novice researcher were searching an index with a controlled vocabulary.

Also, because there is no real "publication cycle" for Internet materials, there are no editors, fact checkers, proofreaders, and no accurate way for the reader to determine the authority of the author, as there is in traditional publishing. A huge amount of information exists on the Internet, some erroneous, outdated, slanted, and even harmful. The websites of hate groups, Holocaust revisionists, conspiracy theorists, and other biased authors are the more extreme examples, but one can also find such things as a free online *Webster's Dictionary*—copyright 1913!

It is often more difficult to determine the worth of a website than that of a print source because many personal sites look every bit as professional and authoritative as a governmental or educational site. One place to start is to consider the end of the address. Sites ending in .edu or .gov are education or government sites, which tend to have more credibility than sites ending in .com or .org or .net. Many libraries and organizations provide lists of subject-specific websites for researchers. They usually serve as excellent starting points, such as the Illinois State University library's Education Resources page (http://www.mlb.ilstu.edu/ressubj/subject/educat/home.htm). Eventually, however, the researcher will need to branch out.

Evaluating Internet Sources

When you begin to evaluate a source on the Internet, you first need to consider what the Internet is—and what it is not. The Internet is not created equal; that is, even though all the information found on the web appears on the computer desktop, some is provided by authoritative sources, using the technology to serve as the medium for the message, and some is not. The online version of ERIC or *Psychological Abstracts* is free to a student, and the student can access it from home and can download or e-mail portions of the database, but the information comes from an established provider or has been purchased for use by the university library. It is thus a credible, authoritative source, using the Internet as a publication medium. This is one reason why it is important to pay careful attention to the address of the websites used, and their authors and sponsors, because saying "I found it on the Internet" is rather like saying "I read it on a piece of paper." (Was it an authoritative piece of paper?)

You can also find many web pages on education-related topics by using a search engine such as Yahoo!, AltaVista, or Hotbot. You can find a great deal of information on nearly any topic by doing this global kind of search. A January 2005 search for the exact phrase "character education" using the Google search engine results in 690,000 matches. Examination of the first link in the search results finds an online organization dedicated to promoting moral development. The second link in the list of results is a site offering instructional resources for principals, teachers, and other educators. Other findings from the search results include web pages of hundreds of links to other character education sites, lesson plans for teachers, listserv memberships, and even poetry. Truly, an insurmountable amount of information can be found from a single, simple web search. Because the Internet is a means by which a great deal of information of varying quality can be presented—the worthy and suspect side by side—it is important that the researcher has criteria by which to judge Internet sources. Determining the quality of a given nonelectronic journal's articles has traditionally focused on the following criteria:

Reputation of the journal

Stringency of its editorial policies

Reporting of primary research, as opposed to feature articles synthesizing or summarizing bodies of research for the lay audience

Use of blind reviews

Reputation of its reviewers

Journal's affiliation with distinguished learned societies

Presence or absence of advertising

Audience for which the journal is intended, scholarly versus the lay audience

All these criteria have been used as ways to determine the relative worth of a particular journal source. These criteria help a novice researcher determine whether the article he or she is looking at is likely to be of high quality. However, when accessing research from web versions of formerly print-based journals, journals that exist solely in electronic form, or accessing the full-text of articles from a variety of sources using a database such as ERIC as a gateway to full-text content, these criteria become less easily applied, even irrelevant. A web-based magazine for the general reader may look as professional and authoritative as a governmental or educational site, and the standards used or editorial policies can be difficult to determine. In particular, it is increasingly common to access articles through aggregated databases such as ERIC, in which the database provider removes the traditional quality markers, so that an article from the popular *Psychology Today* is presented exactly like one from the scholarly *Journal of Developmental Psychology*. In these cases, it becomes especially important that the student look beyond the traditional "markers" to judge the substance, the content, and the source material.

Authority

Is the author of the resource identified? Is a "snail mail" address or e-mail address given so that you can contact him or her? Is the author affiliated with a university, professional organization, or community organization? Is there a link to the sponsoring group's home page, a description of the group, or contact information? For information found on the web, what is the site extension? Web addresses end in a suffix such as ".edu" or ".com." This suffix gives the researcher an idea of who is hosting the website, as follows:

.com	A commercial site
.edu	A college or university
.gov	The U.S. government
.us	Usually a state government, community college, or school district site
.org	An organization
.net	A community network or Internet service provider

Although you cannot be assured of the quality of information in any kind of site, educational and governmental sites usually contain authoritative information. Information provided by companies may be slanted to sell the company's products. In fact, it may be hard to distinguish between an advertisement and a source of objective information.

Accuracy

Is the resource part of an edited publication; has it been selected by a reviewer or editor? Are factual statements supported with bibliographies, endnotes, or links to the sources used? Are statistics given dates or are the sources cited?

Timeliness

Is it clear when the information was originally published? For web-based information, is there a date listed when the page was last updated? If there are links given to outside web pages, are the links still active or are they linking to sites that have moved or changed address?

Online Journals

In recent years, many journals have been produced in a strictly online format and are frequently referred to as e-journals. That is, these journals are not available in print but are only available on the Internet. In education, the premier research association is the American Educational Research Association (AERA). Within AERA, there are subgroups that address particular interests in educational research. These are called divisions and special-interest groups (SIGs). One such SIG is the Communication of Research SIG. This SIG maintains a website listing many of the online journals in the field of education. The SIG and the listing of e-journals are available at http://aera-cr.asu.edu/index.html. Through the website the content of nearly 200 e-journals can be accessed.

ORGANIZING THE RELATED LITERATURE

Once you are satisfied that you have carried out a reasonably comprehensive search of the literature in the field, you can proceed to the task of organizing it. A useful approach is to arrange the studies by topic and determine how each of these topics relates to your own study.

Avoid the temptation to present the literature as a series of abstracts. Rather, it should lay a systematic foundation for the study. Present the literature in such a way as to justify carrying out your study by showing what is known and what remains to be investigated in the topic of concern. The hypotheses provide a framework for such organization. Like an explorer proposing an expedition, the researcher maps out the known territory and points the way to the unknown territory to be explored. If your study includes several facets or investigates more than a single hypothesis, the organization process is done separately for each one.

It is almost inevitable that a number of the reports you have carefully studied and included in your notes will, on reflection, prove only peripherally related to the topic. It is neither necessary nor desirable to include in a proposal every study encountered in the search through the literature. Your readers will not be impressed by mere quantity. Relevance and organization of the material are of prime importance.

The researcher who fails to approach the task of assembling the related literature in a systematic manner from the beginning can become very disorganized. The following suggestions may be of assistance. Your university, department, or research adviser may offer help sessions or minicourses, and the librarians at most institutions can also provide helpful suggestions.

1. *Begin reading the most recent studies in the field and then work backward through earlier volumes.* An obvious advantage of this approach is that you start with studies that have already incorporated the thoughts and findings of previous research. Earlier misunderstandings have been corrected, and unprofitable approaches have been identified. Another advantage is that these studies include references to earlier works and therefore direct you to sources you might not otherwise encounter. Obviously, limits must be set to the process of gathering related research. On the one hand, laying meaningful groundwork for a study entails including all the important works

in the field. On the other hand, devoting excessive time to this endeavor could result in boring the readers of your own report with superfluous detail. Make sure the related literature serves, but does not dominate, your own work.

2. *Read the abstract or summary sections of a report first to determine whether it is relevant to the question*. Doing so can save much time that might be wasted reading unhelpful articles.
3. *Before taking notes, skim the report quickly to find those sections that are related to the question—another way to save reading time.*
4. *Make notes, either on file cards, in a word processing program, or in some format that can be accessed easily, or moved around to cluster with other notes on related research; this begins to organize the review.*
5. *Write out a separate complete bibliographic reference for each work. For the sake of recordkeeping, include the reference in the bibliography list and with the individual notecard with the notes on the source*. A bibliography typically includes author, title, publisher, year, issue and volume numbers, and/or the universal resource locator (URL) or web address, the date you accessed an electronic source, and other information depending on the type of sources. Follow the most recent edition of the chosen style manual for citing references. There are websites that provide help in using the American Psychological Association (APA) and Turabian style manuals (see Chapter 19), which may be good places to begin. Add the library call number, location of the terminal, or URL of the source, to facilitate finding the work again, should it be necessary.
6. *To facilitate sorting and organizing, do not put more than one reference on each page, entry, or card*. It is not possible to arrange references alphabetically or in any other way unless they are recorded singly.
7. *Be sure to indicate which parts of the notes are direct quotations from the author and which are your own paraphrases*. Failure to make this distinction can lead to inadvertent plagiarism. It is also wise to clearly separate the author's evaluation of his or her research from your own conclusions.
8. *If you have searched online databases, keep the search strategies (often called "search histories") on file*. Typically, any given database will give the option of printing out a search history, the list of searches typed in, along with the results. This information will help retrieve information and reduce cost and time in case an update is needed.

SUMMARY

Related literature has several important functions in research. It enables investigators to (1) define the frontiers of their fields, (2) place their questions in perspective, (3) limit their research question and clarify and define the scope of their study, (4) develop insight concerning reasons for contradictory results in an area, (5) learn which methodologies have proven useful and which seem less promising, (6) avoid unintentional replication of previous studies, and (7) be in a better position to interpret the importance of their own results. If the researcher covers the

Table 4.2 Important Sources of Related Literature in Education

Source	Content
Child Development Abstracts and Bibliography	Abstracts of journal articles in the field of child development
Dissertation Abstracts International	Abstracts of doctoral dissertations in the United States, Canada, and Europe
Education Index/Education Abstracts	Citations of journal articles related to education. The *Index*, the print version, is indexed by subject and title. No abstracts. The *Abstracts*, an online version, contains abstracting and indexing coverage for all 478 periodicals included in *Education Index* and 133 additional periodicals. Fully searchable.
Encyclopedia of Educational Research	Summaries and evaluations of published research at the end of each decade
ERIC database	Abstracts of articles from more than 800 education-related journals and thousands of other related documents
Exceptional Child Education Resources	Abstracts of journal articles and other sources in special education
Mental Measurements Yearbooks	Information and evaluations of commercially available tests
Monthly Catalog of Government Publications	Subject listing of U.S. federal government publications
National Center for Educational Statistics (nces.ed.gov)	Provides links to all major educational statistics collected by the U.S. government
Psychological Abstracts	Abstracts of journal articles in psychology
Review of Educational Research	Reviews on various topics in each quarterly issue
Social Sciences Citation Index	Bibliographic information for cited authors and topics
Test Critiques	Reviews of measurement instruments, including critiques of tests, and technical aspects
Test in Print VI	Index and supplement to the first 15 *Mental Measurements Yearbooks*
Thesaurus of ERIC Descriptors	Terms for classifying and indexing ERIC documents
U.S. Department of Education website http://www.ed.gov	Collection of information about federal initiatives, grant opportunities, offices, and full text and ordering information for publications, research, and statistics

avenues to information in his or her area as suggested, the result should provide a reasonably complete picture of the place the study occupies within the field. Table 4.2 lists important sources and contents of related literature in education.

Boolean logic is an efficient way to search databases for useful sources. The Internet has broadened the scope of available related research. Organizing the related research is a challenging task, but there are many strategies that make this less time consuming and more efficient.

KEY CONCEPTS

abstracting sources
Boolean logic
citation indexes
ERIC system
indexes of dissertations and theses
Internet
periodical indexes
specialized dictionaries
statistical source
test sources
World Wide Web

EXERCISES

1. Which of the following are recommended strategies for organizing a literature search?
   a. Organize studies by topic.
   b. Begin with early articles and work forward in time.
   c. Read the abstract or summary sections of a report first.
   d. Skim the report to find those sections that are related to the chosen questions.
   e. Write out a complete bibliographic reference for each work.
2. According to the text, what are three important roles of incorporating related literature in a research project? In your opinion, which role seems most important to you in your current or future research?
3. Conduct a search on the same general topic in both ERIC and in *Education Index*. Compare the usefulness of ERIC and *Education Index* in finding related research on your topic. Compare and contrast two of the following: the quality of abstracts, the journals covered, and the subject terms or descriptors used by the index. Which index do you predict would be the most useful in finding research on your topic?
4. Explain the organization and the purpose of the *Mental Measurements Yearbook* (see Plake, Impara, & Spies, 2002). How does the information differ from that in *Tests* (Maddox, 2003) or *Test Critiques* (Keyser, 1994)?
5. What purposes might searching the *Social Science Citation Index* serve? In addition to information about an article's citation record, what conclusions might the *SSCI* help you draw about an author or about a journal itself?
6. What conclusion could be drawn regarding a work, published in 1959, that was cited in 20 articles listed in the 1999 *SSCI*?
7. If you were interested in the effect of teachers' stereotyping on the achievement of girls in math classes, what are some terms for which you might search? Illustrate how you might combine them into online search statements with Boolean operators AND, OR, or NOT.
8. Describe the differences among the purposes and content of handbooks, encyclopedias, and yearbook sources. For which audiences are they intended, what kind of information do they seem to provide, and at what point would they be most useful to the researcher?
9. If you wanted more information on the concept of multiple intelligence, which type of source might you consult to get an overview of the concept? Where would you go to see the more current research on the topic?
10. Find two web resources on an education-related topic of your choice, one from a commercial (.com) site and one from an educational (.edu) site. Evaluate them using the criteria of authority, accuracy, and timeliness. Are there notable differences between the sources? Explain.

ANSWERS

1. a, c, d, and e
2. Knowledge of related research enables the researcher to define the frontiers of the field, place the question in perspective, and avoid unintentional replication of previous studies. Defining the frontiers of research is especially important for a relatively inexperienced researcher, but any well-reasoned choice is acceptable.
3. Both provide a means to locate relevant journal articles. *Education Index* covers journals from 1929 on and lists new articles more quickly than ERIC. ERIC includes more journals. Begun in 1966, it indexes articles using the ERIC thesaurus of subject descriptors and provides annotations. *Education Index*, though older, does not index unpublished literature, though there are still periodicals that only *Education Index* covers, which tend to be newsletters, and so on. As *Education Abstracts*, the electronic version of the index, tends

to have shorter abstracts and also uses a controlled vocabulary that is less specific than the ERIC descriptors, most students will consider ERIC more useful, unless the student is doing historical research.

4. The editions of *MMY* provide the most comprehensive listing and description of standardized tests available, given its long publication history and the length and authority of its reviews. The critical reviews of the tests assist one in selecting an appropriate test. *Test Critiques* (Keyser, 1994) is easier to use and may be better for a layperson or a beginner who only wants to read a description of a test, and *Tests* (Maddox, 2003) serves as a listing of tests in print and does not offer much evaluative content.
5. The *SSCI* provides a way to see what subsequent research has followed a particular article. You can draw tentative conclusions about the influence of an author by looking at how often his or her work has been cited, and in turn, you can draw conclusions about the influential journals in a field by seeing how often those articles that are heavily cited seem to come from a cluster of important journal titles.
6. If an older article becomes heavily cited several years later, there may be several explanations; the research may have been treated by a noted scholar in a new way, a seminal piece of research may have recently been disproved, or the field of study may be experiencing a surge of interest because of a news event or finding.
7. Answers will vary, but terms mentioned would include *Females* (not *Girls*) AND *Teacher Attitudes* (not *Teacher Stereotypes*, which refers to stereotypes of teacher behavior and attributes) AND *Mathematics Instruction*, *Mathematics Education*, or *Mathematics*. *Sex Discrimination* or *Sex Stereotypes* might also be used successfully.
8. An encyclopedia or handbook would give a more or less detailed overview, usually with history, the names of major researchers, and so on. Encyclopedias tend to offer more brief and general information, and handbooks tend to assume that the audience is not made up of casual readers but of students and researchers. Handbooks tend to focus on more specific topics. Yearbooks and yearbook-type sources (such as, e.g., *Review of Research in Education* or the *Educational Media and Technology Yearbook*) focus on "hot topics" and more recent research, although they are, of course, secondary sources. These reference sources could be used at many points in the research process; students will usually use them in the beginning while formulating a research question, or during the literature review to introduce themselves to related topics. However, periodical indexes, which give access to more recent primary works, would be the best source to look for recent research on the topic.
9. Students may pick up on the fact that this topic will be present in both psychology and education indexes, and that it has appeared in the news media, making it possible to find some periodical sources on the topic in general-interest databases. ERIC, the *Cumulative Index to Nursing and Allied Health Literature*, *PsycInfo*, and so forth, would all be good places to look for the more recent research on the topic. Sources such as the *AERA Encyclopedia of Educational Research* or specialized sources such as the *Encyclopedia of Special Education* or the *Encyclopedia of Higher Education* would be good places to find overview information.
10. Answers will vary.

INFOTRAC COLLEGE EDITION

Use InfoTrac College Edition to search for references useful for writing the related literature section of a required paper for a research methods class or for another class. Look for different kinds of references on your topic such as research articles, discussions, books, and so on.

Chapter 5

The Hypothesis

A HYPOTHESIS TRANSFORMS A GENERAL IDEA INTO A PLAN FOR WHAT TO LOOK FOR.

INSTRUCTIONAL OBJECTIVES

After studying this chapter, the student will be able to:

1. Define *hypothesis.*
2. Describe the purposes of the hypothesis(es) in quantitative and qualitative research.
3. List the criteria of a theory useful for a research study.
4. Distinguish between an inductive and a deductive hypothesis.
5. State the criteria used to evaluate hypotheses for research.
6. Define *operational definition* and give an example.
7. Identify a testable hypothesis from given examples.
8. Define *null hypothesis* and explain its purpose in a research study.
9. Write a research hypothesis and a null hypothesis for a research study.
10. Distinguish between a directional and a nondirectional hypothesis.
11. Describe the steps in testing a hypothesis.
12. State the purpose of the research plan and list the elements to be included.
13. State the purpose of a pilot study.

After stating the research question and examining the literature, the quantitative researcher is ready to state a hypothesis based on the question. The quantitative researcher should state a hypothesis before beginning the research project. Recall that the quantitative problem asks about the relationship between two (or more) variables. The hypothesis states the expected answer to the research question. It presents the researcher's expectations about the relationship between variables within the problem. Hence it is put forth as a suggested solution to the problem, with the understanding that the ensuing investigation may lead to either support for the hypothesis or lack of support for it.

The hypothesis is a powerful tool in scientific inquiry. It enables researchers to relate theory to observation and observation to theory. The use of hypotheses enables people, in the search for knowledge, to employ both the ideas of the inductive philosophers, with their emphasis on observation, and the logic of the deductive philosophers, with their emphasis on reason. The use of hypotheses has united experience and reason to produce a powerful tool for seeking knowledge.

For instance, a researcher might posit that the gender of the teacher is related to how well boys and girls learn. Deductive reasoning leads to the conclusion that if this is true, then boys who have male primary teachers will show greater achievement than boys who have female teachers. Then the inductive stage follows. A researcher compares the achievement of boys with male teachers with a comparable group of boys with female teachers. If a meaningful difference is found, it supports the hypothesis. If a meaningful difference is not found, the hypothesis is not supported.

Or a researcher might begin with the question "What is the role of children's perceptions of themselves in the process of learning to read?" The researcher might then hypothesize that there is a positive relationship between children's perceptions of themselves and their achievement in reading in the first grade. Or one might begin with a question such as "What is the effect of preschool training on the achievement of culturally disadvantaged children in first grade?" The hypothesis would read "Culturally disadvantaged children who have had preschool training achieve at a higher level in first grade than culturally disadvantaged children who have not had preschool training." In both examples you can see that the hypothesis is a proposition relating two variables. In the first hypothesis the variables are self-perception and reading achievement; in the second, the variables are having or not having preschool training and achievement in first grade.

Although hypotheses serve several important purposes, some research studies may proceed without them. Hypotheses are tools in the research process, not ends in themselves. Studies are often undertaken in areas where there is little accumulated background information. If an investigator lacks insight into the scope of a problem, the major variables that influence a phenomenon, or the settings in which the variables occur, then it is very difficult to state a meaningful hypothesis. For example, surveys that seek to describe the characteristics of particular phenomena, or to ascertain the attitudes and opinions of groups, often proceed without hypotheses. In qualitative research, hypotheses are rarely formulated at the beginning of the research. They are usually generated as data accumulate and the researcher gains more insight and understanding about the phenomenon under investigation.

Two reasons for stating a hypothesis before the data-gathering phase of a quantitative study are (1) a well-grounded hypothesis indicates that the researcher has sufficient knowledge in the area to undertake the investigation, and (2) the hypothesis gives direction to the collection and interpretation of the data; it tells the researcher what procedure to follow and what type of data to gather and thus may prevent a great deal of wasted time and effort on the part of the researcher.

PURPOSES OF THE HYPOTHESIS

Principal purposes served by the hypothesis include the following:

1. *The hypothesis brings together information to enable the researcher to make a tentative statement about how the variables in the study may be related.* By integrating information based on experience, related research, or theory, the researcher states the hypothesis that provides the most satisfactory prediction or the best solution to a problem.
2. *Because hypotheses propose tentative explanations for phenomena, they stimulate a research endeavor that results in the accumulation of new knowledge.* Hypothesis testing research permits investigators to validate or fail to validate theory through an accumulation of data from many studies. In this way, knowledge is extended.
3. *The hypothesis provides the investigator with a relational statement that is directly testable in a research study.* That is, it is possible to collect and analyze data that will confirm or not confirm the hypothesis. Questions cannot be tested directly. An investigation begins with a question, but only the proposed relationship between the variables can be tested. For instance, you do not test the question "Do teachers' comments on students' papers cause a significant improvement in student performance?" Instead, you test the hypothesis that the question implies: "Teachers' comments on students' papers result in a significant improvement in performance"; or more specifically, "The performance scores of students who have had teacher comments on previous papers will exceed those of students who have not had teacher comments on previous papers." You then proceed to gather data about the relationship between the two variables (teachers' comments and student performance).
4. *The hypothesis provides direction to the research.* The hypothesis posits a specific relationship between variables and thus determines the nature of the data needed to test the proposition. Very simply, the hypothesis tells the researcher what to do. Facts must be selected and observations made because they have relevance to a particular question, and the hypothesis determines the relevance of these facts. The hypothesis provides a basis for selecting the sampling, measurement and research procedures to use, as well as the appropriate statistical analysis. Furthermore, the hypothesis helps keep the study restricted in scope, preventing it from becoming too broad or unwieldy.

   For example, consider again the hypothesis concerning preschool training of culturally disadvantaged children and their achievement in first grade. This hypothesis indicates the research method required and the sample to use, and it even directs the researcher to the statistical test that would be necessary for analyzing the data. It is clear from the statement of the hypothesis that the researcher will conduct an ex post facto study that compares the first-grade achievement of a sample of culturally disadvantaged children who went through a preschool program and a similar group of disadvantaged children who did not have preschool training. Any difference in the mean achievement of the two groups could be analyzed for statistical significance by the t test or analysis-of-variance technique. (We discuss these procedures in Chapter 7.)

5. *The hypothesis provides a framework for reporting the findings and conclusions of the study.* The researcher will find it very convenient to take each hypothesis separately and state the conclusions that are relevant to it; that is, the researcher can organize this section of the written report around the provision of answers to the original hypotheses, thereby making a more meaningful and readable presentation.

SUGGESTIONS FOR DERIVING HYPOTHESES

As explained in Chapter 3, a study might originate in a practical problem, in some observed behavioral situation in need of explanation, in previous research, or even more profitably in some educational, psychological, or sociological theory. Thus, researchers derive hypotheses inductively from observations of behavior or deductively from theory or from the findings of previous research. Induction and deduction are complementary processes. In induction, one starts with specific observations and reaches general conclusions; in deduction, one begins with generalizations and makes specific predictions.

INDUCTIVE HYPOTHESES

In the inductive procedure, the researcher formulates an **inductive hypothesis** as a generalization from apparent observed relationships—that is, the researcher observes behavior, notices trends or probable relationships, and then hypothesizes an explanation for this observed behavior. He or she should accompany this reasoning process by examining previous research to determine what findings other investigators have reported on the question.

The inductive procedure is a particularly fruitful source of hypotheses for classroom teachers. Teachers observe learning and other student behavior every day and try to relate it to their own behavior, to the behavior of other students, to the teaching methods used, to changes in the school environment, and so on. Teachers might observe, for example, that when they present particularly challenging activities in the classroom, some students get motivated and really blossom, while others withdraw from the challenge. Some students learn complex concepts best from primarily verbal presentations (lectures), whereas others learn best from discussions and hands-on activities.

After reflecting on such experiences, teachers may inductively formulate generalizations that seek to explain the observed relationship between their methods and materials and students' learning. These tentative explanations of why things happen as they do can become the hypotheses in empirical investigations. Perhaps a teacher has observed that classroom tests arouse a high degree of anxiety and believes this adversely affects student performance. Furthermore, the teacher has noted that when students receive an opportunity to write comments about objective questions, their test performance seems to improve. The teacher reasons that this freedom to make comments must somehow reduce anxiety and, as a result, the students score better. This observation suggests a hypothesis: Students who are encouraged to write comments about test items on their answer sheets will make higher test scores than students who have no opportunity to make comments.

The teacher could then design an experiment to test the validity of this hypothesis. Note that the hypothesis expresses the teacher's belief concerning the relationship between the two variables (writing or not writing comments about test items and performance on the test). Note also that the variable *anxiety* that was part of the reasoning chain leading to the hypothesis is not part of the final hypothesis. Therefore, the results of the investigation would provide information concerning only the relation between writing comments and test performance. The relationships between anxiety and comments, and anxiety and test performance, could be subjects for subsequent hypotheses to investigate. Frequently an original idea involves a series of relationships that you cannot directly observe. You then reformulate the question to focus on relationships that are amenable to direct observation and measurement.

The following are some other examples of hypotheses that might be arrived at inductively from a teacher's observations:

Students' learning of computer programming in the middle grades increases their development of logical thinking skills.

Using advance organizers increases high school students' learning from computer-assisted instruction in chemistry.

Students trained to write summaries of a lecture will perform better on an immediate posttest on lecture comprehension than will students who simply take notes.

Children score higher on final measures of first-grade reading achievement when they are taught in small groups rather than large groups.

The cognitive and affective development of first-grade children is influenced by the amount of prior preschool experience.

After-school tutoring programs increase the achievement of at-risk students.

In the inductive process, the researcher makes observations, thinks about the problem, turns to the literature for clues, makes additional observations, and then formulates a hypothesis that seeks to account for the observed behavior. The researcher (or teacher) then tests the hypothesis under controlled conditions to examine scientifically the assumption concerning the relationship between the specified variables.

DEDUCTIVE HYPOTHESES

In contrast to hypotheses formulated as generalizations from observed relationships, some are derived by deduction from theory. These hypotheses have the advantage of leading to a more general system of knowledge because the framework for incorporating them meaningfully into the body of knowledge already exists within the theory itself. A science cannot develop efficiently if each study results in an isolated bit of knowledge. It becomes cumulative by building on the existing body of facts and theories. A hypothesis derived from a theory is known as a **deductive hypothesis**.

THEORY

A **theory** is defined as a set of interrelated statements and propositions that specify the relationships among variables. Theories are proposed as general explanations that apply to a wide range of empirical findings. From the interrelationships proposed in the theory, you can state specific consequences that could logically be assumed to follow. A scientific theory must imply conclusions that can be verified through empirical investigation; that is, from the theory you should be able to predict certain events that will or will not be observed. These deduced consequences become the hypotheses that are subjected to empirical investigation. Because theories are general, one theory may give rise to a number of hypotheses. As the hypotheses derived from a theory receive support in research, the theory also receives support. Hypotheses thus direct people to seek the evidence that supports, expands, contradicts, or leads to revision of the theories from which they derived.

CHOOSING A THEORY

You have probably encountered a number of theories in your coursework that you find interesting. Not all theories are equally useful to a beginning researcher. Some theories are very well known and have stimulated a lot of research; others are less well known and have resulted in little research. Some theories are broad and contain many abstract principles, whereas others are composed of more concrete propositions about phenomena. You will, of course, want to choose a theory in your area of interest. Let us examine some of the characteristics one looks for in a "good" theory for a research study:

1. An essential characteristic of a good theory is that it is testable. The theory chosen should be one from which the researcher can make concise predictions (hypotheses) about what will happen in new situations and can verify these predictions through empirical observation. As the hypotheses are supported in research studies, they then become part of the theory which adds to the body of knowledge. But, if the theory cannot be tested, it serves no useful purpose.
2. A good theory is not only testable, but it must also be falsifiable. Being falsifiable means that it is capable of being proven wrong. It is possible to gather evidence that contradicts the theory. A theory that explains why a tornado touched down in a certain area of a town by saying that the people there are being punished for their sins is not a theory that can be proven wrong. Thus, it is not a useful theory.

   Students sometimes find this concept of **falsifiability** difficult to understand. This concept came from the philosopher, Sir Karl Popper, who in his *Logic of Scientific Discovery* (1965) argued that claims to knowledge "can never be proven or fully justified, they can only be refuted" (p. 40). A theory cannot ever be proved to be true because theories are generalizations that apply to all possible instances of the phenomena they are trying to explain, and it is not possible to test it against all possibilities. We say only that a theory has been supported; the more support it gets in a variety of research studies, the more confidence we have in the usefulness of the theory. But it is possible to disprove a theory by gathering negative evidence that contradicts the theory. According to Popper, this is how most scientific progress is achieved. Neuman and Kreuger (2003) give a classic example: "If I want to test the claim that all swans are white, and I find 1,000 white swans, I have not totally confirmed the causal law or pattern. All it takes is locating one black swan to refute my claim—one piece of negative evidence" (p. 40). Negative evidence indicates that the theory needs to be rejected or at least revised. To summarize, a good theory is one where evidence can be gathered that will either support or refute the theory. Both outcomes must be possible.

3. A good theory deals with some significant phenomenon or behavior that needs explanation, such as learning or motivation.
4. A good theory provides the simplest, clearest, and most plausible explanation for the phenomenon. A good theory follows the principle of parsimony, which says that a theory should explain the largest number of facts with the smallest number of principles.
5. A good theory has internal consistency; its propositions do not contradict one another. For example, a "commonsense" theory of human separation may say "Absence makes the heart grow fonder" but also "Out of sight, out of mind." One could find evidence to support both of these propositions; thus the theory would not be useful for predicting what might happen when people are separated.

GOING FROM THEORY TO HYPOTHESIS

Next you use deductive reasoning to arrive at the logical consequences of the theory. If A is true, then we would expect B to follow. These deductions then become the hypotheses in the research study. For example, social comparison theory suggests that students form academic self-concepts by comparing their self-perceived academic accomplishments to some standard or frame of reference. The frame of reference for most students would be the perceived academic abilities of their classmates. If this is true, then one might hypothesize that gifted students would have lower academic self-concepts if they were placed in selective homogeneous groups than if they were in heterogeneous or mixed-ability groups where they compare themselves to less able students. One could investigate this hypothesis by looking at the change over time in the academic self-concept of gifted students in homogeneous classes as compared with matched gifted students placed in regular, heterogeneous classes.

Another useful theory from which an educational researcher might make deductions is Piaget's classic theory on the development of logical thinking in children. Piaget (1968) suggested that children pass through various stages in their

Table 5.1 Some Well-Known Theories and a Hypothesis Based on the Theory

Theory	Hypothesis
Achievement motivation (McClelland, 1953)	
People have a tendency to strive for success and to choose goal-oriented, success/failure activities.	There is a positive relationship between achievement motivation and success in school.
Attribution theory (Weiner, 1994)	
People attempt to maintain a positive self-image; people explain their success or failure in a way that preserves their self-image.	If students are given a task and told that they failed or succeeded (even though all actually succeed), those who are told they failed will say it is due to bad luck; those who are told they are successful will attribute it to skill and intelligence.
Theory of multiple intelligences (Gardner, 1993)	
People have a number of separate intelligences that may vary in strength.	Teaching science concepts using a variety of approaches will result in greater achievement than when using only linguistic and mathematical approaches.
Cognitive dissonance theory (Festinger, 1957)	
People experience discomfort when a new behavior clashes with a long-held belief or with our self-image. To resolve the discomfort, they may change their beliefs or behavior.	Requiring middle school students who smoke to write an essay on why young people should not smoke will change their attitudes about smoking.
Expectancy theory (Atkinson and Birch, 1978)	
Peoples' motivation to achieve depends on their expectations of reward and the value they place on the reward.	When presented with a difficult task, students' motivation increases up to a point at which they decide that success is unlikely or the goal is not worth the effort.
Vygotsky's theory of learning (1978)	
Cognitive development is strongly linked to input from other people.	Tutoring by more able peers will have a positive effect on the learning of at-risk students.
Maslow's human needs theory (1954)	
In a hierarchy of needs, people must satisfy their lower-level needs (hunger or safety) before they are motivated to satisfy higher-level needs (self-esteem or need to know).	Children from economically disadvantaged homes who are given breakfast at school will show higher achievement than similar students not given breakfast.
Behaviorism (Skinner, 1953)	
Behavior that is positively reinforced will increase in strength.	On-task behavior will increase when teachers positively reinforce it.

mental development, one of which is the stage of concrete operations, which begins at age 7 or 8 and marks the transition from dependence on perception to an ability to use some logical operations. These operations are on a concrete level but do involve symbolic reasoning. Using this theory as a starting point, you might therefore hypothesize that the proportion of 9-year-old children who will be able to answer correctly the transitive inference problem "Frank is taller than George; George is taller than Robert; who is the tallest?" will be greater than the proportion of 6-year-olds who are able to answer it correctly. Such research has implications for the importance of determining students' cognitive capabilities and structuring educational tasks that are compatible with their developmental level.

Piaget's cognitive theory also emphasizes that learning is a highly active process in which learners must construct knowledge. This tenet that knowledge must be constructed by learners rather than simply being ingested from teachers is the basis for much of the research on discovery-oriented and cooperative learning.

In a study designed to test a deduction from a theory, it is extremely important to check for any logical gaps between theory and hypothesis. The researcher must ask, "Does the hypothesis logically follow from the theory?" If the hypothesis does not really follow from the theory, then the researcher cannot reach valid conclusions about the adequacy of the theory. If the hypothesis is supported, but not rigorously deduced from the theory, the researcher cannot say that the findings furnish credibility to the theory. Conversely, if the data do not support the hypothesis, the theory from which it originated will not necessarily be any less credible. Table 5.1 shows a proposition from some well-known theories and a hypothesis based on the theory.

CHARACTERISTICS OF A USABLE HYPOTHESIS

After tentatively formulating the hypothesis, but before attempting any actual empirical testing, you must evaluate the hypothesis. The final worth of a hypothesis cannot be judged prior to empirical testing, but there are certain **criteria for evaluating hypotheses**, and the researcher should use them to judge the adequacy of the proposed hypothesis.

A HYPOTHESIS STATES THE EXPECTED RELATIONSHIP BETWEEN VARIABLES

A hypothesis should conjecture the relationship between two or more variables. For example, suppose you attempt to start your car and nothing happens. It would be unprofitable to state, "The car will not start and it has a wiring system," because no relationship between variables is specified, and so there is no proposed relationship to test. A fruitful hypothesis would be "The car will not start because of a fault in the wiring system." This criterion may seem patently obvious, but consider the following statement: "If children differ from one another in self-concept, they will differ from one another in social studies achievement." The statement appears to be a hypothesis until you note that there is no statement of an expected relationship. An expected relationship could be described as "Higher self-concept is a likely antecedent to *higher* social studies achievement." This hypothesis would then be stated as "There will be a *positive* relationship between self-concept and social studies achievement." If the opposite is predicted—that is, higher self-concept leads to *lower* social studies achievement—then the hypothesis would be "There will be a *negative* relationship between self-concept and social studies achievement." Either statement would meet this first criterion.

A HYPOTHESIS MUST BE TESTABLE

The most important characteristic of a "good" hypothesis is testability. A testable hypothesis is verifiable; that is, deductions, conclusions, or inferences can be drawn from the hypothesis in such a way that empirical observations either support or do not support the hypothesis. If the hypothesis is on target, then certain predictable results should be manifest. A testable hypothesis enables the researcher to determine by observation and data collection whether consequences that are deductively implied actually occur. Otherwise, it would be impossible either to confirm or not to confirm the hypothesis. In the preceding example, the hypothesis "The car's failure to start is a punishment for my sins" is apparently untestable in this world.

Many hypotheses—or propositions, as they may initially be stated—are essentially untestable. For instance, the hypothesis "Preschool experience promotes the all-around adjustment of the preschool child" would be hard to test because of the difficulty of operationalizing and measuring "all-around adjustment." To be testable, a hypothesis must relate variables that can be measured. If no means are available for measuring the variables, then no one could gather the data necessary to test the validity of the hypothesis. We cannot emphasize this point too strongly. Unless you can specifically define the indicators of each variable and subsequently can measure these variables, then you cannot test the hypothesis.

The indicators of the variables are referred to as *operational definitions*. Recall from Chapter 2 that variables are operationally defined either by specifying the steps the investigator takes to measure the variable (measured operational definition) or the steps a researcher takes to produce an experimental condition (experimental operational definition). Consider the hypothesis "High-stressed nursing students will perform less well on a nursing test than will low-stressed students." The experimental operational definition of stress is as follows: One group of students is told that their performance on the nursing test will be a major determinant of whether they will remain in the nursing program (high stress), and the other group is told that they need to do as well as they can but that their scores will not be reported to the faculty or have any influence on their grades (low stress). The measured operational definition of test performance would be scores from a rating scale that assessed how well the students did on the various tasks making up the test. Or consider this hypothesis: "There is a positive relationship between a child's self-esteem and his or her reading achievement in first grade." For this hypothesis to be testable, you must define the variables operationally. You might define *self-esteem* as the scores made on the Self-Image Profile for Children, SIP-C (Butler, 2001), and reading achievement as scores on the California Reading Test, or as first-grade teachers' ratings of reading achievement.

A primary consideration in formulating a hypothesis is to make sure the variables can be given operational definitions. Avoid the use of constructs for which it would be difficult or impossible to find adequate measures. Constructs such as *creativity*, *authoritarianism*, *democracy*, and the like have acquired such diverse meanings that reaching agreement on operational definitions of such concepts would be difficult, if not impossible. Remember that the variables must be defined in terms of identifiable and observable behavior.

It is important to avoid value statements in hypotheses. A statement such as "A counseling program in the elementary school is desirable" cannot be investigated in a research study. However, you could test the hypothesis "Elementary pupils who have had counseling will verbally express greater satisfaction with their school than those who have not had counseling." You can measure verbal expressions of satisfaction, but whether they are desirable is a value judgment.

PICTURE THIS

Joe Rocco

THINK ABOUT IT 5.1

Which of the explanations in the cartoon are not testable hypotheses about why there are more boys than girls in remedial reading classes?

Answer
The one about the "wiring" in the brain and the one about the devil's activities are not testable.

A HYPOTHESIS SHOULD BE CONSISTENT WITH THE EXISTING BODY OF KNOWLEDGE

Hypotheses should not contradict previously well-established knowledge. The hypothesis "My car will not start because the fluid in the battery has changed to gold" satisfies the first two criteria but is so contrary to what is known about the nature of matter that you would not pursue it. The hypothesis "The car will not start because the fluid in the battery has evaporated to a low level" is consistent with previous knowledge and therefore is worth pursuing. It would probably be unprofitable to hypothesize an *absence* of relationship between the self-concept of adolescent boys and girls and their rate of physical growth because the preponderance of evidence supports the *presence* of such a relationship. Historians of science find that people such as Einstein, Newton, Darwin, and Copernicus developed truly revolutionary hypotheses that conflicted with what was accepted knowledge in their time. However, remember that the work of such pioneers was not really so much a denial of previous knowledge as a reorganization of existing knowledge into more satisfactory theory. In most cases, and especially for the beginning researcher, it is safe to suggest that the hypothesis should agree with knowledge already well established in the field. Again, this points up the necessity for a thorough review of the literature so that hypotheses are formulated on the basis of previously reported research in the area.

A HYPOTHESIS SHOULD BE STATED AS SIMPLY AND CONCISELY AS POSSIBLE

A hypothesis should be presented in the form of a concise declarative statement. A complete and concisely stated hypothesis makes clear what the researcher needs to do to test it. It also provides the framework for presenting the findings of the study. If a researcher is exploring more than one relationship, he or she will need to state more than one hypothesis. The general rule is to state only one relationship in any one hypothesis. For example, if you were investigating the effect of a new teaching method on student achievement and student satisfaction, you would state two hypotheses, one for effect on achievement and one for effect on satisfaction. You need not worry about the verbal redundancy inevitable in stating multiple hypotheses. Remember that the goals of testability and clarity will be served better by more specific hypotheses.

THINK ABOUT IT 5.2

Which of the explanations used to explain the greater number of boys in remedial reading in the cartoon on the previous page is not consistent with the existing body of knowledge?

Answer

The one that posits that in the primary grades boys mature more rapidly than girls. There is overwhelming evidence that at that stage girls mature more rapidly than boys. Boys finally catch up at about age 17.

The terms used in the hypothesis should be the simplest acceptable for conveying the intended meaning; avoid ambiguous or vague constructs. Use terms in the way that is generally accepted for referring to the phenomenon. When two hypotheses are of equal explanatory power, prefer the simpler one because it will provide the necessary explanation with fewer assumptions and variables to be defined. Remember that this principle of parsimony is important in evaluating hypotheses.

TYPES OF HYPOTHESES

There are three categories of hypotheses: research, null, and alternate.

THE RESEARCH HYPOTHESIS

The hypotheses we have discussed thus far are called *research*, or substantive, *hypotheses*. They are the hypotheses developed from observation, the related literature, and/or the theory described in the study. A research hypothesis is a statement about the relationship one expects to find as a result of the research. It may be a statement about the expected *relationship* or the expected *difference* between the variables in the study. A hypothesis about children's IQs and anxiety in the classroom could be stated "There is a positive relationship between IQ and anxiety in elementary school children," or "Children classified as having high IQs will exhibit more anxiety in the classroom than children classified as having low IQs." Research hypotheses may be stated in a **directional** or **nondirectional** form. A directional hypothesis specifies the direction of the predicted relationship or difference. The preceding two hypotheses about IQ and anxiety are directional. A nondirectional hypothesis, in contrast, states that a relationship or difference exists but without specifying the direction or nature of the expected finding—for example, "There is a relationship between IQ and anxiety in children."

THE NULL HYPOTHESIS

It is impossible to test research hypotheses directly. The only way you can judge the credibility of a research hypothesis is to state a null hypothesis (symbolized H_0) and assess the probability that this null hypothesis is true. It is called the **null hypothesis** because it states that there is *no* relationship between the variables in the population. A null hypothesis states a negation (not the reverse) of what the experimenter expects or predicts. A researcher may hope to show that, after an experimental treatment, two populations will have different means, but the null hypothesis would state that after the treatment the populations' means will *not* be different.

What is the point of the null hypothesis? A null hypothesis lets researchers assess whether apparent relationships are genuine or are likely to be a function of chance alone. It says, "The results of this study could easily have happened by chance." Statistical tests are used to determine the probability that the null hypothesis is true. If the tests indicate that observed relationships had only a slight probability of occurring by chance, the null hypothesis becomes an unlikely explanation. Therefore, it can be rejected in favor of an alternative hypothesis. Testing a null hypothesis is analogous to the prosecutor's work in a criminal trial. To establish guilt, the prosecutor (in the U.S. legal system) must provide sufficient evidence to enable a jury to reject the presumption of innocence beyond reasonable doubt. It is not possible for a prosecutor to prove guilt conclusively, nor can a researcher obtain unequivocal support for a research hypothesis. The defendant is presumed innocent until sufficient evidence indicates that he or she is not, and the null hypothesis is presumed true until sufficient evidence indicates otherwise.

For example, you might start with the expectation that children develop greater mastery of mathematical concepts through individual instruction than through group instruction. In other words, you are positing a relationship between the independent variable (method of instruction) and the dependent variable (mastery of mathematical concepts). The research hypothesis is "Students taught through individual instruction will exhibit greater mastery of mathematical concepts than students taught through group instruction." The null hypothesis, the statement of no relationship between variables, will read "The mean mastery scores (population mean μ_i) of all students taught by individual instruction will equal the mean mastery scores (population mean μ_g) of all those taught by group instruction." H_0: $\mu_i = \mu_g$.*

THE ALTERNATE HYPOTHESIS

Note that the hypothesis "Children taught by individual instruction will exhibit less mastery of mathematical concepts than those taught by group instruction" also posits a relationship between variables, and therefore is *not* a null hypothesis. It is an example of what is called an **alternative hypothesis**.

In the example, if the sample mean of the measure of mastery of mathematical concepts is higher for the individual instruction students than for the group instruction students, and inferential statistics indicate that the null hypothesis is unlikely to be true, you reject the null hypothesis and tentatively conclude that individual instruction results in greater mastery of mathematical concepts than does group instruction. If, in contrast, the mean for the group instruction students is higher than the mean for the individual instruction students, and inferential statistics indicate that this difference is not likely to be a function of chance, then you tentatively conclude that group instruction is superior.

If inferential statistics indicate that observed differences between the means of the two instructional groups could easily be a function of chance, the null hypothesis is retained, and you decide insufficient evidence exists for concluding there is a relationship between the dependent and independent variables. The retention of a null hypothesis is *not* positive evidence that the null hypothesis is true. It indicates that the evidence is insufficient and that the null hypothesis, the research hypothesis, and the alternative hypothesis are all possible.

TESTING THE HYPOTHESIS

A quantitative study begins with a research hypothesis, which should be a simple, clear statement of the expected relationship between the variables. We explained earlier that hypotheses must be testable, that is, amenable to empirical verifica-

*The Greek letter mu, μ, is used to symbolize population mean.

tion. When researchers speak of testing a hypothesis, however, they are referring to the null hypothesis. Only the null hypothesis can be directly tested by statistical procedures. **Testing a hypothesis** involves the following steps:

1. State, in operational terms, the relationships that should be observed if the research hypothesis is true.
2. State the null hypothesis.
3. Select a research method that will enable the hypothesized relationship to be observed if it is there.
4. Gather and analyze the empirical data.
5. Determine whether the evidence is sufficient to reject the null hypothesis.

Many hypotheses that are formulated are rejected after empirical testing. Their predictions are not supported by the data. Many beginning researchers believe that if the data they collect do not support their hypothesis, then their study is a failure. This is not the case. In the history of scientific research, hypotheses that failed to be supported have greatly outnumbered those that have been supported. Experienced researchers realize that unconfirmed hypotheses are an expected and useful part of the scientific experience. They can lead to reconsideration or revision of theory and the generation of new hypotheses, which often brings science closer to a correct explanation of the state of affairs. Darwin (1887) wrote:

> I have steadily endeavored to keep my mind free so as to give up any hypothesis, however much beloved (and I cannot resist forming one on every subject), as soon as facts are shown to be opposed to it. Indeed, I have had no choice but to act in this manner, for with the exception of the Coral Reefs, I cannot remember a single first-formed hypothesis which had not after a time to be given up or greatly modified. (p. 293)

Even though you may find support for a hypothesis, the hypothesis is not *proved* to be true. A hypothesis is never proved or disproved; it is only supported or not supported. Hypotheses are essentially probabilistic in nature; empirical evidence can lead you to conclude that the explanation is probably true or that it is reasonable to accept the hypothesis, but it never proves the hypothesis.

CLASSROOM EXAMPLE OF TESTING A HYPOTHESIS

A teacher is interested in investigating reinforcement theory in the classroom. From her understanding of reinforcement theory, this teacher hypothesizes that teachers' positive comments on students' papers will lead to greater achievement.

Step 1. The deduced implication is stated as follows: "Teachers' positive comments on students' papers during a specified unit will result in higher scores on the end-of-unit test for those students, compared with students who received no comments." It is the relationship between the two variables—teachers' positive comments and pupil performance on the end-of-unit test—that will be investigated.

Step 2. For statistical testing, the research hypothesis must be transformed into a null hypothesis: "The population mean achievement score for students receiving positive comments (experimental group) will be the same as the population mean achievement score for students receiving no comments (control group)."

Step 3. The teacher would select students to be randomly assigned to the experimental and control groups. For those students in the experimental group, she would write positive comments on their papers, whereas the students assigned to the control group would receive no comments. (The comments to the experimental group should simply be words of encouragement such as "Excellent," "Keep up the good work," or "You're doing better." These comments should have nothing to do with content or the correction of particular errors; otherwise, any improvement could be attributed to the instructional usefulness of such comments.

Step 4. After completing the specified unit, the teacher would administer a common end-of-unit test to both groups and derive average (mean) achievement scores on the test for each group.

Step 5. Inferential statistics (see Chapter 7) can then be used to indicate whether any difference in mean achievement scores is real or is likely to be merely a function of chance. If the difference is not likely to be a function of chance, the researcher tentatively concludes that it results from the different treatments given to the two groups.

THE RESEARCH PLAN

After identifying the problem and formulating the research hypothesis, you are ready to develop a tentative research plan. The **research plan** at this stage is only a preliminary proposal; many changes will probably be needed before the final, formal proposal is written (see Chapter 18). Developing this tentative research plan is essential because it forces you to set down ideas in a concrete form. Many initial ideas seem promising until you must spell them out in black and white; then the difficulties or the inadequacies become obvious.

Another advantage of a written plan is that you can give it to others for their comments and criticism. In a research methods class, for example, the professor would certainly need to see what research students are planning. The director of a thesis or dissertation would want to see a written plan rather early in the process. It is much easier for another person to detect flaws and problems in a proposal that is written out than in one communicated orally. Another point to keep in mind is that the more complete and detailed this initial proposal, the more useful it will be to the researcher and the more time may be saved later.

A research plan should include the following elements: the problem, the hypothesis, the research methodology, and data analysis. The following list briefly describes each component.

1. *Problem*. The plan begins with a clear statement of the research problem. A quantitative problem asks about the relationship between specified variables; a qualitative problem is stated in terms of the purpose of the study.

Include the rationale for the study and a brief description of the background of the problem in theory and/or related research.

2. *Hypothesis*. A quantitative question is followed by a concise statement of the research hypothesis. Provide operational definitions of the variables. Qualitative researchers do not state hypotheses at the beginning of the study. Instead, they may generate hypotheses during the process of data collection and analysis.
3. *Methodology*. This section explains how you will conduct the study. Include the proposed research design, the population of concern, the sampling procedure, the measuring instruments, and any other information relevant to the conduct of the study. The qualitative researcher will need to describe the setting for the research, the people involved, and the various data sources to be used.
4. *Data analysis*. Indicate how you will analyze the data to test the hypothesis and/or answer the research question. Beginning quantitative researchers may find it difficult to write this section because they are not yet familiar with statistics. You might look at the related literature to see what type of statistical analysis other researchers used, or you might consult with your professor or an expert in statistics.

THE PILOT STUDY

After the tentative research plan is approved, it may be helpful to try out the proposed procedures on a few subjects. This trial run, or **pilot study**, will, first of all,

THINK ABOUT IT 5.3

State a hypothesis to test the notion that teachers assign rowdy students to remedial reading classes to get rid of them. State the null hypothesis and list the steps for testing it.

Answer

1. Research hypothesis: Students assessed as rowdy on a behavioral assessment scale are more often assigned to remedial reading classes than are nonrowdy students with equivalent reading skills as measured on the California Achievement Test.
2. Null hypothesis: Rowdy and nonrowdy students with the same reading skills are equally likely to be assigned to remedial reading classes.
3. Administer the Reading subtest of the California Achievement Test to all students. Match students in remedial reading classes with students with the same reading skills who are in regular classes. Use a behavioral assessment scale to identify which students are rowdy and which are not.
4. Calculate the proportion of rowdy and nonrowdy students in remedial reading classes and the proportion of rowdy and nonrowdy students in regular classes.
5. Test the null hypothesis by using a statistical test to see if the difference in the proportions could easily be a function of chance alone.

help the researcher to decide whether the study is feasible and whether it is worthwhile to continue. It provides an opportunity to assess the appropriateness of the operational definitions and the research methodology. It also permits a preliminary testing of the hypothesis, which may give some indication of its tenability and suggest whether further refinement is needed.

Unanticipated problems that appear can be solved at this stage, thereby saving time and effort later. A pilot study is well worth the time required and is especially recommended for the beginning researcher.

SUMMARY

To proceed with the confirmatory phase of a quantitative research study, it is important to have one or more clearly stated hypotheses. The hypothesis is the researcher's prediction about the outcome of the study. Hypotheses are derived inductively from observation or deductively from a known theory. A good theory explains phenomena and permits one to make predictions that further empirical studies will either support or refute. Experience and knowledge in the area and familiarity with previous research are important factors in formulating a satisfactory hypothesis.

The hypothesis serves a multipurpose function in research. It provides direction to the researcher's efforts because it determines the research method and the type of data relevant to the solution of the problem. It also provides a framework for interpreting the results and for stating the conclusions of the study.

A good hypothesis must satisfy certain criteria. It must be testable, which means that it is possible to gather evidence that will either support or fail to support the hypothesis. It must agree with the preponderance of existing data. It must be stated as clearly and concisely as possible. And it must state the expected relationship between variables that can be measured.

Once formulated and evaluated in terms of these criteria, the research hypothesis is ready to be subjected to an empirical test. The null hypothesis—the negation of what the researcher expects—is stated. It is important to remember that a research hypothesis cannot be proved or disproved, only supported or not supported. Even if it is not supported, a hypothesis may still serve a useful purpose because it can lead the researcher to reevaluate rationale and procedures and to consider other approaches to the problem.

KEY CONCEPTS

alternative hypothesis
criteria for evaluating hypotheses
deductive hypothesis
directional hypothesis
falsifiability
inductive hypothesis
nondirectional hypothesis
null hypothesis
pilot study
purposes of hypotheses
research plan
testable hypotheses
theory

EXERCISES

1. What are the purposes of the hypothesis in research?
2. What is the difference between an inductive and a deductive hypothesis?
3. State a hypothesis based on each of the following research questions:
   a. What would be the effect of using the Cuisenaire method in teaching elementary arithmetic?
   b. Is there a relationship between the gender of the tutor and the gains made in

reading achievement by black male elementary students?

   c. Does living in interracial housing affect attitudes toward members of another race?
   d. Is there any relationship between the type of reinforcement (tangible or intangible) and the amount of learning achieved by socioeconomically disadvantaged children?
   e. Does preschool training reduce the educational gap separating advantaged and disadvantaged children before they enter first grade?
   f. Do teacher expectations of children's intellectual performance have any effect on the children's actual performance?

4. Rewrite the following hypothesis in null form: "Children who read below grade level will express less satisfaction with school than those who read at or above grade level."

5. Evaluate the adequacy of each of the following hypotheses. If a hypothesis is inadequate, state the reason for the inadequacy and write an adequate hypothesis.
   a. "Teachers deserve higher pay than administrators."
   b. "Students who take a middle school government course will be capable of more enlightened judgments concerning local political affairs than will those who do not take the course."
   c. "Computer-based drill and practice is a better way to teach slow learners multiplication combinations than is flash cards."
   d. "If students differ in their socioeconomic status, they will differ in their English proficiency scores."
   e. "Children who show high achievement motivation will show high anxiety as measured by the Children's Manifest Anxiety Scale."
   f. "Positive verbal reinforcement of student responses by the teacher will lessen the probability of future responses."

6. Write a directional and a nondirectional hypothesis based on the research question "What is the relationship between the rate of maturation of adolescent boys and their self-concepts?"

7. Why should a hypothesis be clearly stated before a quantitative research study is initiated?

8. Label the following hypotheses as research hypotheses or null hypotheses:
   a. "Students will receive lower scores on achievement tests that measure the higher levels of Bloom's taxonomy."
   b. "There is no difference in the performance of students taught mathematics by method A and those taught mathematics by method B."
   c. "The mean retention scores of children receiving experimental drug X will not differ from the scores of children who do not receive drug X."
   d. "Students taught by laissez-faire teachers will show higher problem-solving skills than students taught by highly structured teachers."

9. Locate a research study stating a hypothesis and try to identify the theory from which the hypothesis originated.

10. Evaluate the following statements as possible research hypotheses:
   a. "Asian high school students are better in mathematics than American high school students."
   b. "Do SAT prep courses improve students' scores on the SAT?"
   c. "Students who participate in the high school volunteerism program become better adult citizens than students who do not."

11. A researcher has a theory about children's ordinal position in the family and their achievement motivation. Write a research hypothesis that might be based on existing theory. Then write the hypothesis in null form.

12. Formulate a tentative research plan for your class project.
   a. What is the general research problem under consideration for investigation?
   b. State the preceding general research problem as a research question.
   c. Explain the rationale for such a study. What are its theoretical or practical applications?
   d. State the hypothesis (or hypotheses) for this study.

e. Was this hypothesis derived deductively from theory or inductively from experience and observation? Explain.
f. Identify the variables in the study and operationally define each.
g. What kind of research methodology will be required for this study?
h. What subjects (sample) will you select for the study?
i. Have you located any published research related to your problem? If so, briefly summarize the findings.

13. Which of the following evidence contributes to the development of a theory?
 a. Evidence that supports a hypothesis
 b. Evidence that contradicts a hypothesis
 c. Both of the above
14. Select a theory that you find interesting and derive a research hypothesis from this theory. You might choose a learning theory, motivational theory, theory of cognitive dissonance, or any other educational or psychological theory.

ANSWERS

1. The purposes of hypotheses are to provide a tentative proposition suggested as a solution to a problem or as an explanation of some phenomenon, stimulate research, provide a relational statement that is directly testable, and provide direction for research.
2. With an inductive hypothesis, the researcher makes observations of relationships and then hypothesizes an explanation for the observed behavior. With a deductive hypothesis, the researcher formulates a hypothesis based on known theory, accompanied by a rationale for the particular proposition.
3. a. "Elementary students taught by the Cuisenaire method will score higher on an arithmetic test than students taught by an alternative method."
 b. "Black male elementary students tutored by another male will achieve higher reading scores than will black male elementary students tutored by a female."
 c. "People living in interracial housing will express more favorable attitudes toward those of another race than will people living in segregated housing."
 d. "Socioeconomically disadvantaged children reinforced with tangible rewards will exhibit greater learning achievement than will children reinforced with intangible rewards."
 e. "Advantaged and disadvantaged children of preschool age receiving preschool training will be separated by a smaller educational gap than will advantaged and disadvantaged children of preschool age not receiving preschool training." (*Note:* The terms advantaged and disadvantaged children, preschool training, and educational gap would need to be defined.)
 f. "Children whose teachers have high expectations of their intellectual performance will perform at a higher level than will children whose teachers have low expectations of their intellectual performance."
4. There is no difference in the satisfaction with school expressed by children who read below grade level and children who read at or above grade level.
5. a. The hypothesis is inadequate because it is a value statement and cannot be investigated in a research study. A legitimate hypothesis would be "Teachers who receive higher pay than their administrators will express greater job satisfaction than will teachers who do not receive higher pay than their administrators."
 b. The hypothesis is inadequate because enlightened judgments is a value term. An acceptable hypothesis would be "Students who take a middle school government course will evidence more knowledge concerning local political affairs, and will more often arrive at inferences based on this knowledge, than will students who do not take a middle school government course."
 c. The hypothesis is inadequate because *better* is a value term and because it

lacks clear and concise operational definitions. A testable hypothesis would be "Those students performing below grade level in math who practice multiplication combinations through computer drill and practice will, on average, score a higher proportion of correct answers on a criterion test than will students performing below grade level who spend the same amount of time practicing multiplication combinations with flash cards."

d. The hypothesis is inadequate because there is no statement of an expected relationship between variables. An acceptable hypothesis would be "Students classified as having high socioeconomic status will have higher scores on an English proficiency test than will students classified as having low socioeconomic status."

e. The hypothesis is inadequate because there are no independent or dependent variables. An acceptable hypothesis would be "Children who show high achievement motivation will have higher scores on the Children's Manifest Anxiety Scale than children with low achievement motivation."

f. The hypothesis is inadequate because it is inconsistent with the existing knowledge of positive reinforcement and its effect on student responses.

6. Directional hypothesis: "Early-maturing boys will exhibit more positive self-concepts than late-maturing boys." Nondirectional hypothesis: "There is a difference in the self-concepts of early- and late-maturing adolescent boys."

7. The hypothesis gives direction to the collection and interpretation of data. Clearly stating the hypothesis reveals flaws that were not apparent while developing the vague idea of the study in mind.

8. a. Research
b. Null
c. Null
d. Research

9. Answers will vary.

10. a. "Better in math" needs to be operationally defined.
b. A hypothesis is not stated in question form.
c. It is not testable as stated. How would you define and measure "better adult citizens"?

11. *Research hypothesis*: "Achievement motivation and ordinal birth position in the family are positively related; or first-born children have greater achievement motivation than their siblings." *Null hypothesis*: "There is no relationship between children's birth position in the family and their achievement motivation."

12. Answers will vary.

13. c

14. Answers will vary

INFOTRAC COLLEGE EDITION

Use the keywords *hypothesis* and *research* to locate a research article that states a hypothesis. How was the hypothesis stated? Was the hypothesis based on deduction from a theory or was it derived inductively from observation? Were operational definitions provided for the variables in the hypothesis?

Chapter 6

Descriptive Statistics

DESCRIPTIVE STATISTICS SIMPLIFY OUR LIVES BY ORGANIZING AND SUMMARIZING DATA.

INSTRUCTIONAL OBJECTIVES

After studying this chapter, the student will be able to:

1 Describe the nature and uses of descriptive statistics.

2 Identify the characteristics, uses, and limitations of four types of measurement scales—nominal, ordinal, interval, and ratio.

3 Organize research data into frequency distributions, present them as frequency polygons and histograms, and interpret polygons and histograms occurring in the professional literature.

4 Distinguish between the measures of central tendency and the situations in which each should be used. Calculate and interpret the mean, the median, and the mode for any given data.

5 Describe appropriate applications of measures of variability and compute variance, standard deviation, quartile deviation, and range for any given set of data.

6 Calculate and explain why *z* scores have universal meaning and how this is useful in interpreting the position of a single observation in a distribution.

7 Explain why *z* scores are often transformed into other standard scores.

8 Convert a *z* score to a stanine score and use this to give a verbal description of the score's meaning. Explain why stanine scores are easy to interpret.

9 Transform raw scores into standard scores.

10 Explain advantages and disadvantages of percentile ranks. Calculate percentile rank for a given score.

11 Identify the characteristics of the normal curve. Explain why it is useful in descriptive research.

12 Use the normal curve table to find the percentile rank of a given *z* score or a given percentile rank.

13 Identify appropriate applications of Pearson *r* correlation for describing the relationship between variables. Explain why it shows both the direction and the strength of the relationship.

14 Describe the meaning of coefficient of determination and its application in interpreting the coefficient of correlation.

15 Identify the components of effect size and what increases and what decreases effect size. Explain why number in sample does not influence effect size.

16 Explain how effect size assesses the strength of relationships between variables.

17 Calculate effect size for a difference between means. Explain why the Pearson *r* is a form of effect size.

18 Perform a meta-analysis and explain the meaning of a meta-analysis outcome.

Statistical procedures are basically methods of handling quantitative information. These procedures have two principal advantages. First, they enable researchers to organize, summarize, and describe observations. Techniques used for these purposes are called **descriptive statistics**. Second, they help determine how reliably researchers can infer that phenomena observed in a limited group—a *sample*—are likely to occur in the unobserved larger *population* of concern from which the sample was drawn—in other words, how accurately you can employ inductive reasoning to infer that what you observe in the part will be observed in the whole. Techniques used for such purposes are called **inferential statistics**.

Knowledge of some basic statistical procedures is essential for researchers proposing to carry out quantitative research, so that they can analyze and interpret their data and communicate their findings to others. In addition, it is desirable that educators keep abreast of research and use research findings in their own setting. To do this they need to be familiar with statistical procedures so they can understand and evaluate research studies conducted by others. The proper administration and interpretation of tests used in schools also requires some understanding of statistical procedures. Teachers who are unfamiliar with these procedures may have difficulty evaluating their students' abilities and performance. They also may find it difficult to review research in their areas of specialization and to acquire up-to-date information. Knowledge of statistics is vital for making evidence-based decisions in education.

SCALES OF MEASUREMENT

A fundamental step in the conduct of quantitative research is measurement: the process through which observations are translated into numbers. S. S. Stevens (1951) is well remembered for his definition: "In its broadest sense, measurement is the assignment of numerals to objects or events according to rules" (p. 1). Quantitative researchers first identify the variables they want to study; then they use rules to determine how to express these variables numerically. The variable *religious preference* may be measured according to the numbers indicated by students who are asked to select among (1) Catholic, (2) Jewish, (3) Protestant, (4) Muslim, or (5) other. The variable *weight* may be measured as the numbers observed when subjects step on a scale. The variable *social maturity* may be operationally defined as scores on the Vineland Social Maturity Scale. The nature of the measurement process that produces the numbers determines the interpretation that can be made from them and the statistical procedures that can be meaningfully used with them. The most widely quoted taxonomy of measurement procedures is Stevens' scales of measurement in which he classifies measurement as nominal, ordinal, interval, and ratio.

NOMINAL SCALE

The most primitive scale of measurement is the **nominal scale**. Nominal measurement involves placing objects or individuals into categories that are qualitatively rather than quantitatively different. Measurement at this level requires only that you be able to distinguish two or more relevant, mutually exclusive categories and know the criteria for placing an individual or object into the appropriate category. The required empirical operation at this level of measurement involves only recognizing whether an object or individual does or does not belong in a given category. The only relationship between categories is that they are *different* from each other; there is no suggestion that one category represents "more" or "less" of a characteristic. For example, classifying students according to gender constitutes nominal measurement. The example of religious preference is also an example of nominal measurement.

Numbers may be used at the nominal level, but only when arbitrarily assigned to serve as labels to identify the categories. There is no empirical relationship between the numbers used in nominal measurement that corresponds to the actual mathematical relationship between the numbers used. For example, the numeral 0 might be used to represent males and the numeral 1 to represent females—but the 1 does not indicate more of something than the 0, and numbers could be interchanged without affecting anything but the labelling scheme used. School District 231 is not necessarily more or less of anything than School District 103. The numbers used at the nominal level do not represent either absolute or relative amounts of any characteristic but merely serve to identify members of a given category.

The identifying numbers in a nominal scale cannot, of course, be arithmetically manipulated through addition, subtraction, multiplication, or division. You may use only those statistical procedures based on mere counting, such as reporting the numbers of observations in each category or expressing those numbers as percentages of the total number of subjects.

ORDINAL SCALE

Next on the hierarchy of measurement scales is the **ordinal scale**, which ranks objects or individuals with respect to how much or how little of the attribute under consideration they possess. Objects or individuals are placed in order according to the degree to which they possess that attribute—but without indicating the degree of difference, or distance, between them. Ordinal measurement occurs, for example, when teachers rank students in a class from highest to lowest on characteristics such as social maturity, leadership skills, or cooperativeness.

The essential requirement for measurement at this level is that the relationship must be such that if object X is greater than object Y and object Y is greater than object Z, then object X is greater than object Z and is written thus: If $(X > Y)$ and $(Y > Z)$, then $(X > Z)$. When appropriate, other wording may be substituted for "greater than" such as "stronger than," "precedes," "has more of," and so on.

When numbers are assigned in ordinal measurement, they indicate only the *order* of the observations and nothing more. Neither the difference between the numbers nor their ratio has meaning. Thus, if the numerals 1, 2, and 3 are used to label observations, there is no implication that the distance between ranks is equal—that is, that 1 is as much higher in rank than 2 as 2 is higher than 3. In an untimed footrace, you only know who came in first, second, and third; you have no way of knowing how much faster one runner was than any other. The difference between first and second place would not necessarily be the same as the difference between second and third; nor could you say that the runner who came in second was twice as fast as the runner who came in fourth. A ranking of students on the basis of math scores or a ranking of high school seniors on the basis of grades represents an ordinal scale.

Statistics employing ordinal scale data provide more information than statistics employing nominal data. However, they produce less information than statistics employing interval or ratio data. Statistics that indicate the points below which certain percentages of the cases fall are appropriate with an ordinal scale.

INTERVAL SCALE

A more precise measurement system is the **interval scale**, which not only orders objects or events according to the amount of the attribute they represent but also has equal intervals between the units of measure. Equal differences in the numbers represent equal differences in the attribute being measured. Fahrenheit and Celsius thermometers are examples of interval scales. There is no true zero on an interval scale. Zero on the Fahrenheit scale is as cold as Fahrenheit could get in his laboratory. Zero on the Celsius scale is arbitrarily set at the temperature water freezes at sea level. With an interval scale both the order of and the distance between the numbers are meaningful. Therefore, with both Fahrenheit and Celsius scales you can say that the difference between $+60°$ and $+50°$ is the same as the distance between $-10°$ and $-20°$, but you cannot say that $+60°$ is twice as warm as $+30°$. Zero on an interval scale is just another point on the scale. It does not indicate an absence of the variable being measured.

Likewise, the zero point on a psychological or educational scale test is arbitrary. When intelligence tests were first developed, the average raw score for each age group was arbitrarily assigned a scale score of 100, and the raw score standard deviation was given the standard score of 16. A student may occasionally receive a score of 0 on a statistics test, but this does not mean that he or she has zero knowledge of statistics. If you had three students who made scores of 15, 30, and 45 on a statistics test, you could not say that the score of 30 represents twice as much knowledge of statistics as the score of 15 or that the score of 45 represents three times as much knowledge as the score of 15. To understand the reason why, let us assume that 15 very simple items are added to the test so that all three students can answer them correctly. The three scores would now become 30, 45, and 60 for the three students. If you attempted to form ratios between the values on this interval-type scale, you would (mistakenly) report that the student with a score of 60 had twice as much knowledge of statistics as the student with a score of 30—but in the earlier ratio you had already (incorrectly) assumed that the same student had three times as great a knowledge of statistics as the other student. Neither of these conclusions makes sense.

Numbers on an interval scale may be manipulated by addition and subtraction, but because the zero is arbitrary, multiplication and division of the numbers are not appropriate. As noted, ratios between the numbers on an interval scale are meaningless. However, the difference between positions on an interval scale may be reported or the numbers may be added. Any statistical procedures based on adding may be used with this level scale along with the procedures appropriate for the lower-level scales. These include most of the common descriptive and inferential statistical procedures.

It is important to point out that in most academic measures, the intervals are equal in terms of the measuring instrument itself but not necessarily in terms of the performance being measured. To illustrate, consider a spelling test with the following words: *cat*, *dish*, *ball*, *loquacious*, *schizophrenia*, and *pneumonia*. Here the distance between one correct and three correct is the same as the distance between three correct and five correct. However, when considered in terms of spelling performance, the difference between three and five correct suggests a greater difference in ability than does the difference between one and three correct. Unless you can say that the distance between three and five on the spelling test represents the same amount of spelling performance as does the distance between one and three, then these scores indicate nothing more than the rank order of the students.

However, through careful construction it is possible to produce an instrument where the intervals observed between scores on the test give a reasonable approximation of ability intervals. The better intelligence tests are an example of this. The difference in ability between an IQ of 90 and an IQ of 95 may not be precisely the same as the difference between an IQ of 105 and an IQ of 110, but you will not be greatly misled if you assume that the two differences are approximately equal.

It has become common practice to treat many educational variables, such as classroom tests and grades ($A = 4$, $B = 3$, and so on), as if they were interval data, even when that assumption is not well justified. It would be difficult to maintain that the difference between $F = 0$ and $D = 1$ represents the same difference in academic achievement as the difference between $C = 2$ and $B = 3$, or to justify treating scores on our spelling test example as interval data. Be cautious when interpreting statistics derived from such data. The statistics imply interval-level information when the information is actually often somewhere between ordinal and interval.

However, grade point average is almost always calculated as if the data are interval. Scores on teacher-made tests are usually quasi-interval, somewhere between interval and ordinal data. Although scores on teacher-made tests are probably rarely as far from interval data as our spelling test example, they almost always vary from true interval data to some extent.

RATIO SCALE

A **ratio scale**, the highest level of measurement scale, has a true zero point, as well as equal intervals. Ratios can be formed between any two given values on the scale. A yardstick used to measure length in units of inches or feet is a ratio scale because the origin on the scale is an absolute zero corresponding to no length at all. Thus, it is possible to state that a stick 6 feet long is twice as long as a stick 3 feet long. With a ratio scale, it is possible to multiply or divide each of

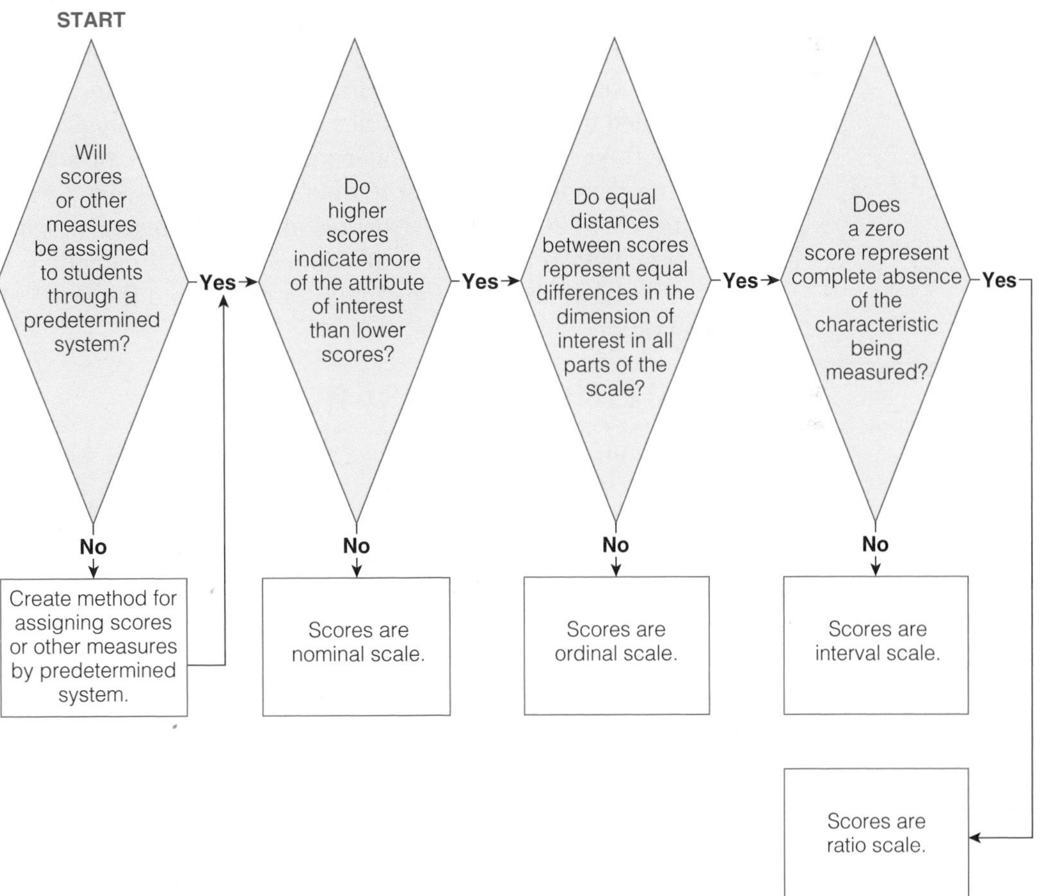

Figure 6.1 Determining Scales of Measurement

THINK ABOUT IT 6.1

You are buying a used car. You consider (a) its make (Ford, Toyota, etc.), (b) the miles on the odometer, (c) the year it was made, and (d) its rating in *Consumers Report*.

1. Which of the above is nominal data?
2. Which of the above is ordinal data?
3. Which of the above is interval data?
4. Which of the above is ratio data?

Answers

1: a; 2: d; 3: c (the year 2006 is not twice the year 1003); 4: b.

the values by a certain number without changing the properties of the scale. For example, you can multiply 2 pounds by 16 to change the unit of measurement to 32 ounces, or you can multiply 6 feet by 12 to change the unit to inches. You can multiply and maintain the same ratio as before the multiplication. For another example, you can multiply 4 quarts of milk and 2 quarts of milk by 2 and change the unit of measurement to pints. In pints, 8 pints is still twice as much as 4 pints.

Only a few variables of interest in education are ratio in nature. These are largely confined to motor performance and other physiological measures. A shot put score of 16 yards is twice as far as a shot put score of 8 yards, but you cannot say that a person who scores 40 on a math test is twice as good at math as a person who scores 20 on a math test because math test scores are interval data. All types of statistical procedures are appropriate with a ratio scale.

Figure 6.1 shows the decisions made to determine the scale of measurement of an observation.

ORGANIZING RESEARCH DATA

Describing data that have not been arranged in some kind of order is very difficult, if not impossible. Therefore, organizing research data is a fundamental step in descriptive statistics. The most familiar ways of organizing data are (1) arranging the measures into frequency distributions and (2) presenting them in graphic form.

FREQUENCY DISTRIBUTIONS

A systematic arrangement of individual measures from highest to lowest is called a **frequency distribution**. The first step in preparing a frequency distribution is to list the scores in a column from highest at top to lowest at bottom. Include all possible intermediate scores even if no one scored them; otherwise the distribution will appear more compact than it really is. Several identical scores often occur in a distribution. Instead of listing these scores separately, it saves time to add a second column where the frequency of each measure is recorded. Table 6.1 shows the test scores of a group of 105 students in an Ed 101 lecture class. Section A of the table lists the scores in an unorganized form. Section B arranges these scores in a frequency distribution with the *f* column showing how many made each score. Now it is possible to examine the general "shape" of the distribution. With the scores so organized, you can determine their spread, whether they are distributed evenly or tend to cluster, and where clusters occur in the distribution. For example, looking over the frequency distribution of the scores presented in Table 6.1, it is easy to see that they range from 21 to 36, that 29 is the most frequent score, and that scores tend to cluster more near the top of the distribution than the bottom. None of this would be apparent had the scores not been organized. Organizing data into frequency distributions also facilitates the computation of various useful statistics.

Table 6.1 The Test Scores of 105 Students on Ed 101 Test

Part A. Unorganized Scores

33	29	30	30	33	29	33	32	28	24	34	31	27	29	23
25	29	24	27	26	33	33	26	30	28	26	29	32	32	31
28	34	30	31	33	21	29	31	30	32	36	30	31	27	29
26	29	33	32	29	28	28	30	28	27	30	31	34	33	22
30	29	27	29	24	30	21	31	31	33	28	21	31	29	31
31	33	22	29	31	32	32	31	28	29	30	22	33	30	30
32	33	31	33	28	29	27	33	27	21	30	29	28	27	33

Part B. Frequency Distribution

Scores (X)	Tallies	Frequencies (f)	fX	cf
36	/	1	26	105
35		0		104
34	///	3	102	104
33	~~////~~ ~~////~~ ~~////~~	15	405	101
32	~~////~~ ///	8	256	80
31	~~////~~ ~~////~~ ////	14	434	78
30	~~////~~ ~~////~~ ////	14	420	64
29	~~////~~ ~~////~~ ~~////~~ /	16	464	50
28	~~////~~ ~~////~~	10	280	34
27	~~////~~ ///	8	216	29
26	////	4	104	16
25	/	1	25	12
24	///	3	72	11
23	/	1	23	8
22	///	3	66	7
21	////	4	84	4
		$N = 105$		

We will get to the fX and cf columns later.

THINK ABOUT IT 6.2

Here are the scores that Mr. Li's 18 physics class students made on their first exam: Al: 20; Ali: 21; Ann: 20; Ben: 23; Cal: 20; Dan: 20; Ed: 21; Ima: 22; Jan: 19; Kay: 16; Joe: 20; Mae: 18; Mia: 23; Ned: 19; Ona: 21; Sam: 22; Sue: 19; Ted: 16; Van: 18. Do a frequency distribution of these scores. For answer see the first two columns in Table 6.2.

Table 6.2 Mr. Li's Physics Class Exam Scores

(1) *X*	(2) *f*	(3) *fX*	(4) *cf*
23	2	46	18
22	2	44	16
21	4	84	14
20	4	80	10
19	2	38	6
18	2	36	4
17	0	0	2
16	2	32	2

GRAPHIC PRESENTATIONS

It is often helpful and convenient to present research data in graphic form. Among various types of graphs, the most widely used are the **histogram** and the **frequency polygon**. The initial steps in constructing the histogram and the frequency polygon are identical:

1. Lay out the score points on a horizontal dimension (abscissa) from the lowest value on the left to the highest on the right. Leave enough space for an additional score at both ends of the distribution.
2. Lay out the frequencies of the scores (or intervals) on the vertical dimension (ordinate).
3. Place a dot above the center of each score at the level of the frequency of that score.

From this point you can construct either a histogram or a polygon. In constructing a histogram, draw through each dot a horizontal line equal to the width representing a score, as shown in Figure 6.2. A score of 26 is thought of as ranging from 25.5 to 26.5, a score of 27 is thought of as ranging from 26.5 to 27.5, and so forth.

To construct a polygon, connect the adjacent dots, and connect the two ends of the resulting figure to the base (zero line) at the points representing 1 less than

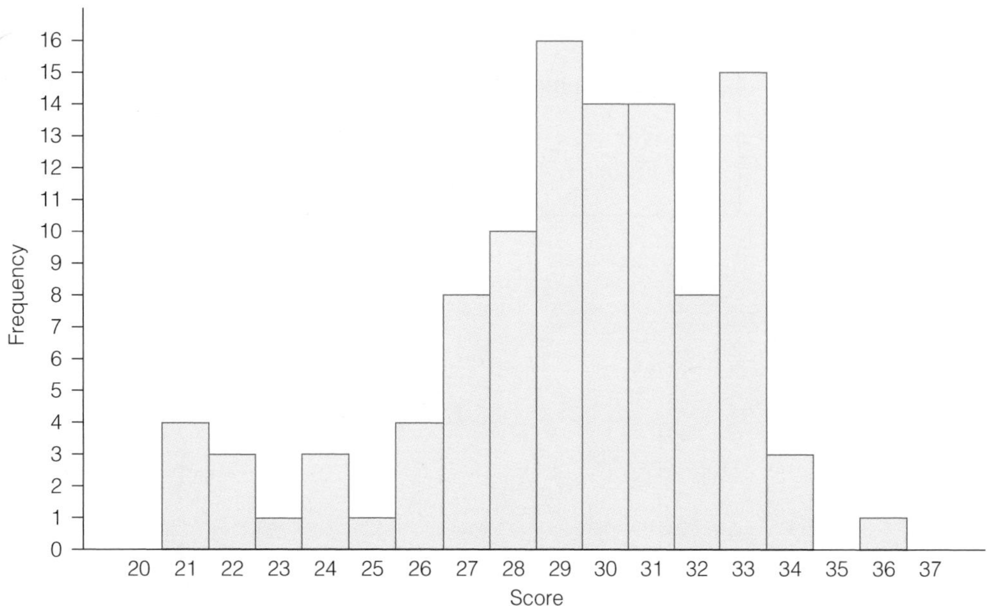

Figure 6.2 Histogram of 105 Test Scores from Table 6.1

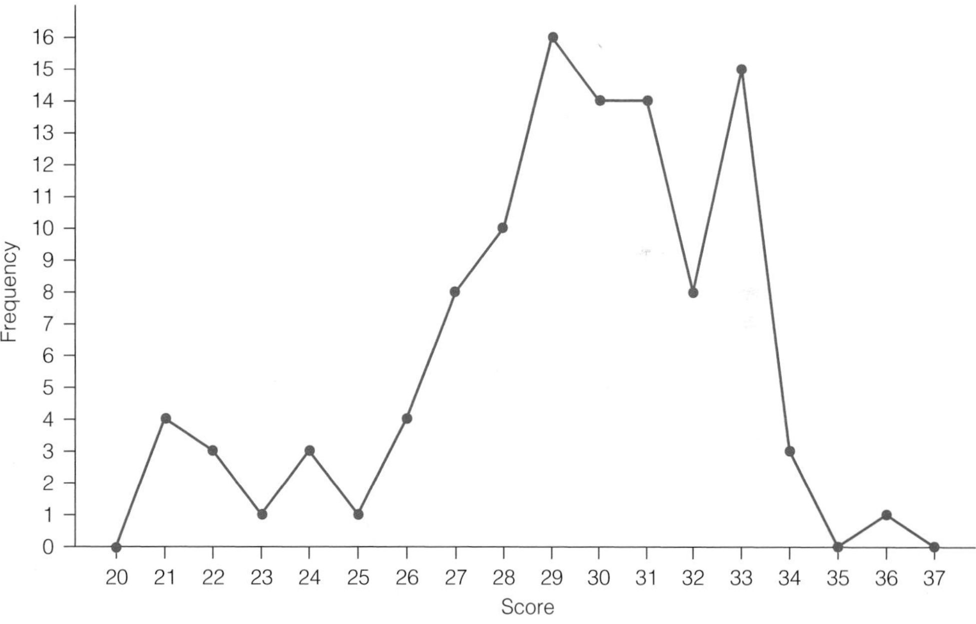

Figure 6.3 Frequency Polygon of 105 Test Scores from Table 6.1

the lowest score and 1 more than the highest score, as shown in Figure 6.3. Histograms are preferred when a researcher wants to indicate the discrete nature of the data, such as when a nominal scale has been used. Polygons are preferred to indicate the continuous nature of the data.

THINK ABOUT IT 6.3

Construct a histogram and a polygon of the scores of Mr. Li's first physics exam.

Answer
See Figure 6.4.

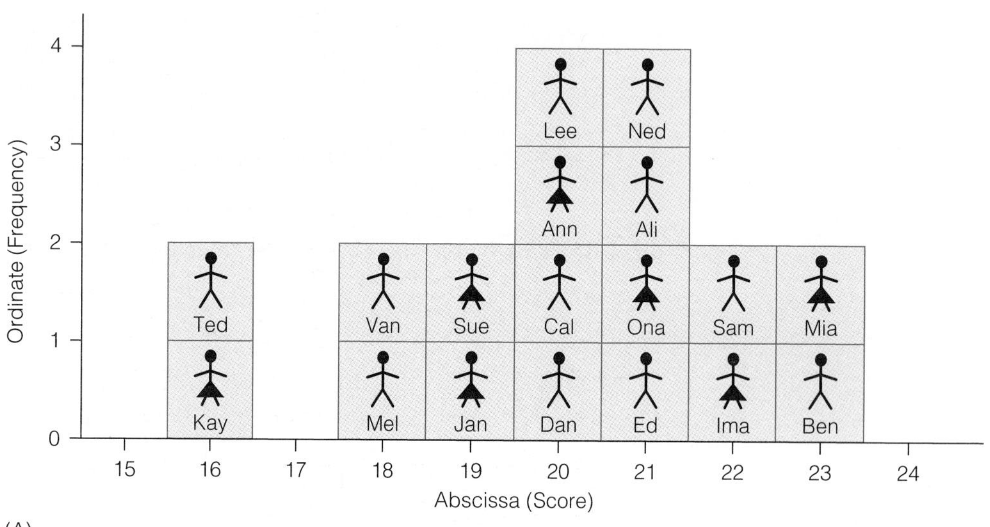

(A)

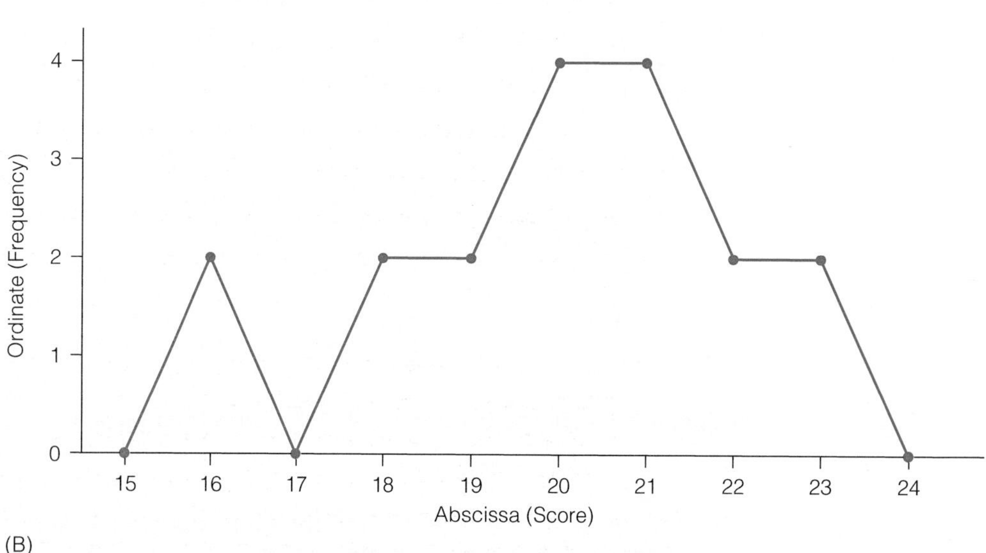

(B)

Figure 6.4 (A) Histogram of Mr. Li's Physics Exam and (B) Polygon of Mr. Li's Physics Exam

MEASURES OF CENTRAL TENDENCY

A convenient way of summarizing data is to find a single index that can represent a whole set of measures. For example, finding a single score that can give an indication of the performance of a group of 300 students on an aptitude test would be useful for comparative purposes. In statistics three indexes are available for such use. They are called **measures of central tendency**, or *averages*. To most laypeople, the term *average* means the sum of the scores divided by the number of scores. To a statistician, the average can be this measure, known as the *mean*, or one of the other two measures of central tendency, known as the *mode* and the *median*. Each of these three can serve as an index to represent a group as a whole.

THE MEAN

The most widely used measure of central tendency is the **mean**, or *arithmetic average*. It is the sum of all the values in a distribution divided by the number of cases. In terms of a formula it is

$$\overline{X} = \frac{X_1 + X_2 + X_3 + \cdots + X_n}{N} \tag{6.1}$$

which is usually written as

$$\overline{X} = \frac{\Sigma X}{N} \tag{6.2}$$

where

$\overline{X}$ = mean
Σ = sum of
X = raw score
N = number of cases

Applying Formula 6.2 to the following IQ scores, we find that the mean is 111:

IQ scores: 112 121 115 101 119 109 100

$$\overline{X} = \frac{112 + 121 + 115 + 101 + 119 + 109 + 100}{7} = \frac{777}{7} = 111$$

Note that in this computation the scores were not arranged in any particular order. Ordering is unnecessary for calculation of the mean.

Some think of formulas as intimidating incantations. Actually they are time savers. It is much easier to write $\overline{X} = \Sigma X/N$ than to write "add all the scores in a distribution and divide by the number of cases to calculate the mean."

Although it is not necessary to put the scores in order to calculate the mean, with larger sets of numbers it is usually convenient to start with a frequency distribution and multiply each score by its frequency. This is shown in column 3 (Xf)

in Table 6.2, Mr. Li's physics class exam scores. Adding the numbers in this column will give us the sum of the scores.

$$\Sigma X = 360$$

The mean of the physics exam scores is

$$\overline{X} = \frac{\Sigma X}{N} = \frac{360}{18} = 20$$

We will use the *cf* column later to calculate the median.

THE MEDIAN

The **median** is defined as that point in a distribution of measures below which 50 percent of the cases lie (which means that the other 50 percent will lie above this point). Consider the following distribution of scores where the median is 18:

14 15 16 17 18 19 20 21 22

In the following 10 scores we seek the point below which 5 scores fall:

14 16 16 17 18 19 20 20 21 22

The point below which five scores, or 50 percent of the cases, fall is halfway between 18 and 19. Thus the median of this distribution is 18.5.

Consider the following scores:

18 20 22 25 25 30

Any point from 22.5 to 24.5 fits the definition of the median. By convention in such cases the median is defined as half way between these lowest and highest points, in this case 22.5 + 24.5/2 = 23.5.

To find the median of Mr. Li's physics exam scores we need to find the point below which 18/2 = 9 scores lie. We first create a cumulative frequency column (*cf*, column 4 in Table 6.2). The cumulative frequency for each interval is the number of scores in that interval plus the total number of scores below it. Since the interval between 15.5 and 16.5 has no scores below it, its *cf* is equal to its *f*, which is 2. Since there were no scores of 17, the *cf* for 17 is still 2. Then adding the two scores of 18 yields a cumulative frequency of 4. Continuing up the frequency column, we get *cf*s of 10, 14, 16, and finally 18, which is equal to the number of students.

The point separating the bottom nine scores from the top nine scores, the median, is somewhere in the interval 19.5 to 20.5. Statistics texts say to partition this interval to locate the median. The *cf* column tells us that we have six scores below 19.5. We need to add three scores to give us half the scores (9). Since there are four scores of 20, we go three fourths of the way from 19.5 to 20.5 to report a median of 20.25. Note that many computer programs, including the Statistical Package for the Social Sciences (SPSS) and the Statistical Analysis System (SAS), simply report the midpoint of the interval, in this case 20, as the median.

Notice that the median does not take into account the size of individual scores. In order to find it, you arrange your data in rank order and find the point that divides the distribution into two equal halves. The median is an ordinal statistic because it is based on rank. You can compute a median from interval or ratio data, but in such cases the interval characteristic of the data is not being used. One circumstance in which the median may be the preferred measure of central tendency arises when there are some extreme scores in the distribution. In this case the use of a measure of central tendency that takes into account the size of each score results in either overestimation or underestimation of the typical score. The median, because of its insensitivity to extreme scores, is the appropriate index to be applied when you want to find the typical score. For illustration, consider the following distribution:

49 50 51 53 54 55 56 60 89

The score of 54, which is the median of this distribution, is the most typical score. The mean, which takes into account the individual values of the scores 60 and 89 will certainly result in an overestimation of the typical score.

THE MODE

The **mode** is the value in a distribution that occurs most frequently. It is the simplest to find of the three measures of central tendency because it is determined by inspection rather than by computation. Given the distribution of scores

14 16 16 17 18 19 19 19 21 22

you can readily see that the mode of this distribution is 19 because it is the most frequent score. In a histogram or polygon the mode is the score value of the highest point (the greatest frequency), as you can see in Figures 6.2 and 6.3, where the mode is 29. Sometimes there is more than one mode in a distribution. For example, if the scores had been

14 16 16 16 18 19 19 19 21 22

you would have two modes: 16 and 19. This kind of distribution with two modes is called *bimodal*. Distributions with three or more modes are called *trimodal* or *multimodal*, respectively.

The mode is the least useful indicator of central value in a distribution, for two reasons. In the first place, it is unstable. For example, two random samples drawn from the same population may have quite different modes. In the second place, a distribution may have more than one mode. In published research the mode is seldom reported as an indicator of central tendency. Its use is largely limited to inspectional purposes. A mode may be reported for any of the scales of measurement, but it is the only measure of central tendency that may legitimately be used with nominal scales.

COMPARISON OF THE THREE INDEXES OF CENTRAL LOCATION

Because the mean is an interval or ratio statistic, it is generally a more precise measure than the median (an ordinal statistic) or the mode (a nominal statistic). It takes into account the value of *every* score. It is also the most stable of the three measures of central tendency in that if a number of samples are randomly drawn from a parent population, the means of these samples will vary less from one another than will their medians and their modes. For these reasons the mean is more frequently used in research than the other two measures.

The mean is the best indicator of the combined performance of an entire group. However, the median is the best indicator of *typical* performance. Consider, for example, a school board whose members have the following annual incomes: $140,000, $60,000, $50,000, $40,000, and $40,000. The mean, $66,000, is the sum of their incomes divided by the number of members, but it is higher than all but one of the board members' incomes. The median, $50,000, gives a better picture of the typical income in the group.

SHAPES OF DISTRIBUTIONS

Frequency distributions can have a variety of shapes. A distribution is symmetrical when the two halves are mirror images of each other. In a **symmetrical distribution** the values of the mean and the median coincide. If such a distribution has a single mode, rather than two or more modes, the three indexes of central tendency will coincide, as shown in Figure 6.5.

If a distribution is not symmetrical, it is described as **skewed**, pulled out to one end or the other by the presence of extreme scores. In skewed distributions the values of the measures of central tendency differ. In such distributions the value of the mean, because it is influenced by the size of extreme scores, is pulled toward the end of the distribution in which the extreme scores lie, as shown in Figures 6.6 and 6.7. The effect of extreme values is less on the median because this index is influenced not by the size of scores but by their position. Extreme values have no impact on the mode because this index has no relation with either of

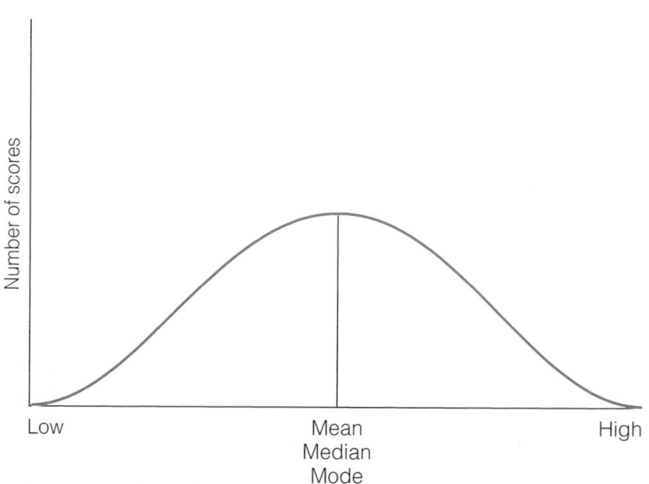

Figure 6.5 Symmetrical Distribution

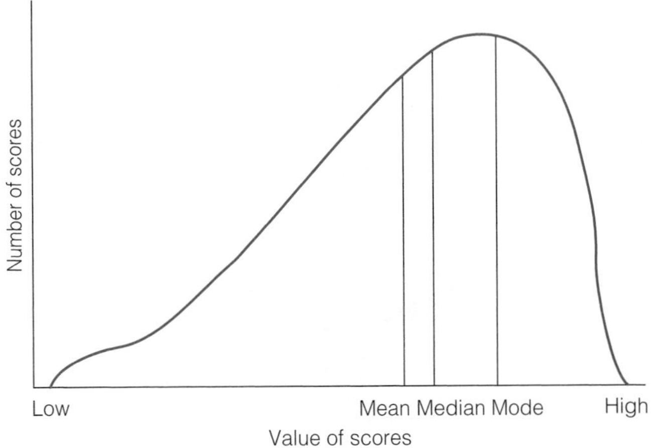

Figure 6.6 Negatively Skewed Distribution

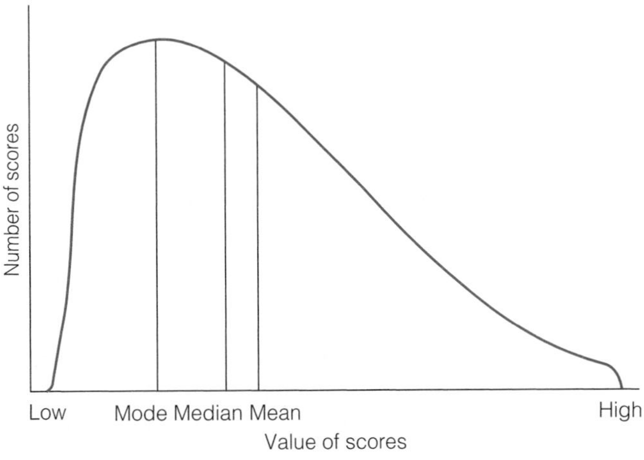

Figure 6.7 Positively Skewed Distribution

the ends of the distribution. Skews are labeled according to where the extreme scores lie. A way to remember this is "The tail names the beast." Figure 6.6 shows a **negatively skewed distribution**, while Figure 6.7 shows a **positively skewed distribution**.

MEASURES OF VARIABILITY

Although indexes of central tendency help researchers describe data in terms of average value or typical measure, they do not give the total picture of a distribution. The mean values of two distributions may be identical, whereas the degree of dispersion, or **variability**, of their scores might be different. In one distribution

PICTURE THIS

Joe Rocco

the scores might cluster around the central value; in the other they might be scattered. For illustration, consider the following distributions of scores:

(a) 24, 24, 25, 25, 25, 26, 26 $\overline{X} = 175/7 = 25$
(b) 16, 19, 22, 25, 28, 30, 35 $\overline{X} = 175/7 = 25$

The value of the mean in both these distributions is 25, but the degree of scattering of the scores differs considerably. The scores in distribution (a) are obviously much more homogeneous than those in distribution (b). There is clearly a need for indexes that can describe distributions in terms of *variation*, *spread*, *dispersion*, *heterogeneity*, or *scatter* of scores. Several indexes are available for this purpose. The most commonly used are range, variance, and standard deviation.

RANGE

The simplest of all indexes of variability is the **range**. It is the difference between the upper real limit of the highest score and the lower real limit of the lowest score. For example, 15 is the range of the following distribution:

2 10 11 12 13 14 16

Recall from a previous discussion that each score in a distribution represents an interval from halfway between that score and the next lowest score up to halfway between that score and the next highest score. For example, the number 16 represents the midpoint of the interval 15.5 to 16.5, and the interval width is 1. In the example just given, you find the range by subtracting 1.5 (the lower limit of the lowest score) from 16.5 (the upper limit of the highest score), which is equal to 15. It is simpler to use Formula 6.3:

$$R = (X_h - X_l) + I \qquad (6.3)$$

THINK ABOUT IT 6.4

1. **a.** What is the range of Mr. Li's physics exam scores?
   b. What is the range of the Ed 101 scores?

Answers

1. **a.** 23.5 − 15.5 = 8 or using Formula 6.3 $H - L + I = 23 - 16 + 1 = 8$.
   b. 36.5 − 20.5 = 16 or $H - L + I = 36 - 21 + 1 = 15 + 1 = 16$. (Note that the highest occurring score was 36; the lowest occurring score was 21.)

where

$$R = \text{range}$$
$$X_h = \text{highest value in a distribution}$$
$$X_l = \text{lowest value in a distribution}$$
$$I = \text{interval width}$$

Subtract the lower number from the higher and add 1 (16 − 2 + 1 = 15). In frequency distribution, 1 is the most common interval width.

The range is an unreliable index of variability because it is based on only two values, the highest and the lowest. It is not a stable indicator of the spread of the scores. For this reason the use of the range is mainly limited to inspectional purposes. Some research reports refer to the range of distributions, but such references are usually used in conjunction with other measures of variability, such as variance and standard deviation.

VARIANCE AND STANDARD DEVIATION

Variance and standard deviation are very useful and frequently used indexes of variability. They are both based on **deviation scores**—scores that show the difference between a raw score and the mean of the distribution. The formula for a deviation score is

$$x = X - \overline{X} \tag{6.4}$$

where

$$x = \text{deviation score}$$
$$X = \text{raw score}$$
$$\overline{X} = \text{mean}$$

Scores below the mean will have negative deviation scores, and scores above the mean will have positive deviation scores. By definition, the sum of the deviation scores in a distribution is always 0. Thus, to use deviation scores in calculating measures of variability, you must find a way to get around the fact that $\Sigma x = 0$. The technique used is to square each deviation score so that they all become positive numbers. If you then sum the squared deviations and divide by the number of scores, you have the mean of the squared deviations from the mean, or the **variance**. In mathematical form, variance is

$$\sigma^2 = \frac{\Sigma x^2}{N} \tag{6.5}$$

Table 6.3 Variance of Mr. Li's Physics Exam Scores

(1) X	(2) f	(3) fX	(4) x	(5) x^2	(6) fx^2	(7) X^2	(8) fX^2
23	2	46	+3	9	18	529	1058
22	2	44	+2	4	8	484	968
21	4	84	+1	1	4	441	1764
20	4	80	0	0	0	400	1600
19	2	38	−1	1	2	361	722
18	2	36	−2	4	8	324	648
17	0	0					
16	2	32	−4	16	32	256	512
$N = 18$	$\Sigma X = 360$	$\Sigma x = 0$	$\Sigma x^2 = 72$	$\Sigma X^2 = 7272$	$\overline{X} = \frac{\Sigma X}{N} = \frac{360}{18} = 20$		

where

σ^2 = variance
Σ = sum of
x^2 = deviation of each score from the mean $(X - \overline{X})$ squared, otherwise known as the deviation score squared
N = number of cases in the distribution

In column 4 of Table 6.3 we see the deviation scores, differences between each score, and the mean. Column 5 shows each deviation score squared (x^2) and column 6 shows the frequency of each score from column 2 multiplied by x^2. Summing column 6 gives us the sum of the deviation scores squared $\Sigma x^2 = 72$. Dividing this by the number of scores gives us the mean of the squared deviation scores, the variance.

$$\sigma^2 = \frac{\Sigma x^2}{N} = \frac{72}{18} = 4$$

The forgoing procedure is convenient only when the mean is a whole number. This rarely occurs except in textbook examples. We have chosen to do our examples with whole number means so you can understand the concept and not get bogged down with the mathematics.

The following formula, 6.6, avoids the tedious task of working with squared mixed-number deviation scores such as 7.6667^2. Using Formula 6.6 yields the desired result with much less labor. Thus, we recommend that students always use this formula for computing standard deviation if the computation must be done "by hand":

$$\sigma^2 = \frac{\Sigma X^2 - \frac{(\Sigma X)^2}{N}}{N} \tag{6.6}$$

where

σ^2 = variance
ΣX^2 = sum of the squares of each score (i.e., each score is first squared, then these squares are summed)
$(\Sigma X)^2$ = sum of the scores squared (the scores are first summed, then this total is squared)
N = number of cases

Column 7 in Table 6.3 shows the square of the raw scores. Column 8 shows these raw score squares multiplied by frequency. Summing this fx^2 column gives us the sum of the squared raw scores:

$$\sigma^2 = \frac{\Sigma X^2 - \frac{(\Sigma X)^2}{N}}{N} = \frac{7272 - \frac{360^2}{18}}{18} = \frac{7272 - \frac{129600}{18}}{18} = \frac{7272 - 7200}{18} = \frac{72}{18} = 4$$

Note that this result is the same as what we got with Formula 6.5.

Because each of the deviation scores is squared, the variance is necessarily expressed in units that are squares of the original units of measure. For example, you might find that the variance of the heights of children in a class is 9 square inches. This would tell you that this class is more heterogeneous in height than a class with a variance of 4 square inches and more homogeneous than a class with a variance of 16 square inches.

In many cases educators prefer an index that summarizes the data in the same unit of measurement as the original data. **Standard deviation** (σ), the positive square root of variance, provides such an index. It is by far the most commonly used measure of variability. By definition, the standard deviation is the square root of the mean of the squared deviation scores. Rewriting this definition using symbols, you obtain

$$\sigma = \sqrt{\frac{\Sigma x^2}{N}} \tag{6.7}$$

For Mr. Li's physics exam scores the standard deviation is

$$\sqrt{\frac{72}{18}} = \sqrt{4} = 2$$

The standard deviation belongs to the same statistical family as the mean; that is, like the mean, it is an interval or ratio statistic, and its computation is based on the size of individual scores in the distribution. It is by far the most frequently used measure of variability and is used in conjunction with the mean.

Formulas 6.5, 6.6, and 6.7 are appropriate for calculating the variance and the standard deviation of a population. In the example, if you are only interested in describing the heterogeneity of Mr. Li's physics students on his first exam, these formulas are appropriate. If scores from a finite group or sample are used to estimate the heterogeneity of a population from which that group was drawn, research has shown that these formulas more often underestimate the population variance and standard deviation than overestimate them. Mathematically, to get unbiased estimates $N - 1$ rather than N is used as the denominator.

The formulas for variance and standard deviation based on sample information are

$$s^2 = \frac{\Sigma x^2}{N - 1} \tag{6.8}$$

$$s = \sqrt{\frac{\Sigma x^2}{N - 1}} \tag{6.9}$$

$$s = \sqrt{\frac{\Sigma X^2 - \frac{(\Sigma X)^2}{N}}{N - 1}} \tag{6.10}$$

Following the general custom of using Greek letters for population parameters and Roman letters for sample statistics, the symbols for variance and standard deviation calculated with $N - 1$ are s^2 and s.

With the data in Table 6.3,

$$\frac{72}{18 - 1} = 4.24 \quad \text{and} \quad s = \sqrt{4.24} = 2.06$$

Formulas 6.8, 6.9, and 6.10 are often used to calculate variance and standard deviation even when there is no intention to estimate population parameters. Many computer and calculator programs calculate variance and standard deviation this way unless instructed to do otherwise.

Spread, scatter, heterogeneity, dispersion, and volatility are measured by standard deviation, in the same way that volume is measured by bushels and distance is measured by miles. A class with a standard deviation of 1.8 on reading grade level is more heterogeneous than a class with a standard deviation of 0.7. A month when the daily Dow Jones Industrial Average has a standard deviation of 40 is more volatile than a month with a standard deviation of 25. A school where the teachers' monthly salary has a standard deviation of $900 has more disparity than a school where the standard deviation is $500.

MEASURES OF RELATIVE POSITION

Measures of relative position indicate where a score falls in relation to all other scores in the distribution. Researchers often want to assess an individual's relative position in a group or to compare the relative position of one individual on two or more measures or of two or more individuals on the same measure. The most widely used statistics for these purposes are z scores, stanines, other standard scores, and percentile rank.

z SCORE

The most widely used measure of relative position is the ***z* score**, which indicates the positive or negative difference between an individual score and the mean as measured in standard deviation units. It and other indexes derived from it are known as **standard scores**. The z score is defined as the distance of a score from the mean as measured by standard deviation units. The formula for finding a z score is

$$z = \frac{x}{\sigma} = \frac{X - \overline{X}}{\sigma} \tag{6.11}$$

where

X = raw score
$\overline{X}$ = mean of the distribution
σ = standard deviation of the distribution
x = deviation score $(X - \overline{X})$

Applying this formula, a score exactly one standard deviation above the mean becomes a z of $+1$, a score exactly one standard deviation below the mean becomes a z of -1, and so on. A score equal to the mean will have a z-score value of 0. For illustration, suppose a student's score on a psychology test is 72 where the mean of the distribution is 78 and the standard deviation equals 12. Suppose also that the same student has made a score of 48 on a statistics test where the mean is 51 and the standard deviation is 6. If you substitute these figures for the appropriate symbols in Formula 6.11, you can derive a z score for each test:

Psychology $$z_1 = \frac{72 - 78}{12} = -0.50$$

Statistics $$z_2 = \frac{48 - 51}{6} = -0.50$$

Both these standard scores belong to the z distribution, where by definition the mean is always 0 and the standard deviation is 1, and therefore they are directly comparable. It is apparent in this example that the score of 72 on the psychology test and the score of 48 on the statistics test are equivalent—that is, both scores indicate the same relative level of performance. In other words, the standing of the student who has obtained these scores is the same in both tests when compared with the performance of the other students. It would be very difficult to make such a comparison without employing the z-score technique.

Let us use another example: Suppose a student who has taken the same tests has obtained a score of 81 on the psychology test and a score of 53 on the statistics test. As before, it is difficult to compare these raw scores to show on which test this student has done better. Converting the scores to z scores makes the comparison easy. Using Formula 6.11, we find the values of z_1 and z_2 in this case to be as follows:

Psychology $$z_1 = \frac{81 - 78}{12} = +0.25$$

Statistics $$z_2 = \frac{53 - 51}{6} = +0.33$$

This result shows that the score of 53 on the statistics test actually indicates a slightly better relative performance than the score of 81 on the psychology test. Compared with the other students, this student has done somewhat better in statistics than in psychology.

Because the mean of the z scores in any distribution is zero and the standard deviation is 1, they have universal meaning. A z score of -0.1 is slightly below average in a distribution of statistics test scores, a distribution of weights of people in a weight control program, a distribution of pork belly prices, or any other distribution. A z score of $+2.4$ is very high, whether you are talking about achievement scores, scores on a measure of depression, corn yield per acre, or any other measure.

STANINE SCORES

During World War II the U.S. Army Air Corps developed a standard system of nine scores called **stanine scores** to help its personnel interpret z scores. Stanines avoid negative numbers and decimals. A stanine score of 5 represents z scores that are average or a little above or a little below average, that is, equivalent to z scores between -0.25 and $+0.25$. From there, stanine scores go up to 9 and down to 1 in increments of 0.5 as shown in Table 6.4. A z score of 0.12 (stanine 5) is just a tad above dead average. This is the case whether you are looking at a vocabulary test score, a measure of paranoia, or weight. A z score of -1.38 (stanine 2) is very well below average. Stanines are standardized with the mean of 5 and a standard deviation of 2. The formula for stanines is $2z + 5$. You convert a z score to a stanine by multiplying by 2 and adding 5. Stanines are always rounded to the nearest whole number. Whenever this formula yields a result greater than 9, the value 9 is assigned. Whenever the result is less than 1, the value 1 is assigned. Because all z scores above 1.75 are assigned a stanine score of 9 and all z scores below -1.75 are assigned a score of 1, stanine scores are not useful for comparing extreme scores. Stanines are easy to comprehend. Like all transformations of the z score, they have universal meaning. A stanine score of 4 always means below average but not too far below average. Stanines are often used in school systems for reporting students' standardized test scores.

Table 6.4 Conversion of z Scores to Stanines

z-Score	Stanine	Interpretation	Percent in Stanine
Above +1.75	9	Among the very highest scores	4
+1.25 to +1.75	8	Quite well above average	7
+0.75 to +1.25	7	Quite noticeably above average	12
+0.25 to +0.75	6	Above average	17
−0.25 to +0.25	5	Near dead average	20
−0.75 to −0.25	4	Below average	17
−1.25 to −0.75	3	Quite noticeably below average	12
−1.75 to −1.25	2	Quite well below average	7
Below −1.75	1	Among the lowest scores	4

THINK ABOUT IT 6.5

Recall the scores in Mr. Li's physics class in Think About It 6.2.

1. What is the z score of a raw score of 21 in Mr. Li's exam?
2. What is the z score of a raw score of 18 in Mr. Li's exam?
3. What is the z score of a raw score of 20 in Mr. Li's exam?
4. What is the stanine for each of these scores?

Answers

(1), +0.5: (2), −1.0:(3), 0
Stanines (1), 6: (2), 3: (3), 5

OTHER STANDARD SCORES

Scores can also be transformed into other standard-score scales that do not involve negative numbers or decimals. One of the most common procedures is to convert to ***T* scores** by multiplying the z scores by 10 and adding 50. This results in a scale of positive whole numbers that has a mean of 50 and a standard deviation of 10. The T score formula is

$$T = 10(z) + 50 = 10\left(\frac{X - \overline{X}}{\sigma}\right) + 50 \tag{6.12}$$

Suppose a student's score on a Spanish test is 21. Given that the mean of the scores in this test is 27 and the standard deviation is 6, the z score will be (21 − 27)/6, which can be inserted directly into the T-score formula as follows:

$$T = 10\left(\frac{21 - 27}{6}\right) + 50 = 40 \tag{6.13}$$

The transformation of z scores into T scores not only enables one to work with whole numbers, but it also avoids the adverse psychological implications of describing subjects' performances with negative numbers. In the preceding example, it would be easier to report that the student's score is 40 where the mean score is 50 than to report a score of −1.00 with an average of zero.

Teachers who wish to compare the standings of their students on successive tests, or to add all the scores obtained on different tests in the same course to make a general distribution, can convert the students' raw scores to z scores or T scores in order to give equal weight to each set of scores. Adding and averaging scores that belong to different distributions and have different means and different standard deviations can only be done by converting them to some kind of standard score. In addition to T, there are other transformed standard-score distributions. To transform a distribution of scores to a new standardized distribution, it is only necessary to multiply the z score by the desired standard deviation and add the desired mean. The general formula is as follows:

$$A = \sigma_A(z) + \mu_A$$

where

A = standard score on the new scale
μ_A = mean for the new standard scale
σ_A = standard deviation for the new standard scale

For example, College Entrance Examination Board (CEEB) scores have a mean of 500 and a standard deviation of 100 for its transformed distribution. If you were 1.5 standard deviations above the mean ($z = 1.5$) on the verbal section of the Scholastic Assessment Test (SAT), your score would be reported as 650, which is 500 + (100)(1.5). If your quantitative score were 500, you would have scored exactly at the mean.

The Wechsler Adult Intelligence Test (WAIS) scores are standard scores with a mean of 100 and a standard deviation of 15. A raw score on the mean is reported as 100. A raw score one standard deviation below the mean is reported as 85. A raw score two standard deviations above the mean is reported as 130.

Transforming a set of scores to standard scores does not alter the shape of the original distribution. If a distribution of scores is skewed, the derived standard scores also produce a skewed distribution. Only if the original distribution is normal do the standard scores produce a normal distribution.

PERCENTILE RANK

A measure of relative position that most people find easy to understand and interpret is the percentile rank. A **percentile rank** (PR) indicates the percentage of scores in a distribution that fall below a given score point. It is easy to picture a score with a percentile rank of 32 as having 32 percent of the scores in its distribution below it and a score with a percentile rank of 89 having 89 percent of the scores below it. Percentile rank is defined as the percentage of scores below a specific score plus half the percentage of scores tied at that score.

In the case of the following 10 scores, each individual's score represents 10 percent of the distribution:

24 26 26 27 27 27 28 30 30 35

There are no scores below 24. The score of 24 is halfway between the lower real limit (23.5) and the upper real limit (24.5) of 24, so half of this score, 5 percent of the total, is considered to be below 24 and 24 is assigned a percentile rank of 5. The scores of 26 have 10 percent of the distribution below them, and 20 percent tied at 26 so the percentile rank of 10% + 20%/2 = 20 is assigned to both scores of 26. The percentile rank for 27 is 30% + 30%/2 = 45. For 28, PR = 65; for 30, PR = 80; and for 35, PR = 95.

A simple way to calculate percentile rank is to (1) arrange the scores in a frequency distribution, (2) determine the cumulative frequency of scores below the interval containing the score of interest and add one half of the frequency of scores within the interval containing the score of interest, and (3) divide this sum by the total number of scores and multiply by 100.

Consider Mr. Li's physics exam scores (Table 6.2). To calculate the percentile rank of 21, we start with the cumulative frequency below a score of 21 ($cf = 10$) and add one half of the number scoring 21 ($f_w = 2$). We then divide this number by the total number of students who took the test ($N = 18$). Finally, we multiply the result by 100 and round to the nearest whole number:

$$\text{PR} = \frac{cf_b + \frac{f_w}{2}}{N}(100) = \frac{10 + \frac{4}{2}}{18}(100) = 66.67$$

which is rounded to 67.

A score of 18 is assigned the following PR:

$$\text{PR} = \frac{cf_b + \frac{f_w}{2}}{N}(100) = \frac{2 + \frac{2}{2}}{18}(100) = \frac{3}{18}(100) = 16.67$$

which is rounded to 17.

The major advantages of percentile ranks are as follows:

1. They have universal meaning. A score with a percentile rank of 89 is high in any distribution. A score with a percentile rank of 32 is somewhat low in any distribution.
2. The familiar concept of 0 to 100 percent applies to the interpretation of percentile rank. Schools often report percentile ranks to parents.

The major difficulties of percentile rank are as follows:

1. As with other ordinal statistics, percentile ranks cannot be added, subtracted, multiplied, or divided.
2. As with all ordinal indexes, equal differences between percentile ranks do not represent equal differences between the scores in the original distribution. If there are many scores near a particular score, a small change in score will produce a major change in percentile rank. If there are few scores near a particular score, a considerable change in raw score will be necessary to produce a change in position relative to other scores and thus a change in percentile rank. For example, a professor has recorded the weights of the students in his Physical Education 202 class and used them to illustrate the computation of percentile rank. The result is the polygon shown in Figure 6.8.

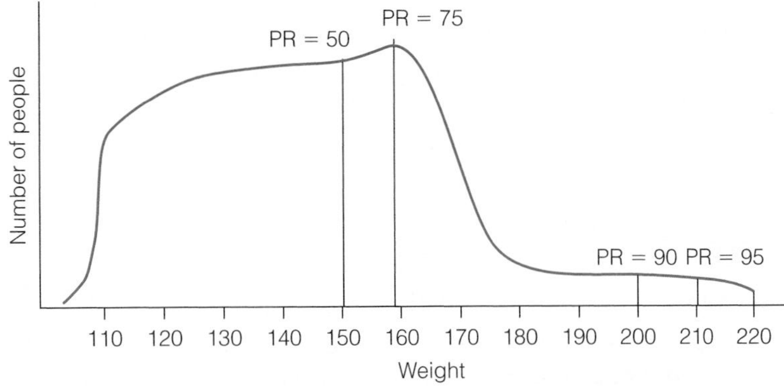

Figure 6.8 Weights of Students in Physical Education 202 Class

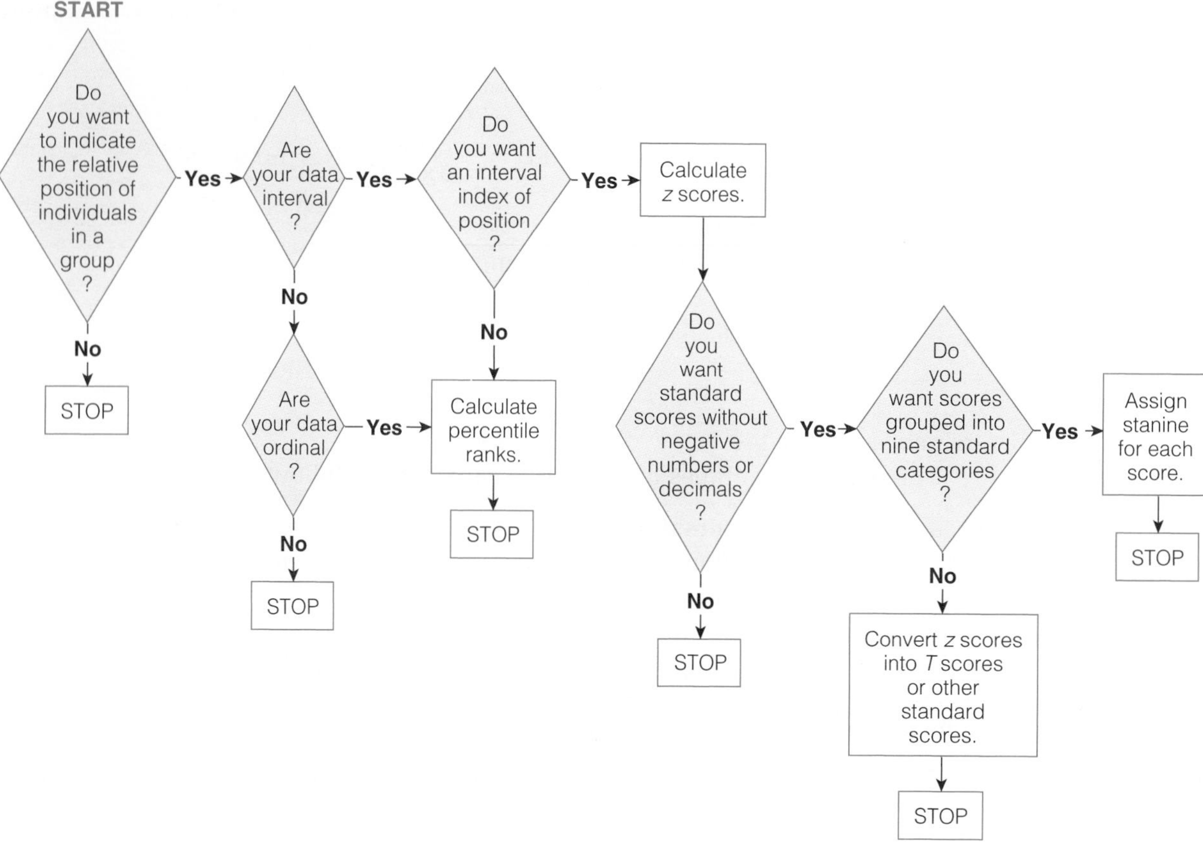

Figure 6.9 Measures of Relative Position

A 160-pound student and a 210-pound student both resolve to lose weight and actually lose 10 pounds each. The 10-pound loss moves the 160-pound student from a percentile rank of 75 to a percentile rank of 50. The same weight loss only changes the heavier student's percentile rank from 95 to 90. More often than not one finds a concentration of cases near the middle of a distribution, then a tapering off of cases at either end. In such distributions, minor differences in raw scores will appear as major differences in percentile ranks among those scores that are near the center of the distribution, where a large number of the scores typically are located. At the extreme ends of the distribution, where there are few scores, major differences in raw score will have only minor effects on percentile rank. We will look at the phenomenon more closely when we consider the normal curve.

Figure 6.9 shows the process of deciding which index to choose for indicating relative position.

THE NORMAL CURVE

Recall the example of deductive reasoning in Chapter 1 where we concluded that if the probability of the birth of either a single son or daughter is 50 percent, the probability of two daughters is 25 percent, the probability of two sons is 25 percent, and the probability of one of each is 50 percent. Abraham DeMeivre (1667–1754) pondered the probabilities of various outcomes when the percent of likelihood in each trial is 50/50 as in heads and tails in honest coin flips. He came up with a formula to predict the probabilities of various number of heads (or tails) when a coin is flipped an infinite number of times. The most frequent score is half infinity, the next most frequent scores are half infinity plus one and half infinity minus one, and so forth. When a polygon of the expected proportions of various *z* scores is made, the outcome is the normal curve. This model proved very useful for gamblers interested in predicting the probability of various gaming outcomes.

Soon after the normal curve was developed, it was noticed that many naturally occurring distributions formed polygons resembling the normal curve. For a contemporary example, if you measure American boys on their tenth birthday, you will find many whose height is near the mean and slightly fewer boys who are a bit above or a bit below the mean. The further you get from the mean, the fewer boys you will find at each height. As in the normal curve probability model, *z* scores near 0 will be expected to occur more frequently than other *z*-score values, and the farther from 0 a *z* score is, the less frequently it will be expected to occur.

Inasmuch as so many naturally occurring distributions resemble the normal curve, this theoretical model has proved very useful in research and other endeavors. Whenever actual data are known or believed to resemble the normal curve in distribution, you can deduce many useful estimates from the theoretical properties of the normal curve.

Note in Figure 6.10 that the normal curve is a symmetrical distribution with the same number of cases at specified *z*-score distances below the mean as above the mean. Its mean is the point below which exactly 50 percent of the cases fall and above which the other 50 percent of the cases are located. Since the curve is symmetrical, the mean, the median, and the mode are identical. In a **normal distribution**, most of the cases concentrate near the mean. The frequency of cases decreases as you proceed away from the mean in either direction. Approximately 34 percent of the cases in a normal distribution fall between the mean and one standard deviation above the mean, and approximately 34 percent are between the mean and one standard deviation below the mean. Between one and two standard deviations from the mean on either side of the distribution are about 14 percent of the cases. Only about 2 percent of the cases fall between two and three standard deviations from the mean, and only about one tenth of 1 percent of the cases fall above or below three standard deviations from the mean.

These characteristics can be seen in Figure 6.10. You can see visually that about one sixth of the curve falls to the left of one standard deviation below the mean. The first line under the curve shows standard deviations from −4 to +4. These are equivalent to *z* scores from −4.00 to +4.00. The cumulative percentage line tells you that 15.9 percent of scores fall below −1 and 97.7 percent falls below +2, and so on. The line following cumulative percentage shows these cumulative percentage scores rounded to the nearest whole percentage. Multiplying each of these numbers by 100 gives you percentile rank.

Percentile equivalents are shown in the next line, which also shows the first quartile (Q_1), the median (Md), and the third quartile (Q_3). Note how slowly the

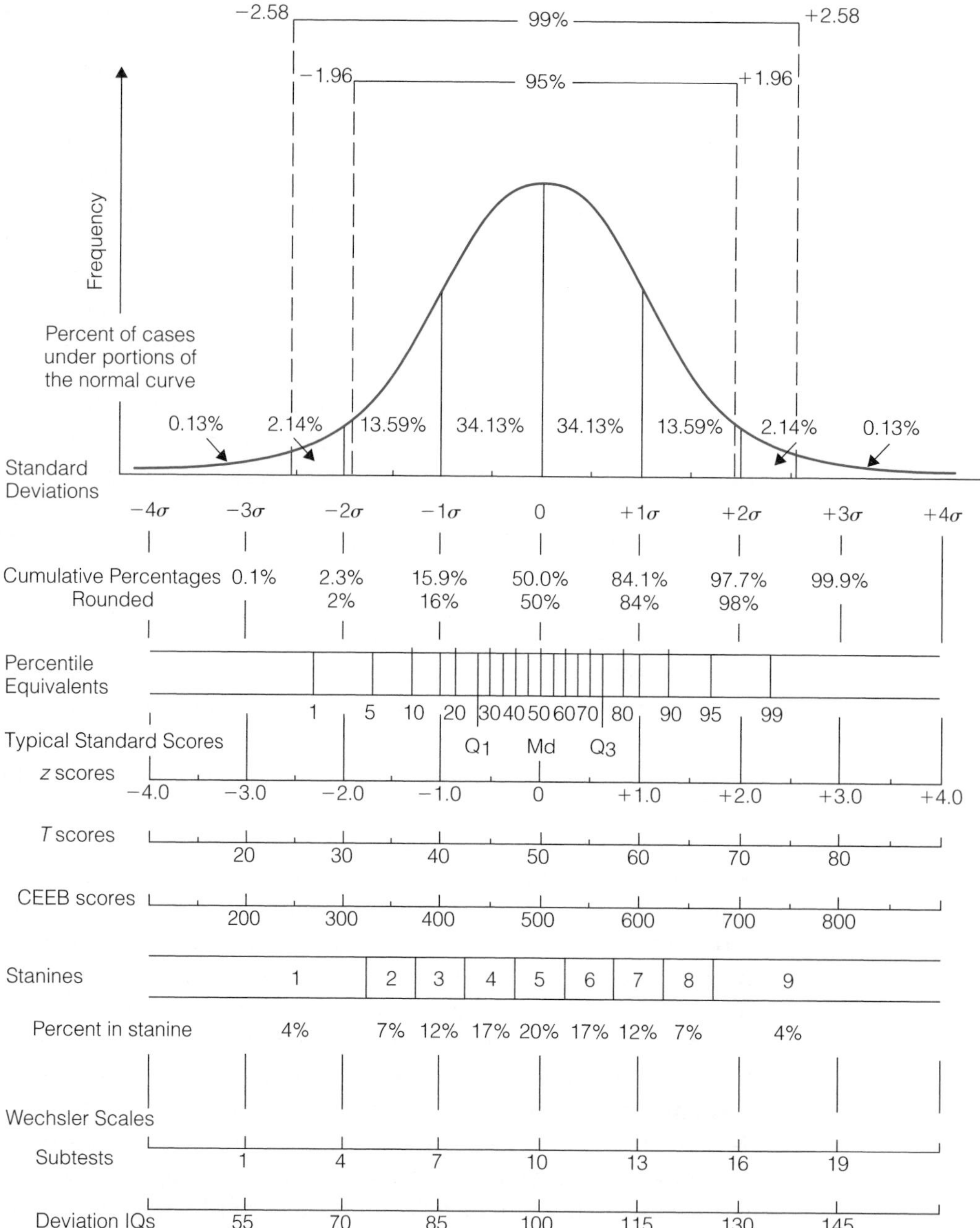

Figure 6.10 Normal Curve and Equivalents

Source: Adapted from H. D. Seashore (Ed.), Methods of expressing test scores, Test Service Bulletin No. 48, Jan. 1955. Reprinted by permission of The Psychological Corporation.

percentile equivalents change below Q_1 and above Q_3, and how rapidly they change between these two points. The next line after percentile equivalents shows *z* scores, which are identical to the scores on the standard deviation line. Following the *z*-score line are various standard scores transformed from *z* scores, including *T* scores, CEEB scores, stanines, percent in stanine, Wechsler subtest scores, and Weschsler deviation IQs. Note that 95 percent of the normal curve falls between plus and minus $z = 1.96$ and 99 percent falls between plus and minus $z = 2.58$. These boundaries become important when we discuss the use of the normal curve in inferential statistics. The normal curve is often described as the *bell-shaped curve*. We have never seen a bell that flares out like this.

To determine the exact percentage of the cases below and above each z score in the normal distribution, consult Table A.1 in the Appendix, which gives the areas of the normal curve. Column (1) of Table A.1 contains different z values. Column (2) gives the area under the curve between the mean and each z value. Column (3) shows the remaining area from each z score to the end of the curve. Therefore, the areas in column (2) and column (3) add up to .5000. Take as an example the z value of +0.70. The area between this z value and the mean can be found in column (2); it is .2580. This figure indicates that 26 percent of the cases fall between this z value and the mean of the distribution. Because the mean of the normal distribution coincides with the median, 50 percent of the cases lie below the mean. Add 0.50 to the .2580, and the result tells you that you can expect 75.8 percent of the cases to fall below the z value of +0.70. Column (3) indicates that the other 24.2 percent of the cases fall above the z value of +0.70.

This procedure is reversed when the z value is negative. Suppose you want to find the percentage of cases below the z value of −0.70. The area between the mean and a z score of −0.70 is .2580 or, in terms of percentage, 25.8 percent of the cases. Subtracting 25.8 from 50, you obtain 24.2. This result would indicate that only 24.2 percent of the scores lie below a z value of −0.70 in a normal distribution. This value can also be found in column (3) of the table, which gives a value of .2420 for a z score of 0.70. The percentage of scores above −0.70 is 100 − 24.2, or 75.8 percent. Since the normal curve is absolutely symmetrical, we do not need separate tables for positive and negative z scores. You just have to remember the sign of the z score with which you are working.

Among other applications, the normal curve can be used to help people who are unfamiliar with standard scores to interpret them. For example, how high is a score of 110 on the WAIS? The WAIS has a mean of 100 and a standard deviation of 15, so the z score here is 0.67. Consulting Table A.1, column (2), you find .2486 of the normal curve falls between the mean and $z = 0.67$. Adding the 50 percent below the mean, you can say that a WAIS score of 110 exceeds the scores of 75 percent of WAIS scores. A WAIS score of 98 has a z score of −0.13, higher than about 45 percent of the scores.

Because it is known that the population distribution of WAIS scores closely resembles the normal curve, PR (percentile rank) approximations based on the normal curve will be quite near to the actual PRs. With other scores, as actual distributions become less and less like the normal curve, the PR approximations become less and less on target. Where the shape of a distribution is not known, it is usually reasonable to assume a distribution similar to the normal curve and to use the normal curve table to find reasonable approximations of the PRs of various z scores. The more the actual shape differs from the normal, the less useful the approximations become.

The most common use of the normal curve in descriptive statistics is going from a given z score to a percentile rank as described in the previous paragraph.

We can also use it to go in the opposite direction, from a given percentile rank to its z-score equivalent.

CORRELATION

After completing the second unit in physics class, Mr. Li gave a second exam. Table 6.5 lists his students in column 1. Their z scores on test 1 are shown in column 2, and their z scores on test 2 are shown in column 3. Recall that z scores are a way to indicate the relative positions of scores. They have universal meaning and can be used with any interval or ratio data.

Looking at Table 6.5 you can see that there is a tendency for those who had positive z scores on test 1 to have positive z scores on test 2, and for those with negative z scores on test 1 to have negative z scores on test 2. Four students have identical z scores on both tests. The others have z scores with the same sign but different values, except Ali who had a positive z score on test 1 and a negative z score on test 2.

Figure 6.11 shows a histogram of the first test scores on the abscissa (x) and a histogram of the second test scores turned sideways on the ordinate (y). In the upper right part of Figure 6.11 you find each student's position on both the first and second tests. This gives a picture of how the students tend to have similar z scores on the two tests, but there is some shifting of their relative positions. There is a strong but not perfect positive relationship between the relative positions of each student's scores on the two tests.

Table 6.5 Mr. Li's First and Second Test z Scores

Student	Test 1 z Scores z_x	Test 2 z Scores z_y	z-Score Products $(z_x z_y)$
Ali	+0.5	−1	−0.5
Ann	0	0	0
Ben	+1.5	+1	1.5
Cal	0	−1	0
Dan	0	+0.5	0
Ed	+0.5	+0.5	0.25
Ima	+1.0	+1.5	1.5
Jan	−0.5	0	0
Kay	−2.0	−1.5	3.0
Lee	0	−1	0
Mel	−1	−0.5	0.5
Mia	+1.5	+1.0	1.5
Ned	+0.5	+1.5	0.75
Ona	+0.5	+1	1.0
Sam	+1.0	+1	1.0
Sue	−0.5	−0.5	0.25
Ted	−2.0	−1.0	2
Van	−1.0	−1.5	1.5
			$\Sigma = 13.75$

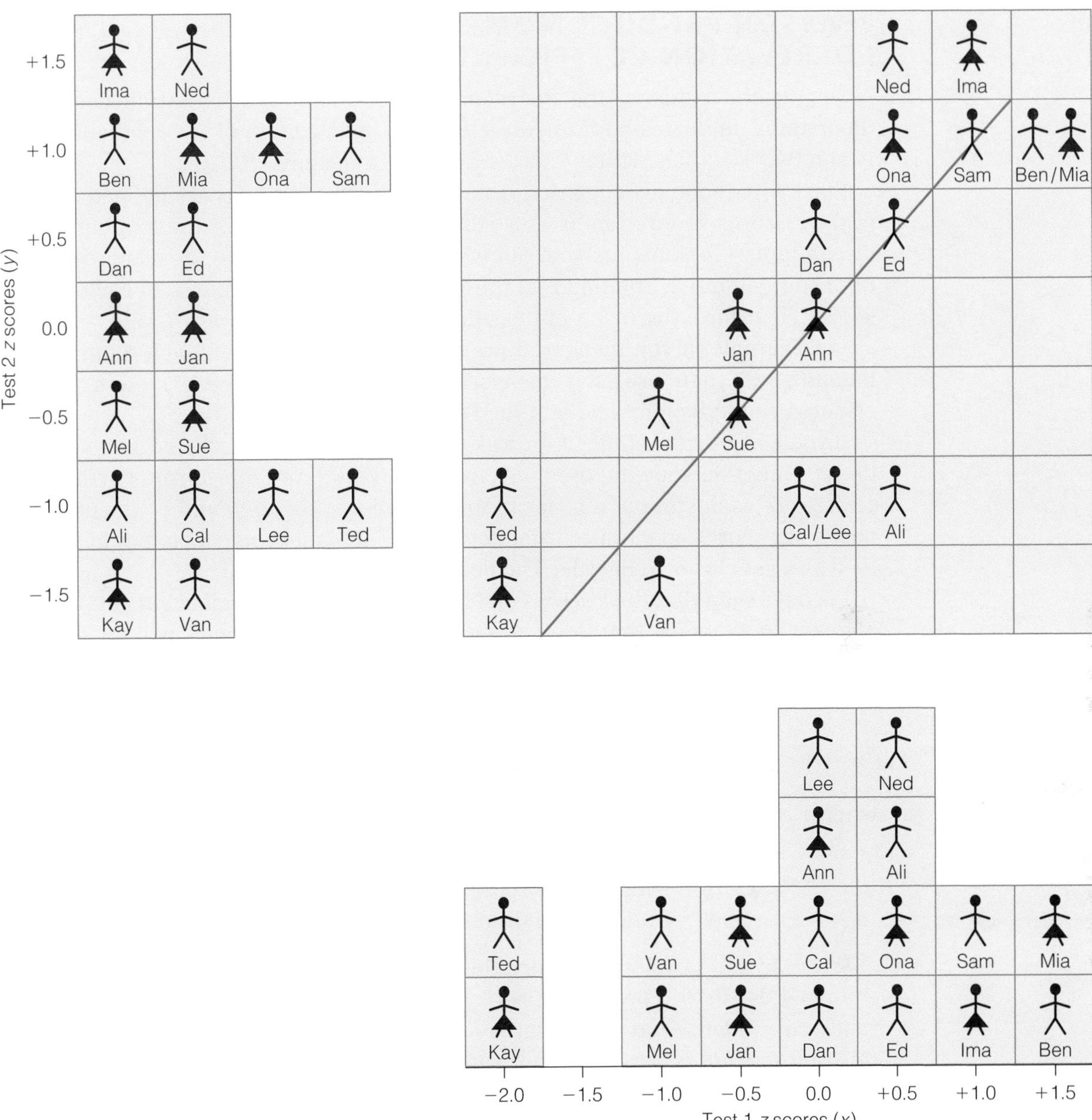

Figure 6.11 Mr. Li's Students' *z* Scores on First and Second Exam Scores

Correlations indicate the relationship between paired scores. The correlation indicates whether the relationship between paired scores is positive or negative and how strong this relationship is. The pairs may be two scores for the same individual, natural pairs such as husbands and wives, or two individuals matched on some measure such as reading test scores. In addition to looking at correlation through visual means, the researcher can calculate a **correlation coefficient** that represents the correlation.

PEARSON PRODUCT MOMENT CORRELATION COEFFICIENT

A very useful statistic, the **Pearson product moment correlation coefficient** (Pearson r), indicates both the direction and the strength of the relationship between two variables without needing a picture to show it.

Start with the knowledge that because of the way z scores are defined the sum of the z scores squared in any distribution will always equal the number in that distribution. (To convince yourself of this, you could square the z scores in column 1 or column 2, and find that the sum of the z scores squared in each column is 18.) Therefore, the mean of the squared deviations is always 1.

For example, if you measured precisely the square feet in each room in your building (x), then precisely measured each room in square meters (y), the z-scores would be identical and the Pearson r would be $+1.0$.

If you look at a schedule of Amtrak trains between Portland, Oregon, and Seattle, Washington, showing the miles from Seattle (x) and miles from Portland (y), z scores of each station in terms of miles from Seattle (x) would be the exact opposite of z scores on y (miles from Portland). Each mile you get farther from Portland you get closer to Seattle. The Pearson r would be -1.0.

We have seen that the z scores on Mr. Li's two tests are similar but not perfectly aligned, so we know that the x and y z-score product averages will be less than $+1.0$ but approaching $+1.0$.

The definition of the Pearson r is simplicity itself. It is the mean $z_x z_y$ product:

$$r = \frac{\Sigma z_x z_y}{N} \tag{6.15}$$

where

r = Pearson product moment coefficient of correlation
$\Sigma z_x z_y$ = sum of the z-score products
N = number of paired scores

With Mr. Li's physics test score the sum of the z-score products in Table 6.5, column 4, is 13.75. Therefore $r = 13.75/18 = .76$. This confirms what we had already concluded. That the z scores on the two tests *are positively related, and this relationship is strong* but not perfect.

Whenever individuals tend to have z scores of the same sign but do not have exactly the same z score on X that they have on Y, the sum of the z scores will be positive but less than N. Therefore, the mean z-score product, the Pearson r, will be less than $+1$. If positive z_x scores tend to be paired with negative z_y scores, but they are not perfect mirror images of each other, the sum of the $z_x z_y$ products will be a negative number, nearer zero than negative N. Therefore, the mean will be between -1 and 0. If there is a strong but not perfectly negative relationship, the r will be near to -1.00. If there is no overall relationship between the paired z scores, their product will be zero, and their mean will be zero.

Here we have an index that indicates not only the direction of relationships between variables but the strength of the relationships. And this index is never greater that $+1.00$ or less than -1.00. It has universal meaning.

Means and standard deviations that are whole numbers almost never occur except in textbooks. Typical z scores are awkward decimal or mixed numbers such as .4716 or 1.6667. Formula 6.15 is useful for understanding what the Pearson r means, but it is hopeless for calculation. Formula 6.16 avoids the need for calculating z scores and multiplying awkward decimals and mixed numbers. It also avoids rounding errors. Its result is the same as that of Formula 6.15:

$$r = \frac{\Sigma XY - \dfrac{(\Sigma X)(\Sigma Y)}{N}}{\sqrt{\left(\Sigma X^2 - \dfrac{(\Sigma X)^2}{N}\right)\left(\Sigma Y^2 - \dfrac{(\Sigma Y)^2}{N}\right)}} \qquad (6.16)$$

where

r = Pearson r
ΣX = sum of scores in X distribution
ΣY = sum of scores in Y distribution
ΣX^2 = sum of the squared scores in X distribution
ΣY^2 = sum of the squared scores in Y distribution
ΣXY = sum of products of paired X and Y scores
N = number of paired X and Y scores (subjects)

Table 6.6 provides the data needed to calculate the Pearson r for Mr. Li's tests 1 and 2 using Formula 6.16. Column 1 lists the students, column 2 shows each student's raw score on test 1 (X). Column 3 shows these raw scores squared (X^2). Column 4 shows each student's raw score on test 2 (Y), column 5 shows these scores squared (Y^2). Column 6 shows the product of each student's X raw score multiplied by his/her Y raw score (XY).

Table 6.6 Mr. Li's Physics Class Raw Scores Illustrating the Calculation of the Pearson r

(1) Name	(2) X	(3) X^2	(4) Y	(5) Y^2	(6) XY
Ali	21	44	22	484	462
Ann	20	400	26	676	520
Ben	23	529	30	900	690
Cal	20	400	22	484	440
Dan	20	400	28	784	560
Ed	21	441	28	784	588
Ima	22	484	32	1024	704
Jan	19	361	26	676	494
Kay	16	256	20	400	320
Lee	200	400	22	484	440
Mel	18	824	24	576	432
Mia	23	529	30	900	690
Ned	21	361	32	1024	672
Ona	21	331	30	900	630
Sam	22	484	30	900	660
Sue	19	361	32	1024	672
Ted	16	256	22	484	352
Van	18	324	20	400	360
	$\Sigma X = 360$	$\Sigma X^2 = 7272$	$\Sigma Y = 468$	$\Sigma Y^2 = 12456$	$\Sigma XY = 9470$

Using Formula 6.16 we get

$$r = \frac{9470 - \dfrac{(360)(468)}{18}}{\sqrt{\left(7272 - \dfrac{(360)^2}{18}\right)\left(12456 - \dfrac{(468)^2}{18}\right)}}$$

$$= \frac{9470 - \dfrac{168480}{18}}{\sqrt{\left(7272 - \dfrac{129600}{18}\right)\left(12456 - \dfrac{219024}{18}\right)}}$$

$$= \frac{9470 - 9360}{\sqrt{(7272 - 7200)(12456 - 12168)}}$$

$$= \frac{9470 - 9360}{\sqrt{(72)(288)}} = \frac{9470 - 9360}{\sqrt{20736}} = \frac{9470 - 9360}{144} = \frac{110}{144} = .76$$

SCATTERPLOTS

In the upper right part of Figure 6.11 we pictured people with their names to illustrate the concept that each figure represents an individual's z scores on both dimensions, test 1 and test 2. It is easier in practice to represent each individual's position on both dimensions with a dot, as shown in Figure 6.12. Such figures are

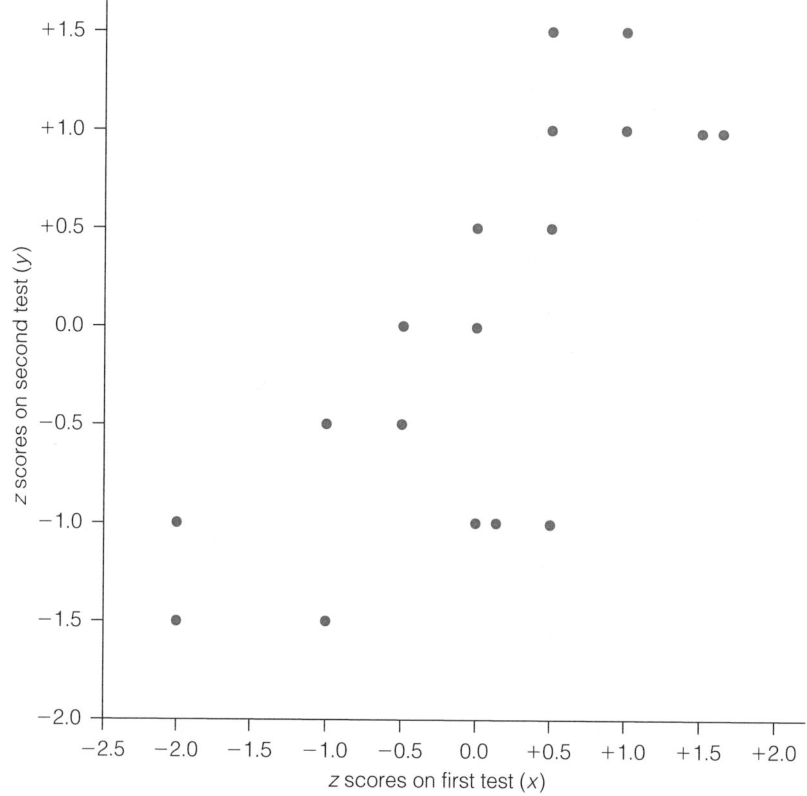

Figure 6.12 Scatterplot of Mr. Li's Students' First and Second Test Scores

called **scatterplots**. In a research situation the z scores on the horizontal axis will be those of the independent variable, with the lowest z score on the left and the highest z score on the right. The z scores on the vertical axis will be those of the dependent variable (y) with the lowest z score at the bottom and the highest z score at the top.

A scatterplot with dots going from lower left to upper right indicates a **positive correlation** (as variable x goes up, variable y also goes up). One with dots going from upper left to lower right indicates a **negative correlation** (as variable x goes up, variable y goes down).

A scatterplot of z scores also reveals the strength of the relationship between variables. If the dots in the scatterplot form a narrow band, so that when a straight line is drawn through the band the dots will be near the line, there is a strong **linear relationship** between the variables. However, if the dots in the z score scatterplot scatter widely, the relationship between variables is relatively weak. The scatterplots in Figure 6.13 show various positive and negative and strong and weak relationships, expressed mathematically by r.

You can see in comparing these scatterplots that the tilt of the "cloud" of dots gets less and less as r moves from a 45° angle for $r = +1.00$ or $r = -1.00$ to less and less tilt until, when it reaches $r = 0$, it is flat and matches the line for the mean of the xy scores.

Once you get used to correlations, you will be able to picture a scatterplot for any Pearson r you encounter.

Like the mean and standard deviation, the Pearson r is an interval statistic that can also be used with ratio data. An assumption underlying the product moment coefficient of correlation is that the relationship between the two variables (X and Y) is linear, that is, that a straight line provides a reasonable expression of the relationship of one variable to the other. If a curved line is needed to express this relationship, it is said to be a **curvilinear relationship**.

A practical way of finding out whether the relationship between two variables is linear or curvilinear is to examine a scatterplot of the data. Figure 6.14 shows two diagrams, one of which (A) indicates a linear relationship and the other (B), a curvilinear one.

THINK ABOUT IT 6.6

After scoring test 2 and entering these exam scores in his computer, Mr. Li also entered each student's days absent during the second unit. He instructed the computer to calculate the Pearson r for these two variables (days absent and test 2 scores). The r was $-.4$.

1. What would he conclude?

Answers

1. There was a moderate tendency for those with high days absent to have lower test 2 scores and those with low days absent to have higher scores on test 2.

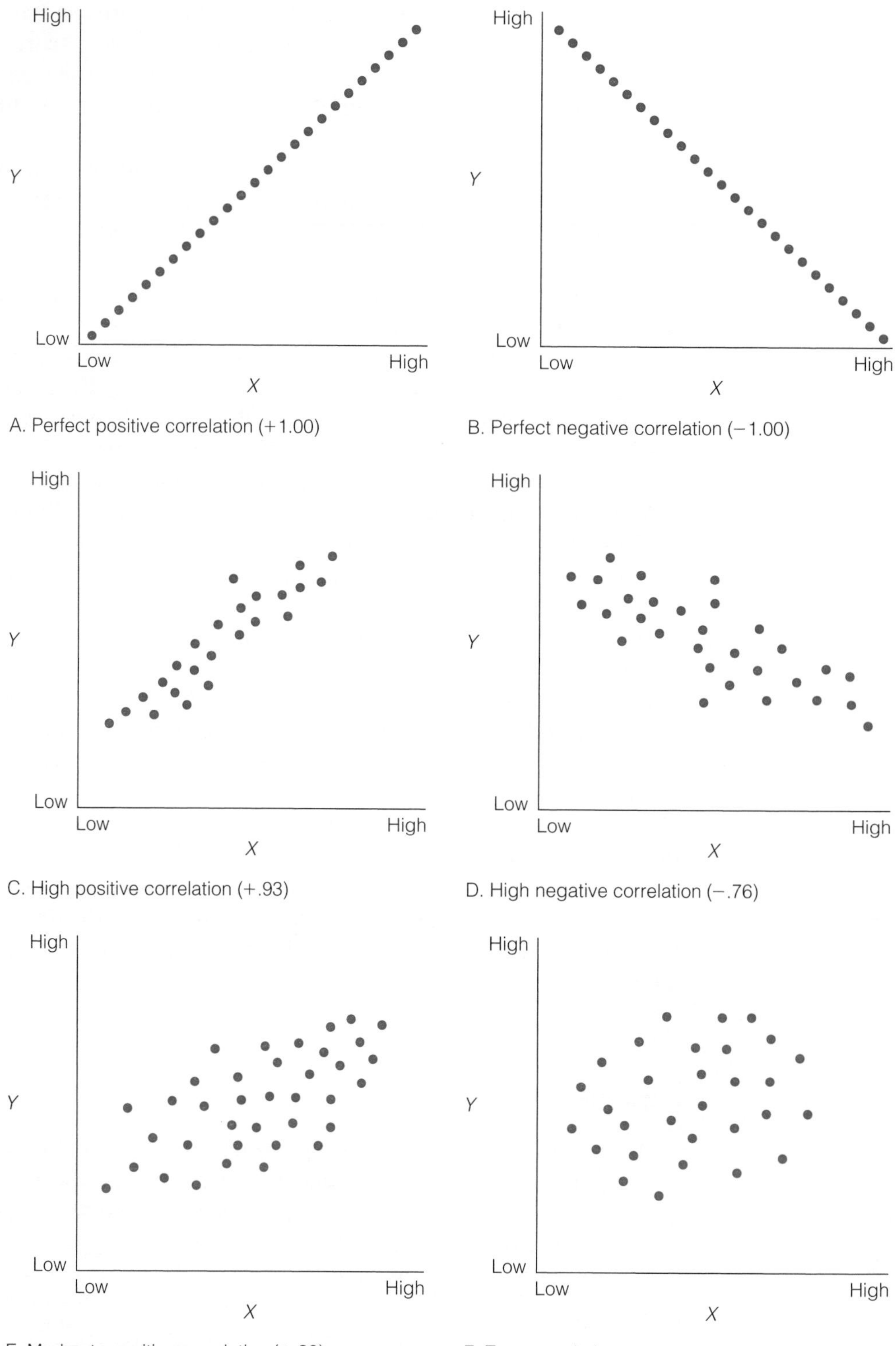

Figure 6.13 Scatterplots of Selected Values of r

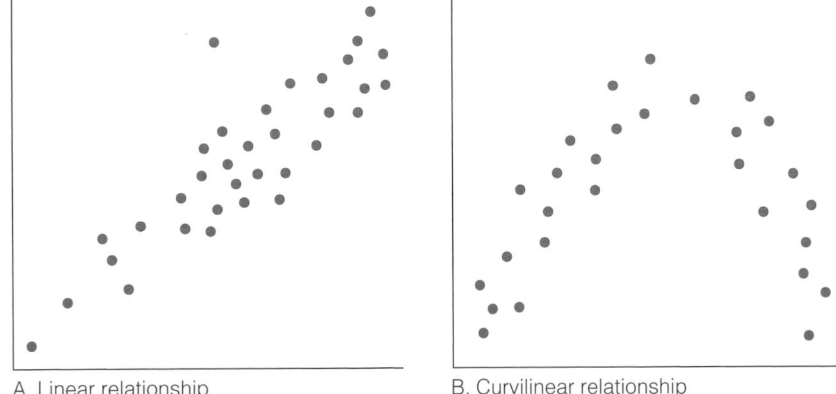

Figure 6.14 Linear and Curvilinear Relationships

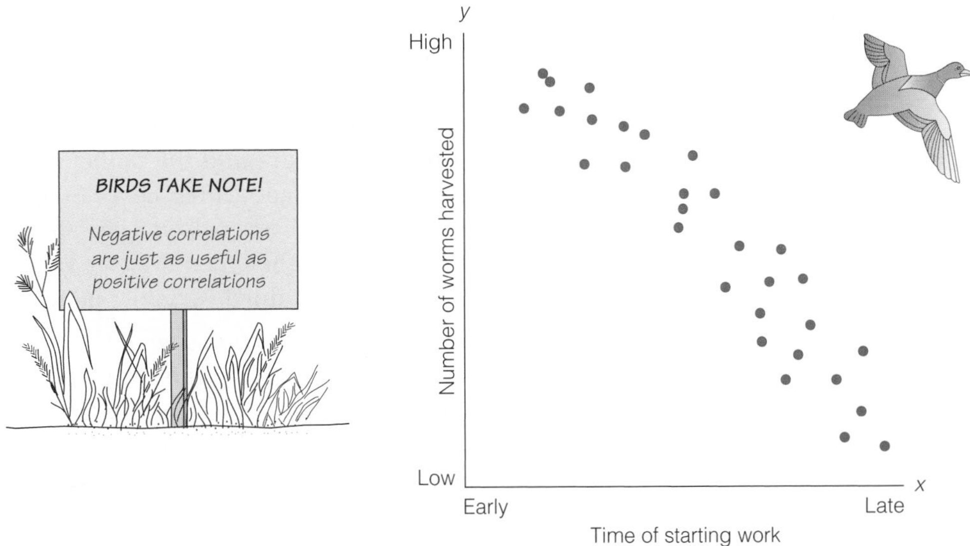

Figure 6.15 A Useful Negative Correlation

If the relationship between variables is curvilinear, the computation of the Pearson *r* will result in a misleading underestimation of the degree of relationship. In this case another index, such as the correlation ratio (Δ) should be applied. A discussion of the correlation ratio appears in Chapter 13.

THINK ABOUT IT 6.7

1. What is the best estimate of the Pearson *r* in Figure 6.15?
   (a) .8, (b) .6, (c) 0, (d) −.6, (e) −.9.
2. What old saying does it represent?

Answers

1. (e)
2. The early bird gets the worm.

INTERPRETATION OF PEARSON *r*

You have seen that when two variables are highly related in a positive way, the correlation between them approaches +1.00. When they are highly related in a negative way, the correlation approaches −1.00. When there is little relation between variables, the correlation will be near 0. Pearson *r* provides a meaningful index for indicating relationship, with the sign of the coefficient indicating the direction of the relationship, and the difference between the coefficient and 0 indicating the degree of the relationship.

However, in interpreting the correlation coefficient keep the following points in mind:

1. *Correlation does not necessarily indicate causation.* When two variables are found to be correlated, this indicates that relative positions in one variable are *associated* with relative positions in the other variable. It does not necessarily mean that changes in one variable are *caused* by changes in the other variable.

   We may find a correlation between two variables not because there is an intrinsic relationship between these variables but because they are both related to a third variable. For example, if we correlate the average teachers' salary for each of the last 20 years and the dollar value of hard liquor sold during each of these years, we get a high correlation. This does not mean that as soon as teachers' salaries are raised, they spend the extra money on booze. We observe a correlation between the two variables because each of them is highly correlated with a third variable, general inflation.

2. *The size of a correlation is in part a function of the variability of the two distributions to be correlated.* Restricting the range of the scores to be correlated reduces the observed degree of relationship between two variables. For example, people have observed that success in playing basketball is related to height: The taller an individual is, the more probable that he or she will do well in this sport. This statement is true about the population at large, where there is a wide range of heights. However, within a basketball team whose members are all tall, there may be little or no correlation between height and success because the range of heights is restricted. In a college that accepts students with a wide range of scores on a scholastic aptitude test, you would expect a correlation between the test scores and college grades. In a college that accepts only students with very high scholastic aptitude scores, you would expect very little correlation between the test scores and grades because of the restricted range of the test scores in this situation.

   If we correlate shoe size and reading vocabulary scores for a single grade level, we would expect a correlation of approximately zero. But, if we correlated this variable for all elementary students, we would get a high correlation because as children mature their feet get larger and their vocabulary increases.

3. *Correlation coefficients should not be interpreted in terms of percentage of perfect correlations.* Because correlation coefficients are expressed as decimal fractions, people who are not trained in statistics sometimes interpret correlation coefficients as a percentage of perfect correlation. An *r* of .80

does not indicate 80 percent of a perfect relationship between two variables. This interpretation is erroneous because, for example, an *r* of .80 does not express a relationship that is twice as great as an *r* of .40. A way of determining the degree to which you can predict one variable from the other is to calculate an index called the **coefficient of determination**. The coefficient of determination is the square of the correlation coefficient. It gives the percentage of variance in one variable that is associated with the variance in the other. For example, if you find a correlation of +.80 between achievement and intelligence, 64 percent of the variance in achievement is associated with variance in intelligence test scores. Probably the best way to give meaning to the size of the correlation coefficient is to picture the degree of scatter implied by correlations of different sizes (as illustrated in Figure 6.13) and to become familiar with the size of correlations commonly observed between variables of interest.

4. *Avoid interpreting the coefficients of correlation in an absolute sense*. In interpreting the degree of correlation, keep in mind the purpose for which it is being used. For example, it may not be wise to use a correlation of .5 for predicting the future performance of an individual. However, if you could develop a measure that you could administer to high school seniors that correlated with their subsequent college freshman grade point average, you could make a fortune because both ACT and SAT scores correlate about .4 with subsequent freshman GPAs. You will find more on correlations and their use in research in Chapter 13.

EFFECT SIZE

We have seen that the Pearson *r* indicates both the direction and strength of a relationship between variables. We have seen that the Pearson *r* has universal meaning in that an *r* near +1.00 always indicates a strong positive relationship no matter what the variables we are considering. An *r* near −1.00 always means a strong negative relationship, and an *r* near 0 always means a weak relationship. Smith and Glass (1977) originated the concept of **effect size**, a statistic that also has universal meaning to assess both the direction and strength of a difference between two means. They subtract the mean of the control group from the mean of the experimental group and then divide this difference by the standard deviation of the control group, as seen in Formula 6.17:

$$\Delta = \frac{\overline{X}_e - \overline{X}_c}{s_c} \tag{6.17}$$

where

Δ = effect size for a difference between means
$\overline{X}_e$ = mean of the experimental group
$\overline{X}_c$ = mean of the control group
s_c = standard deviation of the control group

In experimental studies effect size can be used to compare the direction and the relative strength of different independent variables (intervention) on the same dependent variable.

Consider an experiment in which on-task behavior is the dependent variable. The experimental group receives contingent reinforcement while the control group does not. (We explain this contrast more fully in Chapter 11.) The control group has a mean of 90 and a standard deviation of 10. The experimental group has a mean of 96. The effect size is 96 − 90/10 = .6. Consider another experiment with the same dependent variable (on-task behavior) but with a drug treatment versus a placebo as the independent variable. The control group (which received the placebo) has a mean of 95 and a standard deviation of 8. The experimental group (which received a drug) has a mean of 97. The effect size here is 97 − 95/8 = .25. The evidence suggests that contingent reinforcement has had a greater effect on on-task behavior than the drug did.

Effect sizes are interpreted in the same way that *z* scores are interpreted. Effect size can be used to compare the direction and the relative magnitude of the relationships various independent variables have with a common dependent variable. In addition, it can be used to help decide whether the difference an independent variable makes on the dependent variable is strong enough to recommend its implementation in practice.

One approach is to ask if a given effect size is larger or smaller than effect sizes found in other studies with the same dependent variable. Or you can assess the utility of an effect size by relating the cost in time, money, and other resources needed to implement the independent variable in relation to the importance of the dependent variable. A school of nursing would be interested in a brief, inexpensive procedure that produced an effect size of .20 on state nursing licensure exam scores. A researcher would hesitate to recommend an expensive, time-consuming independent variable with an effect size of .50 on a relatively unimportant dependent variable. Effect size is a useful statistic for assessing the strength and utility of a treatment or other independent variable. Cohen (1988) has suggested the following interpretations:

An effect size of .20 is small

An effect size of .50 is medium

An effect size of .80 is large

Cohen also developed an alternate definition of effect size symbolized by lowercase *d*:

$$d = \frac{\overline{X}_1 - \overline{X}_2}{\sqrt{\dfrac{\Sigma x_1^2 + \Sigma x_2^2}{n_1 + n_2 - 2}}} \tag{6.18}$$

where

d = effect size
$\overline{X}_1$ = mean of one group
$\overline{X}_2$ = mean of the other group
Σx_1 = sum of deviation scores squared in the first group
Σx_2 = sum of deviation scores squared in the second group
n_1 = number in first group
n_2 = number in second group

For example, we compare the scores of 28 students taught method A (group 1) and 22 students taught method B (group 2) with the following statistics. The d is .56, indicating that the group 1 mean is higher than the group 2 mean by an effect size of .56, a medium effect size.

$$d = \frac{\overline{X}_1 - \overline{X}_2}{\sqrt{\dfrac{\Sigma x_1^2 + \Sigma x_2^2}{n_1 + n_2 - 2}}} = \frac{82 - 79}{\sqrt{\dfrac{1390}{28 + 22 - 2}}}$$

$$= \frac{3}{\sqrt{\dfrac{1390}{48}}} = \frac{3}{\sqrt{28.9583}} = \frac{3}{5.3513} = .56$$

Many researchers prefer Cohen's d to Smith and Glass's Δ. **Cohen's *d*** does not require designating one group as the control group in the numerator. Also the denominator is an estimate of the population standard deviation based on the variance within both groups and the number in both groups

As a form of z scores, effect sizes have universal meaning. An effect size of $-.50$ always means that the group 1 mean was half a standard deviation below the group 2 mean. Effect size is important for evaluating the results of any quantitative study. The concept of effect size that originated in education is now widely used in other disciplines. *The Publication Manual of the American Psychological Association* (5th ed., 2001, p. 5) asserts: "For the reader to fully understand the importance of your findings, it is almost always necessary to include some index of effect size or strength of relationship in your results section."

Effect size can be calculated for various statistics other than $\overline{X}_1 - \overline{X}_2$. Cohen's (1988) book and many other books include such measures. Onwuegbuzic (2003) has proposed ways to apply effect size in qualitative research. The reporting of effect sizes is becoming more frequent in education and other fields. We hope it will soon be universal.

A note of caution. Effect size is independent of sample size. Therefore, large effect sizes can easily be observed through chance alone with very small samples. For example, an effect size of $d = .70$ between two samples of 4 each is essentially meaningless. A rule-of-thumb is that samples of less than 30 are considered small. (Yes, we know that most of our examples are less than 30. We did that so you would not get bogged down by the math.) In Chapter 7 we will present ways of taking into account size of sample as well as effect size in evaluating results.

META-ANALYSIS

Having formulated the concept of effect size, Smith and Glass (1977) proceeded to develop **meta-analysis**, which uses effect size to combine the results of studies with the same (or similar) independent and dependent variables. The result provides an overall summary of the outcomes of these studies by calculating a weighted average of their effect sizes. The average effect size as a formula is

$$\overline{\Delta} = \frac{\Delta_1 n_1 + \Delta_1 n_2 + \cdots + \Delta_k n_k}{N} \qquad (6.19)$$

where

$$\begin{aligned}
\overline{\Delta} &= \text{average effect size} \\
\Delta_1 &= \text{effect size for group 1} \\
\Delta_k &= \text{effect size of the last group} \\
n_1 &= \text{number in first group} \\
n_k &= \text{number in last group} \\
N &= \text{total number of subjects}
\end{aligned}$$

Suppose we have four studies investigating the effect of phonics instruction on reading proficiency. Their statistics are as follows:

Study 1: effect size = .9, $n = 60$

Study 2: effect size = .4, $n = 40$

Study 3: effect size = −.2, $n = 30$

Study 4: effect size = .1, $n = 70$

The average effect size is

$$\overline{\Delta} = .9(60) + .4(40) + -.2(30) + .1(70) = \frac{54 + 16 + -6 + 7}{200} = \frac{71}{200} = .36$$

This is about halfway between what Cohen describes as a small effect size and a medium effect size. Another way of looking at it is to use the normal curve. Consulting Table A.1 in the Appendix, you see that a z score of .36 has a percentile rank of 64. The mean in a treatment group is equivalent to a score with a percentile rank of approximately 64 in the control group. If treatment is relatively inexpensive, you would be inclined to recommend it in practice. If treatment is expensive and/or the dependent variable is relatively unimportant, you would not be inclined to recommend it.

In a ground-breaking study, Smith and Glass (1977) used meta-analysis to investigate the broad question: Does psychotherapy make a difference in the mental health of those receiving it? A standard literature search located 1000 experiments focused on this topic. Experiments selected as appropriate for a complete analysis yielded a total of 833 effect sizes. The selected studies included ego, dynamic, behavioral, and humanistic treatment strategies, related experimentally to such outcome variables as self-esteem, adjustment, fear/anxiety, and school performance. The average effect size was .68; that is, the average posttreatment mean for treated subjects was equivalent to a score of .68 of a standard deviation above the mean for untreated subjects. Smith and Glass concluded that the typical outcome of psychotherapy is a gain on the dependent variable equivalent to a move from the mean to the 75th percentile of the control group (see Figure 6.16). Some previous, less organized, attempts to summarize the literature on this subject had concluded that psychotherapy does not make a difference.

Meta-analysis is also used to integrate the findings of nonexperimental studies. Hyde, Fennema, and Lamon (1990) did a meta-analysis of 100 studies comparing male and female mathematics performance on standardized tests. For the total of 3,175,188 subjects in these 100 studies, the average mean for males was .20 of a standard deviation higher than the mean for females. When the researchers excluded studies that represented samples selected for low performance or

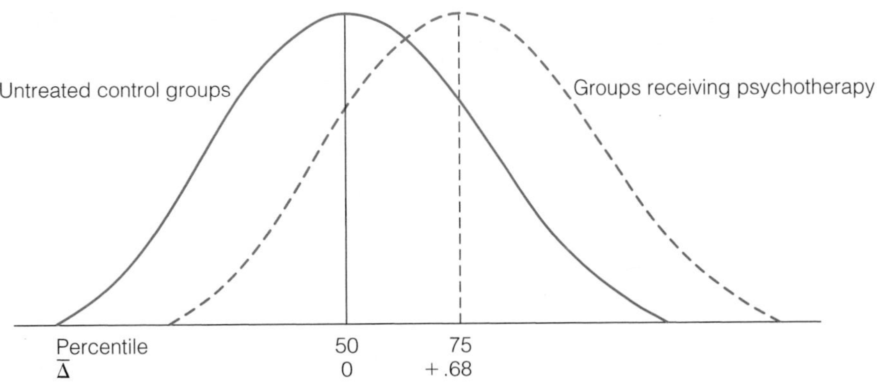

Figure 6.16 Estimated Average Effect Size for Therapies Compared to Untreated Groups

Source: Adapted from Figure 1 in *American Psychologist, 32,* 1977, p. 754. Copyright © 1977 by the American Psychological Association. Adapted with permission.

high performance (such as college or college-bound youth), the average difference was .05 higher for females. The authors concluded that in general, gender differences in mathematics performance are small.

Meta-analysis has sometimes been criticized for including the results of poorly designed, poorly conducted studies along with the results of more credible studies (criteria for evaluating research designs are in Chapter 10). This problem can be resolved by first calculating the average effect size of all studies and then calculating the average effect size of well-designed studies to see if the latter agree with the former. Qin, Johnson, and Johnson (1995) did this in the meta-analysis of studies comparing problem-solving performance of subjects under cooperative versus competitive conditions. In 55 cases cooperation outperformed competition, whereas in 8 competition outperformed cooperation. The average effect size was .55 in favor of cooperation. The average effect size of the 33 studies judged as being of high methodological quality was .68. Meta-analyses can be made for various subclasses of studies. Qin, Johnson, and Johnson found average effect sizes of .37 for linguistic problems and .72 for nonlinguistic problems. They found average effect sizes of .52 for well-defined problems and .60 for ill-defined problems. The reader is referred to Becker and Hedges (1992) for a discussion of other meta-analysis approaches and applications. Effect size and meta-analysis, originally developed in education, are now widely used in medicine and many other fields.

USING TECHNOLOGY TO ANALYZE DATA

We have provided a number of formulas for calculating the statistics covered in this chapter. However, we recognize that many researchers will use technological tools to help them describe data and calculate the relevant statistics. Graphing calculators and other handheld calculators are capable of managing many of the statistical procedures described in this chapter. Common spreadsheet software, such as Microsoft Office's Excel, can be used to create graphic presentations of data and to calculate basic statistics. Database software, such as Microsoft's Access, also can be used for basic data management and analysis. And, of course, statistical software can be used to calculate the statistics described in this chapter as well as more complicated statistical procedures described in later chapters.

The two most common statistical programs used in the social sciences, including education, are SPSS (Statistical Package for the Social Sciences) and SAS (Statistical Analysis System). Both SPSS and SAS were initially developed in the 1960s. Both can import data from most spreadsheet software (such as Excel) and from databases (such as Access).

SAS (see http://www.sas.com) is commonly used by social science researchers and has analytical, data manipulation, and reporting capabilities. It is available for use in PC, Unix, and mainframe environments. SAS/STAT can be used to analyze most types of data and can produce linear models as well as multivariate and categorical statistics. SAS/ETS is available for more sophisticated analyses, such as time-series design. Another SAS product that can be used for common statistical analyses is JMP, which is available for use on PC or MacIntosh platforms.

SPSS (see http://www.spss.com) was developed for use in social science research and is the most common analysis package used for education survey research. SPSS is available for use on all major computer platforms (PC and MacIntosh) as well as Unix environments. This data management and analysis product can provide common statistical analyses and graphical presentation of data as well as more sophisticated statistical procedures. Different modules are necessary for different statistical approaches. The Base system provides descriptive statistics, crosstabs, tables, *t* tests, correlation, ANOVA, regression, cluster and factor analysis, and nonparametric statistics. SPSS has a student package available that will meet the needs of most students in introductory research and statistics courses. Another statistical package owned by SPSS is SYSTAT, which is also available on PC or MacIntosh platforms and is capable of producing most common statistical analyses.

SUMMARY

Descriptive statistics serve to describe and summarize observations. The descriptive technique to be employed is selected according to the purpose the statistic is to serve and the scale of measurement used.

Scales of measurement are means of quantifying observations and are of four types: (1) Nominal scales classify observations into mutually exclusive categories; (2) ordinal scales sort objects or classes of objects on the basis of their relative standing; (3) interval scales use equal intervals for measurement and indicate the degree to which a person or an object possesses a certain quality; and (4) ratio scales use equal intervals for measurement and measure from an absolute zero point. Once observations are quantified, the data can be arranged into frequency distributions and shown graphically in histograms or polygons.

Measures of central tendency—the mode, the median, and the mean—provide a single index to represent the average value of a whole set of measures. The mode, which is a nominal statistic, is the least stable and least useful measure in educational research. The median is an ordinal statistic that takes into account the ranks of scores within a distribution but not the size of the individual scores. The mean, which is an in-

TABLE 6.7 Summary of Descriptive Statistics Presented in This Chapter

	Nominal	Ordinal	Interval
Indexes of central tendency	Mode	Median	Mean
Indexes of variability	Range		Variance and standard deviation
Indexes of location	Label or classification	Percentile rank	*z* score, *T* scores, and other standard scores
Correlation indexes	ϕ[a]	Spearman ρ[a]	Pearson *r*

[a] The ϕ and Spearman ρ correlation coefficients are described in Chapter 14.

terval (or ratio) statistic, is the most stable and most widely used index of central tendency. Another way of describing observations is to indicate the variation, or spread, of the values within a distribution. The range, the variance, and the standard deviation are three indexes used for this purpose. The range, a nominal statistic, is the distance between the highest and the lowest values in a distribution, plus 1. Variance is the mean of the squared deviations of scores from the mean. It is an interval (or ratio) statistic. Standard deviation—the square root of the variance—is the most widely used index of variability.

Standard scores are used to indicate the position of a single score in a distribution. The most widely used is the *z* score, which converts values into standard deviation units. The *z* scores are often converted into stanines, *T* scores, or other standard scores. An ordinal index of location shows a score's position in percentile rank (PR), which indicates what percentage of scores fall below the midpoint of the score's interval. Using the characteristics and the areas of the normal curve, you can approximate the percentage of cases below and above each *z* score in a normal distribution.

Correlation techniques enable researchers to describe the relationship between two sets of measures. Product moment correlation (Pearson *r*), the most widely used index of relationships, is used with interval or ratio data. Table 6.7 summarizes correlation indexes appropriate for data of interval, ordinal, and nominal data.

Effect size—the difference between the means of the experimental and control groups divided by the standard deviation of the control group—is a useful measure of the strength or magnitude of their relationship. A small effect size indicates a trivial relationship. A large effect size indicates a substantial relationship.

Meta-analysis combines data from many studies into a single index. It enables researchers to succinctly summarize results of many studies on a particular question. The most widely used index is the average effect size.

KEY CONCEPTS

coefficient of determination
Cohen's *d*
correlation
correlation coefficient
curvilinear relationship
descriptive statistics
deviation scores
effect size
frequency distribution
frequency polygon
histogram
inferential statistics
interval scale
linear relationship
mean
measures of central tendency
median
meta-analysis
mode
negative correlation
negatively skewed distribution
nominal scale
normal curve
normal distribution

ordinal scale
Pearson product moment correlation coefficient
percentile rank
positive correlation
positively skewed distribution
range
ratio scale
scatterplot
skewed distribution
standard deviation
standard score
stanine score
symmetrical distribution
T score
variability
variance
z score

EXERCISES

1. Identify the type of measurement scale—nominal, ordinal, interval, or ratio—suggested by each statement:
 a. John finished the math test in 35 minutes, while Jack finished the same test in 25 minutes.
 b. Jack speaks French, but John does not.
 c. Jack is taller than John.
 d. John is 6 feet 2 inches tall.
 e. John's IQ is 120, whereas Jack's IQ is 110.

2. Draw a histogram and a frequency polygon for the following frequency distribution:

X	f	X	f	X	f	X	f
80	1	76	6	73	20	70	7
79	2	75	15	72	17	69	3
78	3	74	22	71	9		
77	10						

3. Provide answers as requested, given the following distribution: 15, 14, 14, 13, 11, 10, 10, 10, 8, 5.
 a. Calculate the mean.
 b. Determine the value of the median.
 c. Determine the value of the mode.

4. Briefly explain the relationship between the skewness of a distribution of scores and the resulting values of the mean, median, and mode.

5. Identify the measure—mode, mean, or median—that best suits each type of scale:
 a. Ordinal
 b. Nominal
 c. Interval

6. Identify the measure—mode, mean, or median—that each term defines:
 a. The middle score
 b. The arithmetic average
 c. The most frequently occurring score

7. Discuss the benefits and disadvantages of range and standard deviation as measures of variability of the scores.

8. **a.** Calculate the *z* score for a score of 5 in a distribution with a mean of 7 and a standard deviation of 0.5.
 b. What would the stanine score for this score be?

9. Using Table A.1, what is the estimated percentile rank for a *z* score of +1.20?

10. To minimize the effect of an extreme score, should you choose the mean or median as the measure of central tendency?

11. In an analysis of National Assessment of Educational Progress scores, Hedges and Nowell (1995) found that male scores were more heterogeneous, more spread from low to high, than female scores.
 a. Which statistics would be greater for males?
 b. Which gender had more stanine scores of 9?
 c. Which gender had more stanine scores of 1?
 d. Which gender had more stanine scores of 5?

12. The mean score on a test is 40, and the standard deviation is 4. Express each of the following raw scores as a *z* score:
 a. 41
 b. 30
 c. 48
 d. 36
 e. 46

13. **a.** What would be the *T* score for the raw score of 46 in Exercise 12?
 b. What would the stanine score for the raw score of 46 be?

14. In a normal distribution, what percentage of the scores would fall below a *z* score of −1.0? A *z* score of 0? A *z* score of +.67?

15. Describe the relationship shown by these scatterplots. Then estimate the correlation coefficients.

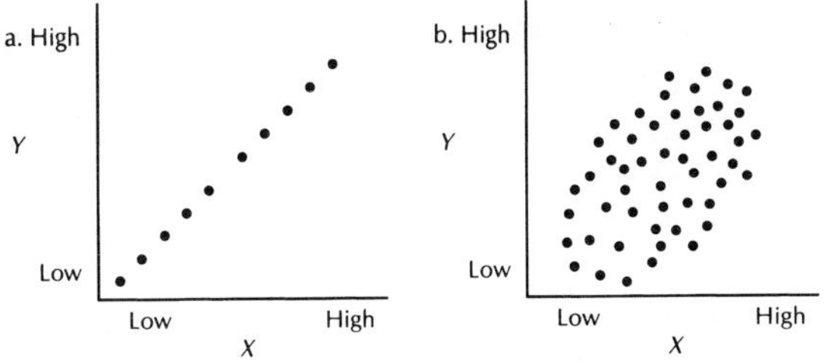

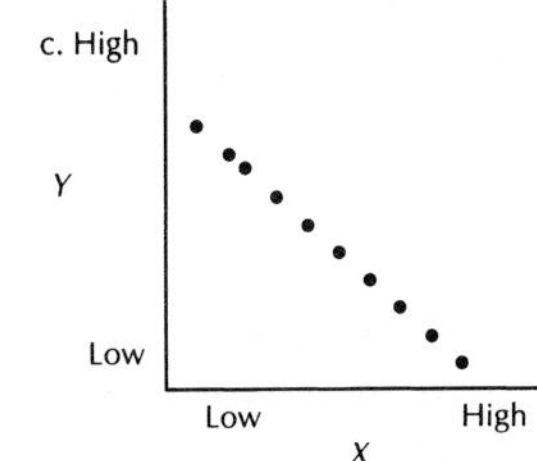

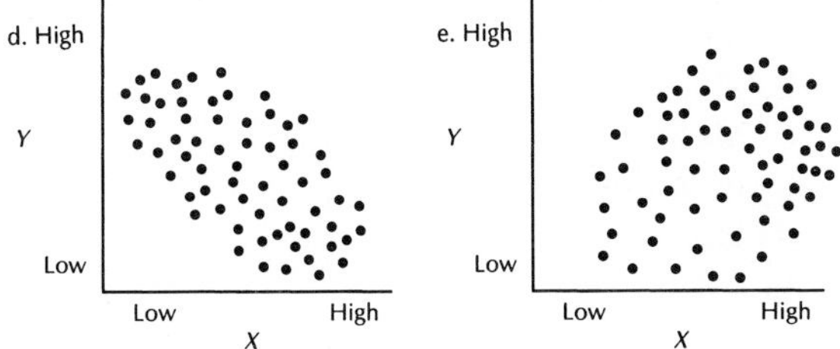

16. Each dot in a scatterplot represents _____.

17. Five girls took a history test and a geography test, with the following results:

	History		Geography	
	Raw Score	*z Score*	*Raw Score*	*z Score*
Ann	28	.5	85	1.5
Nesa	32	1.5	65	.5
María	26	0	55	0
Benazir	20	−1.5	45	−.5
Yoko	24	−.5	25	−1.5

History	Geography
$\Sigma X = 130$	$\Sigma X = 275$
$\sigma = 4$	$\sigma = 20$

a. What is the mean of the history test?
b. Whose performance in history is most in agreement with her performance in geography?
c. What is the correlation between the history and geography scores?

18. Given that the history test mean in Exercise 17 is lower than the geography test mean, which of the following conclusions would be correct?
a. These girls are better in history than in geography.
b. These girls are better in geography than in history.
c. Their teacher has probably spent twice as much time on geography as on history.
d. Their teacher knows more geography than history.
e. None of the above.

19. If the coefficient of correlation between variable *X* and variable *Y* is found to be −.98, which of the following would be indicated?
a. Variable *X* and variable *Y* are closely related.
b. Variable *X* and variable *Y* are unrelated.
c. Variable *X* and variable *Y* are perfectly related.
d. Variable *Y* is a result of variable *X*.

20. For each of the following cases, indicate which statistic should be used—mean, standard deviation, *z* score, or Pearson *r*.
a. We want to know how spread out or heterogeneous the scores of a class are.
b. We want to determine how Joe's score compares with the scores of the rest of the class.
c. We want to know how well the class as a whole did on an examination.
d. We want to predict the future achievement of students from their IQ.

21. Smith and Glass's Δ and Cohen's *d* are two ways of defining what?

22. Interpret the following: "On the College Board exam ($\mu = 500$, $\sigma = 100$), the mean of this year's Central High School seniors was 490, the standard deviation 110. The correlation between the exam scores and high school grade point average was +.40."

23. Interpret the following: "Parents of Central High students were asked to rank ten problems statements from 10 = most serious to 1 = least serious. The median for the problem 'physical safety' was 5.21."

24. Define *effect size*, and tell how it is used.

25. What is the purpose of meta-analysis?

ANSWERS

1. **a.** Ratio
   b. Nominal
   c. Ordinal
   d. Ratio
   e. Interval
2. Figures may be expanded or contracted vertically or horizontally or both and be correct if the relationships between scores and frequencies are maintained.

HISTOGRAM

Frequency

25 20 15 10 5 0

68 69 70 71 72 73 74 75 76 77 78 79 80 81

Scores

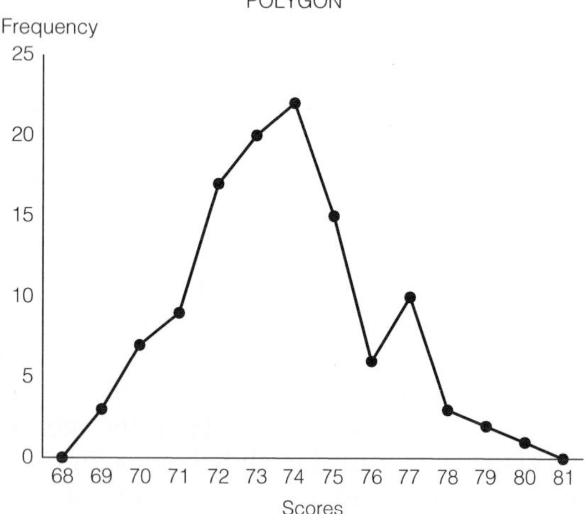

3. **a.** Mean = 11
   b. Median = 10.5
   c. Mode = 10
4. The three measures are not equal in a skewed distribution. The mean is pulled in the direction of the skewed side. Thus, in a positively skewed distribution the mean is always higher than the median, and the mode is usually lowest in value. In a negatively skewed distribution, the mean is always lower than the median, and the mode is usually highest in value.
5. **a.** Median
   b. Mode
   c. Mean
6. **a.** Median
   b. Mean
   c. Mode
7. The range is easy to calculate and to explain. The standard deviation takes into account all the scores and is more stable.
8. **a.** $z = (5 - 7)/.5 = .4$
   b. stanine = 1
9. 88 (rounded from 88.49)
10. Median because extreme scores do not influence the median.
11. **a.** Male scores had higher variance, standard deviation, and range.
    b. Males
    c. Males
    d. Females
12. **a.** .25
    b. −2.5
    c. 2
    d. −1
    e. 1.5
13. **a.** $T = 10z + 50 = 10(1.5) + 50 = 65$
    b. Stanine score $2z + 5$ rounded $= (2)(1.5) + 5 = 8$
14. 16%; 50%; 75%
15. **a.** Perfect positive, +1 correlation
    b. Positive, +.75
    c. Perfect negative, −1
    d. Negative, −.75
    e. No correlation, 0
16. An individual's score on two dimensions or other paired z scores.
17. **a.** 26
    b. Maria; she had the same z score on both test.
    c. $r = \dfrac{\Sigma z_x z_y}{N} = \dfrac{3}{5} = .6$
18. e
19. a
20. **a.** Standard deviation
    b. z score
    c. Mean
    d. Pearson r

21. Effect size.
22. As a group the Central High seniors were slightly below the national average (effect size = −.10). Their scores were a bit more heterogeneous than usual. Those with high scores tended to have high GPAs. Those with low scores tended to have low GPAs. The relationship between scores and GPAs was moderate positive.
23. Parents ranked "physical safety" about average.
24. Effect size (a form of z score) is the difference between experimental and control groups divided by the standard deviation of the control group. It indicates the strength of the relationship between independent and dependent variables.
25. It combines the result of studies with similar independent and dependent variables to produce an average effect size, a mathematical summary of the results.

INFOTRAC COLLEGE EDITION

Use InfoTrac College Edition to locate a research article on a topic of interest to you. Describe the level of measurement associated with each of the measures used in the research. What descriptive statistics were used to summarize the data? Was the statistic appropriate for the level of measurement?

Chapter 7

Sampling and Inferential Statistics

STATISTICAL THINKING WILL ONE DAY BE AS NECESSARY FOR EFFICIENT CITIZENSHIP AS THE ABILITY TO READ AND WRITE.
H. G. WELLS (1866–1946)

INSTRUCTIONAL OBJECTIVES

After studying this chapter, the student will be able to:

1. Describe the meaning, rationale, and steps involved in sampling and distinguish between probability and nonprobability sampling.
2. List the characteristics, uses, and limitations of each kind of probability and nonprobability sampling.
3. Explain the meaning of sampling error and its relationship to making statistical inferences.
4. Describe random assignment and its use in research.
5. Explain the meaning of statistical significance.
6. Explain the general strategy of statistical significance testing.
7. Explain how a null hypothesis is used in scientific research.
8. Describe Type I and Type II errors.
9. Define alpha and beta.
10. Explain the difference between directional and nondirectional tests of significance and the appropriate use of each of these tests.
11. Describe the process of determining sample size.
12. Apply the *t* test to find the significance of a difference between independent means and a difference between dependent means.
13. Understand the concept of degrees of freedom.
14. Know what statistical tests are available for ranked data.
15. Describe the purpose of the *t* test for the Pearson *r* and determine if a given correlation coefficient differs significantly from zero.
16. Describe the uses of *F* tests.
17. Apply the *F* test for finding the significance of the differences between groups in one-way and two-way analysis of variance.

18 Apply the chi-square test for finding the significance of the differences between proportions in one-way and two-way classifications.

19 Select the kind of inferential statistical procedures appropriate for use in testing a given research hypothesis.

20 Demonstrate comprehension of the basic technical statistical terms used in reporting research results.

The statistics discussed in the previous chapter are used for organizing, summarizing, and describing data. In research, however, we often need to go further than describing data. After making observations of a sample, researchers employ induction or inference to generalize findings to the entire population from which the sample was drawn. To do this they need techniques that enable them to make credible inferences from samples to whole populations.

SAMPLING

An important characteristic of inferential statistics is the process of going from the part to the whole. For example, you might study a randomly selected group of 500 students attending a university in order to make generalizations about the entire student body of that university.

The small group that is observed is called a *sample*, and the larger group about which the generalization is made is called a *population*. A **population** is defined as all members of any well-defined class of people, events, or objects. For example, in a study where students in American high schools constitute the population of interest, you could define this population as all boys and girls attending high school in the United States. A **sample** is a portion of a population. For example, the students of Arlington High School in Indianapolis constitute a sample of American high school students.

Statistical inference is a procedure by means of which you estimate **parameters** (characteristics of populations) from **statistics** (characteristics of samples). Such estimations are based on the laws of probability and are best estimates rather than absolute facts. In making any such inferences, a certain degree of error is involved. Inferential statistics can be used to test hypotheses about populations on the basis of observations of a sample drawn from the population.

RATIONALE OF SAMPLING

Inductive reasoning is an essential part of the scientific approach. The inductive method involves making observations and then drawing conclusions from these observations. If you can observe all instances of a population, you can, with confidence, base conclusions about the population on these observations (perfect induction). In Chapter 6 we treated the 18 students in Mr. Li's physics class as a population. Therefore, we could be confident that we had the true means, standard deviations, and so forth (the parameters). However, if you observe only some instances of a population, then you can do no more than infer that these observations will be true of the population as a whole (imperfect induction). This is the concept of sampling, which involves taking a portion of the population, making observations on this smaller group, and then generalizing the findings to the parent population, the larger population from which the sample was drawn.

Sampling is indispensable to the researcher. Usually, the time, money, and effort involved do not permit a researcher to study all possible members of a population. Furthermore, it is generally not necessary to study all possible cases to understand the phenomenon under consideration. Sampling comes to your aid by enabling you to study a portion of the population rather than the entire population.

Because the purpose of drawing a sample from a population is to obtain information concerning that population, it is extremely important that the individuals included in a sample constitute a representative cross section of individuals in the population. Samples must be representative if you are to be able to generalize with reasonable confidence from the sample to the population. For example, the researcher may assume that the students at Arlington High School are representative of American adolescents. However, this sample may not be representative if the individuals who are included have some characteristics that differ from the target population. The location of their school, their socioeconomic backgrounds, their family situations, their prior experiences, and many other characteristics of this group may make them unrepresentative of American adolescents. An unrepresentative sample is termed a **biased sample**. The findings on a biased sample in a research study cannot legitimately be generalized to the population from which it is taken. For example, if the population of interest is all students in a particular urban school district, but the researchers sampled only students from the district's two magnet schools, the sample would be biased.

STEPS IN SAMPLING

The first step in sampling is the identification of the **target population** to be represented in the study. If the researcher is interested in learning about the teachers in the St. Louis public school system, all those who teach within that system constitute the target population. In a study of the attitudes and values of American adolescents, the target population would be all American boys and girls in the age range of 12 to 21, given that adolescence is operationally defined as the period between ages 12 and 21.

Two major types of sampling procedures are available to researchers: probability and nonprobability sampling. **Probability sampling** involves sample selection in which the elements are drawn by chance procedures. The main characteristic of probability sampling is that every member or element of the population has a known probability of being chosen in the sample.

Nonprobability sampling includes methods of selection in which elements are not chosen by chance procedures. Its success depends on the knowledge, expertise, and judgment of the researcher. Nonprobability sampling is used when the application of probability sampling is not feasible. Its advantages are convenience and economy.

PROBABILITY SAMPLING

Probability sampling is defined as the kind of sampling in which every element in the population has an equal chance of being selected. The possible inclusion of each population element in this kind of sampling takes place by chance and is attained through random selection. When probability sampling is used, inferential statistics enable researchers to estimate the extent to which the findings based on the sample are likely to differ from what they would have found by studying the whole population. The four types of probability sampling most frequently used in educational research are simple random sampling, stratified sampling, cluster sampling, and systematic sampling.

Simple Random Sampling

The best known of the probability sampling procedures is **simple random sampling**. The basic characteristic of simple random sampling is that all members of the population have an equal and independent chance of being included in the **random sample**. The steps in simple random sampling comprise the following:

1. Define the population.
2. List all members of the population.
3. Select the sample by employing a procedure where sheer chance determines which members on the list are drawn for the sample.

The first step in drawing a random sample from a population is to assign each member of the population a distinct identification number. Let us illustrate this procedure by showing how to obtain a sample of 50 students from the population attending Arlington High School. First, you need to enumerate all the individuals in the population. The principal's office could supply a list of all students enrolled in the school. You would then assign a number to each individual in the population, for identification purposes. If there are 800 students in the school, you use the numbers 000, 001, 002, 003, . . . , 799 for this purpose. Many schools have already assigned identification numbers to all their students. The next step is to enter a table of random numbers to obtain numbers of three digits each, using only those numbers that are less than or equal to 799. For each number chosen, the corresponding member of the population falls into the sample. Continue the process until the desired number for the sample has been chosen, in this case the first 50 numbers.

In earlier editions of this book, we included a five-page table of random numbers. We decided this is no longer needed as there are so many tables available on the Internet, in statistics texts, and so forth. Next, we describe a procedure that is an absolutely random way to enter the table.

First, roll a die to determine which page to use. We rolled a 3, so we pulled the third page from a table of random numbers (Table 7.1). Then we noted the last two digits from the serial number on a dollar bill. They were 03, so we went to row 3. Then we took the last two digits from a second dollar bill, which were 25,

Table 7.1 Page from a Table of Random Numbers

	COLUMN NUMBER							
	00000	00000	11111	11111	22222	22222	33333	33333
ROW	01234	56789	01234	56789	01234	56789	01234	56789
				3rd Thousand				
00	89221	02362	65787	74733	51272	30213	92441	39651
01	04005	99818	63918	29032	94012	42363	01261	10650
02	98546	38066	50856	75045	40645	22841	53254	44125
03	41719	84401	59226	01314	54581	40398	49988	65579
04	28733	72489	00785	25843	24613	49797	85567	84471
05	65213	83927	77762	03086	80742	24395	68476	83792
06	65553	12678	90906	90466	43670	26217	69900	31205
07	05668	69080	73029	85746	58332	78231	45986	92998
08	39202	99718	49757	79519	27387	76373	47262	91612
09	64592	32254	45879	29431	38320	05981	18067	87137
10	07513	48792	47314	83660	68907	05336	82579	91582
11	86593	68501	56638	99800	82839	35148	56541	07232
12	83735	22599	97977	81248	36838	99560	32410	67614
13	08595	21826	54655	08204	87990	17033	56258	05384
14	41273	27149	44293	69458	16828	63962	15864	35431
15	00473	75908	56238	12242	72631	76314	47252	06347
16	86131	53789	81383	07868	89132	96182	07009	86432
17	33849	78359	08402	03586	03176	88663	08018	22546
18	61870	41657	07468	08612	98083	97349	20775	45091
19	43898	65923	25078	86129	78491	97653	91500	80786
20	29939	39123	04548	45985	60952	06641	28726	46473
21	38505	85555	14388	55077	18657	94887	67831	70819
22	31824	38431	67125	25511	72044	11562	53279	82268
23	91430	03767	13561	15597	06750	92552	02391	38753
24	38635	68976	25498	97526	96458	03805	04116	63514

taking us to the intersection of row 3 and column 25. The first three digits from that intersection were 403, so we wrote 403 on our list. The next three digits are above 799 (the size of the sample) so we could not use them. We could use 579 so we wrote that down. Then we went to line 4 and wrote down 287, 337, 248, skipped 900, wrote down 785, and so forth.

You probably will not actually have to do all this as you are likely to have access to a computer program that will draw a random sample of your desired size from your list of population IDs. However, we wanted to show a way the numbers drawn from a table of random numbers can be absolutely without bias. If you are really lucky you may find a school whose record keeping system allows for drawing a random sample using its computer.

The generally understood meaning of the word *random* is "without purpose or by accident." However, **random sampling** is purposeful and methodical. It is apparent that a sample selected randomly is not subject to the biases of the researcher. Rather, the researchers commit themselves to selecting a sample in such a way that their biases are not permitted to operate. They are pledging themselves to avoid a deliberate selection of subjects who will confirm the hypothesis. They are allowing chance alone to determine which elements in the population will be in the sample.

You would expect a random sample to be representative of the target population sampled. However, a random selection, especially with small samples, does not absolutely guarantee a sample that will represent the population well. Random selection does guarantee that any differences between the sample and the parent population are only a function of chance and not a result of the researcher's bias. The differences between random samples and their parent population are not systematic. For example, the mean reading achievement of a random sample of sixth-graders may be higher than the mean reading achievement of the target population, but it is equally likely that the mean for the sample will be lower than the mean for the target population. In other words, with random sampling the sampling errors are just as likely to be negative as they are to be positive.

Furthermore, statistical theorists have shown, through deductive reasoning, how much a researcher can expect the observations derived from random samples to differ from what would be observed in the population when the null hypothesis is true. All inferential statistical procedures have this aim in mind. Remember that characteristics observed in a small sample are more likely to differ from population characteristics than are characteristics observed in a large sample. When random sampling is used, the researcher can employ inferential statistics to estimate how much the population is likely to differ from the sample. The inferential statistics in this chapter are all based on random sampling and apply directly only to those cases in which the sampling has been random.

Unfortunately, simple random sampling requires enumeration of all individuals in a finite population before the sample can be drawn—a requirement that often presents a serious obstacle to the practical use of this method. Now let us look at other probability sampling methods that approximate simple random sampling and may be used as alternatives in certain situations.

Stratified Sampling

When the population consists of a number of subgroups, or strata, that may differ in the characteristics being studied, it is often desirable to use a form of probability sampling called **stratified sampling**. For example, if you were conducting a poll designed to assess opinions on a certain political issue, it might be advisable to subdivide the population into subgroups on the basis of age, neighborhood, and occupation because you would expect opinions to differ systematically among various ages, neighborhoods, and occupational groups. In stratified sampling, you first identify the strata of interest and then randomly draw a specified number of subjects from each stratum. The basis for stratification may be geographic or may involve characteristics of the population such as income, occupation, gender, age, year in college, or teaching level. In studying adolescents, for example, you might be interested not merely in surveying the attitudes of adolescents toward certain phenomena but also in comparing the attitudes of adolescents who reside in small towns with those who live in medium-size and large cities. In such a case you would divide the adolescent population into three groups, based on the size of the towns or cities in which they reside and then randomly select independent samples from each stratum.

An advantage of stratified sampling is that it enables the researcher to also study the differences that might exist between various subgroups of a population. In this kind of sampling you may either take equal numbers from each stratum or select in proportion to the size of the stratum in the population. The latter procedure is known as **proportional stratified sampling**, which is applied when the characteristics of the entire population are the main concern in the study. Each stratum is represented in the sample in exact proportion to its frequency in the total population. For example, if 10 percent of the voting population are college students, then 10 percent of a sample of voters to be polled would be taken from this stratum.

In some research studies, however, the main concern is with differences among various strata. In these cases the researcher chooses samples of equal size from each stratum. For example, if you are investigating the difference between the study habits of graduate and undergraduate students, you include equal numbers in both groups and then study the differences that might exist between them. You choose the procedure according to the nature of the research question. If your emphasis is on the types of differences among the strata, you select equal numbers of cases from each. If the characteristics of the entire population are your main concern, proportional sampling is more appropriate. When the population to be sampled is not homogeneous but consists of several subgroups, stratified sampling may give a more representative sample than simple random sampling. In simple random sampling, certain strata may by chance be over- or underrepresented in the sample. For example, in the simple random sample of high school students it would be theoretically possible (though highly unlikely) to obtain female subjects only. This could not happen, however, if males and females were listed separately and a random sample were then chosen from each group. The major advantage of stratified sampling is that it guarantees representation of defined groups in the population.

Cluster Sampling

As mentioned earlier, it is very difficult, if not impossible, to list all the members of a target population and select the sample from among them. The population of American high school students, for example, is so large that you cannot list all its members for the purpose of drawing a sample. In addition, it would be very expensive to study a sample that is scattered all around the United States. In this case it would be more convenient to study subjects in naturally occurring groups, or clusters. For example, a researcher might choose a number of schools randomly from a list of schools and then include all the students in those schools in the sample. This kind of probability sampling is referred to as **cluster sampling** because the unit chosen is not an individual but a group of individuals who are naturally together. These individuals constitute a cluster insofar as they are alike with respect to characteristics relevant to the variables of the study. To illustrate, let us assume a public opinion poll is being conducted in Atlanta. The investigator would probably not have access to a list of the entire adult population; thus, it would be impossible to draw a simple random sample. A more feasible approach would involve the selection of a random sample of, say, 50 blocks from a city map and then the polling of all the adults living on those blocks. Each block represents a cluster of subjects, similar in certain characteristics associated with living in proximity. A common application of cluster sampling in education is the use of intact classrooms as clusters.

It is essential that the clusters actually included in your study be chosen at random from a population of clusters. Another procedural requirement is that once a cluster is selected, *all* the members of the cluster must be included in the sample. The sampling error (see discussion later) in a cluster sample is much greater than in true random sampling. It is also important to remember that if the number of clusters is small, the likelihood of sampling error is great—even if the total number of subjects is large.

Systematic Sampling

Still another form of probability sampling is called **systematic sampling**. This procedure involves drawing a sample by taking every *K*th case from a list of the population.

First, you decide how many subjects you want in the sample (n). Because you know the total number of members in the population (N), you simply divide N by n and determine the sampling interval (K) to apply to the list. Select the first member randomly from the first K members of the list and then select every *K*th member of the population for the sample. For example, let us assume a total population of 500 subjects and a desired sample size of 50: $K = N/n = 500/50 = 10$.

Start near the top of the list so that the first case can be randomly selected from the first 10 cases, and then select every tenth case thereafter. Suppose the third name or number on the list was the first selected. You would then add the sampling interval, or 10, to 3—and thus the 13th person falls in the sample, as does the 23rd, and so on—and would continue adding the constant sampling interval until you reached the end of the list.

Systematic sampling differs from simple random sampling in that the various choices are not independent. Once the first case is chosen, all subsequent cases to be included in the sample are automatically determined. If the original population list is in random order, systematic sampling would yield a sample that could be statistically considered a reasonable substitute for a random sample. However, if the list is not random, it is possible that every *K*th member of the population might have some unique characteristic that would affect the dependent variable of the study and thus yield a biased sample. Systematic sampling from an alphabetical list, for example, would probably not give a representative sample of various national groups because certain national groups tend to cluster under certain letters, and the sampling interval could omit them entirely or at least not include them to an adequate extent.

Note that the various types of probability sampling that have been discussed are not mutually exclusive. Various combinations may be used. For example, you could use cluster sampling if you were studying a very large and widely dispersed population. At the same time, you might be interested in stratifying the sample to answer questions regarding its different strata. In this case you would stratify the population according to the predetermined criteria and then randomly select the cluster of subjects from among each stratum.

NONPROBABILITY SAMPLING

In many research situations, the enumeration of the population elements—a basic requirement in probability sampling—is difficult, if not impossible. In these instances the researcher may use nonprobability sampling, which involves nonrandom procedures for selecting the members of the sample. The major forms of nonprobability sampling are convenience sampling, purposive sampling, and quota sampling.

Convenience Sampling

Convenience sampling, which is regarded as the weakest of all sampling procedures, involves using available cases for a study. Interviewing the first individuals you encounter on campus, using the students in your own classroom as a sample, or taking volunteers to be interviewed in survey research are various examples of convenience sampling. There is no way (except by repeating the study using probability sampling) of estimating the error introduced by the convenience sampling procedures. If you do use convenience sampling, be extremely cautious in interpreting the findings.

Purposive Sampling

In **purposive sampling**—also referred to as **judgment sampling**—sample elements judged to be typical, or representative, are chosen from the population. Researchers often use purposive sampling for forecasting national elections. In each state they choose a number of small districts whose returns in previous elections have been typical of the entire state. They interview all the eligible voters in these districts and use the results to predict the voting patterns of the state. Using similar procedures in all states, the pollsters forecast the national results.

The critical question in purposive sampling is the extent to which judgment can be relied on to arrive at a typical sample. There is no reason to assume that the units judged to be typical of the population will continue to be typical over a period of time. Consequently, the results of a study using purposive sampling may be misleading. Because of its low cost and convenience, purposive sampling has been useful in attitude and opinion surveys. Be aware of the limitations, however, and use the method with extreme caution.

Quota Sampling

Quota sampling involves selecting typical cases from diverse strata of a population. The quotas are based on known characteristics of the population to which you wish to generalize. Elements are drawn so that the resulting sample is a miniature approximation of the population with respect to the selected characteristics. For example, if census results show that 25 percent of the population of an urban area lives in the suburbs, then 25 percent of the sample should come from the suburbs.

Here are the steps in quota sampling:

1. Determine a number of variables, strongly related to the question under investigation, to be used as bases for stratification. Variables such as gender, age, education, and social class are frequently used.
2. Using census or other available data, determine the size of each segment of the population.
3. Compute quotas for each segment of the population that are proportional to the size of each segment.
4. Select typical cases from each segment, or stratum, of the population to fill the quotas.

The major weakness of quota sampling lies in step 4, the selection of individuals from each stratum. You simply do not know whether the individuals chosen are representative of the given stratum. The selection of elements is likely to be based on accessibility and convenience. If you are selecting 25 percent of the households in the inner city for a survey, you are more likely to go to houses that are attractive rather than dilapidated, to those that are more accessible, to those where people are at home during the day, and so on. Such procedures automatically result in a systematic bias in the sample because certain elements are going to be misrepresented. Furthermore, there is no basis for calculating the error involved in quota sampling.

Despite these shortcomings, researchers have used quota sampling in many projects that might otherwise not have been possible. Many feel that speed of data collection outweighs the disadvantages. Moreover, years of experience with quota samples have made it possible to identify some of the pitfalls and to take steps to avoid them.

You can find further discussion of sampling techniques in works by Cochran (1985) and Sudman (1976) listed in the References at the end of the book.

RANDOM ASSIGNMENT

When the primary goal of a study is to compare the outcomes of two treatments with the same dependent variable, **random assignment** is used. Here a chance procedure such as a table of random numbers is used to divide the available subjects into groups. Then a chance procedure such as tossing a coin is used to decide which group gets which treatment.

As with random sampling, any bias the researcher has will not influence who gets what treatment, and the groups will be statistically equivalent before treatment. Group 1 may have more highly motivated subjects than group 2, but it is just as likely that group 2 will have more highly motivated subjects than group 1. The same is true of all possible known or unknown variables that might influence the dependent variable. Therefore, the same lawful nature of sampling errors that are true of random sampling are true of random assignment.

THE SIZE OF THE SAMPLE (FUNDAMENTALS)

Laypeople are often inclined to criticize research (especially research whose results they do not like) by saying the sample was too small to justify the researchers' conclusions. How large should a sample be? Other things being equal, a larger sample is more likely to be a good representative of the population than a smaller sample. However, the most important characteristic of a sample is its representativeness, not its size. A random sample of 200 is better than a random sample of 100, but a random sample of 100 is better than a biased sample of 2,500,000.

Size alone will not guarantee accuracy. A sample may be large and still contain a bias. The latter situation is well illustrated by the *Literary Digest* magazine poll of 1936, which predicted the defeat of President Roosevelt. Although the sample included approximately 2.5 million respondents, it was not representative of the voters; thus, the pollsters reached an erroneous conclusion. The bias resulted from selecting respondents for the poll from automobile registrations, telephone directories, and the magazine's subscription lists. These subjects would certainly not represent the total voting population in 1936, when many people could not afford automobiles, telephones, or magazines. Also, because the poll was conducted by mail, the results were biased by differences between those who responded and those who did not. We have since learned that with mailed questionnaires those who are against the party in power are more likely to return their questionnaires than those who favor the party in power. The researcher must recognize that sample size will not compensate for any bias that faulty sampling techniques may introduce. Representativeness must remain the prime goal in sample selection.

Later in this chapter we will introduce a procedure for determining appropriate sample size, on the basis of how large an effect size is considered meaningful and on statistical considerations. Such procedures, known as **power calculations**, are the best way to determine needed sample sizes.

THE CONCEPT OF SAMPLING ERROR

When an inference is made from a sample to a population, a certain amount of error is involved because even random samples can be expected to vary from one to another. The mean intelligence score of one random sample of fourth-graders will probably differ from the mean intelligence score of another random sample of fourth-graders from the same population. Such differences, called **sampling errors**, result from the fact that the researcher has observed only a sample and not the entire population.

Sampling error is "the difference between a population parameter and a sample statistic." For example, if you know the mean of the entire population (symbolized μ) and also the mean of a random sample (symbolized $\overline{X}$) from that population, the difference between these two ($\overline{X} - \mu$) represents sampling error (symbolized e). Thus, $e = \overline{X} - \mu$. For example, if you know that the mean intelligence score for a population of 10,000 fourth-graders is $\mu = 100$ and a particular random sample of 200 has a mean of $\overline{X} = 99$, then the sampling error is $\overline{X} - \mu = 99 - 100 = -1$. Because we usually depend on sample statistics to estimate population parameters, the notion of how samples are expected to vary from populations is a basic element in inferential statistics. However, instead of trying to determine the discrepancy between a sample statistic and the population parameter (which is not often known), the approach in inferential statistics is to estimate the variability that could be expected in the statistics from a number of different random samples drawn from the same population. Because each of the sample statistics is considered to be an estimate of the same population parameter, any variation among sample statistics must be attributed to sampling error.

The Lawful Nature of Sampling Errors

Given that random samples drawn from the same population will vary from one another, is using a sample to make inferences about a population really any better than just guessing? Yes, it is because sampling errors behave in a lawful and predictable manner. The laws concerning sampling error have been derived through deductive logic and have been confirmed through experience.

Although researchers cannot predict the nature and extent of the error in a single sample, they can predict the nature and extent of sampling errors in general. Let us illustrate with reference to sampling errors connected with the mean.

Sampling Errors of the Mean

Some sampling error can always be expected when a sample mean is used to estimate a population mean μ. Although, in practice, such an estimate is based on a single sample mean, assume that you drew several random samples from the same population and computed a mean for each sample. You would find that these sample means would differ from one another and would also differ from the population mean (if it were known). Statisticians have carefully studied sampling errors of the mean and found that they follow known laws.

1. *The expected mean of sampling errors is zero.* Given an infinite number of random samples drawn from a single population, the positive errors can be expected to balance the negative errors so that the mean of the sampling errors will be zero. For example, if the mean height of a population of college freshmen is 5 feet 9 inches and several random samples are drawn from that population, you would expect some samples to have mean heights greater than 5 feet 9 inches and some to have mean heights less than 5 feet 9 inches. In the long run, however, the positive and negative sampling errors will balance. If you had an infinite number of random samples of the same size, calculated the mean of each of these samples, and then computed the mean of all these means, this mean would be equal to the population mean.

   Because positive errors equal negative errors, a single sample mean is as likely to underestimate a population mean as to overestimate it. Therefore, we can justify saying that a sample mean is an unbiased estimate of the population mean and is a reasonable estimate of the population mean.

2. *Sampling error is an inverse function of sample size.* As the size of a random sample increases, there is less fluctuation from one sample to another in the value of the mean. In other words, as the size of a sample increases, the expected sampling error decreases. Small samples produce more sampling error than large ones. You would expect the means based on samples of 10 to fluctuate a great deal more than the means based on samples of 100. In the height example, it is much more likely that a random sample of 4 will

include 3 above-average freshmen and 1 below-average freshman than that a random sample of 40 would include 30 above-average and 10 below. As sample size increases, the likelihood that the mean of the sample is near the population mean also increases. There is a mathematical relationship between sample size and sampling error. This relationship has been incorporated into inferential formulas, which we will discuss later.

3. *Sampling error is a direct function of the standard deviation of the population.* The more spread, or variation, there is among members of a population, the more spread there will be in sample means. For example, the mean weights of random samples of 25, each selected from a population of professional jockeys, would show relatively less sampling error than the mean weights of samples of 25 selected from a population of schoolteachers. The weights of professional jockeys fall within a narrow range; the weights of schoolteachers do not. Therefore, for a given sample size, the expected sampling error for teachers' weights would be greater than the expected sampling error for jockeys' weights.
4. *Sampling errors are distributed in a normal or near-normal manner around the expected mean of zero.* Sample means near the population mean will occur more frequently than sample means far from the population mean. As you move farther and farther from the population mean, you find fewer and fewer sample means occurring. Both theory and experience have shown that the means of random samples are distributed in a normal or near-normal manner around the population mean. Because a sampling error in this case is the difference between a sample mean and the population mean, the distribution of sampling errors is also normal or near normal in shape.

   The distribution of sample means will resemble a normal curve even when the population from which the samples are drawn is not normally distributed. For example, in a typical elementary school you will find about equal numbers of children of various ages included, so a polygon of the children's ages would be basically rectangular. If you took random samples of 40 each from a school with equal numbers of children aged 6 through 11, you would find many samples with a mean age near the population mean of 8.5, sample means of about 8 or 9 would be less common, and sample means as low as 7 or as high as 10 would be rare. Note that the word *error* in this context does not mean "mistake"—it refers to what is unaccounted for.

Standard Error of the Mean

Because the extent and the distribution of sampling errors can be predicted, researchers can use sample means with predictable confidence to make inferences concerning population means. However, you need an estimate of the magnitude of the sampling error associated with the sample mean when using it as an estimate of the population mean. An important tool for this purpose is the standard error of the mean. Sampling error manifests itself in the variability of sample means. Thus, if you calculate the standard deviation of a collection of means of random samples from a single population, you would have an estimate of the amount of sampling error. It is possible, however, to obtain this estimate on the basis of only one sample. We have noted that two things affect the size of sampling error: the size of the sample and the standard deviation in the population. When these two things are known, you can predict the standard deviation of sampling errors. This expected standard deviation of sampling errors of the mean is called the **standard error of the mean** and is represented by the symbol $\sigma_{\overline{X}}$. Deductive logic shows that the standard error of the mean is equal to the standard deviation of the population (σ) divided by the square root of the number in each sample ($\sqrt{n}$). As a formula,

$$\sigma_{\overline{X}} = \frac{\sigma}{\sqrt{n}} \tag{7.1}$$

where

$\sigma_{\overline{X}}$ = standard error of the mean
σ = standard deviation of the population
n = number in each sample

In Chapter 6 we noted that standard deviation (σ) is an index of the degree of spread among individuals in a population. In the same way, standard error of the mean ($\sigma_{\overline{X}}$) is an index of the spread expected among the means of samples drawn randomly from a population. As you will see, the interpretation of σ and $\sigma_{\overline{X}}$ is very similar.

Because the means of random samples have approximately normal distributions, you can also use the normal-curve model to make inferences concerning population means. Given that the expected mean of sample means is equal to the population mean, that the standard deviation of these means is equal to the standard error of the mean, and that the means of random samples are distributed normally, you can compute a ***z* score** for a sample mean and refer that z to the normal-curve table to approximate the probability of a sample mean occurring through chance that far or farther from the population mean. The z is derived by subtracting the population mean from the sample mean and then dividing this difference by the standard error of the mean:

$$z = \frac{\overline{X} - \mu}{\sigma_{\overline{x}}} \tag{7.2}$$

To illustrate, consider a college admissions officer who wonders if her population of applicants is above average on the verbal subtest of the College Board examination. The national mean for College Board verbal scores is 500, and the standard deviation is 100. She pulls a random sample of 64 from her population and finds the mean of the sample to be 530. She asks the question, How probable is it that a random sample of 64 with a mean of 530 would be drawn from a population with a mean of 500? Using Formula 7.1, the admissions officer calculates the standard error of the mean as 12.5:

$$\begin{aligned} \sigma_{\overline{x}} &= \frac{\sigma}{\sqrt{n}} \\ &= \frac{100}{\sqrt{64}} \\ &= 12.5 \end{aligned}$$

Calculating the z score for her sample mean with Formula 7.2, she obtains the following result:

$$z = \frac{\overline{X} - \mu}{\sigma_{\overline{x}}}$$
$$= \frac{530 - 500}{12.5}$$
$$= 2.4$$

Thus, the sample mean deviates from the population mean by 2.4 standard error units. What is the probability of having a sample mean that deviates by this amount ($2.4\sigma_{\overline{X}}$) or more from the population mean? It is only necessary to refer to the normal curve table in order to express this deviation (z) in terms of probability. Referring to the normal curve table, the admissions officer finds that the probability of a $z = 2.4$ or higher is .0082. This means that a z score that great or greater would occur by chance only about 8 times in 1000. Because the probability of getting a sample mean that far from the population mean is remote, she concludes that the sample mean probably did not come from a population with a mean of 500, and therefore the mean of her population, applicants to her college, is very probably greater than 500.

THE STRATEGY OF INFERENTIAL STATISTICS

Inferential statistics is the science of making reasonable decisions with limited information. Researchers use what they observe in samples and what is known about sampling error to reach fallible but reasonable decisions about populations. The statistical procedures performed before these decisions are made are called **tests of significance**. A basic tool of these statistical tests is the null hypothesis.

THE NULL HYPOTHESIS

Suppose you have 100 fourth-graders available to participate in an experiment concerning the teaching of certain number concepts. Further, suppose that your research hypothesis is that method B of teaching results in a greater mastery of these concepts than method A. You randomly assign 50 students to be taught these concepts by method A and the other 50 to be taught by method B. You arrange their environment in such a way that the treatment of the two groups differs only in method of instruction. At the end of the experiment you administer a measure that is considered to be a suitable operational definition of mastery of the number concepts of interest. You find that the mean for the students taught by method B is higher than the mean for those taught by method A. How do you interpret this difference?

Assuming you have been careful to make the learning conditions of the two groups equivalent, except for the method of teaching, you could account for the difference by deciding that (1) the method of teaching caused the difference or (2) the difference occurred by chance. Even though the subjects were randomly assigned to the treatments, it is possible that through chance the method B group had students who were more intelligent, more highly motivated, or for some other reason were more likely to learn the number concepts than the students in the method A group, no matter how they were taught.

The difference between the groups therefore could be a result of (1) a relationship between the variables, method of teaching, and mastery of the concepts, or (2) it could be the result of chance alone (sampling error). How are you to know which explanation is correct? In the ultimate sense you cannot positively prove that the method of teaching caused the difference. However, you can estimate the likelihood of chance alone being responsible for the observed difference and then determine which explanation to accept as a result of this estimate.

The chance explanation is known as the **null hypothesis**, which, as you recall from Chapter 5, is a statement that there is *no* actual relationship between the variables and that any observed relationship is only a function of chance. In the example, the null hypothesis would state that there is no relationship between teaching method and mastery of the number concepts.

Another way of stating the null hypothesis in the example is to declare that the mean for all fourth-graders taught by method A is equal to the mean for all fourth-graders taught by method B. In formula form, using the symbol μ for population mean, this statement becomes

$$H_0: \mu_{\mathrm{A}} = \mu_{\mathrm{B}} \tag{7.3}$$

where

H_0 = null hypothesis
μ_{A} = mean of all fourth-graders taught by method A
μ_{B} = mean of all fourth-graders taught by method B

Note that the assumption is made that the 50 pupils taught by method A are a representative sample of the population of fourth-graders who might be taught by method A and the 50 pupils taught by method B are a representative sample of the population who might be taught by method B. The investigator hopes to use the data from the experiment to infer what would be expected when other fourth-graders are taught by method A or B.

In interpreting the observed difference between the groups, the investigator must choose between the chance explanation (null hypothesis) and the explanation that states there is a relationship between variables (research hypothesis)—and must do so without knowing the ultimate truth concerning the populations of interest. This choice is based on incomplete information and is therefore subject to possible error.

TYPE I AND TYPE II ERRORS

The investigator will either retain or reject the null hypothesis. Either decision may be right or wrong. If the null hypothesis is true, the investigator is correct in retaining it and in error in rejecting it. The rejection of a true null hypothesis is labeled a **Type I error**. If the null hypothesis is false, the investigator is in error in retaining it and correct in rejecting it. The retention of a false null hypothesis is labeled a **Type II error**. The four possible states of affairs are summarized in Table 7.2.

Table 7.2 Schematic Representation of Type I and Type II Errors

		Real Situation in the Population	
		H_0 is true	H_0 is false
Investigator's Decision after Making Test of Significance	Rejects H_0	Type I error	Correct
	Retains H_0	Correct	Type II error

Let us consider some possible consequences of the two types of errors, using the example we have been following.

Type I Error

A Type I error, symbolized by a Greek lowercase letter alpha (α), is a "false alarm"—the investigator thinks he or she has something when there is nothing there. For example, the investigator rejects the null hypothesis and declares that there is a relationship between teaching method and mastery of the numerical concepts and therefore recommends method B as the better method. Schools discard textbooks and other materials based on method A and purchase materials based on method B. Inservice training is instituted to train teachers to teach by method B. After all this expenditure of time and money, the schools do not observe an increase in mastery of the numerical concepts. Subsequent experiments do not produce the results observed in the original investigation. Although the ultimate truth or falsity of the null hypothesis is still unknown, the evidence supporting it is overwhelming. The original investigator is embarrassed and humiliated.

Type II Error

A Type II error symbolized by a lowercase Greek letter beta (β) is a "miss"—the investigator concludes there is nothing when there really is something. In the example, the investigator concludes that the difference between the two groups may easily be attributed to chance and that the null hypothesis may well be true. She thus retains the null hypothesis and declares that there is insufficient evidence for concluding that one method is better than the other. Subsequent investigators conclude that method B is better than method A, and schools that change from method A to method B report impressive gains in student mastery. Although the ultimate truth still remains unknown, a mountain of evidence supports the research hypothesis. The original investigator is embarrassed (but probably not humiliated). Figure 7.1 provides a way of remembering the difference between Type I and Type II errors.

Comparison of Type I and Type II Errors

Type I errors typically lead to changes that are unwarranted. Type II errors typically lead to a maintenance of the status quo when a change is warranted. The consequences of a Type I error are generally considered more serious than the consequences of a Type II error, although there are certainly exceptions.

A fable for the remembrance of Type I and Type II errors

by Donald Ary and John W. Sloan

A beautiful maiden was married to Alpha, the handsome and favorite number one son of the king. Alas, she discovered her husband was impotent. The king's ugly, despised number two son, Beta, became her lover.

In order to escape being stoned to death, she had to declare to the world that with number one, Alpha, there was a relationship when in truth there was none. Concerning number two, Beta, she had to declare that there was no relationship when in truth there was.

The Gods took pity on her and forgave both Type I and Type II errors. They promised her immortality with these words: "Our revered statisticians shall sing of your tragedy to generation after generation throughout all time to come, and the understanding of your dilemma shall cause scholars of all nations to sigh."

Source: From The CEDR Quarterly (1977). 10. (4) p. 19

Figure 7.1

LEVEL OF SIGNIFICANCE

Recall that all scientific conclusions are statements that have a high probability of being correct, rather than statements of absolute truth. How high must the probability be before an investigator is willing to declare that a relationship between variables exists? In other words, how unlikely must the null hypothesis be before a researcher rejects it? The consequences of rejecting a true null hypothesis, a Type I error, vary with the situation. Therefore, investigators usually weigh the relative consequences of Type I and Type II errors and decide, before conducting their experiments, how strong the evidence must be before they would reject the null hypothesis. This predetermined level at which a null hypothesis would be rejected is called the **level of significance**. The probability of a Type I error is directly under the control of the researcher, who sets the level of significance according to the type of error he or she wishes to guard against.

Of course, a researcher could avoid Type I errors by always retaining the null hypothesis or avoid Type II errors by always rejecting it. Neither of these alternatives is productive. If the consequences of a Type I error would be very serious but a Type II error would be of little consequence, the investigator might decide to risk the possibility of a Type I error only if the estimated probability of the observed relationship's being caused by mere luck is one chance in a thousand or less. This is testing the hypothesis at the .001 level of significance, which is considered to be a quite conservative level. In this case the investigator is being very careful not to declare that a relationship exists when there is no relationship.

However, this decision means accepting a high probability of a Type II error, declaring there is no relationship when in fact a relationship does exist.

If the consequences of a Type I error are judged to be not serious, the investigator might decide to declare that a relationship exists if the probability of the observed relationship's being caused by mere luck is 1 chance in 10 or less. This is called "testing the hypothesis at the .10 level of significance." Here the investigator is taking only moderate precautions against a Type I error, yet is not taking a great risk of a Type II error.

The *level of significance* is the probability of a Type I error that an investigator is willing to risk in rejecting a null hypothesis. It is symbolized by the lowercase Greek alpha (α). If an investigator sets the level of significance at .01, it means that the null hypothesis will be rejected if under the assumption that chance alone is responsible, the obtained probability is equal to or less than 1 time in 100. The investigator is saying that he or she is willing to limit the probability of rejecting the null hypothesis when it is true (Type I error) to 1 in 100. If the level of significance is set at .0001, the probability of making a Type I error is 1 in 10,000 or less. The most commonly used levels of significance in the behavioral sciences are the .05 and the .01 levels.

Traditionally, investigators determine the level of significance after weighing the relative seriousness of Type I and Type II errors but before running the experiment. If the data derived from the completed experiment indicate that the probability of the null hypothesis being true is equal to or less than the predetermined acceptable probability, the investigators reject the null hypothesis and declare the results to be statistically significant. If the probability is greater than the predetermined acceptable probability, the results are described as nonsignificant—that is, the null hypothesis is retained.

The familiar meaning of the word *significant* is "important" or "meaningful." In statistics, this word means "less likely to be a function of chance than some predetermined probability." Results of investigations can be statistically significant without being inherently meaningful or important.

We are sorry the phrase "statistically significant" was chosen to indicate when results were less likely to be chance than a previously chosen α. If a phrase such as "statistically not chance" had been chosen, people would not think statistically significant had anything to do with importance.

DIRECTIONAL AND NONDIRECTIONAL TESTS

In testing a null hypothesis, researchers are not usually concerned with the direction of the differences. Rather, they are interested in knowing about the possible departure of sample statistics from population parameters. When comparing the effectiveness of competing treatments, an investigator usually wants to learn if treatment A is better than treatment B or if treatment B is better than treatment A. This kind of test is called **nondirectional** (two-tailed) because the investigator is interested in differences in either direction. The investigator states only that there will be a difference. Note in Figure 7.2 that the region of rejection is equally divided between the two tails of the distribution. Thus, if a sample mean is observed that is *either* sufficiently greater or sufficiently less than the

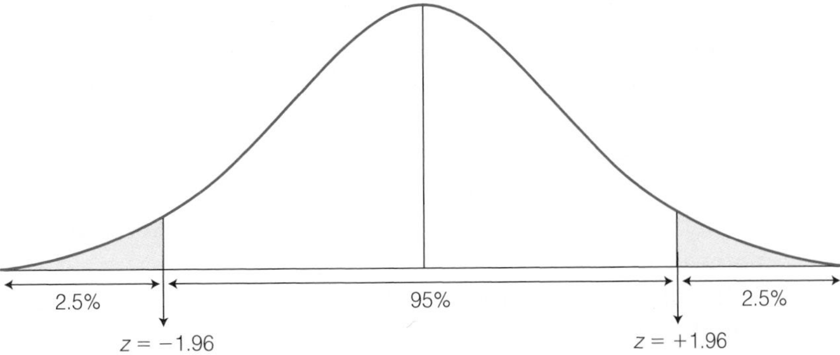

A. Curve showing the critical region for a nondirectional test (two-tailed test)

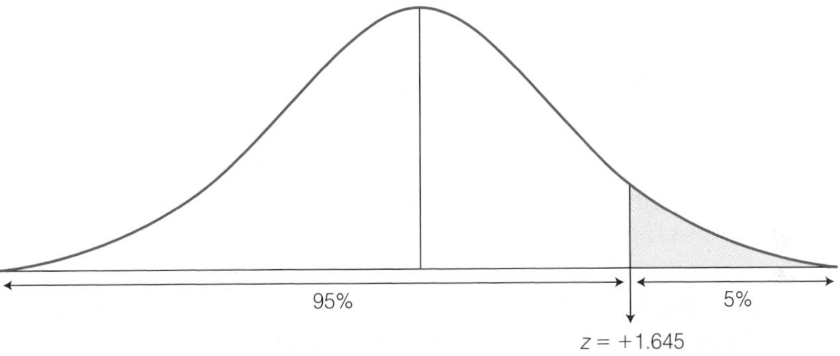

B. Curve showing the critical region for a directional test (one-tailed test)

Figure 7.2 Curves Showing the Critical Regions of Directional and Nondirectional Tests

hypothesized value, the null hypothesis would be rejected. The direction of the difference is not important.

However, if only one alternative to the null hypothesis is of interest, a **directional test** (one tailed) is used. For example, an investigator studying the effects of a specific diet among obese people would only be interested in assessing the probability that the diet reduces weight. Or, if a basketball coach is investigating the effects of a practice regimen on the success rate for shooting from the foul line, he (or she) would only implement the regimen if there is reasonable evidence that it increases success. Results indicating that the regimen decreases success would lead to the same decision as would a retained null hypothesis: Forget the regimen.

If on the basis of experience, previous research, or theory the researcher chooses to state the direction of possible differences, then she or he would perform a directional test. A directional hypothesis would state *either* that the parameter is greater than *or* that the parameter is less than the hypothesized value. Thus, in directional tests the critical region is located in only one of the two tails of the distribution. For a .05 level of significance, this region in a normal curve is the point equal to $z = 1.645$. You do not, as you would in nondirectional tests, divide the 5 percent between the two sides of the curve. Rather, you place the whole

5 percent of chance error on one side of the curve. This means that the null hypothesis will be retained unless the observed difference is in the hypothesized direction. It is obvious that for rejecting a null hypothesis at a given level, a directional test requires a smaller z value than a nondirectional test (compare $z = 1.645$ with $z = 1.96$, the z value required for a two-tailed test). So a directional test makes it easier to reject the null hypothesis and thus increases the probability that the null hypothesis will be rejected if the difference is in the hypothesized direction.

In statistical terminology, a nondirectional test is often referred to as a **two-tailed test of significance**, a directional test as a **one-tailed test**. The decision to use either a one-tailed test or a two-tailed test should be made early in the study, before any statistical tests are performed. You do not wait to see what the data look like and then select a one-tailed or two-tailed test.

DETERMINING THE APPROPRIATE SAMPLE SIZE

Now that we have considered Type I and Type II errors and level of significance, let us return to the question of the size of the sample needed in a research study. A scientific method of determining the sample size needed is to specify a meaningful **effect size** (Δ or d) and then determine the sample size needed to reach a desired probability of rejecting the null hypothesis at a given level of significance. Recall that effect size is the difference between experimental and control groups divided by the standard deviation of the control group (Δ) or the difference between two groups divided by the estimated population standard deviation (d).

To illustrate, let us return to the college admissions officer who wonders if her population of applicants is above average. To determine the number of subjects needed to test her hypothesis, she first specifies what effect size would be meaningful. She decides that an effect size of .33 (one-third of a standard deviation) or more would be meaningful, but an effect size of less than .33 would not be meaningful.

The specification of what is a meaningful effect size is a judgment call. However, professionals in their fields are usually able to specify an effect size that serves as a reasonable dividing line between meaningful and trivial differences. Cohen's (1988) verbal labels for effect sizes (see Chapter 6) are useful guides for this purpose. In this example an effect size of .33 on the verbal subtest of the College Board examination might be considered a reasonable dividing line. It is saying that a mean score of 533 or greater [500 + (.33)(100)] on the verbal subtest of the College Board examination is enough to matter, whereas a smaller effect size has little or no practical importance. Consulting the normal curve table (Table A.1 in the Appendix), we see that a z score of .33 has 62.93 percent below it. Therefore, the admissions officer is saying that if approximately 63 percent of the general population have scores less than the average for her population of applicants, the difference is considered meaningful, whereas less difference would not be considered meaningful.

Next the admissions officer determines her level of significance, designated as α, and her desired probability of rejecting the false null hypothesis ($1 - \beta$). Let us say that she decides she wants a 90 percent chance of rejecting the null hypothesis with a one-tailed .05 α. Now she has all the ingredients needed to determine the needed sample size, as shown by the following formula:

$$N = \left(\frac{1}{\Delta}\right)^2 (z\alpha + z\beta)^2 \tag{7.4}$$

where

N = number needed in the sample
Δ = specified effect size
$z\alpha$ = z score for the level of significance
$z\beta$ = z score for the desired probability of rejecting the null hypothesis $(1 - \beta)$

In Table A.1 you find that the z score for a one-tailed .05 α is 1.645. The z score for a one-tailed probability of 90 percent (the desired probability of rejecting the null hypothesis) is 1.28. Substituting these z values and the specified Δ, you have the following:

$$\begin{aligned} N &= \left(\frac{1}{.33}\right)^2 (1.645 + 1.28)^2 \\ &= 3^2(2.925)^2 \\ &= 9(8.56) \\ &= 77.04 \end{aligned}$$

With a random sample of 78 subjects from her population of applicants, the admissions officer has a 90 percent chance of rejecting the null hypothesis at the one-tailed .05 level if the true effect size in her population is .33 or greater.

Note that as effect size gets smaller, the number needed gets larger. If the investigator had wanted an effect size of .10 to have a 90 percent probability of rejecting the null hypothesis at the one-tailed .05 level, she would need 856 subjects in her sample. Note also that as $(1 - \beta)$, the desired probability of rejecting the null hypothesis gets larger and as α gets smaller (more demanding), the number of subjects needed gets larger.

Determining the number needed in a sample is really a function of how precise you want to be—that is, how large or small an effect size you want to be statistically significant, how much chance of Type I error you are willing to live with, and how much probability of rejecting a false null hypothesis you want. These are all judgment calls, but they can all be made on a rational basis. We would defend the specifications of $\Delta = .33$, $\alpha = .05$, and $(1 - \beta) = .90$ in the example as reasonable. Therefore, we consider a sample size of 78 sufficient in this case.

Although it may be heresy to suggest a sample might ever be too large, it is true that as sample size increases, tinier and tinier effect sizes become statistically significant. We recommend that when planning research, both effect size and statistical significance be considered.

POWER

Power is the ability to reject a null hypotheses when it is false. Formula 7.4 is an example of a power formula. It indicates the number of subjects needed to give the investigator the desired power to reject the null hypothesis for specified effect size and level of significance. Many statistics books describe calculations for determining numbers needed when effect size is defined in terms of proportion, correlation, or other statistics. Borenstein and Cohen's *Statistical Power Analysis* (1989) provides extensive information on these procedures.

THINK ABOUT IT 7.1

Complete each line with either (a) goes up, (b) goes down, or (c) stays the same.

I. As you choose to put α up from .01 to .05,
   1. Probability of Type I error _________.
   2. Probability of Type II error _________.
   3. Power _________.

II. As you increase the number in the samples,
   1. Probability of Type I error _________.
   2. Probability of Type II error _________.
   3. Power _________.

III. As the true difference between means goes up from 3 to 7,
   1. Probability of Type I error _________.
   2. Probability of Type II error _________.
   3. Power _________.

IV. As effect size increases,
   1. Probability of Type I error _________.
   2. Probability of Type II error _________.
   3. Power _________.

V. As the heterogeneity (variance) within the samples increases,
   1. Probability of Type I error _________.
   2. Probability of Type II error _________.
   3. Power _________.

VI. If you do a one-tailed test instead of a two-tailed test and if you correctly predicted the direction of the difference
   1. Probability of Type I error _________.
   2. Probability of Type II error _________.
   3. Power _________.

Answers

I. 1. a
   2. b
   3. a

II. 1. c
   2. b
   3. a

III. 1. c
   2. b
   3. a

IV. 1. c
   2. b
   3. a

V. 1. c
   2. a
   3. b

VI. 1. c
   2. b
   3. a

THE GENERAL STRATEGY OF STATISTICAL TESTS

A statistical test compares what is observed (a statistic) with what we would expect to observe through chance alone. What we would expect through chance alone is called the error term. A ratio is formed:

$$\frac{\text{observation}}{\text{chance expectation}} = \frac{\text{statistic}}{\text{error term}}$$

When the observed statistic is equal to or less than the average value expected through chance alone (the **error term**), the most plausible explanation for the statistic is that it was due to chance alone. If the statistic is greater than the error term, then the chance explanation becomes less and less plausible as this ratio becomes greater and greater than one.

THE *t* TEST FOR INDEPENDENT SAMPLES

In our math concepts example the statistic is the difference between the mean of the group taught by method B and the group taught by method A ($\overline{X}_B - \overline{X}_A$). Through deductive logic statisticians have determined the average difference between the means of two randomly assigned groups that would be expected through chance alone. This expected value (the error term) is derived from the variance within each of the two groups and the number of subjects in each of the two groups. It is called the standard error of the difference between two independent means ($s_{\bar{x}_1-\bar{x}_2}$). Its definition formula is

$$s_{\bar{x}_1-\bar{x}_2} = \sqrt{\frac{\Sigma x_1^2 - \Sigma x_2^2}{n_1 + n_2 - 2}\left(\frac{1}{n_1} + \frac{1}{n_2}\right)} \qquad (7.5)$$

where

$s_{\bar{x}_1-\bar{x}_2}$ = standard error of the difference between two means
n_1 = number of cases in group 1
n_2 = number of cases in group 2
Σx_1^2 = sum of the squared deviation scores in group 1
Σx_2^2 = sum of the squared deviation scores in group 2

The standard error of the difference between two means is sometimes referred to as the "error term for the independent *t* test"

The ***t* test for independent samples** is a straightforward ratio that divides the observed difference between the means by the difference expected through chance alone. In formula form

$$t = \frac{\overline{X}_1 - \overline{X}_2}{s_{\bar{x}_1-\bar{x}_2}} \qquad (7.6)$$

If this *t* ratio is equal to 1.00 or less, the observed difference between means is very probably due to chance alone. Recall the investigator doing the math concepts teaching study comparing a randomly assigned group that did method A

Table 7.3 Computing the t Value for Two Independent Means

Group 1 Frequent Feedback		Group 2 Infrequent Feedback	
X_1	X_1^2	X_2	X_2^2
18	324	15	225
17	289	13	169
16	256	12	144
16	256	12	144
16	256	11	121
15	225	11	121
15	225	10	100
15	225	10	100
14	196	10	100
14	196	10	100
13	169	9	81
12	144	8	64
11	121	7	49
10	100	6	36
8	64	6	36
$\frac{\Sigma X_1}{n_1} = \frac{210}{15}$	$\Sigma X_1^2 = 3046$	$\frac{\Sigma X_2}{n_2} = \frac{150}{15}$	$\Sigma X_2^2 = 1590$

with a randomly assigned group that did method B set his α at .05. Suppose he found that the group 1 mean was 2.05 higher than the group 2 mean and his error term was 2.85. The observed/chance expectation ratio is .83. The observed difference is less than the difference expected by chance. Therefore, the null hypothesis is retained. There is not sufficient evidence to draw a tentative conclusion.

A physical education teacher conducted an experiment to see if archery students perform better if they get frequent feedback concerning their performance or do better with infrequent feedback. She randomly divided her class into two groups of 15 and flipped a coin to determine which group got frequent feedback and which group got infrequent feedback. She set her α at .05 for a two-tailed test. At the end of her study she administered a measure of archery performance. The results are shown in Table 7.3.

The computation formula for the independent t test is

$$t = \frac{\overline{X}_1 - \overline{X}_2}{\sqrt{\frac{\Sigma X_1^2 - (\Sigma X_1)^2/n_1 + \Sigma X_2^2 - (\Sigma X_2)^2/n_2}{n_1 + n_2 - 2}\left(\frac{1}{n_1} + \frac{1}{n_2}\right)}} \qquad (7.7)$$

Inserting the numbers from Table 7.3 into this formula gives us

$$t = \frac{(210/15) - (150/10)}{\sqrt{\dfrac{3046 - \dfrac{(210)^2}{15} + 1590 - \dfrac{(150)^2}{15}}{15 + 15 - 2}\left(\dfrac{1}{15} + \dfrac{1}{15}\right)}}$$

$$= \frac{14 - 10}{\sqrt{\dfrac{3046 - \dfrac{44100}{15} + 1590 - \dfrac{22500}{15}}{28}(.0667 + .0667)}}$$

$$= \frac{4}{\sqrt{\dfrac{(3046 - 2940) + (1590 - 1500)}{28}(.1333)}}$$

$$= \frac{4}{\sqrt{\left(\dfrac{196}{28}\right)(.1333)}}$$

$$= \frac{4}{\sqrt{(7)(.1333)}} = \frac{4}{\sqrt{.9331}} = \frac{4}{.966} = 4.14$$

Here we have an observed difference that is 4.14 times as large as the average difference expected by chance. Is it large enough to reject the null hypothesis? To answer this question we must consider the *t curves* and *degrees of freedom.*

THE *t* DISTRIBUTIONS

For generations researchers used the normal curve to asses the probability of an observation/chance expectation ratio. Consulting Table A.1, we find that a ratio of 4.0 has only 3 chances in 100,000 of occurring by chance.

In the 18th century a quality control officer for Guinness brewery who used the pen name “Student” showed that the normal curve was appropriate for assessing observation/chance expectation ratios only when the population standard deviation formula, $\sigma = \sqrt{\Sigma x^2/N}$, was known. In most research the population standard deviation is not known and must be estimated by $s = \sqrt{\Sigma x^2/(N - 1)}$. When s is used instead of σ, each statistical test has its unique probability distribution based on the number of subjects and the number of population estimates used, its degrees of freedom.

DEGREES OF FREEDOM

The number of **degrees of freedom (df)** is the number of observations free to vary around a constant parameter. To illustrate the general concept of degrees of freedom, suppose a teacher asks a student to name any five numbers that come into his or her mind. The student would be free to name any five numbers he or she chooses, so we would say that the student has 5 degrees of freedom. Now suppose the teacher tells the student to name five numbers but to make sure that the mean of these five numbers is 20. The student now is free to name any numbers for the first four, but for the last number must name the number that will make the total for the five numbers 100 in order to arrive at a mean of 20. If the student names, as the first four numbers, 10, 16, 20, and 35, then the fifth number must be 19. The student has five numbers to name and one restriction, so his or her degrees of freedom are 5 − 1 = 4. We can show this as a formula:

$$\begin{aligned} df &= n - 1 \\ &= 5 - 1 \\ &= 4 \end{aligned} \tag{7.8}$$

Now suppose the teacher asks the student to name seven numbers in such a way that the first three have a mean of 10 and all seven have a mean of 12. Here we have seven numbers and two restrictions, so

$$\begin{aligned} df &= n - 2 \\ &= 7 - 2 \\ &= 5 \end{aligned}$$

When the unknown population standard deviation is estimated from the sample standard deviation, $s = \sqrt{\Sigma x^2/(N - 1)}$, one degree of freedom is lost. The one degree of freedom is lost because the sample statistic (s) is derived from the deviations about the sample mean that must always sum to 0. Thus, all but one of the deviations is free to vary, or $df = N - 1$.

The concept of degrees of freedom is involved in most of the procedures in inferential statistics. An appropriate method of computing the degrees of freedom is associated with each procedure. Often, the number of degrees of freedom on which a sample statistic is based depends on the sample size (N) and the number of sample statistics used in its calculation. In the archery example the error term was calculated using the deviation of the frequent feedback scores around the frequent feedback mean and the deviation of the individual infrequent feedback scores around the infrequent feedback mean. The degrees of freedom for the t test for independent means is $n_1 + n_2 - 2$. In our example $df = 15 + 15 - 2 = 28$. Each degree of freedom has its own probability distribution, its t curve. As the degrees of freedom become larger, the t distribution becomes more like the normal curve. The most frequently needed areas of the ***t* curves** are to be found in Table A.2 in the Appendix. The t curve does not approach the baseline as rapidly as does the normal curve. Some of the t curves are shown in Figure 7.3 along with the normal curve, the solid line labeled $df = \infty$. The t curves are labeled according to their degrees of freedom.

Now we can use Table A.2 in the Appendix to determine the significance of the results. The first column in this table is labeled *df* (degrees of freedom). For the archery example, consult the row for 28 *df*. The remaining columns show the t values associated with certain probabilities for directional and nondirectional tests. Because the independent variable in this example could affect archery performance in either a positive or negative direction, we need to perform a nondirectional test. In the row for 28 *df*, we find 1.701 in the column labeled .10 for

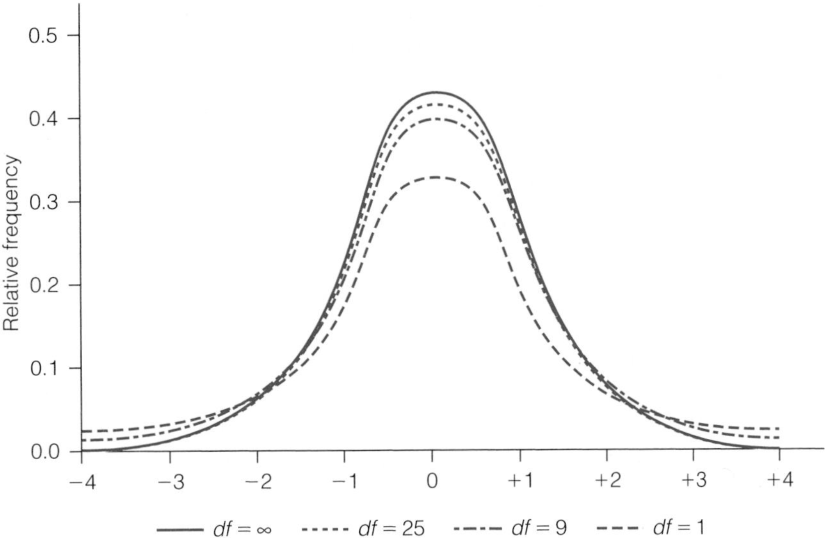

Figure 7.3 *t* Curves for Various Degrees of Freedom

a nondirectional test, which tells you that with a true null hypothesis and 28 *df*, a *t* ratio of +1.701 or more or −1.701 or less will occur by chance 1 time in 10. The number 2.048 in the column labeled .05 indicates that under a true null hypothesis and 28 *df*, a *t* ratio of ±2.048 or more will occur by chance 5 percent of the time.

The observed ratio of 4.14 is greater than 2.048, which means that the difference between the groups is greater than the value required to reject the null hypothesis at the .05 level of significance. The estimated probability of the null hypothesis being true is less than 5 percent ($p < .05$). Thus, we would reject the null hypothesis. Although we do not know for certain that the variables frequent feedback versus infrequent feedback and archery performance are related, the evidence is significant enough according to our previously set criteria to enable us to conclude that the observed relationship is probably not just a chance occurrence. If the observed *t* ratio had been less than 2.048, we would have concluded that the evidence was not good enough to lead us to declare that a relationship exists between the variables. In other words, we would have retained the null hypothesis.

Notice that as we proceed from left to right in the *t* table we find the *t* values required for rejecting the null hypothesis at increasingly rigorous levels of significance. For 28 *df*, a value of 2.763 or greater would lead to the rejection of a null hypothesis at the .01 level. A value of 3.674 or greater would lead to the rejection of the null hypothesis at the .001 level. So the value of 4.14 is significant not only at the .05 level ($p < .05$) but also at the .01 level ($p < .01$) and the .001 level ($p < .001$). If the ratio of observed difference (numerator) divided by error term (denominator) equals or exceeds the value indicated in Table A.2, you can reject the null hypothesis at the indicated level of significance. If you want to report an effect size, first calculate Cohen's *d*, then multiply it by the square root of the sample size. With this approach it is easy to see the relationship of effect size and number on the one hand and statistical significance on the other. The larger the effect size, the larger the t and the more likely that the results are statistically significant.

With two independent samples when the dependent variable is ranked data, the Mann–Whitney test serves the same purpose as the t test for independent samples. For example, if archery proficiency had been assessed by having a judge rank the 30 subjects from 1st to 30th, the Mann–Whitney test would be used to test the hypothesis.

Recall that much data that appears to be interval, such as grade point averages, actually does not meet the requirement of equal intervals between scores. This would probably be the case if a judge rated archery performance on a scale of 1 to 10. In such a case it would be advisable to convert the 1 to 10 scores to ranks and do a Mann–Whitney test. Siegel and Castellan's (1988) book is an excellent, very easy to read, text about statistical tests for ordinal and nominal data including the Mann–Whitney test.

THE *t* TEST FOR DEPENDENT SAMPLES

So far, our discussion has centered on comparing the means obtained from two independent samples. In an independent sample, each member is chosen randomly from the population and the composition of one group has no bearing on the composition of the other group. Sometimes, however, investigators may wish to match the subjects of their two groups on some qualities that are important to the purpose of their research, or they may wish to compare the means obtained from the same subjects under two different experimental conditions. In such cases the groups are no longer independent, inasmuch as the composition of one group is related to the composition of the other group. You would expect the dependent variable scores to be correlated. Therefore, the ***t* test for dependent samples** must be used. This test is also known as the correlated, or nonindependent, or paired t test. The measure to be analyzed by the dependent t test is the mean difference between the paired scores. Pre- and posttest scores of the same individuals are an example of paired scores.

Let us consider an example. Suppose you wish to know whether taking a research course affects the attitudes of the students toward research. To investigate this, you select a research class and obtain attitude measures toward research from the students on the first and last days of class. Let us suppose you have collected such data, and the results are as presented in Table 7.4.

Columns 2 and 3 of Table 7.4 show the scores of each student in the first and second measures. Column 4 presents the difference between the first and second scores of each student. The sum of these differences amounts to +30. The mean of the differences, 2, is found by dividing +30 (ΣD) by the number of paired observations, or 15. Column 5 shows the squares of the differences.

The standard deviation of the difference scores s_D is

$$s_D = \sqrt{\frac{\Sigma D^2 - \dfrac{(\Sigma D)^2}{n}}{N - 1}} \tag{7.9}$$

Table 7.4 Before-and-After Attitude Scores of 15 Students in an Introduction to Research Class

(1) Subject Number	(2) Pretest	(3) Posttest	(4) D	(5) D^2
1	10	12	+2	+4
2	9	13	+4	+16
3	8	12	+4	+16
4	11	9	−2	+4
5	10	8	−2	+4
6	7	9	+2	+4
7	10	12	+2	+4
8	9	11	+2	+4
9	8	10	+2	+4
10	6	10	+4	+16
11	10	12	+2	+4
12	7	13	+6	+36
13	10	6	−4	+16
14	9	13	+4	+16
15	10	14	+4	+16
			$\Sigma D = +30$	$\Sigma D^2 = 164$

In the example, this is

$$s_D = \sqrt{\frac{164 - \frac{(30)^2}{15}}{15 - 1}} = \sqrt{\frac{164 - 60}{14}} = \sqrt{\frac{104}{14}} = \sqrt{7.4286} = 2.7255$$

Effect size, the mean difference divided by the standard deviation ($d = \overline{D}/s_D$), is 2/2.7255 = .7338. Since there is only one sample standard deviation, d and d are equal. By Cohen's (1988) definition, this is nearer a "large" (.8) than a "moderate" (.6) effect size.

To determine the likelihood that the effect size is a function of chance, first calculate a t ratio by multiplying effect size by the square root of the number of pairs:

$$t = \Delta\sqrt{N}$$

In this example the t is $.7338\sqrt{15} = (.7338)(3.87) = 2.84$. The t ratio tells you that the observed difference is 2.84 times as great as the difference that would be expected under a true null hypothesis. Now consult the table of t values (Appendix Table A.2) to determine the statistical significance of the observed ratio. A more commonly used formula for the dependent t test is

$$t = \frac{\overline{D}}{\sqrt{\frac{\Sigma D^2 - \frac{(\Sigma D)^2}{N}}{N(N-1)}}} \tag{7.10}$$

where

$$t = t \text{ ratio}$$
$$D = \text{average difference}$$
$$\Sigma D^2 = \text{different scores squared, then summed}$$
$$(\Sigma D)^2 = \text{difference scores summed then squared}$$
$$N = \text{number of pairs}$$

The number of degrees of freedom for the dependent t test equals $N - 1$, N being the number of *pairs* of observations. In the example you have $15 - 1 = 14$ degrees of freedom. In the table of t values you find that with 14 degrees of freedom a t value of 2.145 is needed for the t to be significant at the .05 level, and a t value of 2.977 for significance at the .01 level when a nondirectional test is performed. The obtained value of 2.84 exceeds the given value for the .05 level but does not reach the given value for the .01 level. This means that the difference between the two means is significant at the .05 level but not at the .01 level. If we had set our level of significance at .05, we could conclude that the attitude of the students toward research had changed.

When the dependent variable is rank data, the Wilcoxon paired sample test serves the same purpose as the dependent t test. This test can also be found in Siegel and Castellan (1988).

THE *t* TEST FOR PEARSON *r* CORRELATION COEFFICIENTS

Another important use for the t test is in testing hypotheses concerning a population correlation rho (ρ). The most common null hypothesis in such cases is that the population correlation is zero and that the correlation observed in the sample (r) is a function of chance. For example, an investigator might draw a sample of 27 college freshmen, administer vocabulary and spatial orientation tests to them, and find a **Pearson *r*** of .20 between the two measures. The next step is to decide whether this observed correlation coefficient could easily be a result of chance in a population where the true correlation in the population (ρ) is zero. To test the hypothesis that the population correlation is zero, you do not have to calculate a t test. These calculations have been done for various sample sizes and sample correlations and are shown in Table A.3 (critical values of Pearson's r).

Whereas with the dependent t test the degrees of freedom are the number of paired observations minus 1, it has been shown mathematically that with the Pearson r the degrees of freedom are the number of paired observations minus 2. A significant r is equal to or larger than the tabled value with $N - 2$ degrees of freedom, where $N =$ the number of *pairs* of scores. Table A.3 indicates that with $df = 25$ (the number in the sample minus 2) when a two-tailed test is performed, an observed Pearson r above +.3809 or less than −.3801 is required to reject the null hypothesis at the two-tailed .05 level. Thus, the correlation of .20 obtained in the study involving college freshmen is not significant at the .05 level.

With a reasonably large number of cases, a coefficient of correlation may be relatively low in value and yet be statistically significant (although not necessarily important). For example, Jackson and Lahaderne (1967), with a sample of 292 sixth-graders, found a correlation of +.25, a correlation statistically significant at the .01 level, between the students' response on a questionnaire measuring students' satisfaction with school and their teachers' prediction of how these students would respond to the questionnaire. The findings indicate that in the population represented by the sample, the correlation is not likely to be 0. However, recall that the coefficient of determination (r^2) indicates the extent of relationship between variables. Only $.25^2$, or 6.25 percent, of the variance of teachers' predictions is in common with the students' actual responses. Although teachers can predict student satisfaction at greater than chance level, the teachers' predictions of satisfaction have only a weak relationship with actual student satisfaction. Statistical significance does not necessarily mean important.

The t test can also be used to test hypotheses about population correlations other than zero. You can also use it to test the hypothesis that the correlations observed in two samples could have arisen from the same population. Because this is an introductory text, we have chosen not to include such tests here. A useful description of these tests may be found in Glass and Hopkins (1996) and in various other texts.

ANALYSIS OF VARIANCE

Analysis of variance (ANOVA) is a statistical test used to analyze the data from a study with more than two groups. In **analysis of variance**, as in the t test, a ratio comparing observed differences to the error term is used to test hypotheses about differences among groups. This ratio, called the ***F* ratio**, employs the variance (σ^2) of group means as a measure of observed differences among groups. This means that ANOVA is a more versatile technique than the t test. A t test can be used only to test a difference between *two* means. ANOVA can test the difference between *two or more* means.

The general rationale of ANOVA is that the *total variance* of all subjects in an experiment can be subdivided into two sources: *variance between groups* and *variance within groups*. Variance between groups is incorporated into the numerator in the F ratio. Variance within groups is incorporated into the error term or denominator, as it is in the t test. As variance between groups increases, the F ratio increases. As variance within groups increases, the F ratio decreases. The number of subjects influences the F ratio: The larger the number, the larger the numerator becomes. When the numerator and denominator are equal, the differences between group means are no greater than would be expected by chance alone. If the numerator is greater than the denominator, you consult the table of F values (Table A.4 in the Appendix) to determine whether the ratio is great enough to let you reject the null hypothesis at the predetermined level.

COMPUTING THE *F* RATIO (SIMPLE ANALYSIS OF VARIANCE)

Suppose you have the three experimental conditions of high stress, moderate stress, and no stress, and you wish to compare the performance on a simple problem-solving task of three groups of individuals, randomly assigned to these three conditions. Assume that the data presented in Table 7.5 summarize your

Table 7.5 Measures Obtained in Three Random Samples after Performance of a Task under Conditions of High Stress, Moderate Stress, and No Stress

Group 1 High Stress		Group 2 Moderate Stress		Group 3 No Stress	
X_1	X_1^2	X_2	X_2^2	X_3	X_3^2
19	361	22	484	15	225
18	324	20	400	14	196
17	289	19	361	14	196
16	256	18	324	13	169
15	225	17	289	13	169
15	225	16	256	12	144
14	196	16	256	12	144
13	169	15	225	11	121
12	144	14	196	11	121
11	121	12	144	10	100
$\Sigma X_1 = 150$	$\Sigma X_1^2 = 2310$	$\Sigma X_2 = 169$	$\Sigma X_2^2 = 2935$	$\Sigma X_3 = 125$	$\Sigma X_3^2 = 1585$
$\overline{X}_1 = 15.0$		$\overline{X}_2 = 16.9$		$\overline{X}_3 = 12.5$	$\overline{\overline{X}} = 14.8$
$\Sigma X_t = 444$			$\Sigma X_t^2 = 6830$		

observations of the performance of these three groups and that you are now going to test the null hypothesis that there is no significant difference among these three groups at the .01 level.

The means can be seen to differ from one another and from the overall mean for all 30 subjects ($\overline{\overline{X}}$, the *grand mean* or overall mean). Are the differences among these means great enough to be statistically significant, or is it likely that they occurred by chance? To answer this, compute the F ratio. Computing the F ratio requires several steps.

The first step is to find the sum of the squared deviation of each of the individual scores from the grand mean. This index is called the "total sum of squares" and reflects all treatment effects plus sampling error. It is expressed by the following formula:

$$SS_t = \Sigma X_t^2 - \frac{(\Sigma X_t)^2}{N} \tag{7.11}$$

SS_t = sum of squares total
ΣX_t^2 = each score squared, then summed
$(\Sigma X_t)^2$ = all the scores summed first, then this sum squared
N = number of scores

(Note that SS is the same as Σx^2, which you first encountered in Chapter 6. We do not know why SS is used instead of Σx^2 in analyses of variance but it is standard operating procedure.)

In this example, this value is

$$SS_t = 6830 - \frac{(444)^2}{30} = 258.8$$

Next, find the part of the total sum of squares that is due to the deviations of the group means from the grand mean. This index is called the "sum of the squares between groups." (To be grammatically correct, we should say "the sum of squares *among* groups" when more than two groups are involved. However, it is a long-standing tradition to use the term "sum of squares between groups," and to be consistent with other texts we are retaining this usage here.) This index is found by applying the formula

$$SS_b = \Sigma x_b^2 = \frac{(\Sigma X_1)^2}{n_1} + \frac{(\Sigma X_2)^2}{n_2} \cdots - \frac{(\Sigma X)^2}{N} \tag{7.12}$$

In our example, this value is

$$SS_b = \Sigma X_b^2 = \frac{(150)^2}{10} + \frac{(169)^2}{10} + \frac{(125)^2}{10} - \frac{(444)^2}{30} = 97.4$$

Then, you find the part of the total sum of squares that is caused by the deviations of each individual score from its own group mean. This index, called the "sum of the squares within groups," is found by applying the raw-score formula for the sum of squared deviations to each group and then summing across groups ($SS_w = SS_1 + SS_2 + \cdots$).

The computation formula is

$$SS_w = \Sigma x_w^2 = \left[\Sigma X_1^2 - \frac{(\Sigma X_1)^2}{n_1}\right] + \left[\Sigma X_2^2 - \frac{(\Sigma X_2)^2}{n_2}\right] + \cdots \tag{7.13}$$

In the example, this value is

$$SS_w = \Sigma x_w^2 = \left[2310 - \frac{(150)^2}{10}\right] + \left[2935 - \frac{(169)^2}{10}\right] + \left[1585 - \frac{(125)^2}{10}\right] = 161.4$$

A shortcut to finding the sum of the squares within groups is to subtract the sum of squares between groups from the total sum of the squares, expressed as follows:

$$SS_w = SS_t - SS_b \tag{7.14}$$

In the example,

$$SS_w = 258.8 - 97.4 = 161.4$$

The sum of squares between groups is a systematic variation, possibly due to effects of treatment. Dividing the between groups sum of squares (97.4) by the total sum of squares, you get .376. Therefore, 37.6 percent of the variation is associated with differences between group means (systematic variation). The other 161.4/258.8 = 62.4 percent is associated with spread within groups (error variation).

An approach to conceptualizing analysis of variance is to picture SS_t as reflecting what you observe, SS_b (sum of squares between) as reflecting what you can explain, and SS_w (sum of squares within) as what you cannot explain. The next step is to see if our systematic knowledge is enough greater than what would be expected by chance to reject the null hypothesis.

THE *F* TEST OF SIGNIFICANCE

Table 7.6 summarizes the results of the calculations so far, together with the results of further calculations. Column 1 of the table lists the three sources of variation: between-groups variance, within-groups variance, and total variance. Column 2 contains the sums of squares, which you have already calculated. Column 3 lists the number of degrees of freedom associated with each source of variance. The number of degrees of freedom for between-groups variance is equal to $(G - 1)$, G being the number of groups. In our example this value is $3 - 1 = 2$. The degrees of freedom for within-groups variance is $[N - G]$, total number of scores $[N]$ minus the number of groups $[G]$ or $30 - 3 = 27$. The number of degrees of freedom for total variance equals $N - 1$; in our example $30 - 1 = 29$. This last value could also be obtained by adding the between-groups and within-groups degrees of freedom.

The next step, then, is to calculate the *between-groups mean square* (MS_b) and the *within-groups mean square* (MS_w) by dividing the between-groups and within-groups sums of squares by their respective degrees of freedom. The resulting mean squares are independent estimates of the parent population variance. It has been shown mathematically that if the null hypothesis is true, the population variance estimates mean square between and mean square within will be approximately equal, and the ratio MS_b/MS_w will be approximately 1. As differences among group means increase, the value of MS_b increases. As the number of subjects increase, the value of MS_w decreases. Therefore, as the ratio MS_b/MS_w (called the *F* ratio) increases, the likelihood that group differences were a function of chance decreases. In the example, the mean square between groups is $97.4/2 = 48.7$ and the mean square within groups is $161.4/27 = 5.98$. The mean square within groups is the error term for your *F* ratio. By applying the following formula, you finally arrive at the end product of the analysis-of-variance procedure, the *F* ratio:

$$F = \frac{MS_b}{MS_w} = \frac{SS_b/df_b}{SS_w/df_w} \tag{7.15}$$

In your example, this value is

$$F = \frac{48.70}{5.98} = 8.14$$

The MS_b is 8.14 times what we would expect through chance alone.

Table 7.6 Summary of the Analysis of Variance of the Three Groups

(1) Source of Variance	(2) *SS*	(3) *df*	(4) *MS*	(5) *F*	(6) Level of Significance
Between groups	97.4	2	48.70	8.14	0.01
Within groups	161.4	27	5.98		
Total	258.8	29			

THINK ABOUT IT 7.2

Match SS_w, SS_b, SS_t, MS_b, and MS_w to the following phrases:

1. The numerator in the F ratio ________.
2. All the variation ________.
3. Systematic variation ________.
4. Unexplained variation ________.
5. A population variance estimate based on differences among group means ________.
6. The degrees of freedom is $N - G$ for ________.

Answers

1. MS_b, 2. SS_t, 3. SS_b, 4. SS_w, 5. MS_b, 6. SS_w

Now consult Table A.4 in the Appendix to determine whether the F ratio is statistically significant. You find the column headed by the between-groups (numerator) degrees of freedom and go down this column to the row entry corresponding to the number of within-groups (denominator) degrees of freedom. At this point in the column you find two values, one in lightface type and one in boldface type. If the F ratio is equal to or greater than the value given in lightface, it is significant at the .05 level. If the obtained F ratio is equal to or greater than the value given in boldface, it is also significant at the .01 level. In the example, with 2 and 27 degrees of freedom you need an F ratio of 3.35 to reject the null hypothesis at the .05 level and an F ratio of 5.49 to reject the null hypothesis at the .01 level. Because the obtained F ratio is greater than both of these values, it is significant at the .01 level and the null hypothesis is rejected at that level.

When the null hypothesis is rejected as a result of this analysis-of-variance procedure, you cannot say more than that the measures obtained from the groups involved differ and that the differences are greater than you would expect to exist by chance alone. Where there are more than two groups, you cannot yet determine *which* groups differ significantly from each other.

A significant F ratio does not necessarily mean that all groups differ significantly from all other groups. But, if the overall F is significant, then at least one out of all possible comparisons between pairs of means or combinations of means will be significant. The significant F may be a result of a difference between one group and the rest of the groups. For instance, in your problem it might be that group 3 is significantly different from group 1 and group 2, but groups 1 and 2 do not differ significantly from each other. Many statistics texts, including the Glass and Hopkins text (1996), describe several of these tests and their applications.

If the dependent variable is in the form of ranks, the Kruskal–Wallis one-way analysis by ranks test can assess the statistical significance of differences among groups. This test may also be found in the Siegel and Castellan (1988) text.

MULTIFACTOR ANALYSIS OF VARIANCE

In the complex world we live in, it often is not the case that X has a consistent influence on Y. Often X influences Y in certain circumstances but not in others. For instance, phonics instruction is useful in teaching reading with children with normal hearing but worthless with the deaf. The independent variable, method of teaching reading, does not have the same effect on the dependent variable, reading proficiency, when the variable normal hearing versus deaf is taken into account.

In the language of research we say, "Is there an *interaction* between the independent variable method of teaching reading (X_1) and the independent variable normal hearing vs. deaf (X_2) and the dependent variable reading proficiency (Y)?"

You may want to investigate the combined effect of stress level and achievement need on performance in a problem-solving task. To investigate this problem you will vary both the level of stress and the achievement need. The layout for an experiment investigating the combined effects of two or more independent variables is called a **factorial design**, and the results are analyzed by means of a **multifactor analysis of variance**.

Let us assume that you have carried out this experiment using five subjects in each group and that the data shown in Table 7.7 represent a summary of your observations of the performance of the subjects. Applying multifactor analysis of variance will enable you to learn (1) whether there is a significant difference between the performance of all the subjects under a high-stress condition and all

Table 7.7 Measures on Problem-Solving Tasks of Subjects with Low and High Achievement Need under High and Low Conditions of Stress

		Stress: High	Stress: Low	
Achievement Need	High	20 20 Group 1 19 19 $\overline{X} = 19$ 17 ΣX 95	23 22 Group 3 21 20 $\overline{X} = 21$ 19 ΣX 105	$\Sigma X_{r_1} = 200$ $\overline{X}_{r_1} = 20.0$
	Low	22 21 Group 2 20 19 $\overline{X} = 20$ 18 ΣX 100	18 16 Group 4 15 14 $\overline{X} = 15$ 12 ΣX 75	$\Sigma X_{r_2} = 175$ $\overline{X}_{r_2} = 17.5$
		$\Sigma X_{c_1} = 195$ $\overline{X}_{c_1} = 19.5$	$\Sigma X_{c_2} = 180$ $\overline{X}_{c_2} = 18.0$	ΣX Total $= 375$ $\overline{\overline{X}}$ (grand mean) $= 18.75$

those under a low-stress condition, (2) whether there is a significant difference between the performance of all the subjects with high achievement need and all those with low achievement need, and (3) whether the difference between performance under high- and low-stress conditions is the same for both subjects with high need for achievement and subjects with low need for achievement. The effects investigated by the first and second analyses are called **main effects**, whereas the third is referred to as an **interaction effect**. The end products of these analyses will be three *F* ratios, two of which indicate the significance of the two main effects and the third, that of the interaction effect.

The computation of these *F* ratios involves the following steps:

1. Find the total sum of squares, the sum of squares between groups, and the sum of squares within groups, using the same procedures and formulas applied in simple analysis of variance. These values, derived from the data in Table 7.7, are as follows:

$$SS_t = 7181 - \frac{(375)^2}{20} = 149.75$$

$$SS_b = \frac{(95)^2}{5} + \frac{(100)^2}{5} + \frac{(75)^2}{5} + \frac{(105)^2}{5} - \frac{(375)^2}{20} = 103.75$$

$$SS_w = 149.75 - 103.75 = 46.00$$

2. Partition the sum of the squares between groups into three separate sums of squares—(a) the sum of squares between columns, (b) the sum of squares between rows, and (c) the sum of squares for interaction between columns and rows—as shown next:

   a. The between-columns sum of squares represents the sum of the squared deviations caused by the difference between the column means and the grand mean. Find it by using the formula

$$SS_{bc} = \frac{(\Sigma X_{c_1})^2}{n_{c_1}} + \frac{(\Sigma X_{c_2})^2}{n_{c_2}} + \cdots - \frac{(\Sigma X)^2}{N} \quad (7.16)$$

   With this formula, the sum of squares between the columns for the data shown in Table 7.7 is

$$SS_{bc} = \frac{(195)^2}{10} + \frac{(180)^2}{10} - \frac{(375)^2}{20} = 11.25$$

   b. The between-rows sum of squares is the sum of the squared deviations caused by the difference between the row means and the grand mean. Find it by applying the formula

$$SS_{br} = \frac{(\Sigma X_{r_1})^2}{n_{r_1}} + \frac{(\Sigma X_{r_2})^2}{n_{r_2}} + \cdots - \frac{(\Sigma X)^2}{N} \quad (7.17)$$

   For the data presented in Table 7.7, this value is

$$SS_{br} = \frac{(200)^2}{10} + \frac{(175)^2}{10} - \frac{(375)^2}{20} = 31.25$$

c. The sum-of-squares interaction is the part of the deviation between the group means and the overall mean that is due neither to row differences nor to column differences. Expressed as a formula, it becomes

$$SS_{\text{int}} = SS_{\text{b}} - (SS_{\text{bc}} + SS_{\text{br}}) \tag{7.18}$$

Expressed in words, the interaction sum of squares is equal to the between-groups sum of squares minus the sum of the between-columns sum of squares and the between-rows sum of squares.

For the data presented in Table 7.7, this interaction sum of squares is

$$SS_{\text{int}} = 103.75 - (11.25 + 31.25) = 61.25$$

3. Determine the number of degrees of freedom associated with each source of variation. They are found as follows:

$$\begin{aligned} df \text{ for between-columns sum of squares} &= C - 1 \\ df \text{ for between-rows sum of squares} &= R - 1 \\ df \text{ for interaction} &= (C - 1)(R - 1) \\ df \text{ for between-groups sum of squares} &= G - 1 \\ df \text{ for within-groups sum of squares} &= N - G \\ df \text{ for total sum of squares} &= N - 1 \end{aligned}$$

where

C = number of columns
R = number of rows
G = number of groups
N = number of subjects in all groups

4. Find the mean-square values by dividing each sum of squares by its associated number of degrees of freedom.

5. Compute the F ratios for the main and the interaction effects by dividing the between-groups mean squares by the within-groups mean square for each of the three components.

The results of the calculations based on the data presented in Table 7.7 are summarized in Table 7.8. Three F ratios are listed in this table. To find the significance of each of these values, consult Table A.4 (the table of F values) as before. To enter this table, use the number of degrees of freedom associated with each F ratio (*df* for the numerator) and the number of degrees of freedom associated with the within-groups mean square (*df* for the denominator). For example, the between-columns F ratio is 3.913. Consulting the table, you see that, with 1 and 16 *df*, an F ratio of 4.49 or more is needed for significance at the .05 level. Because the F ratio is smaller than the value shown in the table, you can conclude that the high-stress versus low-stress difference is not statistically significant.

Because the between-rows degrees of freedom are the same as the degrees of freedom between columns, the same levels of 4.49 (.05 level) and 8.53 (.01 level) apply. Because the obtained value of 10.869 exceeds both of these values, it is significant at the .01 level.

Table 7.8 Summary of a 2 × 2 Multifactor Analysis of Variance

Source of Variance	*SS*	*df*	*MS*	*F*	Level of Significance
Between columns (stress)	11.25	1	11.25	3.913	—
Between rows (achievement need)	31.25	1	31.25	10.869	.01
Columns by rows (interaction)	61.25	1	61.25	21.304	.01
Between groups	103.75	3	34.583		
Within groups	46.00	16	2.875		
Total	149.75	19			

In the example, the degrees of freedom for interaction are the same (1 and 16). Therefore, the same values of F are required. The F value of 21.304 is greater than 8.35; therefore, the interaction is significant at the .01 level. You can reject the null hypothesis—that the difference between the high-stress minus low-stress group means among the subjects with low need for achievement is the same as the difference between the high-stress minus low-stress group means among the subjects with high need for achievement.

Interpreting the *F* Ratios

The first F ratio (between columns) in Table 7.8 is not significant and shows that the stress conditions do not differ significantly from one another in their effect on the performance of the subjects in the experiment. This analysis, a comparison of the combined performance of groups 1 and 2 ($\overline{X} = 19.5$) with the combined performance of groups 3 and 4 ($\overline{X} = 18.0$), was not statistically significant, so we do not have sufficient evidence to make any conclusions about the stress conditions.

The second F ratio (between rows), which is significant at the .01 level, is based on comparing the performance of the subjects in groups 1 and 3 ($\overline{X} = 20.0$) with those in groups 2 and 4 ($\overline{X} = 17.5$). From the significance of this F ratio you can infer that the difference between the performance of those subjects with high achievement need and those with low achievement need is beyond chance expectation. Because you have a significant F ratio for the difference, you conclude that under conditions similar to those of your experiment, a higher level of task performance can be expected from people with high achievement need than people with low achievement need.

The third F ratio shows the interaction effect between the two variables: stress level and achievement need. The significance of the F ratio in this case means that the effect of stress level on performance in a problem-solving task depends on the degree of achievement need.

Among the students with a high need for achievement, the difference between high stress and low stress was only 2 points (21 − 19). Among the students with a low need for achievement, you find a difference between high stress and low stress of 5 points (20 − 15). Because your F test indicated that the interaction was significant, you can conclude that high stress makes more difference when combined with low achievement need than when combined with high achievement need.

Multifactor analysis has been of great value in educational research because many questions educators need to investigate are inherently complex in nature. These techniques enable educators to analyze the combined effects of two or more independent variables in relation to a dependent variable. For example, a simple comparison of the dependent variable means of two groups of pupils taught by different methods may yield insignificant results. But, if you incorporate intelligence into the experiment as a measured independent variable, you may find that one method works better with the less intelligent pupils, whereas the other works better with the more intelligent pupils. (We present more on interpreting factorial analysis of variance in Chapter 11.)

Multifactor analysis of variance is not limited to two independent variables as in our example. Any number of independent variables may be incorporated in this technique. Several intermediate statistics books, including Glass and Hopkins (1996), explain the computation and interpretation of these procedures.

THE CHI-SQUARE TESTS OF SIGNIFICANCE

When dealing with nominal data, the most widely used **tests of significance** are **the chi-square tests**. They compare **observed frequencies** and **expected frequencies**. Observed frequencies, as the name implies, are the actual frequencies obtained by observation. Expected frequencies are theoretical frequencies that would be observed when the null hypothesis is true.

THE ONE-VARIABLE CHI SQUARE (GOODNESS OF FIT)

Consider the hypothesis that the proportion of male and female students in statistics courses is different from that of male and female students in a school of education as a whole. If you know that 40 percent of the total enrollment in the school is male and that 300 students are enrolled in statistics courses, the expected frequencies of male and female students enrolled in statistics will be 120 males and 180 females. Now suppose that the observed frequencies are found to be 140 males and 160 females.

	f Observed	*f* Expected
Male	140	120
Female	160	180
Total	300	300

There is a difference between observed and expected frequencies. Is it likely that this difference is due to chance alone?

To determine whether the difference between the expected and observed frequencies is statistically significant, apply the chi-square formula:

$$\chi^2 = \sum\left[\frac{(f_o - f_e)^2}{f_e}\right] \tag{7.19}$$

where

$$\chi^2 = \text{value of chi square}$$
$$f_o = \text{observed frequency}$$
$$f_e = \text{expected frequency}$$

Applying this formula to the data, you obtain

$$\chi^2 = \frac{(140 - 120)^2}{120} + \frac{(160 - 180)^2}{180} = 5.55$$

To determine whether this chi-square value is significant, consult the table of χ^2 values in the Appendix (Table A.5). The first column in this table shows the number of degrees of freedom involved in any given chi-square problem. The remaining columns present the values needed for different levels of significance. The number of degrees of freedom, as we have discussed previously, is based on the number of observations that are free to vary once certain restrictions are placed on the data. When you have a fixed number of observations divided into only two categories, as soon as the number falling into one category has been determined, the other is fixed. Thus, when you find that the number of male students is 140, the number of female students in the total of 300 must be 160. In this example, there is only 1 degree of freedom. In the one-variable chi-square, the number of degrees of freedom equals $K - 1$, where K is the number of categories used for classification. By consulting the table of χ^2 values, you find that your observed value of 5.55 is statistically significant at the .05 (and .02) level. You would reject the null hypothesis that there is no difference in the proportion of male and female students taking statistics and the proportion of male and female students in the entire school of education.

Interpreting this result, you can now state that the proportion of males who take statistics courses is significantly greater than the proportion in the entire college of education at the .05 level of confidence. The significance level of .05 means that there are less than 5 chances in 100 of observing such a difference between the proportions of male and female students through chance alone. Thus, the data lend support to your research hypothesis that the proportions of male and female students who take statistics courses is significantly different from the proportion of males and females in the entire school of education.

The use of the chi-square test is not limited to situations in which there are only two categories of classification; this test can also be used to test a null hypothesis stating that there is no significant difference between the proportion of the subjects falling into any number of different categories. Suppose, for example, you asked a random sample of 120 undergraduate students whether they prefer to live in a dormitory or in town or have no preference, with the results shown in Table 7.9.

If there were no difference between the three categories of response, you would have 40 responses in each category. These are your expected frequencies, as shown in Table 7.9.

A comparison of the two sets of frequencies presented in Table 7.9 shows that there are differences between your expected and observed data. To determine

Table 7.9 Observed and Expected Frequencies of Responses of 120 Undergraduate Students on Their Preference for Living Accommodations

	Dormitory	Town	No Preference	Total
Observed	40	50	30	120
Expected	40	40	40	120

whether they are significant, apply the chi-square test. The value of χ^2 for these data, using Formula 7.19, would be

$$\chi^2 = \frac{(40-40)^2}{40} + \frac{(50-40)^2}{40} + \frac{(30-40)^2}{40} = 5.00$$

The degrees of freedom, again, equal the number of categories minus 1 ($K - 1$) or, in this case, $3 - 1 = 2$. Referring to the table of χ^2 values, you can see that with 2 degrees of freedom, a χ^2 value of 5.991 or greater is required for significance at the .05 level. However, your obtained χ^2 value is smaller than this value and therefore is not statistically significant. This means that the observed differences between categories could easily have happened by chance. Consequently, the null hypothesis—that there is no significant difference between the frequencies of the three categories—cannot be rejected. In other words, if the proportions of preferences for the three categories in the entire undergraduate population were equal, you would expect to observe sample differences as great as those in your sample more often than 5 times in 100 through chance. We conclude that there is insufficient evidence that the undergraduates have a preference among the living accommodations.

THE TWO-VARIABLE CHI SQUARE (CHI-SQUARE TEST OF INDEPENDENCE)

So far we have only considered examples in which observations were classified along a single dimension. Sometimes, however, researchers wish to use more than one dimension for classification. The two-variable chi-square design uses two independent variables, each with two or more levels, and a dependent variable in the form of a frequency count. The purpose of the test is to determine whether or not the two variables in the design are independent of one another. Suppose, for example, you add another dimension to the previous problem and ask both graduate and undergraduate students to state their preferences as to their living accommodations. Assume the frequencies shown in Table 7.10 were the result.

In this case the null hypothesis is that the preference for living accommodations is the same for graduates as it is for undergraduates—that is, the variables "student status" and "preference for living accommodations" are unrelated, or independent. The null hypothesis in this ***chi-square test of independence*** is always that the variables are independent in the population. Your observations show that 30 percent of all students prefer dormitories, 45 percent prefer town, and 25 percent state no preference. If the null hypothesis is true, you would expect to find these same proportions among both graduates and undergraduates.

Table 7.10 Observed Frequencies of Responses of 200 Undergraduate and Graduate Students on Their Preference for Living Accommodations

Subjects	Dormitory	Town	No Preference	Total
Undergraduate students	40	50	30	120
Graduate students	20	40	20	80
Total	60	90	50	200

Table 7.11 Expected Frequencies of Responses of 200 Undergraduate and Graduate Students as to Their Preference with Respect to Living Accommodations

Subjects	Dormitory	Town	No Preference	Total
Undergraduate students	36	54	30	120
Graduate students	24	36	20	80
Total	60	90	50	200

You can compute expected cell frequencies by multiplying the row frequency associated with a cell by the column frequency associated with that cell, then dividing this product by the grand total ($E = f_r f_c / N$). For example, the expected frequency of response for undergraduate students who want to live in a dormitory is $120 \times 60 \div 200 = 36$; for those undergraduate students who prefer to live in town, it is $120 \times 90 \div 200 = 54$; and for graduate students who want to live in a dormitory, it is $80 \times 60 \div 200 = 24$. Using this approach, you can find the expected frequencies for each cell as shown in Table 7.11.

Note that all the row and column totals in Table 7.11 are exactly the same as those shown in Table 7.10. Now you ask if the observed frequencies differ enough from the expected frequencies to enable you to reject the likelihood that these differences could have occurred merely by chance. Applying the formula, you obtain

$$\begin{aligned}\chi^2 &= \frac{(40-36)^2}{36} + \frac{(50-54)^2}{54} + \frac{(30-30)^2}{30} + \frac{(20-24)^2}{24} \\ &\quad + \frac{(40-36)^2}{36} + \frac{(20-20)^2}{20} \\ &= 1.8518\end{aligned}$$

The number of degrees of freedom for a two-way table is found by applying the formula

$$df = (C - 1)(R - 1)$$

where

df = number of degrees of freedom
C = number of columns
R = number of rows

Applying this formula to the problem under consideration, you obtain

$$df = (3 - 1)(2 - 1) = 2$$

Referring to Table A.4, you can see that with 2 degrees of freedom, a χ^2 value of 5.991 is needed for significance at the .05 level. But your obtained χ^2 value of 1.8518 is smaller than this tabled value and is therefore not significant. This means that the differences between expected and observed frequencies are not beyond what you would expect by chance. In other words, you do not have reliable evidence that there is a relationship between the variables "student status" and "living accommodation preference" in the population from which your sample was drawn. The null hypothesis of independence cannot be rejected.

ASSUMPTIONS OF CHI SQUARE

Chi square is so easy to use that researchers may forget that there are assumptions that must be met if valid interpretations are to be made.

1. Observations must be independent—that is, the subjects in each sample must be randomly and independently selected.
2. The categories must be mutually exclusive: Each observation can appear in one and only one of the categories in the table.
3. The observations are measured as frequencies.

SUMMARY

Investigators hope to form generalizations about populations by studying groups of individuals selected from populations. These generalizations will be sound only if the selected groups (the samples) used in these studies are representative of the larger groups (the populations) from which they are chosen.

Statisticians distinguish between two major types of sampling procedures: probability sampling and nonprobability sampling. Probability sampling is characterized by random selection of population elements. In nonprobability sampling, the researcher's judgment replaces random selection. Simple random sampling, stratified sampling, cluster sampling, and systematic sampling are forms of probability sampling. In simple random sampling, all members of a population have an equal chance of being included within the sample. In stratified sampling, researchers select independent samples from different subgroups, or strata, of a population. In cluster sampling, researchers randomly select naturally occurring groups, or clusters, from a population; then they use as the sample all individuals within the selected clusters. Finally, in systematic sampling, researchers take as the sample every *K*th case from a list of the population. Forms of nonprobability sampling are convenience sampling, purposive sampling, and quota sampling. In accidental sampling, researchers use the available cases as the sample. In purposive sampling, cases judged as typical of the population of interest constitute the sample. Finally, in quota sampling, quotas are assigned to various strata of a population; then cases judged to be typical of each stratum are selected.

Inferential statistics provide tools by means of which researchers can estimate how confident they can be in inferring that phenomena observed in samples will also appear in the populations from which the samples were drawn. In other words, they tell you how much trust to put in what your observations seem to be telling you.

A basic strategy in inferential statistics is to

compute the difference among observations that would be likely to arise by chance alone. The result of this computation is called the error term. Then the observed differences among observations are compared with the error term. If the observed differences are similar to the differences that could arise by chance, the researcher cannot reject the likelihood that the observed differences were merely a function of chance. If the observed differences are greater than the error term, the researcher consults the tabled values of the statistic to determine whether the ratio of observation to error is great enough to reject the chance explanation at a predetermined level of significance. Inferential statistics are used when individuals are randomly assigned to treatments as well as when individuals are randomly selected from a population.

Effect size and sample size determine statistical significance. Power calculations determine the sample size needed to give a specified probability of rejecting the null hypothesis at a specified level of significance for a given effect size.

The indexes most commonly used in inferential statistics are the *t* test, analysis of variance (ANOVA), and the chi-square test. The *t* test is used to determine whether the difference between two sample means is statistically significant. There are three types of *t* tests: (1) the *t* test for independent groups, which is used to compare two sample means (2 groups) when the samples have been drawn independently from a population; (2) the *t* test for dependent groups, which is employed with two samples in which the subjects are matched (e.g., twins) or with two repeated measures such as pre- and posttests obtained from the same subjects; and (3) the *t* test for Pearson product moment correlation.

Analysis of variance is used to compare the means of two or more samples and to test the null hypothesis that no significant differences exist between the means of these samples. Multifactor analysis of variance enables researchers to test the effect of more than one independent variable and the interaction effect of such variables. There are other inferential statistics available to test hypotheses when the data are in the form of ranks.

The chi-square statistic is an index employed to find the significance of differences between proportions of subjects, objects, events, and so forth that fall into different categories (nominal data), by comparing observed frequencies and frequencies expected under a true null hypothesis.

KEY CONCEPTS

analysis of variance (ANOVA)
biased sample
chi-square tests
cluster sampling
convenience sampling
critical values for Pearson *r*
degrees of freedom
directional test
effect size
error term
expected frequency
factorial design
F ratio
F test
interaction effect
level of significance
main effect
multifactor analysis of variance
nondirectional test
nonprobability sampling
null hypothesis
observed frequency
one-tailed test
parameter
Pearson *r*
population
power calculation
power formulas
probability sampling
proportional stratified sampling
purposive (judgment) sampling
quota sampling
random assignment
random sample
random sampling
sample
sampling error
simple random sampling
standard error of the mean
statistic
stratified sampling
systematic sampling
table of random numbers
target population

tests of significance
tests of significance for ranked data
t curve
t test for dependent samples
t test for independent samples
two-tailed test
Type I error
Type II error

EXERCISES

1. Does the accuracy of a sample in representing the characteristics of the population from which it was drawn always increase with the size of the sample? Explain.
2. You have been asked to determine whether teachers in the Springfield School District favor the "year-round school" concept. Because the district is rather large, you are asked to contact only 500 teachers. Determine the number you would choose from each of the following levels to draw a proportional stratified random sample:

Level	Total number
Elementary	3500
Middle School	2100
High School	1400
Total	7000

3. You are asked to conduct an opinion survey on a college campus with a population of 15,000 students. How would you proceed to draw a representative sample of these students for your survey?
4. A national magazine has one million subscribers. The editorial staff wants to know which aspects of the magazine are liked and which are not. The staff decides that a personal interview is the best method to obtain the information. For practical and economic reasons, only 500 people in 5 cities will be surveyed. In this situation, identify the following:
   a. The population
   b. The sample
5. Which of the following are probability samples? Which are nonprobability samples?
   a. Random sample
   b. Convenience sample
   c. Cluster sample
   d. Stratified sample
   e. Purposive sample
   f. Quota sample
   g. Systematic sample
6. What is the difference between random sampling and random assignment?
7. Do the laws of probability apply in both?
8. Investigators wish to study the question "Do blondes have more fun?"
   a. What is the null hypothesis in this question?
   b. What would be a Type I error in this case?
   c. What would be a Type II error in this case?
   d. If one investigator uses a .05 level of significance in investigating this question and another investigator uses a .001 level of significance, which would be more likely to make a Type I error?
   e. If one investigator uses a .05 level of significance in investigating this question and another investigator uses a .001 level of significance, which would be more likely to make a Type II error?
9. Inferential statistics enable researchers to do which of the following?
   a. Reach infallible conclusions
   b. Reach reasonable conclusions with incomplete information
   c. Add an aura of legitimacy to what is really sheer guesswork
10. What two conditions are necessary for a Type I error to occur?
11. Which of the following statements describes the role of the null hypothesis in research?
    a. It enables researchers to determine the probability of an event occurring through chance alone when there is no real relationship between variables.
    b. It enables researchers to prove there is a real relationship between variables.
    c. It enables researchers to prove there is no real relationship between variables.

12. A Type II error occurs when a researcher does which of the following?
    a. Rejects a false null hypothesis.
    b. Rejects a true null hypothesis.
    c. Has already made a Type I error.
    d. Retains a false null hypothesis.
    e. Retains a true null hypothesis.
13. The phrase "level of significance" refers to which of the following situations?
    a. The probability of an event being due to chance alone, which is calculated after the data from an experiment are analyzed
    b. The probability of a Type I error that an investigator is willing to accept
    c. The actual probability of a Type II error
    d. The probability of reporting there is no relationship when there really is one
14. How do you determine the level of significance to use in an experiment?
15. A pharmaceutical company has employed researchers to investigate the frequency of heart attacks among those who have taken their drug regularly and those who have not. Would the manufacturer urge the researchers to be especially careful to avoid making a Type I error or a Type II error?
16. What is concluded when the results of a study are not statistically significant?
17. Compare stratified sampling with quota sampling.
18. What are the three elements to consider in determining sample size?
19. How large a sample would be needed for an effect size of .10 or greater to have an 80 percent chance of being statistically significant at the two-tailed .05 level of significance?
20. Find the chi-square value for the following set of data. Then indicate if the obtained value of chi square is significant at the .05 level of significance.

2	8	10
6	4	10
8	12	

21. You have the responses of two groups of students (education and noneducation majors) to an item in an attitude scale. Find the chi-square value for this problem and indicate whether your obtained chi-square value is statistically significant.

	Strongly Agree	Agree	Undecided	Disagree	Strongly Disagree
Education Students	7	8	10	9	6
Noneducation Students	8	10	7	8	7

22. For testing each of the following hypotheses, indicate which of the following statistical procedures would be appropriate:
    Test for independent means
    Test for nonindependent means
    Factorial analysis of variance
    Chi-square one-variable or goodness-of-fit test
    Chi-square test of independence
    a. The proportion of students in the class who receive *A*'s will be the same as the proportion of students who receive *B*'s.
    b. The mean score of the 1 P.M. section on the final examination will be significantly higher than the mean score of the 7 P.M. section.
    c. Attending the evening class instead of an afternoon class is an advantage, gradewise, for female students and a disadvantage for male students.
    d. If the same statistics quiz that was given to students on the first day of class were administered on the last day of class, students would show a significant gain in achievement.
    e. There is a relationship between a student's passing or failing the class and whether that student expresses satisfaction or dissatisfaction with the course.
    f. Any differences among the mean scores of the fall semester classes and the summer session classes of the same instructor can easily be accounted for by chance.
    g. There is a significant interaction effect between teaching experience and research experience and success in a research course.
23. Are there statistical tests that can be used when the data are in ranks?
24. A directional test differs from a nondirectional test in that in a directional test the

researcher is interested in changes that take place in which of the following ways:
a. Only in a positive direction
b. Only in a negative direction
c. In both positive and negative directions
d. Either in a positive or negative direction, but not both

25. Two randomly selected groups have been used in an experiment in which group I received treatment and group II received no treatment. The researcher's hypothesis is that the mean performance of group I will be higher than the mean performance of group II. Apply the *t* test to the following information and state if the researcher's hypothesis could be supported with a two-tailed .01 α.

	$\overline{X}$	N	ΣX^2
Group I	45.32	30	382.02
Group II	41.78	30	264.32

26. A researcher wants to test the hypothesis that the correlation between variable *A* and variable *B* is significantly greater than zero. He has obtained an $r = .21$ between the two variables using 22 subjects. Use Table A.8 to find if the hypothesis can be rejected at the .05 level (two tailed).

27. The following data are for a 2 × 3 experimental design. Apply the multifactor analysis of variance to test the significance of the main effects and the interaction effect.

	Columns		
Rows	A	B	C
A	25, 23, 20, 17, 15	22, 20, 18, 16, 14	20, 18, 16, 14, 12
B	16, 14, 12, 10, 8	18, 16, 14, 12, 10	19, 18, 16 14, 13

Provide a table in which the sums of squares (*SS*), degrees of freedom (*df*), mean squares (*MS*), and *F* values are shown. Then answer the following questions:
a. Which *F* values are significant and at what level?
b. How many null hypotheses are being tested in this problem?
c. How many of these hypotheses can the researcher reject?

28. Explain the logic of the *t* test.

ANSWERS

1. A larger randomly drawn sample is more likely to be representative of the population than is a smaller random sample. A large sample obtained with a method that permits systematic bias will not be any more representative than a small biased sample.
2. To obtain a proportional stratified sample, divide the 500 teachers in proportion to their representation in the population, as follows:
   Elementary 3500/7000 × 500 = 250
   Middle school 2100/7000 × 500 = 150
   High school 1400/7000 × 500 = 100
   Total sample 500
3. Obtain a list of all students and assign a number to each one. Then select a random sample of a given number by using a table of random numbers. Starting at a random point in the table, go up or down the column and include those students whose numbers are drawn.
4. a. All subscribers to the magazine
   b. Five hundred individuals who are interviewed
5. Probability samples: a, c, d, g
   Nonprobability samples: b, e, f
6. In random sampling a chance procedure is used to select a sample from a list of all those in a population. In random assignment a chance procedure is used to decide which of the available subjects will get which treatment.
7. Yes
8. a. There is no relationship between hair color and how much fun a person has.
   b. The investigators make a Type I error if they declare that blondes have more fun than nonblondes or that blondes have less fun than nonblondes, when in fact the two groups have an equal amount of fun.

c. The investigators make a Type II error if they fail to conclude that blondes have more fun or less fun, when in fact they do.
d. The investigator with the .05 level of significance
e. The investigator with the .001 level of significance

9. b
10. The null hypothesis must be true, and the investigator must reject it.
11. a
12. d
13. b
14. By weighing the consequences of Type I and Type II errors
15. A Type I error
16. The results could easily be a function of chance: the evidence is insufficient to justify a conclusion.
17. In stratified sampling, representativeness in each stratum is achieved through random selection, whereas in quota sampling representativeness in various strata is attained by way of judgment.
18. (1) The effect size considered to be the boundary between a meaningful and a nonmeaningful difference, (2) level of significance (α), and (3) desired probability of rejecting a false null hypothesis (β)
19. $N = (1/.10)^2\,(1.96 + .84)^2$
$= 100(7.84)$
$= 784$
(Note that with a small effect size a large number is required.)
20. 3.33 $df = 1$—nonsignificant
21. 0.954 $df = 2$—nonsignificant
22. a. Chi-square one-variable fit test
b. t Test for independent means, or one-way ANOVA
c. Factorial analysis of variance
d. t Test for dependent means
e. Chi-square test of independence
f. t Test for independent means
g. Factorial analysis of variance
23. Yes
24. d
25. $t = 4.11$, $df = 58$, significant at .001 level
26. With 20 degrees of freedom, an r of .4227 or greater is needed to reject the null hypothesis. Therefore the null hypothesis is retained.
27.

Source of Variance	SS	df	MS	F
Between columns	0	2	0	0
Between rows	120	1	120	11.34
Interaction	*80*	*2*	*40*	*3.78*
Between groups	200	5	40	3.78
Within groups	254	24	10.58	—

a. Between rows at .01 and interaction at .05
b. Three
c. Two

28. Sample statistics are used to determine the difference between two means that is expected due to pure chance when the null hypothesis is true. The observed difference is compared to this expected difference to determine the likelihood that the observed difference is due only to chance.

INFOTRAC COLLEGE EDITION

Use the keywords *probability sampling* or *nonprobability sampling* and locate a research study that used either of these sampling techniques. What was the population sampled? If a nonprobability sample was used, why did the researcher use it instead of a probability sampling technique?

Chapter 8

Tools of Research

OPERATIONAL DEFINITIONS TRANSFORM CONSTRUCTS INTO OBSERVABLE MEASURES.

INSTRUCTIONAL OBJECTIVES

After studying this chapter, the student will be able to:

1. Explain the role of measurement in research.
2. Use the *Mental Measurements Yearbooks* to obtain data necessary in evaluating standardized tests and other measuring instruments.
3. State the difference between a test and a scale.
4. Distinguish between norm-referenced and criterion-referenced tests.
5. Distinguish between measures of aptitude and achievement.
6. Distinguish between ceiling effect and floor effect and discuss why these may be of concern.
7. Describe the steps to follow in preparing a Likert scale for measuring attitudes.
8. Define performance assessment and discuss its advantages and disadvantages.
9. Describe the characteristics of a bipolar adjective scale.
10. State the kinds of errors that are common to rating scales.
11. State advantages and disadvantages of self-report personality measures.
12. List at least five guidelines that a researcher should follow when using direct observation as a data-gathering technique.
13. Define a situational test, and tell when it might be used in research.
14. State the essential characteristic of a projective technique and name at least two well-known projective techniques.

One aim of quantitative research is to obtain greater understanding of relationships among variables in populations. For example, you might ask: What is the relationship between intelligence and creativity among 6-year-olds? You cannot directly observe either intelligence or creativity. Nor can you directly observe all 6-year-olds. But this does not mean that you must remain in ignorance about this and similar questions. There are indicators that approximate the constructs of intelligence and of creativity; that is, there are observable behaviors that are accepted as being valid indexes of these constructs. Using indicators to approximate constructs is the measurement aspect of research.

Some measurement is very straightforward, using a single indicator to represent a variable. For example, you could measure a person's educational background by asking about the highest grade he or she had completed. Similarly, such variables as grade level, nationality, marital status, or number of children could be measured by a single indicator simply because these variables refer to phenomena that are very clear and for which a single indicator provides an acceptable measure. Other variables, however, are more complex and much more difficult to measure. In these cases using a single indicator is not appropriate.

Selecting appropriate and useful measuring instruments is critical to the success of any research study. One must select or develop scales and instruments that can measure complex constructs such as intelligence, achievement, personality, motivation, attitudes, aptitudes, interests, self-concept, and so on. There are two basic ways to obtain these measures for your study: Use one that has already been developed or construct your own.

To select a measuring instrument, the researcher should look at the research that has been published on his or her problem to see what other researchers have used to measure the construct of interest. These reports will generally indicate whether the instrument worked well or whether other procedures might be better. Other useful sources for identifying published instruments for one's research purposes are the *Mental Measurements Yearbooks* and *Tests in Print*, described in Chapter 4. Another good source of information about both published and unpublished tests is the Educational Testing Service (ETS) Test Collection. The ETS Test Collection is a library of more than 20,000 commercial and research tests and other measuring devices designed to provide up-to-date test information to educational researchers. It is available on the World Wide Web.

If researchers cannot find a previously developed instrument, then they must develop their own. The procedure involves identifying and using behavior that can be considered an indicator of the construct. To locate these indicators, researchers should turn first to the theory behind the construct. A good theory generally suggests how the construct will manifest itself and the changes that can be observed; that is, it suggests ways to measure the construct(s). For example, the general (*g* factor) theory of intelligence influenced the choice of tasks in the construction of early intelligence tests. Shavelson, Huber, and Stanton's (1976) multidimensional theory of self-concept served as the blueprint for a number of self-concept measures that have had a major influence on both theory and classroom practice. For instance, the Shavelson model was the basis for Marsh's (1988) widely used SDQ (Self-Description Questionnaire), which measures self-concept in preadolescents, adolescents, and late adolescents/young adults. Following construction of an instrument, additional research is used to support or revise both the instrument and the theory upon which it is based. Researchers can also use their own experiences and expertise to decide on the appropriate indicators of the construct. In this chapter, we briefly discuss some of the kinds of measuring instruments used in educational research.

TESTS

Tests are valuable measuring instruments for educational research. A **test** is a set of stimuli presented to an individual in order to elicit responses on the basis of which a numerical score can be assigned. This score, based on a representative sample of the individual's behavior, is an indicator of the extent to which the subject has the characteristic being measured.

The utility of these scores as indicators of the construct of interest is in large part a function of the objectivity, validity, and reliability of the tests. Objectivity is the extent of agreement among scorers. Some tests, such as multiple-choice and true–false tests, are described as objective because the scoring is done by comparing students' answers with the scoring key, and scorers need make no decisions. Essay tests are less objective because scores are influenced by the judgment and opinions of the scorers. In general, validity is the extent to which a test measures what it claims to measure. Reliability is the extent to which the test measures accurately and consistently. We discuss validity and reliability in Chapter 9.

ACHIEVEMENT TESTS

Achievement tests are widely used in educational research, as well as in school systems. They measure mastery and proficiency in different areas of knowledge by presenting subjects with a standard set of questions involving completion of cognitive tasks. Achievement tests are generally classified as either standardized or teacher/researcher made.

STANDARDIZED TESTS

Standardized tests are published tests that have resulted from careful and skillful preparation by experts and cover broad academic objectives common to the majority of school systems. These are tests for which comparative norms have been derived, their validity and reliability established, and directions for administering and scoring prescribed. The directions are contained in the manuals provided by the test publishers. To establish the norms for these tests, their originators administer them to a relevant and representative sample. The norm group may be chosen to represent the nation as a whole or the state, city, district, or local school. The *mean* for a particular grade level in the sample becomes the norm for that grade level. It is important to distinguish between a norm and a standard. A *norm* is not necessarily a goal or a criterion of what should be. It is a measure of what *is*. Test norms are based on the actual performance of a specified group, not on standards of performance. The skills measured are not necessarily what "ought" to be taught at any grade level, but the use of norms does give educators a basis for comparing their groups with an estimate of the mean for all children at that grade level.

Standardized achievement tests are available for single school subjects, such as mathematics and chemistry, and also in the form of comprehensive batteries measuring several areas of achievement. An example of the latter is the California Achievement Test (CAT/5), which contains tests in the areas of reading, language, and mathematics and is appropriate for grades K to 12. Other widely used batteries include the Iowa Tests of Basic Skills (ITBS), the Metropolitan Achievement Tests (MAT-8), the SRA Achievement Series, and the Stanford Achievement Test Series (SAT-9). Some well-known single-subject achievement tests are the Gates–MacGinitie Reading Test, the Nelson–Denny Reading Test, and the Modern Math Understanding Test (MMUT). If one is interested in measuring achievement in more than one subject area, it is less expensive and time consuming to use a battery. The main advantage of the test battery is that each subtest is normed on the same sample, which makes comparisons across subtests, both within and between individuals, easier and more valid (Kubiszyn & Borich, 2003).

In selecting an achievement test, researchers must be careful to choose one that is reliable and is appropriate (valid) for measuring the aspect of achievement in which they are interested. The test must also be valid and reliable for the type of subjects included in the study. Sometimes a researcher is not able to select the test but must use what the school system has already selected. The *Mental Measurements Yearbooks* present a comprehensive listing, along with reviews of the different achievement tests available. Other references for commercially available tests are described in Chapter 4.

If an available test measures the desired behavior and if the reliability, validity, and the norms are adequate for the purpose, then there are advantages in using a standardized instrument. In addition to the time and effort saved, investigators realize an advantage from the continuity of testing procedures—the results of their studies can be compared and interpreted with respect to those of other studies using the same instrument.

RESEARCHER-MADE TESTS

When using standardized tests of achievement is not deemed suitable for the specific objectives of a research study, research workers may construct their own tests. It is much better to construct your own test than to use an inappropriate standardized one just because it is available. The advantage of a **researcher-made test** is that it can be tailored to the specific research question. For example, suppose a teacher wants to compare the effects of two teaching methods on students' achievement in mathematics. Although there are excellent standardized tests in mathematics, they are generally designed to measure broad objectives and may not focus sufficiently on the particular skills the teacher wishes to measure. It would be wise in this case for the teacher to construct the measuring instrument, paying particular attention to evidence of its validity and reliability. The teacher should administer a draft of the test to a small group who will not participate in the study but who are similar to those who will participate. An analysis of the results enables the teacher to check on the test's validity and reliability and to detect any ambiguities or other problems before employing the test. For suggestions on achievement test construction, refer to specialized texts in measurement, such as those by Linn and Gronlund (2000), Popham (2000), Kubiszyn and Borich (2003), and Haladyna (2004).

NORM-REFERENCED AND CRITERION-REFERENCED TESTS

On the basis of the type of interpretation made, standardized and teacher-made tests may be further classified as **norm referenced** or **criterion referenced**. Norm-referenced tests permit researchers to compare individuals' performance on the test to the performance of other individuals. An individual's performance is interpreted in terms of his or her relative position in a specified reference group known as the *normative group*. Performance is reported in terms of percentiles, standard scores, and similar measures.

In contrast, criterion-referenced tests enable researchers to describe what a specific individual can do, without reference to the performance of others. Performance is reported in terms of the level of mastery of some defined content or skill domain. Typically, the level of mastery is indicated by the percentage of items answered correctly. Predetermined cutoff scores may be used to interpret the individual's performance as pass–fail.

Before measuring instruments are designed, you must know the type of interpretation that is to be made. In norm-referenced tests, items are selected that will yield a wide range of scores. A researcher must be concerned with the difficulty of the items and the power of the items to discriminate among individuals. In criterion-referenced tests, items are selected solely on the basis of how well they measure a specific set of instructional objectives. They may be easy or difficult, depending on what is being measured. The major concern is to have a representative sample of items measuring the stated objectives so that individual performance can be described directly in terms of the specific knowledge and skills that these people are able to achieve.

TEST PERFORMANCE RANGE

One aspect of achievement tests that researchers should consider is the range of performance that the test permits. Ideally, researchers want a test designed so that the subjects can perform fully to their ability level without being restricted by the test itself. For example, gifted students may all score near the top and thus show little variability. This restriction in range at the upper end, which prevents subjects from performing to their maximum ability, represents a **ceiling effect**.

Ceiling Effect

A test with a low ceiling is one that is too easy for some of the subjects to whom it was administered. No one can know what their scores might have been if there had been a higher ceiling. Why is this a problem? In experimental research the effect of a treatment could be underestimated because the test used does not measure subjects' achievement accurately at the upper end of the range.

Assume a researcher wishes to compare the effect of two teaching methods, A and B, with two different populations of students—a gifted group and a learning-disabled group. A test composed of 40 questions is used as the measure of the learning that has occurred. The possible score range is thus 0 to 40. Assume the researcher calculates the mean score on the test for each group taught by each method. The results are graphed in Figure 8.1A.

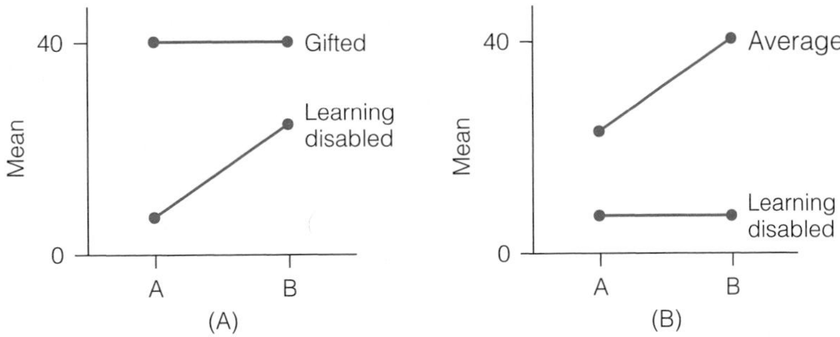

Figure 8.1 Graphs Showing Ceiling Effect (A) and Floor Effect (B)

Figure 8.1A apparently shows that method B is more effective than method A with learning-disabled students, but that there is no difference in effectiveness for gifted students. But note that the mean for the gifted students is very near the maximum score of 40; thus, a large number of those students must have gotten all 40 items answered correctly. The researcher does not know how many correct responses they might have made if there had not been a ceiling. Consequently, the researcher does not know whether methods A and B are really equally effective for gifted students or whether the range on the test was so restricted that gifted students could not perform to their maximum ability. Researchers can easily reach incorrect conclusions if they ignore this ceiling effect.

Floor Effect

Likewise, performance may be restricted at the lower end of the range, resulting in a **floor effect**. Floor effect is influenced by the difficulty of the test. On a very difficult test, you cannot get real evidence about how subjects could perform because the difficulty of the test itself rather than subjects' ability determines their performance. Consider the hypothetical data shown in Figure 8.1B. In this case, it appears that method B is more effective than method A for average students but are equally effective for learning-disabled students. Is this really the case, or was the test so difficult that these students all tended to score near the bottom (zero)? If a less difficult test had been used, the students would probably have shown more variability in performance, and there would not have been a floor effect. When selecting a test, a researcher should look for an instrument that permits a wide range of performance. Standardized test manuals often provide information about ceiling and floor effects because much data on subjects' performance have been gathered during the test standardization process. Researchers who construct their own tests can try them out with various groups and look at the results for evidence of ceiling and floor effects. If it appears that performance range is restricted, then the researcher needs to revise the test.

PERFORMANCE ASSESSMENTS

Another way to classify achievement tests is whether they are paper-and-pencil or **performance tests**. The most common achievement tests are paper-and-pencil tests measuring cognitive objectives. Everyone is familiar with this format that requires the person to compose answers or choose responses on a printed sheet. In some cases, however, a researcher may want to measure performance—what an individual can *do* rather than what he or she *knows*. Performance assessment is a popular alternative to traditional tests among educators. A performance test is a technique in which a researcher directly observes and assesses an individual's performance of a certain task and/or judges the finished product of that performance. The test taker is asked to carry out a *process* such as playing a musical instrument or tuning a car engine or to produce a *product* such as a written essay. The performance or product is judged against established criteria. An everyday example of a performance test is the behind-the-wheel examination taken when applying for a driver's license. A paper-and-pencil test covering knowledge of signs and rules for driving is not sufficient to measure driving skill. Stiggins (2001), an early advocate of performance assessment, defines it in terms of four components: (1) a reason for the assessment, (2) a particular performance to be evaluated, (3) exercises that elicit the performance, and (4) systematic rating procedures. In investigating a new method of teaching science, for example, you would want to know the effect of the method not only on students' cognitive behavior but also on their learning of various laboratory procedures and techniques or their ability to complete experiments. In this case, the researcher's test would require the students to perform a real task or use their knowledge and skills to solve a science problem. Performance assessment is important in areas such as art, music, home economics, public speaking, industrial training, and the sciences, which typically involve individuals' ability to do something or produce something. Portfolios that contain a collection of student work such as poetry, essays, sketches, musical compositions, audiotapes of speeches, and even mathematics worksheets are a popular tool in performance assessment. Portfolios provide an opportunity for teachers and others to gain a more holistic view of changes in students' performance over time.

Constructing a Performance Test

When a performance assessment is desired, the researcher should follow three basic steps in constructing the test.

1. Begin with a clear statement of the objectives or what individuals should do on the test and the conditions under which the task will be performed. A set of test specifications listing the critical dimensions to be assessed will lead to a more comprehensive coverage of the domain. State whether there will be time limits, whether reference books will be available, and so on.
2. Provide a problem or an exercise that gives students an opportunity to perform—either a simulation or an actual task. All individuals should be asked to perform the same task.
3. Develop an instrument (checklist, rating scale, or something similar) that lists the relevant criteria to use in evaluating the performance and/or the product. To maximize objectivity, the instrument should ensure that the same criteria are used for each individual's performance or product.

Performance tests provide a way to measure abilities and skills that cannot be measured by paper-and-pencil tests. They are, however, time intensive and thus more expensive to administer and score.

APTITUDE TESTS

Aptitude tests differ from achievement tests in that the former attempt to measure general ability, whereas the latter attempt to measure skills and knowledge in specific areas. Aptitude tests attempt to measure the subject's ability to perceive relationships, solve problems, and apply knowledge in a variety of contexts.

Aptitude tests were formerly referred to as *intelligence tests*, but the latter term has declined in use because of controversy over the definition of intelligence and because people tend to associate intelligence with inherited ability. Aptitude tests should *not* be considered as measures of innate (or "pure") intelligence. Performance on such tests partly depends on the background and schooling of the subject.

Educators have found aptitude tests useful and generally valid for the purpose of predicting school success. In fact, many of the tests are referred to as **scholastic aptitude tests**, a term pointing out specifically that the main function of these tests is to predict school performance. Well-known aptitude tests are the ACT (American College Testing Assessment) and the SAT (Scholastic Assessment Test) for high school students, and the GRE (Graduate Record Exam) and MAT (Miller Analogies Test) for college seniors.

Researchers also use aptitude tests extensively. Aptitude or intelligence is often a variable that needs to be controlled in educational experiments. To control this variable, the researcher may use the scores from a scholastic aptitude test. Of the many tests available, some have been designed for use with individuals and others for use with groups.

INDIVIDUAL APTITUDE TESTS

The most widely used individually administered instruments for measuring aptitude are the Stanford–Binet Intelligence Scale (4th ed.) and the three Wechsler tests. The Stanford–Binet currently in use is the outcome of several revisions of the device first developed in France in 1905 by Alfred Binet and Theodore Simon, for identifying children who were not likely to benefit from normal classroom instruction; it was made available for American use in 1916. This test was originally used for measuring an individual's *mental age*. Later the concept of *intelligence quotient* (*IQ*) was introduced. This quotient was derived by dividing mental age (MA) by chronological age (CA) and multiplying the result by 100. The present revision of the Stanford–Binet no longer employs the MA/CA ratio for determining IQ. Instead, the IQ is found by comparing an individual's performance (score) with norms obtained from his or her age group through the use of standard scores (see Chapter 6). The latest revision of the test has 15 subtests organized into 4 areas: Verbal Reasoning, Quantitative Reasoning, Abstract/Visual Reasoning, and Short-Term Memory. Subtests scores are standard scores with a mean of 50 and a standard deviation of 8. Area scores and a composite, overall

IQ score have means of 100 and standard deviations of 16. The Stanford–Binet is appropriate for ages 2 through adult.

The tests David Wechsler developed to measure aptitude now come in several forms: the Wechsler Intelligence Scale for Children—Third Edition (WISC–III, 1991), the Wechsler Adult Intelligence Scale-III (WAIS–III,1997), and the Wechsler Preschool and Primary Scale of Intelligence-Revised (WPPSI–R,1989), which was introduced for the 4- to 6½-year age group. The Wechsler tests yield verbal IQ scores, performance IQ scores, and full-scale IQ scores arrived at by averaging the verbal subtest scores, the performance subtest scores, and all subtest scores, respectively. The Wechsler scales are more popular than the Stanford–Binet primarily because they take less time to administer.

GROUP TESTS OF APTITUDE

A Stanford–Binet or Wechsler test must be given by a trained psychometrician to an individual subject, a procedure expensive in both time and money. Thus, they are impractical as aptitude measures for large groups of individuals. In this situation, group tests are used. The first group test of mental ability was developed during World War I for measuring the ability of men in military service. One form of this test, the Army Alpha, was released for civilian use after the war and became the model for a number of group tests. Today many group tests of mental aptitude are available. Among the most widely used are the Cognitive Abilities Tests (CogAT), Test of Cognitive Skills (TCS/2), and the Otis–Lennon School Ability Tests (OLSAT-7). The CogAT and the OLSAT-7 are appropriate for grades K to 12, while the TCS/2 is used for grades 2 to 12.

TESTING AND TECHNOLOGY

Quantitative tests and scales have traditionally been given in pencil-and-paper form. New technologies are presenting opportunities for alternate delivery systems. For example, the PRAXIS I test designed to assess acquisition of basic skills prior to entry into teacher education is given electronically with immediate scoring and feedback on performance provided to the student. A computer is also used to administer the GRE and a number of other well-known tests. Researcher-developed tests can be administered online using various websites. Many of you may have encountered computer-based testing when you took the knowledge portion of your test to obtain a driver's license.

MEASURES OF PERSONALITY

Educational researchers may also need measures of personality. There are several different types of personality measures, each reflecting a different theoretical point of view. Some reflect trait and type theories, whereas others have their origins in psychoanalytic and motivational theories. Researchers must know precisely what they wish to measure and then select the instrument, paying particular attention to the evidence of its validity. There are two approaches used to measure personality: objective personality assessment and projective personality assessment.

OBJECTIVE PERSONALITY ASSESSMENT

Objective personality assessment typically uses the self-report **inventory** in which subjects are presented with an extensive collection of statements describing behavior patterns and are asked to indicate whether or not each statement is characteristic of their behavior by checking *yes*, *no*, or *uncertain*. Other formats used are checklists, multiple choice, and true–false. Their score is computed by counting the number of responses that agree with a trait the examiner is attempting to measure. For example, someone with paranoid tendencies would be expected to answer *yes* to the statement "People are always talking behind my back" and *no* to the statement "I expect the police to be fair and reasonable." Of course, similar responses to only two items would not indicate paranoid tendencies. However, such responses to a large proportion of items could be considered an indicator of paranoia.

Some of the self-report inventories measure only one trait, such as the California F-Scale, which measures authoritarianism. Others, such as Cattell's Sixteen Personality Factor Questionnaire, measure a number of traits. Other well-known inventories in research are the Minnesota Multiphasic Personality Inventory (MMPI-2), the Guilford–Zimmerman Temperament Survey, the Mooney Problem Check List, the Edwards Personal Preference Schedule (EPPS), the Myers–Briggs Type Indicator, and the Strong Interest Inventory. A popular inventory, the Adjective Checklist, asks individuals to check from a list of adjectives those that are applicable to themselves. It is appropriate for individuals in grade 9 through adults and only takes 15 minutes to complete. The Checklist yields scores on self-confidence, self-control, needs, and other aspects of personality adjustment.

Inventories have been used in educational research to obtain trait descriptions of certain defined groups, such as underachievers, dropouts, and so forth. They are useful for finding out about students' self-concepts, their concerns or problems, and their study skills and habits. Inventories have also been used in research concerned with interrelationships between personality traits and such variables as aptitude, achievement, and attitudes.

Inventories have the advantages of economy, simplicity, and objectivity. They can be administered to groups and do not require trained psychologists to administer. Most of the disadvantages are related to the problem of validity. Inventories are self-report instruments, thus their validity depends in part on the respondents' being able to read and understand the items, their understanding of themselves, and especially their willingness to give frank and honest answers. As a result, the information obtained from inventories may be superficial or biased. This possibility must be taken into account when using results obtained from such instruments. Some inventories, however, have validity scales built in to detect faking, attempts to give socially desirable responses, or reading comprehension problems.

PROJECTIVE PERSONALITY ASSESSMENT

Projective techniques are measures in which an individual is asked to respond to an ambiguous or unstructured stimulus. They are called *projective* because a person is expected to project into the stimulus his or her own needs, wants, fears, beliefs, anxieties, and experiences. On the basis of the subject's interpretation of the stimuli and his or her responses, the examiner attempts to construct a comprehensive picture of the individual's personality structure.

Projective methods are used mainly by clinical psychologists for studying and diagnosing people with emotional problems. They are not frequently used in educational research because of the necessity of specialized training for administration and scoring and the expense involved in individual administration. Furthermore, many researchers question their validity primarily because of the complex scoring. The two best known projective techniques are the Rorschach Inkblot Technique and the Thematic Apperception Test (TAT). The Rorschach consists of 10 cards or plates each with either a black/white or a colored inkblot. Individuals are asked what they "see." Their responses are scored according to whether they used the whole or only a part of the inkblot or if form or color was used in structuring the response, whether movement is suggested, and other aspects. In the TAT the respondent is shown a series of pictures varying in the extent of structure and ambiguity and asked to make up a story about each one. The stories are scored for recurrent themes, expression of needs, perceived problems, and so on. The TAT is designed for individuals age 10 through adult. There is also a form available for younger children (Children's Apperception Test) and one for senior citizens (Senior Apperception Test).

SCALES

Scales are used to measure attitudes, values, opinions, and other characteristics that are not easily measured by tests or other measuring instruments. A **scale** is a set of categories or numeric values assigned to individuals, objects, or behaviors for the purpose of measuring variables. The process of assigning scores to those objects in order to obtain a measure of a construct is called *scaling*. Scales differ from tests in that the results of these instruments, unlike those of tests, do not indicate success or failure, strength or weakness. They measure the degree to which an individual exhibits the characteristic of interest. For example, a researcher may use a scale to measure the attitude of college students toward religion or any other topic. A number of scaling techniques have been developed over the years.

ATTITUDE SCALES

Attitude scales, which we will discuss first, use multiple responses—usually responses to questions—and combine the responses into a single scale score. Rating scales, which we discuss a little later in this chapter, use judgments—made by the individual under study or by an observer—to assign scores to individuals or other objects to measure the underlying constructs.

Attitudes of individuals or groups are of interest to educational researchers. An attitude may be defined as a positive or negative affect toward a particular group, institution, concept, or social object. The measurement of attitudes presumes the ability to place individuals along a continuum of favorableness–unfavorableness toward the object.

If researchers cannot locate an existing attitude scale on their topic of interest, they must develop their own scales for measuring attitudes. On the following pages we discuss two types of attitude scales: summated or Likert (pronounced *Lik'ert*) scales and bipolar adjective scales.

Likert Scales: Method of Summated Ratings

The Likert scale (1932), named for Rensis Likert who developed it, is one of the most widely used techniques to measure attitudes. A **Likert scale** (a **summated rating scale**) assesses attitudes toward a topic by presenting a set of statements about the topic and asking respondents to indicate for each whether they strongly agree, agree, are undecided, disagree, or strongly disagree. The various agree–disagree responses are assigned a numeric value, and the total scale score is found by summing the numeric responses given to each item. This total score represents the individual's attitude toward the topic.

A Likert scale is constructed by assembling a large number of statements about an object, approximately half of which express a clearly favorable attitude and half of which are clearly unfavorable. Neutral items are not used in a Likert scale. It is important that these statements constitute a representative sample of all the possible opinions or attitudes about the object. It may be helpful to think of all the subtopics relating to the attitude object and then write items on each subtopic. To generate this diverse collection of items, the researcher may find it helpful to ask people who are commonly accepted as having knowledge about and definite attitudes toward the particular object to write a number of positive and negative statements. Editorial writings about the object are also good sources of potential statements for an attitude scale. Figure 8.2 shows items from a Likert scale designed to measure attitudes toward capital punishment.

For pilot testing, the statements, along with five response categories arranged on an agreement–disagreement continuum, are presented to a group of subjects. This group should be drawn from a population that is similar to the one in which the scale will be used. The statements should be arranged in random order so as to avoid any response set on the part of the subjects.

The subjects are directed to select the response category that best represents their reaction to each statement: *strongly agree* (SA), *agree* (A), *undecided* (U), *disagree* (D), or *strongly disagree* (SD). There has been some question of whether the undecided option should be included in a Likert scale. Most experts in the field recommend that the researcher include a neutral or undecided choice because some respondents actually feel that way and do not want to be forced into agreeing or disagreeing.

Scoring Likert Scales To score the scale, the response categories must be weighted. For favorable or positively stated items, the numeric values 5, 4, 3, 2, and 1, respectively, are assigned to the response categories beginning at the favorable end. For example, *strongly agree* with a favorable statement would receive a weight of 5, *agree* would receive a 4, and *strongly disagree* a weight of 1. For unfavorable or negatively stated items, the weighting is reversed because disagreement with an unfavorable statement is psychologically equivalent to agree-

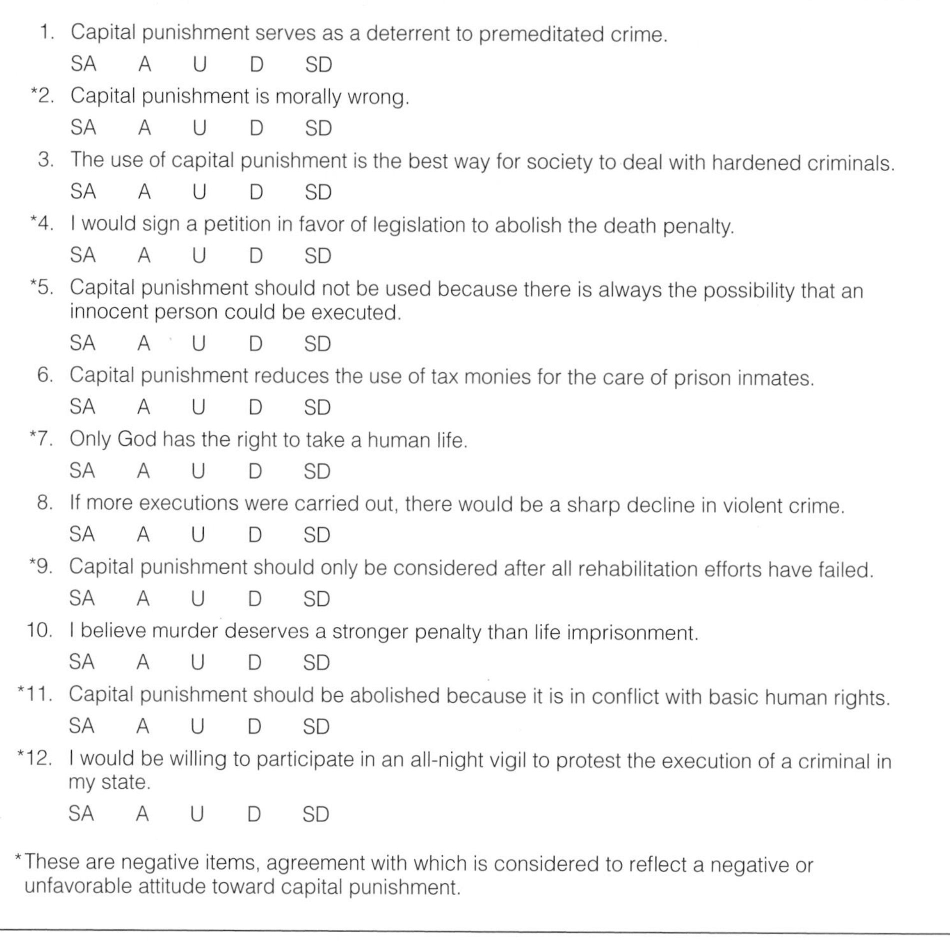

1. Capital punishment serves as a deterrent to premeditated crime.
   SA A U D SD
*2. Capital punishment is morally wrong.
   SA A U D SD
3. The use of capital punishment is the best way for society to deal with hardened criminals.
   SA A U D SD
*4. I would sign a petition in favor of legislation to abolish the death penalty.
   SA A U D SD
*5. Capital punishment should not be used because there is always the possibility that an innocent person could be executed.
   SA A U D SD
6. Capital punishment reduces the use of tax monies for the care of prison inmates.
   SA A U D SD
*7. Only God has the right to take a human life.
   SA A U D SD
8. If more executions were carried out, there would be a sharp decline in violent crime.
   SA A U D SD
*9. Capital punishment should only be considered after all rehabilitation efforts have failed.
   SA A U D SD
10. I believe murder deserves a stronger penalty than life imprisonment.
   SA A U D SD
*11. Capital punishment should be abolished because it is in conflict with basic human rights.
   SA A U D SD
*12. I would be willing to participate in an all-night vigil to protest the execution of a criminal in my state.
   SA A U D SD

*These are negative items, agreement with which is considered to reflect a negative or unfavorable attitude toward capital punishment.

Figure 8.2 Example of a Likert Scale

Source: These items were taken from an attitude scale constructed by a graduate student in an educational research class.

ment with a favorable statement. Thus, for unfavorable statements *strongly agree* would receive a weight of 1 and *strongly disagree* a weight of 5. (The weight values do not appear on the attitude scale presented to respondents.)

The sum of the weights of all the items checked by the subject would represent the individual's total score. This weighting system means that a high scale score (SA or A to favorable items; SD or D to unfavorable items) indicates a positive attitude toward the object. The highest possible scale score is $5 \times N$ (the number of items); the lowest possible score is $1 \times N$.

Let us consider an example of scoring a Likert scale by looking at just the first six statements of the scale shown in Figure 8.2. An individual would complete this scale by circling the appropriate letter(s) for each statement.

The weights assigned to the options for items 1, 3, and 6, which are positive toward capital punishment, would be

SA = 5 A = 4 U = 3 D = 2 SD = 1

The weights assigned to the options for items 2, 4, and 5, which are negative toward capital punishment, would be

SA = 1 A = 2 U = 3 D = 4 SD = 5

The following are the responses circled by the hypothetical respondent and the score for each item:

Response	Score
1. D	2
2. SA	1
3. D	2
4. A	2
5. A	2
6. U	3

The individual's total score on the 6 items is 12 (out of a possible 30), a low score that indicates a negative attitude toward capital punishment. We can divide the total score by the number of items to arrive at a mean attitude score: $(2 + 1 + 2 + 2 + 2 + 3)/6 = 2.0$. Because the mean score is less than 3, we conclude again that this individual has a negative attitude toward capital punishment.

After administering the attitude scale to a preliminary group of respondents, the researcher does an **item analysis** to identify the best functioning items. The item analysis typically yields three statistics for each item: (1) an item discrimination index, (2) the number and/or percentage of respondents marking each choice to each item, and (3) the item mean and standard deviation. The item discrimination index shows the extent to which each item discriminates among the respondents in the same way as the total score discriminates. If high scorers on an individual item have high total scores and if low scorers on this item have low total scores, then the item is discriminating in the same way as the total score. The item discrimination index is calculated by correlating item scores with total-scale scores, a procedure usually done by computer. To be useful, an item should correlate at least .25 with the total score. Items that have very low correlation or negative correlation with the total score should be eliminated because they are not measuring the same thing as the total scale and hence are not contributing to the measurement of the attitude. The researcher will want to examine those items that are found to be nondiscriminating. The items may be ambiguous or double barreled (containing two beliefs or opinions in one statement), or they may be factual statements not really expressing feelings about the object. Revising these items may make them usable. The other statistics from the item analysis (2 and 3) indicate the extent to which the respondents have used the various options. Items on which the respondents are spread out among the response categories are preferred over items on which the responses are clustered in only one or two categories.

After selecting the most consistent items as indicated by the item analysis, the researcher should then try out the revised scale with a different group of subjects and again check the items for discrimination.

Validity Validity concerns the extent to which the scale really measures the attitude construct. It is often difficult to locate criteria to be used in obtaining evidence for the validity of attitude scales. Some researchers have used observations of actual behavior as the criterion for the attitude being measured, but this procedure is not often used because it is difficult to determine what behavior would be the best criterion for the attitude and also because it is difficult to secure measures of the behavior.

One of the easiest ways to gather validity evidence is to determine the extent to which the scale is capable of discriminating between two groups whose members are known to have different attitudes (see Chapter 9). To validate a scale that measures attitudes toward organized religion, a researcher would determine if the scale discriminated between active church members and people who do not attend church or have no church affiliation. A scale measuring attitudes toward abortion should discriminate between members of pro-life groups and members of pro-choice groups. By "discriminate," we mean that the two groups would be expected to have significantly different mean scores on the scale. Another method of assessing validity is to correlate scores on the attitude scale with those obtained on another attitude scale measuring the same construct and whose validity is well established.

Reliability The reliability of the new scale must also be determined. Reliability is concerned with the extent to which the measure would yield consistent results each time it is used. The first step in ensuring reliability is to make sure that the scale is long enough—that it includes enough items to provide a representative sampling of the whole domain of opinions about the attitudinal object. Other things being equal, the size of the reliability coefficient is directly related to the length of the scale. Research shows, however, that if the items are well constructed, scales having as few as 20 to 22 items will have satisfactory reliability (often above .80). The number of items needed depends partly on how specific the attitudinal object is; the more abstract the object, the more items are needed.

You would also want to calculate an index of reliability. The best index to use for an attitude scale is coefficient alpha (see Chapter 9), which provides a measure of the extent to which all the items are positively intercorrelated and working together to measure one trait or characteristic (the attitude). Many statistical computer programs routinely calculate coefficient α as a measure of reliability.

Bipolar Adjective Scales

Another approach to measuring attitudes is the **bipolar adjective scale**. This scale presents a respondent with a list of adjectives that have opposite or bipolar meanings. Respondents are asked to place a check mark at one of the seven points in the scale between the two opposite adjectives to indicate the degree to which the adjective represents their attitude toward an object, group, or concept. Figure 8.3 shows a bipolar adjective scale designed to measure attitude toward school.

Notice in Figure 8.3 that the respondent checked the extreme right position for item a and the extreme left position for item d. The adjective pairs making up a scale are listed in both directions; on some pairs the rightmost position is the

School

a. bad							✓	good
b. fast		✓						slow
c. dull						✓		sharp
d. pleasant	✓							unpleasant
e. light			✓					heavy
f. passive							✓	active
g. worthless						✓		valuable
h. strong				✓				weak
i. still					✓			moving

Figure 8.3 Bipolar Adjective Scale Showing Responses of One Subject Toward the Concept "School"

most positive response, and on other pairs the leftmost position is the most positive. This is done to minimize a response set or a tendency to favor certain positions in a list of options. An individual might have a tendency to choose the extreme right end and would check that position for each item. However, if the direction of the scale is changed in a random way so that the right end is not always the more favorable response, then the individual is forced to read each item and respond in terms of its content rather than in terms of a positional preference. The responses are scored by converting the positions checked into ratings (1 to 7). Seven represents the most positive and 1 the least positive response on each scale. The weights on each item would then be summed and averaged. In Figure 8.3, item weights are $7 + 6 + 6 + 7 + 3 + 7 + 6 + 4 + 5 = 51/9 = 5.67$. The score of 5.67 indicates a positive attitude toward school.

The bipolar adjective scale is a very flexible approach to measuring attitudes. A researcher can use it to investigate attitudes toward any concept, person, or activity in a school or other type setting. It is also much easier and less time consuming to construct than a Likert scale. Instead of having to come up with 20 or so statements, you need only select 4 to 8 adjective pairs. It is also easy to administer because very little reading time is required on the part of the participants. The main difficulty is the selection of the adjectives to use. If one has a problem with this task, there are references such as Osgood, Suci, and Tannenbaum (1967) that provide lists of bipolar adjectives. It is probably better, however, to think of adjective pairs that are especially relevant to one's own project.

RATING SCALES

One of the most widely used measuring instruments is the **rating scale**. Rating scales present a number of statements about a behavior, an activity, or a phenomenon with an accompanying scale of categories. Observers or respondents are asked to indicate their assessment or judgment about the behavior or activity on the rating scale. For example, a teacher might be asked to rate the leadership ability of a student. The teacher would indicate his or her assessment of the student's characteristic leadership behavior by checking a point on a continuum or choosing a response category. It is assumed that raters are familiar with the

	Low	Medium	High
Personal appearance	______	______	______
Social acceptability	______	______	______
Speaking skills	______	______	______

Figure 8.4 Example of a Graphic Scale

behavior they are asked to assess. A numeric value may be attached to the points or categories so that an overall score could be obtained.

There are several different formats used for rating scales. One of the most widely used is the **graphic scale** in which the rater indicates the rating by placing a check at the appropriate point on a horizontal line that runs from one extreme of the behavior in question to the other. Figure 8.4 is a typical example of a graphic scale. The rater can check any point on the continuous line. Some graphic scales assign numeric values to the descriptive points. Such scales are referred to as *numeric rating scales*. The speaking skills item in Figure 8.4 could look like this in a numeric scale:

1	2	3	4	5	6	7
one of the poorest speakers			an average speaker			one of the very best speakers

Category Scales

A second type of rating scale is the **category scale**, which consists of a number of categories that are arranged in an ordered series. Five to seven categories are most frequently used. The rater picks the one that best characterizes the behavior of the person being rated. Suppose a student's abilities are being rated and one of the characteristics being rated is creativity. The following might be one category item:

How creative is this person? (check one)

exceptionally creative ________
very creative ________
creative ________
not creative ________
not at all creative ________

To provide greater meaning, brief descriptive phrases are sometimes used to make up the categories in this type of scale. Clearly defined categories contribute to the accuracy of the ratings. For example,

How creative is this person? (check one)

always has creative ideas ________
has many creative ideas ________
sometimes has creative ideas ________
rarely has creative ideas ________

Comparative Rating Scales

In using the graphic and category scales, raters make their judgments without directly comparing the person being rated to other individuals or groups. In **comparative rating scales**, in contrast, raters are instructed to make their judgments

Area of Competency (to be rated)	Unusually low	Poorer than most students	About average among students	Better than most	Really superior	Not able to judge
1. Does this person show evidence of clear-cut and worthy professional goals?						
2. Does this person attack problems in a constructive manner?						
3. Does he or she take well-meant criticism and use it constructively?						

Figure 8.5 Example of a Comparative Rating Scale

with direct reference to the positions of others with whom the individual might be compared. The positions on the rating scale are defined in terms of a given population with known characteristics. A comparative rating scale is shown in Figure 8.5. Such a scale might be used in selecting applicants for admission to graduate school. Raters are asked to judge the applicant's ability to do graduate work as compared with all the students the rater has known. If the rating is to be valid, the judge must understand the range and distribution of abilities in the total group of graduate students.

Errors in Rating Because ratings depend on the perceptions of human observers, who are susceptible to various influences, rating scales are subject to considerable error. Among the most frequent systematic errors in rating people is the **halo effect**, which occurs when raters allow a generalized impression of the subject to influence the rating given on very specific aspects of behavior. This general impression carries over from one item in the scale to the next. For example, a teacher might rate a student who does good academic work as also being superior in intelligence, popularity, honesty, perseverance, and all other aspects of personality. Or, if you have a generally unfavorable impression of a person, you are likely to rate the person low on all aspects.

Another type of error is the **generosity error**, which refers to the tendency for raters to give subjects the benefit of any doubt; that is, when raters are not sure, they are likely to speak favorably about the people they are rating. In contrast, there is the **error of severity**, which is a tendency to rate all individuals too low on all characteristics. Another source of error is the **error of central tendency**, which refers to the tendency to avoid either extreme and to rate all individuals in the middle of the scale.

One way of reducing such errors is to train the raters thoroughly before they are asked to make ratings. They should be informed about the possibility of making these "personal bias" types of errors and how to avoid them. It is absolutely essential that raters have adequate time to observe the individual and his or her behavior before making a rating. Another way to minimize error is to make certain that the behavior to be rated and the points on the rating scale are clearly defined. The points on the scale should be described in terms of overt behaviors that can be observed, rather than in terms of behaviors that require inference on the part of the rater.

The accuracy or reliability of ratings is usually increased by having two (or more) trained raters make independent ratings of an individual. These independent ratings are pooled, or averaged, to obtain a final score. To assess the extent of agreement (reliability) of the raters the phi coefficient and kappa are useful indexes (see pages 272–273).

DIRECT OBSERVATION

In many cases, systematic **direct observation** of behavior is the most desirable measurement method. Observation is used in both quantitative and qualitative research. When observations are made in an attempt to get a comprehensive picture of a situation, and the product of those observations is notes or narratives, the research is qualitative. In Chapter 15 we discuss the use of observation in qualitative research. The present chapter focuses on observation in quantitative research where the product of using the various observational instruments is numbers. The purpose of direct observation is to determine the extent to which a particular behavior(s) is present. An investigator identifies the behavior of interest and devises a systematic procedure for identifying, categorizing, and recording the behavior in either a natural or a contrived situation. Systematic observation has been used extensively in research on infants and preschool children. In educational research, one of the most common uses of direct observation is in studying classroom behavior. For example, if you were interested in investigating the extent to which elementary teachers use positive reinforcement in the classroom, you could probably obtain more accurate data by actually observing classrooms rather than asking teachers about their use of reinforcement. Or if you wanted to study students' disruptive behavior in the classroom and how teachers deal with it, direct observation would provide more accurate data than reports from students or teachers.

There are five important preliminary steps to take in preparing for quantitative direct observation:

1. *Select the aspect of behavior to be observed.* Because it is not possible to collect data on everything that happens, the investigator must decide beforehand which behaviors to record and which not to record.
2. *Clearly define the behaviors falling within a chosen category.* The observers must understand what actions will be classified as, for instance, cooperative behavior or disruptive behavior. Make sure the categories are mutually exclusive.
3. *Develop a system for quantifying observations.* The investigator must decide on a standard method for counting the observed behaviors. For in-

stance, establish beforehand whether an action and the reaction to it are to count as a single incident of the behavior observed or as two incidents. A suggested approach is to divide the observation period into brief time segments and to record for each period—say, 10 seconds—whether the subject showed the behavior or not.

4. *Develop specific procedures for recording the behavior.* The memory of most observers is usually not reliable enough for meaningful research. The best solution is a coding system that allows the immediate recording of what is observed, using a single letter or digit. A coding system is advantageous in terms of the observers' time and attention.
5. *Train the people who will carry out the observations.* Training and opportunity for practice are necessary so that the investigator can rely on the observers to follow an established procedure in observing and in interpreting and reporting observations. Having the observers view a videotape and discuss the results is a good training technique.

DEVICES FOR RECORDING OBSERVATIONS

Researchers use checklists, rating scales, and coding sheets to record the data collected in direct observation.

Checklists

The simplest device used is a **checklist**, which presents a list of the behaviors that are to be observed. The observer then checks whether each behavior is present or absent. A checklist differs from a scale in that the responses do not represent points on a continuum but nominal categories. For example, a researcher studying disruptive behavior would prepare a list of disruptive behaviors that might occur in a classroom. An observer would then check items such as "Passes notes to other students" or "Makes disturbing noises" each time the behavior occurs. The behaviors in a checklist should be operationally defined and readily observable.

Rating Scales

Rating scales, which we discussed in a previous section, are often used by observers to indicate their evaluation of an observed behavior or activity. Typically, rating scales consist of three to five points or categories. For example, an observer studying teachers' preparation for presentation of new material in a classroom might use a scale with the following points: 5 (*extremely well prepared*), 4 (*well prepared*), 3 (*prepared*), 2 (*not well prepared*), or 1 (*totally unprepared*). A three-point scale might include 3 (*very well prepared*), 2 (*prepared*), or 1 (*not well prepared*). Scales with more than five rating categories are not recommended because it is too difficult to accurately discriminate among the categories.

Coding Systems

Coding systems are used in observational studies to facilitate the categorizing and counting of specific, predetermined behaviors as they occur. The researcher does not just indicate whether a behavior occurred as with a checklist but rather uses agreed-on codes to record what actually occurred. Whereas rating scales can be completed after an observation period, coding is completed at the time the observer views the behavior.

There are two kinds of coding systems typically used by researchers: sign coding and time coding. *Sign coding* uses a set of behavior categories; each time one of the behaviors occurs, the observer codes the happening in the appropriate category. If a coding sheet used in classroom observational research listed "summarizing" as a teacher behavior, the observer would code a happening every time a teacher summarized material.

A classic coding system for recording classroom observations was developed by Flanders (1970). Flanders's system provides the following categories of teacher talk: (1) *accepts feelings*, (2) *praises or encourages*, (3) *accepts ideas of students*, (4) *asks questions*, (5) *lectures*, (6) *gives directions*, and (7) *criticizes or justifies authority*. Trained observers can very quickly record each of these categories of behavior as a single digit. The chain of digits produced can easily be analyzed to provide not only a record of the proportions of teacher verbal behavior falling into each category but also a picture of which behaviors preceded or followed which other behaviors. There are also categories in Flander's system for coding pupil talk.

In a study using sign coding, Skinner, Buysee, and Bailey (2004) investigated how total duration and type of social play of preschool children with disabilities varied as a function of the chronological and developmental age of their social partners. They hypothesized that developmental age of each partner would better predict the duration of social play than chronological age. The 55 focal children were preschool children with mild to moderate developmental delays who were enrolled in some type of inclusive developmental day program. Each focal child was paired with 4 different same-sex partners in a standardized dyadic play situation. The observations took place outside the classroom in a specially designed and well-equipped play area. The observation consisted of two 15-minute sessions with each of the 4 play partners, or a total of 120 minutes per focal child over a period of 2 days. A video camera recorded the play behavior and trained coders used Parten's (1932) seven categories of play to code the extent to which children were engaged socially. The Battelle Developmental Inventory (Newborg, Stock, Wnek, Guidubaldi, & Svinicki, 1988) was used to assess the overall developmental status of both focal children and their social partners. A mixed-model regression analysis was employed with the independent variables being the chronological and developmental ages of both the focal children and the partners; the dependent variable was the total duration of the category called associative play. No impact was observed for the focal children's chronological age once they accounted for developmental age. Also, they found that the influence of partner's developmental age on social play was different depending on the developmental age of the focal child. The researchers concluded that advantages accrued to preschoolers with disabilities from mixed-aged play groupings depend on the child's developmental age and those of available social partners.

In the second type of coding, called *time coding*, the observer identifies and records all predetermined behavior categories that occur during a given time period. The time period might be 10 seconds, 5 minutes, or some other period of time. Miller, Gouley, and Seifer (2004) used time coding in a study designed to document observed emotional and behavioral dysregulation in the classroom and to investigate the relationships between observed dysregulation and teachers' ratings of children's classroom adjustment and their social engagement with peers. Dysregulation was defined as emotional and behavioral displays disruptive to the preschool classroom setting. The participants were 60 low-income children attending Head Start classes. Each child was observed in a naturalistic context for two sessions of 10 minutes each, or a total of 20 minutes. The researchers used handheld computers with *The Observer* (Noldus Information Technology, 1995) software, which permitted coding of behavior along several dimensions. Analysis of the data that consisted of the frequency of observed dysregulated behavior and teachers' ratings of children's classroom adjustment showed that, while the majority of children did not display a great deal of dysregulated emotion or behavior in the classroom, almost one-fourth of children did display high levels of dysregulation in the observation period. High levels of classroom dysregulation were related to teacher ratings of poor classroom adjustment and observed peer conflict behaviors, as well as negative emotional displays.

Coding has the advantage of recording observations at the time the behavior occurs, and it may yield more objective data than do rating scales. The disadvantage is that a long training period may be required for observers to learn to code behavior reliably. A number of standardized coding systems and observation forms are available. Beginning researchers should check references such as the ETS Test Collection Database for a suitable one before attempting to construct their own.

EVALUATION OF DIRECT OBSERVATION

As with other types of measures, the value of direct observation is related to its validity and reliability. The best way to enhance validity is to carefully define the behavior to be observed and to train the people who will be making the observations. Observers must be aware of two sources of bias that affect validity: observer bias and observer effect. **Observer bias** occurs when the observer's own perceptions, beliefs, and biases influence the way he or she observes and interprets the situation. Having more than one person make independent observations helps to detect the presence of bias. **Observer effect** occurs when people being observed behave differently just because they are being observed. One-way vision screens may be used in some situations to deal with this problem. In many cases, however, after an initial reaction the subjects being observed come to pay little attention to the observer, especially one who operates unobtrusively.

Some studies have used interactive television to observe classrooms unobtrusively. Videotaping for later review and coding may also be useful. Researchers who have used videotapes, for example, have found that, while the children initially behaved differently with the equipment in the room, after a few days, they paid no attention and its presence became routine. Handheld technologies, such as a palm pilot, can be used to record data during observations rather than the traditional pencil-and-paper recording techniques.

The accuracy or reliability of direct observation is investigated by having at least two observers independently observe the behavior and by then checking the extent to which the observers' records agree. Reliability is enhanced by providing extensive training for the observers so that they are competent in knowing what to observe and just how to record the observations.

CONTRIVED OBSERVATIONS

In **contrived observations**, the researcher arranges for the observation of subjects in simulations of real-life situations. The circumstances have been arranged so that the desired behaviors are elicited.

One form of contrived observation is the *situational test*. A classic example of a situational test—although not labeled as such at the time—was used in a series of studies by Hartshorne and May (1928) for the Character Education Inquiry (CEI). These tests were designed for use in studying the development of such behavior characteristics as honesty, self-control, truthfulness, and cooperativeness. Hartshorne and May observed children in routine school activities but also staged some situations to focus on specific behavior. For example, they gave vocabulary and reading tests to the children, collected the tests, and without the children's knowledge made duplicate copies of their answers. Later the children were given answer keys and were asked to score their original papers. The difference between the scores the children reported and the actual scores obtained from scoring the duplicate papers provided a measure of cheating. Another test asked the children to make a mark in each of 10 small, irregularly placed circles, while keeping their eyes shut. Previous control tests under conditions that prevented peeking indicated that a score of more than 13 correctly placed marks in a total of 3 trials was highly improbable. Thus, a score above 13 was recorded as evidence that the child had peeked.

Hartshorne and May (1928) found practically no relationship between cheating in different situations, such as on a test and in athletics. They concluded that children's responses were situationally specific—that is, whether students cheated depended on the specific activity, the teacher involved, and other situations rather than on some general character trait.

DATA COLLECTION IN QUALITATIVE RESEARCH

Qualitative researchers also have a number of data-gathering tools available for their investigations. The most widely used tools in qualitative research are interviews, document analysis, and observation. We discuss these methods in Chapter 15.

SUMMARY

Because a research study can be no better than the instruments used to collect the data, one of the most important tasks of researchers in the behavioral sciences is the selection and/or development of dependable measuring instruments. A variety of tests, scales, and inventories is available for gathering data in educational research, especially for quantitative studies. Researchers need to be aware of the strengths and limitations of these data-gathering instruments so that they can choose the one(s) most appropriate for their particular investigation. If an appropriate standardized instrument is available, the researcher would be wise to choose it because of the advantage in terms of validity, reliability, and time saved.

A test is a set of stimuli presented to an individual to elicit responses on the basis of which a numerical score can be assigned. Achievement tests measure knowledge and proficiency in a given area and are widely used in educational research. Standardized achievement tests permit the researcher to compare performance on the test to the performance of a normative reference group. Tests may be classified as paper-and-pencil or as performance tests, which measure what someone can *do*, rather than what he or she *knows*. Aptitude tests are used to assess an individual's verbal and nonverbal capacities. Personality inventories are designed to measure the subject's personal characteristics and typical performance.

Attitude scales are tools for measuring individuals' beliefs, feelings, and reactions to certain objects. The major types of attitude scales are Likert-type scales and the bipolar adjective scale.

Rating scales permit observers to assign scores to the assessments made of observed behavior or activity. Among the types of rating scales are the graphic scale, the category scale, and comparative rating scales.

Rating scales, checklists, and coding systems are the most common procedures used to record the data in direct observation quantitative research. In coding systems, behavior can be categorized according to individual occurrences (sign coding) or number of occurrences during a specified time period (time coding).

KEY CONCEPTS

achievement test
aptitude test
attitude scale
bipolar adjective scale
category scale
ceiling effect
checklist
coding system
comparative rating scales
contrived observation
criterion-referenced test
direct observation
error of central tendency
error of severity
floor effect
generosity error
graphic scale
halo effect
interrater reliability
inventory
item analysis
Likert scale
norm-referenced test
observer bias
observer effect
performance test
projective technique
rating scale
researcher-made test
scale
scholastic aptitude test
standardized test
summated rating scale
teacher-made test
test

EXERCISES

1. What is the meaning of the term *standardized* when applied to measuring instruments?
2. What is the difference between comparative rating scales and graphic and category scales?
3. List some of the common sources of bias in rating scales.
4. What type of instrument would a researcher choose in order to obtain data about each of the following?
   a. How college professors feel about the use of technology in their teaching
   b. The potential of the seniors at a small college to succeed in graduate school
   c. To see if high school chemistry students can analyze an unknown chemical compound
   d. How well the students at Brown Elementary School compare to the national average in reading skills
   e. The advising-style preferences of a group of college freshmen
   f. How well students perform in a public speaking contest
   g. How middle school students feel about a school's new dress code
   h. The general verbal and nonverbal abilities of a student with attention-deficit disorder

i. The extent to which elementary teachers use negative reinforcement in the classroom, and the effect of that reinforcement on students' behavior
j. The problems faced by minority students during the first year at a large research university
k. How parents in a school system feel about moving the sixth grade from the elementary school to the middle school

5. How would you measure parents' attitudes toward a new dress code proposed for a middle school?
6. What are some procedures for increasing the accuracy of direct observation techniques?
7. Construct a five-item Likert scale for measuring peoples' attitudes toward stem cell research.
8. Construct a five-item semantic differential scale for measuring middle school students' attitudes toward school sports programs.
9. Intelligence tests can most accurately be described as
   a. Measures of innate mental capacity
   b. Academic achievement measures
   c. Reading tests
   d. Scholastic aptitude tests
10. List and briefly describe the instruments available for recording data in observational research.
11. What type of instrument would be most appropriate to measure each of the following?
   a. To determine if high school chemistry students can use laboratory scales to weigh specified amounts of a given chemical compound
   b. How students in the various elementary schools in Brown county compare in math skills
   c. How parents feel about an extended school day for elementary schools in the district
   d. The general verbal and nonverbal abilities of a child with dyslexia
   e. To study bullying in an elementary classroom
   f. To get a major professor's evaluation of the potential of a student for advanced work in chemistry
   g. To get a quick measure of students' attitudes toward the extracurricular programs available at the school

ANSWERS

1. *Standardized* refers to instruments for which comparative norms have been derived, their reliability and validity have been established, and directions for administration and scoring prescribed.
2. In judging an individual on a comparative rating scale, the rater must have knowledge of the group with which the individual is being compared. In judging an individual on graphic and category scales, raters do not make a direct comparison of the subject with other people.
3. Raters may be less than objective in judging individuals when influenced by such tendencies as the halo effect, the generosity error, the error of severity, or the error of central tendency.
4. a. Attitude scale
   b. Aptitude test (group)
   c. Performance test
   d. Standardized achievement test
   e. Inventory
   f. Rating scale (performance test)
   g. Attitude scale
   h. Aptitude or intelligence test (individual)
   i. Direct observation
   j. Inventory
   k. Attitude scale
5. Construct a Likert scale containing approximately 20 statements expressing positive and negative feelings about the proposed dress code or construct a bipolar adjective scale.
6. The behaviors to be observed must be specified; behaviors falling within a category must be defined; a system for quantification must be developed; and the observers must be trained to carry out the observations according to this established procedure.
7. Answers will vary.
8. Answers will vary.

9. d
10. Checklists indicate the presence or absence of certain behaviors. Rating scales and coding schemes both yield quantitative measures. In ratings, the person indicates his/her judgment of the behavior on a continuum. Ratings are sometimes completed in retrospect. Coding schemes are used to categorize observed behavior as it occurs.

11. **a.** performance test
    b. standardized achievement
    c. attitude scale
    d. individual intelligence test, such as the Wechsler
    e. observation
    f. comparative rating scale
    g. bipolar adjective scale

INFOTRAC COLLEGE EDITION

Use InfoTrac College Edition and locate a quantitative research article on a topic that interests you. What measuring instruments (tests, scales, etc.) were used to gather the data in this study? Were the instruments standardized or researcher made? Did the researcher believe that the tools were satisfactory for the purpose?

Chapter 9

Validity and Reliability

INFORMATION DERIVED FROM MEASURING INSTRUMENTS RANGES FROM EXCELLENT TO USELESS TO DOWNRIGHT MISLEADING. THERE ARE SYSTEMATIC WAYS TO ASSESS THE USEFULNESS OF THE SCORES DERIVED FROM MEASURING INSTRUMENTS.

INSTRUCTIONAL OBJECTIVES

After studying this chapter, the student will be able to:

1. Distinguish between validity and reliability.
2. List the major types of evidence used to support the valid interpretation of test scores.
3. Define construct underrepresentation and construct-irrelevant variance and explain their relevance to the validity of test scores.
4. Distinguish between convergent and discriminant evidence of validity.
5. Distinguish between random and systematic errors of measurement and their relationship to validity and reliability of test scores.
6. State the different sources of random error in educational and psychological measures.
7. Describe the different procedures (test–retest, equivalent forms, split-half, Kuder–Richardson, and others) for estimating the reliability of a measure.
8. Compute reliability coefficients from given data.
9. Define interobserver reliability and explain how it is calculated.
10. Apply the Spearman–Brown formula to determine the effect of lengthening a test on test reliability.
11. Explain the factors affecting the size of a reliability coefficient.
12. Compute the standard error of measurement and interpret score bands as indications of reliability.
13. Compute indexes to show the reliability of a criterion-referenced test.

Quantitative research always depends on measurement. Chapter 8 introduced you to some of the measuring instruments typically used in research. There are two very important concepts that researchers must understand when they use measuring instruments. These are *validity* and *reliability.* Validity is defined as the extent to which scores on a test enable one to make meaningful and appropriate interpretations. Reliability indicates how consistently a test measures whatever it does measure. Researchers must be concerned about the validity and reliability of the scores derived from instruments used in a study and must include this information in the research report. If a researcher's data are not obtained with instruments that allow valid and reliable interpretations, one can have little faith in the results obtained or in the conclusions based on the results.

VALIDITY

Validity is the most important consideration in developing and evaluating measuring instruments. Historically, **validity** was defined as the extent to which an instrument measured what it claimed to measure. The focus of recent views of validity is not on the instrument itself but on the interpretation and meaning of the scores derived from the instrument. The most recent *Standards for Educational and Psychological Testing* (1999), prepared by the American Educational Research Association (AERA), National Council on Measurement in Education (NCME), and the American Psychological Association (APA) defines validity as "the degree to which evidence and theory support the interpretations of test scores entailed by proposed uses of tests" (p. 9). Measuring instruments yield scores; but the important thing is the interpretation we make of the scores, which may or may not be valid. For example, a fourth-grade math test that might allow a teacher to make valid interpretations about the math achievement of her fourth-grade students would not yield valid interpretations about the fourth-graders' abilities to solve algebra problems. If one tried to use the math achievement test for this purpose, it would be the interpretations about the students' ability to solve algebra problems that would be invalid, not the test itself. Thus, we no longer speak of the validity of the instrument itself but rather speak of the validity of the interpretations or inferences that are drawn from the instrument's scores. Validity does not travel with the instrument. A test may be valid for use with one population or setting but not another.

Assessing the validity of score-based interpretations is important to the researcher because most instruments used in educational and psychological investigations are designed for measuring hypothetical constructs. Recall that constructs such as intelligence, creativity, anxiety, critical thinking, motivation, self-esteem, attitudes, and the like represent abstract variables derived from theory or observation. Researchers have no direct means of measuring these constructs such as exist in the physical sciences for the measurement of characteristics such as length, volume, and weight. To measure these hypothetical constructs, you must move from the theoretical domain surrounding the construct to an empirical level that operationalizes the construct. That is, we use an operational definition to measure the construct. We do this by selecting specific sets of observable tasks believed to serve as indicators of the particular theoretical construct. Then we assume that performance (scores) on the tasks reflects the particular construct of interest as distinguished from other constructs. Essentially, validity deals with how well the operational definition fits with the conceptual definition. Tests may be imprecise measures of the constructs they are designed to assess because they either leave out something that theory says should be included or else include something that should be left out, or both. Messick (1995) identified two problems that threaten the interpretation (validity) of test scores: construct underrepresentation and construct-irrelevant variance. The term **construct underrepresentation** refers to assessment that is too narrow and fails to include important dimensions of the construct. The test may not adequately sample some kinds of content or some types of responses or psychological processes and thus fails to adequately represent the theoretical domain of the construct. Individuals might make low scores on a math test because the test missed some of the relevant skills that, if present, would have allowed the individuals to display their competence. Or a scale designed to measure general self-concept might measure only social self-concept and not academic and physical components of self-concept.

The term **construct-irrelevant variance** refers to the extent to which test scores are affected by processes that are extraneous to the construct. Low scores should not occur because the test contains something irrelevant that interferes with people's demonstration of their competence. Construct-irrelevant variance could lower scores on a science achievement test for individuals with limited reading skills or limited English skills. Reading comprehension is thus a source of construct-irrelevant variance in a science achievement test and would affect the validity of any interpretations made about the individuals' science achievement.

VALIDATION

The process of gathering evidence to support (or fail to support) a particular interpretation of test scores is referred to as validation. We need evidence to establish that the inferences, which are made on the basis of the test results, are appropriate. Numerous studies may be required to build a body of evidence about the validity of these score-based interpretations. The *Standards for Educational and Psychological Testing* lists three categories of evidence that can be used to establish the validity of score-based interpretations: evidence based on content, evidence based on relations to a criterion, and construct-related evidence of validity. Using these categories does not imply that there are distinct types of validity, but rather that different types of evidence may be gathered to support the intended use of a test. The categories overlap and all are essential to a unitary concept of validity.

1. Evidence Based on Test Content

Evidence based on test content involves the test's content and its relationship to the construct it is intended to measure. The *Standards* define content-related evidence as "The degree to which the sample of items, tasks, or questions on a test are representative of some defined universe or domain of content." That is, the researcher must seek evidence that the test to be used represents a balanced and adequate sampling of all the relevant knowledge, skills, and dimensions making up the content domain. This type of evidence is especially important in evaluating achievement tests. Brennan (2001) writes that "In educational achievement tests, content-related validity evidence is absolutely essential. If the content can't be defended, little else matters" (p. 12). Validation of an achievement test, for instance, would look at the material covered, the wording of the questions, and the adequacy of the sample of items to measure the achievement in question. One would not attempt to measure chemistry students' knowledge of oxidation, for example, with only two questions.

A researcher who wished to develop a test in fourth-grade mathematics for a particular school system would need to determine what kinds of content (skills and objectives) are covered in fourth-grade classes throughout the system. After examining textbooks and talking with teachers, the researcher would prepare an

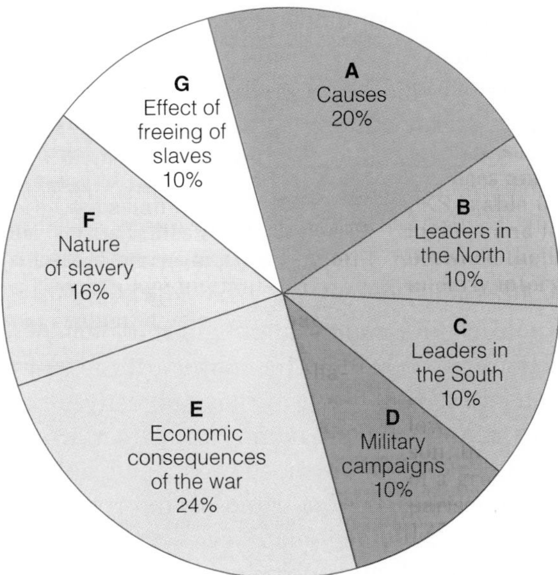

Figure 9.1 Unit on the American Civil War

outline of the topics, skills, and performances that make up fourth-grade mathematics (content domain) in that system, along with an indication of the emphasis given to each. Using the outline as a guide, the researcher would write a collection of test items that cover each topic and each objective in proportion to the emphasis given to each in the total content domain. The result should be a representative sample of the total domain of knowledge and skills included in that school system's fourth-grade math classes.

If the test were designed to be used nationally, the researcher would need to examine widely used textbooks, curriculum guides, syllabi, and so on across the country to determine what content is included in fourth-grade math. Subject matter experts could be asked to judge the adequacy of the test for measuring fourth-grade math achievement. If you were developing a test to select among applicants for a particular job, you would need to specify all the major aspects of the job and then write test items that measure each aspect. Qualified experts would look at the test content to judge the appropriateness and representativeness of the items making up the test.

To ensure content validity in a classroom test, a teacher would define what topics make up the content domain of the unit to be measured and would determine the relative importance of each topic within the unit. If the pie chart in Figure 9.1 represents a teacher's assessment of the relative importance of topics within a unit on the American Civil War, a 50-item exam should include 10 items on topic A, 5 each on B, C, D, and G, 12 on E, and 8 on F.

There is no numerical index to indicate content validity evidence. As we have seen, evidence based on content is mainly the result of a logical examination or analysis that shows whether the instrument adequately represents the content and objectives making up the domain. Brennan (2001) says, "For test users, the single best thing to do in advancing proper score use and interpretation is to take the test, or at least, study its content" (p. 12). Publishers of standardized achievement tests must provide extensive validity evidence of this type. If a publisher says a test measures reading comprehension, then the publisher should provide evidence that higher scores on the test are attributable to higher levels of comprehension rather than, say, better memory. However, we must stress again that an achievement test may permit valid interpretations if used for the purposes defined by the test maker but not yield valid interpretations for a user who defines the content domain in a different way. Only the user of a test can ultimately judge its validity for his or her own purpose. For example, assume that a literature teacher emphasized an understanding of the ideas of selected authors and the relevance of those ideas in the 21st century. If the test the teacher later administered to measure achievement of these objectives contained mostly items asking students to match authors' names with their works and to recall their birth dates, pen names, and so forth, the teacher has failed to obtain a representative sample of the content domain and the interpretation of the scores would have little validity for the intended purpose.

Although **content-related validity evidence** is especially important for achievement tests, it is also a concern for other types of measuring instruments such as personality and aptitude measures. An instrument for measuring attitudes toward capital punishment, for example, would be examined to make sure that it contains, in sufficient number, a balanced set of positive and negative statements about capital punishment. An academic aptitude test should measure skills and abilities judged to be important to success in academic tasks.

2. Evidence Based on Relations to a Criterion

Criterion-related validity evidence shows that test scores are systematically related to one or more outcome criteria. The emphasis is on the criterion because one will use the test scores to infer performance on the criterion. Historically, two types of criterion-related validity evidence have been distinguished: concurrent and predictive. The distinction is made on the basis of the time the criterion data are collected.

Concurrent Validity **Concurrent validity evidence** is the relationship between scores on the measure and criterion scores obtained at the same time. Assume a researcher has developed a foreign language aptitude test and needs evidence that the test really measures foreign language aptitude. The researcher could select a well-known and previously validated foreign language aptitude test and administer it and the new test to a group of students. He or she would then determine the correlation between the two sets of scores. If there is a substantial correlation between the new test and the widely accepted test, then one has some evidence that the new test is also measuring foreign language aptitude. Other criteria available at the time might be current grades in a foreign language class or scores on a teacher-made test. Or assume a researcher at Educational Testing Service (ETS) has developed a new scholastic aptitude test that might replace the more expensive Scholastic Assessment Test (SAT). In order to obtain evidence about the meaningfulness of the scores from this new test, the researcher would administer both the new test and the SAT (the criterion) to a representative

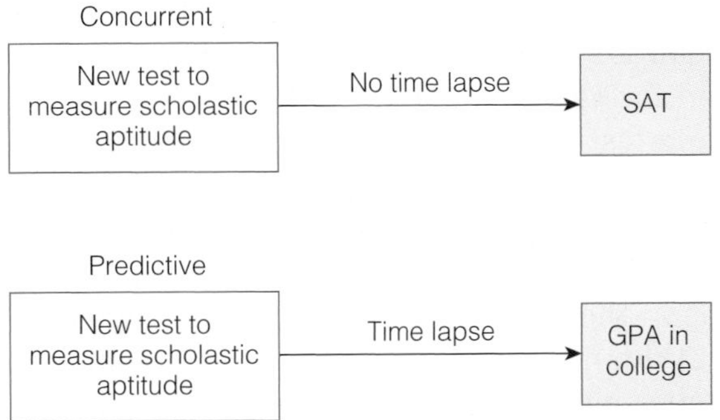

Figure 9.2 Criterion-Related Evidence of Validity

sample of high school students. A substantial correlation between the two sets of scores would indicate that inferences made on the basis of the new test's scores would have validity for measuring scholastic aptitude. A low correlation would indicate that the validity of the inferences based on the new test's scores would be suspect. One would not consider the test a worthwhile replacement for the SAT.

Predictive Validity **Predictive validity evidence** is the relationship between scores on the measure and criterion scores available at a future time. In gathering predictive validity evidence of a foreign language aptitude test, one would look at the relationship between scores on the test and the grades students eventually earned in a future foreign language course (criterion). If a relationship is demonstrated, the scores on the aptitude test could be used later to predict performance in foreign language courses. In the case of a new scholastic aptitude test, predictive validity evidence would involve administering the test to a sample of high school juniors or seniors and then putting the scores away until the students complete their first semester or two of college. When the students' college GPA becomes available, one would correlate the test scores and GPA. If the correlation were high, one has evidence for the usefulness of the aptitude test for predicting college achievement. Large numbers of high school students take the SAT or the ACT test each year because evidence has revealed a correlation between SAT and ACT scores and freshman college grade point average. Likewise, the GRE is used in the selection process for admission to graduate school because there is evidence that scores on the GRE are correlated with achievement in graduate school and thus have validity for predicting future achievement. Figure 9.2 illustrates concurrent- and predictive-related evidence used in the validation of an aptitude test.

Choosing the Criterion The choice of the criterion and its measurement are crucial in criterion-related evidence. What does one look for when choosing a criterion?

1. The worth of the whole procedure depends first and foremost on the *relevance* of the criterion. The criterion must well represent the attribute being

measured or else it would be meaningless to use it. For example, GPA is considered a relevant measure of success in college and is generally chosen as the criterion for validation studies of scholastic aptitude tests. A relevant criterion for a test designed to select salespeople might be the dollar value of sales made in a specified time. Supervisor ratings might be used as a criterion in the validation of a test designed to predict success in data-entry positions at a corporation. It is sometimes difficult to find a relevant criterion measure, as in the validation of measures designed to predict teacher effectiveness. With neither an agreed-on description of teacher effectiveness nor an effective method of measuring that variable, it is extremely difficult to validate such instruments.

2. The criterion must also be *reliable*, which means that it is a consistent measure of the attribute over time or from situation to situation. If the criterion itself is not consistent, you would not expect it to relate consistently to any tests.
3. The criterion should also be *free from bias*, which means that the scoring of the criterion measure itself should not be influenced by any factors other than actual performance on the criterion. For example, if ratings are used as the criterion, it is essential that the raters be trained and be very careful not to let any factors other than actual performance influence their ratings. The criterion may also be biased through contamination, which occurs when scores on the criterion are influenced by the scorer's knowledge of the individuals' predictor test scores. For example, assume that the criterion used to validate an art aptitude test is grades in art class. If the teachers who grade the students' work are aware of the students' scores on the aptitude test, this awareness may influence the teachers' evaluation of the students and hence the grades. This type of contamination of the criterion can be prevented by not permitting the person who grades or rates the criterion to see the original scores on the test.

Validity Coefficient

The coefficient of correlation between test scores and criterion is called a **validity coefficient** (r_{xy}). Like any correlation coefficient, the size of a validity coefficient is influenced by the strength of the relationship between test and criterion and the range of individual differences in the group. As usual, the nearer the coefficient is to 1.00 (+ or −), the stronger the evidence is that the test is useful for the stated purpose.

Validity coefficients indicate whether the test will be useful as a predictor or as a substitute measure. If it has been shown that a test has a high correlation with a future criterion, then that test can later be used to predict that criterion. As we have indicated, criterion-related validity evidence is especially important for scholastic aptitude tests because they are generally used to predict future academic performance. Any tests used for selection purposes need to have criterion-related predictive evidence. Accumulating predictive evidence requires time and patience. In some cases researchers must wait for several years to determine whether performance on a measure is useful for predicting success on a criterion.

Concurrent criterion-related validity evidence is important in tests used for classification, certification, or diagnosis. For example, one would seek concurrent validity evidence for a new psychiatric screening device by looking at its correlation with a well-established instrument already available. If there is a substantial correlation between the new test and the established instrument, one would assume they are measuring the same construct, and the new test could be used as a substitute for the older instrument. Concurrent validity evidence is necessary when new tests are designed to replace older tests that may be more expensive or more difficult and time consuming to administer. Students often ask, "How high does a validity coefficient need to be?" As a general rule, the higher the validity coefficient, the better the evidence. But whether high or low, useful or not useful, depends on the purpose of the test and the context in which it is to be used. A correlation coefficient of .40 could be very helpful in cases for which no predictive instrument has previously been available. In other cases a correlation of .65 might be considered low and unsatisfactory if other predictors are available that have a higher relationship with the criterion. In general, an instrument has "good" validity as a selection device if evidence shows it has a higher correlation with the criterion than do competing instruments.

3. Construct-Related Evidence of Validity

Construct-related evidence of validity focuses on test scores as a measure of a psychological construct. To what extent do the test scores reflect the theory behind the psychological construct being measured? Recall that psychological constructs such as intelligence, motivation, anxiety, or critical thinking are hypothetical qualities or characteristics that have been "constructed" to account for observed behavior. They cannot be seen or touched or much less measured directly. How does one know that a measure of a particular construct really reflects this hypothetical characteristic? The test developer of such a measure would have to provide evidence that the scores really reflect the construct in question. The process begins with a definition of the construct based on the theory and previous research. The test developer then specifies the aspects of the construct that are to be measured in the test and develops items that require test takers to demonstrate the behaviors that define the construct. One collects any logical and empirical evidence that supports the assertion that a test measures the construct as defined and not something else. Construct-related evidence is more comprehensive than content- and criterion-related and really subsumes the other types. In general, any information that sheds light on the construct being measured is relevant.

Let us consider some of the strategies used to gather construct-related evidence.

1. *Related Measures Studies* The aim is to show that the test in question measures the construct it was designed to measure and not some other theoretically unrelated construct. The *Standards* (1999) distinguish two types of evidence based on relations to other variables: **convergent** and **discriminant**. "Relationships between test scores and other measures intended to assess *similar* constructs provide convergent evidence, whereas relationships between test scores and measures purportedly of *different* constructs

provide discriminant evidence" (*Standards*, p. 14). In the case of convergent evidence, the researcher tries to show that the intended construct is being measured; in divergent evidence, he or she shows that the wrong construct is not being measured. A mathematical reasoning test would be expected to correlate with grades in mathematics or with other math reasoning tests (convergent evidence). The math test and these other measures correlate because they all converge on the same construct. Conversely, the scores on the math reasoning test would be expected to have little or no relationship (discriminant evidence) with measures of other skills, such as reading. If a substantial correlation is found between the math test and the reading test, then the math test is being affected by reading ability, and, instead of measuring mathematical reasoning, it is really measuring reading ability. Such evidence would lead one to conclude that the math test is not measuring the intended construct (math reasoning) and thus would not yield valid interpretations about math reasoning.

Of course, a mathematical reasoning test will inevitably involve some reading skill, so one would not expect a zero correlation with a reading test. But if two mathematical reasoning tests are alike in all other aspects, the one with a correlation of .15 with a reading test would be preferred over the one with a correlation of .35.

2. *Known-Groups Technique* Another procedure for gathering construct-related evidence is the **known-groups technique**, in which the researcher compares the performance of two groups already known to differ on the construct being measured. One hypothesizes that the group known to have a high level of the construct will score higher on the measure than the group known to have a low level of the construct. If the expected difference in performance is found, one concludes that the test is measuring that construct. You would expect that scores on a musical aptitude test, for instance, would differ for students currently enrolled in a school of music versus an unselected group of college students. If an inventory measures psychological adjustment, the scores of a group previously identified as adjusted and a group previously identified as maladjusted should be markedly different on the inventory.

3. *Intervention Studies* Another strategy for gathering construct-related evidence is to apply an experimental manipulation and see if the scores change in the hypothesized way. You would expect the scores on a scale designed to measure anxiety to increase if individuals are put into an anxiety-provoking situation. The scores of a control group not exposed to the experimental manipulation should not be affected. If anxiety were manipulated in a controlled experiment and the resulting scores change in the predicted way, you have evidence that the scale is measuring anxiety.

4. *Internal Structure Studies* Analyzing the internal structure of a test is another source of evidence that the test is measuring the construct it is supposed to be measuring. This procedure involves showing that all the items making up the test or scale are measuring the same thing, that is, that the test has internal consistency. We would expect that individuals who answer some questions in a certain way would also answer similar questions in the

same way. In a scale measuring attitudes toward stem cell research, for instance, one would look to see if individuals who support stem cell research were consistent in their agreeing with positive statements and disagreeing with the negative statements in the scale. In gathering **evidence based on internal structure**, we look at the intercorrelations among the items; high intercorrelations indicate that the test is measuring a single construct. You then decide if the observed intercorrelations conform to the theory behind the construct being measured. If the theory suggests a single one-dimensional construct, then we look for high intercorrelations among all the items. If the theory suggests more than one dimension, we should have subscales to measure each separate dimension. In that case, the subscales should have high internal consistency, but they should not correlate highly with other subscales. A measure of feminism, for example, would probably have several subscales covering family, work, pay, politics, authority relations, and the like. The extent to which the observed item intercorrelations agree with the theoretical framework provides evidence concerning the construct being measured.

5. *Studies of Response Processes* Another way to obtain evidence about how well a test is measuring the construct of interest is to look at the **evidence based on response processes** of individuals actually taking the test. Questioning test takers about the mental processes and skills that they use when responding to the items of a test can provide information about what construct is being measured. If one were gathering validity evidence about a new verbal reasoning test, for instance, one might ask individuals to "think aloud" as they work through the test. This procedure may reveal that the test is measuring verbal reasoning, or it may reveal that other factors such as vocabulary or reading comprehension are being measured. Examining response processes may indicate certain construct-irrelevant factors that differentially influence the performance of different subgroups. Thus, it provides evidence about whether the test scores have the same meaning or can be interpreted in the same way across different subgroups.

Let us look at a historical example that illustrates the use of various types of evidence in the validation of an instrument to measure social maturity. Doll (1935) designed the Vineland Social Maturity Scale to measure the abstract construct *social maturity*. Doll first defined the construct *social maturity* as a combination of interrelated elements of self-help, self-direction, locomotion, occupation, communication, and social relations. Reviewers of the first revised version of the test in Buros's *Mental Measurements Yearbook* (1949) tended to agree that these elements are aspects of the construct that should be incorporated in a test of social maturity. The next step in the validation process was to examine the items to see if they were appropriate for assessing the various elements of social maturity (evidence based on test content). For example, the parent of a 6-year-old is asked if the subject uses skates, sled, wagon (occupation); goes to bed unassisted (self-help); prints simple words (communication); plays simple table games (locomotion); and is trusted with money (self-direction). If the original scale had included items concerning the child's preference for certain foods or whether he or she is right-handed, these items would have been deleted as they are not di-

Table 9.1 Types of Evidence for Validity of a Test

Type	Question	Method
Content related	Is the test a representative sample of the domain being measured?	Make a logical analysis of the test's content to see how well it covers the domain
Criterion related (concurrent)	Does a new test correlate with a currently available test (criterion), so that the new test could be a substitute?	Correlate scores from new test with scores of a criterion measure available at the time.
Criterion related (predictive)	Does a new test correlate with a future criterion, so that the test can be used to predict later performance on the criterion?	Correlate test scores with a measure (criterion) available at a future time.
Construct related	Does the test really measure the intended construct?	Gather various kinds of evidence: convergent and divergent evidence, known-groups technique, intervention study, internal structure, and response processes.

rectly related to the elements in the construct. The internal structure of the scale was examined to see if it conformed to the definition of the construct (evidence based on internal structure). Doll showed that Vineland scores for occupation, self-help, and so forth correlated positively with one another. These observations provided internal support for the theory that the construct *social maturity* consists of interrelated elements and provided evidence that the Vineland scale was measuring these interrelated elements.

Another source of validity evidence was the relationship of scores to other variables external to the scale. Doll and others have shown that scores on the Vineland scale do correlate with chronological age, mental age, and with independent assessments of social maturity.

Sometimes researchers disagree on what the elements of a construct are. For example, if you think of the construct *intelligence* as primarily a combination of skills that enable an individual to cope with an academic environment, you would expect such skills to be measured in an intelligence test. If you define *intelligence* as a set of skills that are no more related to school environments than to other environments, you would not want school-specific skills incorporated into the test. Table 9.1 summarizes the three major types of evidence for validity.

Application of the Validity Concept

Validity is always specific to the particular purpose for which the instrument is being used. "It is incorrect to use the unqualified phrase 'the validity of the test.' No test is valid for all purposes or in all situations" (*Standards*, 1999, p.17). A test that has validity in one situation and for one purpose may not be valid in a different situation or for a different purpose. A teacher-made achievement test in high school chemistry might be useful for measuring end-of-year achievement in chemistry but might be useless for predicting achievement in college chemistry. A German proficiency test might be appropriate for placing undergraduates in German classes at a university but not be a valid exit exam for German majors. Thus, validation is always a responsibility of the test user as well as of the test developer.

Validity Generalization

A concern in validity studies of educational and employment tests is the extent to which evidence of validity based on test–criterion relationships can be generalized to new settings without further investigations of validity in the new setting. Research shows that test–criterion correlations may vary greatly from time to time and place to place because of the type of criterion measure used, the way the predictor is measured, the type of test takers, and the time period involved.

Validity generalization studies have used meta-analysis, which provides statistical summaries of past validation studies in similar situations. Research provides support for validity generalization in cases where the meta-analytic database is large, where the data adequately represent the type of situation to which a researcher wishes to generalize, and where there is a consistent pattern of validity evidence. In other circumstances where the findings of the meta-analytic studies are less consistent and where there are more differences between the new and old settings, it is more risky to generalize. Local validation studies providing situation-specific evidence would be more valuable.

THINK ABOUT IT 9.1

Identify the type of validity evidence (content, concurrent criterion, predictive criterion, or construct related) being gathered in each of the following examples:

a. A test administered to applicants for law school correlates .65 with first-semester grades in law school.

b. A group of math professors examine the math placement test administered to freshmen at the university. They conclude that the test is an excellent sample of the math skills students need to succeed in college-level courses.

c. A high school teacher administers a standardized chemistry test and correlates the scores with the scores students earned the next day on a teacher-made chemistry test.

d. As predicted, the scores for a group of Young Republicans on a scale measuring political conservatism were markedly higher than those for a group of Young Democrats.

e. Scores on a new scale to detect depression is correlated with scores on a well-established scale measuring personality adjustment. The correlation was negligible.

Answers

a. predictive criterion related

b. content related

c. concurrent criterion related

d. construct related

e. construct related (theory would predict that measures of depression would not be correlated with measures of personality adjustment; this is divergent construct-related validity evidence)

RELIABILITY

As we mentioned at the beginning of this chapter, the **reliability** of a measuring instrument is the degree of consistency with which it measures whatever it is measuring. This quality is essential in any kind of measurement. A post office will soon take action to repair a scale if users find that the scale sometimes underestimates and sometimes overestimates the weight of packages. A bathroom scale would be reliable if it gives you nearly the same weight on five consecutive days. But if you got vastly different readings on each of the five days, you would consider the scale unreliable as a measure of your weight and would probably discard it. Psychologists and educators are equally concerned about the consistency of their measuring devices when they attempt to measure such complex constructs as scholastic aptitude, achievement, motivation, anxiety, and the like. They would not consider a scholastic aptitude test worthwhile if it yielded markedly different results when administered to the same students on two occasions. People who use such measuring instruments must identify and use techniques that will help them determine to what extent their measuring instruments are consistent and reliable.

On a theoretical level, reliability is concerned with the effect of error on the consistency of scores. In this world measurement always involves some error. There are two kinds of errors: *random errors of measurement* and *systematic errors of measurement*. Random error is error that is a result of pure chance. Random errors of measurement may inflate or depress any subject's score in an unpredictable manner. Systematic errors, on the other hand, inflate or depress scores of identifiable groups in a predictable way. Systematic errors are the root of validity problems; random errors are the root of reliability problems.

SOURCES OF RANDOM ERROR

Chance or random error that leads to inconsistency in scores can come from three sources:

1. *The individual being measured may be a source of error*. Fluctuations in individuals' motivation, interest, level of fatigue, physical health, anxiety, and other mental and emotional factors occur and affect test results. As these factors change randomly from one measurement to the next, they result in a change or inconsistency in one's scores. Individuals may make more lucky guesses at one time than another. A student's breaking a pencil point on a timed test would increase the error component in the test results.
2. *The administration of the measuring instrument may introduce error*. An inexperienced person may depart from standardized procedures in administering or scoring a test. Testing conditions such as light, heat, ventilation, time of day, and the presence of distractions may affect performance. Instructions for taking the test may be ambiguous. The scoring procedure may be a source of error. Objectivity and precise scoring procedures enhance consistency, whereas subjectivity and vague scoring instructions depress it.
3. *The instrument itself may be a source of error.* Brevity of a test is a major source of unreliability. A small sample of behavior results in an unstable

score. For example, if a test is very short, those subjects who happen to know the few answers required will get higher scores than they deserve, whereas those who do not know those few answers get lower scores than they deserve. For example, if a test is given to assess how well students know the capitals of the 50 states, but only 5 questions are asked, it is possible that a student who knows only 10 capitals could get all 5 correct, whereas a student who knows 40 could get none correct. In a short test, luck is more of a factor than in a long test.

If a test is too easy and everyone knows most of the answers, students' relative scores again depend on only a few questions and luck is a major factor. If questions are ambiguous, "lucky" examinees respond in the way the examiner intended, whereas "unlucky" subjects respond in another equally correct manner, but their answers are scored as incorrect.

One element in a physical fitness test for elementary students is the baseball throw. Subjects are instructed to throw a baseball as far as they can, and the distance of the throw is measured. Although the object of the test is to get a score that is typical of a subject's performance, certainly if you had a single subject throw a baseball on several occasions, you would find that the child does not throw it the same distance every time.

Assume you had each student make a throw on two consecutive days. If you then compared the two scores (distance thrown) for each student, you would find that they were almost never exactly the same. Most of the differences would be small, but some would be moderately large, and a few, quite large. The results are inconsistent from one day's throw to the next. One throw is not completely reliable as a measure of a student's throwing ability. Three types of chance, or random, influences lead to inconsistency between scores on the two days:

1. The student may change from one time to another. On one day he or she may feel better than on the other. On one day the student may be more motivated or less fatigued. Maybe the student loses balance when starting to throw the ball, or maybe his or her fingers slip while gripping the ball. Perhaps the student's father, hearing about the task, decides to coach the child in throwing a baseball before the next day.
2. The task may change from one measurement to the next. For example, the ball used one day may be firm, whereas on the second day, it may be wet and soggy. One day perhaps the examiner permits the students to take a running start up to the throwing line, whereas on the second day a different examiner permits only a couple of steps. There may be gusts of wind at certain times that help some students more than others.
3. The limited sample of behavior results in a less reliable score. As we have seen, a small sample of behavior is subject to all kinds of chance influences. The average of a student's baseball throw scores on two days would yield a better estimate of his/her true baseball throwing skill than one day's score. The average of three days' scores would be a still better estimate and so on.

Reliability is concerned with the effect of such random errors of measurement on the consistency of scores. But some errors involved in measurement are predictable or systematic. Using the example of the baseball throw, imagine a situation in which the instructions for the throw are given in English—but not all the subjects understand English. The scores of the non-English-speaking subjects could be systematically depressed because the subjects do not comprehend what they are expected to do. Such systematic errors of measurement are a validity problem. The validity of score-based inferences is lowered whenever scores are systematically changed by the influence of anything other than what you are trying to measure (irrelevant variance). In this instance you are measuring not only baseball-throwing skill but also, in part, English comprehension.

To decide whether you are dealing with reliability or validity, you determine whether you are considering random errors or systematic errors. If a class is being given the baseball throw test and two balls are being employed, one firm and one soggy, and it is purely a matter of chance who gets which ball, the variation caused by the ball used is a reliability problem. The variation caused by the ball represents random error that affects the consistency of the measurements. If the girls are tested using a dry, firm ball and the boys get a wet, soggy ball, scores are a function of gender as well as of skill, resulting in systematic errors that give rise to a validity problem.

RELATIONSHIP BETWEEN RELIABILITY AND VALIDITY

Reliability is concerned with how consistently you are measuring whatever you are measuring. It is not concerned with the meaning and interpretation of the scores, which is the validity question. We express the relationship between these two concepts as follows: A measuring instrument can be reliable without being valid; but it cannot be valid unless it is first reliable. For example, someone could decide to measure intelligence by determining the circumference of the head. The measures might be very consistent from time to time (reliable), but this method would not yield valid inferences about intelligence because circumference of the head does not correlate with any other criteria of intelligence, nor is it predicted by any theory of intelligence. So a test can be very reliable but consistently yield scores that are meaningless.

To be able to make valid inferences from a test's scores, the test must first of all be consistent in measuring whatever is being measured. Reliability is a necessary but not a sufficient condition for valid interpretations of test scores.

EQUATIONS FOR RELIABILITY

It is generally accepted that all measurements of human qualities contain random error. Although scientists cannot remove all this error, they do have ways to assess the aggregate magnitude of measurement errors. Reliability procedures are concerned with determining the degree of inconsistency in scores caused by random error.

When you administer a test to a student, you get a score, which is called the *observed score*. If you had tested this student on some other occasion with the same instrument, you probably would not have obtained exactly the same observed score because of the influence of random errors of measurement. Assuming that test scores have an error component implies that there is a hypothetical error-free score for an individual that would be obtained if the measurement were perfectly accurate. This error-free value is called the individual's **true score** on the test. The true score is conceptualized as "the hypothetical average score resulting from many repetitions of the test or alternate forms of the instrument" (*Standards*, p. 25).

We conclude, therefore, that every test score consists of two components: the *true score* plus some *error of measurement*. As we noted earlier, this error component may be caused by any one, or a combination, of a number of factors associated with variations within the examinee from time to time or with the test and its administration.

The reliability of a test is expressed mathematically as the best estimate of what proportion of the total variance of scores on the test is true variance. As we explained in Chapter 6, variance is an index of the spread of a set of scores. If you administer a test to a group of students, some of the spread (variance) of the students' scores is due to true differences among the group and some of the spread (variance) is due to errors of measurement.

The idea of error component and true component in a single test score may be represented mathematically by Formula 9.1:

$$X = T + E \tag{9.1}$$

where

X = observed score
T = true score component
E = error-of-measurement component

The true-score component may be defined as the score an individual would make under conditions in which a perfect measuring device is used. The error-of-measurement component can be either positive or negative. If it is positive, the individual's true score will be overestimated by the observed score; if it is negative, the person's true score will be underestimated. Because researchers assume that an error of measurement is just as likely to be positive as it is to be negative, then researchers can conclude that the sum of the errors and the mean of the errors would both be 0 if the same measuring instrument or an equivalent form of the instrument were administered an infinite number of times to a subject. Under these conditions, the true component would be defined as the individual's mean score on an infinite number of measurements. The true score is a theoretical concept because an infinite number of administrations of a test to the same subject is not feasible.

In the usual research situation, the investigator has one measure on each of a group of subjects. In other words, the researcher has a single set of test scores to consider. Each observed score has a true-score component and an error-score component. It has been shown mathematically that the variance of the observed scores of a large group of subjects (σ_x^2) is equal to the variance of their true scores (σ_t^2) plus the variance of their errors of measurement (σ_e^2) or

$$\sigma_x^2 = \sigma_t^2 + \sigma_e^2 \tag{9.2}$$

Reliability may be defined theoretically as the ratio of the true-score variance to the observed-score variance in a set of scores, as expressed by the following formula:

$$r_{xx} = \frac{\sigma_t^2}{\sigma_x^2} \tag{9.3}$$

where

r_{xx} = reliability of the test
σ_t^2 = variance of the true scores
σ_x^2 = variance of the observed scores

Reliability is the proportion of the variance in the observed scores that is free of error. This notion can be expressed in the following formula, derived from Formulas 9.2 and 9.3:

$$r_{xx} = 1 - \frac{\sigma_e^2}{\sigma_x^2} \tag{9.4}$$

The **coefficient of reliability** r_{xx} can range from 1, when there is no error in the measurement, to 0, when the measurement is all error. When there is no error in the measurement, σ_e^2 in the reliability formula is 0 and $r_{xx} = 1$.

$$r = 1 - \frac{\sigma_e^2}{\sigma_x^2} \qquad r = 1 - \frac{0}{\sigma_x^2} = 1 - 0 = 1$$

If measurement is all error, $\sigma_e^2 = \sigma_x^2$ and $r_{xx} = 0$.

$$r = 1 - \frac{\sigma_e^2}{\sigma_x^2} = 1 - 1 = 0$$

The extent of error is indicated by the degree of departure of the reliability coefficient from 1. A coefficient of .80 on a test, for example, indicates the best estimate is that 80 percent of the observed variance in the scores is true variance and 20 percent is error. Thus, the greater the error, the more the reliability coefficient is depressed below 1 and the lower the reliability. Conversely, if the reliability coefficient is near 1, the instrument has relatively little error and high reliability.

APPROACHES TO RELIABILITY

A test is reliable to the extent that the scores made by an individual remain nearly the same in repeated measurements. That is, individuals will have the same, or nearly the same, rank on the repeated administrations. There are two ways to express the consistency of a set of measurements.

1. The first method indicates the amount of variation to be expected within a set of repeated measurements of a *single* individual. If it were possible to weigh an individual on 200 scales, you would get a frequency distribution of scores to represent his or her weight. This frequency distribution would have an average value, which you could consider the "true" weight. It would also have a standard deviation, indicating the spread. This standard deviation is called the **standard error of measurement** because it is the standard deviation of the "errors" of measuring the weight for one person. With psychological or educational data, researchers do not often make repeated measurements on an individual. Time would not permit such repetition, and, in addition, the practice and fatigue effects associated with repeated measurement would have an influence on the scores. Thus, instead of meas-

uring one person many times, researchers measure a large, diverse group on two occasions. Using the pair of measurements for each individual, they can estimate what the spread of scores would have been for the average person had the measurement been made again and again.

2. The consistency of a set of scores is also indicated by the extent to which each individual maintains the same relative position in the group. With a reliable test, the person who scores highest on a test today should also be one of the highest scorers the next time the same test is given. Each person in the group would stay in approximately the same relative position. The more individuals shift in relative position, the lower the test's reliability. You can compute a coefficient of correlation between two administrations of the same test to determine the extent to which the individuals maintain the same relative position. This coefficient is called a **reliability coefficient** (r_{xx}). A reliability coefficient of 1.00 indicates that each individual's relative position on the two administrations remained exactly the same and the test would be perfectly reliable.

Thus, the consistency of a measure is indicated by (1) its standard error of measurement or (2) by its reliability coefficient. We will look at standard error of measurement later in the chapter. Let us now consider the various reliability coefficients.

RELIABILITY COEFFICIENTS

There are three broad categories of reliability coefficients: (1) coefficients derived from correlating individuals' scores on the same test administered on different occasions (test-retest coefficients); (2) coefficients derived from correlating individuals' scores on different sets of equivalent items (parallel or equivalent-forms coefficients); and (3) coefficients based on the relationship among scores derived from individual items or subsets of items within a test (internal-consistency coefficients). The internal-consistency coefficient requires only a single administration of a test, whereas the other coefficients require two administrations.

Test–Retest Reliability

An obvious way to estimate the reliability of a test is to administer it to the same group of individuals on two occasions and correlate the two sets of scores. The correlation coefficient obtained by this procedure is called a **test–retest reliability coefficient**. For example, a physical fitness test may be given to a class during one week and the same test given again the following week. If the test has good reliability, each individual's relative position on the second administration of the test will be near his or her relative position on the first administration of the test.

The test–retest reliability coefficient, because it indicates consistency of subjects' scores over time, is sometimes referred to as a **coefficient of stability**. A high coefficient tells you that you can generalize from the score a person receives on one occasion to a score that person would receive if the test had been given at a different time.

A test–retest coefficient assumes that the characteristic being measured by the test is stable over time, so any change in scores from one time to another is caused by random error. The error may be caused by the condition of the subjects themselves or to testing conditions. The test–retest coefficient also assumes there is no practice effect or memory effect. For example, students may learn something just from taking a test and thus will react differently on the second taking of the test. These practice effects from the first testing will not likely be the same across all students, thus lowering the reliability estimate. If the interval of time is short, there may also be a memory effect; students may mark a question the same way they did previously just because they remember marking it that way the first time. This memory effect tends to inflate the reliability estimate, but it can be controlled somewhat by increasing the time between the first test and the retest. However, if the time between testings is too long, differential learning may be a problem—that is, students will learn different amounts during the interval, which would affect the reliability coefficient. Thus, the period of time between the two administrations is an issue that must be considered.

Because of these problems, the test–retest procedure is not usually appropriate for tests in the cognitive domain. Use of this procedure in schools is largely restricted to measures of physical fitness and athletic prowess.

Equivalent-Forms Reliability

Researchers use the **equivalent-forms technique** of estimating reliability, which is also referred to as the **alternate-forms technique** or **parallel-forms technique**, when it is probable that subjects will recall their responses to the test items. Here, rather than correlating the scores from two administrations of the same test to the same group, the researcher correlates the results of alternate (equivalent) forms of the test administered to the same individuals. If the two forms are administered at essentially the same time (in immediate succession), the resulting reliability coefficient is called the **coefficient of equivalence**. This measure reflects variations in performance from one specific set of items to another. It indicates whether you can generalize a student's score to what the student would receive if another form of the same test had been given. The question is, to what extent does the student's performance depend on the particular set of items used in the test?

If subjects are tested with one form on one occasion and with an equivalent form on a second occasion and their scores on the two forms are correlated, the resulting coefficient is called the **coefficient of stability and equivalence**. This coefficient reflects two aspects of test reliability: variations in performance from one time to another, as well as variations from one form of the test to another. A high coefficient of stability and equivalence indicates that the two forms are measuring the same skill and measuring consistently over time. This is the most demanding and the most rigorous measure available for determining the reliability of a test.

Designing alternate forms of a test that are truly equivalent is the major problem with this technique of estimating reliability. If a successful design is not achieved, then the variation in scores from one form to another could not be considered error variance. Alternate forms of a test are independently constructed tests that must meet the same specifications—that is, they must have the same number of items, instructions, time limits, format, content, range, and level of difficulty—but the actual questions are not the same. Ideally, you should have pairs of equivalent items and assign one of each pair to each form. In a world geography test, for example, form A might ask, "On what continent is the Nile River?" while form B asks, "On what continent is the Amazon River?" Form A might ask, "What is the capital of Italy?" and form B, "What is the capital of France?" The distribution of the test scores must also be equivalent.

The alternate-forms technique is recommended when you want to avoid the problem of recall or practice effect and in cases when you have available a large number of test items from which to select equivalent samples. Researchers generally consider that the equivalent-forms procedure provides the best estimate of the reliability of academic and psychological measures.

Internal-Consistency Measures of Reliability

Other reliability procedures are designed to determine whether all the items in a test are measuring the same thing. These are called the **internal-consistency procedures** and require only a single administration of one form of a test.

Split-Half Reliability The simplest of the internal-consistency procedures, known as the *split-half*, artificially splits the test into two halves and correlates the individuals' scores on the two halves. Researchers administer the test to a group and later divide the items into two halves, obtain the scores for each individual on the two halves, and calculate a coefficient of correlation. This **split-half reliability coefficient** is like a coefficient of equivalence because it reflects fluctuations from one sample of items to another. If each subject has a very similar position on the two halves, the test has high reliability. If there is little consistency in positions, the reliability is low. The method requires only one form of a test, there is no time lag involved, and the same physical and mental influences will be operating on the subjects as they take the two halves. A problem with this method is in splitting the test to obtain two comparable halves. If, through item analysis, you establish the difficulty level of each item, you can place each item into one of the two halves on the basis of equivalent difficulty and similarity of content. The most common procedure, however, is to correlate the scores on the odd-numbered items of the test with the scores on the even-numbered items.

The correlation coefficient computed between the two halves systematically underestimates the reliability of the entire test. If everything else is equal, longer tests are more reliable than shorter tests. Therefore, the correlation between the 50 odd-numbered and 50 even-numbered items on a 100-item test is a reliability estimate for a 50-item test, not a 100-item test. To transform the split-half correlation into an appropriate reliability estimate for the entire test, the **Spearman–Brown prophecy formula** is employed:

$$r_{xx} = \frac{2r_{\frac{1}{2}\frac{1}{2}}}{1 + r_{\frac{1}{2}\frac{1}{2}}} \tag{9.5}$$

where

r_{xx} = estimated reliability of the entire test

$r_{\frac{1}{2}\frac{1}{2}}$ = Pearson r correlation between the two halves

For example, if we find a correlation coefficient of .65 between two halves of a test, the estimated reliability of the entire test, using the Spearman–Brown formula, would be

$$r_{xx} = \frac{(2)(.65)}{1 + .65} = .79$$

The Spearman–Brown procedure is based on the assumption that the two halves are parallel. As this assumption is seldom exactly correct, in practice, the split-half technique with the Spearman–Brown correction tends to overestimate the reliability that would be obtained with test–retest or equivalent-forms procedures. Bear this in mind when evaluating the reliabilities of competing tests.

Split-half reliability is an appropriate technique to use when time-to-time fluctuation in estimating reliability is to be avoided and when the test is relatively long. For short tests the other techniques, such as test–retest or equivalent-forms, are more appropriate. The split-half procedure is not appropriate to use with speed tests because it yields spuriously high coefficients of equivalence in such tests. A speed test is one that purposefully includes easy items so that the scores mainly depend on the speed with which subjects can respond. Errors are minor, and most of the items are correct up to the point where time is called. If a student responds to 50 items, his or her split-half score is likely to be 25–25; if another student marks 60 items, his split-half score is likely to be 30–30, and so on. Because individuals' scores on odd- and even-numbered items are very nearly identical, within-individual variation is minimized and the correlation between the halves would be nearly perfect. Thus, other procedures are recommended for use with speed tests.*

Homogeneity Measures Other internal-consistency measures of reliability do not require splitting the test into halves and scoring each half separately. These procedures assess the interitem consistency, or *homogeneity*, of the items. They reflect two sources of error: (1) the content sampling as in split-half and (2) the heterogeneity of the behavior domain sampled. The more heterogeneous the domain, the lower the interitem consistency and, conversely, the more homogeneous the domain, the higher the interitem consistency.

Kuder–Richardson Procedures Kuder and Richardson (1937) developed procedures that have been widely used to determine homogeneity or internal consistency. Probably the best known index of homogeneity is the **Kuder–Richardson formula** 20, which is based on the proportion of correct and incorrect responses to each of the items on a test and the variance of the total scores:

$$r_{xx} = \frac{K}{K-1}\left(\frac{s_x^2 - \Sigma pq}{s_x^2}\right) \qquad \text{K–R 20} \quad (9.6)$$

*There are computer programs for calculating all the reliability formulas in this chapter. We included the formulas and worked examples so you can see *how* the procedures are working.

where

r_{xx} = reliability of the whole test
K = number of items on the test
s_x^2 = variance of scores on the total test (squared standard deviation)
p = proportion of correct responses on a single item
q = proportion of incorrect responses on the same item

The product pq is computed for each item, and the products are summed over all items to give Σpq. Kuder–Richardson 20 is applicable to tests whose items are scored dichotomously (0 or 1); thus, it is useful with test items that are scored as true/false or right/wrong. Many machine-scoring procedures for tests routinely provide a K–R 20 coefficient along with a split-half coefficient.

Another formula (Kuder–Richardson 21) is computationally simpler but requires the assumption that all items in the test are of equal difficulty. This assumption is often unrealistic:

$$r_{xx} = \frac{Ks_x^2 - \overline{X}(K - \overline{X})}{s_x^2(K - 1)} \qquad \text{K–R 21} \quad (9.7)$$

where

r_{xx} = reliability of the whole test
K = number of items in the test
s_x^2 = variance of the scores
$\overline{X}$ = mean of the scores

This method is by far the least time consuming of all the reliability estimation procedures. It involves only one administration of a test and employs only easily available information. As such, it can be recommended to teachers for classroom use.

For example, suppose a teacher has administered a 50-item test to a class and has computed the mean as 40 and the standard deviation as 6. Applying Formula 9.7, the reliability could be estimated as follows:

$$r_{xx} = \frac{(50)6^2 - 40(50 - 40)}{6^2(50 - 1)} = \frac{1800 - 400}{1764} = .79$$

Because the Kuder–Richardson procedures stress the equivalence of all the items in a test, they are especially appropriate when the intention of the test is to measure a single trait. For a test with homogeneous content (e.g., math test covering fractions), the reliability estimate will be similar to that provided by the split-half. For a test designed to measure several traits, the Kuder–Richardson reliability estimate is usually lower than reliability estimates based on a correlational procedure.

Analysts have shown through deductive reasoning that the Kuder–Richardson reliability for any test is mathematically equivalent to the mean of the split-half reliability estimates computed for every possible way of splitting the test in half. This fact helps explain the relationship between the two procedures. If a test is of uniform difficulty and is measuring a single trait, any one way of splitting that test in half is as likely as any other to yield similar half scores. Therefore, the Spearman–Brown and Kuder–Richardson methods will yield similar estimates. If a test has items of varying difficulty and is measuring various traits, the Kuder–Richardson estimate is expected to be lower than the split-half estimate. For example, suppose a secretarial skills test samples typing, shorthand, spelling, and English grammar skills. In applying the split-half method, the test maker would assign equal numbers of items from each subtest to each half of the test. If the test is doing a good job of measuring this combination of skills, the split-half reliability will be high. The Kuder–Richardson method, which assesses the extent to which all the items are equivalent to one another, would yield a considerably lower reliability estimate.

Coefficient Alpha Another widely used measure of homogeneity is **coefficient alpha**, also called **Cronbach alpha** after Lee Cronbach who developed it (1951). Coefficient alpha has wider applications than the K–R 20 formula. When items are scored dichotomously, it yields the same result as the K–R 20, but it can also be used when items are not scored dichotomously. The formula for alpha is as follows:

$$\alpha = \left(\frac{K}{K-1}\right)\left(\frac{s_x^2 - \Sigma s_i^2}{s_x^2}\right) \tag{9.8}$$

where

K = number of items on the test
Σs_i^2 = sum of variances of the item scores
s_x^2 = variance of the test scores (all K items)

The formula for alpha is similar to the K–R 20 except that the Σpq is replaced by Σs_i^2, the sum of the variances of item scores. To calculate, you determine the variance of all the scores for *each* item and then add these variances across all items to get Σs_i^2.

Researchers use Cronbach alpha when measures have items that are not scored simply as right or wrong, such as attitude scales or essay tests. The item score may take on a range of values as, for example, on a Likert attitude scale the individual may receive a score from 1 to 5 depending on which option was chosen. Similarly, on essay tests a different number of points may be assigned to each answer. Many computer programs for reliability, such as the one included in SPSS, provide a coefficient alpha as the index of reliability.

If the test items are heterogeneous—that is, they measure more than one trait or attribute—the reliability index as computed by either coefficient alpha or K–R 20 will be lowered. Furthermore, these formulas are not appropriate for timed tests because item variances will be accurate only if each item has been attempted by every person.

Table 9.2 presents a summary of the different types of reliability coefficients arranged according to the number of forms and number of administrations required.

Table 9.2 Summary of Reliability Coefficients

		Number of Test Forms Required	
		One	Two
Number of Administrations Required	One	Split-half K–R 20 Coefficient alpha	Equivalent forms (no time lapse)
	Two	Test–retest	Equivalent-forms (time lapse)

INTERPRETATION OF RELIABILITY COEFFICIENTS

The interpretation of a reliability coefficient should be based on a number of considerations. Certain factors affect reliability coefficients, and unless these factors are taken into account, any interpretation of reliability will be superficial.

1. *The reliability of a test is in part a function of the length of the test.* Other things being equal, the longer the test, the greater its reliability. A test usually consists of a number of sample items that are, theoretically, drawn from a universe of test items. You know from what you have studied about sampling that the greater the sample size, the more representative it is expected to be of the population from which it is drawn. This is also true of tests. If it were possible to use the entire universe of items, the score of a person who takes the test would be his or her true score. A theoretical universe of items consists of an infinite number of questions and is obviously not a practical possibility. You, therefore, construct a test that is a sample from such a theoretical universe. The greater the length of this test (i.e., the greater the number of items included in the test), the more representative it should be of the true scores of the people who take it. Because reliability is the extent to which a test represents the true scores of individuals, the longer the test, the greater its reliability, provided that all the items in the test belong in the universe of items.
2. *Reliability is in part a function of group heterogeneity.* The reliability coefficient increases as the spread, or heterogeneity, of the subjects who take the test increases. Conversely, the more homogeneous the group is with respect to the trait being measured, the lower will be the reliability coefficient. One explanation of reliability is that it is the extent to which researchers can place individuals, relative to others in their groups, according to certain traits. Such placement is easier when you are dealing with measures that fall in a large range rather than those that fall in a small range. It does not take a sensitive device to determine the placement of children in a distribution according to their weights when the age range of these children is from 5 to 15. In fact, this placement is possible with some degree of accuracy even

without using any measuring device. It does take a sensitive device, however, to carry out the same placement if all those who are to be compared and placed in the distribution are 5 years old. Thus the heterogeneity of the group with whom a measuring instrument is used is a factor that affects the reliability of that instrument. The more heterogeneous the group used in the reliability study, the higher the reliability coefficient. Keep this fact in mind when selecting a standardized test. The publisher may report a high reliability coefficient based on a sample with a wide range of ability. However, when the test is used with a group having a much narrower range of ability, the reliability will be lower.

3. *The reliability of a test is in part a function of the ability of the individuals who take that test.* A test may be reliable at one level of ability but unreliable at another level. The questions in a test may be difficult and beyond the ability level of those who take it—or the questions may be easy for the majority of the subjects. This difficulty level affects the reliability of the test. When a test is difficult, the subjects are guessing on most of the questions and a low reliability coefficient will result. When it is easy, all subjects have correct responses on most of the items, and only a few difficult items are discriminating among subjects. Again, we would expect a low reliability. There is no simple rule by which you can determine how difficult, or how easy, a test should be. That depends on the type of test, the purpose, and the population with which it will be used.

4. *Reliability is in part a function of the specific technique used for its estimation.* Different procedures for estimating the reliability of tests result in different coefficients of reliability. The alternate forms with time lapse technique gives a lower estimation of reliability than either test–retest or split-half procedures because in this technique form-to-form as well as time-to-time fluctuation is present. The split-half method, in contrast, results in higher reliability coefficients than do its alternatives because in most tests some degree of speed is involved, and to that extent the reliability coefficient is overestimated. Thus, in evaluating the reliability of a test, you would give preference to a test whose reliability coefficient has been estimated by the alternate-forms technique, rather than by other techniques, when the reported reliabilities are similar. Standardized test manuals report reliability coefficients based on test–retest and alternate-forms techniques, but teachers generally do not use these procedures for estimating reliability. Repeated testing and alternate forms are not feasible in most classroom situations. Instead, teachers use the split-half, the Kuder–Richardson, or one of the other measures of internal consistency as a measures of reliability.

5. *Reliability is in part a function of the nature of the variable being measured.* Some variables of interest to researchers yield consistent measures more often than do other variables. For instance, because academic achievement is relatively easy to measure, most established tests of academic achievement have quite high reliability (coefficients of +.90 or higher). Aptitude

Table 9.3 Factors Affecting Reliability of a Test

Factor	Potential Effect
1. Length of the test	The longer the test, the greater the reliability.
2. Heterogeneity of group	The more heterogeneous the group, the greater the reliability.
3. Ability level of group	Test that is too easy or too difficult for group results in lower reliability.
4. Techniques used to estimate reliability	Test–retest and split-half give higher estimates. Equivalent forms give lower estimates.
5. Nature of the variable	Tests of variables that are easier to measure yield higher reliability estimates.
6. Objectivity of scoring	The more objective the scoring, the greater the reliability.

tests that are designed to predict future behavior—a more difficult task—have somewhat lower reliability (.80 or lower). Reliable measures of personality variables are most difficult to obtain; thus these measures typically have only moderate reliability (.60 to .70).

6. *Reliability is influenced by the objectivity of the scoring.* Inconsistent scoring introduces error that reduces the reliability of a test. The potential unreliability of the scoring of essay tests, for example, means that essay tests are generally considered to be not as reliable as multiple-choice and other types of selected-response tests.

Table 9.3 summarizes the factors affecting reliability.

What is the minimum reliability acceptable for an instrument? Perhaps the best response to this question is that a good reliability is one that is as good as or better than the reliability of competing measures. A spelling achievement test with a reliability of .80 is unsatisfactory if competing tests have reliability coefficients of .90 or better. A coefficient of .80 for a test of creativity would be judged excellent if other tests of the same construct have reliabilities of .60 or less.

The degree of reliability you need in a measure depends to a great extent on the use you will make of the results. The need for accurate measurement increases as the consequences of decisions and interpretation become more important. If the measurement results are to be used for making a decision about a group or for research purposes, or if an erroneous initial decision can be easily corrected, scores with modest reliability (coefficients in the range of .50 to .60) may be acceptable. But if the results are to be used as a basis for making decisions about individuals, especially important or irreversible decisions (such as rejection or admission of candidates to a professional school or the placement of children in special education classes), only instruments with the highest reliability are acceptable. Measurement experts state that in such situations a reliability of .90 is the minimum that should be tolerated, and a reliability of .95 should be the desired standard.

PICTURE THIS

Adding an irrelevant measure will lower reliability and validity.

Joe Rocco

STANDARD ERROR OF MEASUREMENT

The reliability coefficient looks at the consistency of test scores for a group. But it does not tell us anything about the amount of error in individual test scores. Suppose you had an aptitude test score of 105 for an individual child. If we retested, we would probably not obtain that same score. How much variability could we expect in the child's score on retesting? Recall that measurement theory states that any obtained score is made up of the true score plus an error score: $X = T + E$. Because of error, the obtained score is sometimes higher than the true score and sometimes lower than the true score. Returning to the ex-

THINK ABOUT IT 9.2

Indicate the type of reliability coefficient illustrated in each of the following exercises.

a. A teacher prepares two forms of a math achievement test, administers the two forms to a group of students on consecutive days, and correlates the students' scores from the two administrations.

b. A college professor administers a 40-item multiple-choice test in educational psychology. The scoring office provides the professor a reliability index found by dividing the test into two forms and calculating the correlation between the students' scores on the two.

c. A teacher questions the results of a verbal aptitude test administered to her English class. She decides to have the students take the same test on the following day. She then correlates the two sets of scores and finds a coefficient of .90.

d. A commercial test developed two forms of a standardized reading test and administered the two forms of the test to a representative sample of elementary school students in the fall and again in the spring.

e. A teacher wanted a reliability estimate of an essay test in history administered at the end of the semester. She used a computer program that calculated the variance of all the scores for each item and then plugged the total variances across all items into a formula.

Answers

a. Alternate forms (coefficient of equivalence)
b. Split-half reliability coefficient
c. Test–retest (coefficient of stability)
d. Alternate forms (coefficient of stability and equivalence)
e. Coefficient alpha

ample of the aptitude test, you would expect with repeated administration to obtain a number of different scores for the same individual. In fact, you would have a frequency distribution of aptitude scores. The mean of this distribution of scores would be the best approximation of the child's true score, and the standard deviation would be an indicator of the errors of measurement. Because this standard deviation is the standard deviation of the errors of measurement, it is called the **standard error of measurement**. Test theory tells us that the distribution of error scores approximates a normal distribution, and, as we will see, we can use the normal distribution to represent it. Measurement errors are normally distributed with a mean of zero. There may be many small errors, but there will be few very large ones. The standard deviation of this distribution of errors (standard error of measurement, s_M) would give an estimate of how frequently errors of a given size might be expected to occur when the test is administered many times.

In practice, you usually do not have repeated measures for an individual but you can get an estimate of the standard error of measurement from one group administration of a test. The formula for standard error of measurement is:

$$s_M = s_x\sqrt{1 - r_{xx}}$$

where

$$s_M = \text{standard error of measurement}$$
$$s_x = \text{standard deviation of test scores}$$
$$r_{xx} = \text{reliability coefficient}$$

Thus, using the standard deviation of the obtained scores and the reliability of the test, we can estimate the amount of error in individual scores. If the aptitude test has a reliability coefficient of .96 and a standard deviation of 15, then

$$s_M = 15\sqrt{1 - .96} = 15\sqrt{.04} = 3$$

What does the standard error of measurement tell us? It tells us something about how accurate an individual's score is on a test. We have stated that the distribution of error scores approximates a normal distribution. This is a very important concept because it means that we can use what we know about a normal distribution to make statements about the percent of scores that fall between different points in a distribution. Given a student's obtained score, you use the s_M to determine the range of score values that will, with a given probability, include the individual's true score. This range of scores is referred to as a **confidence band.** If we assume that the errors of measurement are normally distributed about a given score and equally distributed throughout the score range, you could be 68 percent confident that a person's true score (the score if there were no errors of measurement) lies within one s_M on either side of the observed score. For example, if a subject has an observed score of 105 on an aptitude test where the standard error of measurement is 3, you could infer at the 68 percent confidence level that the subject's true score lies somewhere between 102 and 108. Or you can state at the 95 percent confidence level that the true score will fall within $+1.96$ (or rounded to 2) s_M of the obtained score (between 99 and 111). You can also use the standard error of measurement to determine how much variability could be expected on retesting the individual. If the subject could be retested on the same aptitude test a number of times, you could expect that in about two-thirds of the retests the scores would fall within a range of 6 points of the observed score, and in 95 percent of retest scores they would fall within a range of 12 points. Figure 9.3 shows (a) the distribution of error scores (standard error of measurement of the test) and (b) the distribution of errors around an obtained score of 105 with $s = 3$.

The standard error of measurement (s_M) and the reliability coefficient (r_{xx}) are alternative ways of expressing how much confidence we can place in an observed score. The reliability coefficients provide an indicator of the consistency of a group of scores or items making up a test. The standard error of measurement provides an estimate of the consistency of an individual's performance on a test. How accurate or precise an estimate of the true score any observed score will provide is indicated by the size of these two indexes of reliability. As the reliabil-

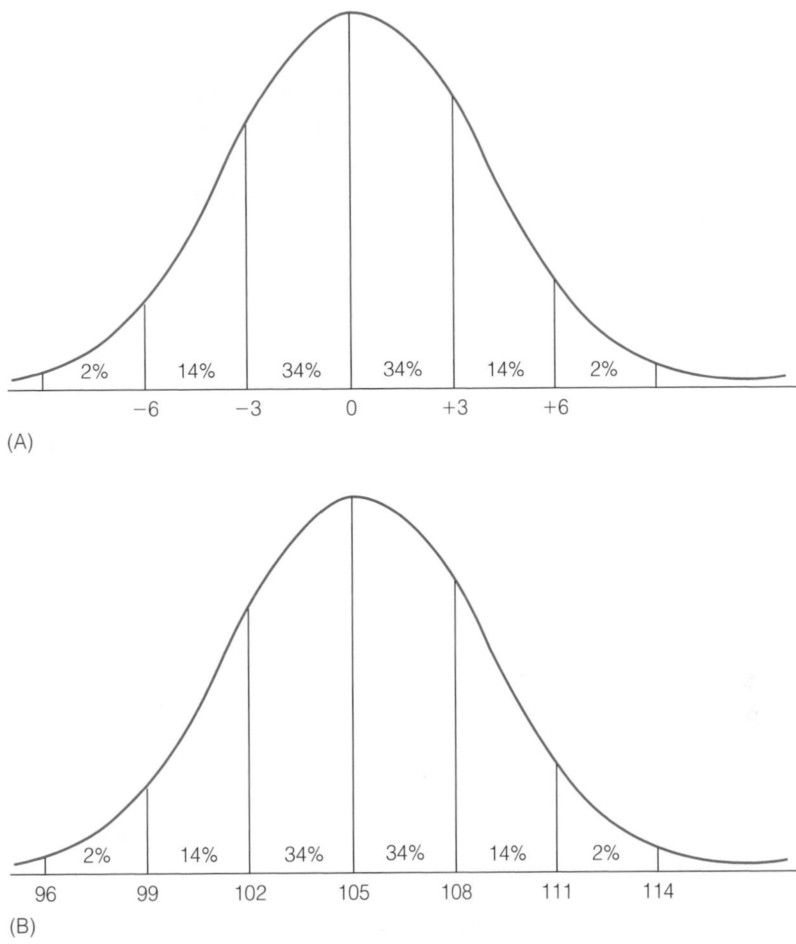

Figure 9.3 (A) The Distribution of Error Scores when $s_M = 3.00$ and (B) the Distribution around an Obtained Score of 105 with $s_M = 3.00$

ity coefficient increases, the standard error of measurement decreases; as reliability decreases, the standard error of measurement increases. Look for a low standard error of measurement or a high reliability coefficient as an indicator of the stability of test scores. No one method of estimating reliability is optimal in all situations. The standard error of measurement is recommended for use when interpreting individual scores and the reliability coefficient for use when comparing the consistency of different tests. You always want scores that are sufficiently consistent to justify anticipated uses and interpretations.

It is meaningless, however, to make a general statement that a test is "reliable." You must report the methods used to estimate the reliability index, the nature of the group from which data were derived, and the conditions under which data were obtained. Potential users of a test then must take responsibility for determining how the reliability data would apply to their population.

THINK ABOUT IT 9.3

a. A standardized test has a reported reliability coefficient of .84 and a standard deviation of 8. Calculate the standard error of measurement for this test.

b. Mary had a score of 100 on this test. Calculate the band within which Mary's true score is likely to fall. (Use the 95 percent confidence level.)

Answers

a. $s_M = s_X\sqrt{1 - r_{xx}}$ $\quad s_M = 8\sqrt{1 - .84} = 8\sqrt{.16} = 8(.4) = 3.2$

b. You can state at the 95 percent confidence level that Mary's true score is between 94 and 106 [$100 \pm (1.96)(3) \approx 100 \pm 6 = 94$ and 106].

RELIABILITY OF CRITERION-REFERENCED TESTS

Developing satisfactory methods for assessing the reliability of criterion-referenced tests has been more difficult. Recall that criterion-referenced tests are used to determine an individual's status with respect to a well-defined set of content objectives. Reliability of this type of test is concerned with the consistency with which this status is estimated. Does the individual have the same level of proficiency on the two administrations of the test? The traditional reliability procedures, such as correlation and K–R 20, are not considered appropriate for criterion-referenced tests because these procedures depend on the variability of the individuals for whom they are computed. On criterion-referenced tests, there is typically little or no variability in scores because training continues until the skill is mastered or nearly mastered. The restricted variability, or spread, of scores will result in low or near-zero estimates of reliability, even though the test may be internally consistent and highly stable.

Several procedures have been suggested for estimating the reliability of criterion-referenced tests. A relatively simple procedure involves administering two equivalent forms of the test, or the same test, on two occasions and finding the consistency of the decisions reached. Researchers determine the consistency of the results by finding the percentage of people for whom the same decision (mastery or nonmastery) is made on both administrations. This index is referred to as the **agreement coefficient** ρ_0.

For example, the results displayed in Table 9.4 were obtained when two equivalent forms of a criterion-referenced test were administered to a sample of 100 students. In this situation, 70 students were consistently classified as masters and 14 students were consistently classified as nonmasters. The agreement coefficient is the proportion of the total subjects consistently classified on the two administrations of the test, or

$$\rho_0 = \frac{b + e}{N} = \frac{70 + 14}{100} = \frac{84}{100} = .84 \qquad (9.10)$$

Table 9.4 Decisions Based on Forms 1 and 2

		Form 1		
		Nonmaster	Master	
Form 2	Master	(b) 70	(a) 10	80
	Nonmaster	(d) 6	(c) 14	20
		76	24	100 (N)

where

ρ_0 = agreement coefficient
a = number classified as masters on both administrations
d = number classified as nonmasters on both administrations
N = total number of subjects

Thus, 84 percent of the subjects were classified consistently, and .84 is the agreement coefficient of this test. If classifications as master or nonmaster are consistent for all examinees on both administrations, the agreement coefficient equals 1, the maximum value.

Some agreement in classifications as master or nonmaster between two administrations is expected merely by chance; that is, even if classifications were made randomly, some individuals would be expected to fall in cells (b) and (c) in Table 9.4. Therefore, we suggest using Cohen's **coefficient kappa**, κ, a statistic that takes *chance agreement* into consideration. The kappa coefficient refers to the proportion of consistent classifications observed *beyond* that expected by chance alone.

The rationale of kappa coefficient is straightforward. First, calculate the percentage of cases expected to have consistent classification even if there were no genuine relationship between the tests—that is, if the classification on the two administrations were completely independent. This index is referred to as the *expected chance agreement*, ρ_c. The expected chance agreement is subtracted from the observed agreement $\rho_o - \rho_c$ to obtain the actual increase over chance consistency; this quantity is then divided by $1 - \rho_o - \rho_c$, the maximum possible increase in decision consistency beyond chance, to yield κ the kappa coefficient. Thus, the expected chance agreement is shown by the following formula:

$$\rho_c = \frac{(a + b)(a + c) + (c + d)(b + d)}{N^2} \quad (9.11)$$

where

ρ_c = proportion of agreement expected by chance

$$\kappa = \frac{\rho_o - \rho_c}{1 - \rho_c} \quad (9.12)$$

where

$$\begin{aligned}\kappa &= \text{proportion of agreement } \textit{above} \text{ that expected by chance}\\ \rho_o &= \text{observed agreement coefficient}\\ \rho_c &= \text{expected chance agreement}\end{aligned}$$

Using the data in the preceding example,

$$\begin{aligned}\rho_c &= \frac{(80)(76) + (20)(24)}{100^2} \\ &= \frac{6080 + 480}{10{,}000} \\ &= .66\end{aligned} \qquad \begin{aligned}\kappa &= \frac{.84 - .66}{1 - .66} \\ &= \frac{.84}{.34} \\ &= .53\end{aligned}$$

You can see that the kappa coefficient (.53) provides a lower estimate of reliability than the agreement coefficient (.84). This is always the case, except when agreement is perfect ($\rho_0 = 1.00$) because the kappa formula begins with ρ_0 and then adjusts for expected chance agreement. The agreement coefficient and kappa require two administrations of a test. There are techniques available for estimating these coefficients from a single test administration. The simplest procedure, however, is to use tables developed by Subkoviak (1988) that permit you to read directly the approximate value of the agreement coefficient or the kappa coefficient after just one administration of a criterion-referenced test.

Another coefficient that is not inflated by chance agreement and yields results similar to kappa is phi(ϕ):

$$\phi = \frac{bc - ad}{\sqrt{(a + b)(c + d)(a + c)(c + d)}}$$

In our example,

$$\begin{aligned}\phi &= \frac{(70)(14) - (10)(6)}{\sqrt{(10 + 70)(14 + 6)(10 + 14)(10 + 6)}} \\ &= \frac{980 - 60}{\sqrt{(80)(20)(24)(76)}} = \frac{920}{\sqrt{2{,}918{,}400}} \\ &= \frac{920}{1705.33} = .54\end{aligned}$$

Note how close phi (.54) and kappa (.53) are. The advantage of phi is that it is a mathematical simplification of the Pearson r (believe it or not) and therefore is a measure of effect size. If you go to Chapter 13, you will find that a Pearson r of .5 is considered to indicate a strong effect size.

RELIABILITY OF OBSERVATIONAL DATA

Reliability is also important in measuring instruments that require ratings or observations of individuals by other individuals. The researcher in these cases must determine the reliability of the ratings—whether different judges/observers have given similar scores or ratings to the same behaviors. A simple way to determine the reliability of ratings is to have two or more observers independently rate the same behaviors and then correlate the observers' ratings. The resulting correlation is called the interrater or interobserver reliability. If the behaviors to be observed are well defined and the observers well trained, the reliability of the observations should be positive and quite high (around .90).

Take the case of two individuals who have rated several students in a performance assessment where the ratings run from 1 (very poor) to 10 (excellent). Here reliability can be assessed through correlational procedures in the same way these procedures are used in test–retest or alternate-forms reliability. The second observer serves the same function as a retest or an alternate form in a paper-and-pencil test. When the scores are only 1 or 0 (behavior occurred versus behavior did not occur), the kappa (Formula 9.12) can be used to assess the reliability of the observers' scores. These procedures are also useful when training observers. Trainees watch and score a videotape that has been scored by an experienced observer, and the agreement coefficient, or kappa, indicates the correspondence between a trainee and the experienced observer. The trainer can go through the tape with the trainee to determine when and why the trainee misclassified observations.

The phi coefficient may also be used to assess the agreement of observers scoring 0 and 1, especially if you want to determine effect size. An extensive discussion of reliability procedures in behavioral observations may be found in Suen and Ary's book (1989).

VALIDITY AND RELIABILITY COMPARED

Validity is a more important and comprehensive characteristic than reliability. Because it is more difficult to measure systematic error than random error, evaluating validity is more challenging. Published research studies often report much more reliability data than validity data. Validity is not obtained as directly as reliability. Assessing validity involves accumulating a great deal of evidence to support the proposed interpretations of scores. The conceptual framework indicates the kinds of evidence that you need to collect to support the meaning and interpretation of test scores. You must answer questions about the appropriateness of test content, the adequacy of criteria, the definitions of human traits, the specification of the behavioral domain, the theory behind the test content, and so forth. All these matters involve judgment and the gathering of data from many sources.

Reliability, in contrast, can be investigated directly from the test data; no data external to the measure are required. The basic issues of reliability lend themselves easily to mathematical analysis, and reasonable conclusions about the amount of error can be stated in mathematical terms.

If a measure is to yield valid score-based interpretations, it must first be reliable. The reliability of an instrument determines the upper limit of its validity. Scores on a test with zero reliability are entirely random and therefore cannot

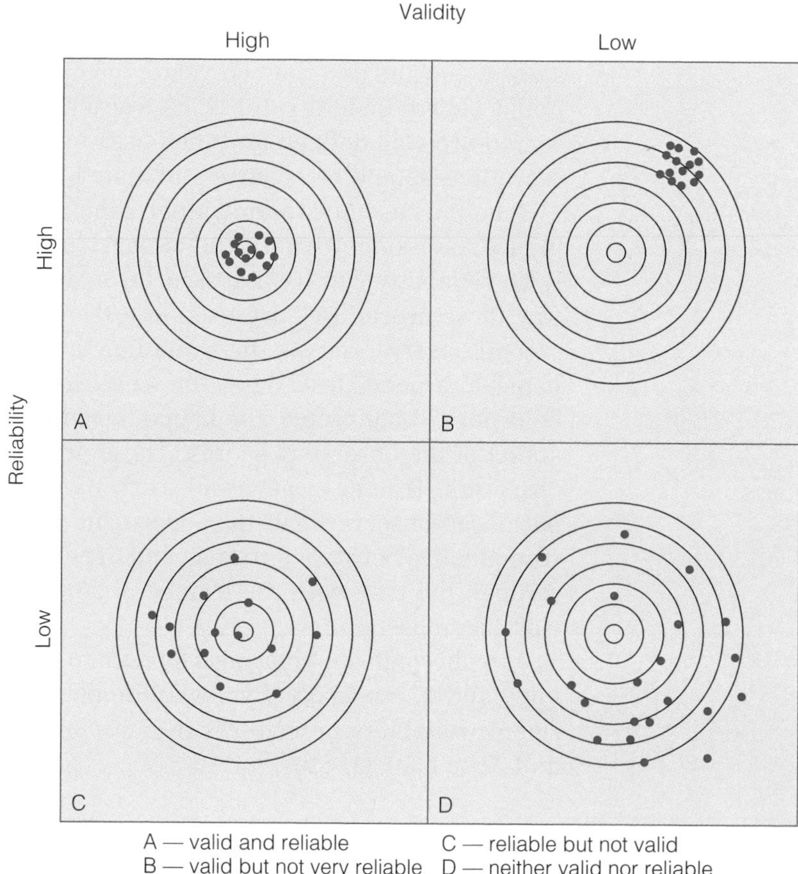

Figure 9.4 Four Rifles Tested by Aiming at Bullseye and Pulling Trigger

Source: http://highered.mcgraw-hill.com/sites/dl/free/0072415444/22503/06044/jpg/. Reproduced with permission of the McGraw-Hill Companies, 2005.

correlate with any criterion. The possible correlation of an instrument with any possible criterion increases as the reliability of the instrument increases. Remember, however, that a measure can have reliability without providing valid interpretations; it can consistently measure the wrong thing. Feldt and Brennan (1989) emphasize the primacy of validity in evaluating the adequacy of an educational measure by stating, "No body of reliability data, regardless of the elegance of the methods used to analyze it, is worth very much if the measure to which it applies is irrelevant or redundant" (p. 143).

Table 9.5 shows an excerpt from the 15th *Mental Measurements Yearbook* (Plake, Impara, & Spies, 2003) showing the kind of validity and reliability data available on published tests. In this case, the test is the Pre-Kindergarten Screen (PKS) designed "to be a quick screening instrument for children between the ages of 4 years 0 months and 5 years 11 months who may be at risk for early academic difficulty" (p. 686). The technical section is from the test manual and the commentary is from an expert the Buros Institute asked to review the test.

Table 9.5 Example of a Test Review From *Mental Measurements Yearbook*

TECHNICAL. The PKS was administered to 854 children between the ages of 3½ and 6 years, from both urban and rural areas in the Northeast, South and West. The measure was subsequently standardized on 679 children ranging in age from 4–0 to 5–11; 70% of these were Caucasian and 30% represented other ethnicities. Norms tables for conversion of raw scores to standard scores and percentile ranks are provided for 2-month age intervals.

Internal consistency was evaluated using Cronbach's alpha, with obtained coefficients ranging from a low of .68 to a high of .83; corrected split-half reliabilities ranged from a low of .67 to a high of .90. The standard error of measurement, another measure of reliability, ranged from a low of 6.18 to a high of 8.49. Interrater reliability was examined across four raters and 12 children for a total of 48 ratings; a concordance rate of 92% was obtained, with examiners rating 9 of the 12 children in identical fashion. Correlations of .99 to 1.0 were also obtained for all possible pairs of examiner ratings. Test–retest reliability was examined for a group of 58 children, ranging in age from 4–0 to 5–11 years, who were tested on two occasions, with intervals between test administrations ranging from 115 to 135 days. An overall temporal stability coefficient of .78 was obtained, with subtest coefficients ranging from .25 to .89.

Content validity of the PKS was evaluated by a group of 12 experts in preschool assessment and instruction. Construct validity evidence was based on expected increases in PKS scores by age. Discriminative validity evidence was obtained through a comparison of scores obtained by three groups of kindergarten students with varying academic needs; results indicated statistically significant differences among mean scores, indicating that the PKS is able to discriminate adequately between the highest and lowest functioning children as well as between the lowest functioning children and those in early intervention programs.

Finally, the predictive validity of the PKS was examined by comparing children's pre-kindergarten PKS scores to (a) their kindergarten outcomes and (b) their teachers' identification of the highest and lowest performing students. On the first comparison, the PKS was able to accurately classify 98.7% of a group of 392 children, and on the second comparison, it was able to accurately classify 91.2% of 125 students.

COMMENTARY. Internal consistency is no more than adequate and the test has an undesirably large standard error of measurement. Interrater reliability is relatively high but was based on a sample of only 12 children. Test–retest reliability is unimpressive, even at the 5-year-old level, when it would be expected to be at its highest. Additional subtest items, and therefore, a longer test, may improve reliability. Construct, discriminative, and predictive validity evidence is encouraging; however, evidence of concurrent validity would have been useful for practitioners, as would more information about the content validation performed by domain experts.

Source: B. Plake, J. Impara, and R. Spies (Eds.), *The fifteenth mental measurements yearbook* (Lincoln: Buros Institute of Mental Measurements, 2003): 687–688.

SUMMARY

Choosing from the multiplicity of measuring instruments available to the researcher requires the use of criteria for the evaluation of these instruments. The two most important criteria for measuring devices are validity and reliability.

Validity is the extent to which theory and evidence support the proposed interpretations of test scores for an intended purpose. In the process of assessing validity, the researcher gathers various types of supporting evidence from many sources. Three types of evidence are gathered: (1) content-related evidence, which assesses how well the instrument samples the content domain being measured; (2) criterion-related evidence, which assesses how well the instrument correlated with other measures of the variable of interest; and (3) construct-related evidence, which assesses how well the instrument represents the construct of interest.

The researcher must also ask how consistently does the test measure whatever it does measure? This is the issue of reliability. No test can permit meaningful interpretations unless it measures consistently—that is, unless it is reliable. Reliability refers to the extent to which the test is consistent in measuring whatever it does measure. Specifically, reliability refers to the extent to which an individual scores nearly the same in repeated measurements, as indicated by a high reliability coefficient. Reliability coefficients can be computed in various ways, depending on the source of error being considered. The reliability coefficient shows the extent to which random errors of measurement influence scores on the test. The standard error of measurement, another index of reliability, enables researchers to employ the normal curve to estimate the limits within which a subject's true score can be expected to lie.

Different types of reliability coefficients are required for norm-referenced and criterion-referenced tests. Establishing reliability of the latter is more problematic, but two procedures that have been used for criterion-referenced tests were presented in this chapter. Procedures are also available for determining the reliability of observations.

KEY CONCEPTS

agreement coefficient
alternate-forms technique
coefficient (Cronbach) alpha
coefficient kappa
coefficient of equivalence
coefficient of reliability
coefficient of stability
coefficient of stability and equivalence
concurrent validity evidence
confidence band
construct-irrelevant variance
construct-related evidence of validity
construct underrepresentation
content-related evidence of validity
convergent evidence of validity
criterion-related validity evidence
discriminant evidence of validity
equivalent-forms technique
evidence based on internal structure
evidence based on response processes
evidence based on test content
internal-consistency procedures
interobserver reliability
interrater reliability
known-groups technique
Kuder–Richardson formulas
parallel-forms technique
predictive validity evidence
reliability
reliability coefficient
Spearman–Brown prophecy formula
split-half reliability coefficient
standard error of measurement
test–retest reliability coefficient
true score
validity
validity coefficient

EXERCISES

1. Compare *validity* and *reliability* with respect to the following:
   a. The meaning of each concept
   b. The relative importance of each concept
   c. The extent to which one depends on the other
2. Explain the statement: A measuring device may be reliable without being valid, but it cannot be valid without being reliable.
3. How would you propose to gather evidence to support the use of a new scholastic aptitude test that had been developed for use with high school seniors?
4. You have been asked to assess the validity of an instrument designed to measure a student's academic self-concept (i.e., the way he or she sees himself or herself as a student). How would you go about this task?
5. What source of evidence supporting the proposed interpretation of test scores is indicated in each of the following situations?
   a. The high school language proficiency test scores of college dropouts and college persisters are compared in order to determine whether the test data correlated with the subjects' college status.

b. A new scholastic aptitude test is found to have a correlation of .93 with the SAT, which has been used to predict college success.

c. A new intelligence test has been developed. The author argues that the mental processes required by the test are congruent with the Z theory of intelligence. Furthermore, he shows that among children the average score on the test increases with each year of age.

d. A teacher carefully examines a standardized achievement test to see if it covers the knowledge and skills that are emphasized in the class.

e. The mean difference between the rankings of members of the Ku Klux Klan and members of the Americans for Democratic Action on the liberalism scale was found to be highly significant.

f. A mathematics test is judged by a group of teachers to be an adequate and representative sample of the universe of test items.

g. Students are asked to verbalize how they solve mathematics problem-solving items.

6. Identify the type of procedure for estimating reliability that is illustrated in each of the following:

a. The same test was given twice to a certain group. The correlation between the scores on the two administrations of the test was .90.

b. The group's scores on the odd items of a test were correlated with their scores on the even items of the same test: $r_{xx} = .95$.

c. Alternate forms of the test were administered after one month, and results of the two administrations were correlated: $r_{xx} = .85$.

d. The variance, the mean, and the number of items are used to estimate reliability.

7. How would you account for the differences in the reliability coefficients in Exercise 6, assuming that the groups tested were the same?

8. How would you gather evidence for the validity of a reading readiness test?

9. What can you do to increase reliability when constructing a test?

10. Indicate the source of evidence that might be most relevant for assessing validity of the following types of tests:

a. A classroom history test

b. An instrument to measure achievement motivation

c. A measure designed to identify potential dropouts

d. A group intelligence test

e. A reading readiness test

11. Explain how a mathematics achievement test could be judged to have high validity in one mathematics class and low validity in another mathematics class.

12. Criticize the following statement: The reliability of the intelligence test is .90. Therefore, you can assume that the test scores can be interpreted as measuring intelligence.

13. Determine the standard error of measurement for a test with a standard deviation of 16 and a reliability coefficient of $r_{xx} = .84$. How would you interpret this standard error of measurement?

14. Select a standardized achievement test that you might use in a research study and obtain the necessary validity data on this test. (You may use Buros *Mental Measurements Yearbook* and the manual that accompanies the test you select.)

15. Check the test manual for the achievement test being used in your school. What type of reliability data are reported there?

16. The following data were obtained when two forms of a criterion-referenced test in mathematics were given to a group of elementary school children. There were 50 items on each form. To pass, a student had to get 80 percent correct on each form. Express the reliability of this test in terms of the kappa coefficient (κ).

Examinee	Form 1	Form 2
1	45	47
2	43	48
3	45	31
4	39	39

Examinee	Form 1	Form 2
5	39	48
6	34	37
7	46	46
8	48	49
9	43	38
10	36	46
11	45	48
12	38	39
13	44	45
14	31	34
15	42	48

17. Criticize the following procedures used to gather validity evidence:

a. A high school English teacher developed a writing test for identifying talented high school students and administered the test to her senior English classes. On the basis of high scores, students were permitted to enroll in an English class at the local university. At the end of the semester the teacher correlated the original test scores with the grades the students earned in the college English class. The teacher was surprised to find a negligible correlation. What was the problem?

b. A school counselor developed a scale to measure need for academic achievement in elementary school children. The scale was administered to two classes of elementary school children, and the results were given to the teachers of these children. The teachers were asked to observe these children carefully for one semester, after which they were asked to rate the children on their need for achievement. The teachers' ratings were then correlated with the scores the children received on the scale. The correlation was quite high, so the counselor concluded that the scale had high validity for measuring need for achievement. Do you agree with the counselor's conclusion?

18. Assume that you wanted to investigate teacher "burnout." Suggest some indicators of this construct that you might use in developing a scale for this purpose.

19. What type of reliability estimate would be most appropriate for the following measuring instruments?

a. A multiple-choice achievement test will be used as the dependent variable in an experimental study.

b. A researcher will study changes in attitude and will administer one form of an attitude scale as both the premeasure and the postmeasure.

c. A researcher has two forms of an achievement test; she administered one form at the beginning of the study and the other at the conclusion of the study. She wants to determine the reliability of the test.

20. A 100-item test was split into two halves, and the split-half coefficient of correlation was found to be .60. Calculate the reliability coefficient for the full-length test.

21. Using a 10-point scale, two judges gave the following ratings to the essays written by a group of students. Calculate an index that indicates the reliability of this rating procedure.

	Judge 1	Judge 2
Kata	10	9
Ashok	8	7
Mary	7	10
Kwaku	9	8
Anil	6	5
Ester	4	3

22. Indicate whether each of the following practices would increase or decrease reliability?

a. The teacher decides to give a weekly quiz instead of one big test at the end of the grading period.

b. Jane Smith brags about her difficult tests where a large percentage of students fail.

c. On Friday afternoon, Miss Jones postponed the big exam until the following Monday when she heard about the big football game after school that day.

d. The teacher decided to add 10 easy test items that everyone could answer correctly.

e. The teacher wrote items having a wide range of difficulty, with most items answered correctly by 40 to 70 percent of students.
f. To save time, Ms. White had the students do only two of the subtests from a standardized test instead of taking the complete test.
g. The teacher decided to give 25 spelling words on the weekly test instead of 10.

23. The following are some comments often heard from students following exams. To what test characteristic are the comments most directly related?
   a. The test measured minute details, not the important concepts emphasized in class.
   b. The test was too long for the time available.
   c. That material was not even covered in class.
   d. The reading level was so complex that the test was really a measure of reading comprehension, not math.
   e. Many students were observed to be cheating.
   f. What does this test have to do with choosing students for the advanced chemistry class?

24. You have the following technical information from two tests:

Test	Mean	Reliability	SD
A	50	.75	6
B	50	.91	15

On which test would a student's score be expected to fluctuate the most on repeated administrations?

25. What are the sources of error that affect the reliability of a test? Give an example of each.

26. The following types of reliability coefficients were calculated for a test. Which coefficient do you think would be highest? Explain why.
   a. Test–retest (one month)
   b. Parallel forms (1 week)
   c. Split-half

ANSWERS

1. Validity is the extent to which an instrument measures what it is designed to measure. Reliability is the extent to which an instrument is consistent in measuring whatever it is measuring. Validity is considered a more important aspect than reliability because lack of validity implies lack of meaning. However, an instrument cannot be valid without first being reliable.
2. A measure may produce consistent scores (reliability) yet may bear no relationship to other accepted measures of the construct or not be able to predict behavior associated with the construct (validity). Scores on a test with zero reliability are entirely random and therefore cannot correlate with any criterion. The extent of reliability sets an upper limit on possible validity.
3. You first must define what is meant by *aptitude*. If you wish to measure general academic ability, gather evidence about its content by examining the test items for representativeness. Do they assess the basic academic skills of reading, spelling, math, and so on? Gather evidence about the correlation between the test scores and senior-year GPA, freshman-college GPA, and other criteria. Correlation with other validated aptitude test scores could also be done.
4. The items of the scale or questionnaire would need to cover aspects of the student behavior that would logically be a part of the construct *academic self-concept* (e.g., I intend to go to college). Criterion measures could be personal interviews with students or independent assessment by teachers. Assuming academic self-concept is related to achievement, self-concept scores could be correlated with GPA and/or achievement test scores.
5. a. Evidence based on correlation with other variables
   b. Evidence based on correlation with other variables
   c. Evidence is construct related
   d. Evidence based on content
   e. Evidence based on known-groups technique

f. Evidence based on content
g. Evidence based on response processes (construct related)

6. a. Test–retest reliability
b. Split-half reliability
c. Alternate-forms with time lapse reliability
d. Internal consistency (Kuder–Richardson formula 21)

7. Split-half reliabilities tend to be higher than test–retest reliabilities because subject variability due to maturation, increase in testing skill, and other random factors is less. Equivalent-forms reliability is lower than same-test reliability because (a) it is impossible to construct exactly equivalent forms and (b) there is an added source of variability when nonidentical forms are used. The internal consistency reliability will be depressed if the test is not homogeneous.

8. You would first identify which specific skills (e.g., letter recognition, left-to-right orientation) comprise reading readiness and then determine if the test incorporated these skills in appropriate proportions. When subjects who have taken the test have begun their reading programs, you would determine how scores on the test and on subtests correlate with reading test scores, teachers' ratings, and other criteria.

9. Rewriting ambiguous items, using items of appropriate difficulty and clarifying instructions will increase reliability. Making a test longer by including additional items drawn from the same universe increases reliability, as does testing on a more heterogeneous group.

10. a. Evidence based on content
b. Evidence based on internal structure of test, correlation with other criteria of achievement motivation, and performance of contrasted groups
c. Evidence based on relationship with some criteria
d. Evidence based on internal structure of the test and relationships with appropriate criteria
e. Evidence based on internal structure of the test and relationship with appropriate criteria of reading achievement

11. A mathematics test that covered only computation would have little validity in a class that stressed concepts and reasoning. If content and emphasis of a different class match the content and emphasis of the test, the test will have high validity in that class.

12. A test can be reliable without measuring what it intends to measure. To determine validity, you need to look at content, constructs, and relations with other measures of the same construct as well as relations with measures of behavior assumed to be correlated with the construct.

13. By Formula 9.9, you interpret the standard error of measurement as a standard deviation. Thus, you can say that there are two chances in three that the individual's true score will fall in the range of 66.4 score points from the observed score.

$$\begin{aligned} s_M &= s_x\sqrt{1 - r_{xx}} \\ &= 16\sqrt{1 - .84} \\ &= 16\,(.4) \\ &= 6.4 \end{aligned}$$

14. Answers will vary.

15. Answers will vary.

16. A score of 40 represents mastery ($50 \times .80 = 40$).

		Form 1		
		Nonmaster	Master	
Form 2	Master	(b) 2	(a) 7	9
	Nonmaster	(d) 4	(c) 2	6
		6	9	15

$$p_0 = \frac{7 + 4}{15} = \frac{11}{15} = .73$$

(73% of the students were classified consistently)

$$p_c = \frac{(9)(9) + (6)(6)}{15^2} = \frac{81 + 36}{225} = \frac{117}{225} = .52$$

$$\kappa = \frac{.73 - .52}{1 - .52} = \frac{.21}{.48} = .44$$

17. a. Selecting just high scorers restricted the variability. The restricted variability lowered the coefficient of correlation.
    b. There was criterion contamination. Letting the teachers see the results of the original measurement of need for achievement contaminated their ratings of the children on need for achievement.
18. There are a number of possible indicators of teacher burnout. You could look at absenteeism from school, lower evaluations by supervisors, incidences of hostility toward students or supervisors, and incidences of challenging of school policies. You might also develop a scale to measure attitudes toward their work; from teachers' own responses to appropriate questions, you might infer the presence of burnout.
19. a. You would be interested in the internal consistency of this one form of the test. A split-half, alpha, or Kuder–Richardson reliability coefficient would be appropriate.
    b. With one form to be used as both a pre- and postmeasure, you would compute a coefficient of stability.
    c. With two forms and two administrations, you would compute the coefficient of stability and equivalence.
20. $r_{xx} = \dfrac{2(.60)}{1 + .60} = .75$
21. Pearson $r = .78$
22. a. Increase
    b. Decrease
    c. Increase
    d. No effect
    e. Increase
    f. Decrease
    g. Increase
23. a. Validity
    b. Reliability
    c. Validity
    d. Validity
    e. Reliability
    f. Validity
24. Fluctuation would be greater on test B because the standard error of measurement is larger. (Calculate the standard error of measurement for each test.)
25. (a) The test itself (too short or ambiguous items); (b) administration of the test (poor directions, distractions during test); and (c) test taker (illness, fatigue, lack of motivation).
26. Split-half because it measures only fluctuation from one-half of the test to another. There is no time lapse; thus only one source of error.

INFOTRAC COLLEGE EDITION

Use the keywords *validity-construct* to locate an article that focuses on the construct validity of some measuring instrument. What procedures were used to investigate construct validity? What conclusions were reached about the validity of that instrument for measuring the construct under consideration?

Chapter 10

Experimental Research

OBSERVATION IS A PASSIVE SCIENCE, EXPERIMENTATION AN ACTIVE SCIENCE.
CLAUDE BERNARD

INSTRUCTIONAL OBJECTIVES

After studying this chapter, the student will be able to:

1. Describe characteristics of experimental research.
2. Distinguish between the independent variable and levels of the independent variable.
3. Explain the concept of control and its importance in experimental research.
4. Distinguish between true control groups and comparison groups in experimental research.
5. Define internal and external validity.
6. Identify threats to internal validity and strategies for avoiding or minimizing them.
7. Identify internal-validity problems in research proposals and reports.
8. Describe the difference between random selection and random assignment and show how they are related to internal and external validity.

An **experiment** is a scientific investigation in which the researcher manipulates one or more independent variables, controls any other relevant variables, and observes the effect of the manipulations on the dependent variable(s). An experimenter deliberately and systematically introduces change and then observes the consequences of that change. Only research problems that permit a researcher to manipulate conditions are appropriate for experimental research. The goal of experimental research is to determine whether a causal relationship exists between two or more variables. Because the experiment involves control and careful observation and measurement, this research method provides the most convincing evidence of the effect that one variable has on another.

Early scientists learned the value of observation in the study of our environment but soon realized that nature's complexity could not always be understood through simply observing its many events. They found that events occurring in their "natural" state were often so complicated by irrelevant factors that the operation of the factor they wished to study was obscured. They solved the difficulty by controlling the conditions under which it occurred, so that the irrelevant factors were eliminated. Then they could deliberately manipulate the independent variables of interest and measure the changes in the dependent variables that resulted from changes in the independent variables. In other words, they began to perform experiments.

Because the application of experimental methods was fruitful in investigating the physical world, investigators applied these methods to other fields. The 19th century saw these methods introduced into the biological sciences, and great advances were made in zoology, physiology, and medicine. Toward the end of the 19th century, scholars began to apply the same methods to psychological problems, thus beginning experimental psychology. In the 1890s the experimental method was first used to study an educational problem. Rice's (1897) investigation of spelling achievement in the schools marks the first attempt at educational field experimentation. Thorndike (1924) and other early investigators extended the experimental method to education.

In its simplest form an experiment has three characteristics: (1) an independent variable is manipulated; (2) all other variables that might affect the dependent variable are held constant; and (3) the effect of the manipulation of the independent variable on the dependent variable is observed. Thus, in an experiment the two variables of major interest are the independent variable and the dependent variable. The *independent variable* is manipulated (changed) by the experimenter. The variable on which the effects of the changes are observed is called the *dependent variable*, which is observed but not manipulated by the experimenter. The dependent variable is so named because its value is hypothe-

THINK ABOUT IT 10.1

Which of the following questions would be appropriate for experimental research?

1. Do students who have 40 minutes of spelling each day score higher on spelling tests than those who have 20 minutes of spelling each day?
2. What do elementary teachers think about retaining low achievers?
3. Are first-born children higher achievers than their younger siblings?
4. Do teachers who are given in-service training in test construction do a better job of evaluating their students than those who are not given the in-service training?

Answers:

Questions 1 and 4 because the independent variables can be manipulated.

sized to depend on, and vary with, the value of the independent variable. For example, to examine the effect of different teaching methods on achievement in reading, an investigator would manipulate method (the independent variable) by using different teaching methods in order to ascertain their effect on reading achievement (the dependent variable).

CHARACTERISTICS OF EXPERIMENTAL RESEARCH

There are three essential requirements for experimental research:

1. Control
2. Manipulation
3. Observation and measurement

CONTROL

Control of variables is the essence of the experimental method. When a study is completed, researchers want to attribute the outcome to the experimental treatment. To do this, researchers must eliminate all other possible explanations.

That is, they must *control* the influence of all variables except the one under investigation. Without control it is impossible to evaluate unambiguously the effects of an independent variable or to make inferences about causality. Let us examine briefly this concept of control in experimentation.

Basically, the experimental method of science rests on two assumptions regarding variables (Mill, 1846): (1) If two situations are equal in every respect except for a variable that is added to or deleted from one of the situations, any difference appearing between the two situations can be attributed to that variable. This statement is called the **law of the single independent variable**. (2) If two situations are not equal, but it can be demonstrated that none of the variables except the independent variable is significant in producing the phenomenon under investigation, or if significant variables other than the independent variable are made equal, then any difference occurring between the two situations after introducing a new variable (independent variable) to one of the systems can be attributed to the new variable. This statement is called the **law of the single significant variable**.

The purpose of control in an experiment is to arrange a situation in which the effect of a manipulated variable on a dependent variable can be investigated. The conditions underlying the law of the single variable are more likely to be fulfilled in the physical sciences than in education. For example, Robert Boyle was able to apply this principle in formulating his law about the effect of pressure on the volume of a gas: When temperature is held constant, the volume of a gas varies inversely with the pressure on it. Likewise, Jacques Charles formulated a law dealing with the effect of temperature: When pressure is held constant, the volume of a gas varies directly with the temperature. Because educational research is concerned with human beings, many variables are always present. To attempt to reduce educational problems to the operation of a single variable is not only unrealistic but perhaps even impossible. Fortunately, such rigorous control is not absolutely essential because many aspects in which situations differ are irrelevant to the purpose of the study and thus can be ignored. It is sufficient to apply the law of the single *significant* independent variable. For example, in a study of the different effects of two methods of teaching arithmetic, an experimenter would wish to have two groups of children who are identical in every respect except the way in which they are taught arithmetic. Because it is impossible to have two absolutely identical groups of children, the experimenter seeks to establish two groups that are as similar as possible with respect to the variables that are related to arithmetic achievement, such as reading ability, motivation, general intelligence, and the like. Other variables that are highly unlikely to be related to arithmetic, such as athletic ability, height, shoe size, or color of hair, are ignored. Although the law of the single variable cannot be followed absolutely, the experiment endeavors to approximate it as closely as possible in all relevant variables. Therefore, in experimental studies in education you need procedures that permit you to compare groups on the basis of significant variables. A number of methods of control have been devised to make such comparisons possible.

Let us assume that you wish to test the hypothesis that children taught by the inductive method (group A) show greater gains in learning scientific concepts than children taught by the deductive method (group B). To draw a conclusion concerning the relationship between teaching method (independent variable) and the learning of scientific concepts (dependent variable), you must control for the effects of any extraneous variables. An **extraneous variable** is a variable that is not related to the purpose of the study but may affect the dependent variable. In this experiment, aptitude is a factor that certainly affects the learning of scientific concepts; therefore, it would be considered a relevant extraneous variable that you must control. Otherwise, if the children in group A had more aptitude than those in group B, the greater gains in learning by group A could be attributed to aptitude and therefore you could not properly evaluate the effects of the teaching method on learning. Aptitude has confounded the relationship between the variables in which you are interested. The term **confounding** refers to the "mixing" of the variables extraneous to the research problem with the independent variable(s) of the research study in such a way that their effects cannot be separated. It could not be clearly stated whether the relation found is (1) between the independent variable and the dependent variable of the study, (2) between the extraneous variables and the dependent variable, or (3) a combination of (1) and (2). Eliminating confounding by controlling for the effect of extraneous variables is the only way to rule out other possible explanations of any observed changes.

In the preceding experiment, the best way to control for aptitude is to randomly assign subjects to the two groups. You could put the names of all the available subjects in a hat and randomly draw one name at a time, assigning the first to group A and the second to group B, the third to A, the fourth to B, and so on. Random assignment increases the probability that the two groups of subjects will be similar on any relevant extraneous variables such as aptitude, gender, socioeconomic level, motivation, and so on and will differ only in their exposure to the independent variable.

MANIPULATION

The **manipulation of an independent variable** is a deliberate operation performed by the experimenter. In educational research and other behavioral sciences, the manipulation of an independent variable involves setting up different *treatment* groups or conditions. In research, treatment is another word for the experimental manipulation of the independent variable. The different treatment conditions administered to the subjects in the experiment are the *levels* of the independent variable. In a study on the effect of using computer simulations on the learning of science concepts, you have one independent variable with two levels: computer simulation and no computer simulation. Do not confuse one independent variable having two levels for two independent variables. The levels represent two or more values of an independent variable and may involve differences in *degree* or differences in *kind*, depending on the nature of the manipulation. An independent variable whose levels differ in degree or amount involves manipulation in the extent of the independent variable. In contrast, manipulation may involve independent variables with levels that differ in kind. For example, assume an experimenter is interested in the effects of a stimulant on college students' learning of nonsense syllables. The researcher would begin by specifying the stimulant to be used and the amount to be administered. If the researcher is interested in the effect of the stimulant amount on learning, he or she would perhaps set up three levels of the independent variable: high, medium, and low dosage. Or the researcher could compare the effects of one stimulant with another stimulant, or with nothing at all. In this case, the levels differ in kind.

Other examples of independent variables where the levels might differ in amount are sleep deprivation or money used as an incentive. Independent variables, such as different teaching methods (lecture versus discussion) or different instructions given to subjects, would have levels differing in kind. The number of levels of an independent variable will equal the number of treatment conditions the experimenter has set up. A researcher may manipulate more than one independent variable in a single study.

OBSERVATION AND MEASUREMENT

After the researcher has applied the experimental treatment, he or she must observe to determine if the hypothesized change has occurred. Researchers use various means of measuring the change in the dependent variable. Some changes can be observed directly, whereas other changes are measured indirectly. Learning, for example, is often the dependent variable in educational research. Note that researchers cannot measure learning directly. They can only estimate learning through scores on an achievement test or other measures chosen according to the operational definition. Therefore, strictly speaking, the dependent variable is observed scores rather than learning per se. Figure 10.1 illustrates the basic design of an experiment.

EXPERIMENTAL COMPARISON

An experiment begins with an experimental hypothesis, a prediction that the treatment will have a certain effect. The research hypothesis expresses expectations as to results from the changes introduced—that the treatment and no-

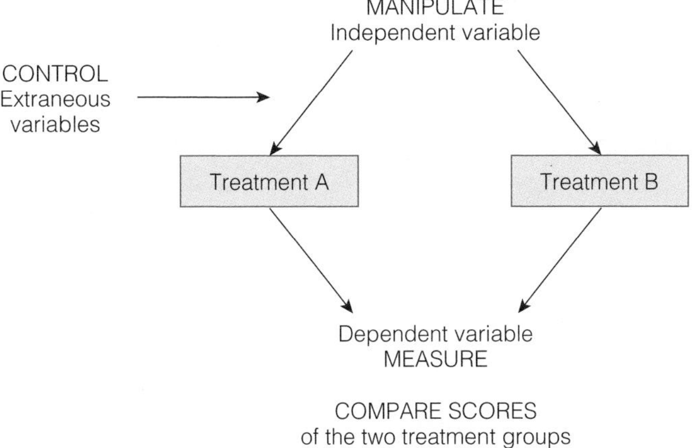

Figure 10.1 Basic Elements of an Experiment

treatment groups will differ because of the treatment's effects. The experiment is planned and carried out to gather evidence relevant to the stated hypothesis. For the simplest experiment, you need two groups of subjects: the **experimental group** and the **control group**. The original definitions designated the experimental group as the one receiving a specific treatment, whereas the control group receives no treatment. Using a control group enables the researcher to discount many alternative explanations for the effect of treatment. For example, a fertilized field might yield a bumper crop only because of benign weather or for other reasons. If equivalent adjacent unfertilized fields yield less, the effect of fertilizer on yield becomes credible.

More common, however, than comparing a treatment group to a group receiving no treatment (*true control group*) is the situation where researchers compare groups receiving different treatments. These are called **comparison groups**. The majority of educational experiments study the difference in the results of two or more treatments rather than the difference in the results of one treatment versus no treatment at all. For example, it would be pointless to compare the spelling achievement of an experimental group taught by method A with a control group that had no spelling instruction at all. Instead, researchers compare groups receiving method A and method B treatments. Comparison of groups receiving different treatments provides the same control over alternative explanations, as does comparison of treated and untreated groups. To simplify subsequent discussions, we will use the term *control group* to refer both to groups with no treatment and to groups with alternative treatments. Comparisons are essential in scientific investigation. Comparing a group receiving treatment with either an equivalent group receiving no treatment or an equivalent group or groups receiving alternative treatment makes it possible to draw well-founded conclusions from the results.

The experimental and control groups must be equivalent in all variables that may affect the dependent variable; they differ only in exposure to the independent variable. After the experimenter has imposed the different conditions on the subjects, he or she measures each subject on the dependent variable.

THINK ABOUT IT 10.2

Match the term on the left with the appropriate term on the right:

1. Outcome variable	**a.** Independent variable
2. Treatment variable	**b.** Extraneous variable
3. Confounding variable	**c.** Dependent variable

Answers

1. c **2.** a **3.** b

Evaluation follows measurement. Is there a difference between the two groups? Is the effect of treatment A different from that of treatment B? This question implies and requires a comparison of the measures of the dependent variable in the first group with the measures of the dependent variable in the other group. The comparison should tell the experimenter whether differences on the dependent variable are associated with differences on the independent variable as represented by the two conditions, A and B.

EXPERIMENTAL DESIGN

The term **experimental design** refers to the conceptual framework within which the experiment is conducted. The experimental design sets up the conditions required for demonstrating cause-and-effect relationships, which is the goal of experimental research. These conditions are: (a) cause precedes effect in time, (b) the cause variable covaries (occurs together) with the effect, and (c) alternative explanations for the causal relationship can be ruled out.

Experimental designs differ in various ways. First, designs differ in the number of independent variables that are manipulated. Some experimental designs have only one independent variable; other designs have two or more. Second, designs differ in the method of assigning subjects to different treatments. In randomized experiments, subjects are randomly assigned to the groups; in other cases, the design uses preexisting groups, or each subject may receive all the treatments. Third, designs also differ in how often dependent variable measures are made and whether all subjects receive all treatments or not. An experimental design serves two functions: (1) It establishes the conditions for the comparisons required to test the hypotheses of the experiment; and (2) it enables the experimenter, through statistical analysis of the data, to make a meaningful interpretation of the results of the study.

The most important requirement is that *the design must be appropriate* for testing the particular hypotheses of the study. The mark of a sophisticated experiment is neither complexity nor simplicity but rather appropriateness. A design that will do the job it is supposed to do is the right design. Does the hypothesis state the expected effect of a single independent variable or the effect of two or more variables and the interaction among them? The first task for the experimenter is to select the design that best arranges the experimental conditions to test the hypotheses of the study.

A second requirement is that *the design must provide adequate control* so that the effects of the independent variable can be evaluated as unambiguously as possible. Unless the design controls extraneous variables, you can never be confident of the relationship between the variables of the study. As you will see, **randomization** is the single best way to achieve the necessary control. Therefore, the best advice is to select a design that uses randomization in as many aspects as possible.

VALIDITY OF RESEARCH DESIGNS

Researchers have to be concerned with the correctness of the inferences they draw about a causal relationship between the variables of the study. In other words, are the inferences drawn from the experiment valid? A very significant contribution to the validity of experiments was made by Campbell and Stanley (1963), who suggested two general categories of validity: *internal validity* and *external validity*. Cook and Campbell (1979) elaborated the previous classification to four types of validity: *internal validity*, *external validity*, *construct validity*, and *statistical conclusion validity*. For a more recent discussion of experimental validity, see Shadish, Cook, and Campbell (2002). Table 10.1 presents the latters' classification of the types of validity.

Validity is not a property of an experimental design but rather refers to the validity of the inferences. Thus, it is not strictly correct to say that an experiment has internal validity or is internally valid, but we may continue to state it that way because of habit.

INTERNAL VALIDITY

Campbell and Stanley (1963) stated that internal validity is the basic requirement if one is to draw correct conclusions from an experiment. **Internal validity** refers to the inferences about whether the changes observed in a dependent variable are, in fact, caused by the independent variable(s) in a particular experimental situation rather than by some extraneous factors. Internal validity is concerned with such questions as: Did the experimental treatment cause the observed change in the dependent variable or was some spurious factor working? Are the findings accurate? These questions of internal validity cannot be answered positively by the experimenter unless the design provides adequate control of extra-

Table 10.1 Four Types of Validity

Internal Validity: The validity of the inferences about whether the effect of variable A (the treatment) on variable B (the outcome) reflects a causal relationship.

Statistical Conclusion Validity: The validity of the inferences about the covariation between treatment and outcome.

Construct Validity: The validity of the inferences about psychological constructs involved in the subjects, settings, treatments, and observations used in the experiment.

External Validity: The validity of the inference about whether the cause–effect relationship holds up with other subjects, settings, and measurements.

Source: From Shadish et al., *Experimental and quasi-experimental designs for generalised causal inference*, Tables 2.1 and 2.2.

neous variables. If the design provides control of variables, you can eliminate alternative explanations of the observed outcome and interpret it as showing an intrinsic relationship between variables. Internal validity is essentially a problem of control. The design of appropriate controls is a matter of finding ways to eliminate extraneous variables that could lead to alternative interpretations. Anything that contributes to the control of a design contributes to internal validity.

Campbell and Stanley (1963) identified eight extraneous variables that frequently represent threats to the internal validity of a research design. These variables are called *threats* because, unless they are controlled, they may very well produce an effect that could be mistaken for the effect of the experimental treatment. If uncontrolled, these extraneous variables raise doubts about the accuracy of the experiment because they permit an alternative explanation of the experimental findings.

Threats to Internal Validity

1. *History.* Specific events or conditions, other than the experimental treatment, may occur in the environment between the beginning of the treatment and the posttest measurement and may produce changes in the dependent variable. Such events are referred to as the **history effect**. In this case, *history* does not refer to past events but to events occurring *at the same time* that the experimental treatment is being applied and that could have produced the observed outcome even without any treatment. These may be major political, economic, or cultural events or some rather minor disruptive factors that occur during the conduct of the experiment. The longer the period of time between the pre- and postmeasurements on the subjects, the greater the history threat becomes.

   Assume that a late summer 2001 study investigated the use of films to change students' attitudes toward immigration. The researchers administer a pretest on September 2 to gauge attitudes, show a series of films over a 2-week period, and then give a posttest to see what changes may have occurred. During those 2 weeks, the tragic 9/11 attacks on our country occur. The effect of the films on students' attitudes would be confounded with the effects of this horrible event, so that the researcher does not know whether the change in attitudes occurred as a result of the films or because of the attacks and the subsequent extensive media coverage. Or, to take another example, during an experiment to measure the effectiveness of a unit on how the stock market works, let us say the stock market drops precipitously and the media devote considerable attention to the stock market. The investigator cannot determine whether the students' greater knowledge at the conclusion of the unit is caused by the unit or by the students' exposure to the media coverage. The effects of the unit and of the students' exposure to the media coverage are confounded, and it is impossible to know how much of the students' learning is caused by the unit and how much by events outside the experiment. In this case, history threatens the internal validity of the research.

2. *Maturation.* The term **maturation** refers to changes (biological or psychological) that may occur within the subjects simply as a function of the pas-

PICTURE THIS

sage of time. These changes threaten internal validity because they may produce effects that could mistakenly be attributed to the experimental treatment. Subjects may perform differently on the dependent variable measure simply because they are older, wiser, hungrier, more fatigued, or less motivated than they were at the time of the first measurements. Maturation is especially a threat in research on children because they are naturally changing so quickly. For example, it can be difficult to assess the effects of treatments for articulation problems among preschoolers because young children often naturally outgrow such problems. It has been difficult to assess the effects of compensatory programs such as Head Start on children's cognitive development because normal development ensures that children's cognitive development will naturally improve over time.

PICTURE THIS

Joe Rocco

3. *Testing*. Taking a test once may affect the subjects' performance when the test is taken again, regardless of any treatment. This is called the **testing effect**. In designs using a pretest, subjects may do better on the posttest because they have learned subject matter from a pretest, have become familiar with the format of the test and the testing environment, have developed a strategy for doing well on the test, or are less anxious about the test the second time around. When an achievement test is used in the research, pretesting is a problem if the same form is used for both the pre- and posttest. We recommend using equivalent forms rather than the very same test. Research has shown that pretesting effects are less threatening in designs in which the interval between tests is large (Menard, 1991).

With attitude and personality inventories, taking a pretest may sensitize the subjects so that they think about the questions and issues raised and subsequently give different responses on the posttest (**pretest sensitization**). For example, assume a researcher administers an attitude scale toward an ethnic group, introduces a diversity awareness program, and then gives a posttest to determine whether attitudes changed. The attitude scale itself may stimulate subjects to think about their attitudes; this self-examination rather than the program itself may lead to improvements in attitudes.

4. *Instrumentation.* The **instrumentation** threat to internal validity is a result of a change in the instruments used during the study. The change in the way the dependent variable was measured from the first time to the second, rather than the treatment, may bring about the observed outcome. Changes may involve the type of measuring instrument, the difficulty level, the scorers, the way the tests are administered, using different observers for pre- and postmeasures, and so on. The best advice is to avoid any changes in the measuring instruments during a study. In classroom research, for example, a teacher should not use a multiple-choice pretest and an essay posttest, and the posttest should not be easier or more difficult than the pretest. Instrumentation is a problem in longitudinal research because the way measures are made may change over a period of time.

5. *Statistical regression.* The term **statistical regression** refers to the well-known tendency for subjects who score extremely high or extremely low on a pretest to score closer to the mean (regression toward the mean) on a posttest, regardless of the treatment. Statistical regression is a threat when a subgroup is selected from a larger group on the basis of the subgroup's extreme scores (high or low) on a measure. When tested on subsequent measures, the subgroup will show a tendency to score less extremely on another measure, even a retest on the original measure. The subgroup will have a mean score closer to the mean of the original group. For example, let us assume that the lowest fourth of the scorers on an English proficiency test are selected for a special experimental program in English. The mean of this group will tend to move up toward the mean of the original population on a second test whether or not an experimental treatment is applied. Similarly, high initial scorers would tend to go down toward the population mean on a second testing.

   Let us illustrate regression with a scattergram (Figure 10.2) that shows the pattern we would get if the correlation of fourth-grade reading test scores and fifth-grade reading test scores is $r = .7$. Each dot represents both z scores for an individual. If you select individuals with a particular z score on the fourth-grade reading test and look at their scores on the fifth-grade reading test, you find that few have the same z score on both tests. If the fourth-grade z score for this subgroup is above the mean, we find that a few of the students score farther above the mean in fifth grade than they did in fourth grade, but the majority of them have z scores closer to the mean and some even fall below the mean.

   For the subgroup with a z score one standard deviation above the mean on X, the mean on Y is $+0.7$; for the subgroup with z scores two standard deviations below the mean on X, the mean on Y is -1.4; the group with a z score of $+2$ on X has a mean z score of $+1.4$ on Y, and so forth. The slanted

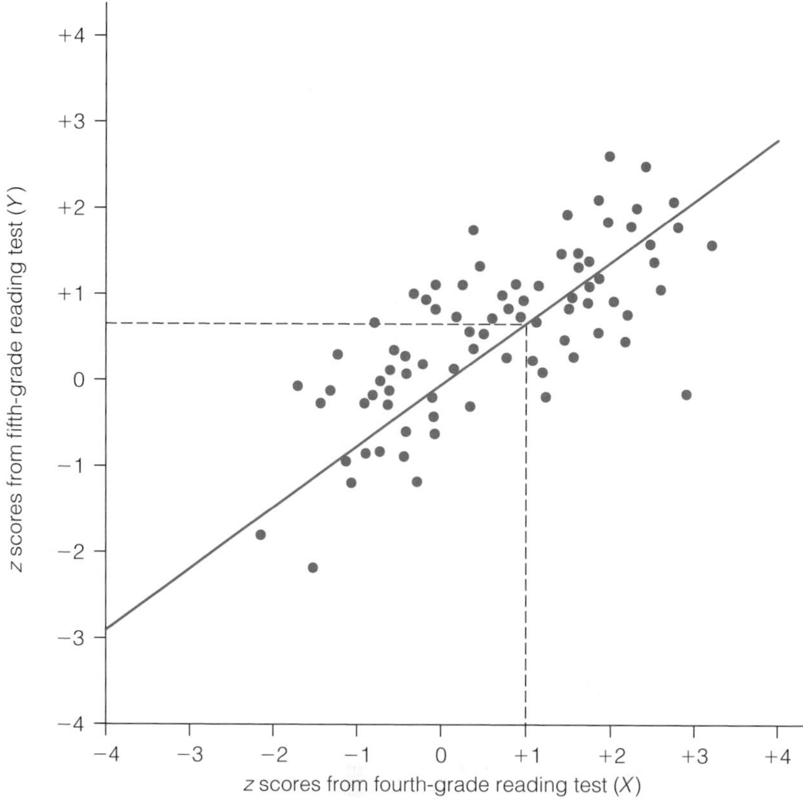

Figure 10.2 Scattergram for Fourth- and Fifth-Grade Reading Test Scores

line on the scattergram connects these means on *Y* for various scores on *X*. Note that for each group with scores above the mean on the fourth-grade reading test, the mean *z* score on *Y* is *lower* on the fifth-grade reading test. For each group with scores below the mean on the fourth-grade reading test, the mean *z* score is *higher* on the fifth-grade reading test. In other words, the average scores for each group move closer to the mean—which is the result of regression.

Regression inevitably occurs when the correlation between two variables is less than perfect. Random error of measurement (Chapter 9) partly explains the imperfect correlation. On a given occasion, high scores will tend to have more positive random error pushing them up, whereas low scores will tend to have more negative random error pulling them down. On the same measure at a later time, or on another measure at the same time, the random error is less likely to be so extreme, and thus the observed score will be less extreme (Shadish, Cook, & Campbell, 2002). An aspect of regression is captured in the adages "When you are at the bottom, you have nowhere to go but up" and "When you are on top, you have nowhere to go but down."

For example, a school establishes a remedial mathematics program and assigns those middle school students who score 2 years or more below

PICTURE THIS

Joe Rocco

grade level on a standardized mathematics test to this program. After a semester the students are given an equivalent form of the standardized test. The majority of them score nearer their grade equivalent and appear to have benefited from the remedial program. Before attributing the gains to the program, remember that when you are at the bottom, you have nowhere to go but up. The lowest scorers on the pretest include those whose scores were depressed because of temporary ill health, emotional problems, inattention, or other random errors of measurement. The majority of these cases would be expected to score better in a subsequent test. Conversely, if those who score highest on any measure are assigned to a special treatment, such as an enrichment program, a posttreatment measure may make it appear that the treatment had a deleterious effect. Those on top have nowhere to go but down.

Because practically none of the variables of interest in education are perfectly correlated, you must always be aware of the effect of regression in designing your experiments. If dealing with extreme scores is an essential part of your research question, the best solution is to select a large group of extreme scorers and then randomly assign these individuals to two different treatments. Regression will occur equally for each group, and you can determine the effect of the treatment unconfounded with regression. You can also reduce regression by using more reliable measures, which are are less influenced by random error of measurement.

6. *Selection.* **Selection** is a threat when there are important differences between the experimental and control groups even before the application of the experimental treatment. This initial difference may account for the result after the experiment that might be attributed to the treatment. Random assignment of subjects to groups controls this selection bias because randomly assigned groups differ only by chance. Selection bias is most likely to occur when the researcher cannot assign subjects randomly but must use intact groups (quasi-experiment). An intact group is a preexisting group such as a class or a group set up independently of the planned experiment. In a learning experiment, if the experimental group is more intelligent than the control group, the former would be expected to perform better on the dependent variable measure even without the experimental treatment. As you will see later, there are ways to control this threat so that intact classes can be used in research.

   Selection is also a threat when volunteers are used. People who volunteer for a study may differ in some important respects from nonvolunteers. If the researcher then compares volunteers with nonvolunteers following the experimental treatment, the researcher does not know if the differences are caused by the treatment or by preexisting differences between the two groups.

7. **Experimental mortality (attrition).** The **experimental mortality (attrition)** threat occurs when there is differential loss of participants from the comparison groups. If a particular type of subject drops out of one group during the course of the experiment, this differential loss would result in differences on the outcome measure even in the absence of treatment. If, for example, several of the lowest scorers on a pretest gradually drop out of the experimental group, this group will have a higher mean performance on the final measure, not because of the experimental treatment but because the low-scoring subjects are absent when the posttest is administered.

   Assume a counselor wanted to compare the effectiveness of two different marital counseling procedures. She administered a pretreatment measure of marital adjustment to couples who had enrolled in her program, then randomly assigned each couple to procedure A or procedure B. With procedure A, which involved considerable soul-searching and confrontation, only 11 of 20 couples persisted in the program and were available for the posttreatment measure. With procedure B, which was relaxed and less demanding, 18 of 20 couples persisted and were available for the posttreatment measure. The posttreatment mean of procedure A was higher than the mean of the procedure B group. This may be evidence that procedure A is

PICTURE THIS

Joe Rocco

more effective, but it may also be evidence that only those couples who were highly motivated to improve their marriage persisted in the program, whereas the posttreatment scores for procedure B included less motivated couples.

Attrition is not usually a serious threat unless the study goes on for a long time or unless the treatment is so demanding that it results in low-performing subjects dropping out.

8. *Selection–maturation interaction.* Some of these threats may interact to affect internal validity. For example, **selection** and **maturation** may interact in such a way that the combination results in an effect on the dependent variable that is mistakenly attributed to the effect of the experimental treat-

ment. Such interaction may occur in a quasi-experimental design where the experimental and control groups are not randomly selected but instead are preexisting intact groups, such as classrooms. Even though a pretest may indicate that the groups are equivalent at the beginning of the experiment, the experimental group may happen to have a higher rate of maturation than the control group, and the increased rate of maturation accounts for the observed effect. More rapidly maturing students are "selected" into the experimental group, and the **selection–maturation interaction** may be mistaken for the effect of the experimental variable.

A group who elected to take a freshman honors English class, for instance, may show more vocabulary growth than a group in a regular freshman English class because their vocabulary growth was at a higher rate both before and during their freshman year. A comparison of pretest and posttest differences of the honors and the regular classes might lead you to conclude erroneously that the independent variable was responsible for a difference in gain that is really only caused by selection–maturation interaction. This problem also frequently arises when volunteers are compared with nonvolunteers. The volunteers may be more motivated to make gains on the dependent variable than are the nonvolunteers, and this difference in gains may be mistakenly attributed to the independent variable—as can happen even when the groups are equivalent on a pretest.

Although Campbell and Stanley (1963) originally listed only eight threats to internal validity, Cook and Campbell (1979) suggest that at least three more should be considered.

9. *Experimenter effect.* The threat of **experimenter effect** involves unintentional effects that the researcher him- or herself has on the study. Personal characteristics of the researcher such as gender, race, age, and position can affect the performance of subjects. Sometimes the actual implementation of the experiment inadvertently gives the experimental group an unplanned advantage over the control group. For example, in an experiment comparing the effectiveness of two teaching methods, the more capable teacher may be assigned to the experimental group. Internal validity is threatened if the experimenter has expectations or a personal bias in favor of one method over another. These preferences and expectancies on the part of the experimenter may be unconsciously transmitted to subjects in such a way that their behavior is affected.

   Assume an experimenter is investigating the effectiveness of a new teaching technique that he or she has developed and believes to be superior. If this experimenter is in a position to influence the experiment, he or she may be friendlier or unintentionally behave in a way that improves the performance of the experimental group but not of the control group. An impartial researcher would not necessarily obtain the same findings. Bias could also result if the experimenter who knows which subjects are in which group is asked to rate the performance of these subjects. The experimenter might unintentionally rate the performance of the experimental group higher. Rosenthal (1966) was a pioneer in investigating the experimenter bias effect.

He showed that rats labeled "bright" outperformed "dull" ones simply by convincing experimenters that the labels were correct. The higher scores for the bright rats were caused by experimenter bias rather than any genuine differences between the rats. Experimenter expectancies in research are similar to the Pygmalion effect in education, where teachers' expectancies about student achievement become self-fulfilling prophecies (Rosenthal, 1973).

We should emphasize, however, that this bias effect does not result from any deliberate action on the part of the experimenter to alter data or to get the experiment to come out a certain way. Instead, the effect comes from subtle, nonverbal cues of which the experimenter may not be aware but that can be detected by the participants, influencing their behavior. The best way to reduce experimenter effect is to standardize all procedures or to let other trained individuals (rather than the investigator him- or herself) work directly with the participants in the study. He or she should also refrain from communicating to the people who administer the experimental treatment any information about the hypotheses of the study. For more information on the experimenter effect, see Rosenthal and Rosnow (1991).

10. *Subject effects.* Subjects' attitudes developed in response to the research situation called **subject effects** can be a threat to internal validity. For instance, in a study of the effects of various levels of lighting on worker productivity at the Hawthorne, Illinois, plant of the Western Electric Company, researchers observed that both increases and decreases in light intensity resulted in increased productivity. The researchers concluded, however, that the attention given to the employees and the employees' knowledge that they were participating in an experiment—rather than any changes in lighting—were the major factors leading to the production gains. This tendency for subjects to change their behavior just because of the attention gained from participating in an experiment has subsequently been referred to as the **Hawthorne effect**.

This effect can be a problem in educational research that compares exciting new teaching methods with conventional methods. Sometimes subjects may react to what they perceive to be the special *demands* of an experimental situation. That is, subjects react not as they normally might but as they think the more "important" researcher wants them to act. Research has shown, for instance, that subjects knowing they are in an experiment tolerate more stress or administer more stress to others than they normally would.

The opposite of the Hawthorne effect is the **John Henry effect**.* This effect, also called **compensatory rivalry**, refers to the tendency of control group subjects who know they are in an experiment to exert extra effort and hence to perform above their typical or expected average. They may

*This effect is named for John Henry, the legendary railroad worker, who died trying to show that he could drive steel railroad spikes as fast as a machine. The experiment was testing the machine as a replacement for human workers.

THINK ABOUT IT 10.3

Identify the potential threat to internal validity in each of the following:

1. A teacher wanted to investigate the effectiveness of new teaching materials designed to increase students' math skills. One of her classes used the new materials, and another class used the conventional materials. Both classes took a math skills test at the end of the semester.
2. Three seventh-grade science teachers used different teaching materials (A, B, and C) for a unit on geology. At the end of the unit, all three classes took the same achievement test. The class that used the A materials had significantly higher scores on the test. The teachers concluded that A material was the best one to use in the future.
3. A teacher administered an attitude scale toward underage drinking among high school students. She then shows a video and uses other materials that show the dangers associated with underage drinking. In order to determine the effectiveness of the video and other materials, she later administered another attitude scale to see if students changed their attitudes toward drinking.
4. After administering a pretest and then implementing a new instructional method designed for low performers, a teacher noted that posttest results showed improvement for the low performers while the high performers who received the control condition remained constant.

Answers

1. There may be several threats to internal validity: differential selection (the groups were not equivalent prior to the study); history; experimenter effect (teacher was more enthusiastic about the new materials); diffusion.
2. Differential selection; history; diffusion.
3. Pretesting (students were sensitized by the initial attitude scale, which influenced the way they responded to the video and other instructional materials.
4. Regression (low scorers on test 1 moved up on test 2).

perceive that they are in competition with the experimental group and they want to do just as well or better. Thus, the difference (or lack of difference) between the groups may be caused by the control subjects' increased motivation rather than by the experimental treatment. This effect is likely to occur in classroom research in which a new teaching technique is being compared to a conventional method that may be replaced by the new method. The students in the conventional classroom may want to show that they can do just as well as the students being taught by the new method. Furthermore, the teacher in the control classroom may want to show that the old method is just as good and is motivated to make a special effort. For example, early research on televised classroom instruction showed that the teachers in the regular classroom (control group) made a special effort, so that their students' performance matched or exceeded the performance of

Table 10.2 Threats to Internal Validity

History	Unrelated events that occur between pre- and posttests affect the dependent variable.
Maturation	Changes occur within the participants just as a function of time.
Testing	Exposure to prior test affects posttest.
Instrumentation	Unreliability or a change in the measuring instrument affects result.
Regression	Extremely high or low scorers on a pretest regress toward mean on a posttest.
Selection	Because of selection methods, subjects in the comparison groups are not equivalent prior to study.
Mortality	A differential loss of participants from the groups affect dependent variable.
Selection–maturation interaction	Subjects with different maturation rates are selected into treatment groups.
Experimenter effect	Unintentional bias or behavior of experimenter affects results.
Subject effect	Attitudes developed during the study affect performance on dependent variable.
Diffusion	Participants in experimental group communicate information about treatment to control group, which may affect the latter's performance.

students receiving televised instruction (experimental group). Teachers in the conventional classroom probably felt threatened by this innovation and wanted to show that they could teach better than television.

Another subject effect, called **compensatory demoralization**, occurs when subjects feel they are receiving less desirable treatment or are being neglected. Consequently, they may become resentful or demoralized and put forth less effort than the members of the other group. There may also be a **novelty effect** where subjects react with increased enthusiasm and motivation simply because the experiment involves something new and different.

11. *Diffusion*. **Diffusion** occurs when participants in one group (typically the experimental group) communicate information about the treatment to subjects in the control group in such a way as to influence the latter's behavior on the dependent variable. Or teachers involved with the experimental group may share information about methods and materials with teachers of the control group. Assume the subjects in the experimental group being taught math by an innovative method get so excited about the project that they share information with their friends in the control group. Later the groups may perform similarly on the dependent variable, not because the new method was ineffective but because its effects were disseminated to the control group as well. Diffusion can be controlled by de-emphasizing the fact that an experiment is going on involving differences between the groups.

In summary, the preceding threats to internal validity represent specific reasons why a researcher's conclusions about a causal relationship between variables may be completely wrong. Researchers must systematically examine how each of the threats may have influenced the results of a study. If the threats can be ruled out, researchers can have more confidence that the observed results were caused by the different treatments. Table 10.2 summarizes the threats to internal validity.

DEALING WITH THREATS TO INTERNAL VALIDITY

An experiment should be designed to avoid or at least minimize the effect of threats to internal validity.* The researcher's first efforts must be directed toward controlling for any relevant preexisting differences between subjects used in an experiment. Only in this way can you be fairly confident that any postexperimental differences can be attributed to the experimental treatment rather than to preexisting subject differences. Six basic procedures are commonly used to increase equivalence among the groups that are to be exposed to the various experimental situations: (1) random assignment, (2) randomized matching, (3) homogeneous selection, (4) building variables into the design, (5) analysis of covariance, and (6) use of subjects as their own controls.

RANDOM ASSIGNMENT

Consider the experimenter's task. There is an available supply of subjects who for experimentation are to be divided into two groups that will be treated differently and then compared. In assigning subjects to groups for the experiment, the experimenter needs a system that operates independently of personal judgment and of the characteristics of the subjects themselves. For example, the known high scorers must not all be assigned to group A and the low scorers to group B. A system that satisfies this requirement is **random assignment**. Random assignment is the assignment of subjects to groups in such a way that, for any given placement, every member of the population has an equal probability of being assigned to any of the groups. Chance alone determines whether subjects are placed in the experimental or the control group, thus eliminating selection bias. The term **randomization** is often used as a synonym for *random assignment*. Randomization is the most powerful method of control because only chance would cause the groups to be unequal with respect to any potential confounding variables. For example, Ms. Brown has 1000 subjects available for an experiment but only has sufficient facilities to include 100 in her experiment. She would first randomly select the 100 for the experiment by numbering all the available subjects and using a table of random numbers to select 100 participants. Thus, she avoids creating systematic differences between the subjects in the experiment and the population from which they were selected. She would then use a random assignment procedure such as a coin toss to put subjects into groups for the experiment. If heads comes up for a subject, than that subject goes into one group; if tails comes up, the subject goes into the other group. A coin toss would then determine which of the two groups is to get treatment A and which is to get treatment B or the control condition.

Note that random assignment is not the same thing as random selection. Random selection (see Chapter 7) is the use of a chance procedure to select a sample from a popultion. Random assignment is the use of a chance procedure to assign subjects to treatments.

*Reichart (2000) states that it is better to speak of "taking account of threats to validity" than "ruling out threats" because the latter implies a finality that can rarely be achieved in practice. "Ruling out" threats implies an all-or-none quality in which threats either do or do not apply. But in many cases threats are a matter of degree rather than being absolute.

PICTURE THIS

Joe Rocco

When subjects have been randomly assigned to groups, the groups can be considered statistically equivalent. **Statistical equivalence** does not mean the groups are absolutely equal, but it does mean that any difference between the groups is a function of chance alone and not a function of experimenter bias, subjects' choices, or any other factor. A subject with high intelligence is as likely to be assigned to treatment A as to treatment B. The same is true for a subject with low intelligence. For the entire sample, the effects of intelligence on the dependent variable will tend to balance or randomize out. In the same manner, subjects' differences in political viewpoints, temperament, achievement motivation, socioeconomic level, and other characteristics will tend to be approximately equally distributed between the two groups. The more subjects in the original subject pool, the more likely that randomization will result in approximately equivalent groups.

When random assignment has been employed, any pretreatment differences between groups are nonsystematic, that is, a function of chance alone. Because these differences fall within the field of expected statistical variation, the researcher can use inferential statistics to determine how likely it is that posttreatment differences are due to chance alone.

RANDOMIZED MATCHING

An alternative procedure for assigning subjects to groups is to match individual subjects on as many extraneous variables as one thinks might affect the dependent variable, and then to use some random procedure to assign one member of each matched pair to treatment A and the other to treatment B. This procedure is called **randomized matching**. If the groups are adequately matched on these variables, then there is reasonable assurance that any postexperimental differences can be attributed to the experimental treatment.

Although matching is a method for providing partial control of intersubject differences, you may encounter several difficulties. The first of these is determining what variable(s) to use for matching. Variables such as IQ, mental age, socioeconomic status (SES), age, gender, reading score, or pretest score may be used. The variables on which subjects are matched must be substantially correlated to the dependent variable or else the matching is useless. As a general rule, we suggest that unless the variable correlates .50 or higher with the dependent variable, the variable should not be employed for the matching procedure because it would do little to increase the precision of the study. Ideally, the experimenter would like to match on two or more variables that correlate well with the dependent variable and do *not* correlate significantly with each other. However, when an experimenter tries to match on more than two variables, it becomes almost impossible to find subjects who are well matched on these several variables. Subjects are lost because no match can be found for them.

Another question that arises is how closely to match the subjects on the variable(s). Matching closely increases the precision of the method, but it also increases the number of subjects who cannot be matched. This, of course, reduces the sample size and introduces sampling bias into the study. Subjects for whom matches cannot be found are usually those with high or low scores. Therefore, these subjects would be underrepresented.

The researcher must decide what matching procedure is feasible in each particular situation. The usual method is to use a person-to-person procedure in which an effort is made to locate two people from among the available subjects who score within the prescribed limits. For example, if the matching variable is IQ, then the researcher locates two subjects who are within, say five points of each other on the IQ scale and then randomly assigns one subject to treatment A and the matching subject to treatment B. It would not be too difficult to match subjects on just the IQ variable. But, if gender and social class were also relevant variables, then it would become extremely difficult to find pairs who match on all three variables. The experimenter loses those subjects for whom no match can be found.

Another method of matching is to place all subjects in rank order on the basis of their scores on the matching variable. The first two subjects are selected from the rank order list (regardless of the actual difference in their scores) to constitute the first pair. One subject of this pair is then randomly assigned to treatment A and the other to treatment B. The next two subjects on the list are selected, and again one is randomly assigned to treatment A and the other to treatment B. This process is continued until all subjects have been assigned. It is somewhat simple to match according to this procedure, but it is less precise than the person-to-person method. Note that randomized matching requires that the subjects be matched first and then randomly assigned to treatments. A study where subjects who are already experiencing one treatment are matched with subjects who are already experiencing another treatment cannot be classified as an experimental study. Such studies (discussed in Chapter 11) where matching is present, but random assignment to groups is not present, can lead researchers to erroneous conclusions.

HOMOGENEOUS SELECTION

Another method that can make groups reasonably comparable on an extraneous variable is to select samples that are as homogeneous as possible on that variable. This is called **homogeneous selection**. If the experimenter suspects that age is a variable that might affect the dependent variable, he or she would select only children of a particular age. By selecting only 6-year-old children, for instance, the experimenter would control for the effects of age as an extraneous independent variable. Similarly, if intelligence is likely to be a variable affecting the dependent variable of the study, then subjects would be selected from children whose IQ scores are within a restricted range, say, 100 to 110. This procedure has controlled the effects of IQ. Then the experimenter randomly assigns individuals to groups from the resulting homogeneous population and can be confident that they are comparable on IQ. Beginning with a group that is homogeneous on the relevant variable eliminates the difficulty of trying to match subjects on that variable.

Although homogeneous selection is an effective way of controlling extraneous variables, it has the disadvantage of decreasing the extent to which the findings can be generalized to other populations. If a researcher investigates the effectiveness of a particular method with such a homogeneous sample, say, of children with average IQs, the results could not be generalized to children in other IQ ranges. The effectiveness of the method with children of low intelligence or very high intelligence would not be known, and the experiment would have to be repeated with subjects from different IQ strata.

As with matching, a true experiment requires that the subjects be selected first and then assigned randomly to treatments.

BUILDING VARIABLES INTO THE DESIGN

Some variables associated with the subjects themselves can be built into the experimental design and thus controlled. For example, if you want to control gender in an experiment and you choose not to use the homogeneous selection technique just discussed, you could add gender as another independent variable. You would include both males and females in the study and then use analysis of variance to determine the effects of both gender and the main independent variable on the dependent variable. This method not only controls the extraneous gender variable but also yields information about its effect on the dependent variable, as well as its possible interaction with the other independent variable(s).

Analysis of covariance (ANCOVA) is a statistical technique used to control for the effect of an extraneous variable known to be correlated with the dependent variable. For example, consider an experiment to study the effects of two methods of teaching reading on reading achievement, the dependent variable. Subjects' reading ability before the experiment would be a variable that would certainly be related to the dependent variable of the study. You would expect that those who are good readers to begin with would score well on the reading posttest, whereas those who are poor readers would tend to score more poorly. After randomly assigning half of the subjects to method A and half to method B, you would administer a reading pretest to both groups. At the end of the experiment, analysis of covariance would statistically adjust the mean reading posttest scores for any initial differences between the groups on the pretest. The ANCOVA technique removes the portion of each subject's posttest score that is in common with his or her pretest score. The resulting F value can then be checked for statistical significance. The variable used in ANCOVA to adjust scores (in this case, the reading pretest) is called the **covariate**.

Using this technique, you are not considering a subject's posttest score per se. Instead, you analyze the difference between posttest scores and what you would expect the posttest score to be, given the score on the pretest and the correlation between pretest and posttest.

By removing that portion of the dependent-variable score variance that is systematically associated with pretest variance, the precision of the experiment improves. With part of the variance in the posttest scores that is *not* caused by treatment removed, any difference caused by treatment stands out more clearly. Using a covariate that is related to the dependent variable reduces the likelihood of Type II error.

Achievement pretest scores are often used as covariates, but other measures such as aptitude or attitude scores can also be used. Aptitude test scores or perhaps grade point average could be used in the previous example. To be useful, a covariate must be correlated with the dependent variable. Therefore, baseball throw scores or shoe sizes would not be useful covariates, as they would be expected to have negligible correlation with the reading posttest.

USING SUBJECTS AS THEIR OWN CONTROLS

Still another procedure involves **using subjects as their own controls**—assigning the same subjects to all experimental conditions and then obtaining measurements of the subjects, first under one experimental treatment and then under another. For example, the same subjects might be required to learn two different lists of nonsense syllables, one list with high association value and the other with low association value. The difference in learning time between the two lists is found for each subject, and the average difference in learning time for all subjects then can be tested for significance.

This method of control is efficient when feasible, but in some circumstances it cannot be used. In some types of studies, exposure to one experimental condition would make it impossible to use the subjects for the other experimental condition. You cannot, for example, teach children how to divide by fractions one way and then erase their memory and teach it another way.

In the foregoing experiment, where one group of subjects was used to investigate the relative ease of learning high-association and low-association nonsense syllables, there could be a "learning to learn" effect, and thus whichever list appeared second would have an advantage over the first. Conversely, fatigue or interference effects might result in poorer performance on the second list. In either case you cannot separate the effect of the independent variable and the effect of order on the dependent variable. A useful strategy for this experiment would be to randomly divide the subjects into two groups: one group learning the high-association syllables first, the other learning the low-association syllables first. This would "balance out" the effects of learning to learn or fatigue. However, if learning high-association syllables first helps subjects to learn low-association syllables later, and the reverse is not true, this can confound the interpretation of the results.

CONTROLLING SITUATIONAL DIFFERENCES

The methods discussed in the preceding section are used to control intersubject differences that threaten internal validity. In addition, extraneous variables may operate in the experimental setting to create **situational differences** that can threaten internal validity. If these extraneous situational variables are not controlled in an experiment, you cannot be sure whether it is the independent variable or these incidental differences operating in the groups that are producing the difference in the dependent variable. These uncontrolled extraneous variables whose effects may mistakenly be attributed to the independent variable are called **confounding variables** or **contaminating variables**. For instance, let us assume that an experimenter is interested in the effectiveness of a film in producing changes in attitude toward some issue. One group of children is selected at random from a classroom and sent off to see the film, leaving a comparable group in the classroom. Unknowingly, the experimenter may have set in motion a large number of forces. The children in the control group may be resentful or feel rejected or inferior to the others. Any of these factors could affect the outcome of the study. The difference that the experimenter wants to attribute to the use of the film could really be caused by one of these incidental features. In this case steps must be taken to ensure that the control subjects also see a film of some sort and that both groups, or neither group, know that they are taking part in an experiment. This precaution is necessary in order to control subject effects, such as the Hawthorne effect or compensatory demoralization.

It is very important to control subjects' attitudes in experiments on drugs. For example, in studying the effect of a drug on the performance of a manipulative skill, all subjects must think they are taking the drug. This is managed by using a *placebo*, which is a chemically inert or neutral substance given to subjects to make them believe they are receiving the actual experimental drug. The experimenter gives every subject a substance that appears to be the same. For some subjects this is the drug under investigation and for the remainder it is the placebo. Thus, the expectation of a drug effect is held constant between experimental and control subjects and is therefore eliminated as a confounding variable. Otherwise, just the knowledge that they had been given a drug might lead the experimental subjects to be either extra cautious or quite reckless—and the experimenter would not know whether it was the effect of the drug or the subjects' behavior, or both, that produced the result.

The use of a placebo as just described illustrates what is called a **single-blind experiment**. The subjects are unaware of the treatment condition they are in, although the researcher does know. Sometimes, however, it is necessary to hold the attitudes of the researcher constant for different independent variable levels. This is done by using a **double-blind experimental** procedure in which neither the experimenter nor the subjects knows which kind of treatment the subjects are getting. Double-blind experiments are more difficult to carry out because the nature of the treatment often makes it obvious which is the experimental group. Another consideration is that in a double-blind situation the experimenter must depend on other people to set up the groups, administer the treatment, and record results.

Three methods are commonly used to control potentially contaminating situational variables: hold them constant, randomize them, or manipulate them systematically and separately from the main independent variable. Holding extraneous variables constant means that all subjects in the various groups are treated exactly alike except for their exposure to the independent variable. For instance, in a reading experiment you would need to control the size of the groups because size of group is known to be a factor affecting reading achievement. You must see that the experimental and control groups have the same number of subjects. And you must also control the teacher variable because teacher efficacy and enthusiasm may affect the outcome of any learning experiment. Thus, the same teacher should be used with two teaching methods that are to be compared. In an experiment, the various assistants must follow the same procedures: Use the same instructions, apparatus, and tests and try to assume the same attitudes with all groups. All groups should meet at the same time of day and in the same type of room. You would not want the experimental group to meet during the first period in the morning of a school day and the control group during the last period of the day. Environmental conditions—such as temperature, light intensity, humidity, furniture in the room, and the presence or absence of distracting noises—should be the same for all groups. If you cannot hold conditions constant, as the experimenter you must attempt to randomize or balance out certain situational variables. For instance, if it is not possible to have the same teacher for both treatments, you might randomly assign half of the available teachers to use method A and half to use method B. You could do the same with other experimental conditions, such as apparatus. In this way you randomize situational variables; a variety of extraneous conditions is represented but not allowed to affect the dependent variable systematically.

Another way to control extraneous situational variables is by manipulating them systematically. Many educational experiments must use a sequence of experimental and control conditions to control progressive effects, such as practice and fatigue effects. Experimenters do this by controlling the order in which experimental conditions are presented, through counterbalancing; half the subjects may receive an AB order and the other half a BA order. In this case an extraneous variable is being systematically manipulated. This procedure not only controls the potentially contaminating effect of order but can also estimate the size of the order effect by determining whether the average A and B values obtained in the two sequences are different.

If a researcher believes that class size may influence the effectiveness of a new instructional method, he or she can control that variable by building it into the design as a second independent variable. The design would provide for two levels of the method variable and two levels of class size, as shown here:

		Class Size	
		Small	Large
Method	A		
	B		

The researcher could then determine the effect of the instructional method itself, the effect of class size, and any interaction effect between method and class size. This method for controlling extraneous variables amounts to the same thing as adding more independent variables to the experiment. Although it increases the complexity of the study, the method has the advantage of furnishing additional information about the effect of relevant variables on the dependent variable and their interaction with the main independent variables. The use of this method of control has been increasing since the introduction of computers to handle data analysis in complex studies. Two-way analysis-of-variance designs and more complex analysis-of-variance designs permit the simultaneous investigation of a number of variables considered singly and in interaction—the latter often being the most significant aspect of the study.

STATISTICAL CONCLUSION VALIDITY

Statistical conclusion validity is closely related to internal validity because both are concerned with the relationship between the experimental treatment and the outcome. Statistical conclusion validity is concerned with errors in statistical interpretations, while internal validity is concerned with errors in reasoning about causation. Statistical conclusion validity is defined as the appropriate use of statistics to infer whether the observed relationship between the independent and dependent variables in a study is a true cause–effect relationship or whether it is just due to chance. Even though a study uses randomization and is carefully conducted, statistical errors can occur and lead to incorrect conclusions. Following an experimental treatment, assume we compare the means of the experimental and control groups on the dependent variable. The null hypothesis in this case is that the difference between the population means which the samples represent is zero. We test the null hypothesis and make a statement of the probability that a difference of the size we found would have occurred by chance in a population where the difference is zero. We then report that the result is either statistically significant ($p < .05$) or not significant. Some naive researchers have been known to conclude that a retained null hypothesis indicates that there is no cause-and-effect relationship between the variables. But this conclusion can be wrong, and this is the concern of statistical conclusion validity. Shadish, Cook, and Campbell (2002) state: "Null hypothesis significance testing tells us little about the size of an effect. Indeed, some scientists wrongly think that nonsignificance implies a zero effect when it is more often true that such effect sizes are different from zero" (p. 43).

Experts in the field are now recommending that researchers report their results first as effect size estimates (see Chapter 6) followed by the exact probability level of a Type I error obtained from a null hypothesis significance testing.

THREATS TO STATISTICAL CONCLUSION VALIDITY

The threats to statistical conclusion validity are basically due to inappropriate use of statistics in analyzing the data. The main problem is reaching an erroneous conclusion about the effect of the independent variable on the dependent variable. A researcher may report that a treatment had no effect, but this conclusion is incorrect because of problems with statistical analysis, the measures used, and other features of the study. "In that case, a difference that is real but small may be lost in the statistical noise" (McBurney & White, 2004, p. 179).

The following is a partial list of the threats to statistical validity taken from Shadish, Cook, and Campbell (2002):

1. *Low statistical power*. An experiment with low power may incorrectly conclude that the relationship between treatment and outcome is not significant.
2. *Violation of assumptions of statistical tests*. Violations of assumptions of tests lead to overestimating or underestimating the size and significance of an effect.
3. *Unreliability of measures*. Measurement error weakens the relationship between two variables.
4. *Restriction of range*. Reduced range on a variable usually weakens the relationship between it and another variable.
5. *Extraneous variance in the experimental setting*. Some features of an experimental setting may inflate error, making detection of an effect more difficult.
6. *Inaccurate effect size estimates*: Some statistics systematically overestimate or underestimate the size of an effect.

The reader is referred to Chapter 2 of Shadish, Cook, and Campbell (2002) for a further discussion of statistical conclusion validity.

CONSTRUCT VALIDITY

Experimental research deals with psychological constructs such as intelligence, motivation, learning, personality, self-concept, creativity, attitudes, anxiety, and so on. You may recall from Chapter 8 that such abstract constructs cannot be measured directly; we choose indicators (operational definitions) that we assume represent the construct. In Chapter 9, we discussed construct validity in connection with tests that are used to measure these psychological constructs. We defined construct validity as the extent to which a test is measuring the psychological construct it is intended to measure. Researchers took the next logical step of applying construct validity to experiments, where it is used to refer to the validity of the inferences made about the construct based on the measures used in the study. More specifically, **construct validity of experiments** is defined as the degree to which inferences are warranted from the study's observed persons, settings, and cause–effect operations to the constructs that these instances represent (Shadish, Cook, & Campbell, 2002). You can see that these writers expanded construct validity to include not only the measures but also the treatment, subjects, and settings used in a study.

Let us give some examples of construct validity of treatments, subjects, and settings. Assume a researcher wants to investigate the effect of anxiety on learning a verbal task. The researcher manipulates anxiety by telling the experimental group "the results will influence your grade," "performance on this task is an indicator of your intelligence," or some similar verbal instructions. The control group receives some benign instructions. Construct validity is concerned with how well this manipulation represents the construct (anxiety) that the researcher claims. The researcher may not be manipulating anxiety at all but something else such as need to achieve. The question is: To what extent are the inferences made from this experiment about the effect of anxiety on verbal learning justified?

Construct validity is also concerned with the subjects chosen for an experiment. Continue with the assumption that a researcher wants to study the effect of level of anxiety on a verbal learning task. The researcher could ask teachers to classify the children in their classrooms as "high anxiety" or "low anxiety" based on their observations. Would the teachers' ratings be an acceptable measure of children's anxiety level? We would probably have more faith in the results of a study where a standardized and well-established measure of anxiety were used to classify high- and low-anxiety children. In other words, such a study would have more construct validity.

How does the researcher define the term "disadvantaged"? Studies will define it differently so that one might find very different kinds of children with that label in different studies. To take another example, assume the subjects of a study are people suffering from depression. People labeled "depressed" might differ greatly depending on whether the diagnosis was made by a competent psychologist or by a counselor using only scores from a personality inventory.

There is also concern about the construct representation of the settings for experimental research. It gets somewhat less attention, however, than the construct representations of treatments and subjects, except for research dealing with the effect of environment and culture. Assume a study wishes to investigate the effect of preschool on first-grade achievement and adjustment. Preschools differ greatly—from Head Start to those in public schools, to Montessori, and to other private and very expensive preschools. It would be important to know the characteristics of the setting in order to make valid inferences from the results.

THREATS TO CONSTRUCT VALIDITY

Construct validity is often difficult to achieve because of the large number of theories that might exist to account for the findings of a study. The threats to construct validity concern how well the study's operations match the constructs used to describe those operations.

The potential threats are:

1. *Inadequate explanation of constructs.* A researcher's failure to explain the construct may lead to incorrect inferences about the match between the study's operations and the construct. In some cases, the wrong construct may be used, as when immigrants to our country were labeled "retarded" due to low scores on intelligence tests. The meaning of the low scores would be better described by lack of knowledge of the English language.
2. *Manipulation of the construct.* The construct was not properly manipulated in the study; faulty manipulation may lead to incorrect inferences.
3. *Measure of the construct.* The measures used were not appropriate (poor operational definition), so the construct was not accurately measured.
4. *Reactivity to the experimental situation.* Subjects' perceptions of the experimental situation become part of the treatment construct actually being tested. Recall the Hawthorne effect from the discussion of internal validity.
5. *Experimenter effect.* The experimenter can convey expectations about desirable responses, and those expectations become part of the treatment construct being tested.

PROMOTING CONSTRUCT VALIDITY

Shadish, Cook, and Campbell (2002) suggest ways to improve construct validity of experiments: (1) start with a clear explanation of the persons, setting, treatment, and outcome constructs of interest; (2) carefully select instances that match those constructs; (3) assess the match between instances and constructs to see if any slippage between the two occurred; and (4) revising construct descriptions accordingly. The reader is referred to Shadish, Cook, and Campbell (2002) for a thorough discussion of construct validity.

EXTERNAL VALIDITY OF RESEARCH DESIGNS

External validity refers to the validity of the inferences about whether the findings of the study would generalize to other subjects, settings, and operations. The experimenter asks questions such as: Would the same results occur with other subjects, in other settings, and at other times? Would a teaching method found to be highly effective in Indianapolis be equally effective in Minneapolis? To what populations, settings, experimental variables, and measurement variables can these findings be generalized? Any single study is necessarily performed on a particular group of subjects, with selected measuring instruments and under conditions that are in some respects unique. Yet researchers want the results of a study to furnish information about a larger realm of subjects, conditions, and operations than were actually investigated. To make generalizations from the observed to the unobserved, researchers need to assess how well the sample of events actually studied represents the larger population to which results are to be generalized. To the extent that the inferences about a causal relationship hold over changes in subjects, settings, and treatments, the experiment has external validity. Let us consider how generalization might be affected by (1) variations in subjects, (2) variations in settings, and (3) variations in treatments.

GENERALIZING TO OTHER POPULATIONS

One must use appropriate sampling procedures so that the participants selected for a study accurately represent the population to which the findings are to generalize. A researcher who has found an apparently effective new method of teaching reading to a sample of first-graders would like to infer that this method is superior for other groups of first-graders, perhaps all first-graders in the United States. To be able to make valid generalizations of the sample experimental results to the larger population, the researcher must show that the sample correctly represents that population.

Relevant to this problem is the distinction between the *experimentally accessible population* and the *target population*. The experimentally accessible population is the population of subjects accessible or available to the researcher for his or her study. The target population is the total group of subjects to whom the researcher wants to apply the conclusions from the findings. In the foregoing example, the experimentally accessible population would likely be all the first-graders in the local school district. The target population would be all first-grade students in the United States.

The researcher's generalizations would occur in two stages: (1) from the sample to the experimentally accessible population and (2) from the accessible population to the target population. If the researcher has randomly selected the sample from the experimentally accessible population (all first-graders in the school district), then the findings can be generalized to this larger group with no difficulty. Inferential statistics indicate the likelihood that what was true of the sample is also true of the population from which it was drawn. In the second stage, the researcher wants to generalize from the accessible to the target population (all first-graders in the United States). This type of generalizing cannot be made with the same degree of confidence as the former type. To make such an inference requires a thorough knowledge of the characteristics of both populations. The more nearly similar the accessible and target populations are, the more confidence the researcher has in generalizing from the one to the other. Generalizing from the accessible population to the target population cannot be done statistically—it is a matter of judgment. The researcher must describe the accessible population as thoroughly as possible and point out any ways this population differs from the target population. Then the researcher and the readers of the research report can make intelligent judgments about how likely the results are to generalize to the target population or to other populations. A noneducational example concerns the extent to which the findings from research on new drugs conducted with subjects in a clinical setting are generalizable to the public. We frequently hear of drugs that were thought to be safe and effective following clinical trials later being removed from the market because of their dangerous side effects.

GENERALIZING TO OTHER SETTINGS

Experimenters are also concerned with generalizing the results of their research to other settings. Before generalizing results, consider the environment in which the research was done. If the experimental environment is very different from the environment to which the results are to generalize, then the generalization is weakened.

Obviously, the first requirement is that the experimenter furnish a complete description of the experimental setting involved in the study. Any artificiality in the research setting that would not be present in other situations limits the generalizability of the results. Experiments are often done in laboratory settings where variables such as lighting, noise, and other distractions can be tightly controlled. Such control is desirable for enhancing internal validity but may reduce external validity because it makes the setting unrepresentative of the subjects' real-world environment. For example, could one generalize the findings from subjects watching a violent movie in a lab setting to the effect of watching violence on television over a long period of time?

Even in classroom research without any artificiality, unique features in the setting may influence generalizability of findings. Size and type of school, technology available to the students, library facilities, and so on would influence generalizing to schools with different characteristics. For example, would results found in a spacious, well-equipped classroom generalize to a crowded, ill-equipped classroom? It is important that researchers sufficiently describe the setting so that readers can reasonably judge the generalizability of results.

GENERALIZING TO OTHER TREATMENTS

How would changes in the way the independent variable is manipulated or the way the variables are measured affect the validity of the inferences? In some learning experiments, anxiety has been induced by electric shock and in others by verbal instructions to subjects.

Could we infer that the effects of anxiety on learning are similar in both cases, so that we could generalize from one situation to the other? In a study of the effect of frustration, one study may manipulate frustration by barring children from desirable toys, whereas another may give them unsolvable problems.

THREATS TO EXTERNAL VALIDITY

1. *Selection–treatment interaction.* A major threat to external validity is the possibility of interaction between subject characteristics and treatment. An effect found with certain kinds of subjects may not hold with different subjects. The results of a reading study that used the first-graders enrolled in an affluent suburban school district as subjects might not be the same if first-graders in a rural school district had been the subjects. When two experimentally accessible populations are not representative of the same tar-

get population, seemingly similar studies can lead to entirely different results. A teaching method that works with college students may not work with high school students. Counseling method A may produce better results than method B in inner-city schools, whereas method B is superior in affluent suburban schools. The best method for teaching quantitative reasoning among second-graders may be the worst method among eighth-graders. As the old saying goes, "One man's meat is another man's poison." Again, a thorough description of the accessible population will help other educators judge whether a particular treatment is likely to be "meat or poison" for their populations of interest.

Using volunteers also presents an external validity problem because volunteers are known to have special characteristics that may not be typical of the population to which generalizations are to be made. No one knows how nonvolunteers would be affected by the experimental treatment. Critics have also questioned the use of college students in so much of the experimental research in psychology and the social sciences. How representative are college students? Whether we can generalize the findings from research with college students to larger groups depends partly on the type of research. We might generalize the findings from research on reaction time or the learning of nonsense syllables but not the findings from research on attitudes.

2. *Setting–treatment interaction.* Any interaction of the treatment with the experimental setting may limit the generalizability of the results. An instructional method that was found to be effective in a rural school may not work in an inner-city school.
3. *Pretest–treatment interaction.* Using a pretest, for instance, may increase or decrease the experimental subjects' sensitivity or responsiveness to the experimental variable and thus make the results obtained for this pretested population unrepresentative of effects of the experimental variable on the unpretested population from which the experimental subjects are selected. In this case you could generalize to pretested groups but not to unpretested ones. Assume that you give a group of seventh-graders a questionnaire concerning their dietary habits and randomly divide the group into experimental and control groups. You expose the experimental group to a series of film presentations concerning good eating habits, whereas the control group sees a series of health films unrelated to eating habits (placebo). The dependent variable is derived by observing the children's food selections in an actual free-choice situation. If the experimental group shows a significantly greater preference for healthful foods, you would like to conclude that the films are effective. Before reaching a conclusion, you must consider the possibility that the pretest caused the students to think about their eating habits and "set them up" to respond to the films. The same effect might not have been observed in an unpretested group.
4. *Subject effects.* Attitudes and feelings of the participants (**subject effects**) that develop during a study may influence the generalizability of the find-

ings to other settings. This threat is also called the **reactive effect** because subjects are reacting to the experimental arrangements or to the experience of participating in an experiment. For example, the Hawthorne effect described earlier as an internal validity problem can also be an external validity problem. Subjects' knowledge that they have been selected for an experiment and are being treated in a special way may affect the way they respond to the treatment. This effect weakens generalization to situations where people do not regard themselves as special. Likewise, the John Henry effect results in atypical behavior on the part of control groups that may affect the application of results.

5. *Experimenter effects.* Another threat to external validity is the **experimenter effect**, which occurs when the experimenter consciously or unconsciously provides cues to subjects that influence their performance. The results of the study could be specific to an experimenter with a certain personality or other characteristics. Sometimes the presence of observers during an experiment may so alter the normal responses of the participating subjects that the findings from one group may not be valid for another group or for the broader population, and it would be hazardous to generalize the findings.
6. *Novelty effect.* A **novelty effect** may threaten external validity. A new instructional method may appear to be successful because it leads to excitement and enthusiasm among subjects. Or a new method may appear less effective because it may be disruptive or subjects are employing unfamiliar materials that they have not learned to use effectively before the dependent variable measures are taken.

Table 10.3 summarizes the threats to external validity.

Table 10.3 Threats to External Validity

Selection–treatment interaction	An effect found with certain kinds of subjects might not apply if other kinds of subjects were used. Researcher should use a large, random sample of participants.
Setting–treatment interaction	An effect found in one kind of setting may not hold if other kinds of settings were used.
Pretest–treatment interaction	Pretest may sensitize subjects to treatment to produce an effect not generalizable to an unpretested population.
Subject effects	Subjects' attitudes developed during study may affect the generalizability of the results. Examples are the Hawthorne and the John Henry effects.
Experimenter effects	Characteristics unique to a specific experimenter may limit generalizability to situations with a different experimenter.
Novelty effect	A novel treatment may lead to excitement (or anxiety) among subjects that causes them to respond differently than they would in a normal or real-world situation.

DEALING WITH THREATS TO EXTERNAL VALIDITY

Controlling the threats to external validity is not as straightforward as with internal validity. With the latter, the research design is the significant factor. Before you can assume external validity, you need to examine carefully and logically the similarities and differences between the experimental setting and the target setting with respect to subjects and treatments. A review of the literature would reveal if research on the same question had used other kinds of subjects, settings, or methodology.

The following suggestions can help control threats to external validity:

1. Randomly sample the target population to select subjects for the study and then randomly assign them to treatment groups. If this is not possible because of the population size, then select subjects randomly from the experimentally accessible population and show the similarity of the experimentally accessible population and the target population.
2. Identify the relevant characteristics of subjects in the target population, and determine the impact of these characteristics by incorporating them into the research study. For example, if you want to generalize to ethnically diverse urban high schools, you could include different ethnic groups in the study and look at the performance of each group separately to see if the experimental treatment worked equally well with all groups or if there were differences. This kind of information would help determine the groups of students to whom the results could be generalized. The same could be done with gender, age, educational levels, and other characteristics. Factorial designs enable researchers to assess the effectiveness of the treatment at different levels of other variables such as race, gender, and so on.
3. You can control problems arising from an interaction of treatment with setting by (a) choosing a design that does not use a pretest or (b) using a second control group that will experience an interaction with the researcher just like the experimental and first control group. The interaction arranged for the second control group, however, is interesting but completely unrelated to the dependent variable of the study. If there is a reactive effect brought on by subjects' participation in a research study, then it will be evident in this second control group just as it would be with the experimental group. In a sense, you have controlled for the Hawthorne effect. If the experimental group performs better on the dependent variable measure, then you have some confidence that the effect is caused by the treatment itself and not by the Hawthorne effect.
4. Provide clearly stated operational definitions for all variables related to subjects or setting.
5. Replicate the research study in a new setting. This is a good way to determine if similar results will be found. If you find the same results with other populations and in other settings, you can have reasonable confidence that generalizations are valid.

RELATIONSHIPS AMONG THE TYPES OF VALIDITY

We have discussed four types of validity of concern in experimental research. You may be wondering how one ever designs a study that has appropriate validity. In practice, researchers prioritize and make trade-offs among the validity types. The most important and most discussed trade-off is that between internal validity and external validity. Internal validity has long been considered the sine qua non ("without which, nothing") of experimentation. As an experiment becomes more rigorously controlled (internally valid), its artificiality tends to increase, and it becomes less generalizable and less externally valid. An experiment conducted in a more natural environment such as a classroom may have greater external validity, but its internal validity may be less. Fortunately, internal and external validity are not incompatible. Most researchers would try first to establish internal validity because unless one can show that a treatment has an unambiguous effect in one setting, it is almost pointless to ask if the treatment would cause the same effect in other settings. Researchers attempt to reach a compromise, which amounts to choosing a design that provides sufficient control to make the results interpretable, while preserving some realism so that the findings will generalize.

External validity is also related to construct validity because valid knowledge about the constructs that are involved in a study is important to generalizing the results. And you notice that some of the same threats to internal validity are also threats to construct validity (subjects' reactivity and experimenter effects).

Lastly, internal validity and statistical conclusion validity are related because both are concerned with the relationship between treatment and outcome. A study may be very carefully designed and well-controlled (internal validity), but a statistical error can occur and lead to incorrect conclusions about statistical significance and effect sizes. "Thus, in quantitative experiments, internal validity depends substantially on statistical conclusion validity" (Shadish, Cook, & Campbell, 2002, p. 63).

SUMMARY

Experimentation is the most rigorous and the most desirable form of scientific inquiry. The controlled conditions that characterize the experiment make it possible to identify verified functional relationships among the phenomena of interest to educators. Experimenters who control the conditions under which an event occurs have distinct advantages over observers who simply watch or study an event without control: (1) they can manipulate or vary the conditions systematically and note the variations in results; (2) they can make the event occur at a time when they are prepared to make accurate observations and measurements; and (3) they can repeat their observations under the same conditions, for verification, and can describe these conditions so that other experimenters can duplicate them and make an independent check on the results.

We discussed four types of validity important in experimental research. These four types of validity correspond to four questions that people ask when interpreting a experimental results:

1. Is there a causal relationship between the variables, or would the outcome have been obtained without the treatment? (internal validity)

2. How large and reliable is the covariation between the presumed cause and effect? (statistical conclusion validity)
3. What constructs are involved in the persons, settings, treatments, and measures used in the experiment? (construct validity)
4. How generalizable is the observed causal relationship to other persons, treatments, and settings? (external validity)

We also discussed the factors that threaten the different types of validity of experimental research and how to minimize their influence.

KEY CONCEPTS

analysis of covariance (ANCOVA)
comparison group
compensatory demoralization
compensatory rivalry
confounding
confounding variables
construct validity of experiments
contaminating variables
control group
control of variables
covariate
diffusion
double-blind experiment
experiment
experimental design
experimental group
experimental mortality (attrition)
experimenter effect
external validity
extraneous variable
Hawthorne effect
history effect
homogeneous selection
implementation threat
instrumentation
internal validity
John Henry effect
law of the single independent variable
law of the single significant independent variable
manipulation of independent variable
maturation
novelty effect
population external validity
pretest sensitization
testing effect
random assignment (randomization)
randomized matching
reactive effect
selection
selection–maturation interaction
single-blind experiment
situational differences
statistical conclusion validity
statistical equivalence
statistical regression (as internal-validity problem)
subject effects
using subjects as their own controls

EXERCISES

1. Which type of validity is being referred to in the following questions?
   a. Is there a relationship between a treatment, variable A, and variable B?
   b. If there is a relationship, did variable A cause variable B or would the relationship be obtained in the absence of the treatment?
   c. If it is a causal relationship, what constructs are involved in the cause–effect relationship?
   d. Can we generalize this causal relationship to other persons, settings, and times?
2. What is the difference between random selection and random assignment? How are they related to internal and external validity?
3. Evaluate the following research designs with respect to methods used and the control provided. Make suggestions for improvements if needed.
   a. A researcher wanted to ascertain if homogeneous grouping improves learning in a first course in biology. The researcher designated one of two high schools in a small city to serve as the experimental school and the other as the control. Both schools had about the same number of students in each of four sections of science. In the experimental school, pupils were grouped homoge-

neously on the basis of aptitude and scores on achievement tests in science. In the control school, pupils were placed in sections at random. At the end of the year, all pupils were given a standardized test in biology. Statistical tests showed the experimental group to be superior on the test. The researcher concluded that homogeneous grouping results in greater learning in biology.

b. A history teacher was concerned about her students' lack of knowledge of their state and national governments and of current events. She decided to experiment with some new materials and methods to see if she could obtain improvement. In classes A and B she introduced the new materials and methods. In classes C and D she used the traditional methods. Classes A and B were administered both the pretest and posttest; classes C and D were administered only the posttest. When comparisons were made on the posttest, classes A and B were found to be superior. Their superior performance was attributed to the new materials and methods.

4. Identify the internal validity threat defined in each of the following:

a. The experimental group performs better because they know they are participating in an experiment.

b. Changes occur within subjects over time that may affect the dependent variable.

c. Extraneous events occur during the research that may influence dependent variable.

d. Subjects differ on the dependent variable even before the experimental treatment.

e. Control group perceives itself in competition with the experimental group and tries harder.

f. Learning about the experiment from people in the experimental group may affect the control group's performance on the dependent variable measure.

5. Identify the threats to internal validity in each of the following experimental studies:

a. At the beginning of the school year, an elementary teacher set up reading stations in her room with supplementary reading materials in each. At the end of the year, she reported that the interest of her class in reading was higher than in any of her previous classes. She recommended that all teachers set up reading stations.

b. A researcher wanted to investigate the effectiveness of new teaching materials designed to increase students' verbal skills. One class used the new materials, and another class used conventional workbooks. Both classes were given a test of verbal skills at the end of the semester.

c. A study was conducted in three third-grade classrooms investigating the effect of three methods of teaching math. The teacher could choose the method she wanted to use but could use only one method with her students. At the end of the semester, all the third-graders were given the same math achievement test.

6. Identify the threat to external validity in the following examples:

a. A teacher read research reporting great results from using a particular remedial reading program. She tried the program in her classroom but did not get the same results.

b. A teacher read about a new method of instruction that was very successful with regular classes. The method did not work when she tried it with her special education students.

c. A research journal reported that a new antismoking film had brought about a significant change in students' attitudes. After viewing the film, students expressed many more negative attitudes toward smoking than they had on a prefilm measure. A teacher decided to use the film with his middle school students but did not want to take time to administer the "pretest." He administered an attitude scale following the film but did not find marked negative attitudes toward smoking.

7. What are the threats to internal validity in the following examples?

a. Very obese individuals who go to a weight control clinic will likely show some loss of weight even if the weight control treatment has no effect.
b. A longitudinal study of the effectiveness of a study skills treatment followed a group of college students. The results showed that the seniors had a final mean GPA higher than they had as freshmen.

8. Distinguish the instrumentation threat to internal validity from the testing threat.

ANSWERS

1. a. Statistical conclusion validity
   b. Internal validity
   c. Construct validity
   d. External validity
2. Random selection is using a chance procedure to draw a sample from a population. Because it addresses the question of how well results drawn from a sample can be generalized to the population from which the sample was drawn, it is a strategy for increasing external validity. Random assignment is using a chance procedure to assign the subjects available for an experiment to treatment. It is a strategy for increasing internal validity.
3. a. Because the researcher could not assign students randomly to the high schools, there are several threats to internal validity. Students in the experimental school may have been brighter or have had more background in science than students in the control school. Differences in the quality of teaching biology in the schools have not been controlled. Because the researcher used only schools in a small city, the results of the study could not be generalized to other high schools in different settings. To improve the study, the researcher could compare initial science achievement and aptitude scores for the schools to see if the groups were equivalent before treatment. Using several high schools, with classes within each high school being randomly assigned to experimental conditions, would control for factors specific to a given school.
   b. Classes not randomly assigned may not be equivalent. Pretesting could have been used to determine equivalence but was only given to the experimental groups. The pretesting of the experimental groups alone may have sensitized the groups and influenced the differences found.
4. a. Hawthorne effect (or subject effect)
   b. Maturation
   c. History
   d. Selection
   e. John Henry effect
   f. Diffusion
5. a. Selection, history, and subjects' attitudes
   b. Selection, history, and subjects' attitudes
   c. Without random assignment, groups may not have been equivalent at the beginning. Teachers chose the method they wanted to use; their enthusiasm rather than the method itself may have been the important factor. If one of the methods was very novel, diffusion may have occurred.
6. a. The Hawthorne effect could be a threat in this situation. The students in the original study may have felt special because they were taking part in an experiment, and thus put forth extra effort. The findings did not generalize to a nonexperimental setting.
   b. The threat in this case is an interaction between selection and treatment. Certain characteristics of the students interacted with the treatment to produce an effect that did not generalize to a group with different characteristics.
   c. The threat is the interaction effect of pretesting. The prefilm measure may have sensitized students so that they responded to the film differently than would a group who did not have the "pretest." It was the interaction that brought about the observed change in attitudes. Thus, the results would prob-

ably generalize to other pretested populations but not to unpretested ones. The teacher should have used the pretest.

7. a. Regression
   b. Attrition; the low performers initially may have dropped out of school

8. Instrumentation involves a change in the measuring instrument; testing involves a change in the subject because of exposure to a prior test (pretest).

Use the keyword *experimental* or *research validity* to locate an article that discusses the concept of validity in experimental research.

Chapter 11

Experimental Research Designs

STATISTICAL DESIGNS ALWAYS INVOLVE COMPROMISES BETWEEN THE DESIRABLE AND THE POSSIBLE.
LESLIE KISH

INSTRUCTIONAL OBJECTIVES

After studying this chapter, the student will be able to:

1. Explain the function of a research design.
2. Explain the relationship between research design and internal validity.
3. Define preexperimental design and discuss its limitations.
4. Describe the most common randomized experimental designs and state the advantages of each.
5. Define factorial design and state its advantages.
6. Distinguish between-groups and within-groups experimental designs.
7. Define quasi-experimental design and discuss its limitations.
8. Describe single-subject experimental research and its uses.

A design is the general plan for carrying out the experimental research study. The purpose of the **experimental design** is to enable researchers to estimate the effect of an experimental treatment. The design functions to (1) make sure that the outcome is a consequence of the manipulation of the independent variable and not some spurious factor and (2) to ensure that the subjects assigned to the treatment and control groups do not differ systematically on any variables except those under consideration. Thus, the experimental design has a significant effect on the validity of any conclusions that might be drawn from the research study.

CLASSIFYING EXPERIMENTAL DESIGNS

There are many types of experimental designs. Designs differ in a number of ways, such as their efficiency and their cost in time, money, and other resources. But as Hoyle, Harris, and Judd (2002, p. 237) note, "The major distinction among designs is how effectively they rule out threats to internal validity." In the following discussion, we classify experimental designs as **preexperimental**, randomized experimental, or quasi-experimental, depending on the degree of control provided. Preexperimental designs do not have random assignment of subjects to groups or other strategies to control extraneous variables. **Randomized experimental designs** use randomization and provide maximum control of extraneous variables. **Quasi-experimental designs** lack randomization but employ other strategies to provide some control over extraneous variables. They are used, for instance, when intact classrooms are used as the experimental and control groups. Thus, randomized experiments have the greatest internal validity, the quasi-experimental somewhat less, and the preexperimental designs the least internal validity.

Before we begin discussing some of the different types of experimental designs, we need to introduce the terms and symbols that we will use:

1. X represents the independent variable, which is manipulated by the experimenter; we will also refer to it as the *experimental variable* or the *treatment*.
2. Y represents the measure of the dependent variable. Y_1 represents the dependent variable *before* the manipulation of the independent variable X; it is usually a pretest of some type administered before the experimental treatment. Y_2 represents the dependent variable *after* the manipulation of the independent variable X; it is usually a posttest administered to subjects after the experimental treatment.
3. S represents the subject or participant used in the experiment; the plural is Ss.
4. E group is the experimental group—the group that is given the independent variable treatment.
5. C group is the control group—the group that does not receive the experimental treatment. It receives a different treatment or no treatment at all.
6. R indicates random assignment of subjects to the experimental groups and the random assignment of treatments to the groups.
7. M_r indicates that the subjects are matched and then members of each pair are assigned to the comparison groups at random.

In the paradigms for the various designs, the Xs and Ys across a given row are applied to the same people.

The left-to-right dimension indicates the temporal order, and the Xs and Ys vertical to one another are given simultaneously. A dash (—) indicates that the control group does *not* receive the X treatment or receives an alternative treatment.

THINK ABOUT IT 11.1

An investigator conducted a study to assess the effectiveness of interactive videotape instruction on learning of high school economics. Forty-five students were picked at random and assigned to one of two groups. Group E received interactive videotape instruction; group C received conventional instruction. It was found that the groups did not differ significantly in knowledge of economics on a pretest. An achievement test was given immediately after completion of the study; four weeks later a retention test was given.

	Group	Mean	t	p
Achievement Test	C	97.55		
	E	125.73	4.02	.01
Retention Test	C	90.52		
	E	112.91	2.19	.05

Match the terms on the right with the description given on the left.

1. Pretest knowledge of economics
2. $p = .01$
3. Random assignment to classes
4. Retention of material over a four-week period showed a significant difference in favor of group E.
5. Use of interactive videotape versus conventional instruction

a. Independent variable
b. Control
c. Finding
d. Level of significance

Answers

1. b; **2.** d; **3.** b; **4.** c; **5.** a

PREEXPERIMENTAL DESIGNS

This section presents two designs that are classified as **preexperimental** because they provide little or no control of extraneous variables. We do not recommend these designs; but we realize they are still sometimes used in educational research. We include these poor designs in our discussion simply because they illustrate quite well the way that extraneous variables may operate to jeopardize the internal validity of a design. If you become aware of these sources of weakness in a design, you should be able to avoid them.

Design 1: One-Group Pretest–Posttest Design

The **one-group pretest–posttest design** usually involves three steps: (1) administering a pretest measuring the dependent variable, (2) applying the experimental treatment X to the subjects, and (3) administering a posttest, again measuring the dependent variable. Differences attributed to application of the experimental treatment are then evaluated by comparing the pretest and posttest scores.

Design 1: One-Group Pretest–Posttest Design

Pretest	Independent Variable	Posttest
Y_1	X	Y_2

To illustrate the use of this design, assume that an elementary teacher wants to evaluate the effectiveness of a new technique for teaching fourth-grade social studies. At the beginning of the school year, the students are given a standardized test that appears to be a good measure of the achievement of the objectives of fourth-grade social studies. The teacher then introduces the new teaching technique and at the end of the year administers the standardized test a second time, comparing scores from the first and second administrations of the test in order to determine what difference the exposure to the new teaching method has made.

Because Design 1 involves only one group and one teacher, it would seem to control intersubject differences and situation variables. The control is only superficial, however. The major limitation of the one-group design is that because no control group is used, the experimenter cannot assume that the change between the pretest and posttest is brought about by the experimental treatment. There is always the possibility that some extraneous variables account for all or part of the change. Thus, this design lacks internal validity.

What are some extraneous variables that could produce the change noted between the pretest and posttest scores? Two obvious extraneous variables not controlled in this design are history and maturation. The term *history* as a source of extraneous variance refers to specific events that can occur between pretest and posttest, other than experimental treatment. In the social studies example, widespread community interest in an election, increased emphasis on social studies in the school, or introducing a particularly effective teacher could increase student achievement in this area. Or a flu epidemic causing increased absences could depress achievement. The term *maturation* refers to changes in the subjects themselves that occur over time. Between pretest and posttest, children are growing mentally and physically, and they may have learning experiences that could affect the dependent variable. History and maturation become increasingly influential sources of extraneous variance with longer time intervals between Y_1 and Y_2. Attitude of subjects, implementation, and regression also present uncontrolled threats to internal validity.

Another shortcoming of Design 1 is that it affords no way to assess the effect of the pretest itself. We know there is a practice effect when subjects take a test a second time or even take an alternate form of the test—subjects do better the second time even without any instruction or discussion during the interval. This is true not only for achievement and intelligence tests but also for personality tests. In the case of personality tests, a trend toward better adjustment is generally observed. As we discussed earlier, pretesting is also a problem in research on attitude change. The pretest may result in subjects' becoming aware of issues and thinking about the topic so they become motivated to change attitudes even without the treatment.

Avoid using Design 1. Without a control group to make a comparison possible, the results obtained in a one-group design are basically uninterpretable.

Design 2: Static Group Comparison

Design 2—**static group comparison**—uses two or more preexisting or intact (*static*) groups, only one of which is exposed to the experimental treatment. The subjects are not randomly assigned to the groups. No pretreatment measures are employed. The researcher makes the assumption that the groups are equivalent in all relevant aspects before the study begins and that they differ only in their exposure to X. The dependent-variable measures for the groups are compared to assess the effect of the X treatment. Although this design has sometimes been used in education, it is basically worthless. The achievement of students taught by a new method is compared with that of a supposedly similar class taught by the old method.

Design 2 has a control group or groups, which permits the comparison that is required for scientific respectability. However, there is a basic flaw in this design. Because neither randomization nor even matching is used to assign subjects to the experimental and control groups, we cannot assume that the groups are equivalent prior to the experimental treatment. They may differ on certain relevant variables, and these differences, rather than X, may be responsible for observed change. Because we cannot be sure that the groups are equal in respect to all factors that may influence the dependent variable, we consider this design lacking in the necessary control and must classify it as preexperimental.

Design 2: Static Group Comparison

Group	Independent Variable	Posttest
E	X	Y_2
C	—	Y_2

RANDOMIZED EXPERIMENTAL DESIGNS

The designs in this category require random assignment of subjects to groups. They are the most highly recommended designs for experimentation in education because of the control they provide.

Design 3: Randomized Subjects, Posttest-Only Control Group Design

Design 3—**randomized subjects, posttest-only control group design**—is one of the simplest yet one of the most powerful of all experimental designs. It has the two essential elements necessary for maximum control of the threats to internal validity, namely randomization and a control group. As the name indicates, it requires that subjects be randomly assigned to groups. The groups are then randomly assigned to different conditions. No pretest is used; the randomization controls for all possible extraneous variables and assures that any initial differences between the groups are attributable only to chance and therefore will follow the laws of probability. After the subjects are randomly assigned to groups, only the experimental group is exposed to the treatment. In all other respects the two groups are treated alike. Members of both groups are then measured on the dependent variable Y_2, and the scores are compared to determine the effect of X. If the obtained means of the two groups differ significantly (i.e., more than would be expected on the basis of chance alone), the experimenter can be reasonably confident that the experimental conditions are responsible for the observed result.

The main advantage of Design 3 is randomization, which assures statistical equivalence of the groups before introduction of the independent variable. Recall that as the number of subjects increases, the likelihood that randomization will produce equivalent groups increases. We recommend at least 30 subjects in each group. Design 3 controls for the main effects of history, maturation, regression, and pretesting; because no pretest is used, there can be no interaction effect of pretest and X. Thus, this design is especially recommended for research on attitudes. It is also useful in studies in which a pretest is either not available or not appropriate—as, for example, in studies with kindergarten or primary grades, where it is impossible to administer a pretest because the learning is not yet manifest. Another advantage of this design is that it can be extended to include more than two groups if necessary. Possible threats to internal validity are subjects' attitudes and experimenter effects.

Design 3: Randomized Subjects, Posttest-Only Control Group Design

	Group	Independent Variable	Posttest
(R)	E	X	Y_2
(R)	C	—	Y_2

Design 3 does not permit the investigator to assess change. If such an assessment is desired, then a design (such as Design 5) that uses both a pretest and a posttest should be chosen.

The lack of a pretest could also be a disadvantage if attrition occurs during the study. Without having pretest information, preferably on the same dependent variable used as the posttest, the researcher has no way of knowing if those who dropped out of the study were different from those who continued (Shadish, Cook, & Campbell, 2002).

Design 4: Randomized Matched Subjects, Posttest-Only Control Group Design

Design 4—**randomized matched subjects, posttest-only control group design**—is similar to Design 3, except that it uses a matching technique to form equivalent groups. Subjects are matched on one or more variables that can be measured conveniently, such as IQ or reading score. Of course, the matching variables used are those that presumably have a significant correlation with the dependent variable. Although a pretest is not included in Design 4, if pretest scores on the dependent variable are available, they could be used very effectively for the matching procedure. The measures are paired so that opposite members' scores are as close together as possible; one member of each pair is randomly assigned to one treatment, and the other, to the second treatment. The flip of a coin can be used to achieve this random assignment.

Design 4: Randomized Matched Subjects, Posttest-Only Control Group Design

	Group	Independent Variable	Posttest
(M_r)	E	X	Y_2
	C	—	Y_2

Matching is most useful in studies where small samples are to be used and where Design 3 is not appropriate. Design 3 depends completely on random assignment to obtain equivalent groups. With small samples the influence of chance alone may result in a situation in which random groups are initially very different from each other. Design 3 provides no assurance that small groups are really comparable before the treatments are applied. The matched-subjects design, however, serves to reduce the extent to which experimental differences can be accounted for by initial differences between the groups; that is, it controls preexisting intersubject differences on variables highly related to the dependent variable that the experiment is designed to affect. The random procedure used to assign the matched pairs to groups adds to the strength of this design.

Design 4 is subject to the difficulties that we mentioned earlier in connection with matching as a means of control. The matching of all potential subjects must be complete, and the members of each pair to the groups must be assigned randomly. If one or more subjects were excluded because an appropriate match could not be found, this would bias the sample. When using Design 4, it is essential to match every subject, even if only approximately, before random assignment. Design 4 can be used with more than two groups by creating matched sets and randomly assigning one member of each set to each group.

Design 5: Randomized Subjects, Pretest–Posttest Control Group Design

Design 5 is one of the most widely used randomized experiments. In this design (**randomized subjects, pretest–posttest control group design**)—subjects are assigned to the experimental and control groups by random assignment and are given a pretest on the dependent variable Y. The treatment is introduced only to the experimental subjects (or two different treatments may be compared), after which the two groups are measured on the dependent variable. The researcher then compares the two groups on the posttest. If there are no differences between the groups on the posttest, the researcher can then look at pretest and posttest scores in each group to determine whether the experimental treatment produced a greater change than the alternative or the control situation. The recommended statistical procedure to use in this case is analysis of covariance (ANCOVA) with posttest scores as the dependent variable and pretest scores as the covariate to control for initial differences on the pretest. A less desirable procedure that is sometimes used is to analyze the average change scores ($Y_2 - Y_1$) for each group using a t test or F test. For reasons beyond the scope of this discussion, measurement experts have pointed out that technical problems arise when comparing change scores. Thus, we do not recommend this procedure. Use analysis of covariance, which is more powerful and gives more interpretable results.

Design 5: Randomized Subjects, Pretest–Posttest Control Group Design

	Group	Pretest	Independent Variable	Posttest
(*R*)	*E*	Y_1	*X*	Y_2
(*R*)	*C*	Y_1	—	Y_2

The main strength of this design is the initial randomization, which assures statistical equivalence between the groups prior to experimentation; also, the fact that the experimenter has control of the pretest can provide an additional check on the equality of the two groups on the pretest, Y_1. Design 5, with its randomization, thus controls most of the extraneous variables that pose a threat to internal validity. For example, the effects of history and maturation are experienced in both groups; therefore, any difference between the groups on the *posttest* measure could probably not be attributed to these factors. Differential selection of subjects and statistical regression are also controlled through the randomization procedure. There is one internal validity issue, however. Although both *E* and *C* groups take the pretest and may experience the sensitizing effect, the pretest can cause the experimental subjects to respond to the *X* treatment in a particular way just because of their increased sensitivity. The result is a difference on the posttest that could mistakenly be attributed to the effect of the treatment alone. The crucial question is would the effect of *X* on the experimental subjects be the same without the exposure to the pretest? This problem has been particularly evident in studies of attitude change. When the first attitude scale is administered as the pretest in a study, it can arouse interest or sensitize subjects to the issues or material included in the scale. Then, when the experimental treatment (a lecture, film, or the like) is administered, the subjects may be responding not so much to the *X* treatment as to a combination of their aroused sensitivity to the issues and the experimental treatment.

The main concern in using Design 5 is external validity. Ironically, the problem stems from the use of the pretest, an essential feature of the design. As mentioned earlier, there may be an interaction between the pretest and the treatment so that the results are generalizable only to other pretested groups. The responses to the posttest may not be representative of how individuals would respond if they had not been given a pretest.

Let us consider an example. Suppose that one criterion for the success of a new teaching method in high school social studies is the number of students who report that they read newspapers such as the *New York Times*. During the course itself, no special emphasis is placed on this particular source; but it, along with several other papers of somewhat less repute, is made available to students. If the study uses a pretest–posttest design, the pretest questionnaire might include an item such as "Do you read the *New York Times* for daily news?" This question alone may be enough to sensitize the experimental students to that newspaper, so when it becomes available during the course, they will be more likely to pick it out from the others. As a result, the experimental group may show greater use of the *New York Times* on the posttest than does the control group—not because of the course content only but because of the combined effect of course content and pretest. A new class taught by the same method, but not pretested and hence not sensitized, may show no greater attentiveness to the *New York Times* than the control group.

Despite this shortcoming, Design 5 is widely used because the interaction between pretest and treatment is not a serious problem in most educational research. The pretests used are often achievement tests of some type and therefore do not significantly sensitize subjects who are accustomed to such testing. However, if the testing procedures are somewhat novel or motivating in their effect, then it is recommended that the experimenter choose a design not involving a pretest. Alternatively, whenever you suspect that the effect of the pretest might be reactive, it is possible to add a new group or groups to the study—a group that is *not* pretested. Solomon (1949) suggested two designs that overcome the weakness of Design 5 by adding an unpretested group or groups. We present these designs next.

Design 6: Solomon Three-Group Design

The first of the Solomon designs uses three groups, with random assignment of subjects to groups. You can see that the first two lines of this design are identical to Design 5. However, this **Solomon three-group design** has the advantage of employing a second control group and thereby overcoming the difficulty inherent in Design 5—namely, the interactive effect of pretesting and the experimental treatment. This second control group, labeled C_2, is *not* pretested but is exposed to the X treatment. Their Y_2 measures are then used to assess the interaction effect.

Design 6: Solomon Three-Group Design

	Group	Pretest	Independent Variable	Posttest
(*R*)	E	Y_1	X	Y_2
(*R*)	C_1	Y_1	—	Y_2
(*R*)	C_2	—	X	Y_2

The interaction effect is assessed by comparing the Y_2 scores for the three groups. Only the posttest scores enter into the analysis. Even though the experimental group has a significantly higher mean on Y_2 than does the first control group (C_1), the researcher cannot be confident that this difference is caused by X. It might have occurred because of the subjects' increased sensitization after the pretest and the interaction of their sensitization and X. However, if the Y_2 mean of the second control group (C_2) is also significantly higher than that of the first control group, then you can assume that the experimental treatment, rather than the pretest–X interaction effect, has produced the difference because the second control group is not pretested. This group, although receiving the X treatment, is functioning as a control and is thus labeled C_2.

Design 7: Solomon Four-Group Design

Design 7 (**Solomon four-group design**) provides still more rigorous control by extending Design 6 to include one more control group. This fourth group receives neither pretest nor treatment. Again group C_3, though receiving the X treatment, is functioning as a control group.

Design 7: Solomon Four-Group Design

	Group	Pretest	Independent Variable	Posttest
(R)	E	Y_1	X	Y_2
(R)	C_1	Y_1	—	Y_2
(R)	C_2	—	X	Y_2
(R)	C_3	—	—	Y_2

Design 7 has strength because it incorporates the advantages of several other designs along with its own unique contribution. It provides good control of the threats to internal validity. The first two lines (Design 5) control extraneous factors such as history and maturation, and the third line (Design 6) provides control over the pretest–X interaction effect. When the fourth line is added to make Design 7, you have control over any possible contemporary effects that may occur between Y_1 and Y_2. The last two lines represent Design 3, so actually you have a combination of the randomized subjects pretest–posttest control group design with the randomized subjects posttest-only control group design. In addition to the strengths of each design taken separately, you also have the replication feature provided by the two experiments. This combination takes advantage of the information provided by the pretest–posttest procedure and at the same time shows how the experimental condition affects an unpretested group of *S*s.

In Design 7 you can make several comparisons to determine the effect of the experimental X treatment. If the posttest mean of the E group is significantly greater than the mean of the first control group, C_1, and if the C_2 posttest mean is significantly greater than that of C_3, you have evidence for the effectiveness of the experimental treatment. You can determine the influence of the experimental conditions on a pretested group by comparing the posttests of E and C_1 or the pre–post changes of E and C_1. You can find the effect of the experiment on an unpretested group by comparing C_2 and C_3. If the average differences between posttest scores, $E - C_1$ and $C_2 - C_3$, are about the same, then the experiment must have had a comparable effect on pretested and unpretested groups.

Design 7 actually involves conducting two experiments, one with pretests and one without pretests. If the results of these two experiments agree, as indicated earlier, the investigator can have much greater confidence in the findings.

The main disadvantage of this design is the difficulty involved in carrying it out in a practical situation. More time and effort are required to conduct two experiments simultaneously, and there is the problem of locating the increased number of subjects of the same kind that would be needed for the four groups.

Another difficulty is with the statistical analysis. There are not four complete sets of measures for the four groups. As noted, you can compare E and C_1, and C_2

and C_3, but no single statistical procedure would use the six available measures simultaneously. Campbell and Stanley (1966) suggest working only with posttest scores in a two-way analysis-of-variance design. The pretest is considered as a second independent variable, along with X. The design is as follows:

	No X	**X**
Pretested	Y_2, control 1	Y_2, experimental
Unpretested	Y_2, control 3	Y_2, control 2

From the column means, you can determine the main effect of X; from row means, the main effect of pretesting; and from cell means, the interaction of testing with X.

FACTORIAL DESIGNS

The designs presented thus far have been the classical single-variable designs in which the experimenter manipulates one independent variable X to determine its effect on a dependent variable Y. However, in complex social phenomena several variables often interact simultaneously, and restricting a study to one independent variable may impose an artificial simplicity on a complex situation. The X variable alone may not produce the same effect as it might in interaction with another, so the findings from one-variable designs may be misleading. For instance, we might ask about the effectiveness of a particular method of teaching on students' learning. The answer may well be that the effectiveness depends on a number of variables, such as the age and ability level of the students, the personality of the teacher, the subject matter, and so on. Computer-assisted instruction, for example, may be more effective with slow students than with bright ones or vice versa. A classical one-variable design would not reveal this interactive effect of method and intelligence level. The information yield of an experiment can be markedly increased by ascertaining the simultaneous effects of two or more independent variables in a factorial design. The main advantage of a factorial design is that we can examine interaction effects of multiple independent variables as well as the separate or main effects of those variables by themselves. In fact, some have said that the real breakthrough in educational research came with Fisher's (1925) development of factorial designs.

You have encountered factorial designs as statistical procedures in Chapter 7. We will now consider them as experimental research designs. A **factorial design** is a design in which the researcher can simultaneously assess the effect of two or more independent variables on the dependent variable as well as the effect of the interaction of the two independent variables on the dependent variable. The independent variables may be one of two types: active or attribute. An active independent variable is one that the researcher can manipulate directly. Method of teaching, method of grouping, and reinforcement procedure are examples of active independent variables. An attribute independent variable is one that the researcher cannot actively manipulate. Such variables are individuals' characteristics such as aptitude, achievement, gender, race, age, and social class. Investigators incorporate attribute variables into their research by assigning subjects to groups on the basis of such preexisting variables. The independent variables of either type are known as factors, hence the name factorial design.

Factorial designs are of two types. In the first type of design, only one of the independent variables is experimentally manipulated. In this case the experimenter is primarily interested in the effect of the active independent variable but must consider subjects' attribute variables that may influence the dependent variable. Their influence can be investigated (and at the same time controlled) by building the attribute variable or variables directly into a factorial design. The experimenter assesses the effect of the active independent variable at each of the "levels" of the one or more attribute independent variables. As noted above, the effect of the active independent variable on the dependent variable may depend on the level of the attribute independent variable. That is, the two variables may be found to interact in producing the effect on Y. The different levels of the attribute variable typically represent naturally occurring selected groups of subjects, as when a study uses high achievers and low achievers to determine the effectiveness of an instructional technique. Building the attribute variables into a factorial design not only increases the precision of the experiment but also its generalizability. Because you can determine whether the treatment has comparable effects over all levels or not, the generalizability of the experimental findings is increased. The second type of factorial design permits the random assignment of subjects to one or more active independent variables. For example, one might randomly assign 40 subjects to a lecture class and 40 to work in groups, and then randomly assign 20 of each group to a high-stress condition and 20 of each group to a low-stress condition. In this study, there would be two levels of one variable (lecture vs. group) and two of the second variable (high stress vs. low stress). Such a design permits analysis of main effects for both independent variables as well as analysis of interaction between the independent variables.

Design 8: Simple Factorial Design

Factorial designs have been developed at varying levels of complexity. The simplest factorial design is the 2 × 2, which is read as 2 by 2. In this design, each of two independent variables has two levels.

Design 8: Simple Factorial Design

Variable 2 (X_2)	**Variable 1** (X_1)	
	Treatment A	**Treatment B**
Level 1	Cell 1	Cell 3
Level 2	Cell 2	Cell 4

To illustrate, let us assume that an experimenter is interested in comparing the effectiveness of two types of teaching methods—methods A and B—on the achievement of ninth-grade science students, believing there may be a differential effect of these methods based on the students' level of science aptitude. The experimenter stratifies the population into high- and low-aptitude scores and

Table 11.1 Example of a Factorial Design

	Instructional method (X_1)		
Aptitude (X_2)	Method A	Method B	Mean
High	75.0	73.0	74
Low	60.0	64.0	62
Mean	67.5	68.5	

randomly selects 60 *S*s from the high-aptitude group and assigns 30 *S*s to method A and 30 *S*s to method B. This process is repeated for the low-aptitude group. Teachers are also randomly assigned to the groups. In this hypothetical experiment there are two experimental treatments and two levels of aptitude. Table 11.1 shows the 2 × 2 factorial design for measuring the effects of the two methods of instruction on the learning of students. Note that a 2 × 2 design requires four groups of subjects; subjects within each of two levels of aptitude are randomly assigned to the two treatments.

The scores in the four cells represent the mean scores of the four groups on the dependent variable, the science achievement test. In addition to the four cell scores representing the various combinations of treatments and levels, there are four marginal mean scores: two for the columns and two for the rows. The marginal column means are for the two methods, or treatments, and the marginal row means are for the two levels of aptitude.

From the data given, you can first determine the *main effects* for the two independent variables. We must point out that the term *main effect* does not mean the most important effect but rather the effect of one independent variable ignoring the other independent variable(s). For example, the main effect for treatments refers to the treatment mean scores without regard to aptitude level. If you compare the mean score of the two method A groups, 67.5, with that of the two method B groups, 68.5, you find that the difference between these means is only one point. Therefore, you might be tempted to conclude that the method used has little effect on the achievement scores, the dependent variable.

Now examine the mean scores for the levels to determine the main effect of X_2, aptitude level, on achievement scores. The main effect for levels does not take into account any differential effect caused by treatments. The mean score for the two high-aptitude groups is 74, and the mean score for the two low-aptitude groups is 62; this difference, 12 points, is the effect attributable to aptitude level. The high-aptitude group has a markedly higher mean score; thus, regardless of treatment, the high-aptitude groups perform better than the low-aptitude groups.

A factorial design also permits the investigator to assess the **interaction** between the two independent variables—that is, the different effects of one of them at different levels of the other. If there is an interaction, the effect that the treatment has on learning will differ for the two aptitude levels. If there is no interaction, the effect of the treatment will be the same for both levels of aptitude. From looking at Table 11.1, you can see that the method A mean is higher than the method B mean for the high-aptitude group, and the method B mean is higher for the low-aptitude group. Thus, some particular combinations of treatment and

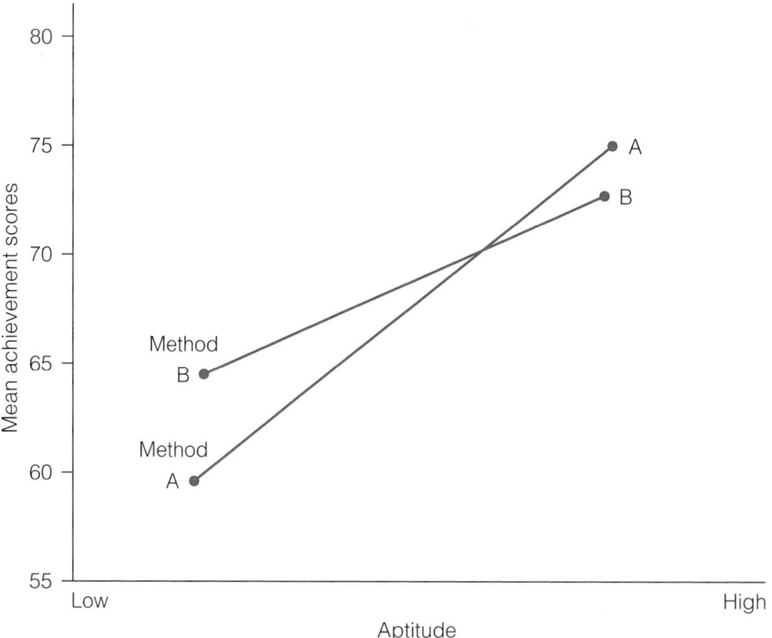

Figure 11.1 Illustration of Interaction between Method and Aptitude Level

level of aptitude interact to produce greater gains than do some other combinations. This interaction effect between method and aptitude levels is shown graphically in Figure 11.1. If this interaction is statistically significant, you conclude that the effectiveness of the method depends on aptitude. Method A is more effective with the high-aptitude students; method B is more effective with the low-aptitude group.

Now examine another set of data obtained in a hypothetical 2 × 2 factorial study. Table 11.2 shows the results of a study designed to investigate the effect of two methods of instruction on achievement. Again, because the investigator anticipates that the method may be differentially effective depending on the aptitude of the subject, the first step is to distinguish two levels of aptitude. The researcher randomly assigns subjects within each level to the two methods. After the experiment, the researcher administers achievement tests and records the scores for every subject. If you compare the mean score of the two groups taught by method B, 53, with that of the two groups taught by method A, 45, you see that the former is somewhat higher. Therefore, method B appears more effective than method A. The difference between the means for the two aptitude levels, on the main effects for aptitude, is 10 (54 − 44). Regardless of treatment, the high-aptitude group performs better than the low-aptitude group. The data reveal no interaction between treatment and levels. Method B appears more effective regardless of the aptitude level. In other words, treatments and levels are independent of each other. The lack of interaction is illustrated graphically in Figure 11.2. It is not possible to demonstrate either the presence or absence of interaction without using a factorial design.

Table 11.2 Example of a Factorial Design

	Treatment (X_1)		
Aptitude (X_2)	Method A	Method B	Mean
High	50	58	54
Low	40	48	44
Mean	45	53	

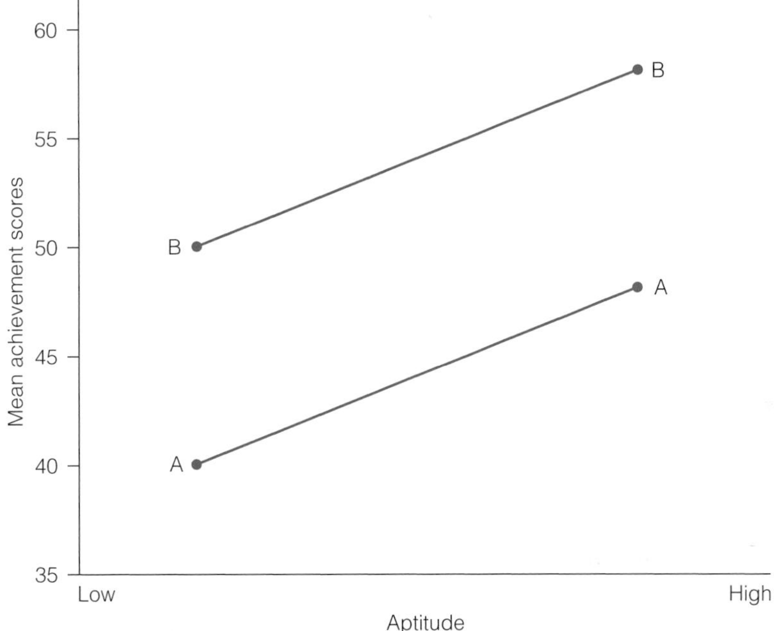

Figure 11.2 Illustration of Lack of Interaction between Method and Aptitude Level

The factorial design can be extended to more complex experiments in which there are a number of independent variables; the numeric values of the digits indicate the number of levels for the specific independent variables. For instance, in a $2 \times 3 \times 4$ factorial design, there are three independent variables with two, three, and four levels, respectively. Such an experiment might use two teaching methods, three ability levels, and four grades. Theoretically, a factorial design may include any number of independent variables with any number of levels of each. However, when too many factors are manipulated or controlled simultaneously, the study and the statistical analysis become unwieldy and some of the combinations may be artificial. The number of groups required for a factorial design is the product of the digits that indicate the factorial design. In the $2 \times 3 \times 4$ design, 24 groups would be required to represent all combinations of the different levels of the multiple independent variables. The mere thought of the complexities involved in arranging for large numbers of subjects under large numbers of conditions will perhaps help the reader to understand why most educational researchers attempt to answer their questions with the simplest possible designs, even though the statistical analysis can be easily handled by com-

THINK ABOUT IT 11.2

Consider the following statements and indicate whether each is true or false.

1. If there is a significant interaction in a factorial design, then at least one of the two main effects also must be significant.
2. A factorial design with two levels of factor A and four levels of factor B would require exactly eight separate groups of subjects.
3. A researcher believes that a special training course will be equally effective for males and females. This researcher is predicting an interaction between training and gender.
4. In a two-factor experimental design, the researcher obtains two separate scores for each subject.
5. Adding an attribute independent variable that is known to be related to the dependent variable can reduce error variance.
6. The mean square within groups is the error term in a 2×2 factorial design.

Answers

1. false; 2. true; 3. false; 4. false; 5. true; 6. true

puter. The advantages of the factorial design are that it accomplishes in one experiment what otherwise might require two or more separate studies, provides an opportunity to study interactions that are often so important in educational research, and provides a more powerful test of hypotheses.

OTHER RANDOMIZED EXPERIMENTAL DESIGNS

The experimental designs we have discussed so far use at least two groups of subjects, one of which is exposed to the treatment (independent variable) and the other that does not receive the treatment or is exposed to another level of the treatment. The researcher then compares the dependent variable scores for the different treatment groups. The essential feature of these designs is that they compare separate groups of subjects in order to determine the effect of the treatment. When the independent variable is manipulated in this way, we have what is called a **between-subjects design**. For example, a researcher who compares reading achievement scores for students taught by one method with scores for an equivalent group of students taught by a different method is using a between-subjects design.

However, the manipulation of an independent variable does not have to involve different groups of subjects. It is possible to use experimental designs where the same participants are exposed to different levels of the independent variable at different times. For example, a researcher might measure the learning of nonsense syllables by one group of students under different levels of anxiety, or the math performance scores of a group of students when music is played in the classroom versus no music. This type of design in which a researcher observes each individual in all of the different treatments is called a **within-subjects design**. It is also called a **repeated-measures design** because the research repeats measurements of the same individuals under different treatment conditions. The main advantage of a within-subjects design is that it eliminates the problem of differences in the groups that can confound the findings in between-subjects research. Remember one is not comparing one group of subjects to another; one is comparing each individual's score under one treatment with the same individual's score under another treatment. Each subject serves as his or her own control. Another advantage of within-subjects designs is that they can be conducted with fewer subjects. The disadvantage of these designs is the carryover effect that may occur from one treatment to another. To deal with this problem, researchers typically arrange for the participants to experience the different treatments in random or counterbalanced order.

Discussion of the different designs for within-subjects experimental research is beyond the scope of this text. Interested readers should consult advanced texts.

QUASI-EXPERIMENTAL DESIGNS

We have looked at various randomized experimental designs all of which require random assignment of subjects. In many situations in educational research, however, it is not possible to randomly assign subjects to treatment groups. Neither the school system nor the parents would want a researcher to decide to which classrooms students were assigned. In this case, researchers turn to quasi-experiments in which random assignment to treatment groups is not used. Quasi-experimental designs are similar to randomized experimental designs in that they involve manipulation of an independent variable but differ in that subjects are not randomly assigned. Because the quasi-experimental design does not provide full control, it is extremely important that the researcher be aware of the threats to both internal and external validity and consider these factors in the interpretation. Campbell and Stanley (1966) stated, however, that quasi-experimental studies are "well worth employing where more efficient probes are unavailable" (p. 205). These designs permit the researcher to reach reasonable conclusions even though full control is not possible.

Design 9: Nonrandomized Control Group, Pretest–Posttest Design

In a typical school situation, schedules cannot be disrupted nor classes reorganized to accommodate a research study. In such a case it is necessary to use groups as they are already organized into classes or other preexisting intact groups.

Design 9 is one of the most widely used quasi-experimental designs in educational research. You can see that it is similar to design 5 but with one important difference; Design 9 does *not* permit random assignment of subjects to the experimental and control groups.

Design 9: Nonrandomized Control Group, Pretest–Posttest Design

Group	Pretest	Independent Variable	Posttest
E	Y_1	X	Y_2
C	Y_1	—	Y_2

A researcher might be allowed to use two sections of freshman English at a high school for a study on vocabulary development. The researcher should select two sections that at least appear to be similar; do not choose a remedial class and an advanced class. Although subjects cannot be randomly assigned, one can flip a coin to determine which of the two intact groups will be the experimental and which the control group. The researcher would give a vocabulary pretest to both classes, administer a program designed to improve vocabulary to the experimental group only, and then give a vocabulary posttest to both groups. If the experimental group shows significantly greater achievement on the posttest, can the researcher conclude that the new program was effective?

Without random assignment of subjects, you do not know if the groups were equivalent before the study began. Perhaps the class designated the experimental group would have done better on the posttest without the experimental treatment. Thus, there is an initial *selection bias* that can seriously threaten the internal validity of this design. The pretest, the design's most important feature, provides a way to deal with this threat. The pretest enables you to check on the equivalence of the groups on the dependent variable before the experiment begins. If there are no significant differences on the pretest, you can eliminate selection as a threat to internal validity and proceed with the study. If there are some differences, the investigator can use ANCOVA to statistically adjust the posttest scores for the pretest differences.

Because both experimental and control groups take the same pre- and posttest, and the study occupies the same period of time, other threats to internal validity such as maturation, instrumentation, pretesting, history, and regression (if groups are not selected on the basis of extreme scores) should not be serious threats to internal validity. Having the same person teach both English classes would be recommended.

There are some possible internal validity threats, however, that this design does not control, namely threats resulting from an interaction of selection and some of the other common threats.

Interaction of Selection and Maturation We have stated that maturation per se is not a serious threat in this design because both groups would mature during the course of the experiment. The problem arises when the two groups differ in their propensity to maturation. If one of the selected groups is more subject to maturation than the other, you have an *interaction of selection and maturation* to threaten internal validity. Suppose Section 1 of freshman English meets at the same hour that the remedial mathematics class meets, whereas Section 3 meets at the same hour as the advanced algebra class. You would expect Section 1 as a group to show the most gain on academic performance on the posttest because many of the poorer students are in the remedial mathematics class. Section 3 would be expected to show the least gain because many of the best students are in the advanced algebra class at the same time. The timing of the mathematics classes influences the makeup of the English sections, and because of the interaction between selection and maturation, the gain to be expected in the sections is affected.

Selection–maturation interaction can be a particularly difficult problem when volunteers are compared with nonvolunteers. For example, let us say you offer an after-school reading improvement program to those who wish it. Reading pretest means show no difference between those who volunteer for the after-school program and those who do not. If the posttreatment scores show greater gain for the treatment group than for the control group, you cannot confidently attribute the greater gain to the treatment. It is quite possible that students who were willing to participate in the after-school program were more concerned about their reading or their parents were more concerned about their reading and were therefore more likely to show greater gain in reading whether they received treatment or not.

Interaction of Selection and Regression A selection–regression interaction could occur in this design if you drew the groups used in the study from populations having different means. Even though the groups are equivalent on a pretest, the regression toward the mean effect that occurs could result in a shift (change) from pre- to posttest that is incorrectly interpreted as an experimental effect.

Let us assume that the experimental group in a study has a mean of 75 on a pretest, which is below the mean of its parent population, whereas the control group with a pretest mean of 75 is above the mean of its population. Because each group will regress toward the mean of the parent population when retested, the experimental group will be expected to have a higher mean on the posttest, whether or not X is introduced; on the other hand, the mean of the control group will regress downward. The experimental group will appear to have made more progress during the course of the study than the control group, which will most likely be erroneously attributed to the effect of the treatment.

Interaction of Selection and Instrumentation As we pointed out in Chapter 8, most educational tests have a ceiling, which means that range of achievement on the test is limited. This characteristic could result in changes occurring for one group that apparently do not occur for the other. The gains are limited by the difference between the posttest's ceiling and the magnitude of the pretest score. If a student answers 92 items correctly on a 100-item pretest, this student can only gain 8 points on the 100-item posttest. However, a student with a score of 42 on the pretest could make a gain of 58 points on the posttest. Thus, because of this ceiling effect, students who score high on the pretest are restricted to a low change score. They may have improved greatly, but the instrument cannot show the gain. In contrast, low-scoring students on the pretest show a large gain because they have room to improve their scores. You might erroneously conclude that the treatment was more effective with the latter group. This illustrates the problem with change or gain scores; an analysis of covariance with the pretest scores as the covariate would be the recommended procedure for analyzing the posttest scores.

In summary, the **nonrandomized control group, pretest–posttest design** is a good second choice when random assignment of subjects to groups is not possible. The more similar the experimental and the control groups are at the beginning of the experiment, and the more this similarity is confirmed by similar group means on the pretest, the more credible the results of the nonrandomized control group pretest-posttest study become. If the pretest scores are similar and selection–maturation and selection–regression interactions can be shown to be unlikely explanations of posttest differences, the results of this quasi-experimental design are quite credible.

Even if the group means are noticeably different before treatment, a nonequivalent control group is better than a preexperimental design that has no control group at all. Design 9 can be extended to employ more than two groups. The threats to external validity in Design 9 are similar to those encountered with Design 5. An advantage of Design 9, however, is that the reactive effects of experimentation are more easily controlled than they are in Design 5. When intact classes are used, subjects are probably less aware of an experiment being conducted than when subjects are drawn from classes and put into experimental sessions. This contributes to the generalizability of the findings.

Design 10: Counterbalanced Design

Design 10, or **counterbalanced design**, another design that can be used with intact class groups, rotates the groups at intervals during the experimentation. For example, groups 1 and 2 might use methods A and B, respectively, for the first half of the experiment and then exchange methods for the second half. The distinctive feature of design 10 is that all subjects receive all experimental treatments at some time during the experiment. In effect, this design involves a series of replications; in each replication the groups are shifted so that at the end of the experiment each group has been exposed to each X. The order of exposure to the experimental situation differs for each group. The counterbalanced design is usually employed when several treatments are to be tested, but it also may be used with only two treatments.

Design 10: A Sample Counterbalanced Design

	Experimental Treatments			
Replication	X_1	X_2	X_3	X_4
1	Group A	B	C	D
2	Group C	A	D	B
3	Group B	D	A	C
4	Group D	C	B	A
	Column mean	Column mean	Column mean	Column mean

Each row in Design 10 represents one replication. For each replication the groups are shifted so that group A first experiences X_1, then X_2, X_3, and finally X_4. Each cell in the design would contain the mean scores on the dependent variable for the group, treatment, and replication indicated. The mean score for each column would indicate the performance of all four groups on the dependent variable under the treatment represented by the column.

A classroom teacher could use a counterbalanced study to compare the effectiveness of two methods of instruction on learning in science. The teacher could choose two classes and two units of science subject matter comparable in the nature of the concepts, difficulty of concepts, and length. It is essential that the units

Table 11.3 Example of a Counterbalanced Design

	Experimental Treatments	
Replication	**Method A**	**Method B**
(Unit) 1	Class 1	Class 2
(Unit) 2	Class 2	Class 1
	Column mean	Column mean

be equivalent in the complexity and difficulty of the concepts involved. During the first replication of the design, class 1 is taught unit 1 by method A and class 2 is taught by method B. An achievement test over unit 1 is administered to both groups. Then class 1 is taught unit 2 by method B and class 2 is taught by method A; both are then tested over unit 2. The arrangement is shown in Table 11.3.

After the study, the column means are computed to indicate the mean achievement for both groups (classes) when taught by the method indicated by the column heading. A comparison of these column mean scores through an analysis of variance indicates the effectiveness of the methods on achievement in science.

Design 10 overcomes some of the weaknesses of Design 9; that is, when intact classes must be used, counterbalancing provides an opportunity to rotate out any differences that might exist between the groups. Because the treatments are administered to all groups, the results obtained for each *X* cannot be attributed to preexisting differences in the subjects. If one group should have more aptitude on the average than the other, each *X* treatment would benefit from this greater aptitude.

The main shortcoming of Design 10 is that there may be a carryover effect from one *X* to the next. Therefore, this design should be used only when the experimental treatments are such that exposure to one treatment will have no effect on subsequent treatments. This requirement may be hard to satisfy in much educational research. Furthermore, one must establish the equivalence of learning material used in various replications. It may not always be possible to locate equivalent units of material. Another weakness of the counterbalanced design is the possibility of boring students with the repeated testings this method requires.

TIME-SERIES DESIGNS

Design 11: One-Group Time-Series Design

Design 11 (**one-group time-series design**) involves periodic measurement on one group and the introduction of an experimental treatment into this time series of measurements. As the design indicates, a number of measurements on a dependent variable are taken, *X* is introduced, and additional measurements of *Y* are made. By comparing the measurements before and after, you can assess the effect of *X* on the performance of the group on *Y*. A time-series design might be used in a school setting to study the effects of a major change in administrative policy on disciplinary incidents. Or a study might involve repeated measurements of stu-

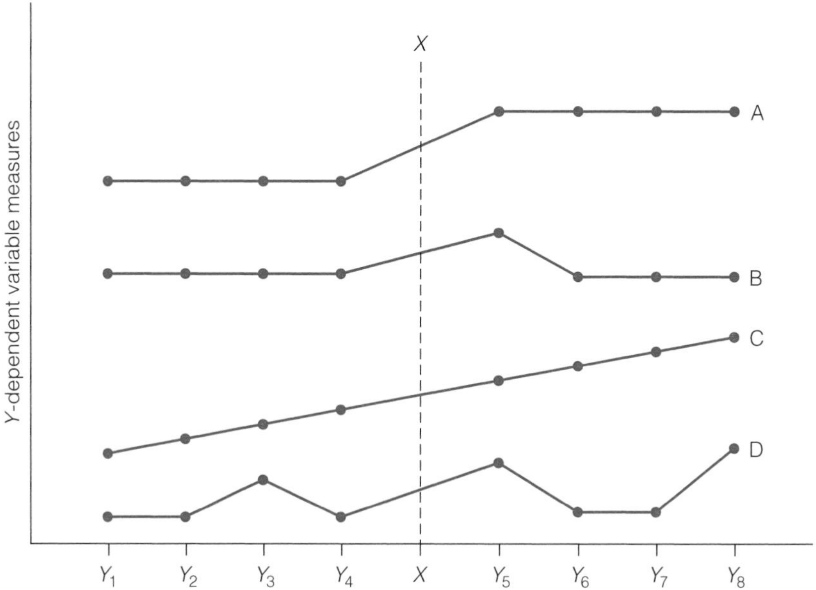

Figure 11.3 Illustration of Possible Outcome Patterns in a Time Design

dents' attitudes and the effect produced by introducing a documentary film designed to change attitudes.

Design 11: One-Group Time-Series Design

Y_1	Y_2	Y_3	Y_4	X	Y_5	Y_6	Y_7	Y_8

Figure 11.3 illustrates some possible patterns from time-series studies into which an experimental treatment is introduced. It shows the series of measurements Y_1 through Y_8, with the introduction of the experimental treatment at point X. You can assess the effect of the X by examining the stability of the repeated measurements.

From examining the difference between Y_4 and Y_5 in pattern A in Figure 11.3, perhaps you would be justified in assuming that X affects the dependent variable. Pattern B suggests the possibility of a temporary experimental effect of X. However, you could not assume that X produces the change in either pattern C or D. Pattern C appears to result from maturation or a similar influence. The erratic nature of pattern D suggests the operation of extraneous factors.

Design 11 is similar to Design 1 in that it uses before-and-after measures and lacks a control group. However, it has certain advantages over Design 1 that make it more useful in educational research. The repeated testing provides a check on some common threats to internal validity. Maturation, testing, and regression could be ruled out as plausible explanations of the shift occurring between Y_4 and Y_5, if such shifts do not occur in the previous time periods under observation. It is recommended that no change in measuring instruments be made during the course of the time study. In this way you eliminate changes in instrumentation as a possible explanation of the $Y_5 - Y_4$ difference.

The major weakness of Design 11 is its failure to control history; that is, you cannot rule out the possibility that it is not *X* but some simultaneous event that produces the observed change. Perhaps such factors as seasonal or weather changes or such school agents as examinations could account for the change. In a study designed to assess the effect of a lecture–film treatment on student attitudes toward minorities, to what extent would the attitude measurements be affected by a nationally publicized minority riot in a distant city? The extent to which history (uncontrolled contemporary events) is a plausible explanatory factor must be taken into account by the experimenters as they attempt to interpret their findings. You must also consider the external validity of the time design. Because there are repeated tests, perhaps there is a kind of interaction effect of testing that would restrict the findings to those populations subject to repeated testing. However, as long as the measurements are of a typical, routine type used in school settings, this is not likely to be a serious limitation. Further, a selection–*X* interaction may occur, especially if you select some particular group that may not be typical.

Statistical interpretation can be a particular problem with time data. The usual tests of significance are not appropriate with a time design because they assume that observations are independent of one another; but time-series data are typically correlated with one another. See Chapter 4 of Shadish, Cook, and Campbell (2002) for a discussion of the statistical tests that may be used with this design.

Design 12: Control Group Time-Series Design

Design 12 (**control group time-series design**) is an extension of Design 11 to include a control group. The control group, again representing an intact class, would be measured at the same time as the *E* group but would not experience the *X* treatment. This design overcomes the weakness of Design 11—that is, failure to control history as a source of extraneous variance. The control group permits the necessary comparison. If the *E* group shows a gain from Y_4 to Y_5 but the *C* group does not show a gain, then the effect must be caused by *X* rather than by any contemporaneous events, which would have affected both groups.

Design 12: Control Group Time-Series Design

Group									
E	Y_1	Y_2	Y_3	Y_4	X	Y_5	Y_6	Y_7	Y_8
C	Y_1	Y_2	Y_3	Y_4	—	Y_5	Y_6	Y_7	Y_8

Other variations of the time-series design include adding more control groups, more observations, or more experimental treatments.

VALIDITY PROBLEMS WITH EXPERIMENTAL DESIGNS

Some sources of invalidity in the one-variable experimental designs are summarized in Table 11.4. This brief summary must not be depended on as the sole guide in selecting a design. It must be accompanied by a thorough consideration

Table 11.4 Factors Jeopardizing the Internal Validity of Experimental Designs

	Designs[a]											
	Preexperimental		True Experimental						Quasi-Experimental			
Sources of Invalidity	1	2	3	4	5	6	7	8	9	10	11	12
History[b]	–	+	+	+	+	+	+	+	+	+	–	+
Maturation	–	?	+	+	+	+	+	+	+	+	+	+
Pretesting	–	+	+	+	+	+	+	+	+	+	+	+
Instrumentation	–	+	+	+	+	+	+	+	+	+	?	+
Statistical regression	?	+	+	+	+	+	+	+	?	+	+	+
Differential selection	+	–	+	+	+	+	+	+	–	+	+	+
Experimental mortality	+	–	+	+	+	+	+	+	+	+	+	+
Interaction of selection and other threats	–	–	+	+	+	+	+	+	–	?	+	+
Subject effects	–	–	?	?	?	–	–	–	–	+	–	–
Experimenter effect	–	–	?	?	?	–	–	–	–	–	–	–
Diffusion	na	–	?	?	?	?	?	?	–	?	na	?

[a]Designs are as follows:
1. One-group pretest–posttest
2. Static group comparison
3. Randomized *S*'s, posttest-only control group
4. Randomized matched *S*'s, posttest-only control group
5. Randomized *S*'s, pretest–posttest control group
6. Solomon, three groups
7. Solomon, four groups
8. Simple factorial
9. Nonrandomized control group, pretest–posttest
10. Counterbalanced
11. One-group time series
12. Control group time series

[b]A plus sign indicates that the factor is controlled; a minus sign indicates lack of control; and a question mark indicates a possible source of concern.

of the qualified presentation appearing in the text so that the reader understands the particular strengths and weaknesses that characterize each design.

SINGLE-SUBJECT EXPERIMENTAL DESIGNS

The single-subject experimental design almost sounds like a contradiction in terms. How can an experiment be run with a sample size of one? Obviously, there can be no random assignment or use of control groups. Yet **single-subject research** has become popular over the past 25 years. Proponents of this particular methodology argue that experimental control can be achieved in other than the traditional ways. After describing the two major approaches to single-subject research and the rationale behind them, we will examine the strengths and limitations of this type of research in comparison with the other more conventional designs.

Study of the individual has always had a place in educational and psychological research. Freud's case studies and Piaget's observations of individual children are notable examples. Although case studies (see Chapter 15) and single-subject experiments both study the individual, in a single-subject experiment, the investigator deliberately manipulates one or more independent variables, whereas in a case study the observer studies the subjects' interaction with events that occur naturally.

Single-case designs have been particularly useful in clinical applications where the focus is on the therapeutic value of an intervention for the client. A teacher of severely learning-disabled children, for example, would want information regarding the effectiveness of a specific procedure with an individual child. Some feel that studies that report mean or average differences for groups may have little meaning when treating a specific individual. Single-subject designs are basically extensions of the quasi-experimental one-group time-series design (Design 11). The two most common are the ABAB and the multiple-baseline design.

ABAB Designs

The **ABAB design** consists of a period of no treatment, or baseline (A), during which the behavior of interest is repeatedly measured. Examples of such behaviors are the number of times a student with cognitive disability leaves her seat or the number of times an autistic child bangs his or her head. This pretreatment assessment serves as a control period with which treatment effects will be compared. After a stable picture of pretreatment behavior has been established, phase B, the treatment, is initiated. In the treatment phase the child might be given tokens (exchangeable for desired privileges) for time periods spent seated or time periods with no self-abusive action. The behavior is consistently monitored throughout the treatment phase, usually until the intervention appears to have taken effect and the rate of behavior stabilizes. Further experimental control is achieved by a second A phase. This is usually a withdrawal of treatment, but in some cases the second A phase is actually a reversal of treatment, reinforcing a behavior incompatible with the desired response. Discontinuing the giving of tokens to the girl constitutes a withdrawal of treatment, whereas giving her tokens when she leaves her seat is a reversal of treatment. In either case removal of treatment is expected to cause the behavior to return to the original (first baseline) level. Ending the experiment with the second A phase has the drawback of leaving the client in the same state as before the experiment started. For ethical reasons and to add strength to the design by replicating the procedure, the treatment phase (B) is again instituted. Many variations on the ABAB design are possible. More than one treatment can be tested—for instance, using an ABCACB format in which A is no treatment and B and C are alternate treatments.

Figure 11.4 illustrates an ABAB design. Mornings were often difficult for the entire family of an 8-year-old developmentally disabled boy, Curt, because he took up to 2 hours to get dressed in the morning. Constant reminders, pleadings, and occasional scoldings had not helped. Once during a week of baseline measurement (A), Curt did get dressed in only 4 minutes, so his parents knew he was capable of dressing himself in a reasonable time.

During the treatment (B) phase, each morning Curt's clothes were laid out in the bathroom, he was awakened, and then a kitchen timer was set for 10 minutes. Curt earned a red sticker to put on the chart on his door if he dressed himself before the timer rang. The sticker entitled him to watch TV that evening. If he did not finish within the 10 minutes, he had to stay in the bathroom until dressed and forfeit TV for the day. Curt was praised when he met the criterion, ignored when he did not.

During the week of baseline, Curt took an average of 59 minutes to get dressed. During 17 days of the first B phase, Curt met the criterion 9 times and his average was 10 minutes. On 3 occasions 0 minutes was recorded because he woke and dressed himself before his parents were awake.

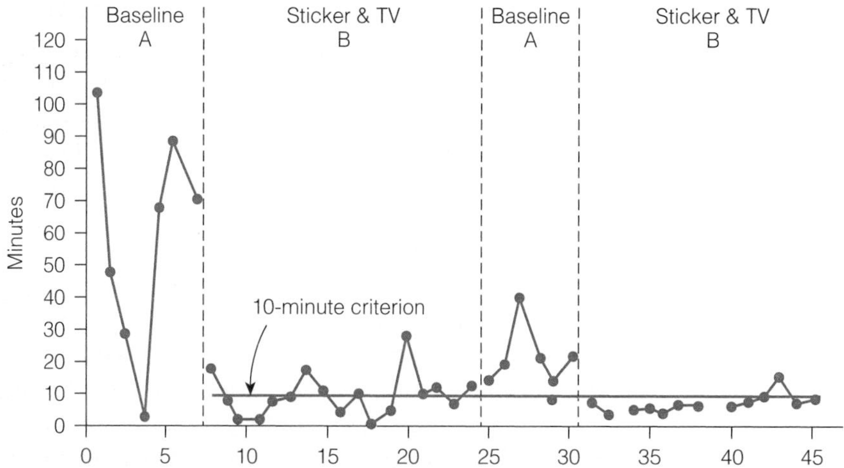

Figure 11.4 ABAB Design (Use of Differential Reinforcement to Decrease Dressing Time of an 8-year-old Boy)

Source: From *Working with Parents of Handicapped Children* (p. 59) by W. Heward, J. C. Dardig, & A. Rossett, 1979, Columbus, OH: Merrill. Copyright 1979 by Bell & Howell Company. Reprinted by permission.

During the following 6 days, Curt's clothes were laid out for him, but the timer was omitted and he was allowed to watch TV no matter how long he took to dress. His dressing time averaged 23 minutes during this second A phase. When treatment was reinstituted for 12 of the next 13 days, Curt's dressing time then averaged 8 minutes.

Because treatment was always accompanied by a change in dressing time, a credible relationship between treatment and dressing time was established. The key element in the ABAB design is the return to former levels of behavior when the baseline condition is reinstated. The assumption that the intervention is the cause of the change can be quite weakened under certain circumstances. If there is considerable variability during the baseline period, you could argue that post-treatment behavior did not differ meaningfully from pretreatment behavior. If the shift from treatment (B) back to baseline (A) is equivocal, much of the power of the ABAB design is gone. The second baseline often does not show the same extreme of behavior as the first, and in some cases there is no return to previous rates. In some cases other factors, such as history or maturation, could cause the observed effect.

Some researchers argue that returning to baseline conditions may be unethical under certain circumstances. Do you really want the autistic child to return to the previous levels of head-banging just to provide evidence that the treatment caused the reduction? Because of these potential problems with the ABAB design, the multiple-baseline design was developed. This design has the clinical advantage of continuing any improvement made without returning to less desired behavior.

Multiple-Baseline Designs

In a **multiple-baseline design**, measures of different behaviors are made simultaneously during the baseline condition. For example, the researcher might record the number of times a student talked in class without permission, the number of worksheets completed, and the number of times the student hit another child. Or the same behavior of several clients, such as amount of eye contact with the teacher, could be recorded for two or more children in a preschool class during the baseline phase. In both cases the treatment (B) is the same across all conditions or students. Experimental control in the multiple baseline results from starting the treatment at a different point in time for each behavior and/or person involved, rather than from returning to baseline. Thus, after the baseline is established, treatment for behavior 1 is instituted and the baseline is continued for behaviors 2 and 3. When treatment for behavior 2 is instituted, treatment for behavior 1 and baseline for behavior 3 are continued. Finally, treatment for behavior 3 is instituted. It is expected that each behavior will change in the desired direction at the point at which treatment is begun, not before or after.

Thus, the multiple-baseline design uses the AB as its basic unit. If some outside event other than the treatment was the actual cause of the changes, it should affect all children or all behaviors at the same point in time. One assumption of this design is that treatment affects different behaviors specifically. Reinforcing one behavior (completing arithmetic problems) is not expected to increase another response (reading rate). The behaviors, or situations, must be independent (uncorrelated) for the multiple-baseline study to show interpretable effects. In actuality, independence of behavior may be difficult to attain. Modifying one behavior (such as talking in class) may influence other targeted behaviors (completing assignments on time).

COMPARISON OF SINGLE-SUBJECT AND GROUP DESIGNS

In both single-subject and group experiments, the goal of the experimenter is to establish as unequivocally as possible the connection between the manipulation of the independent variable (treatment) and its effect on the dependent variable (behavior). In group designs, random assignment of subjects to experimental or control groups eliminates many rival explanations of differences observed after treatment. Treatment effects (between groups) can be assessed relative to intersubject variability effects (within group) by using appropriate statistical tests. These tests determine whether chance alone is a credible explanation for the results. The single-subject design uses other methods to establish credibility. The experimenter controls the amount of time in which baseline and treatment phases are in effect, and the length of the baseline period can be extended until the behavior stabilizes. For unambiguous interpretation, the baseline should be relatively flat or the trend should be in the opposite direction from that expected after treatment. One drawback to experimenter control of the length of the treatment phase is the tendency to continue treatment until "something happens." If behavior change does not closely follow the beginning of treatment, it is possible that another, nonexperimental variable is the cause of the observed change.

Single-subject experimental designs do bypass one source of error of group designs—namely, intersubject variability. Each individual serves as his or her own control, so comparability is not a problem. The major means of control is replication, a feature seldom incorporated into group designs. The ABAB design involves a single replication using the same subject, whereas the multiple-baseline design replicates more than one treatment. Replication of the multiple-baseline design makes it less likely that effects attributed to treatment were in fact caused by extraneous event or subject variables.

Well-designed single-subject research can meet the criteria for internal validity. However, the question of external validity—the generalizability of experimental findings—is not as easily answered by designs that use only one or a few subjects. You can demonstrate that allowing a behaviorally disordered teenager to listen to rock music contingent on completing assignments increases the amount of schoolwork done by that particular teenager, but how can you determine whether this treatment will be successful with other teenagers, or all behaviorally disordered teenagers? Although any one particular single-subject study will be low in external validity, a number of similar studies that carefully describe subjects, conditions, and treatments will build the case for wide application of particular treatment effects.

SUMMARY

The design one chooses to use is very important to the validity of any conclusions that might be drawn from the research. We classified designs as preexperimental, randomized experimental, or quasi-experimental, depending on the degree of control provided. The preexperimental designs provide little or no control of extraneous variables and are not recommended.

Randomized experimental designs are the best for investigating causal relationships among variables. As the name indicates, they require random assignment of subjects to levels of the independent variable. Because of the randomization, they provide the best control of the factors that threaten internal and external validity and are recommended for use whenever possible. Experiments may use different groups of subjects for the different experimental conditions, or the experiment may have each subject experience every condition. The former are called between-subjects experiments and the latter are called within-subjects experiments.

Factorial designs use two or more independent variables, each having at least two levels. Factorial designs enable the researcher to investigate the main effects of each of the independent variables on the dependent variable as well as the interaction effect of the independent variables. An interaction exists when variable A has a different effect on the dependent variable when it is combined with one level of variable B than when it is combined with another level of variable B. Thus, one factorial design experiment can accomplish more than two single, independent variable experiments.

Quasi-experimental designs are used when the investigator cannot randomly assign subjects to treatments. There is less control of extraneous variables in quasi experiments, thus they are subject to a variety of different threats to internal validity. Quasi-experimental designs that study the effect of treatment on a single subject have proven useful in behavioral research.

KEY CONCEPTS

ABAB design
between-subjects design
control group time-series design
counterbalanced design
experimental design
factorial design
interaction
multiple-baseline design
nonrandomized control group, pretest–posttest design
one-group pretest–posttest design
one-group time–series design
preexperimental design
quasi-experimental design
randomized experimental design
randomized matched subjects, posttest-only control group design

randomized subjects, posttest-only control group design
randomized subjects, pretest–posttest control group design
repeated-measures design
single-subject research
Solomon four-group design
Solomon three-group design
static group comparison
within-groups design
within-subjects design

EXERCISES

1. From a group of students enrolled in social studies in a high school, a researcher randomly selected 60 students. The students were then divided into two groups by random assignment of 30 to group A, the traditional social studies curriculum, and 30 to group B, a new program designed to deal with the history of certain ethnic groups. The two groups were compared at the end of the semester on a scale designed to measure attitudes toward ethnic groups. In this study, identify the following:
   a. Independent variable
   b. Dependent variable
   c. Control group
   d. Experimental group
   e. Method(s) used to control for differences between the groups
   f. Research design used
   g. Any threats to internal validity
2. Consider the following research question: Does teaching the first year of French through an oral–aural approach, rather than the grammar–transformational method, alter pupil performance on a standardized year-end test in grammar, reading, and vocabulary?
   a. Design the *ideal* experiment to answer this question, assuming that there are no administrative or other restrictions.
   b. Design the experiment that would most likely be required in the typical high school setting.
   c. State the relative advantages of the ideal experimental design (Exercise 2a) as compared with the design in Exercise 2b.
3. Design the *ideal* experiment to test the following hypothesis: Children who view films of harmonious racial interaction will show a more positive attitude toward racial minorities than will children shown films that depict racial conflict.
4. Returning to the research problem in Exercise 2, suppose you also want to know if the two methods of teaching French have differential effects for boys and girls? Outline the experimental design that would permit you to answer this question at the same time.
5. Assume an investigator used two methods of instruction (A_1 and A_2) with two groups of students (B_1 and B_2) having varying levels of achievement motivation. The groups were compared on an achievement test at the end of the study. The means are presented below. What interpretation would you make of these results?

	Method	
	A_1	A_2
Motivation B_1	35	15
B_2	15	35

6. What must occur to establish credibility of results in a single-subject design?
7. A researcher wants to test the effectiveness of two different computer-based instructional methods on teaching a unit on weather in seventh-grade science. The researcher finds a teacher who will permit three of his classes to participate: Two classes use the computer-based instruction, and the third receives conventional classroom instruction. The researcher administers a pretest to all students, each class has a different method of instruction, and then a posttest as administered.
   a. Specify the design of this study and represent it using the notation system used in this chapter.
   b. What statistics would you choose to analyze the data?

ANSWERS

1. a. Type of social studies curriculum
   b. Scores on an ethnic attitude scale
   c. Group A, the present curriculum
   d. Group B, curriculum with ethnic history
   e. Random selection of the sample from the population and random assignment of the sample to the experimental and control groups
   f. Design 3, the randomized subjects, posttest-only control group design
   g. In the event that randomization does not control for initial group differences, there is no pretest to use to check if there are differences in attitudes before the study.
2. a. Use Design 3—that is, randomly assign first-year French students to either the grammar-transformational (control) or oral–aural (experimental) group. Maintain the same conditions, time spent, teachers, and classroom facilities for both groups so that only the teaching method is different. Administer test at the end of the year and compare group achievement.
   b. Randomly assign intact classes of first-year French students to the two teaching methods. Each teacher has an equal number of the two types of classes.
   c. In the ideal design, threats to external and internal validity are better controlled through randomization of individual students. The design in Exercise 2b could have problems with nonequivalence of subjects before treatment is given, so that test score differences could be caused by factors other than difference in treatment.
3. The ideal experiment would randomly assign students to groups. The results of a posttreatment measure of attitudes toward racial minorities would be used to compare the experimental and control groups.
4. This question requires a factorial design with half of the boys and half of the girls assigned randomly to the control and experimental conditions.
5. It appears that there is an interaction between achievement motivation and type of instruction. Students with achievement motivation at level B_1 did better with method A_1, while those at level B_2 did better with method A_2. The significance of this interaction could be tested with an F test. There is no overall effect of motivation or instructional method because the means for A_1 and A_2, and B_1 and B_2 are the same.
6. There must be an unambiguous change in behavior whenever there is a change in treatment.
7. a. Nonrandomized control group, pretest–posttest design:

E	Y_1	X	Y_2
E	Y_1	X	Y_2
C	Y_1	—	Y_2

   b. If the groups were not significantly different on the pretest, you could use analysis of variance (ANOVA) on the posttest scores. Otherwise, ANCOVA could be used with pretest scores as the covariate.

INFOTRAC COLLEGE EDITION

Use the keywords *quasi-experimental design* to locate a study that uses a quasi-experimental research design. What particular quasi-experimental design was used? Did the investigator discuss the strengths and weaknesses of this design?

Chapter 12

Ex Post Facto Research

NOT ALL IMPORTANT QUESTIONS IN EDUCATION CAN BE ANSWERED WITH EXPERIMENTAL RESEARCH.

INSTRUCTIONAL OBJECTIVES

After studying this chapter, the student will be able to:

1. Describe ex post facto research and compare it to experimental research.
2. State conditions needed to infer a causal relationship.
3. Describe alternative explanations in ex post facto research and identify cases where these are or are not plausible.
4. Describe methods of partial control and identify cases where they would be useful.
5. Design an ex post facto investigation.
6. Identify questions for which ex post facto research would be the method of choice.
7. State the major weakness of ex post factor research.

As researchers probe such educational questions as "Why are some children better readers than others?" "What is the effect of single-parent homes on achievement?" and "Why do some youths become delinquent while others do not?" they find that only some questions can be investigated through experimental research. If you want to investigate the influence of such variables as home environment, motivation, intelligence, parental reading habits, age, ethnicity, gender, disabilities, self-concept, and so forth, you cannot randomly assign students to different categories of these variables. Independent variables such as these are called **attribute independent variables**. An attribute variable is a characteristic that a subject has before a study begins.

In contrast, an independent variable that an investigator can directly manipulate is an **active independent variable**. An investigator can determine which students will have access to a computer laboratory and which will not, which will use program A to study a unit in algebra and which will use program B. When active independent variables are involved, an investigator can employ experimental or quasi-experimental research. When investigation involves attribute independent variables that the researcher cannot manipulate, he or she must turn to *ex post facto* research (also called *causal-comparative research*). Ex post facto research is also appropriate when the variable actually could be manipulated but is not because it would be unethical or irresponsible to do so. For example, it would not be ethical to manipulate illegal drug use or use of alcohol or cigarettes to study their effects on human subjects.To study the effect of retention on subsequent achievement, you would not want to randomly assign some children to be retained and others to be promoted. And you would not manipulate the use of a drug such as Ritalin to study its effects on children's problem-solving behavior. But a researcher could use the ex post facto research method to study the retention question by matching retained students with nonretained students and looking at their subsequent achievement, or he or she could compare the problem-solving behavior of a group of children already taking Ritalin with that of a matched group not taking the drug.

The designation *ex post facto*, from Latin for "after the fact," indicates that **ex post facto research** is conducted after variation in the variable of interest has already been determined in the natural course of events. This method is also called **causal comparative** because its purpose is to investigate cause-and-effect relationships between independent and dependent variables. Researchers use it, however, in situations that do not permit the randomization and manipulation of variables characteristic of experimental research.

The two basic modes of ex post facto research are (1) to begin with subjects who differ on an independent variable (cause) and try to determine the consequences (effect) of these differences, and (2) to begin with subjects who differ on a dependent variable (effect) and try to determine the antecedents (cause) of this difference. An example of the former would be investigating the effect of single-parent households versus that of two-parent households (independent variable) on truancy (dependent variable). An example of the latter would be comparing students who graduated from high school with those who drop out (dependent variable) on independent variables such as motivation, clarity of goals, and self-discipline.

EX POST FACTO AND EXPERIMENTAL APPROACHES COMPARED

In both types of research, interest is focused on discovery or establishment of relationships among the variables. Ex post facto or causal-comparative research, as well as experimental research, can test hypotheses concerning the relationship between an independent variable (X) and a dependent variable (Y). In basic logic, experimental and ex post facto approaches are similar. Thus, much of the same kind of information that an experiment provides can also be obtained through an ex post facto study.

However, with an experiment it is possible to obtain much more convincing evidence for **causal** (functional) **relationships** among variables than can be obtained with ex post facto studies. The effects of extraneous variables in an experiment are controlled by the experimental conditions, and the antecedent independent variable is directly manipulated to assess its effect on the dependent variable. If you observe Y to vary concomitantly with the variation in X in this controlled situation, then you have obtained evidence for the validity of the hypothesized antecedent-consequent relationship between X and Y. In an ex post facto investigation, in contrast, the researcher cannot control the independent variables by manipulation or by randomization: Changes in the variables have already taken place. Because of this lack of control, in an ex post facto study it is more hazardous to infer a genuine relationship between X and Y.

Let us illustrate the difference between ex post facto and an experimental approach by examining these two approaches to the same research question. Consider the question of the effect of students' anxiety, in an achievement-testing situation, on their examination performance. The ex post facto approach would involve measuring the already existing anxiety level at the time of the examination, then comparing the performance of "high anxious" and "low anxious" students. The weakness of such an approach is that you could not necessarily conclude that the students' anxiety produced the observed difference in achievement examination performance. Both sets of scores may have been influenced by a third factor, such as knowledge of the subject matter being examined or general intelligence. Knowledge or aptitude may be the major cause of both the level of anxiety and the achievement test results.

In an experimental approach to the same problem, the investigator could randomly assign subjects to two exam conditions that are identical in every respect except that one is anxiety arousing and the other is neutral. The experimenter can induce anxiety by telling the subjects that their final grade depends on their performance, that the test is extremely difficult, or that the test will be used to identify the incompetent. The neutral group would merely be told that their cooperation is needed for the experiment. The investigator could randomly assign subjects to the two conditions. Then, if the anxious group performed better than the neutral group, it could be concluded that the induced anxiety had a facilitating effect on test performance. Such a conclusion could be legitimately drawn because of the control provided by the random assignment of groups to treatments and by the experimenter's direct manipulation of the independent variable. Anxiety is one of the few variables that can be either an active or an attribute-independent variable. You can manipulate it actively, as described (experimental approach), or you can classify subjects on the basis of their scores on an anxiety measure (ex post facto approach).

In a sense, the ex post facto study can be viewed as a reverse approach to experimentation. Instead of taking groups that are equivalent and exposing them to different treatments, the ex post facto study starts with groups that are already different and tries to determine the consequences of or the antecedents of these differences. Such a procedure does not provide the safeguards, typical in experimentation, that are necessary for making strong inferences about causal relationships. Mistakenly attributing causation based on a relationship between two variables is called the **post hoc fallacy**. An investigator who finds a relationship between the variables in an ex post facto study has secured evidence only of some concomitant variation. Because the investigator has not controlled X or other possible variables that may have determined *why*, there is less basis for inferring a causal relationship between X and Y.

If you wish to reach a conclusion that one variable (X) is the cause of another variable (Y), three kinds of evidence are necessary:

1. A statistical relationship between X and Y has been established.
2. X preceded Y in time.
3. Other factors did not determine Y.

A statistical relationship is one in which a change in one variable can be predicted from a change in the other. However, we must note that such a relationship between two variables, by itself, is not sufficient evidence of cause and effect. You must proceed to look for evidence on the other two criteria.

Therefore, the investigator must also establish the time sequence; that is, you must consider whether Y might have occurred before X and hence could not be an effect of X. If X is a cause of Y, then a change in X must precede a change in Y. Decisions about the time relationship between X and Y can be made either on a logical basis or as a result of measurements that show the groups did not differ on Y before exposure to X.

The third kind of evidence shows that no other plausible explanation can account for the observed effect. It is extremely important that the investigator consider whether factors other than X might have determined Y. This is the most difficult evidence to obtain. You proceed to check this possibility by introducing other relevant variables into the analysis and observing how the relationship be-

THINK ABOUT IT 12.1

1. Why does the current administration of the U.S. Department of Education prefer randomized experimental research to ex post facto research?
2. Why do researchers conduct ex post facto research?

Answers

1. Because active independent variables are factors that one can change; therefore, true experimental research yields information on which proposed programs have sufficient evidence to obtain funding.
2. Because many important independent variables in education cannot be deliberately manipulated; or, in some cases they could be manipulated, but it would be unethical to do so.

tween X and Y is affected by these additional variables. You may find that the relationship between X and Y holds up even when the other variables are introduced. In this case you have some evidence to support a causal inference. However, you may find that other variables may account for the apparent relationship between X and Y. In this case, you would conclude that the relationship between X and Y is spurious. A **spurious relationship** is one in which the two variables really have no effect on each other but are related because some other variable influences both. For example, a positive relationship between the number of churches and the number of armed robberies in the cities within a state does not mean that building more churches will increase armed robberies, nor that increasing armed robberies will cause more churches to be built. Here the **extraneous variable** is city size. Large cities have more churches and more armed robberies, whereas small cities have fewer armed robberies and fewer churches.

CONDUCTING AN EX POST FACTO RESEARCH STUDY

1. *The first step in an ex post facto study is to state the research problem, usually in the form of a question.* What is the relationship between variable A and variable B? Or, what is the effect of variable A on variable B? Again, in this type of research the variables involved are those that the researcher does not directly manipulate. The researcher then states a hypothesis about the expected relationship and defines the variables in operational terms.
2. *Next select the two groups to be compared.* Recall that investigators doing ex post facto or causal-comparative research achieve the variation they want, not by directly manipulating the variable itself, but by *selecting* individuals in whom the variable is present or absent, strong, or weak. Thus, these two groups should differ on the variable of interest in that one group should possess the characteristic and the other group should not, but they should be similar on any relevant extraneous variables. Differential (subject) selections pose a major threat to the internal validity of ex post facto investigations because then you have no control over the selection of subjects into the two groups. They are selected because they already possess the variable of interest, for example, smoker/nonsmoker, retained/not retained and so forth. Whenever assignment is not random, there is always an opening for other variables to enter to explain the observed difference between the groups. The way to deal with this threat is to collect data to show that the groups are similar on other extraneous variables that might affect the variable of interest. For example, if you were looking at the effect of preschool attendance on the social maturity of kindergarteners, you would have to control any other factors that might have been shown to influence social maturity. Some of these might be age, gender, socioeconomic status, aptitude, and so on. You use logic and previous research to determine what factors need to be controlled in an ex post facto study.

3. *Choose between the basic designs for ex post facto research.*

	Independent Variables		Dependent Variables
Design 1	Subjects are already known to differ on independent variable(s).	→	Investigator tests hypothesis concerning possible dependent variable(s).
Design 2	Investigator tests hypothesis concerning possible independent variable(s).	←	Subjects are already known to differ on dependent variable(s).

a. Design 1

Design 1 looks at the consequences of differences on an independent variable. The groups differ in that one group possesses a characteristic and the other does not, or the groups may differ in the degree or extent to which they possess the characteristic. An example would be a study to compare the problem-solving performance of creative and noncreative college students. The hypothesis would read "Creative college students will exhibit greater speed and accuracy on a problem-solving task than will noncreative college students." This hypothesis clearly indicates the need for an ex post facto design because the investigators can neither manipulate creativity nor assign students randomly to groups. They must start with two groups who already differ on the independent variable, creativity, and compare them on the dependent variable, problem-solving performance. The investigators must define "creative college student" and "noncreative college student" in precise operational terms. Creative college students might be defined as those undergraduates scoring above the third quartile both on the Guilford Test of Alternate Uses and Consequences and on an anagram test. Those students scoring below the first quartile on the tests would be defined as noncreative. The investigators should try to identify variables other than creativity that could affect the dependent variable of problem-solving performance and take steps to equate the experimental and control groups on these variables by matching or by statistical means. For example, in this study other independent variables that should be controlled are intelligence, gender, and perhaps college major or college year. A bright male sophomore in the creative group might be matched with his counterpart in the noncreative group. After formation of the matched groups, the researcher would give both groups a measure of the dependent variable, a problem-solving task. Further analysis of the data by means of a *t* test would reveal any significant differences in the problem-solving performance of the two groups and perhaps show a relationship between creativity and problem-solving performance.

b. Design 2

Design 2 looks for the cause(s) of differences in the dependent variable. Consider 10 members of a wrestling team, 3 of whom become ill when returning from a tournament. To investigate the cause of the illness, the

PICTURE THIS

Does the in-school performance of children who get corporal punishment at home differ from the in-school performance of those who do not?

In ex post facto research the investigator cannot control the independent variable.

Joe Rocco

doctor asks what they ate when the team stopped for dinner on their way home. She finds that every item the 3 ill wrestlers chose differed except for creamed chicken. The 7 wrestlers who did not have creamed chicken did not become ill. She concludes that the creamed chicken caused the illness. The doctor is using philosopher John Stuart Mill's *joint method of agreement and difference*:

> If two or more instances in which the phenomenon occurs have only one circumstance in common, while two or more instances in which it does not occur have nothing in common save the absence of that circumstance; the circumstance in which alone the two sets of instances differ, is the effect, or cause, or necessary part of the cause, of the phenomenon. (1846, p. 229)

An example of Design 2 is the research on gender differences in performance on standardized mathematics tests. What factors might account for observed male superiority on these tests? Royer and his colleagues (1999) found support for the hypothesis that males are faster at retrieving basic mathematical facts and hence perform at a higher level on tests. Other researchers have challenged this conclusion. Is the difference in math performance between males and females really due to gender or is it due to a difference in experiences and learned attitudes?

4. *Collect data on the independent and dependent variables and the relevant extraneous variables from the subjects.*
5. *Analyze and interpret the data.* The same statistics commonly used in analyzing experimental research data are used in analyzing ex post facto data. First, calculate the mean and standard deviation of each group. Then use the t test to see if there is a significant difference between the means of the two groups or ANOVA if there are more than two groups. Chi square is used to determine if an event occurs more frequently in one group than another. Next, the researcher states and explores alternative explanations.

ALTERNATIVE EXPLANATIONS IN EX POST FACTO RESEARCH

When investigators can control the treatment (X) and then observe the dependent variable (Y) as in experimental research, they have reasonable evidence that X influences Y. *Ex post facto research, on the other hand, lacks control of the independent variable and thus has lower internal validity.* If researchers cannot control (X), they may be led to inappropriate conclusions. When interpreting ex post facto research, one should consider alternative explanations, such as (1) common cause, (2) reverse causality, and (3) the presence of other independent variables.

Common Cause

In an ex post facto investigation, you must consider the possibility that both the independent and dependent variables of the study are merely two separate results of a third variable—that they have a **common cause**. For example, if you use a school's total budget as an independent variable and cases of diagnosed learning disability as a dependent variable, you would find a positive correlation between the two variables. Does this mean that an increase in total school budget leads to an increase in cases of learning disability? A more plausible explanation is that the relationship is spurious. An increase in school size/number of children attending could account for both the budget and the cases of diagnosed learning disability as funding is tied to the number of students. It is well established that the average income of private high school graduates is much higher than the average income of public and parochial high school graduates. Does this mean that private schools better prepare students for financial success? Or is the difference due to the fact that those families with enough money to send their children to private schools are also able to finance their children's professional training and set them up in business?

When doing ex post facto research, you must always consider the possibilities of common cause or causes accounting for an observed relationship. In our examples fairly obvious common causes could be identified. However, in ex post facto research there is always a nagging doubt that maybe common causes no one has thought of explain a relationship. Research has shown that the injury rate of drivers who use safety belts is lower than the injury rate of drivers who do not. Is this because using safety belts reduces injury or because cautious drivers have fewer injury-causing accidents and also are more likely to use safety belts?

Reverse Causality

In interpreting an observed relationship in an ex post facto study, the researcher must consider the possibility of **reverse causality**—that the reverse of the suggested hypothesis could also account for the finding—instead of saying that X causes Y, perhaps it is the case that Y causes X. For instance, the proportion of Episcopalians listed in *Who's Who in America* is much greater than their proportion in the general population. Does this mean Episcopalianism leads to the kind of success that results in being listed in *Who's Who*? It is just as plausible to hypothesize that successful people tend to gravitate to the Episcopal church. Similarly, if you find that college students who drink have a lower GPA than nondrinkers, you cannot automatically conclude that alcohol consumption depresses academic performance. Perhaps bad grades drive students to drink. (Or, of course, any number of common causes could lead to both drinking and poor grades.)

Investigations on the effects of child-rearing practices have revealed that children who are frequently punished show more aggressive behavior. Can you conclude that parental punishment leads to aggressive children? Or are aggressive children more likely to be punished? A recent study (Hotz, 2002) conducted at the University of Southern California reported that children who are outgoing and adventurous as toddlers have substantially higher IQs and reading ability by the time they are preteens (age 11). The difference in mental ability was true for boys and girls and across variations in ethnic background and income levels. The researchers correctly concluded that the research does not show whether the children's outgoing curiosity as toddlers was the cause of their better scores on later IQ tests, or whether children who have higher IQs are, by nature, more curious and outgoing.

The hypothesis of reverse causality is easier to deal with than the hypothesis of common cause. With the latter, numerous common causes in each case could produce a spurious relationship. With reverse causality, there is only one possibility in each case: Y caused X, instead of X caused Y.

In a situation when X always precedes Y in time, the very nature of the data rules out the possibility of reverse causality. For example, numerous studies have shown that the average annual income of college graduates is higher than the average annual income of nongraduates. You can rule out the hypothesis of reverse causality because graduation or nongraduation precedes the subsequent annual income. You cannot rule out a variety of possible common causes.

A method of establishing the time order of variables is to obtain measurements of the same subjects at different times. Let us assume that you are interested in the relationship between employees' acceptance of the philosophy of a corporation and job promotion within that corporation. If you merely interviewed a sample of the employees and found that those in higher positions held attitudes and opinions more in line with the company's value system, you would not know whether acceptance of company values and objectives was conducive to promotion or whether promotion increased acceptance of the company value system. To rule out reverse causality as an explanation, you could interview a group of new trainees and obtain—by means of a questionnaire, rating scale, or the like—a measure of their acceptance of the corporation philosophy. Then after a period of time, perhaps 18 months, you could determine from company records which employees had been promoted. If the findings showed that a significantly higher proportion of employees who had expressed attitudes and opinions consistent with corporation philosophy had been promoted, as compared with those who had not, you would have better evidence that conformity with company philosophy was conducive to promotion. (You are still left with the possibility that some common cause or causes account for differences in both philosophy and promotion.)

Other Possible Independent Variables

Independent variables other than the one considered in the causal-comparative study may bring about the observed effect on the Y variable; that is, in addition to X_1, other variables, X_2 and X_3, may also be antecedent factors for the variation in the dependent variable. In the example of the relationship between school budget and cases of diagnosed learning disability, it could be that an increase in budget allowed hiring of a school psychologist, which led to more screenings and identification of learning disabled children. The recorded suicide rate in Sweden is among the highest in the world. Does this mean the Swedish environment causes more people to commit suicide? Does it mean that the Swedish people are more suicide prone than others? Perhaps there is truth in one or both of these hypotheses. It is equally possible, however, that the actual independent variable is the honesty of coroners in Sweden compared with the honesty of coroners in other countries. In countries where great social stigma falls on the families of those who commit suicide, coroners may well use every conceivable means to record a death as accidental rather than suicide. Therefore, the difference between reported suicide rates may be a function of coroner behavior and nothing else.

Let us consider some more examples. At a governors' conference, governor X points with pride to the low crime rate in his state. Another governor points out that the police forces in governor X's state are seriously undermanned and the low crime rate may indicate only that very few crimes there are ever reported. An industrialist asks his personnel manager why he does not hire more Old Tuephingen University graduates, asserting that because so many of them are rapidly moving up the promotion ladder, they are obviously more competent than other graduates. The personnel manager tactfully points out that the phenomenon may not be explained by competence but rather by the fact that the indus-

THINK ABOUT IT 12.2

1. The chief of police finds that the proportion of African Americans who are arrested for traffic violations is much higher than the proportion of whites in his city. State a possible explanation the chief should consider before concluding that African Americans are more reckless drivers than others.
2. Why is reverse causality not a credible explanation in this case?

Answer

1. His police officers expect African Americans to be more reckless and thus give them greater surveillance than other drivers. The "hood" expression is "arrested for DWB" (Driving While Black).
2. It is not possible for traffic violations to cause skin color.

trialist is himself an Old Tuephingen University graduate and may be subconsciously favoring his fellow alumni in promotion decisions.

Recent research published in the *Archives of Internal Medicine* (as reported in the *Herald-Times*, 2004) suggests that the arrival of spring can bring about a significant drop in cholesterol levels of people suffering from high cholesterol. Can we conclude that spring weather causes cholesterol levels to fall? A more likely explanation is that with the arrival of spring people get outside to walk and engage in other physical activity and that it is the increased physical activity that results in the drop in cholesterol. We can rule out common cause and reverse causality in this case, but it is plausible that another independent variable (exercise) could account for the finding.

An obvious first task for investigators is to attempt to list all the possible alternative independent variables. Then by holding the others constant, you can test in turn each variable to determine if it is related to Y. If you can eliminate the alternative independent variables by showing that they are not related to Y, you gain support for the original hypothesis of a relationship between X and Y.

AN APPLICATION OF ALTERNATIVE EXPLANATIONS

Is there a relationship between having a car and academic achievement among high school students? Some high school principals have asserted that car ownership has a negative effect on students' school attendance and their grades and have tried to place restrictions on students' use of cars at school. Is such a conclusion justified?

Let us consider the possible alternative hypotheses.

1. *Common cause*. Are there variables that may influence both auto use and scholarship? A possible common cause is student employment. Having a car may require students to work in order to afford the car. Working results in less time spent studying and thus lower grades. Differences in student lifestyle or values could also account for the apparent relationship. If some

THINK ABOUT IT 12.3

A supervisor of student teachers notices that those with pierced tongues get lower ratings from their mentor teachers than do other student teachers. The supervisor might hypothesize the following:

a. The same lifestyle that leads to pierced tongues leads to poor student teaching performance.
b. Pierced tongues lead to poor health, which leads to poor student teaching performance.
c. Student teachers who are not doing well decide to have their tongues pierced.
d. Mentor teachers imagine that pierced tongues indicate antisocial attitudes and give student teachers with pierced tongues lower ratings than they deserve.

Which of the above hypotheses represent the following possibilities:

1. Reverse causality
2. Cause/effect
3. Common cause
4. Alternate independent variable

Answers

1. c **2.** b **3.** a **4.** d

students value driving highly and have little interest in scholarship, denying them access to cars would not necessarily increase their scholarship. You could propose a number of credible common cause hypotheses.

2. *Reverse causality*. Is it possible that poor grades are a cause of car use? You could reasonably hypothesize that students who do poorly in school look for other paths to social acceptance and that car use is one possible path.
3. *Other possible independent variables*. Could having a car lead to an overactive social life that leaves less time for studying?

How could this question be investigated? Instead of considering only present grades and auto use, one could record grades of seniors at the end of the first semester and the grades of the same subjects when they were freshmen. If auto use affects scholarship, then the grades of drivers would be expected to drop between the time they were freshmen—and therefore ineligible for driver's licenses—and the time they were seniors. So the dependent variable would be the difference between freshman and senior GPA. One might also covary (see Chapter 11) on IQ.

PARTIAL CONTROL IN EX POST FACTO RESEARCH

There are strategies for improving the credibility of ex post facto research, although none can adequately compensate for the inherent weakness of such research—namely, lack of control over the independent variable. These strategies provide **partial control** of the internal validity problems of common cause and other possible independent variables. Among these strategies are matching, homogeneous groups, building extraneous variables into the design, analysis of covariance, and partial correlation.

MATCHING

A common method of providing partial control in ex post facto investigations has been to match the subjects in the experimental and control groups on as many extraneous variables as possible. This **matching** is usually done on a subject-to-subject basis to form matched pairs. For example, if you are interested in the relationship between scouting experiences and delinquency, you could locate two groups of boys classified as delinquent and nondelinquent according to specified criteria. In such a study, it would be wise to select pairs from these groups matched on the basis of socioeconomic status, family structure, and other variables known to be related to both choosing the scouting experience and delinquency. The data from the matched samples could be analyzed to determine whether the proportion of those who participated in scouting is greater among nondelinquents than among delinquents. The matching procedure in ex post facto research presents some of the difficulties described in our discussion of its use in experimentation (Chapter 10).

In the first place, using matching in an ex post facto study assumes that you know what the relevant factors are—that is, the factors that may have some correlation with the dependent variable. Even if you are able to match on a few relevant variables, you will leave many other variables unmatched, and these unmatched variables may affect the dependent variable. Furthermore, matching is likely to greatly reduce the number of subjects that can actually be used in the final analysis. Probably there are several variables that need to be controlled. As the number of matching variables grows, it becomes increasingly more difficult to find a match. The loss of cases inherent in the matching process is an even more serious problem in ex post facto research than in experimentation, where matching precedes the introduction of the independent variable.

A more serious problem than loss of subjects is the role of regression in an ex post facto matched-pairs design. Let us illustrate the point. Principal A has introduced a new reading program in the fifth grade, and after it has been in use for a year he wants to compare its effectiveness with the effectiveness of the reading program it replaced. In the same district, principal B's school is still using the old program. Both schools give the same standardized reading test at the end of each school year. Principal A compares the mean grade-equivalent reading scores for fifth-graders in the two schools. He finds the mean grade level equivalent for his fifth-graders is 6.0, whereas the mean for principal B's fifth-graders is 4.0. Is this dramatic evidence of the effectiveness of the new method? Principal A realizes that the difference between means could be caused by differences between the pupils when they began the fifth grade in the two schools. He obtains scores for the reading test administered when the pupils were finishing fourth grade. He finds that his students had a mean grade level equivalent of 4.8, whereas principal B's students had a mean grade level equivalent of only 3.2.

Therefore, he must make an adjustment for the fact that the two groups were not at the same point when they began fifth grade.

Principal A decided to use matching as a way to control for this difference. He selected matched pairs by taking a student from his school with a fourth-grade reading score of 3.1 and matching that student with a student from principal B's school with a fourth-grade reading score of 3.1, a student from his school with a score of 4.8, with a student from B's school with a score of 4.8 and so on. However, because the mean of the B population is lower than the mean of the A population, there will be many low-scoring B students for whom there is no match in A and many high-scoring A students for whom there is no match in the B group. The scores of all the unmatchable students will be excluded from the data analysis. For those who could be matched, the mean score for the pretreatment fourth-grade reading test for group A and group B will be identical. Therefore, it appears the researchers have successfully created a group from school B who are the same as the group from school A in reading achievement.

This all sounds very good. Can you now attribute differences in fifth-grade reading scores to a difference in the effectiveness of the old and new methods? Alas, no! The matched pairs are basically those students with poorer fourth-grade reading scores from population A and those students with higher scores from population B. The matched A students' scores will regress *up* toward the total A mean, and the matched B students' scores will regress *down* toward the total B mean. Thus, when you compare the fifth-grade reading scores of the matched groups, you would expect the A mean to be higher than the B mean even if the new method is no more effective than the old method.

Matching looks good because it provides experimental and control groups that are equal on a pretreatment variable or variables. However, when two matched groups are drawn from different populations, regression toward the original population means will be expected to create spurious results whenever the two populations are not equal. Matching pairs from within a *single* population is often a useful strategy. Matching subjects from one population with subjects from another population is a *bad* strategy. As is the case with change scores, matching only partly adjusts for preexisting differences between groups, and this under-adjustment can be misleading.

HOMOGENEOUS GROUPS

You may recall from the discussion of control in experimentation that it is possible to control for the effects of a variable by selecting samples that are as homogeneous as possible on that variable. A similar procedure can be followed in ex post facto research. Instead of taking a heterogeneous sample and comparing matched subgroups within it, an investigator may control a variable by including in the sample only subjects who are homogeneous on that variable. If academic aptitude is a relevant extraneous variable, the investigator could control its effect by using subjects from only one academic aptitude level. Or if gender is a variable to be controlled, you can use only males or only females in the research. This procedure serves the purpose of disentangling the independent variable in which you may be interested from other variables with which it is commonly associated, so that any effects you find can more justifiably be associated with the independent variable. Using **homogeneous groups** restricts the generalizability of the findings to that homogeneous group, thus reducing external validity of the study. Lee and Loeb (2000) used homogeneous groups in studying the effect of school size on teacher attitudes and student achievement. They avoided any influence the dimension of rural, suburban, and urban settings might have on the dependent variables by studying only schools in the city of Chicago. They found that in small schools (those with fewer than 400 students), teachers had a more positive attitude about their responsibility for students' learning and students learned more than in medium-sized or large schools.

BUILDING EXTRANEOUS VARIABLES INTO THE DESIGN

It may be possible to build relevant extraneous independent variables into the ex post facto design and investigate their effect through the use of two-way and higher-order analyses of variance. For example, suppose an investigator wants to compare the number of truancies among students who have been through an attendance-promoting program and among students who have not been in such a program. If the investigator thinks that ethnic membership and gender influence the number of truancies, the subjects could be classified as Anglo, Hispanic, Asian American, or black and as male or female. An *F* test would first be used to assess the main effect of program versus no program on number of truancies. An *F* test for gender would assess the truancy differences of males and females. The *F* test for ethnicity by program versus no program would assess whether the effect of the program was consistent among the ethnic groups. The *F* test for program by gender would assess the consistency of program effectiveness between genders. The gender by ethnicity *F* test would assess the consistency of gender differences in truancy among ethnic groups. Finally, the $2 \times 4 \times 2$ higher-order interaction *F* test would indicate if the treatment by ethnic group interaction was consistent between males and females. Building other variables into an ex post facto design is a partial solution, but you can never be sure that you have *all* the variables that should have been considered.

ANALYSIS OF COVARIANCE

Analysis of covariance (ANCOVA) is sometimes used to partially adjust for preexisting differences between groups in an ex post facto design. Specifically, it adjusts scores on the dependent variable for any initial differences on the extraneous variable. However, as the adjustment is only partial, ANCOVA does not "solve" the problem of initial differences between groups but only reduces it. When interpreting ex post facto research, it is inappropriate to assume ANCOVA has satisfactorily adjusted for initial differences.

A classic example of the problems inherent in matching and analysis of covariance is the Cicirelli (1969) ex post facto investigation of the effects of the Head Start program. This study compared the academic achievement of students who had been in the Head Start program with the achievement of those who had not been in the Head Start program. Children who had been in the program were matched with non–Head Start children from the same neighborhoods on gender, racial/ethnic groups, and kindergarten attendance. Analysis of covariance was used to adjust for differences in income per capita, educational level of father, and occupational level of father. The results indicated that the achievement of the non–Head Start group was greater than that of the Head Start group even when scores were adjusted for initial differences. The authors concluded that the Head Start program was harmful. Researchers have pointed out that because of regression, both matching and analysis of covariance underadjust for initial differences between groups. One would therefore expect adjusted posttreatment scores of a disadvantaged group to be less than adjusted posttreatment scores of a less disadvantaged group. Because the extent of the underadjustment is unknown, the Cicirelli study (1969) does not determine whether the Head Start experience was harmful or beneficial or had no effect.

PARTIAL CORRELATION

Partial correlation can be used to determine the extent of the relationship between two variables when their relationship to other variables has been removed or "partialed out." For example, partial correlation could show the relationship between need for achievement and academic achievement in science with the influence of science aptitude removed. When both independent and dependent variables are continuous, partial correlation provides an adjustment similar to the adjustment that analysis of covariance provides when independent variable(s) are discrete. We discuss partial correlation in Chapter 13.

THE ROLE OF EX POST FACTO RESEARCH

Given the hazards involved in ex post facto research, many educational researchers feel they should not engage in this type of research at all. Basically, they contend that it is better to admit ignorance than to risk reaching incorrect conclusions. However, others point out that many variables of great interest are not amenable to experimental research. Researchers cannot randomly assign children to broken or intact homes, to high or low social class, to achievement-oriented or non-achievement-oriented peer groups, to high or low self-esteem groups, and so forth. Therefore, if they want to learn anything about relationships between such attribute variables and other variables, the ex post facto method is their only recourse. An ex post facto study is better than no study at all. If researchers use appropriate methods of partial control and consider alternative hypotheses, perhaps they can be right more often than wrong.

Certainly, there have been many highly credible ex post facto studies. The U.S. Surgeon General's study of the relationship between smoking and lung cancer is a well-known example. It is not possible to designate randomly a group of human subjects who are to smoke for years and a group who are not to smoke, so the study had to be done as an ex post facto investigation. The reversed-causality hypothesis that lung cancer causes people to smoke is not plausible. None of the common-cause hypotheses offered seem very likely: Nervous people are prone to both smoking and lung cancer, some genetic predisposition leads to both, and so forth. The Surgeon General controlled for many alternative independent variables—for example, by analyzing separately samples from areas of high air pollution and low air pollution. Experimental evidence with animals who were made to inhale or not inhale cigarette smoke produced evidence of a cause–effect relationship. Given all this, despite the dangers inherent in ex post facto research, most would conclude that it is better to bet there *is* a cause-to-effect relationship between smoking and lung cancer among humans than to bet there is *not* such a relationship. In fact, much medical research is ex post facto in design. Researchers study diseases and try to determine the influence of factors such as eating habits, lifestyle, genes, and so on. The new science of "fetal programming" is looking at the effect of conditions and development—in utero—and adult health. Ex post facto research in education has permitted investigations of the effects of variables such as home background, father absence, early experiences, disabilities, teacher competence, and others that are beyond the control of educators. In some instances, ex post facto research has discovered relationships or raised questions that can later be investigated more systematically in well-controlled experimental studies. Appropriately used and cautiously interpreted, ex post facto, or causal-comparative, research will continue to provide a valuable methodology for the acquisition of knowledge.

SUMMARY

Ex post facto research is used to investigate cause-and-effect relationships when the researcher cannot randomly assign subjects to different conditions or directly manipulate the independent variable. Ex post facto research begins with subjects who differ on an observed dependent variable and tries to determine the antecedents (cause) of the difference. Or the researcher begins with subjects who differ on an independent variable and tries to determine the consequences of the difference.

Although there are many disadvantages of ex post facto design, it nevertheless is frequently the only method by which educational researchers can obtain necessary information about characteristics of defined groups of students or information needed for the intelligent formulation of programs in the school. It permits researchers to investigate situations in which controlled variation is impossible to introduce. Attributes such as academic aptitude, creativity, self-esteem, socioeconomic status, and teacher personality cannot be manipulated and hence must be investigated through ex post facto research rather than through the more rigorous experimental approach.

The possibility of spurious relationships is always present in ex post facto research. Considering the possibilities of common cause, reversed causality, and possible alternate independent variables can help educators evaluate such research more realistically. Several partial control strategies can help researchers avoid gross errors in ex post facto designs, but none can entirely solve the problems inherent in those designs. Always exercise caution in interpreting causal-comparative results.

EXAMPLE OF EX POST FACTO RESEARCH

The following is an abstract of a published ex post facto research study. You may find the complete article in *The High School Journal*, Dec/Jan 2000, 21–27.

Academic Achievement and Parental School Involvement as a Function of High School Size

Pamela W. Gardner
Shulamit N. Ritblatt
James R. Beatty
San Diego State University

The purpose of this research was to examine academic achievement, absenteeism, dropout rate, and parental school involvement as a function of high school size. Previous studies indicated that, generally, students of small schools exhibited greater extracurricular participation, greater satisfaction, lower absenteeism, and lower dropout rate. In terms of academic achievement, findings have been mixed.

Academic achievement was measured by scores on the Scholastic Aptitude Test (SAT), while parent participation was measured by membership in the Parent Teacher Association (PTA) or other parent organization(s). Absenteeism and dropout rate were measured using data provided by the California Department of Education.

Sixty-seven randomly selected large California public high schools (enrollments over 2,000) were compared to sixty randomly selected small California public high schools (enrollments between 200 and 600 students). The t-tests and analyses of covariance were employed to determine the differences between the large and small high schools. Contrary to several hypotheses, the large schools exhibited higher academic achievement on total SAT score, verbal SAT score, and math SAT score. In addition, this cohort had a higher proportion of students taking the SAT. Confirming other hypotheses, the small school cohort displayed lower absenteeism, lower dropout rate, and higher parental school involvement.

The results of this investigation indicate the need for further research, both in size and scope. In addition, the findings carry implications for educational policy decisions. Standard procedures for reporting absenteeism and parental school involvement should be established.

KEY CONCEPTS

active independent variable
analysis of covariance (ANCOVA)
attribute independent variable
causal relationship
common cause
ex post facto (causal-comparative) research
extraneous variable
homogeneous groups
matching
partial control
post hoc fallacy
reverse causality
spurious relationship

EXERCISES

1. What are the two major limitations of ex post facto or causal-comparative designs?
2. Classify the following independent variables as active or attribute:
   a. Kindergarten entrance age
   b. Method of teaching reading
   c. Montessori school attendance versus attendance at public school
   d. Teaching experience
   e. Use of drug A in treating diabetes versus drug B
   f. Learning style
3. What method would you use to investigate the following research hypothesis?
   a. High school students who work during the school year will have lower grades and lower standardized test scores than students who do not work.
   b. First-grade students who are taught reading using phonics will read at a higher level than first-grade students taught by another method.
   c. Beginning teachers who are mentored will be more effective and express more satisfaction with teaching than beginning teachers who are not mentored.
   d. Students who are in small classes (under 15) in grades K to 3 will perform at a higher level in grades 4 to 6 than will students in regular-sized classes (over 20).
4. Interpret this statement: "A statistical relationship between two variables is a necessary but not a sufficient condition for inferring a causal relationship between the variables."
5. Show the design you would use to test the hypothesis stated in Exercise 3(a).
6. What alternative hypotheses would you want to explore if your causal-comparative research indicates that there is a relationship between self-concept and achievement in school?
7. What steps would you take to avoid the post hoc fallacy in your ex post facto research?
8. In the following examples, suggest an alternative explanation for the finding:
   a. A researcher finds a relationship between use of alcohol and unemployment and concludes that using alcohol causes workers to lose their jobs.
   b. A researcher finds that the proportion of the population confined to mental hospitals for manic-depression is greater in the United States than it is in England. He concludes that the American environment is more conducive to the development of depression.
   c. A researcher finds that the increase in the use of cell phones in recent years has been accompanied by an increase in the incidence of brain tumors. He concludes that using a cell phone can result in a brain tumor.
9. Find an example of an ex post facto study in the current literature. Identify (a) the problem, (b) the operational definitions of the variables, (c) the design used, (d) the steps taken to control extraneous variables, (e) the findings, and (f) the conclusions. Did the author include a caveat about the conclusion?
10. A recent study reported that of 4500 women who underwent dental X-rays during pregnancy 1117 had low-birth-weight babies. The researchers concluded that

women who have dental X-rays during pregnancy face an increased risk of having underweight babies. What questions might you want to ask about this research before accepting their conclusion?

11. The following are examples of published studies. Which do you think involve ex post facto research methodology?
    a. Do After-School Programs Help Students Succeed?
    b. The Impact of Hope and Social Activity on Academic Performance of Midwestern College Students.
    c. The Importance of Middle School Math on High School Mathematics Achievement.
    d. The Effect of Using Classroom LapTop Computers on the Writing of Middle School Students.

ANSWERS

1. The two major limitations are lack of randomization and lack of manipulation of the independent variable.
2. a. Attribute
   b. Active
   c. Attribute
   d. Attribute
   e. Active
   f. Attribute
3. a. Ex post facto
   b. Experimental
   c. Experimental
   d. Ex post facto (it is generally not feasible to manipulate class size, although it has been done)
4. To report that one variable (X) is the cause of another variable (Y), the researcher must first show that there is a statistical relationship between the variables. But this finding by itself is not sufficient to establish a causal relationship. The researcher must examine the time (X must precede Y) and must show that no other variables could cause Y.
5. Use ex post facto design 1. That is, you would select two groups of high school students, one of whom works a certain number of hours each week (X), and would compare their grades and scores on standardized tests (Y) with a comparable group of students who do not work. Or, instead of studying the effect of working or not working, you could study the effect of the *extent* of work as measured by the number of hours worked each week. One group could work less than 10 hours a week, and the other group could work 20 or more hours. You would have to control a number of variables, including aptitude scores, previous grades, socioeconomic status, and gender. If you used only one class level (only juniors or only seniors), you could control for the variable of class standing (if relevant).
6. A more positive self-concept could lead to higher achievement in school. Or the reversed causality hypothesis could account for the finding. That is, higher achievement in school could lead to a more positive self-concept. You would also want to explore a common-cause hypothesis. Perhaps another variable, such as intelligence, causes both achievement and self-concept.
7. Try to control any relevant extraneous variables that could affect the measured variable. Methods of control include (a) matching, (b) using homogeneous groups, (c) building extraneous variables into the design, and (d) using ANCOVA or other statistical means to partially control unwanted variables.
8. a. Perhaps unemployment leads to the use of alcohol. Or perhaps profound depression causes people to lose their jobs and also take to drink.
   b. Perhaps depressed people in England receive a different type of treatment and are less likely to be hospitalized than in the United States. Perhaps English psychologists are less inclined to make a diagnosis of depression.
   c. Perhaps there is a common cause. The stress and rapid pace of life at the turn of the century is conducive to the use of

cell phones and may also influence the development of brain tumors.

9. Answers will vary.
10. One would first want to ask why the women received X-rays because, normally, dentists are cautious about using X-rays during pregnancy. Perhaps there was some disease or infection that necessitated the use of X-rays, and it was the disease or infection that caused the low-birth-weight babies. The study's lead author stated that more research is needed to determine if dental X-rays really were the culprit.
11. b and c are ex post facto research.

INFOTRAC COLLEGE EDITION

Use the keywords *theory* + *research* to locate a research study that used an ex post facto design. Hint: Locate the study investigating the effect of maternal child-rearing practices on preschoolers' delay of gratification behavior. Why was an ex post facto design chosen? How were the variables operationally defined? What methods of partial control were used? Were the conclusions justified?

Chapter 13

Correlational Research

CORRELATION REVEALS RELATIONSHIP BUT NOT NECESSARILY CAUSATION.

INSTRUCTIONAL OBJECTIVES

After studying this chapter, the student will be able to:

1. Describe the nature of correlational research.
2. Describe the ways correlational research is used.
3. Describe the design of correlational research.
4. Discuss the limitations of correlational research.
5. Distinguish between correlation and ex post facto research.
6. List different types of correlation coefficients and state the conditions for their appropriate use.
7. Interpret correlation coefficients in terms of sign, magnitude, statistical significance, and practical significance.
8. Test a hypothesis about a correlation coefficient, r.
9. Define predictor and criterion.
10. Define multiple regression, and explain when it is used.
11. Define discriminant analysis and explain its purpose.
12. Define factor analysis and explain its purpose.
13. Distinguish exploratory factor analysis and confirmatory factor analysis.
14. Define partial correlation and explain its purpose.
15. Describe a research study in which *canonical correlation* would be appropriate.
16. Define path analysis and briefly explain its purpose.
17. Define structural equation modeling.

Correlational research is a type of nonexperimental research that investigates whether there is an association between two or more variables. Specifically, it investigates how scores on one or more variables rise and fall as scores on other variables rise or fall. We want to know if high scores on one variable are associated with high scores on another variable (and low scores with low scores), or whether high scores on one are associated with low scores on the other. If the relationship takes either of these forms, we say that there is a correlation between the variables. Educators are interested in the correlation between certain variables and school achievement. For example, what is the relationship between class size and achievement or extent of parental involvement and achievement?

Correlational research differs from experimental research in that there is usually no manipulation of the variables. It simply investigates the extent to which the variables are related and the direction of the relationship. Beginning researchers often confuse correlational research with ex post facto or causal-comparative research. Correlational research relates two (or more) variable measures from the *same group of subjects*, whereas ex post facto research compares two (or more) groups on the *same variable measure*. Although ex post facto research *seeks* to establish cause–effect relationships, correlational research usually does not. Another difference is that the "cause" in ex post facto research is usually a discretely scaled variable (categorical), whereas in correlational research the variables are typically continuous. When correlational research finds a relationship between two variables, researchers say that the variables are *correlated*. The strength and direction of the relationship are described by means of a quantitative index called the **coefficient of correlation**. Recall from Chapter 6 that in interpreting a coefficient of correlation, one looks at both its sign and its size. The sign (+ or −) of the coefficient indicates the direction of the relationship. If the coefficient has a positive sign, this means that as one variable increases, the other also increases. For example, the correlation between height and weight is positive because tall people tend to be heavier and short people lighter. A negative coefficient indicates that as one variable increases, the other decreases. The correlation between outdoor air temperature during the winter months and heating bills is negative; as temperature decreases, heating bills rise.

The size of the correlation coefficient indicates the strength of the relationship between the variables. The coefficient can range in value from +1.00 (indicating a perfect positive relationship) through 0 (indicating no relationship) to −1.00 (indicating a perfect negative relationship). A perfect positive relationship means that for every z-score unit increase in one variable, there is an identical z-score unit increase in the other. A perfect negative relationship indicates that for every unit increase in one variable there is an identical unit decrease in the other. Few

THINK ABOUT IT 13.1

Interpret each of the following:

1. The correlation between time spent watching television and time spent reading is −.44.
2. The correlation between socioeconomic status and number of museums visited is +.21.
3. The correlation between days absent from school and kindergarten reading scores is −.58.

Answers

1. The more time spent watching TV, the less time spent reading; there is a negative relationship.
2. The higher the socioeconomic status, the more museums visited; there is a positive relationship.
3. The more days absent, the lower the reading scores; there is a negative relationship.

variables ever show perfect correlation, especially in relating human traits. Most range somewhere between 0 and ± 1.00, such as $+.40$ for the correlation between a scholastic aptitude measure and grade point average in high school, or $-.40$ for the correlation between days absent from school and spelling test scores. The correlation between aptitude scores and weight for a sample of adult subjects would be expected to be about zero.

USES OF CORRELATIONAL RESEARCH

Correlational research is useful in a wide variety of studies. The most useful applications of correlation are (1) determining relationships, (2) assessing consistency, and (3) prediction.

DETERMINING RELATIONSHIPS

Correlational research methods are used to determine relationships and patterns of relationship among variables in a single group of subjects. For instance, correlational research is used to answer questions such as, Is there a relationship between math aptitude and achievement in computer science? What is the direction and strength of this relationship, if any? You would most likely predict that a positive relationship will be found between scores on a math aptitude test and grades in computer science. A correlational study would determine the extent of any relationship between these variables.

Other examples of questions that could be investigated in a correlational study are: What is the relationship between self-esteem and academic achievement? Is there a relationship between musical aptitude and mathematics achievement among 6-year-olds? What is the relationship between watching media violence and aggression in children?

In some correlational studies, the researcher may be able to state a hypothesis about the expected relationship. For example, from phenomenological theory you might hypothesize that there is a positive relationship between first-grade children's perceptions of themselves and their achievement in reading. In other instances, the researcher may lack the information necessary to state a hypothesis.

You may recall from Chapter 9 that the correlation between test scores and selected external variables is a widely used source of evidence in validity studies.

ASSESSING CONSISTENCY

In Chapter 9 we noted that the reliability (consistency) of a test can be assessed through correlating test–retest, equivalent-forms, or split-half scores. Correlation can be used to measure consistency (or lack thereof) in a wide variety of cases. For example, how consistent are the independently assigned merit ratings given by the principal and the assistant principal to teachers in a school? How much agreement is there among Olympic judges rating the performance of a group of gymnasts? When a researcher asks a group of teachers to rank the severity of disruption created by each item on a list of behavior disorders, to what extent do their rankings agree?

PREDICTION

If you find that two variables are correlated, then you can use one variable to predict the other. The higher the correlation, the more accurate the prediction. Prediction studies are frequently used in education. For example, correlational research has shown that high school grades and scholastic aptitude measures are related to college GPA. If a student scores high on aptitude tests and has high grades in high school, he or she is more likely to make high grades in college than is a student who scores low on the two predictor variables. Researchers can predict with a certain degree of accuracy a student's probable freshman GPA from high school grades and aptitude test scores. This prediction will not hold for every case because other factors such as motivation, initiative, or study habits are not considered. But in general, the prediction is accurate enough to be useful to college admissions officers.

DESIGN OF CORRELATIONAL STUDIES

The basic design for correlational research is straightforward. First, the researcher specifies the problem by asking a question about the relationship between the variables of interest. The variables selected for investigation are generally based on a theory, previous research, or on the researcher's observations. Because of the potential for spurious results, we do not recommend the "shotgun" approach in which one correlates a number of variables just to see what might show up. The population of interest is also identified at this time. In simple correlational studies, the researcher focuses on gathering data on two (or more) measures from *one* group of subjects. For example, you might correlate vocabulary and reading comprehension scores for a group of middle school students. Occasionally, correlational studies investigate relationships between scores on one measure for logically paired groups such as twins, siblings, or husbands and wives. For instance, a researcher might want to look at the correlation between the SAT scores of identical twins.

An example of a typical correlational research question might be, What is the relationship between quantitative ability and achievement in science among high school students? You might state a hypothesis that the two variables are significantly related in the specified group. The hypothesis might be stated in a nondirectional form or in the directional form of a positive or negative relationship. In the preceding example, the researcher would most likely predict a significant positive relationship between students' quantitative ability and their achievement in science.

Next the researcher determines how the constructs, such as ability and achievement in the preceding example, will be quantified. He or she may already be aware of well-accepted operational definitions of the constructs, may seek definitions in sources such as those described in Chapter 4, or may develop his or her own operational definitions and then assess their reliability and validity. In the example, the researcher may decide that quantitative ability will be defined as scores on the School and College Ability Test, Series III (SCAT III), and science achievement will be defined as scores on the science sections of the Sequential Tests of Educational Progress (STEP III).

Figure 13.1 Design of a Correlational Study

It is important in correlational studies to select or develop measures that are appropriate indicators of the constructs to be investigated, and it is especially important that these instruments have satisfactory reliability and are valid for measuring the constructs under consideration. The size of a coefficient of correlation is influenced by the adequacy of the measuring instruments for their intended purpose. For instance, instruments that are too easy or too difficult for the subjects of a study would not discriminate among them and would result in a smaller correlation coefficient than instruments with appropriate difficulty levels. Studies using instruments with low reliability and questionable validity are unlikely to produce useful results.

Next the researcher selects the sample to represent the specified population. Typically, correlational studies do not require extremely large samples. You can assume that if a relationship exists, it will be evident in a sample of moderate size (e.g., 50 to 100). We do not recommend samples with fewer than 30 subjects. If the researcher is interested in generalizing the findings to a large population, he or she will need to draw a random sample from that population. For example, if a researcher wants to generalize the results from the correlational study of quantitative ability and science achievement to all secondary school students in a district, then a random sample of all the secondary students in that district should be drawn.

Finally, the researcher collects the quantitative data on the two or more variables for each of the students in the sample and then calculates the coefficient(s) of correlation between the paired scores. Even before calculating the coefficient, the researcher should look at a scatterplot or a graph of the relationship between the variables. Most correlational procedures assume a linear relationship between the variables (see Figure 6.14). Figure 13.1 illustrates the basic design for a correlational study.

CORRELATION COEFFICIENTS

There are many different kinds of correlation coefficients. The researcher chooses the appropriate statistical procedure primarily on the basis of (1) the scale of measurement of the measures used and (2) the number of variables.

PEARSON'S PRODUCT MOMENT COEFFICIENT OF CORRELATION

In Chapter 6 we introduced you to the Pearson product moment correlation coefficient, symbolized r, which is the most widely used descriptive statistic of correlation. You may recall that the Pearson coefficient is appropriate for use when the variables to be correlated are normally distributed and measured on an interval or ratio scale. We will briefly mention some of the other indexes of correlation without going into their computation. Interested students should consult statistics books for the computational procedures.

SPEARMAN'S RHO COEFFICIENT OF CORRELATION

Spearman's rho (ρ), an ordinal coefficient of correlation, is used when the data are ranks rather than raw scores. For example, assume the principal and assistant principal have independently ranked the 15 teachers in their school from first, most effective, to fifteenth, least effective, and you want to assess how much their ranks agree. You would calculate the Spearman's rho by putting the paired ranks into the Pearson *r* formula or by using a formula developed specifically for rho. Interested readers are referred to a statistics book.

Spearman's rho is interpreted the same as is Pearson *r*. Like the Pearson product moment coefficient of correlation, it ranges from −1.00 to +1.00. When each individual has the same rank on both variables, the rho correlation will be +1.00, and when their ranks on one variable are exactly the opposite of their ranks on the other variable, rho will be −1.00. If there is no relationship at all between the rankings, the rank correlation coefficient will be 0. If you have a computer or calculator program for Pearson *r*, you can calculate Spearman rho by putting the ranks into that program.

THE PHI COEFFICIENT

The **phi (ϕ) coefficient** is used when both variables are genuine dichotomies scored 1 or 0. For example, phi would be used to describe the relationship between the gender of high school students and whether they are counseled to take college preparatory courses or not. Gender is dichotomized as male = 0, female = 1. Being counseled to take college preparatory courses is scored 1, not being so counseled is scored 0. It is possible to enter the pairs of dichotomous scores (1's and 0's) into a program that computes Pearson *r*'s and arrive at the phi coefficient.

If you find the phi coefficient in school A is −.15, it indicates that there is a slight tendency to counsel more boys than girls to take college preparatory courses. If in school B the phi coefficient is −.51, it indicates a strong tendency in the same direction. As with the other correlations, the phi coefficient indicates both direction and strength of relationships.

If a scatterplot shows that the relationship is not linear but curvilinear, the most commonly used correlation coefficients are not appropriate because they underestimate the degree of relationship. The *eta correlation ratio* is appropriate in such cases.

A variety of correlation coefficients are available for use with ordinal and nominal data. These include coefficients for data that are more than just pairs; for example, assessing the agreement of three or more judges ranking the performance of the same subjects. A useful source of such correlations is Siegel and Castellan's (1988) classic text.

CONSIDERATIONS FOR INTERPRETING A CORRELATION COEFFICIENT

The coefficient of correlation may be simple to calculate, but it can be tricky to interpret. It is probably one of the most misinterpreted and/or overinterpreted statistics available to researchers. Various considerations need to be taken into account when evaluating the practical utility of a correlation. The importance of the numerical value of a particular correlation may be evaluated in three ways: (1) according to its absolute size and predictive utility, (2) in relation to other correlations of the same or similar variables, or (3) in terms of its statistical significance.

ABSOLUTE SIZE AND PREDICTIVE VALIDITY

Unsophisticated consumers of research often assume that a correlation indicates percentage of relationship, for example, that an *r* of .60 means the two variables are 60 percent related. No, *r* is the mean *z*-score product for the two variables, not a percentage. The absolute size of the correlation coefficient (how far it is from zero) indicates how strong the relationship is. Thus, a correlation of −.4 indicates a stronger relationship than a +.2 because it is further from zero. The sign has nothing to do with the strength of the relationship. Another way to see how closely two variables are related is to square the correlation coefficient. When you square the Pearson *r*, you get an index called the **coefficient of determination, r^2**, which tells you how much of the variance of *X* is in common with the variance of *Y*. A correlation of +.60 or −.60 means that the two variables have ($.60^2$) or 36 percent of their variance in common with each other. If the two variables were caffeine and reaction time, then the amount of caffeine one has consumed would be associated with 36 percent of the variance in one's reaction time. That leaves 64 percent of the variance in reaction time associated with factors other than variation in caffeine intake. The notion of common variance is illustrated in Figure 13.2, where the total amount of variation in each variable is represented by a circle. The overlap of the circles represents the common variance.

An increase in the *r* results in an accelerating increase in r^2. A correlation of .20 yields a coefficient of determination of .04. An *r* of .4 yields an r^2 of .16. An *r* of .8 yields an r^2 of .64, and so on. The coefficient of determination is a useful index for evaluating the meaning of size of a correlation. It also reminds one that

THINK ABOUT IT 13.2

Criticize the conclusions reached in the following examples:

1. The correlation between two variables in an investigation turned out to be negative. The researcher reported that there was no relationship between the variables.
2. A scatterplot showed that the points were all close to a straight line. The researcher concluded that this indicated a positive correlation between the variables.

Answers

1. There is a relationship; the negative correlation means that high scores on one variable are associated with low scores on the other. As one variable increases, the other decreases.
2. It could also indicate a negative correlation. It depends on the direction of the straight line.

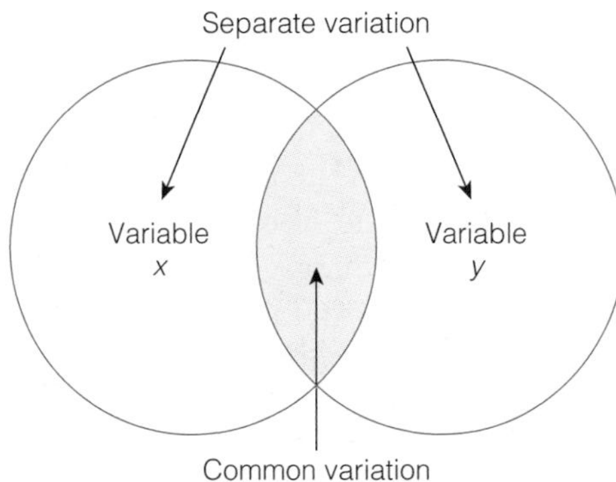

Figure 13.2 The Common Variance between Two Variables

positive and negative correlations of the same magnitude, say $r = .5$ and $r = -.5$, are equally useful for prediction and other uses because both have the same coefficient of determination, $r^2 = .25$. The coefficient of determination ranges from 0 to +1.00. If it is 1.00 ($r = +1.00$), you can predict individuals' scores on one variable perfectly from their scores on the other variable.

CORRELATION AS EFFECT SIZE

The Pearson r as a measure of relationships independent of sample size is a form of effect size. Cohen (1988), employing the same logic used for describing small, medium, and large effect sizes for differences between means (see Chapter 6), has suggested the following conventions for the effect sizes of correlations:

$r = .10$ small
$r = .30$ medium
$r = .50$ large

Obviously, a correlation of .10 with only 1 percent of the variance in common is small. Although an r of .30 with a coefficient of determination indicating only 9 percent common variance may at first seem small, the relationship and the size of the relationship can be seen in a scatterplot (see Figure 6.12). Many correlation coefficients encountered in the behavioral sciences are of this order of magnitude. For example, correlation coefficients between personality tests and real-life criteria typically fall around .30. Correlations within a single variable, such as two measures of the same thing, often exceed .5. Correlations of competing tests of spelling proficiency are typically about .80. Correlations between equivalent forms of a single test are often in excess of .90. However, correlations between different variables in the behavioral sciences rarely approach that level. As Cohen (1988) says, "Thus, when an investigator anticipates a degree of correlation between two different variables 'about as high as they come' this would by our definition be a large effect, $r = .50$" (p. 81). Cohen's conventions for correlations—small $r = .10$ ($r^2 = .01$), medium, $r = .30$ ($r^2 = .09$), and large $r = .50$ ($r^2 = .25$)—are approximately equal in terms of accounted-for variance to his conventions for differences between means effect sizes of .2, indicating small; .5, indicating medium; and .8, indicating large.

COMPARISON TO OTHER CORRELATIONS

The magnitude of a correlation must also be assessed in relation to other correlations of the same or similar variables. For example, an *r* of .75 would be considered low for the relationship between the results of two equivalent forms of an achievement test, but it would be considered high for the relationship between an aptitude measure and grades for college freshmen. Over the years both the SAT and the American College Testing (ACT) tests have typically correlated with subsequent college freshman GPAs by about $r = .40$. A correlation of .40 is less than Cohen's definition of a high correlation. However, the 16 percent of variance in freshman GPAs that can be predicted from either of these tests is sufficiently helpful for making admissions decisions that their use is justified. Anyone who could create a test for high school seniors with a correlation of .50 with college freshman GPA could make a fortune marketing it because it would account for 25 percent ($.50^2$) of freshman GPA as opposed to 16 percent ($.40^2$) for ACT or SAT. A way to assess the size of a correlation is to define a high correlation as one that is higher than its competition and a low correlation as one that is lower than its competition. To help evaluate obtained correlations, the researcher should determine from a review of the literature what levels of correlation are typically found for specific types of data.

STATISTICAL SIGNIFICANCE

In evaluating the size of a correlation, it is important to consider the size of the sample on which the correlation is based. Without knowing the sample size, you do not know if the correlation could easily have occurred merely as a result of chance or is likely to be an indication of a genuine relationship. If there were fewer than 20 cases in the sample (which we would not recommend), then a "high" *r* of .50 could easily occur by chance. You should be very careful in attaching too much importance to large correlations when small sample sizes are involved; an *r* found in a small sample does not necessarily mean that a correlation exists in the population.

To avoid the error of inferring a relationship in the population that does not really exist, the researcher should state the null hypothesis that the population correlation equals 0 (H_0: $\rho_{xy} = 0$) and then determine whether the obtained sample correlation departs sufficiently from 0 to justify the rejection of the null hypothesis. In Chapter 7 we showed you how to use Table A.3 in the Appendix, which lists critical values of *r* for different numbers of degrees of freedom (*df*). By comparing the obtained *r* with the critical values of *r* listed in the table, you can determine the statistical significance of a product moment correlation. For example, assume a correlational study involving 92 students yields a correlation of .45. The critical value listed in Table A.3 is .27 at the .01 level and .21 at the .05 level. Because the obtained correlation of .45 exceeds the tabled values, the researcher can report that the correlation is statistically significant. The null hypothesis would be rejected, and the researcher would tentatively conclude that the two variables are related in the population.

You can see in Table A.3 that the smaller the sample, the larger the absolute size of the correlation must be to reach statistical significance. Table A.3 shows that with 22 cases ($df = 20$), a coefficient of .54 is needed to be significant at the .01 level. With 102 cases, however, a correlation of .25 is significant at the .01 level. When $N = 1000$, an r of .08 is significant at the .01 level. The larger the sample, the more likely a given correlation coefficient is to be statistically significant.

PRACTICAL UTILITY

Always consider the practical significance of the correlation coefficient. Even though a correlation coefficient may be statistically significant, it may have little practical utility. We have seen that with a sample of 1000, a very small coefficient such as .08 would be statistically significant at the .01 level. But of what practical importance would this correlation be? Information on X only accounts for less than 1 percent (.08 = .0064 or 00.64 percent) of the variance in Y (r^2). In this case it would hardly be worth the bother of collecting scores on a predictor variable, X, to predict another variable, Y. You want to avoid the **significance fallacy**, which assumes that a statistically significant correlation also has practical significance. Statistical significance alone is not sufficient. How worthwhile a correlation may be is partly a function of its predictive utility in relation to the cost of obtaining predictor data. A **predictor** with a high correlation that is difficult and expensive to obtain may be of less practical value than a cheap and easy predictor with a lower correlation. Also, note that a correlation coefficient only describes the degree of relationship between given operational definitions of predictor and predicted variables in a particular research situation for a given sample of subjects. It can easily change in value if the same variables are measured and correlated using different operational definitions and/or a different sample.

Failure to find a statistically significant relationship between two variables in one study does not necessarily mean there is *no* relationship between the variables. It only means that in that particular study, sufficient evidence for a relationship was not found. Recall from Chapter 6 that other factors, such as reliability of the measures used and range of possible values on the measures, influence the size of a correlation coefficient.

CORRELATION AND CAUSATION

In evaluating a correlational study, one of the most frequent errors is to interpret a correlation as indicating a cause-and-effect relationship. Saslow (1982) refers to this practice of interpreting correlation as causation as one of the "seven deadly sins" committed by researchers. Correlation is a necessary but never a sufficient condition for causation. For example, if a significant positive correlation is found between number of hours of television watched per week and body weight among middle school pupils, that does not prove that excessive television watching causes obesity. Recall from Chapter 12 that when the independent variable is not under the investigator's control alternate explanations must be considered. In this example, reverse causality is plausible. Perhaps the more overweight a child is, the more he or she is inclined to choose television watching instead of physical activities, games, and interacting with peers. The common-

Table 13.1 Possible Interpretations of a Relationship between Self-esteem and Academic Achievement

Cause		Effect
Self-esteem	→	Achievement (self-esteem causes achievement)
Achievement	→	Self-esteem (achievement causes self-esteem)
Intelligence	→	Self-esteem (a third factor causes both)
	→	Achievement
Home environment	→	Self-esteem (a third factor causes both)
	→	Achievement

Table 13.2 Possible Interpretations of a Relationship between Children's Watching Television Violence and Aggression

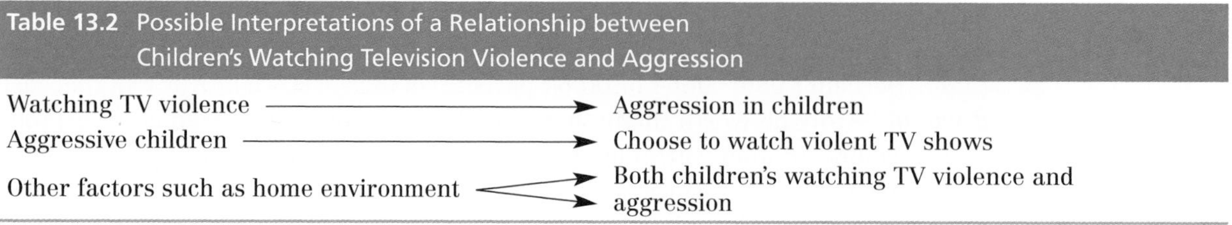

Cause		Effect
Watching TV violence	→	Aggression in children
Aggressive children	→	Choose to watch violent TV shows
Other factors such as home environment	→	Both children's watching TV violence and aggression

cause explanation is also plausible. Perhaps differences in family recreational patterns and lifestyle account for both differences in weight and time spent watching television.

Consider another example. Assume a researcher finds a relationship between measures of self-esteem and academic achievement (grades) for a sample of students. Table 13.1 summarizes the possibilities for interpreting this observed relationship. Any number of factors could act together to lead to both self-esteem and academic achievement: previous academic experiences, parents' education, peer relationships, motivation, and so.

Let us consider the example of the relationship between amount of violence children watch on television and their aggression. Most research has shown a relationship between these two variables, which many people assume is causal. But Table 13.2 shows other explanations for this relationship.

We must stress, however, that correlation can bring evidence to bear for cause and effect. The Surgeon General's warning about the dangers of cigarette smoking are, in part, based on studies that found positive correlations between the number of cigarettes smoked per day and incidence of lung cancer and other maladies. Here, reverse causality (cancer leads to cigarette smoking) is not a credible explanation. Various common-cause hypotheses (such as people who live in areas with high air pollution smoke more and have higher cancer rates) have been shown not to be the case.

Although correlational research does not permit one to infer causality, it may generate causal hypotheses that can be investigated through experimental research methods. For example, finding the correlation between smoking and lung cancer led to animal experiments that allowed scientists to infer a causal link between smoking and lung cancer. Because the correlational studies with humans agree with the results of experimental studies with animals, the Surgeon General's warning is considered well founded.

PARTIAL CORRELATION

The correlation techniques discussed so far are appropriate for looking at the relationship between two variables. In most situations, however, a researcher must deal with more than two variables, and we need procedures that look at the relationship among several variables. **Partial correlation** is a technique used to determine what correlation remains between two variables when the effect of another variable is eliminated. We know that correlation between two variables may occur because both of them are correlated with a third variable. Partial correlation controls for this third variable. For example, assume you are interested in the correlation between vocabulary and problem-solving skills. Both these variables are related to a third variable, chronological age. For example, 12-year-old children have more developed vocabularies than 8-year-old children, and they also have more highly developed problem-solving skills. Scores on vocabulary and problem solving will correlate with each other because both are correlated with chronological age. Partial correlation would be used with such data to obtain a measure of correlation with the effect of age removed. The remaining correlation between two variables when their correlation with a third variable is removed is called a *first-order partial correlation*. Partial correlation may be used to remove the effect of more than one variable. However, because of the difficulty of interpretation, partial correlation involving the elimination of more than one variable is not often used.

MULTIPLE REGRESSION

Multiple regression is a correlational procedure that looks at the relationships among several variables. Specifically, this technique enables researchers to find the best possible weighting of two or more independent variables to yield a maximum correlation with a single dependent variable. For example, colleges use data submitted by prospective freshmen to predict first-semester GPA. The predictor values may be scores on the SAT subtests (SAT verbal and SAT math), along with students' relative high school rank (RHSR). Relative high school rank, found by dividing a student's rank in the high school graduating class by the size of the class, adjusts for the variation in size of graduating classes. Table 13.3 shows the simple correlations between each of the predictors and the criterion.

You can see in Table 13.3 that none of the variables has a very high correlation with freshman GPA; the best single predictor is relative high school rank. But we can use all three variables in a multiple regression analysis to determine the correlation of the best possible weighted *combination* of the three predictor vari-

Table 13.3 Correlations of Each Predictor with the Criterion

	SATV	SATM	RHSR[a]
GPA	0.31	0.39	−0.42

[a]The negative correlation between relative high school rank and GPA is due to the way that rank in class is measured. The highest achiever in the class has a rank of 1 (the lowest number); the lowest achiever in the class has a rank equal to the size of the class (a high number). The students with the lowest *size* rank are predicted to have the highest GPA; hence, the correlation coefficient is negative.

ables with GPA. Computer programs produce a prediction equation with the predictor variables weighted in the appropriate way to yield the highest correlation with GPA and hence the best prediction. The university can use the equation with similar groups of prospective students whose SAT scores and relative high school ranks are known to predict their as-yet-unknown GPA at the university.

The regression equation would look as follows: $Y' = a + b_1X_1 + b_2X_2 + b_3X_3$ where Y' is the predicted score (GPA); a and b_1, b_2, and b_3 are constants provided by the regression analysis; and X_1, X_2, and X_3 are the independent variables (RHSR, SAT verbal, and SAT math). Assume a student has the following scores: SATV = 510, SATM = 540, and RHSR = 21. The student's predicted GPA at the university would be 2.97.

$$Y' = 2.0813 + (-.0131)21 + .0014(540) + .0008(510) = 2.97$$

The regression analysis also yields R, the **coefficient of multiple correlation**, which indicates the relationship between the predictor variables in combination and the criterion. If we square R to get the coefficient of determination, we know the amount of variability in the criterion that is due to differences in scores on the predictor variables. If R, for example, is .50, then 25 percent of the variability in GPA can be accounted for by the combined SATV, SATM, and RHSR scores.

In the development of a multiple regression equation, the variables should be measured on an interval scale. It is possible, however, to put categorical variables such as gender, social class, marital status, political preference, and the like into a prediction equation if they are recoded as binary variables. For instance, if the variable is gender, 1's can be assigned to females and 0's to males. Such recoded variables are referred to in multiple regression as **dummy variables**.

Because the computations are very complex, multiple regression is done by computer. Computer programs are available that provide not only the multiple correlation coefficient (R) and the prediction equation but also the proportion of

THINK ABOUT IT 13.3

Match the procedure listed in the left column with the definition in the right column:

1. Spearman rho
2. Pearson r
3. Multiple regression
4. Phi coefficient
5. Eta correlation

a. Shows sign and magnitude of correlation between two nominal variables
b. Shows sign and magnitude of correlation between two ordinal variables
c. Shows sign and magnitude of correlation between two interval variables
d. Uses a number of independent variables to predict a single dependent variable
e. Used when the relationship between two variables is curvilinear

Answers

1. b; 2. c; 3. d; 4. a; 5. e

variance in the criterion accounted for by the combination of predictors (R^2), and tests of statistical significance for the R and for the contribution of each predictor. For further discussion of multiple regression, see Cohen, Cohen, West, and Aiken (2003).

Several more complex techniques are available to investigate correlation of more than two variables. These analyses require more sophistication with statistics than is usually needed in a beginning research course. We will briefly describe these techniques and refer interested students to other texts.

CANONICAL CORRELATION

Canonical correlation is a generalization of multiple regression that adds more than one dependent variable (criterion) to the prediction equation. Recall that a multiple correlation coefficient shows the correlation between the "best" combination of several independent variables and a single dependent variable. Canonical correlation extends the analysis to more than one dependent variable. In other words, canonical correlation is an analysis with several independent variables and several dependent variables. It takes into account the X and Y scores, the relations between the X variables, between the Y variables, and between the X and Y sets of variables. The result is a canonical correlation coefficient that represents the maximum correlation possible between sets of X scores and sets of Y scores. It also indicates the relative contributions of the separate independent and dependent variables to the canonical correlation, so you can see which variables are most important to the relationships between the sets. For more information on canonical correlation, see Thompson's *Canonical Correlation Analysis* (1984).

DISCRIMINANT ANALYSIS

Discriminant analysis is a statistical procedure related to multiple regression, but it differs in that the criterion is a categorical variable rather than a continuous one. Discriminant analysis uses a number of predictor variables to classify subjects into two or more distinct groups, such as dropouts versus persisters, successful versus unsuccessful students, delinquents versus nondelinquents, and so on. The criterion in discriminant analysis is thus a person's group membership. We might predict teacher retention based on measures of self-efficacy and job satisfaction. The procedure results in an equation, or *discriminant function*, where the scores on the predictors are multiplied by weights to predict the classification of subjects into groups. When there are just two groups, the discriminant function is essentially a multiple-regression equation with the group membership criterion coded 0 or 1. But with three or more groups as the criterion, discriminant analysis goes beyond multiple regression.

For example, discriminant analysis might be used to identify predictors of success in an education doctoral program. You could identify the variables that discriminate membership into one of two groups: those who successfully completed doctoral study and those who did not. A number of different predictors might be used: Miller Analogies Test (MAT) scores, undergraduate GPA, graduate GPA, time lapse between the master's degree and entrance into the doctoral program, doctoral major, age at entrance, gender, and marital status. Complex correlational analysis would produce an equation showing the variables that were significant in predicting the criterion, success or lack of success in a doctoral program. Discriminant analysis is also often used in diagnosis to identify individuals for specialized treatment or intervention. For more information on discriminant analysis, see Huberty (1994).

PATH ANALYSIS

Social scientists are showing increased interest in studying patterns of causation among variables and have proposed various approaches. One popular approach to the analysis of causality is **path analysis**, which Pedhazur (1997) defines as "a method for studying direct and indirect effects of variables hypothesized as causes of variables treated as effects." Pedhazur further states, "Path analysis is intended *not* to discover causes but to shed light on the tenability of the causal models a researcher formulates based on knowledge and theoretical considerations" (p. 769). The hypothesized pattern of causal relations among a set of variables is usually displayed graphically by means of the path diagram. Path analysis is basically an extension of multiple regression in which each dependent variable in the analysis is regressed on every independent variable that is predicted to affect it. Using the resulting correlations, theory, and existing knowledge, the researcher proposes a causal model and then applies path analysis to determine if the hypothesized causal model is consistent with the empirical data. If the model seems to fit the data well, the researcher concludes that the data fit the a priori causal model. Models inconsistent with the data are rejected, whereas those not rejected are viewed as plausible causal patterns. This does not mean that path analysis proves causality but suggests that some causal patterns are plausible and should be subjected to further investigation.

For example, Culver, Wolfle, and Cross (1990) tested a path model of the influences affecting teachers' job satisfaction early in their careers. The model hypothesized that job satisfaction is a function of a teacher's gender, age, father's education, mother's education, the teacher's academic achievement, number of years in teaching, the teacher's perceptions of the principal and coworkers, and the teacher's commitment to the teaching profession. The analysis was done separately for samples of black teachers and white teachers. For both groups, background demographic variables such as age, sex, father's education, and mother's education were found to be of little importance to job satisfaction compared to the more immediate variables of school climate and commitment to teaching. Years of teaching experience also had little influence on level of job satisfaction. In general, the path coefficients were similar for black teachers and white teachers. One exception was found when satisfaction was related to academic achievement. Lower-achieving white teachers tended to be more satisfied in their jobs than did their higher-achieving counterparts; for blacks, no such difference was found. Another observed difference occurred when satisfaction was related to gender. Black men tended to be more satisfied with their jobs than black women, but white women tended to be more satisfied than white men. The researchers concluded that the process leading to teacher job satisfaction may be different for blacks and whites. For further discussion of path analysis, see Chapter 18 in Pedhazur (1997).

FACTOR ANALYSIS

Factor analysis is a family of techniques used to detect patterns in a set of interval-level variables (Spicer, 2005). Factor analysis begins with a table of pairwise correlations (Pearson *r*'s) among all the variables of interest; this table is called a **correlation matrix.** The purpose of the analysis is to try to reduce the set of measured variables to a smaller set of underlying factors that account for the pattern of relationships. The search follows the law of parsimony, which means that the data should be accounted for with the smallest number of factors. This reduction of the number of variables serves to make the data more manageable and interpretable.

There are two types of situations in which factor analysis is typically used. In the first, a researcher is interested in reducing a set of variables to a smaller set. For example, assume a technology company uses 10 different tests to select computer programmers. Factor analysis could be used to identify perhaps 4 underlying dimensions measured by those 10 tests, so that tests of the 4 dimensions could be used just as effectively in the selection process as the 10 original tests.

The second type of situation is when researchers use factor analysis to determine the characteristics or underlying structure of a measuring instrument such as a measure of intelligence, personality, or attitudes. Assume a researcher has developed a new scale to measure self-esteem and claims it is unidimensional (measuring one single dimension). If the claim is true, factor analysis should yield only one factor. In other cases, a researcher may be interested in investigating the nature of the underlying factors in an existing scale. We have earlier (Chapter 9) referred to the use of factor analysis in establishing the construct validity of tests.

Let us illustrate factor analysis with a simple example. Imagine that you have scores on six different subscales of an aptitude measure for 300 subjects. The correlations among all the pairs of scores are shown in Table 13.4.

The question is: Is there a simpler structure underlying these 15 correlations? Table 13.4 shows that all of the subscales are positively correlated, and we assume all of the correlations are statistically significant. The first two subscales (vocabulary and analogies) form a separate subgroup because they correlate .50 with each other but do not correlate with the other subscales. The next two subscales (arithmetic and numerical reasoning) correlate .55 and thus form another subgroup, and likewise the last two subscales (picture completion and block design) have a correlation of .52 with each other but negligible correlations with

Table 13.4 Correlations Among Subscale Scores

	1	2	3	4	5	6
1. Vocabulary	—	.50	.15	.12	.12	.15
2. Analogies	—	—	.12	.15	.10	.18
3. Arithmetic	—	—	—	.55	.15	.12
4. Numerical reasoning	—	—	—	—	.20	.22
5. Picture completion	—	—	—	—	—	.52
6. Block design	—	—	—	—	—	—

Table 13.5 Hypothetical Factor Matrix from an Analysis of Scores on Six Subscales[a]

Test Subscale	Factor 1	Factor 2	Factor 3
Vocabulary	**.91**	.40	.30
Analogies	**.87**	.30	.20
Arithmetic	.25	**.90**	.15
Numerical reasoning	.22	**.80**	.10
Picture	.15	.10	**.85**
Block design	.09	.05	**.75**

[a]The variables loading most strongly on each factor are set in boldface.

other subscales. In other words, the pattern of correlations among these variables seems to reflect three underlying factors, which we label verbal, numerical, and spatial.

In this simple example, we are dealing with only six variables. In most cases, there would be a greater number, and it would not be so easy to discover the factors by inspection. So, researchers turn to factor analysis. The mathematics of factor analysis is beyond the scope of this book. But, basically, it involves searching for the clusters of variables that are all correlated with each other. The first cluster identified is called the first factor, and it represents the variables that are most intercorrelated with each other. Then other factors are identified that account for decreasing amounts of the variance. The factor is represented as a score, which is generated for each subject in the sample. Next, a correlation coefficient is computed between subjects' factor score and their score on the particular variable entered into the factor analysis. This correlation between a variable and a factor is called the **factor loading**. The higher its loading, the more a variable contributes to and defines a particular factor. A factor loading is interpreted like a correlation coefficient: The larger it is (either positive or negative), the stronger the relationship of the variable to the factor. The result of the factor analysis is a factor matrix, which shows the number of important underlying factors, and the weight (loading) of each original variable on the resulting factors. The square of the factor loading is the proportion of common variance between the test and the factor. Table 13.5 shows what the hypothetical factor matrix resulting from a factor analysis of the intelligence test in the above example might look like.

The first two tests load strongly on factor 1; we might call this underlying factor "verbal ability." The next two tests load strongly on factor 2, which we might label "numerical ability." The last two tests load strongly on factor 3, which we might label "spatial ability." Our simple example thus suggests that there were three factors underlying performance on the intelligence test. This procedure did not involve a hypothesis to be tested but rather something to be explored. How does one decide on the "correct" number of factors? The first criterion is that all the factors should be interpretable; an uninterpretable factor serves no practical or theoretical function (Spicer, 2005). Second, the factors should account for a satisfactory amount of shared variance in the data. What is "satisfactory" is defined by the researcher. Some writers suggest that the analysis keep extracting factors as long as a factor accounts for at least another 10 percent of the variance. "There is general agreement that overfactoring is preferable to underfactoring" (Spicer, 2005, p. 195).

This preceding discussion illustrates **exploratory factor analysis** (EFA) because a researcher does not test any formal hypotheses about the number of underlying factors. The number of factors is determined empirically rather than being specified a priori. It is distinguished from the more advanced technique called **confirmatory factor analysis** (CFA), which we describe briefly next.

Confirmatory Factor Analysis

Confirmatory factor analysis, like exploratory factor analysis, "is used to examine the relationships between a set of measured variables and a smaller set of factors that might account for them" (Spicer, 2005, p. 199). Confirmatory factor analysis, however, assumes relatively precise advance knowledge and allows a researcher to specify a priori what these relationships might look like and then to test the accuracy of these formal hypotheses.

The first step then in CFA is to specify a model made up of a number of hypotheses about the number of underlying factors, whether or not they are correlated, and which variables are expected to load on which factors. The output of CFA allows the researcher to evaluate the factor model overall and at the level of individual variable–factor relationships. The researcher can use CFA and compare different models or factor solutions that might be proposed.

Researchers often use both exploratory and confirmatory factor analysis in the construction and evaluation of measuring instruments. They begin with EFA and then move to CFA at later stages in the research. Confirmatory factor analysis is beyond the scope of an introductory text. Interested readers may refer to Pedhazur (1997), Loehlin (2004), or Thompson (2004).

STRUCTURAL EQUATION MODELING

Structural equation modeling (SEM) is a popular technique used in the analysis of causality. SEM combines confirmatory factor analysis and path analysis to test both a measurement model and a structural model. The first step involves a factor analysis to test the measurement model. After determining the underlying constructs, the second step uses path analysis to test the structural model. For example, assume a researcher wanted to investigate the relationship of certain variables such as socioeconomic background, educational background, and academic achievement to career success. The researcher would first select measures of these designated variables and of career success. Socioeconomic status could be measured by family income during formative years, types of school attended and parent's occupation. Academic achievement could be measured by highest level of school completed, grade point average, rank in class, academic honors/awards, and so on. Career success could be measured by income, occupational prestige, job level within organization, and the like. All of these measures represent indicators of the constructs of interest.

The extent to which these specific measures do, in fact, represent the hypothesized constructs in the way predicted is a test of the measurement model. In other words, are they good measures of the constructs? If not, the measurement

THINK ABOUT IT 13.4

Match the procedure in the left column with the definition in the right column:

1. Factor analysis
2. Discriminant analysis
3. Canonical correlation
4. Partial correlation
5. Path analysis

a. Uses multiple independent variables to predict more than one dependent variable
b. Reduces a matrix of correlations among variables to a few underlying constructs
c. Uses a number of variables to predict membership in categories
d. Uses theory to specify and test models of causation among variables
e. Determines the relationship between two variables when the effect of another variable is eliminated

Answers

1. b; **2.** c; **3.** a; **4.** e; **5.** d

model requires more work. If the data indicate support for the measurement model, then the researcher examines the structural model. Path analysis would test the structural model to determine if the variables as measured are related to career success in the way predicted by the researcher. SEM is a very complex and data-intensive procedure. The reader is referred to Bentler and Chou (1988), Pedhazur (1997), or Loehlin (2004) for further discussion of SEM.

SUMMARY

Correlational research is nonexperimental research that studies the direction and strength of relationships among variables. It gathers data on two or more quantitative variables from the same group of subjects (or from two logically related groups) and then determines the correlation among the variables.

Correlational procedures are widely used in educational and psychological research. They enable researchers to better understand certain phenomena and to make predictions. Correlational designs are often valuable for generating hypotheses that can be further investigated in experimental or causal-comparative research. Correlations must be interpreted appropriately. One must look at the sample size, the magnitude of the correlation coefficient, and its statistical and practical significance. The most serious error is to interpret correlation per se as an indicator of causation.

A number of different types of correlation coefficients are used with variables that are measured on different types of scales. Multiple regression is used to find the relationship between two or more independent variables and a dependent variable. It yields a prediction equation that the researcher can use later to predict the dependent variable for a new group of subjects, when the researcher has information only on the independent variables.

Some more sophisticated correlational procedures include partial correlation, discriminant analysis, factor analysis, canonical correlation, path analysis, and structural equation modeling. It is important to know the type of research situation in which each of these techniques would be useful.

KEY CONCEPTS

canonical correlation
coefficient of correlation
coefficient of determination (r^2)
coefficient of multiple correlation
confirmatory factor analysis
correlation matrix
correlational research
discriminant analysis
dummy variable
exploratory factor analysis
factor loading
multiple regression
partial correlation
path analysis
phi coefficient
predictor
significance fallacy
spearman's rho
structural equation modeling (SEM)

EXERCISES

1. Which correlation indicates the greatest extent of relationship between two variables?
   a. +.80 or −.80
   b. +.60 or −.85
   c. +.04 or −.15
2. A state official found a correlation of .65 between the number of bars in cities in the state and the number of crimes reported in those cities. He concluded that legislation to reduce the number of bars would reduce crime. What would you say about the official's conclusion?
3. Why are magnitude interpretations of correlation coefficients alone sometimes misleading?
4. Construct a scatter diagram for the following pairs of scores (X and Y):

X	2	3	10	6	4	9	7	3	6
Y	10	9	1	3	7	1	2	5	4

   Is the relationship
   a. Linear or curvilinear?
   b. High, moderate, or low?
   c. Positive or negative?
5. A study finds a moderate positive relationship between measures of self-esteem and achievement scores for a group of middle school students. Which of the following correlation coefficients would best represent this relationship?
   a. .94
   b. .35
   c. −.62
   d. .20
   e. .62
6. A study finds almost no relationship between two physical fitness scores for a group of elementary school students. Which of the following coefficients would best represent this relationship?
   a. .25
   b. .75
   c. −.10
   d. .60
   e. −.80
7. A researcher administered a series of tests to a group of entering law students at State University. At the end of the first year of law school, the researcher obtained the students' GPAs.
   a. What correlational technique should be used to determine the maximum relationship of these tests to first-year GPA?
   b. What assumptions would have to be made in order to generalize the findings to future applicants to the same law school? To applicants to other law schools?
8. How would you compare the correlations .70 and .35 in terms of magnitude?
9. A researcher is interested in anxiety and how it might affect performance on scholastic aptitude tests. He has a clinical psychologist assess the anxiety of subjects by ranking them from 1 through 20. Then he administers a standardized aptitude test to each of the 20 subjects and converts their IQ scores to ranks. Which correlation coefficient should the researcher calculate for the data? Explain your answer.
10. A researcher demonstrated a correlation of +.35 between principals' ratings of teacher attire and student academic performance across 150 grade schools in his state. He concluded that encouraging teachers to be properly attired will increase academic performance. Comment on his conclusion.

11. Determine the kind of index of correlation appropriate for use in solving each of the following problems:
    a. What is the coefficient of correlation between self-esteem and aptitude scores for a group of subjects?
    b. What is the correlation between gender and being hired or not hired for a job when you have 60 men and 60 women with identical scores on a qualifying test for that job?
    c. What is the correlation between the responses of 180 students to two test items when you know the right and wrong responses of these students on both test items?
    d. What is the relationship between sociometric scores of a group of students and their academic rank in a high school class?
12. To compute a correlation coefficient between traits A and B, which of the following must you have?
    a. One group of subjects, some of whom possess characteristics of trait A and the remainder of whom possess those of trait B
    b. Measures of trait A on one group of subjects and measures of trait B on another group
    c. One group of subjects, some who have both traits A and B, some who have neither trait, and some who have one trait but not the other
    d. Two groups of subjects, one of which could be classified as A or not A, the other as B or not B
    e. Measures of traits A and B on each subject in one group of students
13. An investigation finds a positive correlation between IQ scores and length of attention span among 10-year-olds. From this finding, which of the following would be a reasonable conclusion?
    a. A long attention span is a cause of intelligence.
    b. A high IQ is a cause of long attention span.
    c. There is a high probability that a large sample of high-IQ 10-year-olds will have a shorter mean attention span than a large sample of low-IQ 10-year-olds.
    d. One would predict longer attention spans for high-IQ 10-year-olds than for low-IQ 10-year-olds.
14. Examine the following research topics and decide whether experimental research, ex post facto research, or correlational research is the appropriate research design for each one:
    a. The effect of parents' divorce on the achievement motivation of the children
    b. The effect of a specific program of vocabulary instruction on social studies achievement
    c. The relationship between self-esteem and grade point average
    d. The effect of phonics instruction on the reading grade level of fourth-grade students
    e. The relationship between the verbal aptitude scores of identical twins
    f. The relationship between preschool attendance or nonattendance and academic achievement in first-graders
15. A researcher found a correlation of −.42 between rank in high school class and achievement in college for a sample of 1500 college freshmen. How would you interpret this coefficient in terms of direction, magnitude, and percentage of shared variance?
16. A school administrator wants to predict achievement in foreign languages. She has available scores on an intelligence test, a language aptitude test, and a reading test; she also knows the sex of the students. How would you recommend that she proceed to predict foreign language achievement?
17. Explain how it is possible for the measures of two variables to be associated in a fairly systematic way without the existence of any causal relationship between the variables?
18. A researcher is investigating the validity of an inventory designed to measure teacher stress. He wishes to know if the inventory is measuring the single construct, teacher stress, or more than one construct. What procedure would you recommend that the researcher use to answer this question?
19. A researcher wanted to predict achievement in the first year of law school. He con-

ducted a multiple-regression analysis with a sample size of 1000 and used six predictor variables: undergraduate GPA, undergraduate major, LSAT score, score on a writing test, sex, and time lapse between undergraduate degree and application to law school. The resulting $R = .20$ was significant at the .01 level of significance. How would you interpret the researcher's findings?

20. A researcher wants to investigate the relationship between class size and student satisfaction in sections of beginning psychology at a university. Describe two research methodologies that might be appropriate to answer this question.
21. Distinguish between correlational research and ex post facto research.
22. A researcher found a moderate negative correlation between two variables of interest. He concluded that the negative correlation meant that it would be useless to try to predict one variable from the other. Do you agree? Why or why not?

ANSWERS

1. **a.** The extent of relationship is the same.
   b. −.85
   c. −.15
2. Correlation between the two variables does not indicate causation. In this case, common cause is a likely explanation. Large cities have more bars and more crime; smaller cities have fewer bars and fewer crimes.
3. To interpret the correlation, you need to know the sample size on which it is based and the magnitude of other correlations of the same variables in other studies.
4. The relationship is
   a. linear
   b. high
   c. negative
5. .35
6. −.10
7. **a.** Multiple regression
   b. The researcher would have to assume that the relationship among the variables in the population of applicants to the law school remains similar over time. To apply the results to other law schools, the researcher would have to assume that the relationships among variables among applicants to other law schools are similar to these relationships among applicants to her law school.
8. An r of .70 might be described as being a very high correlation, the r of .35 as being moderate. One must *not* say that the r of .70 is twice as high as the r of .35. A good way to compare them is in terms of the coefficient of determination (r^2). With an r of .70, 49 percent of the variance is shared variance; with an r of .35, only 12 percent of the variance in Y is accounted for by variance in X. Thus, the difference in magnitude of the relationship is more like 4 to 1, instead of 2 to 1 as might have been incorrectly assumed from the absolute size of the coefficients.
9. Because the researcher has ordinal or rank-order data, he should calculate the Spearman rho correlation coefficient.
10. The researcher has no justification for inferring a causal relationship merely on the basis of correlational evidence. Principals' ratings of teacher attire and student academic performance could very well be functions of some other variable.
11. **a.** Pearson product moment
    b. Phi coefficient
    c. Phi coefficient
    d. Spearman rho
12. e.
13. d.
14. **a.** Ex post facto research
    b. Experimental research
    c. Correlational research
    d. Experimental research
    e. Correlational research
    f. Ex post facto research
15. The r of −.42 indicates a moderate negative relationship between rank in high school class and achievement in college; that is, students with a low numeric ranking would tend to have high achievement. The negative correlation is due to the way that rank in class is measured. The highest

achiever in the class has a rank of 1 (the lowest number), the lowest achiever in the class has a rank equal to the size of the class (the highest number). The student with a rank of 1 in a class of 400 would be expected to have a higher GPA in college than the student with a rank of 400. An $r = -.42$ indicates that about 18 percent of the variance in college grades can be accounted for by achievement in high school as indicated by rank.

16. The school administrator would select a sample of students and obtain their scores on the three tests and their grades in foreign languages. Sex would be coded 0 or 1. The data would be entered into a multiple-regression analysis, with the intelligence test, language aptitude test, reading test, and gender as independent variables and grades in foreign language as the dependent variable. Once the multiple-regression equation is developed, it can be used to predict foreign language achievement of similar groups of students when only the independent variables are known.
17. Even when two variables are correlated, you cannot infer that one causes the other. Correlation does not indicate causation. A third variable, unmeasured by the researcher, may account for the observed relationship.
18. The researcher should subject the inventory to factor analysis.
19. With the large sample size, it is not surprising that a coefficient of only .20 would be statistically significant. It is only moderately useful in prediction. $R^2 = .04$; only 4 percent of the variance in law school achievement would be predictable from this combination of predictor variables.
20. You could use ex post facto methodology by selecting already existing sections with different numbers of students and comparing the satisfaction scores in the various sections. Or you could use correlational methodology by correlating class size with student satisfaction scores.
21. Both are nonexperimental quantitative research methods. Correlational research seeks to determine the relationship between two variables. It typically involves correlating two measures for one group of subjects. Ex post facto research seeks to establish a cause–effect relationship. It compares two groups on one variable measure.
22. A negative correlation is just as good for predictive purposes as a positive correlation. It is the magnitude of the correlation that is important in this case.

INFOTRAC COLLEGE EDITION

Use the keyword *multiple regression* to locate an article investigating the prediction of academic achievement among high school students. What variables were found to be significant predictors? What was the multiple-correlation coefficient?

Chapter 14

Survey Research

ASK AND YOU SHALL KNOW.

INSTRUCTIONAL OBJECTIVES

After studying this chapter, the student will be able to:

1. State the purpose of survey research.
2. Describe the four categories of surveys classified according to their scope and focus.
3. Distinguish between longitudinal and cross-sectional surveys.
4. Describe the different types of longitudinal surveys.
5. List the steps involved in carrying out a survey.
6. Explain the importance of probability sampling in survey research.
7. Define margin of error and use sample data to calculate the margin of error and the confidence interval around the population parameter.
8. Calculate the sample size needed to achieve a desired margin of error in a survey.
9. List some of the factors that influence a researcher's decision about sample size.
10. State the merits and disadvantages of the interview as a data-gathering technique.
11. Write both open-ended and closed-ended survey questions.
12. List guidelines for conducting an interview.
13. State the advantages and disadvantages of the questionnaire as a data-gathering technique.
14. State some rules for writing items for a questionnaire.
15. List guidelines to follow for developing the format of a questionnaire.
16. Explain the advantages of field testing a questionnaire.
17. Explain the follow-up procedures a researcher should employ with a mailed survey.
18. Write a cover letter for a questionnaire.
19. Outline procedures for dealing with nonrespondents after follow-up procedures have been used.
20. Discuss the procedures for assessing the validity and reliability of questionnaires and/or interviews.

21 Explain the data analyses that are appropriate for survey data.

22 Explain the statistics used with cross tabulations.

23 Describe issues with electronic surveys.

In **survey research** investigators ask questions about peoples' beliefs, opinions, characteristics, and behavior. The survey questionnaire is widely used as a source of data in studies in sociology, business, psychology, political science, and education. It also provides information used for non-research planning and policy setting in the areas of government, business, health, and education. For example, the U.S. Census Bureau conducts a monthly survey for the Bureau of Labor Statistics that focuses on measuring labor force participation and unemployment. These data are used to produce the monthly unemployment figures for the United States as well as of the individual states. Surveys are taken of consumer choices, use of health services, numbers of women and minority faculty in universities, and so on. A survey researcher may want to investigate associations between respondents' characteristics such as age, education, social class, race, and their current attitudes toward some issue. Survey research typically does not make causal inferences but rather describes the distributions of variables in a large group.

Although researchers want to gather information about the characteristics of populations, they usually study a smaller group (a sample) carefully drawn from the population and then use the findings from the sample to make inferences about the population.

The range of topics covered by surveys and the techniques used have increased significantly in the past several years. Hardly a week goes by that you are not exposed through the news media to the results of some survey. The well-known Gallup poll, for instance, surveys public opinion on a variety of issues. Market researchers ask what products you purchase or might purchase, political pollsters ask whom you are likely to vote for, and television networks want to know what shows you watch.

Surveys are very important in higher education. Many universities have survey research institutes, such as the University of Michigan Institute for Social Research and the UCLA Higher Education Research Institute. Annually since 1966, the latter has surveyed college freshmen in order to gather information on students' reasons for going to college and for choosing a particular college, on their anticipated major, career and graduate school plans, on their attitudes, political views, religious preferences, and many other aspects of their lives. The 2003 survey, based on the responses of 276,449 freshmen entering 413 U.S. institutions, showed that 73 percent of the students said their reason for going to college was to get training for a specific career. Eighty percent expected to get a bachelor's degree with business being the most popular major. A majority (59 percent) expected to get at least a B average, a figure twice as high as in 1971 when the question was first asked. The researchers considered the increased political awareness of entering college students a significant finding. Students' political awareness was at its highest level since 1994. Students said "keeping up to date with political affairs" was a very important life goal. About half of the students considered themselves "middle-of-the-road" in their political views. The survey also showed that self-reported drinking and smoking were down among freshmen, reaching the lowest levels in the survey's history. The researchers state that the data are representative of the total population of first-time, full-time freshmen (*Chronicle of Higher Education*, 2004a).

Many doctoral dissertations and much of the research published in educational journals involve survey methods. Public school districts also conduct surveys to gather data such as average teacher load, number of preschool children in the community, number of students who participate in extracurricular activities, opinions of parents and students and data on a myriad of other topics. The annual Phi Delta Kappan/Gallup poll for 2002 (Rose & Gallup, 2003) surveyed 1011 adults to get their views of the state of public schools and the current efforts to improve them. The data showed that the public has high regard for the public schools and little interest in seeking alternatives. Forty-eight percent of the respondents assigned an A or B to schools in their community, with 31 percent assigning a grade of C. However, they rated schools in general lower than their own schools. The public believes improved student achievement is an important goal but does not support some of the proposed ways to effect improvement. In particular, the survey focused on the No Child Left Behind (NCLB) Act of 2002 and the strategies associated with the implementation of the act. The survey showed that the public saw itself as uninformed on the NCLB Act. Sixty-nine percent of the respondents said that they lacked the information to say whether their impression of the act was favorable or unfavorable.

THINK ABOUT IT 14.1

Which of the following questions would best be answered by survey methods?

1. Do voters in our school district think we should raise taxes in order to build new classrooms?
2. Do people who have taken driver education have fewer accidents than people who have not?
3. What do voters consider the most important issues in the upcoming election?
4. What do school principals consider to be the biggest problems in their schools?
5. Does dividing second-grade math students into ability groups produce greater math achievement than doing math instruction in a single group?

Answers

Questions 1, 3, and 4 would be suitable for survey research. Ex post facto would be appropriate for question 2, and experimental research would be suitable for question 5.

TYPES OF SURVEYS

Before initiating survey research, the investigator must determine the format that is most appropriate for the proposed investigation. Surveys are classified according to their focus and scope (census and sample surveys) or according to the time frame for data collection (longitudinal and cross-sectional surveys). Becoming familiar with the options enables the researcher to select the method that will provide the most useful data.

SURVEYS CLASSIFIED ACCORDING TO FOCUS AND SCOPE

A survey that covers the entire population of interest is referred to as a **census**, an example of which is the U.S. Census, undertaken by the government every 10 years. In research, however, "population" does not refer to all the people of a country. The term **population** is used to refer to the entire group of individuals to whom the findings of a study apply. The researcher defines the specific population of interest. It is often difficult or even impossible for researchers to study very large populations. Hence, they select a smaller portion, a sample, of the population for study. A survey that studies only a portion of the population is known as a **sample survey**.

Surveys may be confined to simple tabulations of *tangibles*, such as what proportion of children rides school buses and the average class enrollment. The most challenging type of survey is one that seeks to measure *intangibles*, such as attitudes, opinions, values, or other psychological and sociological constructs. In such a study you must bring to bear not only the skills involved in proper sampling but also the skills involved in identifying or constructing appropriate measures and employing the scores on these measures to make meaningful statements about the constructs involved. If you classify surveys on the basis of their scope (census versus sample) and their focus (tangibles versus intangibles), four categories emerge: (1) a census of tangibles, (2) a census of intangibles, (3) a sample survey of tangibles, and (4) a sample survey of intangibles. Each type has its own contributions to make and its own inherent problems.

A Census of Tangibles

When you seek information about a small population, such as a single school, and when the variables involved are concrete, there is little challenge in finding the required answers. If a school principal wants to know how many desks are in the school, how many children ride the school bus, or how many teachers have master's degrees, a simple count will provide the information. Because the study covers the entire population, the principal can have all the confidence characteristic of perfect induction. Well-defined and unambiguous variables are being measured, and as long as the enumeration is accurate and honest, the principal can say, without much fear of contradiction, "On the first of September there were 647 children's desks in our school" or "Sixty-five percent of the present faculty have master's degrees." The strength of a census of this type lies in its irrefutability. Its weakness lies in its confinement to a single limited population at a single point in time. The information provided by such a census may be of immediate importance to a limited group, but typically such surveys add little to the general body of knowledge in education.

A Census of Intangibles

Suppose the school principal now seeks information about pupil achievement or aspirations, teacher morale, or parents' attitudes toward school. The task will be more difficult because this census deals with constructs that are not directly observable but must be inferred from indirect measures. Test scores and responses to questionnaires serve to approximate constructs such as knowledge and attitudes. The National Study of School Evaluation (NSSE) publishes an opinion inventory designed to measure student, teacher, and parent attitudes and opinions about schools. Administering the inventory to all the students, teachers, or parents in the school system would represent a census of intangibles.

Another example of this type of census is the achievement-testing program carried out by most schools. All children are tested, and the test scores are used to compare their performance with national norms, their own previous performance, and so on.

The value of a census of intangibles is largely a question of the extent to which the instruments used actually measure the constructs of interest. Reasonably good instruments are available for measuring aptitude and achievement in a variety of academic areas. Many other variables remain very difficult to measure. Because researchers lack instruments that can meaningfully measure the constructs involved, many important questions in education have not been answered. Such variables as teacher success, student motivation, psychological adjustment, and leadership have been difficult to define and measure operationally.

A Sample Survey of Tangibles

When investigators seek information about large groups, the expense involved in carrying out a census is often prohibitive. Therefore, researchers use sampling techniques and use the information they collect from the sample to make inferences about the population as a whole. When sampling is done well, the inferences made concerning the population can be quite reliable.

A classic example of a sample survey of tangibles is the report on equality of educational opportunities commissioned by the U.S. Department of Health, Education, and Welfare. This study, sometimes called the Coleman Report after James Coleman who developed the survey, was conducted in response to Section 402 of the Civil Rights Act of 1964, which directed the Commissioner of Education to conduct a survey of inequalities in educational opportunities among various groups in the United States. The sample survey included more than 600,000 children in grades 1, 3, 6, 9, and 12 of approximately 4000 schools. The schools were considered generally representative of all U.S. public schools, although there was some intentional overrepresentation of schools with minority-group populations. From the data generated by the survey, the researchers concluded that 65 percent of blacks attended schools in which more than 90 percent of students were black and 80 percent of whites attended schools enrolling more than 90 percent white. When comparisons were made concerning class size, physical facilities, and teacher qualifications, relatively little difference was found among schools serving different racial and ethnic groups. However, these variables did differ between metropolitan and rural areas and between geographic regions. Those disadvantaged in regard to these variables appeared to be rural children and those in the South, regardless of race.

A 2003 survey by the U.S. Department of Education focused on the prevalence of distance education in American colleges. The survey of 1600 institutions found that distance education expanded significantly during the late 1990s. Enrollment in for-credit distance-education courses grew to 2.9 million in the 2000–2001 academic year up from 1.3 million in 1997–1998. Fifty-six percent of two- and four-year institutions were offering distance-education courses, up from 44 percent 3 years earlier. Public institutions offered distance-education courses more frequently than did private ones. Based on the survey's results, it was estimated that the number of for-credit courses offered through distance education grew to 118,100 in 2000–2001 from 47,500 in 1997–1998 (*Chronicle of Higher Education*, 2003).

The researchers said that distance education is not replacing traditional higher-education institutions, but "It's allowing these traditional higher-education institutions to make their courses and faculty expertise available to a whole new set of students who otherwise would not be able to participate for whatever reason" (p. A28).

A Sample Survey of Intangibles

The public opinion polls are examples of studies measuring intangible constructs. Opinion is not directly observable but must be inferred from responses made by the subjects to questionnaires or interviews. Opinion polling began in the 1930s and has grown tremendously. Where respondents have been willing to reveal their preferences freely before elections, for instance, pollsters have been quite accurate in inferring public opinion from which they have predicted subsequent election results. These polls have provided excellent examples of the usefulness of sample statistics in estimating population parameters. However, if people who support one candidate are reluctant to reveal their preference, whereas people who support the other candidate feel free to say so, considerable error is introduced into the results of the poll. For example, people are more willing to say they will vote *against* an incumbent than *for* him or her. A classic example occurred before the 1948 presidential election when several polls showed Dewey leading the incumbent, Truman, but with many people indicating they were undecided. Newspapers had already prepared headlines proclaiming Dewey the winner, but Truman won the election. Apparently, most of those who indicated they were undecided actually voted for Truman. Respondents are also reluctant to reveal a choice that may appear based on self-interest, prejudice, or lack of knowledge about the issues.

How someone is going to vote is an intangible, but what is marked on a ballot is tangible. The television network news services have done very well in predicting how states will vote when only a few precincts have reported because they can use tangible measures of a sample (i.e., how some ballots have been marked) to predict the vote of a population. Therefore, the risks are only those involved in

THINK ABOUT IT 14.2

What type of survey is illustrated in the following examples?

1. Randomly selected teachers are asked how many years experience they have teaching?
2. The superintendent of School District 214 has Iowa Test of Basic Skills scores for all second-graders in his district.
3. The state superintendent of schools' list of the enrollment in each of the states' 1143 schools.
4. Some students in Shaw School are given a physical fitness test to get an estimate of the fitness of all the students in the school.

Answers

1. Sample survey of tangibles
2. Census of intangibles
3. Census of tangibles
4. Sample survey of intangibles

estimating population parameters from sample statistics. However, pollsters who estimate how a population *will* vote on the basis of how people *say* they will vote have the additional handicap of measuring what is intangible at the time the measurements are made. Surveys of intangibles are limited by the fact that the data researchers collect are only indirectly measuring the variables they are concerned about. The seriousness of this limitation depends on how well the observations measure the intangible variable.

The same survey may study tangibles and intangibles at the same time. The survey on equality of educational opportunities asked the students to answer questionnaires and administered intelligence and achievement tests in order to make inferences about social class, ability, and achievement, as well as the relationship of these variables to each other and to tangible variables in the study.

SURVEYS CLASSIFIED ACCORDING TO THE TIME DIMENSION

Surveys are also classified according to the time of data collection: longitudinal surveys, which study changes across time, and cross-sectional surveys, which focus on a single point in time.

Longitudinal Surveys

Longitudinal surveys gather information at different points in time in order to study changes over extended periods of time. Three different designs are used in longitudinal survey research: panel studies, trend studies, and cohort research.

Panel Studies In a **panel study**, the *same* subjects are surveyed several times over an extended period of time. For example, a researcher studying the development of quantitative reasoning in elementary school children would select a sample of first-graders and administer a measure of quantitative reasoning. This same group would be followed through successive grade levels and tested each year to assess how quantitative reasoning skills develop over time. Researchers have studied how age affects IQ by measuring the same individuals as adolescents, college-age, middle-age, and beyond. Because the same subjects are studied over time, researchers can see the changes in the individuals' behavior and investigate the reasons for the changes. An example of a panel study is Terman's classic study of intelligence where he followed exceptionally bright children into maturity.

Trend Studies A **trend study** differs from a panel study in that *different* individuals randomly drawn from the same general population are surveyed at intervals over a period of time. For example, researchers who have studied national trends in mathematics achievement sample middle school students at various intervals and measure their math performance. Although the same individuals are not tested each time, if the samples from the population of middle school students are selected randomly, the results each time can be considered representative of the middle school population from which the student samples were drawn. Test scores from year to year are compared to see if any trends are evident. Another example of a trend study is the survey on alcohol, tobacco, and other drug use among Indiana youth conducted annually by the Indiana Prevention Resource Center. The 2003 survey based on 141,342 students in grades 6 through 12 in 450 Indiana schools found a decline in the self-reported use of most drugs since the peak year of 1996. The most notable decrease was in tobacco use, which showed a decline for every grade except sixth. Among seventh, eighth, and ninth grades, cigarette use was one-half the rate reported in 1996. The use of inhalants increased somewhat among the younger students. The rate of use of cocaine and prescription drugs was approximately the same as reported in the 2002 survey. This trend study permits researchers to evaluate the prevention and enforcement efforts directed at the teenage population and to plan future programs.

Cohort Studies In a **cohort study**, a *specific* population is followed over a length of time with different random samples studied at various points. Whereas trend studies sample a general population that changes in membership over time, a cohort study samples a specific population whose members do not change over the duration of the survey. Typically, a cohort group has age in common. For example, a school system might follow the high school graduating class(es) of 2004 over time and ask them questions about higher education, work experiences, attitudes, and so on. From a list of all the graduates, a random sample is drawn at different points in time, and data are collected from that sample. Thus, the population remains the same during the study, but the individuals surveyed are different each time.

Cross-Sectional Surveys

Cross-sectional surveys study a cross section (sample) of a population at a single point in time. In a longitudinal study of vocabulary development, for example, a

THINK ABOUT IT 14.3

1. How would you administer a questionnaire to assess changes in students' political attitudes during college with a (a) cross-sectional approach, (b) panel study, (c) trend study, and (d) cohort study?

Answers

a. In the cross-sectional study, you would draw a random sample from each of the four levels and administer the questionnaire to them at the same time.

b. Panel, trend, and cohort studies are all longitudinal. In all three, you first randomly draw a sample of freshmen from your population of interest. In a panel study, you assess your original sample and study the same individuals again when they are sophomores, juniors, and seniors.

c. In the trend study, you draw a random sample of sophomores from the population. A year later, you draw a random sample of juniors, then in the final year you draw a random sample of seniors.

d. The cohort study would differ from the trend study in that the subsequent samples are drawn only from the population who were enrolled as freshmen when the study began and does not include students who transferred in later.

researcher would compare a measure of first-grade students' vocabulary skills in 2000 with one when they were fourth-grade students in 2003 and seventh-grade students in 2006. A cross-sectional study would compare the vocabulary skills of a sample of children from grades 1, 4, and 7 in 2006. The cross-sectional survey is the method of choice if you want to gather the data at one point in time.

Longitudinal surveys are more time consuming and expensive to conduct because the researcher must keep up with the subjects and maintain their cooperation over a long period of time. Cross-sectional surveys, in contrast, do not require years to complete. Hence, they are less expensive. A major disadvantage of the cross-sectional method is that chance differences between samples may seriously bias the results. You may by chance draw a sample of first-graders who are more mature than average and a sample of fourth-graders who are less mature than average, with the result that the difference between the groups appears much smaller than it really is. However, researchers usually can obtain larger samples for cross-sectional studies than for longitudinal studies, and the larger samples mitigate the problem of chance differences.

SURVEY TECHNIQUE

The survey permits you to gather information from a large sample of people relatively quickly and inexpensively. Conducting a good survey, however, is not as easy as it might initially appear. It requires careful planning, implementation, and analysis if it is to yield reliable and valid information.

SIX BASIC STEPS INVOLVED IN SURVEY RESEARCH

1. *Planning.* Survey research begins with a question that the researcher believes can be answered most appropriately by means of the survey method. For example, "How do elementary teachers feel about retaining students?" and "What is the extent of tobacco use among the high school students in this district?" are questions that a survey could answer. The research question in survey research typically concerns the beliefs, preferences, attitudes, or other self-reported behaviors of the people (respondents) in the study. A literature review reveals what other researchers have learned about the question.

2. *Defining the population.* One of the first important steps is to define the population under study. To whom will you distribute the survey? The population may be quite large, or it may be rather limited. For instance, the population might be all elementary teachers in the United States or all elementary teachers in the state of Indiana. Or you might further restrict the population to "all first-year male elementary teachers in the state of Indiana." Defining the population is essential for identifying the appropriate subjects to select and for knowing to whom the results can be generalized.

   Once the population has been defined, the researcher must obtain or construct a complete list of all individuals in the population. This list, called the **sampling frame**, can be very difficult and time consuming to construct if such a list is not already available.

3. *Sampling.* Because researchers generally cannot survey an entire population, they select a *sample* from that population. It is very important to select a sample that will provide results similar to those that would have been obtained if the entire population had been surveyed. In other words, the sample must be representative of the population. The extent to which this happens depends on the way subjects are selected. The sampling procedure that is most likely to yield a representative sample is some form of probability sampling (see Chapter 7). Probability sampling permits you to estimate how far sample results are likely to deviate from the population values.

4. *Constructing the instrument.* A major task in survey research is constructing the instrument that will be used to gather the data from the sample. The two basic types of data-gathering instruments are interviews and questionnaires.

5. *Conducting the survey.* Once the data-gathering instrument is prepared, it must be field-tested to determine if it will provide the desired data. Also included in this step are training the users of the instrument, interviewing subjects or distributing questionnaires to them, and verifying the accuracy of the data gathered.

6. *Processing the data.* The last step includes coding the data, statistical analysis, interpreting the results, and reporting the findings.

Many considerations are involved in implementing the foregoing steps. The balance of this chapter discusses these considerations in detail.

DATA-GATHERING TECHNIQUES

There are two basic ways in which data are gathered in survey research: interviews and questionnaires. Each has options, thus providing different approaches to collecting data. Interviews may be conducted in person or by telephone or by using other electronic means such as interactive television or synchronous web or e-mail forms. Questionnaires may be directly administered or sent by regular mail, electronic mail, or posted on the World Wide Web.

Although they all use a question-asking approach, each has certain unique characteristics, advantages, and disadvantages that you need to consider before deciding what type of instrument to use.

Personal Interviews

In a **personal interview**, the interviewer reads the questions to the respondent in a face-to-face setting and records the answers. One of the most important aspects of the interview is its flexibility. The interviewer has the opportunity to observe the subject and the total situation in which he or she is responding. Questions can be repeated or their meanings explained in case they are not understood by the respondents. The interviewer can also press for additional information when a response seems incomplete or not entirely relevant.

A greater response rate is another obvious advantage of the personal interview. The term **response rate** refers to the proportion of the selected sample that agrees to be interviewed or returns a completed questionnaire. With interviews, response rates are very high—perhaps 90 percent or better. Personal contact increases the likelihood that the individual will participate and will provide the desired information. With mailed questionnaires, the personal contact is missing, and people are more likely to refuse to cooperate. This results in many *nonreturns* (people who do not complete and return the questionnaire). The low response rate typical for mailed questionnaires (less than 30 percent is common) not only reduces the sample size but also may bias the results (Fowler, 2002). However, an interviewer can get an answer to all or most of the questions. Missing data represent a serious problem for the mailed questionnaire.

Another advantage is the control that the interviewer has over the order with which questions are considered. In some cases it is very important that respondents not know the nature of later questions because their responses to these questions may influence earlier responses. This problem is eliminated in an interview, where the subject does not know what questions are coming up and cannot go back and change answers previously given. For individuals who cannot read and understand a written questionnaire, interviews provide the only possible information-gathering technique.

The main disadvantage of the personal interview is that it is more expensive than other survey methods. The selection and training of the interviewers, their salary, and their travel to the interview site make this procedure costly. It takes a great deal of time to contact potential respondents, set up appointments, and actually conduct the interview. Another disadvantage is the possibility of **interviewer bias**, which occurs when the interviewer's own feelings and attitudes or the interviewer's gender, race, age, and other characteristics influence the way questions are asked or interpreted. As a general rule, interviewers of the same ethnic/racial group get the most accurate answers to race-related questions. On other issues, however, two studies found that blacks reported income from welfare and voting more accurately to white interviewers than to black interviewers (Fowler, 2002). The gender of the interviewer may be a factor in surveys of opinions on abortion and gender equality issues. Women talking to women interviewers may express different opinions than they would if the interviewer were male. Researchers should consider the interaction between the subject matter of a survey and the demographic characteristics of the interviewers and respondents. If race, ethnicity, or some other characteristic is very relevant to the answers to be given, then the researcher should consider controlling the relationship of interviewer and respondent characteristics.

Another problem is **social desirability bias** in which respondents want to please the interviewer by giving socially acceptable responses that they would not necessarily give on an anonymous questionnaire. They may say what they think the interviewer wants to hear. For example, in preference polls in elections involving minority candidates, the proportion of respondents who said they would vote for the minority candidates was often higher than the proportion of votes these candidates actually received in the election. To account for this error, researchers speculate that white voters may have feared they would appear racist if they admitted to interviewers that they preferred a white candidate. Without realizing it, the interviewer also may verbally or nonverbally encourage or reward "correct" responses that fit his or her expectations.

Telephone Interviews

The telephone interview is popular, and studies show that it compares quite favorably with face-to-face interviewing. In fact, the last 50 years have seen a gradual replacement of face-to-face interviewing with telephone interviewing as the dominant mode of survey data collection in the United States (Holbrook, Green, & Krosnick, 2003). Its major advantages are lower cost and faster completion, with relatively high response rates. The average response rate may reach 80 percent or higher (Neuman & Kreuger, 2003). Telephone interviews can be conducted over a relatively short time span with people scattered over a large geographic area. For example, national polling organizations often use the telephone to obtain nationwide opinions among voters near election time. Large-scale surveys in major cities often use the telephone instead of sending interviewers into unsafe areas. The phone permits the survey to reach people who would not open their doors to an interviewer but who might be willing to talk on the telephone. Another advantage is that respondents have a greater feeling of anonymity—and hence there may be less interviewer bias and less social desirability bias than with personal interviews.

The main disadvantage of the telephone interview is that there is less opportunity for establishing rapport with the respondent than in a face-to-face situation. It takes a great deal of skill to carry out a telephone interview so that valid results are obtained. The interviewer often finds it difficult to overcome the suspicions of the surprised respondents. We recommend that you identify yourself right away and explain that you are doing a survey and are not asking for money. An advance letter that informs the potential respondents of the approaching call is sometimes used to deal with this problem, but the letter can induce another problem: The recipient has time to think about responses or to prepare a refusal to participate when the call comes.

Another limitation of telephone interviews is that complex questions are sometimes difficult for respondents to follow. If they misunderstand the questions, the interviewer may not know. It is best that interview questions be short with a limited number of options. The phenomenon of multitasking may affect the quality of telephone interviews. Without the interviewer's knowing, the respondent may be watching television, stirring the soup, or writing checks while answering the survey questions. Telephone interviews can be very time consuming. If the sample is very large, a researcher will need a number of people to help with the interviews. We recommend that telephone interviews be relatively brief.

Another disadvantage is that households without telephones, those with unlisted numbers, and those with cell phones only are automatically excluded from the survey, which may bias results. Almost all American homes now have telephones, so this is not the problem it was years ago. Neuman and Kreuger (2003) state that about 95 percent of the population can be reached by telephone. A technique known as "random-digit dialing" (RDD) solves the problem of unlisted numbers (although it does not reach households without a telephone). In random-digit dialing, a computer randomly generates a list of telephone numbers based on all possible numbers thought to be in use in an area. Because of the random determination, this technique assures that every household with telephone service has an equal chance of being included in the sample. Random-digit dialing has greatly improved the sampling in telephone surveys. See Fowler (2002) for a thorough discussion of random-digit dialing.

Other limitations of telephone surveys arise from new technology that may make it increasingly difficult to reach potential respondents by phone. Services such as caller identification, phone number blocking, and similar procedures enable residential phone customers to have much greater control over incoming calls. People may simply ignore calls from the unfamiliar number of the surveyer and telephone response rates may continue to drop.

A national telephone poll for *The Chronicle of Higher Education* (March 7, 2004b) conducted 1000 telephone interviews of 20 minutes each with a random selection of men and women ages 25 to 65. The sample generated using random-digit dialing methodology was reported to be representative of the U.S. population with respect to gender, race, geography, religious/political affiliation, and income. The poll focused on public opinion of higher education. The results showed that the public's trust in colleges ranks near the top among all kinds of institutions. Nearly 93 percent of respondents agreed that higher-education institutions are one of the most valuable resources to the United States. Sixty percent said that the four-year colleges in their states, both public and private, were of high quality.

Computer-Assisted Telephone Interviewing (CATI)

Computer and telecommunications technology has been applied to telephone surveys. Wearing earphones, the interviewer sits at a computer while it randomly selects a telephone number (through random-digit dialing or from a database) and dials. When the respondent answers, the interviewer reads the first question that appears on the computer screen and types the answer directly into the computer. The computer program displays the next screen containing the next question, and so on through the entire survey. Using CATI saves a great deal of time. The surveyor can fill in forms on a computer screen or type answers to open-ended questions very quickly. The biggest advantage is that CATI software immediately formats responses into a data file as they are keyed in, which saves the researcher time usually spent in coding and manually transferring responses from paper into the computer for analysis.

Conducting the Interview

Whether the interview is conducted in person or by telephone, the interviewer's main job is to ask the questions in such a way as to obtain valid responses and to record the responses accurately and completely. The initial task for the interviewer is to create an atmosphere that will put the respondent at ease. After introducing yourself in a friendly way, briefly state the purpose of the interview but avoid giving too much information about the study, which could bias the respondent. It is well to begin the interview with fairly simple, nonthreatening questions.

The interviewer also has the responsibility of keeping the respondent's attention focused on the task and for keeping the interview moving along smoothly. This can best be done if you are thoroughly familiar with the questions and their sequence so that you can ask the questions in a conversational tone and without constantly pausing to find what question is coming next. Of course, you must refrain from expressing approval, surprise, or shock at any of the respondent's answers.

Interviews can be more or less structured. In a less structured interview, the same questions are asked of all respondents, but the interview is more conversational and the interviewer has more freedom to arrange the order of the questions or to rephrase the questions. If comparable data are to be obtained, however, the interviewer must standardize the procedure by using a structured interview schedule. A structured interview schedule contains specific questions in a fixed order, to be asked of all respondents, along with transition phrases and **probes** (questions used to clarify a response or that push a little further into a topic). For example, if the respondent starts to hedge, digress, or give irrelevant responses, or if he or she has obviously misinterpreted the question, then the interviewer may use a fixed probe such as "Explain your answer a little further" or "Can you tell me a little more about that?" Another important technique besides the probe is the **pause**. A good interviewer needs skill in listening and is quiet at times until the respondent answers. In less structured interviews, any marked deviations from the protocol should be documented so that the information can be taken into account when analyzing the interviewee's response. In using probes, take care not to suggest or give hints about possible responses. It takes less training time to teach interviewers to administer a structured interview than it does an unstructured one because everything they need to say or do is contained in the interview schedule. For this reason, the structured interview is the most widely used format for large studies with numerous interviewers.

Training the Interviewer

It is essential that potential interviewers receive training before being sent out to conduct interviews. Quality of interviewers is probably one of the least appreciated aspects of survey research. "Interviewers have a great deal of potential for influencing the quality of the data they collect" (Fowler, 2002, p. 117).

There are certain aspects of interviews that need to be standardized; thus, they should always be included in interviewer training: (1) procedures for contacting respondents and introducing the study, (2) instructions on asking questions so that interviewers ask all questions in a consistent and standardized way, (3) procedures for probing inadequate answers in a nondirective way, (4) procedures for recording answers to open-ended and closed-ended questions, and (5) rules for handling the interpersonal aspects of the interview in a nonbiasing way (Fowler, 2002). To be able to answer respondents' questions, interviewers should also know the purpose of the project, the sponsorship, the sampling approach used, and the steps that will be taken with respect to confidentiality.

Interviewer trainees should be provided with written manuals on interviewing procedures. They should observe interviews being conducted by trained individuals and should be supervised in conducting practice interviews. In the practice interviews, the interviewees should be individuals drawn from the same population that will be used in the research project.

Mailed Questionnaires

The direct one-on-one contact with subjects in a personal interview is time consuming and expensive. Often much of the same information can be obtained by means of a questionnaire mailed to each individual in the sample, with a request that he or she complete and return it by a given date. Because the questionnaire is mailed, it is possible to include a larger number of subjects as well as subjects in more diverse locations than is practical with the interview.

A mailed questionnaire has the advantage of guaranteeing confidentiality or anonymity, thus perhaps eliciting more truthful responses than would be obtained with a personal interview. In an interview, subjects may be reluctant to express unpopular or politically incorrect points of view or to give information they think might be used against them at a later time. The mailed questionnaire also eliminates the problem of interviewer bias.

A disadvantage of the questionnaire is the possibility of respondents misinterpreting the questions. It is extremely difficult to formulate a series of questions whose meanings are crystal clear to every reader. The investigator may know exactly what is meant by a question, but because of poor wording or different meanings of terms, the respondent makes a significantly different interpretation. Furthermore, large segments of the population may not be able to read or may read only in another language and may not be able to respond to a mailed questionnaire. Only people with considerable education may be able to complete a very complex questionnaire.

Another important limitation of mailed questionnaires is the low return rate. It is easy for the individual who receives a questionnaire to lay it aside and simply forget to complete and return it. A low response rate limits the generalizability of the results of a questionnaire study. It cannot be assumed that nonresponse is randomly distributed throughout a group. Studies have shown that there are usually systematic differences in the characteristics of respondents and nonrespondents to questionnaire studies. Response rate is often higher among the more intelligent, better educated, more conscientious, and those more interested or generally more favorable to the issue involved in the questionnaires. The goal in a questionnaire study is 100 percent returns, although a more reasonable expectation may be 40 to 75 percent returns.

A number of factors have been found to influence the rate of returns for a mailed questionnaire. Some of these are (1) length of the questionnaire, (2) cover letter, (3) sponsorship of the questionnaire, (4) attractiveness of the questionnaire, (5) ease of completing it and mailing it back, (6) interest aroused by the content, (7) use of a monetary incentive, and (8) follow-up procedures used. We discuss these factors in more detail later.

Electronic Mail Surveys

As computers have become common, researchers have used electronic mail (e-mail) to deliver questionnaires. Dillman (2000) found that e-mail surveys have the advantages of prompter returns, lower item nonresponse, and more complete answers to open-ended questions. Electronic surveys can be completed at a pace the respondents choose, and they cannot be mislaid like a mail survey. The main disadvantage is that not everyone has an e-mail address. In 2001, 56.5 percent of U.S. households owned a computer and a total of 50.5 percent had Internet access (Statistical Abstract of the United States, 2003). Because only a portion of the U.S. population can be contacted through e-mail, "there is no possibility for listing general populations and drawing a sample in which nearly every adult in the U.S. population has a known nonzero chance of being selected for participation in a survey" (Dillman, 2000, p. 355). E-mail surveys have been used most successfully on college campuses with faculty and students, with companies and their employees, or with other populations having universal e-mail access. Dillman suggests combining e-mail and regular mail surveys for a maximum return rate. Research shows that some of the factors found to be important for regular mail surveys are also important in e-mail surveys. For example, people who received a prior e-mail notification about the survey were more likely to respond; also, surveys addressed individually to a person (rather than being part of a mailing list) had higher response rates.

Internet Surveys

The Internet has become a popular methodology for survey research. The questionnaire is placed on the World Wide Web where respondents visit the web page, answer the questions, and submit the questionnaire online. **Web-based surveys** have a number of advantages. They have the potential of reaching large populations and permit the collection of larger amounts of data than would be possible with traditional survey methods. They can be conducted quickly and easily and are less expensive than mailed surveys. The cost advantage increases as the size of the sample increases. Dillman (2000) states "Once the electronic data collection has been developed, the cost of surveying each additional person is much less, compared with both telephone interview and postal procedures. In some instances these technologies may result in decisions to survey entire populations rather than only a sample" (p. 353). Another important benefit is in the processing of survey data. Web-based surveys can significantly reduce the amount of time and effort and the costs associated with getting the data into a system for analysis. Furthermore, because they are available 24 hours a day, respondents can reply when and where they choose. In a University of Colorado survey, 55 percent of respondents cited ease of use as one of the things they liked most about answering a web survey (Cook, Heath, & Thompson, 2000).

An obvious limitation of Internet surveys is that samples are restricted to those with access to the technology. Samples are dominated by relatively affluent, well-educated, urban, white-collar, technically sophisticated young males (Flatley, 2001). The large number of potential responses in a web survey does not overcome the problem of sampling error due to lack of representativeness. We need to be sure the survey is reaching the desired respondents.

There is somewhat conflicting evidence about response rates in web-based surveys. The consensus, however, is that response rates for web surveys are lower than rates obtained by other methods. A meta-analysis of 68 web surveys found a mean response rate of 39.6 percent (Cook, Heath & Thompson, 2000). Dillman and Bowker (2001) compared response rates to a questionnaire administered by telephone, mail, or Internet. The response rate for the Internet was 50 percent compared with 80 percent for telephone and mail surveys. To generate enthusiasm and maximize response, one should send an introductory letter separate from the instrument that explains what the survey is about, that requests their cooperation, and provides an incentive for completing the survey. The problem, however, is that the introductory letter is usually sent by e-mail and may be deleted before it is ever read by the potential respondent. Because of the relative anonymity provided by the Internet, it is more difficult to determine if respondents are who they say they are. It would also be possible for people to use different identities and respond more than once to a survey.

Web-based surveys are still relatively new, and we need more research on the types of studies for which they are most appropriate and the factors that affect their success. We do not know if the techniques used to increase response rates in paper and telephone surveys will directly translate to web surveys. Saxon, Garrett, Gilroy, and Cairns (2003) remind us that the biggest long-term threat to the future of Internet survey methodology is the information overload factor. It may become so easy to develop and distribute surveys over the web that no one will have the time or inclination to complete them. Researchers are faced with competition with marketers and spammers on the Internet for the cooperation of respondents (Whitcomb, 2003).

Meister and Melnick (2003) conducted an Internet survey of first and second-year teachers in order to determine their concerns in the areas of classroom management, time management, communication with parents, and academic preparation. Ten flyers each containing a request for new teachers to go to the website and respond to the survey were sent to 1000 principals in all 50 states. They were directed to distribute the flyers to their new teachers. A second mailing via e-mail was sent to 500 principals. They were asked to forward the e-mail to any first or second-year teacher in their building. A total of 273 teachers from 41 states responded. Sixty percent of the respondents were elementary teachers, 27 percent high school, and 13 percent middle school. Rural, suburban, and urban school districts were all represented. The responses were immediately recorded in a database as teachers answered items on the website.

The findings showed that new teachers were less confident of their knowledge and skills in the areas of discipline, time management, and communication skills. They reported needing assistance in handling disruptive students and those with special needs. Eighty-four percent reported that they felt sometimes "overwhelmed" by the paperwork and other noninstructional demands on their time. One in four teachers did not feel well prepared by the student teaching experience, especially in the areas of reading and language arts. Forty percent of beginning elementary teachers responded that they were not prepared to teach reading.

This research example illustrates the advantages and disadvantages of Internet surveys. The survey had the potential of reaching teachers over a wide geographic area and permitted them to respond at their convenience. The fact that the data were put into the system ready for analysis saved time and effort for the researchers. The disadvantage is that the response rate appears to be low, but actually we cannot calculate the response in the usual way. We do not know how many teachers actually received a flyer or got the e-mail message about the survey.

The reader is referred to a book by DeVaus (2002) that discusses a variety of applications for web-based surveys, as well as tips on designing the questionnaire.

Directly Administered Questionnaires

The directly administered questionnaire is given to a group of people assembled at a certain place for a specific purpose. Examples include surveying the freshmen or their parents attending summer orientation at a university. Surveys at universities are often administered in classrooms or in residence halls. For example, the annual survey of freshmen coordinated by UCLA that was referred to earlier is administered during orientation at the various colleges and universities.

The main advantage of directly administering questionnaires is the high response rate, which typically reaches close to 100 percent. Other advantages are the low cost and the fact that the researcher is present to provide assistance or answer questions. The disadvantage is that the researcher is usually restricted in terms of where and when the questionnaire can be administered. Also, when a population is limited (e.g., parents of freshmen in a specific university), then the results of the survey will be equally limited in terms of generalizability.

As we have seen, researchers have a choice among several data collection methods for survey research. They choose the one best suited for their particu-

Table 14.1 Comparison of Data Collection Methods

Method	Advantages	Disadvantages
Personal interview	Researcher is present Can establish rapport Flexibility High response rate Fewer incomplete answers Good for surveys on complicated issues Time for thoughtful answers	Time consuming More expensive Interviewer bias Social desirability bias Need trained interviewers No anonymity Less safe for researchers
Telephone interview	Low cost Convenient High response rate Quick Greater safety for interviewers and respondents	Less rapport Individuals may refuse to talk Questions need to be short and simple
Mailed questionnaire	Low cost Allows anonymity No interviewer bias Convenient Nonthreatening	Slow Low response rate and nonresponse bias Cannot clarify question Missing data Literacy required
Electronic or Internet questionnaires	Low cost Easy for researcher Convenient for respondent Allows anonymity Potential of quick response Time for thoughtful answers Low social desirability bias Greater safety for researcher and respondent	Limited to computer savvy Difficulty getting cooperation Potentially lower response rate Literacy requirement May not be able to identify respondents
Directly administered questionnaire	Low cost High response rate Researcher present	Not as flexible with respect to time and place

lar study. However, a multimode approach in which researchers use combinations of these methods in the same study is quite common. In fact, Fowler (2002) says that mixing modes is one of the best ways to minimize survey nonresponse because it enables researchers to reach people who are inaccessible via a single mode. Table 14.1 provides a summary of the advantages and disadvantages of the various data collection methods.

STANDARD ERROR OF THE SAMPLING PROPORTION

We have seen in Chapter 7 that even with random sampling there will always be some error in estimating a population parameter from sample statistics. The statistic most commonly reported in a sample survey is a proportion or a percentage of the sample that gives a particular response. The discrepancy between the known sample proportion and the unknown population value is referred to as **sampling error**. The first step in assessing how much sample results are likely to deviate from the population values is to calculate the standard error of the sampling proportion.

CALCULATING THE STANDARD ERROR

Using the obtained sample proportions, you can calculate the variance and then the standard error of the proportion. The variance of a proportion is pq, where p is the proportion agreeing or having a certain characteristic and q $(1 - p)$ is the proportion not agreeing or not having the characteristic. If the variance for the proportion is pq, the formula for the standard error of the proportion is

$$\text{SE } (\sigma_p) = \sqrt{\frac{\text{Var}}{n}} = \sqrt{\frac{pq}{n}} \qquad (14.1)$$

where

$$\begin{aligned} \text{SE or } \sigma_p &= \text{standard error of the proportion} \\ p &= \text{proportion agreeing} \\ q &= \text{proportion not agreeing } (1 - p) \\ n &= \text{size of the sample} \end{aligned}$$

For example, assume you survey a random sample of 100 parents of prekindergarten children in a school district and ask if they are in favor of full-day kindergarten in the district. You find that 80 say "Yes" to this question and 20 say "No." The standard error of the proportion is

$$\text{SE} = \sigma_p = \frac{\sqrt{(.80)(.20)}}{\sqrt{100}} = \frac{\sqrt{.1600}}{\sqrt{100}} = \frac{.4}{10} = .04$$

From probability theory, we say that we are 95 percent confident that the sample statistic is within 1.96 standard errors of the parameter.

In our example, standard error of .04 multiplied by 1.96 gives us .0784. Rounding that to .08 and expressing it as a percent, we have 8 percent. Thus, we would report that 80 percent of parents of prekindergarten children are in favor of a full-day with a **margin of error** of 8 percent. This means that we have 95 percent confidence that the population proportion is between 72 and 88 percent.

THINK ABOUT IT 14.4

A community survey asked the question: "Are you in favor of having a Wal-Mart in our community?" From the 899 completed surveys, it was found that 63 percent of the residents answered "Yes" to this question. Calculate the margin of error and set up the 95 percent confidence interval for these data:

Answer

$$\sigma_p = \sqrt{\frac{(.63)(.37)}{899}} = \sqrt{\frac{.2331}{899}} = \frac{.4828}{29.9833} = .0161$$

$1.96 \times .0161 = .0316$ or a 3 percent margin of error. The confidence interval would be 63 ± 3. One would be 95 percent confident that the percent in the population favoring a Wal-Mart in the community is between 60 and 66 percent. In surveys conducted by the major polling organizations, a margin of error of ± 3 percent is generally considered acceptable.

CALCULATING SAMPLE SIZE

How large a sample to draw is one of the early and difficult questions researchers must answer. We know that sampling error decreases as the size of the sample increases. Once you decide on an acceptable margin of error, you can determine the sample size needed to achieve that margin of error by applying Formula 14.2.

$$n = \left(\frac{\frac{1}{E}}{\sqrt{pq}} \right)^2 (z)^2 \tag{14.2}$$

where

n = sample size needed
E = desired margin of error
pq = variance of hypothesized proportion
z = z score of confidence level

For example, if we want a ±3 percent margin of error at the 95 percent confidence level ($z = 1.96$) for a hypothesized $p = .5$, $q = .5$, the required n would be

$$n = \left(\frac{\frac{1}{.03}}{\sqrt{(.5)(.5)}} \right)^2 (1.96)^2 = \left(\frac{1}{.06} \right)^2 (3.8416) = (277.7783)(3.8416)$$
$$n = 1067.1131$$

If the hypothesized population proportions are .50/.50, then 1068 subjects would be needed to yield a margin of error of ±3 percent. Remember that this is 1068 usable responses. If you are using a mailed questionnaire and anticipate a 50 percent return, you would need to mail out twice that number of questionnaires. If a 10 percent margin of error would be acceptable, then only 97 respondents would be needed.

$$n = \left(\frac{\frac{1}{10}}{\sqrt{(.5)(.5)}} \right)^2 (1.96)^2 = \left(\frac{1}{.2} \right)^2 (3.8416) = (25)(3.8416) = 96.04$$

Using $p = .50$ is always a safe way to calculate the needed sample size because pq is at its maximum possible value when p and q each equals .50 and $pq = .25$. Using population estimates of $p = q = .50$ in Formula 14.2, the researcher will be confident that the margin of error will be as small as or smaller than the value specified. If there are compelling reasons to hypothesize unequal population proportions for p and q, these may be substituted for .50 and .50, respectively, and the result will be a lower required number of subjects. For instance, if 20 percent of the high school boys in a school district tried out for intermural sports last year, you might use $p = .20$ and $q = .80$ in calculating the number of subjects needed for a survey of this year's boys. Note that all these statistics are based on the assumption that the sample is a random sample of the population of interest. The credibility of the results are a function of the validity of that assumption.

Table 14.2 shows the sample size needed to have a certain margin of error for a given p. Note that the largest sample is required when the desired margin of error is lowest and $p = .50$. As the acceptable margin of error increases and p varies from .50, the required sample size decreases.

Table 14.2 Minimum Sample Sizes Required for Various Margins of Error around the Parameter Estimation at the .95 Confidence Level (sizes are shown as a function of anticipated sample proportions)

Maximum Margin of Error (%)	Value of p		
	.10 or .90[a]	.25 or .75	.50
1	3462	7212	9616
2	866	1803	2404
3	385	802	1069
5	139	289	385
10	35	73	97

[a]The sample variance, pq, is the same when $pq = (.10)(.90)$ as when $pq = (.90)(.10)$.

As with anything else that relies on sampling, the representativeness of the sample is more important than the size of the sample. An unrepresentative sample leads to inappropriate conclusions regardless of its size. For example, a university wanted to determine the need for evening cafeteria hours. They conducted a random sample of all full-time students enrolled at the university. However, the majority of the students taking evening classes and thus potentially more likely to use the cafeteria in the evening were part-time, not full-time, students. A survey of full-time students could lead to inaccurate conclusions about the demand for evening cafeteria hours.

Another factor influencing the decision about sample size is the variability of the population to be sampled. If the population is fairly homogeneous, then you can use a smaller sample than if the population is more variable. A population of college students, for example, would be expected to show less variability than a population of adults in general, and thus a smaller sample could be used. Check published research studies to learn something about the variability of the population of interest and the sample size used in survey research on the population.

Also consider the statistical analysis that will be used on the survey data. Some statistics require samples of certain sizes. Chi square, for instance, cannot be used if the sample is too small. There is also a financial consideration. Increasing the size of the sample increases the cost. Mailing of questionnaires and follow-ups is costly; interviewing is even more expensive. The researcher must consider the time and money available for the survey and select as large a sample as can be economically managed. But remember: Size alone does not guarantee a representative sample; the sampling procedure is more important in determining whether the sample is representative of the population. Another point to emphasize is that sample size does not need to be a certain percentage of the population. When random sampling is used, a sample size that is only a small percentage of the population can represent the population well. The major public opinion polls, for example, do not use really large samples. The Nielsen rating service uses a sample of only about 5000 TV-watching households in the United States to estimate the popularity of various programs. The Nielsen ratings are a major variable in determining which programs continue and which do not.

CONSTRUCTING THE INSTRUMENT

FORMAT OF QUESTIONS

Once the overall research question has been determined, the next task is to construct an instrument that will provide the desired information. Because survey data consist of peoples' responses to individual questions, it is essential to start with good questions. Two basic types of questions are used in survey instruments: closed-ended or fixed alternative and open-ended or free-response questions. Use **closed-ended questions** when all the possible, relevant responses to a question can be specified, and the number of possible responses is limited. For example, in a survey of undergraduates, a question about class level would be closed-ended. The possible answers are known and are few in number: *freshman*, *sophomore*, *junior*, or *senior*. Other closed-ended questions might ask about residency status (in-state or out-of-state) or sex. **Open-ended questions** are used when there are a great number of possible answers or when the researcher cannot predict all the possible answers. For example, a question about the students' reasons for selecting a particular university would probably be open-ended. A question about the college major would be open ended because the researcher would probably not want to include the long list of possible majors. Both formats can be used in the same question—that is, a number of closed-ended responses can be followed by "Other" as the last possible response. For example, you might ask a professor a question such as:

1. What type of writing assignments do you typically require in your course? (circle as many as apply)

a. Reports

b. Themes or essays

c. Research papers

d. Take-home essay examinations

e. Minute papers

f. Other (please specify)

There are advantages and disadvantages to both these question formats. The open-ended question permits a free response rather than restricting the respondent to a choice from among stated alternatives. Individuals are free to respond from their own frame of reference, thus providing a wide range of responses. Open-ended questions are easier to construct, but analyzing them is very tedious and time consuming. The researcher must read and interpret each response, then develop a coding system that will permit a quantitative analysis of the responses. Some responses may be unclear, and the researcher may be unsure how to classify or code the response. The responses to open-ended questions typically differ in length, and some respondents may give more than one response to a particular question. If asked the most important reason for choosing a certain university, a respondent might answer, "I chose University X because of its academic reputation and because it is in-state and less expensive for me." The researcher must then decide whether to use both answers or only the first one, assuming the first answer is the more important one. An option to consider with such a question is rank ordering, using a combination of closed- and open-ended responses or using new technology to directly enter responses electronically.

Closed-ended questions take more time to construct, but the responses are easier to tabulate. Responses to closed-ended questions can be coded directly on scannable sheets that can be "read" and the data entered into a computer database for analysis. Closed-ended questions can be answered more easily and quickly by respondents. A closed format also ensures that all subjects have the same frame of reference in responding and may also make it easier for subjects to respond to questions on sensitive or private topics.

A limitation of the closed-ended question is that it does not provide much insight into whether respondents really have any information or any clearly formulated opinions about an issue. It is easier for the uninformed respondent to choose one of the suggested answers than to admit to lack of knowledge on an issue. For example, in response to the question "What is the effect of outsourcing on the U.S. economy?" the respondent who has little knowledge of outsourcing and the reasons for it could easily select a reasonable answer from among the alternatives provided. In contrast, respondents who have the knowledge or who have well-informed opinions on the issue may dislike being restricted to simple response categories that do not permit them to qualify their answers. It is possible to get the benefits of both open-ended and closed-ended questions. A researcher can first use the open-ended format with a small sample to identify possible alternative responses to the questions. The researcher can then design closed-ended questions for the final form of the instrument.

STRUCTURE OF QUESTIONS

We have discussed the advantages and disadvantages of the closed-ended and open-ended questions in survey research. Now let us look at the ways these two formats can be used to structure questions for interviews and questionnaires.

1. **Completion, or fill-in, items** are open-ended questions to which respondents must supply their own answers in their own words. For example: "What is the major weakness you have observed in your students' preparation for college?"
2. **Checklists** are questions that present a number of possible answers, and the respondents are asked to check those that apply. For example:

   What type of teaching aids do you use in your classes? (check as many as apply)

   _____ 1) CHALKBOARD

   _____ 2) OVERHEAD PROJECTOR

   _____ 3) COMPUTER PROJECTOR

   _____ 4) VIDEOTAPES

   _____ 5) OTHER (please specify)
3. **Scaled items** ask respondents to rate a concept, event, or situation on such dimensions as quantity or intensity, indicating "how much"; on quality, indicating "how well"; or on frequency, indicating "how often." For example:

How would you rate the writing skills of students you are teaching this semester? (check one)

_____ 1) VERY POOR

_____ 2) LESS THAN ADEQUATE

_____ 3) ADEQUATE

_____ 4) MORE THAN ADEQUATE

_____ 5) EXCELLENT

_____ 6) INSUFFICIENT INFORMATION

or

How well prepared in basic math skills are the students who typically enroll in your course? (check one)

_____ 1) NOT AT ALL PREPARED

_____ 2) SOMEWHAT PREPARED

_____ 3) WELL PREPARED

_____ 4) EXTREMELY WELL PREPARED

4. **Ranking items** ask respondents to indicate the order of their preference among a number of options. Rankings should not involve more than six options because otherwise it becomes too difficult for respondents to make the comparisons. An example of a ranking item follows:

   Please rank the order of difficulty your students have in reading each of the following materials, with 1 being the most difficult and 4 the least difficult.

   _____ 1) TEXTBOOKS

   _____ 2) OTHER REFERENCE BOOKS

   _____ 3) JOURNAL ARTICLES

   _____ 4) OTHER (please specify)

5. **Likert-type items** let subjects indicate their responses to selected statements on a continuum, from *strongly agree* to *strongly disagree*. Likert-type scales were discussed in Chapter 8. An advantage of this type of item is that points can be assigned to the various responses, and thus measures of central tendency, variability, correlation, and the like can be calculated. For example:

   The students who typically enroll in my course are underprepared in basic math skills. (circle one)

   strongly agree   agree   undecided   disagree   strongly disagree

WRITING SURVEY QUESTIONS

Now let us examine the task of formulating good questions. Deciding how to word the questions that are asked in a survey is a challenge. Before beginning to write a structured set of survey questions, it can be helpful to have a focus group discuss the questions in a nonstructured form. You do this by bringing together a

THINK ABOUT IT 14.5

Assume you are conducting a survey of students in the local high school on the extent of alcohol and drug use among students in the school. Construct one item of each of the following types that you might include in this survey: (1) completion, (2) checklist, (3) scaled item, (4) ranking, and (5) Likert type.

Suggested Answer

Completion

How would you describe the extent of alcohol use in your school?

Checklist

Are you (check one)

_____ 1) MALE

_____ 2) FEMALE

Scaled item

On average, how often do the students that you know use alcohol? (check one)

_____ 1) Twice a week

_____ 2) Once a week

_____ 3) Twice a month

_____ 4) Once a month

Ranking

How would you rank the following in terms of extent of use among students you know? (1 most common and 5 least common)

_____ 1) Beer

_____ 2) Wine

_____ 3) Other alcoholic beverages

_____ 4) Marijuana

_____ 5) Hard drugs

Liken-type item

Alcohol consumption is a serious problem among students in this school. (circle one)

SA A U D SD

few groups of 5 to 10 people representative of the study population to discuss the topics covered in the survey. A moderator keeps the discussion focused on a preset agenda and asks questions to clarify comments.

A focus group can be very valuable in questionnaire development. Focus-group discussions help the researcher understand how people talk about the survey issues, which is helpful in choosing vocabulary and in phrasing questions. A focus group often can suggest issues, concerns, or points of view about the topic that the researcher had not considered.

A significant body of research has shown that changes in such things as phrasing, the amount of information offered, and the choice of answers available to respondents can influence the outcome of a survey to a greater or lesser degree. The way you ask a question may prescribe the answer. It is possible for surveyors with competing agendas to come up with entirely different responses. Consider the following three ways to ask a question:

1. Would you support increased taxes to pay for full-day kindergarten?
2. Would you support an increase in your property taxes to pay for full-day kindergarten?
3. Would you support a 5 percent increase in your property taxes to pay for full-day kindergarten?

Individuals who might agree with the first general question would not necessarily agree when they consider that their property taxes would be increased.

Or consider the following ways to ask opinions on abortion:

1. Do you believe in women's right to choose?
2. Do you believe women should be allowed to decide whether to continue a pregnancy?
3. Do you believe women should be allowed to kill their unborn child?

Here are basic guidelines for writing good questions:

1. *Questions should be short, simple, and direct.* Eliminate any words and phrases not essential to the clear meaning of the question. Short questions are easier to understand. A useful rule of thumb is that most of the questions should have fewer than 10 words (one line), and all questions should be under 20 words (Mitchell & Jolley, 2004, p. 198).
2. *Phrase questions so that they can be understood by every respondent.* The vocabulary used should be nontechnical and should be geared to the least educated respondent. At the same time, avoid talking down to respondents or choosing words that sound patronizing. It is a good idea to have some other people, preferably ones whose background is similar to those who will be included in the study, read and give their interpretation of the content of each question. For example, questions using terms such as "authentic assessment," "distance learning," and "total quality management" may not be appropriate in a survey designed for the general public. Also, be careful not to use slang, abbreviations, or acronyms that may not be familiar to all.
3. *Phrase questions so as to elicit unambiguous answers.* The question "Did you vote in the last election?" is ambiguous because it does not specify which election. Quantify responses whenever possible. Words such as *often* and *sometimes* have different meanings for different people. For example, in a survey on how often undergraduates use the main library for studying, the responses should be quantified (*daily*, *five times per week*, *twice per week*, and so on) instead of using responses such as *usually*, *sometimes*, and *often*.
4. *Phrase questions so as to avoid bias that may predetermine a respondent's answer.* The wording of a question should not influence the respondent in a certain direction. For this reason, avoid stereotyped, prestige-carrying, emotionally loaded, or superlative words. Some words have such an emotional appeal in U.S. culture that they tend to bias questions regardless of how they are used. For example, the wording "Have you exercised your American right and registered to vote?" would undoubtedly bias the question. Simply asking, "Are you registered to vote?" would be preferable. Dillman (2000) says that words such as *freedom*, *equality*, *private enterprise*, *justice*, and *honesty* have a strong positive appeal in our culture. Words such as *bureaucratic*, *socialist*, *boss*, and *government planning* have a strong negative appeal. Avoid such words if possible.

5. *Avoid questions that might mislead because of unstated assumptions.* The frame of reference for answering the questions should be clear and consistent for all respondents. If any assumptions must be made before respondents give an answer, then also include questions designed to inquire into these assumptions. For example, in a survey designed for high school seniors, the question "Do you think your high school has adequately prepared you for college?" assumes the student is going to college and knows what is required in the way of preparation. The question "Have you registered to vote for the next presidential election?" assumes the high school student is 18 years of age, which may not be true.

6. *Avoid leading questions, which imply a desired response.* For example, "What do you think of the biased coverage of the Iraq War by the major TV networks?" is a leading question.

7. *Avoid questions that may elicit embarrassment, suspicion, or hostility in the respondent.* Questions should not put the respondent on the defensive. For example, people often resent questions about their age, income, religion, or educational status. Instead of asking a subject's age, the researcher can ask for his or her year of birth. People seem less concerned about giving their year of birth than about giving their age. The question "Do you have a high school diploma?" may embarrass someone who did not graduate from high school. The question might instead ask, "What grade had you completed when you left school?" In fact, it is best to avoid personal questions entirely unless the information is essential to the research.

8. *Avoid **"double-barreled" questions**, which attempt to ask two questions in one.* For example, "Do you feel that the university should provide basic-skills courses for students and give credit for those courses?" is a double-barreled question. When a respondent answers such a question, the researcher does not know whether the answer applies to both parts of the question or just to one. A yes answer to the preceding question may either mean that the respondent believes the university should offer basic-skills courses and give credit for them, or that it should offer the courses but not give credit for them. You can identify a double-barreled question from noting the *and*, *or*, or some other conjunction in the wording.

9. *Make sure the alternatives to each questionnaire item are exhaustive—that they express all the possible alternatives on the issue.* For example, "What is your marital status?" should include not only the alternatives "married" and "single," but also "unmarried cohabiting," "widowed," "divorced," and "separated." In developing the alternatives for questionnaire items designed to identify attitudes or opinions on issues, it is a good idea first to present the questions in an open-ended form to a small sample of respondents. Their answers can then be used as alternatives in the final product. On questions with a wide variety of possible responses, always include the alternative "other," along with a request that the respondent explain that choice. The question "What is your position in the school system?" might be followed by the alternatives "administrator," "teacher," "librarian," and "other (please specify)."

PICTURE THIS

"Next question: I believe that life is a constant striving for balance, requiring frequent tradeoffs between morality and necessity, within a cyclic pattern of joy and sadness, forging a trail of bittersweet memories until one slips, inevitably, into the jaws of death. Agree or disagree?"

10. *Keep the questionnaire as brief as possible so that it requires a minimum of the respondents' time.* Respondents are much more likely to complete and return a short questionnaire. The researcher must make an effort to eliminate all unnecessary items, especially those whose answers are available from other sources. All the items of a questionnaire should serve a research problem function; that is, they should elicit data needed to test the hypotheses or answer the questions of the research study. For example, you can eliminate a question that asks the respondent's age in a study where this information is not needed in the data analysis.
11. *Make sure the respondents have the information necessary to answer the questions.* Avoid questions dealing with experiences or topics you know are unfamiliar to your sample.

See Fowler (2002) for additional suggestions on writing survey questions.

THINK ABOUT IT 14.6

Which of the basic guidelines for writing good questions are violated in the cartoon above?

Answer
1, 2, 3, 8, 10, 11

USING A MAILED QUESTIONNAIRE

As we discussed earlier, it is not always practical to obtain survey data using an interview format—in these cases questionnaires are used, and quite often they are mailed to respondents. A well-constructed questionnaire is an important factor influencing response rate. We have already offered guidelines for writing the questions. In this section, we look at the overall arrangement of the questions, the cover letter, the follow-ups, and other factors that contribute to the success of a mailed questionnaire.

DIRECTIONS

It is very important to begin with precise directions that tell the respondents exactly what to do. Indicate how and where they are to mark their responses; for example, "Please indicate your response to the following questions by placing an X in the box next to the answer of your choice" or "Please use a No. 2 pencil and indicate your answers by blackening in the appropriate bubbles on the separate scannable answer sheet." If the format changes within the questionnaire, include new directions for that section.

ORDER OF QUESTIONS

Once the questions are written, they must be arranged in an appropriate order. The order of questions is important because it can influence the respondent's interest in completing the questionnaire. The very first question should be especially interesting and easy enough for all respondents to interpret and answer. If respondents are motivated to answer the first question, they are more likely to continue with the questionnaire. The first question should seek worthwhile information that is clearly related to the topic under consideration. For this reason, never begin a questionnaire with questions relating to age, gender, education, occupation, ethnic origin, marital status, and the like. The respondents may regard these questions as irrelevant or as an invasion of privacy and may therefore decide not to continue with the questionnaire. It could end up in the nearest wastebasket. Researchers also recommend that the first few questions be of the closed-ended type, which the respondent can complete quickly, instead of open-ended ones that may require a long, written response.

Group together questions that are similar in content. For example, in a questionnaire asking university faculty about the basic academic skills of their students, all the questions on reading would be placed together. Then questions on writing would appear together, followed later by questions related to mathematics skills. Within the content areas, group items according to the type of question. For example, the questions requiring a simple yes or no would be placed together, as would items requiring respondents to rank or to indicate the extent of agreement or disagreement.

Within each of the topic areas, arrange the questions in good psychological order. A logical or psychological arrangement contributes to better-thought-out answers on the part of the respondents. For example, first ascertain whether respondents were satisfied with working conditions before asking them to recommend changes. If both general and specific questions are asked on a topic, place the general questions first. Objective items on an issue or situation should precede the more subjective questions. Questions that are less likely to be objectionable should precede items that are more objectionable. People are sometimes reluctant to answer questions about attitudes, preferences, motives, behavior, personal feelings, and the like, but if objective questions can be used first to clarify and specify the situation, it may be easier for individuals to respond. For example, a researcher who wanted to survey students on the extent of marijuana usage might begin by asking more objective questions first, such as "How would you describe marijuana usage in your school: serious problem, moderate problem, slight problem, or no problem?" This could be followed by the questions "Do you think the frequency of marijuana smoking has increased, stayed about the same, or decreased this year?" and "Do you know students who use marijuana?" Then perhaps "Do you ever smoke marijuana?" could be asked. This principle of placing less objectionable questions before more objectionable ones implies that items dealing with demographic data such as age, gender, and occupation should be placed at the end of the questionnaire rather than at the beginning. The respondent will have fewer objections to giving this personal information after completing the questionnaire and seeing why such data would be relevant.

MATRIX SAMPLING

A procedure called **matrix sampling** is sometimes used when the survey is long and the accessible population is large. This technique involves randomly selecting respondents, each of whom is administered a subset of questions, randomly selected from the total set of items. The practical advantage of using matrix sampling is the decrease in the time required for each individual to respond. This is an important advantage because one obstacle to obtaining a high response rate is the unwillingness of some individuals to take the time to answer a long questionnaire.

FORMAT OF THE QUESTIONNAIRE

The questionnaire should be formatted so that it is attractive, easy for the respondent to read and answer, and convenient for the researcher to code and score. To achieve these ends, incorporate the following suggestions into the design of the survey document:

1. *Number questions consecutively* throughout the questionnaire without any repetitions or omissions. Having a unique number for each question avoids confusion in coding responses.
2. *Differentiate questions from answer categories* by using regular type for the questions and uppercase letters for the answers. Put any specific directions for responding inside parentheses and in lowercase. For example,

   Do you favor setting standards in basic skills as a requirement for high school graduation? (check your response)

   _____ 1) NO

   _____ 2) YES

3. *Use numbers to identify the various response categories.* The numbers assigned to the options represent a form of precoding that will facilitate processing the data. You can place a blank or box in front of the response options and ask the respondent to place an *X* or check mark in the space. For example:

   What is the highest level of education that you have completed? (check one)

   _____ 1) GRADE SCHOOL

   _____ 2) SOME HIGH SCHOOL

   _____ 3) COMPLETED HIGH SCHOOL

   _____ 4) SOME COLLEGE

   _____ 5) COMPLETED COLLEGE

   _____ 6) SOME GRADUATE WORK

   _____ 7) GRADUATE DEGREE

   A check or *X* in front of item 5 indicates that the individual has completed college, and a count can easily be made for category 5. Because of the varying lengths of the options, survey designers recommend placing the numbers for the response options at the beginning, to the left of the response categories rather than at the right, for ease of scoring.

4. *Be consistent in assigning numbers to the various answer categories.* Always use the same number for the same answer throughout the questionnaire. It is conventional to assign low numbers to the negative responses and higher numbers to the positive responses. For example, 1 is assigned to "*no*" and 2 is assigned to "*yes*"; 1 is assigned to "*unfavorable*" and 2 to "*favorable.*" Whatever number scheme is chosen, use it throughout because it is confusing for a respondent to associate 1 with "*no*" in the first part of the questionnaire and then find 1 associated with "*yes*" in another part.

5. *Response categories should be arranged vertically rather than horizontally.* The vertical arrangement makes the questionnaire appear less crowded and eliminates the common error of checking the space on the wrong side of the answer, as might occur for the following:

   What is your present marital status?

   _____ 1) NEVER MARRIED _____ 2) MARRIED _____ 3) DIVORCED

   _____ 4) SEPARATED _____ 5) WIDOWED _____ 6) UNMARRIED, COHABITING

   The above confusing arrangement could be improved in the following way:

   What is your present marital status? (check one)

   _____ 1) NEVER MARRIED

   _____ 2) MARRIED

_____ 3) DIVORCED

_____ 4) SEPARATED

_____ 5) WIDOWED

_____ 6) UNMARRIED, COHABITING

6. *Use contingency questions when not every question will be relevant to all respondents.* A **contingency question** is one whose relevancy depends on the answer to a prior question. For example, in a survey designed to assess faculty interest in using computer-assisted testing, the following question might be used:

   1. Are you interested in using computer-assisted testing in your classes?
      1) NO (if NO, please go to question 6)
      2) YES
      3) UNDECIDED
   2. If YES, would you use the computer-assisted testing for
      1) QUIZZES
      2) TESTS
      3) BOTH

   In the preceding example, the second question is a contingency question because its relevance is contingent on the answer given in the first question. Faculty members who indicated in question 1 that they were not interested in computer-assisted testing would not even have to read the next four questions but could proceed to 6, the next relevant question. Thus, contingency questions save time for the respondent and provide more accurate data for the researcher. Contingency questions can be set off by arrows, indenting, or enclosed boxes.

7. *Have the questionnaire reproduced by a high-quality printing method.* Quality printing gives the questionnaire a more professional appearance and makes a more favorable impression on respondents.
8. *Keep the questionnaire as short as possible.*

RECORDING ANSWERS

The previous discussion has assumed that respondents will mark their answers directly on the questionnaire form. Whenever possible, we recommend that researchers provide scannable sheets and direct the respondents to mark all responses directly on the sheets. General-purpose scannable sheets with either 5 or 10 options per question are available at a nominal cost. The sheets can be read by an optical scanner, and the data put on a disk or sent directly to a computer for analysis. Using scannable answer sheets saves time for the researcher and reduces human error in coding responses. The survey questions would be printed on a separate form, and the scannable sheet included for the responses. For example:

1. How many semesters of the *same* foreign language did you have in high school?

   A. NONE (0)

   B. ONE

   C. TWO

   D. THREE

   E. MORE THAN THREE

The response to the preceding question could be coded directly on the answer sheet. In some cases, it is possible to print survey questions directly on a scannable sheet. Figure 14.1 shows a sample of some survey questions used in a study of freshman students' perceptions of the adequacy of their high school preparation for college.

FIELD TESTING

Before the final printing, the researcher must **field-test** the instrument to identify ambiguities, misunderstandings, or other inadequacies. First, it is a good idea to ask colleagues who are familiar with the study to examine a draft of the questionnaire and give their opinions on whether the instrument will obtain the desired data and whether they see any problems that may have been overlooked.

Next, administer the questionnaire personally and individually to a small group drawn from the population to be considered in the study. Respondents answer the questions one at a time and provide feedback to the researcher on any difficulties they have with the items. Pay attention to such comments as "I don't know what you mean here" and "More than one of these answers apply to me." Try to ascertain whether all respondents interpret the questions in the same way. You might even state some of the questions in different ways to see if different responses are given to different versions of the same question. Observations made of the respondents as they fill out the questionnaire can also be enlightening. Spending an undue amount of time on a question or leaving a question blank and returning to it later can be clues that there are problems with some items.

The results of field tests can be used to clarify the items or perhaps to eliminate some. It is especially important to determine whether the questions will operate equally well in the different social classes and culture groups of the population to be studied. Some specific issues that should be addressed by field testing include the following:

1. Do the respondents seem comfortable with the questionnaire and motivated to complete it?
2. Are certain items confusing?
3. Could some items result in hostility or embarrassment on the part of respondents?
4. Are the instructions clear?
5. How long will it take a respondent to complete the questionnaire?
6. Do all respondents interpret the items in the same way?

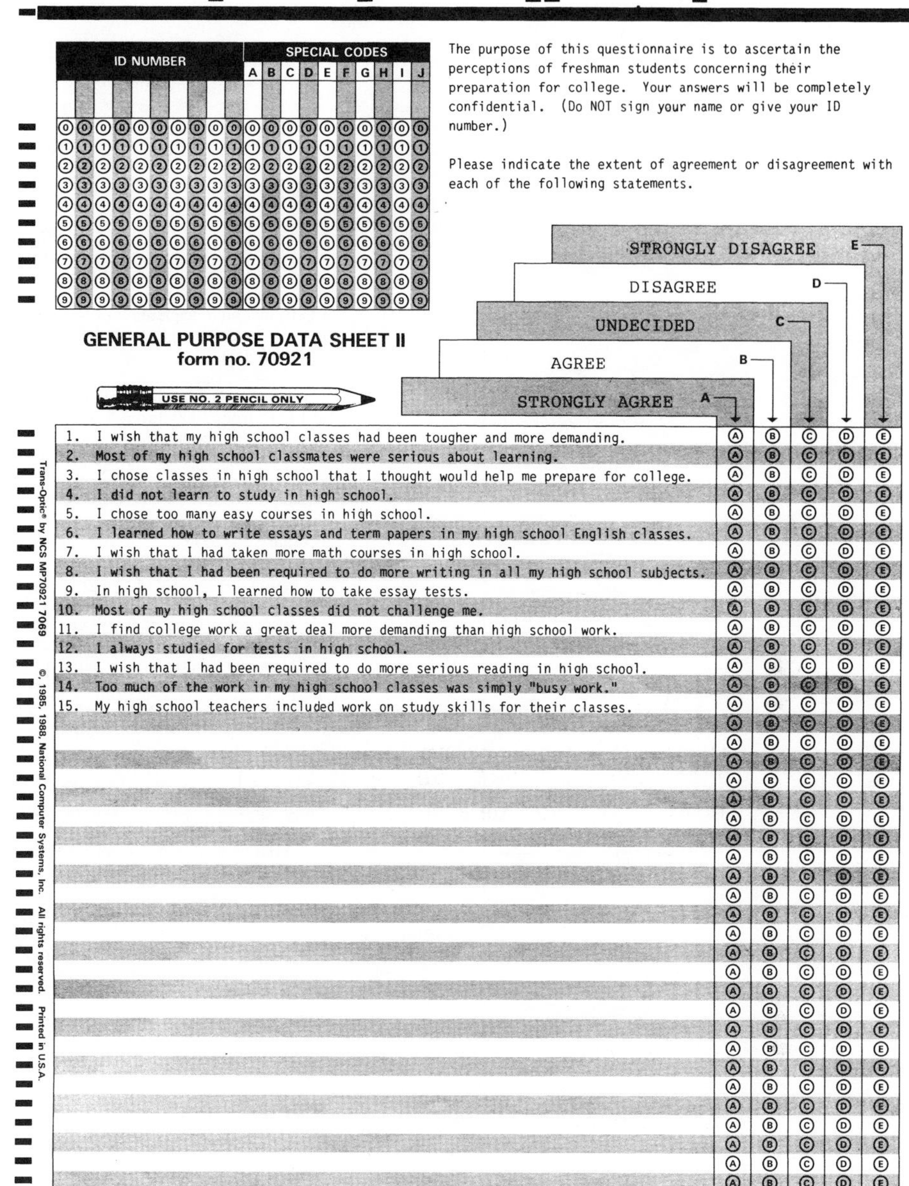

ID NUMBER

SPECIAL CODES
A B C D E F G H I J

The purpose of this questionnaire is to ascertain the perceptions of freshman students concerning their preparation for college. Your answers will be completely confidential. (Do NOT sign your name or give your ID number.)

Please indicate the extent of agreement or disagreement with each of the following statements.

GENERAL PURPOSE DATA SHEET II
form no. 70921

USE NO. 2 PENCIL ONLY

A — STRONGLY AGREE
B — AGREE
C — UNDECIDED
D — DISAGREE
E — STRONGLY DISAGREE

1. I wish that my high school classes had been tougher and more demanding.
2. Most of my high school classmates were serious about learning.
3. I chose classes in high school that I thought would help me prepare for college.
4. I did not learn to study in high school.
5. I chose too many easy courses in high school.
6. I learned how to write essays and term papers in my high school English classes.
7. I wish that I had taken more math courses in high school.
8. I wish that I had been required to do more writing in all my high school subjects.
9. In high school, I learned how to take essay tests.
10. Most of my high school classes did not challenge me.
11. I find college work a great deal more demanding than high school work.
12. I always studied for tests in high school.
13. I wish that I had been required to do more serious reading in high school.
14. Too much of the work in my high school classes was simply "busy work."
15. My high school teachers included work on study skills for their classes.

Trans-Optic® by NCS MP70921 7069

Figure 14.1 Example of a Scannable Sheet with Survey Statements

Source: Reproduced with permission from National Computer Systems Inc.

PREPARING THE COVER LETTER

Researchers may find it useful to mail an introductory letter to potential respondents in advance of the questionnaire itself. This procedure alerts the subject to the study so that he or she is not overwhelmed by the questionnaire package. In any case, a cover letter addressed to the respondent by name and title must accompany the questionnaire. One can use the "mail merge" feature of word pro-

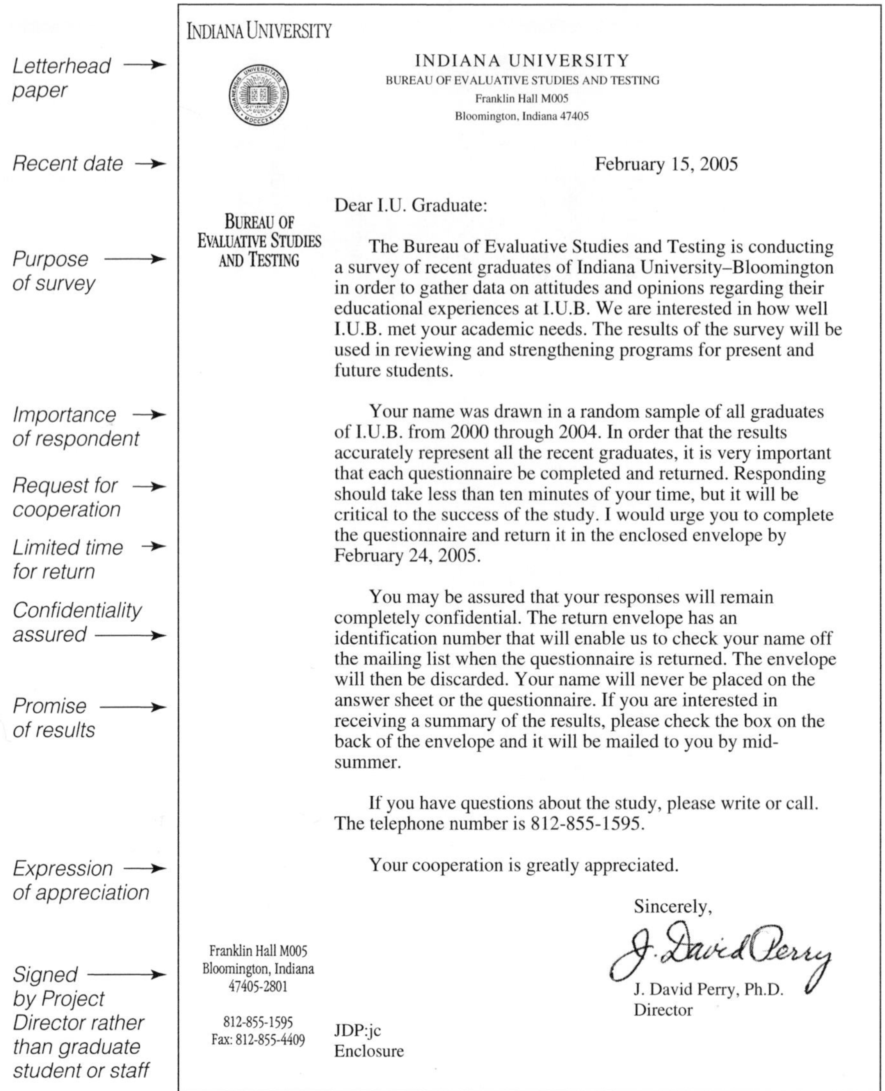

INDIANA UNIVERSITY

INDIANA UNIVERSITY
BUREAU OF EVALUATIVE STUDIES AND TESTING
Franklin Hall M005
Bloomington, Indiana 47405

February 15, 2005

BUREAU OF EVALUATIVE STUDIES AND TESTING

Dear I.U. Graduate:

The Bureau of Evaluative Studies and Testing is conducting a survey of recent graduates of Indiana University–Bloomington in order to gather data on attitudes and opinions regarding their educational experiences at I.U.B. We are interested in how well I.U.B. met your academic needs. The results of the survey will be used in reviewing and strengthening programs for present and future students.

Your name was drawn in a random sample of all graduates of I.U.B. from 2000 through 2004. In order that the results accurately represent all the recent graduates, it is very important that each questionnaire be completed and returned. Responding should take less than ten minutes of your time, but it will be critical to the success of the study. I would urge you to complete the questionnaire and return it in the enclosed envelope by February 24, 2005.

You may be assured that your responses will remain completely confidential. The return envelope has an identification number that will enable us to check your name off the mailing list when the questionnaire is returned. The envelope will then be discarded. Your name will never be placed on the answer sheet or the questionnaire. If you are interested in receiving a summary of the results, please check the box on the back of the envelope and it will be mailed to you by mid-summer.

If you have questions about the study, please write or call. The telephone number is 812-855-1595.

Your cooperation is greatly appreciated.

Sincerely,

J. David Perry

J. David Perry, Ph.D.
Director

Franklin Hall M005
Bloomington, Indiana
47405-2801

812-855-1595
Fax: 812-855-4409

JDP:jc
Enclosure

Figure 14.2 Example of a Cover Letter for a Survey

cessing packages to personalize the letter. Figure 14.2 shows a cover letter with the important parts identified. The cover letter introduces the potential respondents to the questionnaire and "sells" them on responding. The cover letter should include the following elements:

1. *The purpose of the study.* The first paragraph of the letter should explain the purpose of the study and its potential usefulness. It will be helpful to relate the importance of the study to a reference group with which the individuals may identify. For example, a cover letter with a questionnaire for graduate students should stress the importance of the data for improving graduate education at the university.

2. *A request for cooperation.* The letter should explain why the potential respondent was included in the sample and should make an appeal for the respondent's cooperation. Respondents should be made to feel they can make an important contribution to the study.

3. *The protection provided the respondent.* The letter must not only assure the respondents that their responses will be confidential but also explain how that confidentiality will be maintained. To facilitate the follow-up procedure necessary for a high return rate, use identification numbers on the questionnaires. If there is no identification, the problem of nonresponse bias is compounded because there is no way to know who has responded and who has not, and follow-up procedures become very confused. If identification numbers are used, respondents must be told that the numbers are there simply to let the researcher check the respondents' names off the mailing list when the questionnaires are returned. The respondents must be assured that their names will never be placed on the questionnaires themselves; thus there will be no way to associate particular responses with any individuals. If the researcher intends to destroy the questionnaires immediately after the responses have been rostered, this information should be conveyed in the letter, to reassure the respondents of their anonymity.

   Some researchers prefer not to use any identification system at all, especially when the topic is sensitive. In this case, it is recommended that one include in the mail-out package a postcard that the respondent can mail separately to indicate that the questionnaire has also been mailed. This postcard contains a pretyped message that the questionnaire has been returned and a place for the respondent to write his or her name or a coded identifier. In this way, a record can be kept of the returned questionnaires.

4. *Sponsorship of the study.* The signature on the letter is important in influencing the return of the questionnaire. If the study is part of a doctoral dissertation, it is helpful if a person well known to the respondents, such as the head of a university department or the dean of the school, signs or countersigns the letter. Such a signature is likely to be more effective than that of an unknown graduate student. If there is a sponsor for the study, such as a foundation or some agency, mention this. Use a university or agency letterhead.

5. *Promise of results.* An offer may be made to share the findings of the study with the respondents if they are interested. Tell them how to make their request for the results. One method is to provide a place for checking on the back of the return envelope, as well as a place for the respondent's name and address.

6. *Appreciation.* Include an expression of appreciation for their assistance and cooperation with the study.

7. *Recent date on the letter.* Date the cover letter near the day of mailing. A potential respondent will not be impressed by a letter dated several weeks before receipt.

8. *Request for immediate return.* It is also important to urge immediate return of the questionnaire. If a time period such as 2 weeks or a month is suggested, the respondent may lay the questionnaire aside and, in spite of good intentions, forget about it. A questionnaire that fails to receive attention within a week is not likely ever to be returned.

All of the preceding elements should be included, but at the same time the cover letter should be as brief as possible. One page is the maximum recommended length. Enclose the letter in an envelope along with the questionnaire. Always include a self-addressed, stamped return envelope for the respondent's use. This is indispensable for a good return rate.

Research shows that the type of postage used on the mailing can also influence returns. Stamps increase response rate over bulk-printed postage. Evidently, the stamp makes the questionnaire appear more personal and important and less like junk mail.

MAXIMIZING RESPONSE RATES

Research shows that response rates for most American national surveys of all types have been falling during the last four decades (Cook, Heath, & Thompson, 2000). Hegelson, Voss, and Terpening (2002) conceptualize the process of responding to a request to complete a survey as involving four phases through which the researcher must move the potential respondent (see Figure 14.3).

1. *Attention*, the entry point to the response process, is critical for maximizing the probability of a response. If we can gain the respondent's attention, then we have moved the respondents into the process and increased the likelihood that there will be a follow-through to the end.
2. *Intention*, the next phase, involves the potential respondent's estimating the time and effort that must be expended to comply with the researcher's request for information and making a decision to continue with the survey.
3. *Completion* is the phase where the potential respondent moves from the consideration of the survey completion process to the physical and mental activity necessary for actual survey completion.

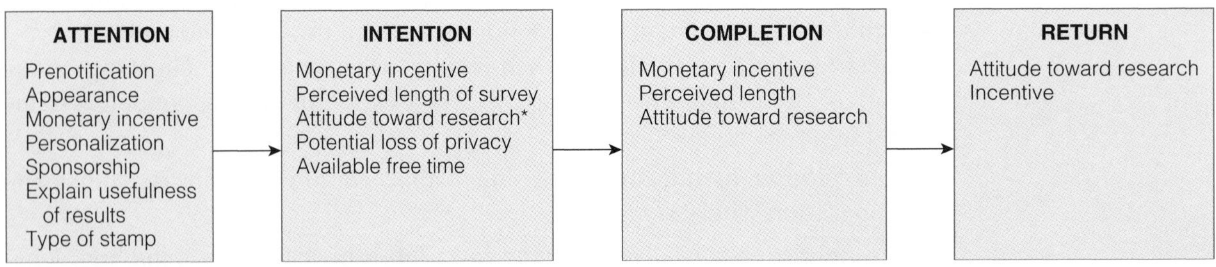

Figure 14.3 Maximizing Response Rates

*Hegelson et al. found that an individual's attitude toward research is an important factor in responding to a survey.
Source: From *Psychology and Marketing, 19*, 303–328, 2002. Reprinted by permission of John Wiley & Sons, Inc.

4. *Return* involves putting the completed survey into a return envelope and mailing it, a relatively low-cost action compared to earlier phases of the decision process.

We will summarize some of the aspects of survey design that may affect the potential respondent at each phase.

MONETARY INCENTIVE

A great deal of research has shown that a token monetary incentive consistently increases response rate. The gratuity offered can be a nickel, a dime, a quarter, or even a dollar or more. Researchers believe that the payment creates a feeling of obligation on the part of the recipient and a need to reciprocate that is satisfied by completing and returning the questionnaire. Monetary incentives are most effective when prepaid rather than promised and when included with the first mailing of the questionnaire rather than with a follow-up. Among several survey design factors examined, Helgeson, Voss, and Terpening (2002) found that the one dollar incentive included with the mailed survey had the most effect on returns. Jobber, Saunders, and Mitchell's (2004) research not only supports the use of a prepaid monetary incentive but also shows that the response rate increases as the value of the incentive increases. They concluded from their studies that the inclusion of any incentive, regardless of amount, raises the response rate by an average of 15 percent. The size of the incentive had an additional effect at the rate of 2 percent per dollar within the observed range of incentives.

Newby, Watson, and Woodliff (2003) also found a monetary incentive to be an effective way to increase rates. Of course, offering a payment is not always possible because even a token amount can greatly increase the cost of the survey. If the sample is not too large, however, it is an option worth considering.

FOLLOW-UPS

To reach the maximum percentage of returns in a mailed questionnaire survey, planned follow-up mailings are essential. Several steps are typically taken in the follow-ups and are explained here.

First Reminder

If the questionnaire has not been returned in a week or 10 days after the initial mailing, send a postcard to the respondent. This card serves as a polite reminder that a questionnaire was sent earlier and that the response is very important to the study. Urge respondents to complete and return the questionnaire immediately ("today"). Of course, express thanks to those who may have already mailed the questionnaire. An offer can be made to send another questionnaire if one is needed by people who may have misplaced or never received it. Usually the postcard reminder brings in a relatively large number of responses.

Second Follow-Up

The follow-up, which should be sent about 3 weeks after the original mailing, involves a letter, another copy of the questionnaire, and an addressed return envelope. The letter should first tell the nonrespondents that their questionnaires have not been received and should reiterate the usefulness of the study. Emphasize that a replacement questionnaire is enclosed and make a strong appeal to complete and return it. Tell the respondents not to respond a second time if they have already mailed the questionnaire.

Third Follow-Up

The third and final follow-up is sent out 6 to 7 weeks after the initial mailing. It is similar to the second, having both a letter and a replacement questionnaire. Many researchers send this follow-up by certified mail. If a researcher has 75 to 90 percent returns after three follow-ups, he or she may be ready to terminate the survey and to declare the remaining subjects nonrespondents. The researcher must decide whether the responses obtained through further follow-up efforts would be worth the cost and time involved. Also, you do not want potential respondents to feel harassed. It is sometimes suggested that the researcher include in the third follow-up a postcard on which subjects could indicate that they do not wish to participate in the survey and will not be returning the questionnaire. Such a procedure permits definite identification of nonrespondents.

DEALING WITH NONRESPONSE

Nonresponse can be a serious problem in survey research. Researchers generally agree that nonresponse can bias survey data especially when it is nonrandom and if it is in some way correlated with the variables measured in the study. Nonrespondents may differ systematically from respondents. Research shows that respondents tend to differ from nonrespondents in characteristics such as education, intelligence, motivation, and interest in the topic of the survey. A survey with low response rate can thus be biased even though the researcher started out by mailing questionnaires to a representative sample. Recent studies, however, suggest that the effect of nonresponse may not be as pronounced as was once thought and that low response rates may not necessarily indicate bias (McCarty, 2003). Teitler, Reichman, & Sprachman (2003) investigated the costs and benefits of improving response rates for a hard-to-reach population. They concluded that efforts to improve response rate were beneficial in obtaining a representative sample, but there was a point of diminishing returns beyond which the benefits were marginal. So where does this leave us? The findings from these studies do not justify low response rates; there is no question that high response rates are preferable to lower ones. They simply indicate that lower response rates do not necessarily translate into biased data.

What does a researcher do about the nonrespondents? We do not want to ignore them. If, after all follow-up attempts, response rate remains below about 75 percent, try to learn something about the characteristics of the nonrespondents and the extent to which they might differ from the respondents. There are several ways to do this:

1. *Compare respondents to population.* If you have access to information on characteristics of the population—such as age, gender, education, ethnicity, socioeconomic status, and so on—you can compare the characteristics of the respondents with those of the population from which they were selected.

If the respondents in general are typical of the population in important characteristics, you can assume the respondents are truly representative of the total population and thus can generalize from the respondents to the total sample. If the respondents are found to differ from the population, results must be limited to the respondents.

2. *Compare early to late respondents.* Research has shown that nonrespondents are often similar to late respondents. Thus, a second way to estimate the responses of nonrespondents is to look at those of the late respondents. Prior to this step, however, categorize the respondents into early and late groups and compare their responses to check for any significant differences. If no significant differences appear between early and late respondents, and late respondents are believed typical of nonrespondents, then you can assume the respondents are an unbiased sample of the recipients and can thus generalize to the total group.
3. *Compare respondents and nonrespondents.* A more systematic approach is to interview either personally or by telephone a small random sample (perhaps 10 percent) of the nonrespondents. This sample of nonrespondents drawn for comparison purposes is sometimes called a "double-dipped sample." Using the questionnaire as an interview schedule, the investigator then gathers responses from the random sample of nonrespondents. The mean responses or the proportion of responses of the nonrespondents can be statistically compared to those of the respondents to see whether the two groups differ significantly. If no significant differences are found when the responses of the initial respondents are compared with those of the interview sample, then the researcher can reasonably assume that the respondents represent an unbiased sample of all who received the questionnaire. The data can be pooled and generalizations made to the total sample and to the population. Without such a check, you have no way of knowing if the respondents are different and therefore biased. Using a double-dipped sample is the preferred method of checking for bias because the direction and the extent of bias that are due to nonresponse can be directly assessed. It is, however, more costly and time consuming.

If you find that certain clearly identifiable subgroups did not return the questionnaire, you may need to change the original research question to exclude these subgroups. For example, if secondary teachers showed a much lower rate of returns than did elementary teachers in a survey, a researcher might conclude that the questionnaire had little relevance or interest for secondary teachers and decide to restrict the study to elementary teachers. The research question would be restated to indicate the change.

VALIDITY

Some attention must be given to the validity of interviews and questionnaires—that is, whether they are really measuring what they are supposed to measure. The survey should have *face validity*: It should *appear* valid for its intended purpose. Subjects are more inclined to respond to questions they perceive to be relevant and meaningful than to questions whose purpose they do not comprehend. Subjects are less inclined to complete and return a questionnaire they perceive as being inappropriate. The most obvious type of scientific validity evidence is based on content, which may be gathered by having some competent colleagues who are familiar with the purpose of the survey examine the items to judge whether they are appropriate for measuring what they are supposed to measure and whether they are a representative sample of the behavior domain under investigation.

Some validity studies have looked at evidence based on the relationship of survey responses to other variables. Direct observation of behavior, for example, has been a criterion used to validate surveys. After responses were obtained, observations were made to see whether the actual behavior of the subjects agreed with their expressed attitudes, opinions, or other answers. If you find agreement between survey responses and actual behavior, you have some evidence for the validity of the survey. Other data sources, such as third parties, may also be used as criteria.

Two important variables influence the validity of a questionnaire. First, how important is the topic to the respondent? You can assume more valid responses from individuals who are interested in the topic and/or are informed about it. And second, does the questionnaire protect the respondents' anonymity? It is reasonable to assume that greater truthfulness will be obtained if the respondents can remain anonymous, especially when sensitive or personal questions are asked.

RELIABILITY

Survey data must have reliability if they are to be useful. If respondents' answers are not consistent, then the validity of the research is also questionable. One procedure for assessing reliability of questionnaires or interviews is having two different interviewers interview the same individuals to check the consistency of the results. Internal consistency may be checked by building some redundancy into the instrument—items on the same topic may be rephrased and repeated in the questionnaire or interview. The more consistent the responses, the higher the reliability.

It is also possible to repeat a questionnaire or interview with the same individuals after a period of time or to administer two different forms of the questionnaire to the same individuals. Such procedures are often expensive and time consuming, however, and somewhat impractical because it is not easy to find subjects willing to repeat the questionnaire or interview. Another problem with this approach is that some answers to questions dealing with less stable aspects of behavior may legitimately change over time.

STATISTICAL ANALYSIS IN SURVEYS

Surveys do not require complex statistical analyses. Data analysis may simply consist of determining the frequencies and percentages of responses for the questions of the study. For example, a survey of library resources may report the number of fiction books, the number of nonfiction books, and so on. A survey

Table 14.3 Students' Attitudes toward Increase in Activity Fee

	Approve	No Opinion	Disapprove	Total
Freshmen and sophomores	60	68	32	160
Juniors and seniors	80	46	66	192
Graduate students	12	10	66	88
Total	152	124	164	440

Table 14.4 Attitudes toward Library Tax by Residence

	City	County	Total
Favor	150	96	246
Oppose	90	164	254
Total	240	260	500

of people's attitudes on an issue may report the number and percentage of the respondents who gave each response, such as "strongly agree," "agree," "disagree," and so on. It is useful to convert numbers to percentages in order to be able to talk about the proportion responding a certain way and to be able to make comparisons. Consider the hypothetical frequency data in Table 14.3, based on a survey of 440 students concerning their opinions of a proposed increase in student activity fees at the university they attend. Looking at the raw frequencies, you might say that upperclassmen (66 juniors and seniors) and graduate students (66) are equally opposed to the increase in fees. But if you calculate *percentages* based on the total number of students *in each group*, you can see that more than twice the proportion of graduate students disapprove of the increase compared to juniors and seniors. This is because 66 of the 88 graduate students (75 percent) disapprove, compared to 66 of 192 (34 percent) juniors and seniors.

Thus, the table shows that graduate students are more likely to disapprove of the activity fee increase than undergraduates. To avoid a misinterpretation, always make sure that the total numbers for different groups are presented in tables such as this one.

CONTROLLING VARIABLES IN A SURVEY ANALYSIS

Consider the hypothetical results of a survey of attitudes toward a new library tax for improving and expanding the county public library. Table 14.4 shows that 63 percent (150/240) of city residents favor the library tax, compared with 37 percent (96/260) of the county residents. It appears from these data that there is a relationship between place of residence and attitude toward the library tax. A chi-square test will show whether there is a statistically significant relationship between the two variables (see Chapter 7 for discussion of chi square). Table 14.5 shows the calculation of chi square for these data. The expected frequencies for each cell are shown in parentheses.

Referring to Table A.4 of the Appendix with 1 degree of freedom, you can see that the chi square of 32.83 is highly significant ($<.01$). You might conclude that

Table 14.5 Observed and Expected Frequencies for Attitude Data

	City	County	Total
Favor	150 (118)	96 (128)	246
Oppose	90 (122)	164 (132)	254
Total	240	260	500

$$\chi^2 = \frac{(150-118)^2}{118} + \frac{(96-128)^2}{128} + \frac{(90-122)^2}{122} + \frac{(164-132)^2}{132}$$

$$\chi^2 = 32.83$$

there is a statistically significant relationship between place of residence and attitude toward the library tax. A more cautious observer, however, might point out that the city (the location of a major state university) has a greater proportion of educated people and that it may be educational level rather than place of residence per se that accounts for the favorable attitude toward the library tax.

To explore this alternative explanation, you can control for the variable of educational level by holding it constant, and then observe whether the relationship between the first two variables continues to exist. The simplest way to hold the variable constant is to divide the subjects into separate groups, each having a different value on that variable, and to look at the crosstabs for each of these groups separately. In this case, you could categorize the 500 respondents into college-educated and non-college-educated (assuming this information is available) and look at the relationship within the two separate groups.

The data in Table 14.6 show that the alternative explanation is correct; if college education is controlled by holding it constant, there is no relationship between the variables "place of residence" and "attitude toward the tax." Among the college educated, 80 percent (144/180) of the city residents favor the tax, and so do 80 percent (80/100) of the county residents. Among the non-college-educated, 10 percent (6/60) of the city residents favor the tax, as do 10 percent (16/160) of the rural residents.

Suppose the data had been as shown in Table 14.7. Even though educational level has been held constant within each table, the relationship between the variables "residence" and "attitude" is evident. Among the college-educated, 67 percent (80/120) of the city residents favor the tax, compared with 33 percent (20/60) of the rural residents. Among the non–college-educated, 58 percent of the city residents favor the tax, compared with 38 percent of the rural residents. In this case, there *is* something about the city and county respondents, other than their education, that leads them to respond differently about the library tax.

You might also want to investigate sex differences in responses to a survey. In this case, the crosstabs would show the frequency of responses to the questions for males and females separately. Social class differences could be examined by categorizing the subjects into separate groups on the basis of appropriate criteria and looking at the responses for each of the groups.

Tables that show frequencies of different groups' responses are often the best way to illustrate the relationship among the variables of a survey. These tables are called cross tabulations, or **crosstabs**, because they permit comparisons

Table 14.6 Attitudes toward Library Tax Related to Education, Not to Residence

	College-Educated		
	City	County	Total
Favor	144	80	224
Oppose	36	20	56
Total	180	100	280
	Non-College-Educated		
	City	County	Total
Favor	6	16	22
Oppose	54	144	198
Total	60	160	220

Table 14.7 Attitudes toward Library Tax Related to Residence, Not to Education

	College-Educated		
	City	County	Total
Favor	80	20	100
Oppose	40	40	80
Total	120	60	180
	Non-College-Educated		
	City	County	Total
Favor	70	76	146
Oppose	50	124	174
Total	120	200	320

across groups. The simplest crosstabs contain two variables with two categories for each variable. More complex forms are possible, however, such as 2×3, 2×4, 3×3, and so on. Cross tabulations are used most often with categorical or nominal data.

STATISTICS FOR CROSSTABS

Crosstabs are a widely used way to graphically show the differences in responses among various groups and whether or not a relationship may exist between the variables. When both variables in the cross tabulation are measured at the nominal level, the chi-square test may be used to determine whether a systematic relationship exists between the two variables. Chi square, however, indicates *only* whether the variables are related or are independent. It does not tell the extent to which they are related. For example, the value of χ^2 for the "college-educated" versus the "non-college-educated" data in Table 14.6 is 17.09, which is statistically significant at the .01 level. Thus, you know that there is a significant relationship between place of residence and attitude toward the tax among the college educated, but you do not know how strongly the two variables are related.

To learn the extent of the relationship, you must calculate a coefficient of correlation. A coefficient that is frequently used with nominal data in 2 × 2 tables is the *phi coefficient* (ϕ). The phi coefficient is a mathematical simplification of the Pearson product moment coefficient for 2 × 2 tables. Thus, phi has a value of 0 when no relationship exists, +1.00 when a perfect positive relationship exists, and −1.00 when a perfect negative relationship exists. The phi coefficient for the college-educated in Table 14.6 is .32. The phi coefficient is interpreted like any other Pearson coefficient. The .32 indicates a moderate positive relationship between place of residence and attitude toward the library tax among the college educated.

For tables larger than 2 × 2, an appropriate measure of relationship is the kappa statistic (κ) (Siegel & Castellan, 1988, p. 284). If there is a perfect relationship between the variables, κ will equal 1.00. If agreement between variables is exactly what would be expected through chance, κ equals 0. If agreement is less than what is expected by chance, κ will be a negative number. If the two variables in the cross tabulation are ordinal, statistics such as the Kendall coefficient of concordance (W) or the gamma statistic can be used to indicate the strength of the relationship between variables. [You can find comprehensive discussion of correlation procedures for nominal and ordinal variables in Chapter 9 of Siegel and Castellan's (1988) text.]

SUMMARY

The survey is a widely used research method for gathering data ranging from physical counts and frequencies to attitudes and opinions. Surveys are classified according to their focus, scope, and time of data collection. They should involve careful planning, unbiased sampling of a population, thoughtful development of data-gathering instruments, and careful analysis of the results.

If researchers use some type of probability sampling, they can infer population values from the sample results. The usual procedure is to set up an interval or range that has a high probability of including the population value. The width of this interval is a function of the risk they are willing to take of being wrong and the sample size. The interval narrows as the acceptable probability of error increases and as sample size increases. You can also use this procedure to estimate the sample size needed for any desired margin of error.

Interviews and questionnaires are the major means of data collection for a survey. Both procedures involve asking questions of selected subjects, but each has unique advantages and disadvantages. It is important that the instruments used be as valid and reliable as possible. Various follow-up procedures have proved effective in increasing returns from mailed questionnaires.

Cross tabulations provide an excellent way to show the relationship existing among the variables in a survey.

KEY CONCEPTS

census
checklists
closed-ended question
cohort study
completion (fill-in) items
contingency question
cross-sectional survey
crosstabs
double-barreled question
field test
interview
interviewer bias
Likert-type item
longitudinal survey
margin of error
matrix sampling
nonresponse
open-ended question

panel study
pause
population
probe
ranking items
response rate
sample survey
sampling error
sampling frame
scaled items
social desirability bias
survey research
trend study
web-based survey

EXERCISES

1. Suggest a research question that can best be answered by means of a survey. Write two open-ended items, two closed-end items, and two Likert-scale items that would provide data relevant to the question.
2. What data-gathering technique would you use for each of the following surveys?
   a. A survey of a sample of high school teachers throughout the state concerning the use of mandatory competency exams for high school graduation
   b. A survey of the opinions of people in a major metropolitan area on the way juveniles who commit violent crimes are presently handled in the state's court system
   c. A survey of the opinions of a sample of professors on the campus of State University about the use of pass/fail grades instead of letter grades (You want a very high response rate.)
   d. A freshman survey of certain noncognitive characteristics that might relate to academic achievement in the first year of college
   e. A survey of 500 people from throughout the United States about their attitudes toward the administration's immigration policy
3. How does the proportion of yes/no responses influence the sample size needed?
4. The evening news on television reported the following: In a recently conducted survey of the American public, 37 percent of the respondents said they approve of the president's performance. What else would you want to know before you interpreted this report?
5. How would you interpret the following report? "A poll of 1000 randomly selected registered voters in Indiana found that 45 percent favored using state lottery profits for education. Figures from this poll are subject to a sampling error of ±3 percent. The confidence level is 95 percent."
6. For each of the following three sample sizes, calculate the 95 percent margin of error for the population proportion. Assume the sample proportion is .40 for each. What effect does an increase in sample size have on the width of the interval? Why?
   n of sample A = 100
   n of sample B = 1000
   n of sample C = 10,000
7. A school superintendent wants to determine what proportion of the 5000 middle and high school students in the district use cigarettes. He will distribute a questionnaire to a random sample of the students. How many students will he need to sample in order to have a 95 percent margin of error of ±5 percent in his estimate?
8. A national polling organization wants to be able to predict the outcome of the 2004 presidential election to within ±3 percent. How large a random sample will be needed to achieve this level of precision? Assume a 95 percent confidence level.
9. A survey had an initial response rate of 51 percent. What would you suggest to the researcher for dealing with this low response rate?
10. The administration at State University wants to estimate the incoming freshman class's interest in a computer science major. Not having the financial resources to survey all 5000 freshmen, they survey a random sample of 500. They find that 100 students report they are interested in such a major.
    a. Calculate the margin of error in this survey.
    b. What is the best estimate of the number of freshmen who would be interested in majoring in computer science?

11. Which of the following would be biased samples of the population of college students at a large university?
    a. A random sample of students entering the library on Friday evening
    b. A random sample of students registered for classes
    c. A random sample of students buying season tickets for basketball
    d. A sample composed of students who volunteered for a project after seeing a notice in the school newspaper
12. Assume you are conducting a survey to determine how elementary school teachers in a district feel about the policy of retaining students.
    a. Write two closed-ended questions for this survey.
    b. Write two open-ended questions for this survey.
    c. Write a contingency question.
13. On the basis of the time of data collection, classify each of the following surveys:
    a. Terman's study of adults who were intellectually gifted as children
    b. A comparison of math achievement in public middle schools in the United States in 1990, 1995, and 2000
    c. A follow-up of the 1995 graduates of the Indiana University School of Business
    d. A survey of reading achievement at different grade levels in a school system in 2000
14. Which of the following is an advantage of the longitudinal type of survey?
    a. More intensive individual study
    b. Providing data for different age groups at the same time
    c. Prompt data gathering
    d. No sampling errors
15. A popular weekly news magazine included a detailed questionnaire on attitudes about crime. The editors invited readers to fill out the questionnaire and return it to the magazine. The magazine subsequently printed an article on the widespread fear of crime among U.S. citizens, especially older people. How would you evaluate this survey?
16. A graduate student is planning to use a survey to gather data for her dissertation but is unsure whether to use mailed questionnaires or telephone interviews. Examine the following list of considerations and indicate whether a questionnaire or an interview would be more appropriate.
    a. She is on a tight financial budget for her data collection.
    b. Her goal is a 90 percent response rate from the sample.
    c. Some of the questions may involve sensitive issues.
    d. She hopes to minimize the time needed for coding and organizing data and getting it ready for computer analysis.

ANSWERS

1. Answers will vary. *Example*: How do adults in a community feel about the building of a new elementary school?
2. a. Mailed questionnaire
    b. Telephone interview
    c. Personal interview
    d. Directly administered questionnaire
    e. Telephone interview
3. The nearer the proportions are to .50–.50, the larger the sample size needed.
4. One would want to know the size of the sample, how it was drawn, the width of the interval around the estimated population parameter (the margin of error), and the confidence level.
5. The .95 confidence interval for the proportion of registered voters who favor using lottery funds for education is between 42 and 48 percent.
6. **Sample A**

$$\sigma_p = \frac{\sqrt{(.40)(.60)}}{\sqrt{100}} = \frac{\sqrt{.24}}{\sqrt{100}} = \frac{.4899}{10} = .04899$$

$.04899 \times 1.96 = .0960$ or .10 margin of error

Sample B

$$\sigma_p = \frac{\sqrt{(.40)(.60)}}{\sqrt{1000}} = \frac{\sqrt{.24}}{\sqrt{1000}} = \frac{.4899}{31.62} = .0155$$

$.0155 \times 1.96 = .03$ margin of error

Sample C

$$\sigma_p = \frac{\sqrt{(.40)(.60)}}{\sqrt{10{,}000}} = \frac{\sqrt{.24}}{\sqrt{10{,}000}} = \frac{.4899}{100} = .004899$$

$$.0049 \times 1.96 = .01 \text{ margin of error}$$

An increase in sample size decreases the width of the interval. As n increases, the sample error decreases and hence the size of the interval.

7. Use Formula 14.2. Assume $p = q = .50$

$$n = \left(\frac{1}{\frac{E}{\sqrt{pq}}}\right)^2 (1.96)^2 = \left(\frac{1}{\frac{.05}{\sqrt{(.5)(.5)}}}\right)^2 (1.96)^2$$

$$= \left(\frac{1}{.10}\right)^2 (1.96)^2 = 100(3.8416) = 384$$

8. Assume $p = q = .50$

$$n = \left(\frac{1}{\frac{E}{\sqrt{pq}}}\right)^2 (1.96)^2 = \left(\frac{1}{\frac{.03}{\sqrt{(.5)(.5)}}}\right)^2 (1.96)^2$$

$$= \left(\frac{1}{.06}\right)^2 (1.96)^2 = (277.78)(3.8416) = 1067$$

9. The researcher should follow up with a postcard reminder and then another mailing or two of the questionnaire. After follow-up efforts have been completed, the researcher should try to interview some of the remaining nonrespondents to find out about their characteristics and to obtain their responses, to determine if they differ significantly from the respondents.

10. **a.** $p = .20$

$$q = .80 \qquad \sigma_p = \frac{\sqrt{pq}}{\sqrt{n}}$$

$$\sigma_p = \frac{\sqrt{(.20)(.80)}}{\sqrt{500}}$$

$$= \frac{.4}{22.36} = .0178$$

margin of error $= 1.96 \times .0178 = .03$ or $\pm 3\%$

b. Between 17 and 23 percent or between 850 and 1150 students would be interested in a computer science major.

11. Samples a, c, and d would not be representative of the population of college students at a large university.

12. Answers will vary.

13. **a.** Longitudinal panel study
b. Longitudinal trend study
c. Longitudinal cohort study
d. Cross-sectional survey

14. a

15. Those who completed and returned the questionnaire would not be a representative sample of all U.S. citizens. A number of factors would bias this sample, such as socioeconomic level, educational level, sufficient interest in the topic to complete the questionnaire, and payment of postage to return it.

16. **a.** Mailed questionnaire
b. Telephone interview
c. Mailed questionnaire
d. Telephone interview

INFOTRAC COLLEGE EDITION

Using the keyword *mailed questionnaire*, locate a survey that used this methodology for data collection. Why do you think the researcher(s) chose a mailed questionnaire rather than a personal interview? What return rate was reported? If the return rate is acceptable, identify some aspects of the survey that may have contributed to a good return. Can you think of any other techniques, such as a monetary incentive, that the researcher might have used to increase the return rate?

Chapter 15

Qualitative Research: Defining, Selecting, and Planning

THE RESEARCH METHODS WE CHOOSE SAY SOMETHING ABOUT OUR VIEWS ON WHAT QUALIFIES AS VALUABLE KNOWLEDGE AND OUR PERSPECTIVE ON THE NATURE OF REALITY.
GLESNE AND PESHKIN (1992)

INSTRUCTIONAL OBJECTIVES

After studying this chapter, the student will be able to:

1. Define qualitative research and identify the critical aspects of this methodology.
2. Distinguish between quantitative and qualitative research.
3. Describe ways qualitative inquirers gather data.
4. Identify some of the different types of qualitative research.
5. Distinguish between participant and nonparticipant observation.
6. Identify ethical issues associated with qualitative research.
7. Define content or document analysis and give an example of its use in educational research.
8. Define ethnography and give an example of an ethnographic study in education.
9. Define case study and give an example of a case study in education.
10. Define grounded theory and describe its role in qualitative research.
11. Explain phenomenological research and how it can be used in educational research.
12. Describe historical research.
13. Distinguish between primary and secondary sources in historical research.
14. Distinguish between internal and external criticism in historical research.

The research methods described in Chapters 10 through 14 use numeric data to answer questions. Such procedures are classified as quantitative research because they employ such quantitative measures as frequencies, means, correlations, and statistical tests. In contrast, qualitative research employs words to answer questions. One form of research is not superior to the other. They are designed to answer different questions, have different assumptions, and different ways of inquiring into realities. Qualitative research investigates the quality of relationships, activities, situations, and materials.

DISTINGUISHING QUALITATIVE INQUIRY FROM QUANTITATIVE INQUIRY

The phrase **qualitative inquiry** is a generic term for a variety of educational research approaches variously labeled as ethnography, naturalistic inquiry, case studies, interpretive research, fieldwork, field studies, and participant observation among others. These approaches use different methodologies, but certain features are typical of all kinds of qualitative research. These characteristics set qualitative research apart from the quantitative approach to educational research outlined in Chapter 5 and the methodology described in Chapters 10 through 14. Both qualitative and quantitative researchers approach their studies by stating a purpose, posing a problem or question, defining a research population, collecting and analyzing data, and presenting results. Both use theories and both are concerned with the rigor of their inquiry. They differ in their views about the nature of reality, their assumptions about the role of the researcher, and in how they define knowledge.

APPROACH

The quantitative approach to the study of social and behavioral phenomena holds that the aim and methods of the social sciences are, at least in principle, the same as the aim and methods of the natural or physical sciences. **Quantitative research** strives for testable and confirmable theories that explain phenomena by showing how they are derived from theoretical assumptions (see the discussion of scientific theory in Chapter 1). It seeks scientific explanation that includes the discovery of laws governing not only the behavior of the physical world but also human behavior.

Qualitative inquiry begins from a different assumption, namely, that the subject matter of the social or human sciences differs fundamentally from the subject matter of the physical or natural sciences and therefore requires a different goal for inquiry and a different set of methods for investigation. Qualitative inquirers argue that human behavior is always bound to the context in which it occurs, that social reality (e.g., cultures, cultural objects, institutions, etc.) cannot be reduced to variables in the same manner as physical reality, and that what is most important in the social disciplines is understanding and portraying the meaning that is constructed by the participants involved in particular social settings or events.

Qualitative inquiry seeks to understand human and social behavior not from the **"etic"** or "outsider's" perspective, but from the **"emic"** or "insider's" perspective, that is, as it is lived by participants in a particular social setting (e.g., a culture, school, community, group, or institution). It is an intensely personal kind of research, one that freely acknowledges and admits the subjective perceptions and biases of both participants and researcher (Goetz & LeCompte, 1993). Defenders of qualitative approaches argue that, in contrast, quantitative inquiry is principally concerned with the discovery of "social facts" devoid of subjective perceptions of intentions and divorced from particular social and historical contexts.

GENERALIZATION

Quantitative approaches in the human sciences rely on a **hypothetico-deductive model** of explanation. Inquiry begins with a theory of the phenomenon to be investigated. From that theory any number of hypotheses are deduced that, in turn, are subjected to a test using a predetermined procedure such as an experimental, ex post facto, or correlational design. The ultimate goal of researchers using this hypothetico-deductive model is to revise and support theories, or law-like statements, of social and behavioral phenomena based on the results of hypothesis testing. Theories are refined and extended (and sometimes abandoned) to account for the results of testing their implications or instances (deductions).

Qualitative inquiry relies on a different model of explanation and argues for a different goal of inquiry. In general, its practitioners hold that the search for generalizations is misguided. Human behavior is always bound to a particular historical, social, temporal, and cultural context; therefore, such researchers reject the "law and its instances" kind of explanation in favor of a "cases and their interpretations" kind of explanation (Geertz, 1980). Qualitative inquirers seek to interpret human actions, institutions, events, customs, and the like, and in so doing construct a "reading," or portrayal, of what is being studied. The ultimate goal of this kind of inquiry is to portray the complex pattern of what is being studied in sufficient depth and detail so that someone who has not experienced it can understand it. When qualitative inquirers interpret or explain the meaning of events, actions, and so forth, they generally use one of the following types of interpretation: (1) construction of patterns through analysis and resynthesis of constituent parts, (2) interpretation of the social meaning of events, or (3) analysis of relationships between events and external factors. These interpretations may lead to the generation of theories that may later be tested by quantitative researchers.

METHODS

Quantitative methods use well-planned empirical approaches, experimental designs, and often statistical testing as compared to the more naturalistic, emergent, and field-based methods typical of qualitative research. The primary instrument used for data collection in qualitative research is the researcher him or herself, often collecting data through direct observation or interviews. Quantitative research more typically relies on measurement tools such as scales, tests, observation checklists, and questionnaires. The selection of subjects for study also differs. The ideal selection in quantitative research is random sampling, which allows for control of variables that may influence findings. Qualitative studies more typically use nonrandom or purposive selection techniques based on particular criteria.

VALUES

Quantitative inquirers admit that the inquirer's values may play a role in deciding what topic or problem to investigate but maintain that the actual investigation itself must be value free, that is, the inquirer must follow procedures specifically designed to isolate and remove all subjective elements, such as values, from the inquiry situation so that what remains are just the "objective facts." For example, imagine an experimental study involving two different classes of third-graders in which one third-grade class is the experimental group and the other is the control group. Imagine further that observers are placed in each classroom to record interactions between teachers and students. Quantitative inquirers prefer that the observers be unaware of whether they are observing the experimental or the control group, that they be unaware of subject characteristics (their social class, IQ, previous academic achievement, etc.), and that they use highly structured observational protocols that require only low-level inferences and as little as possible interpretation about what is happening in the interactions between teacher and students. These procedures are used in quantitative inquiry to ensure that the observers' values and beliefs will not influence or contaminate the observations that they make. By following these procedures for making observations, the quantitative inquirer provides strong assurance that the inquiry is value free.

In contrast, the qualitative approach argues that inquiry is always value bound; it can never be considered value free; and inquirers must be explicit about the roles that values play in any given study. Qualitative inquirers argue that inquiry is value bound in the choice of a problem to investigate, in the choice of whether to adopt a quantitative or qualitative approach to a problem, in the choice of methods used to investigate that problem, in the choice of a way to interpret results or findings, and by the values inherent in the context where the study takes place (Lincoln & Guba, 1985). Qualitative inquirers believe that it is impossible to develop a meaningful understanding of human experience without taking into account the interplay of both the inquirers' and participants' values and beliefs. They believe that rather than try to eliminate bias, it is important to

THINK ABOUT IT 15.1

For each statement below, indicate whether it is more descriptive of qualitative (QL) or quantitative (QT) research. Which method:

1. Relies more on the inductive approach
2. Is more likely to use random sampling
3. Relies more on the deductive approach
4. Is more likely to use purposive sampling
5. Is more likely to include a statistical report
6. Is more likely to include extensive quotations
7. Is more interested in generalizing
8. Is more likely to include intense interactions between the researcher and the subject
9. Is more likely to allow the researcher to modify, delete, or add interview questions during the interview
10. Is more likely to investigate a topic about which little is known

Answers:

1. QL, **2.** QT, **3.** QT, **4.** QL, **5.** QT, **6.** QL, **7.** QT, **8.** QL, **9.** QL, **10.** QL

Table 15.1 Comparison of Quantitative Inquiry and Qualitative Inquiry

Quantitative Inquiry	Qualitative Inquiry
Purpose	
To generalize findings	To contextualize findings
To predict behavior	To interpret behavior
To provide causal explanations	To understand perspectives
Approach	
Begins with hypotheses (hypothesis testing)	Ends with hypotheses (hypothesis generating)
Uses theory to ground the study	May create theory grounded in the findings
Uses manipulation and control of variables	Portrays the natural context
Deductive then inductive	Inductive then deductive
Seeks to analyze discrete components	Searches for larger patterns
Looks for the norm	Looks for complexity
Reduces data to numbers	Relies on words and only minor use of numbers
Reports written in precise, abstract language	Reports written in descriptive, holistic language
Assumptions	
There is an objective reality	Reality is socially constructed
The world is stable	The world is not stable
Variables can be identified and measured	Variables are complex and difficult to measure
Rooted in logical empiricism	Rooted in symbolic interactionism
Research from the "etic" or outsider's view	Research from the "emic" or insider's view
Role of Researcher	
Detached and impartial	Personally involved
Objective portrayal	Empathic understanding
Inquiry should be as value free as possible	Inquiry is always value bound
Methods	
Focused on quantity (how much, how many)	Focused on quality (nature, essence)
Experimental, empirical, statistical focus	Fieldwork, ethnographic, naturalistic focus
Predetermined, structured methods, precise	Flexible, evolving, emergent methods
Random sampling is the ideal	Typically uses purposive sampling
Uses inanimate instruments (scales, tests, questionnaires, observation checklists, etc..)	Researcher as the primary instrument (observations, interviews, document analysis)

Source: Portions adapted from Merriam (1998). Also adapted from Glesne and Peshkin, *Becoming qualitative researchers*, p. 7. Published by Allyn & Bacon, Boston. Copyright © 1992 by Pearson Education. Adapted by permission of the publisher.

identify and monitor biases and how they may affect data collection and interpretation. Furthermore, qualitative inquirers argue that human inquiry requires frequent, continuing, and meaningful interaction between inquirers and their respondents (subjects) and that inquiry must maximize rather than minimize this kind of contact. Because qualitative inquiry openly acknowledges the role of values in inquiry and demands involvement and interaction of inquirers and respondents, some claim that the findings (results) of such studies are simply a matter of opinion. To counter that charge, qualitative inquirers employ a variety of techniques to demonstrate the trustworthiness of their findings. (These techniques are discussed in Chapter 16.) Table 15.1 summarizes key differences between qualitative inquiry and quantitative inquiry.

MAJOR CHARACTERISTICS OF QUALITATIVE RESEARCH

Although qualitative inquirers work in many different ways, their studies have certain characteristics in common that set this approach apart from quantitative research. Some of the more important aspects of qualitative research are discussed next.

CONCERN FOR CONTEXT AND MEANING

Qualitative inquiry shows **concern for context and meaning**. It assumes that human behavior is context bound, that human experience takes its meaning from and, therefore, is inseparable from social, historical, political, and cultural influences. Thus inquiry is always bounded by a particular context or setting. Qualitative researchers focus on how people make sense of their experience. There is no attempt to predict what will happen in the future but rather to understand a unique and particular context. Proponents of qualitative inquiry argue that the quantitative approach to the study of human experience seeks to isolate human behavior from its context; it engages in "context stripping."

NATURAL SETTING

Qualitative research studies real-world behavior as it occurs naturally in a classroom, an entire school, a playground, or in an organization. Qualitative inquiry takes place in the field, in **natural settings** as they are found. It is not contrived or artificial, and there is no attempt to manipulate behavior. The researcher goes physically to the people, the setting, or the institution to observe behavior. In addition, qualitative inquiry places no prior constraints on what is to be studied. It does not identify, define, and investigate or test the relationship between independent and dependent variables in a particular setting; rather, it studies human experience holistically, taking into account all factors and influences in a given situation.

HUMAN INSTRUMENT

One of the distinguishing characteristics of qualitative research is the methods used to collect and analyze data. In qualitative studies, the human investigator is the primary instrument for the gathering and analyzing of data. Lincoln and Guba (1985) introduced the concept of **human as instrument** to emphasize the unique role that qualitative researchers play in their inquiry. Because qualitative research studies human experiences and situations, researchers need an instrument flexible enough to capture the complexity of the human experience, an instrument capable of adapting and responding to the environment. Lincoln and Guba believed that only a human instrument was capable of this task. He or she talks with people in the setting, observes their activities, reads their documents and written records, and records this information in field notes and journals. Qualitative inquiry relies on fieldwork methods (interviewing, nonstructured observation, and document analysis) as the principal means of collecting data, avoiding the use of paper-and-pencil tests, mechanical instruments, and highly structured observational protocols.

DESCRIPTIVE DATA

The qualitative inquirer deals with data that are in the form of words or pictures, rather than numbers and statistics. Data in the form of quotes from documents, field notes, and interviews or excerpts from videotapes, audiotapes, or electronic communications are used to present the findings of the study. The data collected are the subjects' experiences and perspectives; the qualitative researcher attempts to arrive at a rich description of the people, objects, events, places, conversations, and so on. From time to time some numeric data may be collected. Managing the large volume of descriptive data generated from interviews, observations, and the collection of documents is an important consideration in qualitative studies. Qualitative investigators also typically keep a personal or reflexive log or journal in which they record accounts of their thoughts, feelings, assumptions, motives, and rationale for decisions made. This is one way the qualitative inquirer addresses the issue of the inquiry being value bound.

EMERGENT DESIGN

In quantitative studies, researchers carefully design all aspects of a study *before* they actually collect any data; they specify variables, measures for those variables, statistics to be used to analyze data, and so forth. This is possible because these researchers know in advance what they are looking for. They have specific hypotheses or questions in mind and can imagine what a test of the hypothesis or an answer to the question might look like. Regardless of the particular problem or phenomena being investigated, quantitative researchers insist that this careful specification of elements in a study's design is extremely important. In contrast, while qualitative inquirers broadly specify aspects of a design before beginning a study, the design continues to *emerge* as the study unfolds, hence the name **emergent design**. They adjust their methods and way of proceeding (design) to the subject matter at hand. This is necessary because the qualitative inquirer is never quite sure just what will be learned in a particular setting because what can be learned in a particular setting depends on the nature and types of interactions between the inquirer and the people and setting, and those interactions are not fully predictable, and because important features in need of investigation cannot always be known until they are actually witnessed by the investigator.

INDUCTIVE ANALYSIS

In most qualitative studies, data collection and data analysis take place simultaneously. In other words, the inquirer does not wait until all the data are "in" before beginning to interpret them. From the outset of the first interview or observation, the qualitative inquirer is reflecting on the meaning of what he or she has heard and seen, developing hunches (working hypotheses) about what it means, and seeking to confirm or disconfirm those hunches in subsequent interviews or observations. It is a process of **inductive data analysis**; it proceeds from data to hypotheses to theory. As the inquirer reduces and reconstructs the data through the processes of coding and categorization, he or she aims at the development of theory about the phenomena being observed that is directly tied to, *grounded*, in the data about those phenomena (Strauss & Corbin, 1998).

THINK ABOUT IT 15.2

For each research question listed below, indicate whether you would choose a qualitative (QL) or quantitative (QT) research approach. (Note: In some cases, the question could be answered using more than one approach. Select the one you believe would be most appropriate.)

1. How are the social relations of adolescents who use illicit drugs different from those who do not use them?
2. How do school attendance and grades earned in school differ between adolescents who use illicit drugs and those who do not?
3. To what extent does family income predict whether a student will choose to attend a commuter or residential campus?
4. How do Hispanic and Latino students experience their first year in an urban community college?
5. Do students who have high scores on reading tests also have high scores on writing tests?
6. How do middle school students of differing ability levels approach reading?
7. What are the characteristics of mathematics lessons in Japanese and U.S. middle school textbooks?
8. How do U.S. middle school students compare to Japanese middle school students in performance on standardized mathematics examinations?
9. Do mainstreamed students in science classes using cooperative grouping differ in their performance from those not exposed to cooperative groups?
10. What are the helping behaviors of students in cooperative learning groups?
11. What are the personal and educational interactions in a group of teachers developing a high school chemistry curriculum?
12. How do gangs recruit members in schools?

Answers:

1. QL, **2.** QT, **3.** QT, **4.** QL, **5.** QT, **6.** QL,
7. QL, **8.** QT, **9.** QT, **10.** QL, **11.** QL, **12.** QL

Janesick (1994, p. 212) summarizes the characteristics of qualitative research design as follows:

1. Qualitative design is holistic. It looks at the larger picture, the whole picture, and begins with a search for understanding of the whole.
2. Qualitative design looks at relationships within a system or culture.
3. Qualitative design refers to the personal, face to face, and immediate.
4. Qualitative design is focused on understanding a given social setting, not necessarily on making predictions about that setting.
5. Qualitative design demands that the researcher stay in the setting over time.
6. Qualitative design demands time in analysis equal to the time in the field.

7. Qualitative design demands that the researcher develop a model of what occurred in the social setting.
8. Qualitative design requires the researcher to become the research instrument. This means the researcher must have the ability to observe behavior and must sharpen the skills necessary for observation and face-to-face interview.
9. Qualitative design incorporates informed consent decisions and is responsive to ethical concerns.
10. Qualitative design incorporates room for description of the role of the researcher as well as description of the researcher's own biases and ideological preference.
11. Qualitative design requires ongoing analyses of the data.

Topics that are often investigated through qualitative methods include those that defy quantification, those that are best understood in a natural setting, those that involve studies of group activities over time, those that involve the study of roles and behaviors, those that involve studying an organization in its entirety, those about which little is known, and those that involve closed cultures. Types of questions asked in qualitative studies include: What is happening? What does something mean? How are events organized or related? What are the perspectives of the participants? How do participants interact? What are the relationships among structure, events, and participants? Answering qualitative questions can help to illuminate everyday life, provide specific details to help understand a particular setting, examine interpretations of local meanings, and illuminate differences across settings.

TYPES OF QUALITATIVE RESEARCH

Different authors have produced various taxonomies for qualitative research (see Creswell, 2005; Lancy, 1993; Patton, 1990; Denzin & Lincoln, 2000; Merriam & Associates, 2002). We have elected to focus on seven of the most common types of qualitative research. It is important to remember that although these qualitative research approaches differ in context and participants, they overlap in many aspects. They all share the general characteristics described earlier in this chapter.

CASE STUDIES

Case studies provide an "intensive description and analysis of a phenomenon or social unit such as an individual, group, institution, or community" (Merriam & Associates, 2002, p. 8). Case studies can be of an individual, group, site, class, program, policy, process, institution, or community. The unit of analysis determines whether the study is a case study or a different form of qualitative research, although at times other forms of qualitative research may be combined with the case study approach, for example an ethnographic case study. Case studies provide an in-depth description of a specific unit that may be selected because it is unique or typical or for a variety of other reasons. The unit is defined within specific boundaries, referred to as a "bounded system."

In comparing a case study with single-subject experiments (see Chapter 11) both may study a single individual. However, single-subject experiments focus on a single behavior or a very limited number of behaviors, whereas case studies attempt to describe the subject's entire range of behaviors and the relationship of these behaviors to the subject's history and environment. In a case study the investigator attempts to examine an individual or unit in depth. The emphasis is on understanding why the individual does what he or she does and how behavior changes as the individual responds to the environment. This requires detailed study for a considerable period of time; that is, it is a longitudinal approach. The investigator gathers data about the subject's present state, past experiences, environment, and how these factors relate to one another.

The greatest advantage of a case study is the possibility of depth; it seeks to understand the whole individual in the totality of that individual's environment. Not only the present actions of an individual but his or her past, environment, emotions, and thoughts can be probed. The researcher tries to determine *why* an individual behaves as he or she does and not merely to record behavior. Case studies often provide an opportunity for an investigator to develop insight into basic aspects of human behavior. The intensive probing characteristic of this technique may lead to the discovery of previously unsuspected relationships.

However, case studies need not be limited to the study of individuals. Case studies are made of communities, institutions, and groups of individuals. A classic case study of a community was Lynd and Lynd's *Middletown* (1929), which described life in Muncie, Indiana, a typical average-size midwestern city. This first study was followed by *Middletown in Transition* in 1937. Another classic was Hollingshead's *Elmtown's Youth* (1949), which studied the life of adolescents in a small Illinois community. Other case studies have focused on communities ranging from the isolated mountain villages of Appalachia to life among ethnic and minority groups in inner sections of large cities.

Institutions such as schools, churches, colleges, fraternal organizations, and businesses have been the focus of case studies. Case studies have been made of groups of individuals such as gays, drug addicts, delinquents, street gangs, migratory workers, CEOs, medical students, teachers, and many others. Members of religious groups such as the Amish, the Shakers, and various other denominations have been studied.

Case studies are anchored in real life and can provide rich detailed accounts of phenomena. The case study permits an in-depth examination of factors that explain present status and that influence change over time. The advantages of the case study, however, are also its weaknesses. Although it can have depth, it inevitably lacks breadth. The dynamics of one individual or social unit may bear little relationship to the dynamics of others. Some argue, however, that what we learn in a particular case can be transferred to similar situations with the reader, rather than the researcher, determining what might apply to his or her context.

The opportunities for insights in a case study are also opportunities for subjectivity or even prejudice. The preconceptions of an investigator can determine which behaviors are observed and which are ignored, as well as the way in which the observations are interpreted. The reputation of the case study approach has suffered because some investigators in the past have explained their observations in constructs that are impossible either to confirm or refute through empirical study. Because the extent to which case studies can produce valid generalizations is limited, their major usefulness is not as tools for testing hypotheses but rather in producing hypotheses, which can then be tested through more rigorous investigation. For example, the insights Jean Piaget gained in his famous case studies on the maturation of intellect provided useful hypotheses that have since been investigated through other methods.

In those instances when case studies result from attempts to learn about individuals in order to help them, the research aspects of the study take second place. However, case studies are also frequently conducted with the primary aim of gaining knowledge. Itard's classic case study on the "wild boy" of Aveyron (1962) was an effort to learn about the effects of civilization through studying (from documents) a boy who had grown up in isolation from civilization in 18th-century France. Piaget's case studies were conducted in order to learn about mental growth in children rather than to benefit the subjects involved.

Case studies may employ multiple methods of data collection and do not rely on a single technique. Testing, interviewing, observation, review of documents and artifacts, and other methods may be used. The distinction is that whatever techniques are used, all are focused on a single phenomenon or entity (the case) and attempt to collect information that can help understand or interpret the focus of the study. Readers interested in doing a case study are referred to Merriam (1998) and Stake (1995).

ETHNOGRAPHIC STUDIES

Ethnography is the in-depth study of naturally occurring behavior within a culture or social group. It seeks to understand the relationship between culture and behavior, with culture referring to the beliefs, values, and attitudes of a specific group of people. The ethnographic research method was developed by anthropologists (such as Margaret Mead) as a way of studying and describing human cultures. In Mead's classic study, *Coming of Age in Samoa* (1928), she studied adolescent girls in Samoa and analyzed the differences in development between Samoan and American girls. Anthropologists immerse themselves in the lives of the people they study, using primarily extended observation (participant and nonparticipant) and occasionally in-depth interviewing to gain clarification and more detailed information. The ethnographer undertakes the study without any a priori hypotheses to avoid predetermining what is observed or what information is elicited from informants. The ethnographer explores and tests hypotheses, but the hypotheses evolve out of the fieldwork itself. Ethnographers refer to the people from whom they gather information as "informants" rather than participants, and they study "sites" rather than individuals.

Ethnographic research has advantages and disadvantages. The advantage is its observation of behavior in a real-life setting, the assumption being that human behavior can be fully understood only by knowing the setting in which it occurs. The main limitation is that the findings depend heavily on the particular researcher's observations and interpretations of the data. For example, researchers now suggest that Margaret Mead's interpretations of the data collected on the Samoan culture were completely wrong. Later research did not support her conclusions about the sexual behavior of young Samoan women but found almost the exact opposite. Mead was criticized for spending too little time in Samoa, seeing only what she wanted to see, and accepting the responses of a few young girls at face value without corroboration from other sources (Freeman, 1983). Later in this text, we will discuss some strategies for enhancing the validity of interpretations made of qualitative data.

Spindler and Hammond (2000) describe some of the characteristics of good ethnography: (1) extended participant observation; (2) long time at the site (a year would be a short time for a community study); (3) collection of large volumes of material such as notes, artifacts, audio- and videotapes, and so on; and (4) openness, which means having no specific hypotheses or even highly specific categories of observation at the start of the study.

The term *ethnography* is used to refer to both the work of studying a culture and also the end product of the research. Ethnography has moved from anthropology to other disciplines, including education, where it has become a valuable tool in understanding the process of schooling. It has provided basic information on the nature of cultural transmission and the formal process of education that has resulted in insights and generalizations useful to educational practitioners (Chilcott, 1992). Ethnographic research on immigrant children and other minority populations in U.S. schools, for example, has helped educators understand these students' cultural backgrounds and the discontinuity that may exist between family and school culture that affects the success or failure of these diverse students in schools. Spindler and Hammond (2000) write that ethnography "can help teachers separate their personal cultural values from those of their students in order to see both themselves and their students more clearly" and to understand the voices of the "other" (p. 44).

Peshkin's work is an example of ethnographic research in education. In his 1991 work, *The Color of Strangers, the Color of Friends*, Peshkin presented a year-long, in-depth study of Riverview High School, a school in a working-class community in California with large numbers of students from different ethnic groups. He used participant observation and interviews to explore the role of ethnicity in this multiethnic school. Although Riverview had experienced ethnicity-based disorder and violence a few years earlier, Peshkin found the school characterized by ethnic peace. He described Riverview High School as a social success story, a place where strangers and friends were not sorted out on the basis of color. Social interactions that usually occur only within an ethnic group routinely took place across ethnic groups at Riverview. The students' level of academic success, however, did not match their success in social interactions. Peshkin found a persistently low level of academic success, especially among the black and Hispanic students.

In another ethnographic study, *The Imperfect Union: School Consolidation and Community Conflict*, Peshkin (1982) focused on a midwestern rural school district that was resisting state-mandated consolidation. After thorough study of the school district and its history, Peshkin illustrated how, when viewed through the eyes of the people in the district, their behavior was quite reasonable and not at all "irrational" as had been suggested. That is what ethnographic research attempts to do, build a complete understanding of a group from the perspectives of the members of that group. Other ethnographic research has provided insights on immigrant children and ethnic minorities in our schools, special-needs children in schools, and teacher–pupil relationships in inner-city schools and other types of schools. Nozaki (2000) conducted an ethnographic study of Japanese children in an American school.

As in case studies, a variety of data collection techniques may be used as part of the ethnographic study. Common means of collecting data include interviewing, document analysis, participant observations, researcher diaries, and life stories. It is not the data collection techniques that determine whether a study is an ethnography but rather the "sociocultural interpretation" that sets it apart from other forms of qualitative inquiry. "Ethnography is not defined by how data are collected, but rather by the lens through which the data are interpreted" (Merriam & Associates, 2002, p. 9).

Spradley (1980) identified the sequence of steps making up the methodology of ethnographic research:

1. *Selecting an ethnographic project.* The scope of these projects can vary greatly, from studying a whole complex society, such as an Inuit hunting group in Alaska, to a single social situation or institution, such as an urban bar, a fraternity, or a school playground. The beginner would be wise to restrict the scope of his or her project to a single social situation so that it can be completed in a reasonable time. A social situation always has three components: a place, actors, and activities.
2. *Asking ethnographic questions.* The researcher needs to have questions in mind that will guide what he or she sees and hears and the collection of data.
3. *Collecting ethnographic data.* The researcher does fieldwork to find out the activities of the people, the physical characteristics of the situation, and what it feels like to be part of the situation. This step generally begins with an overview comprising broad descriptive observations. Then, after looking at the data, you move on to more focused observations. Here you use participant observation, in-depth interviews, and so on to gather data.
4. *Making an ethnographic record.* This step includes taking field notes and photographs, making maps, and using any other appropriate means to record the observations.
5. *Analyzing ethnographic data.* The fieldwork is always followed by data analysis, which leads to new questions and new hypotheses, more data collection and field notes, and more analysis. The cycle continues until the project is completed.
6. *Writing the ethnography.* The ethnography should be written so that the culture or group is brought to life, making readers feel they understand the people and their way of life. The ethnographic report can range in length from several pages to a volume or two. You can greatly simplify this task by beginning the writing early as data accumulate instead of waiting until the end. The writing task will also be easier if, before writing, you read other well-written ethnographies.

PHENOMENOLOGICAL STUDIES

A **phenomenological study** is designed to describe and interpret an experience by determining the *meaning* of the experience as perceived by the people who have participated in it. Rooted in philosophy and psychology, the assumption is that there are many ways of interpreting the same experience and that the meaning of the experience to each person is what constitutes reality. This belief is characteristic of all qualitative studies, but the element that distinguishes **phenomenology** from other qualitative approaches is that the subjective experience is at the center of the inquiry. The central research question aims to determine the essence of the experience as "perceived by the participants." Phenomenology addresses questions about common human experience. A phenomenological researcher who was asked to study, for example, the integration of special-needs children into a regular classroom would focus on asking what this experience means to the parties involved: the special-needs children, other students, and the teacher. Whether or not the integration plan is working is not the important issue; what matters is how the students and the teacher experience it. "In the same way that ethnography focuses on culture, a phenomenological study focuses on the essence or structure of an experience. Phenomenologists are interested in showing how complex meanings are built out of simple units of direct experience" (Merriam & Associates, 2002, p. 7).

The following examples of education topics have been studied by phenomenological researchers (Langenbach, Vaughn, & Aagaard, 1994, p. 155):

Coping styles of children

Being labeled "learning disabled"

The urban classroom

Children whose parents are unemployed

The anxious math student

The student athlete

Novice teachers

The schooling experience

Teaching neglected and abused children

Homework in the lives of children

Racial integration of an elementary school

Home schooling

First-time-computer users

Televised worship experiences

The participants in a phenomenological study are chosen because they have been through the experience being investigated and can share their thoughts and feelings about it. The distinguishing data collection method in a phenomenological study is the personal, unstructured interview. The interviews may be lengthy (1 to 2 hours), and there may be more than one interview with each participant. The researcher typically interviews 10 to 25 individuals who may come from a single site or different sites. Tape-recording the interviews facilitates the subsequent analysis. Phenomenological researchers also typically explore their own experiences related to the topic of interest prior to conducting interviews in order to examine their own biases and assumptions.

Maykut and Morehouse (1994) write, "The human instrument is the only data collection instrument which is multifaceted enough and complex enough to capture the important elements of a human or human experience" (p. 27). Lincoln and Guba (1985) concur, stating that a human investigator can explore the idiosyncratic responses in ways that are not possible with any instrument that is constructed in advance of the study. Because of the importance of the interview in this research, it is critical that the investigator be a skilled interviewer. The questions used need to focus on meaning and be designed to elicit the "essence" of the experience from the perspective of the participants. The interviewer must be able to listen, prompt when necessary, and encourage subjects to expand and elaborate on their recollections of the experience.

From an analysis of the interview data, the researcher writes descriptions of the participants' experiences and how those experiences were perceived. In Chapter 16 we discuss analysis of qualitative data. From the analysis, the researcher derives an overall description of the general meaning of the experience.

For further discussion of phenomenological research, see Hycner (1999, Vol. 3, pp. 143–164) or Moustakas (1994).

GROUNDED THEORY STUDIES

The aim of a **grounded theory** study is to discover or build a theory in an area. This emphasis on theory distinguishes it from other qualitative approaches. Glaser and Strauss (1967) developed grounded theory as a way of formalizing the operations needed to develop theory from empirical data. This research approach focuses on gathering data about peoples' experiences in a particular context and then inductively building a theory "from the bottom up." The theory is grounded in the data, and the researcher has no preconceived ideas about what the theory will be. The desired theory is "conceptually dense"; that is, it presents many conceptual relationships that are stated as propositions pertaining to a particular context, situation, or experience.

In the role as the primary data-gathering instrument, the researcher asks questions about some event, experience, or social phenomenon. He or she collects data through observations and interviews and then analyzes data by looking for similarities/differences among the participants' responses about the experience. Documentary materials (letters, speeches, etc.) and literature can also be potential data sources. After forming categories having similar units of meaning, the researcher looks for underlying themes and relationships among the categories. This analysis of the data results in insights, conditional propositions, and questions that are pursued through further data collection. The researcher constructs tentative theoretical statements about the relationships among constructs, explores these theoretical propositions through further data collection, and so on. This cyclical process of testing the explanatory adequacy of the theoretical constructs by comparing with additional empirical data continues until the comparative analysis no longer contributes anything new (theoretical saturation). Thus, through induction and verification techniques, the researcher progressively elaborates a general theoretical statement well grounded in the data. The constant-comparative method of analysis is typically used in grounded theory. In this method, the researcher compares units of data with each other to generate tentative categories, eventually reducing these to conceptual categories that evolve into an overall framework or theory. Generating the theory is not easy; it requires insight and understanding and, as indicated, many reviews of the data.

The personal open-ended interview is the primary method of data collection. The interviewer asks questions about what happened to individuals, why it happened, and what it means to them. Choose a sample where each individual has had the experience and can contribute to theory development. The study may include as many as 20 to 25 subjects who are interviewed on the topic until no new information is forthcoming (data saturation). To confirm or refute the theory that has developed, researchers sometimes interview another group that has had different experiences.

Grounded theory studies of a sociological nature have focused on victims of Alzheimer's disease and how families accommodate to the different stages, drug addiction in women, chronic illness, alcoholism, eating disorders, pain management, how families make decisions about placing members in a nursing home, and so on. A grounded theory study in education might focus on mainstreaming, mentoring new teachers, integrating minorities in private prep schools, classroom discipline, and many other topics. In education, an example of a grounded theory study was that of Brott and Myers (1999) who conceptualized the development of professional school counselor identity. The research sought to identify counselors' self-conceptualizations or personal guidelines that provide a framework for carrying out their professional roles. The theory developed through the study describes the context, conditions, and phases for a process called the *blending of influences*. Readers who are interested in grounded theory methodology are referred to Strauss and Corbin (1998) and to Dey (1999).

BASIC INTERPRETIVE STUDIES

Interpretive studies are basic qualitative research. They contain all of the characteristics described earlier and may use data collected through a variety of means: interviews, observations, review of documents, focus groups, and the like. They provide rich descriptive accounts targeted to understanding a phenomenon, a process, or a particular point of view from the perspective of those involved. The central purpose of basic interpretive studies is to understand the world or the experience of another. This explanation may seem similar to others described earlier, but interpretive studies are more simplistic. They are not restricted to a particular phenomenon as in case studies. They do not seek to explain sociocultural aspects as in ethnography. They do not seek to enter the subject's conceptual world to explain the "essence" as in phenomenology. They do not seek to define theory as in grounded theory research.

Basic interpretive studies are the most common qualitative studies and are used in a variety of disciplines, including education. They may use a variety of data collection techniques, including interviews and observations as well as review of documents, and may draw from diverse theoretical orientations. Data analysis typically involves categorization and development of patterns, interpreted by the researcher through his or her own disciplinary lens. Often these studies may also be shorter in duration than some of the other qualitative forms, with the researcher not as fully involved in the context. To reiterate, the basic goal of interpretive studies is to understand the meaning people make of their experiences.

CONTENT OR DOCUMENT ANALYSIS

Content or **document analysis** is a research method applied to written or visual materials for the purpose of identifying specified characteristics of the material. The materials analyzed can be textbooks, newspapers, speeches, television programs, advertisements, musical compositions, or any of a host of other types of documents. Content analysis is widely used in education. The following are some of the purposes of content analysis in educational research:

1. *To identify bias, prejudice, or propaganda in textbooks.* For example, a researcher might analyze high school history texts in a particular school district to see how often women are mentioned and how much discussion is given in each mention.
2. *To analyze types of errors in students' writings.* For example, you could look at students' written work to classify spelling or grammatical errors and their nature and frequency.
3. *To describe prevailing practices.* For example, you could identify the entrance requirements of Big Ten universities by analyzing their bulletins.
4. *To discover the level of difficulty of material in textbooks or other publications.* For example, you could ask, "What is the vocabulary level of the fourth-grade social studies textbooks in this district?"
5. *To discover the relative importance of, or interest in, certain topics.* For example, you might analyze popular educational research textbooks to see the coverage given to qualitative research.

Content analyses may be done in an emergent design framework. Or they may be done in a quantitative research framework with variables that are specified a priori and numbers that are generated to enable the researcher to draw conclusions about these specified variables. For example, Allen, Allen, and Sigler (1993) investigated gender–role stereotyping in children's books that had won the Caldecott Medal award. The purpose of the analysis was to determine if these books presented stereotypical or gender-dependent role behaviors to children through the characters in their text and pictures. They compared books from 1938 to 1940 and from 1986 to 1988 on 11 categories where gender–role stereotyping could occur, including the characters in text and picture, the occupation of the main characters, whether the characters were active or passive, indoor or outdoor, in traditional or nontraditional roles, and so on. They found a weak trend toward equal representation in 7 of the 11 categories, although males still comprised the majority of the characters in each category. Males were characterized as active, outdoors, nontraditional, and in diverse occupations more often than females in both time periods. The researchers concluded that gender–role stereotyping had decreased, but it remained prevalent in each category of investigation.

The preceding study illustrates the steps involved in a content analysis:

1. *Specifying the phenomenon to be investigated* (such as gender–role stereotyping).
2. *Selecting the media from which the observations are to be made* (such as the Caldecott Medal books for specified time periods).
3. *Formulating exhaustive and mutually exclusive coding categories* so that the verbal or symbolic content can be counted (such as the 11 categories where gender–role stereotyping could occur).
4. *Deciding on the sampling plan to be used* in order to obtain a representative sample of the documents (such as the sample consisting of all the Caldecott winners for two 2-year periods). You might decide to look at three issues per week of a newspaper over a period of a year, for instance, or every issue of a weekly newsmagazine for a year.
5. *Training the coders* so that they can consistently apply the coding scheme that has been developed and thus contribute to the reliability of the content analysis. Some coding is not so straightforward but may require inferences about whether a minority group, for example, is being portrayed positively or negatively. Several coders should be able to code the documents using the scheme and obtain consistent results. If the interrater reliability is satisfactory, you can proceed to the next step. If it is less than satisfactory, the coders themselves may be useful in revising the category definitions to make them clearer and more complete.
6. *Analyzing the data*, which may involve just the frequencies and percentages in the various categories or may involve more descriptive accounts. This step can be slow and time consuming. Fortunately, computers can now carry out a content analysis quickly and accurately. Most universities have image scanners that can read printed pages and transfer the text to electronic files. Then, a computer program can be used to search through the scanned text and find words or phrases that meet specified criteria. You can obtain a listing of specified words, for example, and the frequency with which the words appear in the printed documents. Even more sophisticated computer programs, including ones that will be able to classify content and interpret meaning of words according to the context, can be expected to become available as research continues into the area known as *artificial intelligence*.

An advantage of content analysis is that it is unobtrusive. The presence of the observer does not influence what is being observed. You do not need to enlist the cooperation of subjects or get permission to do the study. Another advantage of content analyses is that they are easily replicated. For more information on content analysis, see Krippendorff's second edition of *Content Analysis: An Introduction to Its Methodology* (2003).

HISTORICAL STUDIES

Historical studies are oriented to the past rather than to the present and thus use different data collection methods from those used in other qualitative approaches. Historical research is included in qualitative research because of its emphasis on interpretation and its use of nonnumeric data. **Historical research** is the attempt to establish facts and arrive at conclusions concerning the past. The historian systematically locates, evaluates, and interprets evidence from which people can learn about the past. Based on the evidence gathered, conclusions are drawn regarding the past so as to increase knowledge of how and why past events occurred and the process by which the past became the present. The hoped-for result is increased understanding of the present and a more rational basis for making choices.

The historian operates under different handicaps from those of researchers in other fields. Control over treatment, measurement, and sampling is limited, and there is no opportunity for replication. Although historians have no choice concerning what documents, relics, records, and artifacts survive the passage of time, they do have some limited control over what questions they will ask of these sources and what measures they will apply to them. When interviewing witnesses of past events and when searching the historical record, researchers can decide what questions to ask and what is to be measured. But they can measure only those things that witnesses remember or the record contains. In descriptive and experimental research, investigators can attempt to control sampling; that is, they can decide for themselves whom they are going to study. Historians can study only those people for whom records and artifacts survive. If newspapers ignore a particular segment of a community and no other sources for that community exist, then historians cannot directly assess the contributions that a particular segment of a population made to the life of that community. Another limitation impinging on historical researchers is that no assumption about the past can be made merely because no record can be found, nor can it be assumed, on the contrary, that a conspiracy of silence has distorted the historical record.

Primary and Secondary Sources

The historian classifies materials as **primary and secondary sources**. Primary sources are original documents (correspondence, diaries, reports, etc.), relics, remains, or artifacts. These are the direct outcomes of events or the records of participants. Examples would be the minutes of a school board meeting, an unedited videotape of a basketball game, or a collection of the artwork completed by a third-grade class. Relics, remains, and artifacts are direct outcomes of events. Records of eyewitnesses are also classified as primary sources. If only the mind of an eyewitness comes between the event and the source of information about the event, it is still classified as a primary source. For example, an eyewitness or participant decided what would or would not be recorded in the school board minutes, and someone decided when the camera would be on or off and where it would be focused during the basketball game.

With secondary sources the mind of a **nonobserver** also comes between the event and the user of the record. If a newspaper reporter has been present at a school board meeting, the published report is a primary source. If the reporter relies on the minutes of the meeting or an interview with a participant to prepare the report, then the published report is a secondary source. Common examples of secondary sources are history books, articles in encyclopedias, and reviews of research. Historians seek to employ primary sources whenever possible.

External and Internal Criticism

Two ideas that have proved useful in evaluating historical sources are the concepts of external (or lower) criticism and internal (or higher) criticism. Basically, **external criticism** asks if the evidence under consideration is authentic and, depending on the nature of the study, may involve such techniques as authentication of signatures, chemical analysis of paint, or carbon dating of artifacts. Suppose a historian has a letter describing Massachusetts schools that is believed to have been written by Horace Mann. Using external criticism, the investigator would ask: Is the paper of the right age? Is the handwriting Mann's? Are the point of view and the writing style consistent with Mann's other writings? After the authenticity of a piece of evidence has been established, the historical investigator proceeds to **internal criticism**, which requires evaluating the worth of the evidence, for instance, whether a document provides a true report of an event. Such a question can best be answered by comparing it with others that throw light on an event or provide further information about an event and the people or circumstances surrounding it. In the example, the investigator would ask: Is Mann's description of the schools unbiased? Does it agree with other contemporary descriptions of the schools?

Because historical research does have limitations, you could very well ask why it should be attempted. The fundamental reason is that there is no other way to investigate many questions. How else might you attempt to assess the effect of the Kent State shootings and other campus disorders in the spring of 1970?

An advantage of historical research, and sometimes a reason for using this approach, is that it is unobtrusive. The researcher is not physically involved in the situation studied. There is no danger of experimenter–subject interaction, nor is there any need to get the permission of school authorities for the research. The historian locates appropriate documents, gathers suitable data, and draws conclusions at a distance from the situation being studied. In addition, historical research may provide new perspectives to a crisis situation. The uninvolved nature of historical research may make it acceptable in an emotionally charged situation where other types of research would be impossible.

Because of its limitations, however, caution must be exercised in generalizing the results of historical research. Students who plan to do historical study should consult appropriate bibliographies and sources on historical methodology such as Howell and Prevenier's (2001) introduction to historical methods.

OTHER QUALITATIVE TYPES

While we have chosen to focus on the seven types of qualitative research described above and compared in Table 15.2, there are a few other types worth mentioning. **Narrative studies**, also called biography, life stories, life narratives, or oral histories, are first-person accounts of experiences. They use documents

Table 15.2 Characteristics of Common Qualitative Research Types

Type of Qualitative Research	Key Characteristics
Case study	Focuses on a single unit Has multidisciplinary roots (business, law, medicine) Produces an in-depth description Is anchored in real life Provides a rich, holistic description of context, themes, issues Uses multiple data collection techniques Time spent examining the "unit" is important Can be combined with other qualitative approaches The basic question is "What are the characteristics of this particular entity, phenomenon, person, setting?"
Ethnography	Studies the naturally occurring behavior of a group Focuses on culture and societal behavior Has roots in anthropology Describes the beliefs, values, and attitudes of a group Participant observation is the primary data collection tool Immersion in the site is important Provides a holistic description of context and cultural themes The basic question is "What are the cultural patterns and perspectives of this group in its natural setting?"
Phenomenology	Is concerned with the essence of a phenomenon Interprets the meaning of the participant's experience Has roots in philosophy Includes the investigator's firsthand experiences Interview is the primary data collection tool Typically interviews multiple subjects Attempts to determine the meaning of statements Provides a rich description of invariant structures (common characteristics or essences) The basic question is "What is the experience of an activity or concept from the perspective of these particular participants?"
Grounded theory	Its goal is to inductively build a theory about a practice or phenomenon It is "grounded" in the real world Has its roots in sociology Is a cyclical process of building a tentative theory and testing it against the data Interviews and observation are the primary data collection tools Typically involves observations and interviews with multiple participants or settings Uses a coding process that ends in description and presentation of theory and propositions The basic question is "How is an inductively derived theory about a phenomenon grounded in the data in a particular setting?"
Basic interpretive	Describes and interprets a phenomenon or process Seeks to understand participants' point of view Has its roots in the social sciences Identifies recurrent patterns or themes Can be based on a variety of disciplinary lenses May use a variety of data collection techniques The basic question is "How are events, processes, and activities perceived by participants?"
Content/ document analysis	Uses analysis of written or visual materials Describes the characteristics of the materials Has its roots in communication studies The basic question is "What meaning is reflected in these materials?"
Historical	Focuses on the past Written documents and artifacts are the primary data sources Has its roots in the study of history Seeks to authenticate sources and determine their consistency with other artifacts and documents The basic question is "How can historical events and reports be interpreted?"

and other sources of personal information to illuminate a person's life. Written in a story format, these studies attempt to communicate the meaning of an experience and have become increasingly popular. Data may be gathered via interviews or from written records such as diaries, journals, or letters and analyzed from a variety of disciplinary perspectives. The analysis may be approached through a biographical lens, a psychological lens, or through a linguistic approach. For more discussion on narrative analysis, see Denzin's (1989) text *Interpretive Biography*, or Atkinson's (1998) *The Life Story Interview*.

Portraiture is a form of qualitative research that seeks to join science and art in its attempt to describe complex human experiences within an organizational culture. The "portrait" is shaped by the dialogue between the researcher (portraitist) and the subject and attempts to reveal the "essence" of the subject and to tell the "central story." As Lawrence-Lightfoot and Davis (1997) explain in the book *The Art and Science of Portraiture*, "Portraiture is a method framed by the traditions and values of the phenomenological paradigm, sharing many of the techniques, standards, and goals of ethnography. But it pushes against the constraints of those traditions and practices in its explicit effort to combine empirical and aesthetic description, in its focus on the convergence of narrative and analysis, in its goal of speaking to broader audiences beyond the academy. . ." (p.13). The goal of portraiture is to paint a vivid portrait or story that reflects meaning from the perspectives of both the participants and the researcher. Data can be collected using in-depth interviews and observations over a period of time and typically results in a personal relationship between the researcher and participants.

Critical research seeks to empower change through examining and critiquing assumptions. Questions focus on power relationships and the influence of race, class, and gender. Whereas other forms of qualitative research we have described have as a key purpose the understanding of a phenomenon and the meanings people attach to events, the purpose in critical research is to critique and challenge the status quo. Critical research may analyze texts or artifacts such as film or other communication forms such as drama or dance to reveal underlying assumptions. Feminist research and participatory research are sometimes classified as critical research. Some resources for more information on this approach include Carspecken's (1995) text on critical ethnography, *Feminism and Method* by Nancy Naples (2003), or *Feminist Methodology* by Caroline Ramazanoglu and Janet Holland (2002).

Semiotics and **discourse analysis** study linguistic units to look at the relationship between words and their meanings. These approaches stress the system of relations between words as a source of meaning and view language as a social construction. Words are viewed as signs that bring together a concept and an image, derive their meaning from their place within an articulated system, are arbitrary (e.g., different languages use different terms for the same concepts), can be put together in combinations and patterns, and their use excludes other choices. Questions investigated through discourse analysis focus on verbal interaction and dialogue, and data collection strategies focus on recoded dialogue—text based, audio, or video recorded. One text, *Semiotics: The Basics* (Chandler, 2001) provides an introduction to semiotics. Paul Gee (1999) provides an *Introduction to Discourse Analysis*.

THINK ABOUT IT 15.3

For each description of a study below, determine which type of qualitative research is represented.

1. A study of in-church and televised worship sought to understand the perspectives of worshippers and to interpret how they describe the experience or worship through firsthand descriptions captured through interview processes
2. A study to investigate identity development of minority teachers during the first 3 years of their teaching career
3. A study of how a particular school assimilated immigrant children and transmitted values, beliefs and customs of American society
4. A study to understand the experience of good supervision from the supervisees' perspective to determine what central factors need to be present for good supervision experiences to occur
5. A study to understand the communities created and sustained in cyberspace
6. A study of a nursing student who changed her major to elementary education and how memories of childhood experiences framed her adult schooling
7. A study to look at the effect of an impoverished, rural environment on the creativity of a gifted black child
8. A study of the extent to which discursive and nondiscursive elements of character education curricula reflected attention to multicultural aspects.
9. A study of the lives (from their earliest memories) of inner-city African American and Latino American young men previously involved in destructive behavior (i.e., illegal drug marketing) who had made positive behavioral changes to examine personal and environmental transitions that contributed to the change.
10. A study about student perceptions of the influence of race on professor credibility through nonparticipant observation, interviews, and questionnaires.

Answers:

1. Phenomenology
2. Grounded theory
3. Case study
4. Phenomenology
5. Ethnography
6. Narrative study
7. Case study
8. Content analysis
9. Basic interpretive
10. Basic interpretive

DESIGNING QUALITATIVE RESEARCH

The research design is the researcher's plan of how to proceed to gain an understanding of some group or some phenomenon in its natural setting. The design begins with a general statement of a research problem or topic. Lincoln and Guba (1985) refer to this initial topic that a qualitative researcher chooses for investigation as the *focus of inquiry*. To develop the focus of inquiry, the beginning researcher needs to think about some topic in which he or she has an interest and wants to know more about. The research question may be one that comes from the investigator's observations and experiences with particular topics, settings, or groups. Qualitative problems look at the context of events, natural setting, subjects' perspectives, unfolding and uncontrolled events, reasons for the events, and phenomena needing exploration and explanation. For example, qualitative researchers may ask the following questions: How do social workers cope with the stress of their jobs? How do teachers in rural schools react to distance-learning technologies? How do chronically ill children deal with pain? What is the relationship of rural schools to their communities? What is the mentoring relationship like for a beginning teacher? What is the first-year college experience like for students who have been home schooled?

CHOOSING A PROBLEM

The following are some practical suggestions for choosing a qualitative research problem (Bogdan & Biklen, 1998). Choose a problem that (1) is not only interesting to you but also is one for which your skills are adequate, (2) is significant because it will contribute to the body of knowledge or to solving some educational problem, (3) is reasonable in size and complexity so that you can complete a study of it within the time and with the resources to which you will have access, and (4) is one in which you are not directly involved. A researcher should not choose his or her own school, for example, because it is difficult to remain neutral and to assume the role of researcher with friends.

A review of the relevant literature at this step will help familiarize the researcher with theory in the area and with previous research designs and findings related to the problem. It will be most useful if you find related research that is *qualitative*. Although quantitative studies may provide background information on the topic, beginning qualitative researchers especially need to see how the qualitative paradigm has been used in research on relevant topics.

The choice of the research question is crucial because the question determines the design. Yin (1991) gives three standards that researchers can use to help them decide if qualitative methods are appropriate for their particular research question: (1) the phenomenon under investigation is contemporary, (2) the boundaries and context of the study are not distinct, and (3) the researcher has little control over the phenomenon being studied. Using these criteria, you would determine that a problem such as violence in schools, for example, could be appropriately investigated with qualitative methodology. Maxwell (1996) describes two types of research questions posed in qualitative research. *Particularizing* questions ask about a specific context—what is happening in this particular school?—and are less concerned about generalizing, but rather focus on developing rich descriptions and interpretations. *Process* questions look at how things happen, the process by which a phenomenon takes place. Questions asking about meaning, influences, and context are process oriented.

After deciding that qualitative methodology is indeed appropriate, next make decisions about the particular qualitative approach, the main data collection tools, setting for the study, the participants, size of sample, and the behaviors to study. A qualitative design, however, is flexible and may be changed as the researcher gets into the setting. Marshall and Rossman (1989) list three criteria for evaluating the qualitative design to be used to answer the research question: The first criterion is *informational adequacy*. That is, does the research plan maximize the possibilities that the researcher will understand the setting thoroughly, precisely, and accurately? Will the research strategy elicit the desired information? The second criterion is *efficiency*. Does the plan allow adequate data to be collected at the least cost in terms of time, access, and cost to participants? The third criterion to use is *ethical considerations*. Will the proposed method violate the participants' privacy or put them at risk? Will the procedure violate their human rights in any way? We will have more to say about ethics in a later section.

SAMPLING

Sampling is important in qualitative research just as it is in quantitative research. Qualitative researchers cannot observe everything about the group or site that might be relevant to the research problem, but they try to obtain a sample of observations believed to be *representative* of everything they could observe. Although the sample may be representative, it is typically not a random sample.

Qualitative researchers select *purposive* samples believed to be sufficient to provide maximum insight and understanding of what they are studying. They use their experience and knowledge to select a sample of participants that they believe can provide the relevant information about the topic or setting. In a classic work, Guba and Lincoln (1981) wrote, "Sampling is almost never representative or random but purposive, intended to exploit competing views and fresh perspectives as fully as possible" (p. 276).

The qualitative researcher should first decide what in the situation is essential to a study of the problem. Let us say a qualitative study focuses on discipline in a school system. In this case, the researcher decides what personnel to interview (principals, assistant principals, teachers, coaches, students) and what settings (classroom, playground, cafeteria) to observe. The researcher must develop a plan to sample personnel and settings that in his or her judgment will provide an accurate picture of attitudes and disciplinary techniques employed in the school system.

Because of the depth and extent of the information sought in qualitative studies, purposive samples are typically small. How large should the sample be? There is no general rule about the number of participants to include in a qualitative study. Of course, practical considerations such as time, money, and availability of participants influence the size of the sample. But Lincoln and Guba (1985) state that the primary criterion of sample size is redundancy of information. Sampling should be terminated when no new information is forthcoming from new units (p. 202). This point is referred to as *data saturation*.

Several variations on **purposive sampling** are used in qualitative research:

1. **Comprehensive sampling**. In comprehensive sampling, every unit is included in the sample. For example, a study of physically disabled students in a high school would include all such students in the school. Comprehensive sampling is used when the number of units is small.

2. **Critical case sampling**. A critical case sample is selecting a single unit (person, event, organization, etc.) that provides a crucial test of a theory or program.
3. **Maximum variation sampling**. In maximum variation sampling, units are included that maximize differences on specified characteristics. For example, a study of American high school students might include students from schools that differ in location, student characteristics, parental involvement, and other factors. This type of sampling reveals differences but may also identify commonalities across the units.
4. **Extreme, deviant, or unique case sampling**. Extreme case sampling selects units that are atypical, special, or unusual. For example, you might choose to study an inner-city elementary school that has achieved exemplary reading and other achievement test scores. Such a study might identify practices, teaching methods, and student characteristics that may be relevant to their superior performance.
5. **Typical case sampling**. Typical case sampling selects units that are considered typical of the phenomenon to be studied. In a study of an elementary school, you would select a school considered typical rather than a very high achieving school or a very low achieving school.
6. **Negative or discrepant case sampling**. This method of sampling selects units that are examples of exceptions to expectations. The researcher would intentionally look for examples that appear not to confirm the theory being developed.
7. **Homogeneous sampling**. Homogeneous sampling selects a subgroup that is considered homogeneous in attitudes, experiences, and so on. For example, you might choose only a sample of special education teachers from a population of teachers.
8. **Snowball, chain, or network sampling**. Snowball, chain, or network sampling occurs when the initially selected subjects suggest the names of others who would be appropriate for the sample. These next subjects might then suggest others and so on. Such sampling occurs when potential respondents are not centrally located but scattered in different sites. For example, a researcher might ask one teacher who has been nominated for an environmental science teaching award to name another teacher who he or she considers to be an exemplary environmental educator.
9. **Intensity or stratified sampling**. Intensity sampling involves selecting participants who exhibit different levels of the phenomenon of interest to the researcher. Stratified sampling attempts to ensure that subgroups are represented with several cases at each of several levels of variation of the phenomenon. For example, the researcher may select some high-achieving, average-achieving, and low-achieving students or in a study of teaching practices select experienced and inexperienced teachers.
10. **Theoretical sampling**. In theoretical sampling, the researcher continues to select new cases to include as the research unfolds and the theory emerges. The researcher does not know ahead of time what or who might be selected as the next sample.

11. **Convenience sampling**. Convenience sampling is choosing a sample based on availability, time, location, or ease of access. Convenience sampling is not recommended as it may produce evidence that is not credible. A study of your own children or your own workplace would be examples of convenience sampling.

DATA COLLECTION METHODS

The next step is to choose the data collection method(s) that will be used. The most common data collection methods used in qualitative research are (1) observation, (2) interviewing, and (3) document analysis. The researcher may use one or more of these methods in a study.

Observation

Observation is the basic method for obtaining data in qualitative research. It is a more global type of observation than the systematic, structured observation used in quantitative research. The qualitative researcher's goal is a complete description of behavior in a specific natural setting rather than a numeric summary of occurrence or duration of observed behaviors. Qualitative observation usually takes place over an extended period of time and proceeds without any prior hypotheses. Quantitative observations often use checklists and behavior observation tools developed prior to the observation to record or document observed behaviors. Qualitative observations rely on narrative or words to describe the setting, the behaviors, and the interactions.

Choosing an Observation Site Guided by the research question, the qualitative investigator must select a site in which to observe. You must seek to gain access to a particular site or group of people in which the topic of interest can be studied and then negotiate entry by adopting a role either as a full **participant observer**, just an observer, or some combination of the two. Some sites are very specific to the research question. For example, if you want to investigate college majors in gender studies and how they have developed, you must find universities that offer majors in gender studies.

In many cases, once the site is selected, the researcher has to get permission to conduct the study in that setting. It may take a long time from the first contact with a site until final approval is given. Most school systems, for instance, have specific procedures they follow before giving approval to researchers. Bogdan and Biklen (1998) list some questions that the researcher should be prepared to answer: (1) What are you actually going to do? (2) Why us? (3) Will you be disruptive? (4) What are you going to do with the findings? (5) What will we get out of this? Negotiating entry, adopting a role, and developing and maintaining trust with the participants in a study are fairly complex topics about which much has been written.

Observer Roles The qualitative researcher may be a participant in the situation being observed or a nonparticipant. Five stances toward observation have been identified: (1) complete participant, (2) participant as observer, (3) observer as participant, (4) complete observer, and (5) collaborative partner. A **complete or covert participant** is a member of the group or context under study and focuses on the natural activity of the group without informing them that they are under study. Sociological researchers have pretended to join street gangs or pretended to be homeless in order to learn about such groups' feelings, relationships, and problems. Another example might be a researcher who becomes a certified teacher and takes a position in a school for the purpose of conducting research without telling anyone. In the Internet world, a researcher may join a listserve or chat room in order to examine the online world of a particular subgroup. The ethics of the covert approach, however, may be questionable. Before undertaking such a study, you must submit your plan to your Institutional Review Board (IRB) for approval (see Chapter 18).

In the **participant as observer** stance, the observer actively participates and becomes an insider in the event being observed so that he or she experiences events in the same way as the participants. The researcher's role is known to the people being observed. Anthropologists often are participant observers when they conduct a study of a particular culture. In most educational research, however, it is difficult for the investigator to pretend to be a member of a group and play the same role as the subjects who are being studied. It might be possible for a young researcher to be accepted in a group of college freshman in order to gather data on the freshman experience but not to become a participating member of a junior high school club.

In the **observer as participant** stance, researchers may interact with subjects enough to establish rapport but do not really become involved in the behaviors and activities of the group. Their status as observer/researcher is known to those under study. Their role is more peripheral rather than the active role played by the participant observer. For example, a researcher could focus on observing a vocational training class for welfare recipients or an organization such as Alcoholics Anonymous. The **complete observer** is typically hidden from the group or may be simply in a public setting observing public behavior. In studies that involve the use of one-way mirrors or hidden cameras, for example, in studies of preschool child behaviors, the researcher is a complete observer. On the playground, the researcher could observe from some distance so that his or her presence is not noticeable to the children. Or a study of greeting behaviors of travelers at an airport may be conducted as a complete observer. The qualitative researcher simply observes and records events as they naturally occur. No attempt is made to alter the situation in any way. These are considered **naturalistic observations**.

Simple naturalistic observation can take a great deal of time because you must wait for the behavior to occur naturally. For this reason, some researchers set up a contrived naturalistic situation to elicit the behavior to be observed. Although the setup is contrived, the researcher tries to maintain the naturalness of the situation and makes the observations in a way not noticeable to the subjects. Hartshorne, May, and Shuttleworth (1928) used naturalistic contrived observation in their classic study of classroom cheating (see Chapter 8).

The **collaborative partner** stance has been described in action research (Chapter 17) and feminist research and has as a defining characteristic an equal partnership in the research process between the researcher and participants.

PICTURE THIS

Joe Rocco

The degree of participation in an observation study is thus a continuum ranging from a complete participant at one end to a complete observer at the other. The observer must decide what degree of participation will provide the most appropriate data. It is easier to ask questions and record observations if members of the group know your purpose; furthermore, it may be more ethical to make people aware of what is going on. Being open, however, may present problems. Knowing they are being observed, group members may behave differently from the way they usually do, or they may not be truthful when answering questions. This impact of the observer on the participants being studied is called **observer effect** and can result in an inaccurate picture of the group and its interactions. There is a risk that the observer will destroy the very naturalness of the setting that he or she wants. **Observer expectation** may occur when the researcher knows the participants are associated with certain characteristics and may expect certain behaviors. In other words, expectations may cause you to see or interpret actions or events in a particular way.

Another problem with observation as a data-gathering tool is the possible effect that the observer him- or herself might have on the results. **Observer bias** occurs when the observer's personal attitudes and values affect the observation and/or the interpretation of the observation. In participant observation, there may also be a problem of the observer's getting emotionally involved in the group and hence losing objectivity. The nonparticipant observer can be more objective and emotionally detached from the group. A major question with observation is the extent to which the observations of another researcher might be different.

Field Notes

The most common method of recording the data collected during observation is **field notes**. The researcher may make brief notes during the observation but then later expands his or her account of the observation as field notes. These notes may supplement information from other sources, including documents and interviews, or they may comprise the main research data. Field notes contain what the researcher has seen and heard. They have two components: (1) the *descriptive* part, which includes a complete description of the setting, the people and their reactions and interpersonal relationships, and accounts of events (who, when, what was done); and (2) the *reflective* part, which includes the observer's personal feelings or impressions about the events, comments on the research method, decisions and problems, records of ethical issues, and speculations about data analysis. Field notes may also include photographs and audio and video recordings.

The researcher's reflections are identified as *observer comments* (OC) to distinguish them from the descriptive information. Exhibit 15.1 shows an excerpt from field notes collected as part of a study of students with disabilities in an urban high school.

The researcher's field notes present the data that will later be analyzed to provide an understanding of the research setting and the behavior of people within that setting. It can be said that the successful outcome of the study relies on detailed, accurate, and extensive field notes. Record everything you see, hear, or experience during the observation session. Observation sessions typically should last not more than 1 to 2 hours at a time; otherwise, so many data accumulate that it is difficult to record them all. Make the field notes as soon as possible following the observation, while the experience is still fresh in your mind. You may also use audio and video tapes to facilitate data collection. See Bogdan and Biklen (1998) for guidelines to writing field notes.

While field notes are the most common data collection technique used in observations, other techniques may include video recordings or photographs. A disadvantage of these methods is that participants may be conscious of the camera and behave differently or may try to avoid being filmed or photographed.

Joe McCloud
11:00 a.m. to 12:30 p.m.
Westwood High
6th Set of Notes

THE FOURTH-PERIOD CLASS IN MARGE'S ROOM

I arrived at Westwood High at five minutes to eleven, the time Marge told me her fourth period started. I was dressed as usual: sport shirt, chino pants, and a Woolrich parka. The fourth period is the only time during the day when all the students who are in the "neurologically impaired/learning disability" program, better known as "Marge's program," come together. During the other periods, certain students in the program, two or three or four at most, come to her room for help with the work they are getting in other regular high school classes.

It was a warm, fortyish, promise of a spring day. There was a police patrol wagon, the kind that has benches in the back that are used for large busts, parked in the back of the big parking lot that is in front of the school. No one was sitting in it and I never heard its reason for being there. In the circular drive in front of the school was parked a United States Army car. It had insignias on the side and was a khaki color. As I walked from my car, a balding fortyish man in an Army uniform came out of the building and went to the car and sat down. Four boys and a girl also walked out of the school. All were white. They had on old dungarees and colored stenciled t-shirts with spring jackets over them. One of the boys, the tallest of the four, called out, "oink, oink, oink." This was done as he sighted the police vehicle in the back.

> O.C.: This was strange to me in that I didn't think that the kids were into "the police as pigs." Somehow I associated that with another time, the early 1970s. I'm going to have to come to grips with the assumptions I have about high school due to my own experience. Sometimes I feel like Westwood is entirely different from my high school and yet this police car incident reminded me of mine.

Classes were changing when I walked down the halls. As usual there was the boy with girl standing here and there by the lockers. There were three couples that I saw. There was the occasional shout. There were no teachers outside the doors.

> O.C.: The halls generally seem to be relatively unsupervised during class changes.

Two African American girls I remember walking down the hall together. They were tall and thin and had their hair elaborately braided with beads all through them. I stopped by the office to tell Mr. Talbot's (the principal) secretary that I was in the building. She gave me a warm smile.

> O.C.: I feel quite comfortable in the school now. Somehow I feel like I belong. As I walk down the halls some teachers say hello. I have been going out of my way to

Exhibit 15.1 Example of Field Notes

say hello to kids that I pass. Twice I've been in a stare down with kids passing in the hall. Saying "How ya' doin?" seems to disarm them.

I walked into Marge's class and she was standing in front of the room with more people than I had ever seen in the room save for her homeroom which is right after second period. She looked like she was talking to the class or was just about to start. She was dressed as she had been on my other visits—clean, neat, well-dressed but casual. Today she had on a striped blazer, a white blouse and dark slacks. She looked up at me smiled and said: "Oh, I have a lot more people here now than the last time."

O.C.: This was in reference to my other visits during other periods when there are only a few students. She seems self-conscious about having such a small group of students to be responsible for. Perhaps she compares herself with the regular teachers who have classes of thirty or so.

There were two women in their late twenties sitting in the room. There was only one chair left. Marge said to me something like: "We have two visitors from the central office today. One is a vocational counselor and the other is a physical therapist," but I don't remember if those were the words. I felt embarrassed coming in late. I sat down in the only chair available next to one of the women from the central office. They had on skirts and carried their pocketbooks, much more dressed up than the teachers I've seen. They sat there and observed.

Alfred (Mr. Armstrong, the teacher's aide) walked around but when he stood in one place it was over by Phil and Jeff. Marge walked about near her desk during her talk which she started by saying to the class: "Now remember, tomorrow is a fieldtrip to the Rollway Company. We all meet in the usual place, by the bus, in front of the main entrance at 8:30. Mrs. Sharp wanted me to tell you that the tour of Rollway is not specifically for you. It's not like the trip to G.M. They took you to places where you were likely to be able to get jobs. Here, it's just a general tour that everybody goes on. Many of the jobs that you will see are not for you. Some are just for people with engineering degrees. You'd better wear comfortable shoes because you may be walking for two or three hours." Maxine and Mark said: "Ooh," in protest to the walking.

She paused and said in a demanding voice: "OK, any questions? You are all going to be there. (Pause) I want you to take a piece of paper and write down some questions so that you have things to ask at the plant." She began passing out paper and at this point Jason, who was sitting next to me, made a tutting sound of disgust and said: "We got to do this?" Marge said: "I know this is too easy for you, Jason." This was said in a sarcastic way but not like a strong putdown.

O.C.: It was like sarcasm between two people who know each other well. Marge has known many of these kids for a few years. I have to explore the implications of that for her relations with them.

Exhibit 15.1 *Continued*

Source: From R. C. Bogdan and S. K. Biklen, *Qualitative research for education*, 3rd ed., pp. 109–111. Published by Allyn & Bacon, Boston.

THINK ABOUT IT 15.4

Select a setting in which you regularly participate (e.g., office, classroom, restaurant, etc.). Observe and take field notes for 15 minutes. What sort of activities does the physical setting encourage or discourage? How do people use the space? How do they interact and communicate with one another? How do people behave when they are on their own, in pairs, in groups? What themes, features, or patterns do you see in your field notes?

INTERVIEWS

The interview is one of the most widely used methods for obtaining qualitative data. Interviews are used to gather data on subjects' opinions, beliefs, and feelings about the situation in their own words. Interviews provide information that cannot be obtained through observation, or they can be used to verify the observation. The qualitative interview is typically more probing and open ended and less structured than the interview used in quantitative research but varies considerably in the way it is conducted.

The structure of the interview follows the extent to which the questions to be asked are developed prior to the interview. At one extreme is the unstructured conversational type of interview where the questions arise from the situation. It is sometimes described as "a conversation with a purpose." The interview is not planned ahead of time; the researcher asks questions as the opportunity arises and then listens closely and uses the subjects' responses to decide on the next question. The subjects in the setting may not even realize they are being interviewed. At the other end of the continuum lies the more structured interview, scheduled for the specific purpose of getting certain information from the subjects. Each respondent is asked the same set of questions, but with some latitude in the sequence. Both approaches may be used in the same study. In between is the semi or partially structured interview where the area of interest is chosen and questions are formulated, but the interviewer may modify the format or questions during the interview process. One characteristic that all qualitative interview formats share is that the questions are open ended (cannot be answered with a yes or no or simple response) and designed to reveal what is important to understand about the phenomenon under study (Maykut & Morehouse, 1994, p. 81).

An interview has the advantage of supplying large volumes of in-depth data rather quickly. Interviews provide insight on participants' perspectives, the meaning of events for the people involved, information about the site, and perhaps information on unanticipated issues. Interviews allow immediate follow-up and clarification of participants' responses. One disadvantage of the interview as a data-gathering tool is that interviewees may not be willing to share information or may even offer false information. Interviews require a great deal of time to conduct and later to transcribe the audio tapes or other notes. Interviewers need skill and practice to carry out a successful interview: they must be tactful, well prepared (so that they know what questions to ask), and listen well. Careful listening is crucial to successful interviewing. Be on guard to eliminate any personal biases that could threaten the accuracy of the data collected.

The most efficient way to collect interview data is to use an audio tape recorder. This is much less distracting than taking notes, and it also provides a verbatim record of the responses. Informal interviews in the field are reconstructed later and included in the field notes. Video taping can also be used to collect interview data. In recent years, interviews conducted via e-mail or chat areas have been used in studies. A good source for additional information on interviewing is Maykut and Morehouse (1994, Chapter 7).

Qualitative interviews might involve one-time interviews with a subject or subjects, multiple interviews with the same subject or subjects, or group interviews or focus groups. A **focus group**, which is like a group interview, typically centers on a particular issue; the trained interviewer elicits the views of the group members while noting interactions within the group. Focus groups are helpful because they bring several different perspectives into contact. The researcher gains insight into how the participants are thinking and why they are thinking as they do. Focus groups make more economical use of time and money than do individual interviews. And they are helpful when a researcher is studying a topic that is new or one for which little information is available. The topics and ideas expressed in the focus group can help the researcher to identify questions and other important aspects of the phenomenon to pursue in the study.

A focused interview is much more flexible and open in form than the survey interview discussed in Chapter 14. The respondents are free to answer in their own words and can answer either briefly or at length. The questions asked may even vary from individual to individual. The responses are recorded by taking notes, either during the interview or immediately afterward, or with an audiotape. Focus groups are more socially oriented than individual interviews and can increase the sample size in the study, but they allow less control than individual interviews, and data can be more difficult to analyze. Focus groups should not be used in emotionally charged environments.

For both individual and focus group interviewing, some key rules are important. You must take care not to impose your own agenda or bias. You must be open to responses that are contrary to your own knowledge, beliefs, or perspectives. Care should be taken not to mention specific terms or to over-cue interviewees. Interviewers should direct responses to concrete, detailed accounts rather than generalizations. You should also watch for discrepancies between the interviewee's verbal and nonverbal behaviors and note these. Strategies useful in interviewing include the probe and the pause. The probe is a comment that leads to more detail such as "Can you tell me more?" "I'm not sure I understand." and "Can you give me an example?" The pause involves learning to be silent longer than the interviewee. The pause is at least 5 seconds and may be coupled with eye contact.

Focused interviews were used by Kagan, Dennis, Igou, and Moore (1993) to examine the effects of a staff development program on the professional lives of four elementary teachers who participated in it. The program took experienced

These questions were designed to be used in a study of teacher understanding of a change to block scheduling in a high school.

1. Describe your involvement in making the decision and planning to implement block scheduling in the school.
2. How do you feel about the amount and type of communication you received during the decision and planning process?
3. How has the change to block scheduling affected your curriculum?
4. How has the change to block scheduling affected your classroom instruction practices?
5. How have the changes affected teacher attitudes in the school?
6. What effect do you think the change has had on students?
7. What feedback have you heard from students and parents about the change?
8. Think back to last year, before block scheduling. What is different in the school this year?
9. What things are going well or not so well with the new block schedule?
10. If you had a magic wand, what is the one thing you would change about the school?

Exhibit 15.2 Sample Focus Group Questions

elementary teachers to a university college of education for 2-year terms, during which they functioned as adjunct faculty. The teachers interviewed said that they did not learn radically new things in the program, but that it enabled them to clarify what they already knew about teaching and to recommit themselves to the role of career teacher. This qualitative research showed the potential of school–university partnerships for enhancing teachers' professional lives.

Focus groups typically consist of 6 to 12 people. The group should be small enough that everyone can take part in the discussion, but large enough to provide diversity in perspective. Focus group discussions usually need to last at least 1 hour and possibly 2 hours. Groups should be homogenous in terms of prestige and status to ensure comfort in expressing opinions. Exhibit 15.2 provides some sample focus group questions. For more information on conducting focus groups, see Krueger and Casey (2000).

STUDY OF DOCUMENTS

Qualitative researchers may also use written documents to gain an understanding of the phenomenon under study. The term *documents* here refers to a wide range of written, physical, and visual materials, including what other authors may term artifacts. Documents may be personal, such as autobiographies, diaries, and letters; official, such as files, reports, memoranda, or minutes; or documents of popular culture, such as books, films, and videos. **Document analysis** can be of written or text-based artifacts (textbooks, novels, newspapers, transcripts, birth certificates, letters, etc.) or of nonwritten records (photographs, audiotapes, videotapes, computer files). The analysis may be of existing artifacts or records, or in some cases the researcher may ask subjects to produce artifacts or documents, for example, asking participants to keep a journal about personal experiences, to tell family stories, to draw pictures to express memories, or to explain thinking aloud as it is audiotaped.

Merriam (1998) describes documents in four categories: (1) public records, (2) personal documents, (3) physical materials, and (4) researcher-generated documents. You are likely familiar with a wide range of public records. If you were interested in examining the changing role of the federal government in education, for example, you might examine such public records as the *Congressional Record*, federal reports, websites of congressional committees, agency reports, *Education Week*, and the *Chronicle of Higher Education* to name a few. Personal documents are typically first-person narratives and include such items as diaries, letters, home videos, scrapbooks, and more. While these may be reliable sources of information about the individual's beliefs and perspectives, they are highly subjective and not necessarily objective or reliable. Physical materials may include many objects such as equipment, paintings, photographs, and other physical traces. For example, a researcher interested in student pride in their school might document the amount of trash left in hallways and classrooms. Researcher-generated documents are prepared by the researcher or for the researcher by the participants, as in the example above when participants are asked to keep a journal.

As discussed earlier, if a document is written by someone who has had first-hand experience with the phenomenon under study, it is considered a primary source. For example, researchers have used diaries and letters written by pioneer women to understand what life was like for such women in the early years of our country. A secondary source is a secondhand description written by someone who may have heard about an event from others but did not directly experience it. You cannot assume that documents always provide accurate accounts of events or settings. Other sources of data should be used whenever possible to corroborate the conclusions presented in the document.

It is important to establish the authenticity of documents used in research. The researcher should attend to such issues as the history of the document, its completeness, and the original purpose of the document. Even public records may have built-in biases that need examination, and personal documents may be subject to deception or distortion (intentional or unintentional). Another limitation is that documents were generally not produced for research purposes and may be incomplete or unrepresentative. Despite limitations, documents are a good source of data. They can provide good descriptive information, are stable sources of data, and can help ground a study in its context.

ETHICAL CONSIDERATIONS IN QUALITATIVE RESEARCH

In Chapters 3 and 18 we discuss ethical issues pertaining to all types of educational research. Here we consider ethical issues inherent in qualitative research.

1. *Kind of information obtained.* One ethical issue may result from the lengthy and personal interaction that the qualitative researcher often has with the subjects and the research site. The data collection methods involve personal interviews and observations of participants during a prolonged time at a

site. Depending on the nature of the research, there is a great likelihood of situations arising that present ethical dilemmas to the researcher. A researcher may come into unforeseen possession of knowledge about illegal activities or in some cases may have actually participated in the illegal behavior. For example, a researcher studying a high school may learn about the use and sale of illegal drugs. An educational researcher investigating teaching styles may observe emotionally abusive teachers. What should a researcher do with such "guilty knowledge" (as it is sometimes called)? Do you have an ethical responsibility to report this information to the appropriate authorities? The researcher must decide whether his or her main responsibility is to the research study, to the participants, or to society as a whole. You must balance the benefit of continuing the study after acquiring such guilty knowledge against your responsibilities as a good citizen. One rule that researchers must always follow is that they are legally obligated (mandated) to report any evidence of child abuse.

2. *Researcher's relationship to participant.* After spending a great amount of time observing or interviewing, the **researcher's relationship to participants** may gradually become less that of researcher and researched and more like friendship. Because the researcher is regarded as a friend, the participants trust him or her and may forget a research study is going on. Some field researchers say they obtain their best data at this point, but at the same time are most ethically vulnerable (Langenbach, Vaughn, & Aagaard, 1994). Through such interactions, Peshkin said, he "donned masks in order to remove the masks of those I wanted to observe and interview" (1984, p. 258). The reader is referred to Peshkin's account of his ethical concerns about the deceptive role he played during an 18-month study of a fundamentalist Christian school.

   Somewhat related are the issues of anonymity and confidentiality in qualitative research. Participants may expect and have a right to anonymity, but it can be problematic in qualitative research. The researcher cannot promise anonymity if, as is usually the case, he or she knows the names of the participants. If a researcher has promised confidentiality, then he or she must try to keep that promise if at all possible. Be aware, however, that your records can be subpoened if a court discovers that you may have evidence about criminal activity. For this reason, researchers who conduct sensitive research do not keep records that identify individuals unless absolutely necessary. In field notes, they can use false names or code numbers to keep track of what information came from whom without revealing identities.

   The confidentiality issue may arise in educational research. Let us say you have conducted a study of the teachers in a particular school and assured them confidentiality. At the end of the study, the principal asks to see your data on one or more of the teachers. What would you do? Do you have a responsibility to the teacher(s) to whom you promised confidentiality, to the principal, or perhaps to the students who are exposed to this teacher?

3. *Reciprocation.* Another issue about which the researcher should be concerned is the issue of **reciprocity**. The people in the research setting have given of themselves to help the researcher, and he or she is indebted. Qual-

itative researchers need to give participants something in return for their time, effort, cooperation, and just tolerating their extended presence. For example, assume a researcher has conducted a lengthy study of students' achievement, parental involvement, and the teachers in an elementary school. At the end of the study, it would be appropriate for the researcher and his or her team to give something back to the school. They might offer to provide a written report, present the findings at a school or neighborhood meeting, give advice or assistance on other research projects at the school, or help with grant writing, and so forth. Marshall and Rossman (1995) write, "Of course, reciprocity should fit within the constraints of research and personal ethics, and within the constraints of maintaining one's role as a researcher" (p. 71).

4. *Getting permission to conduct research.* Like the quantitative researcher, the qualitative researcher must get approval for the project from his or her institution's Human Subjects Research Committee, especially if minors are included in the research. Beginning researchers should get a copy of the application form used at their institutions to see what questions they must answer. It is often more difficult for a qualitative researcher to inform the committee about the specifics of the research project because in qualitative research you do not always know what is going to happen. The problem you think you are going to investigate may not be the one you actually end up studying. Qualitative research plans may be altered as you get the study underway, and unanticipated ethical issues may arise that you will need to resolve. Usually qualitative researchers inform the committee in a general way about the project. If it is necessary to change the focus or design of the study, then the researcher needs to get an amendment from the committee.

SUMMARY

Qualitative studies are a distinctive type of research in education and the social sciences that can produce vivid and richly detailed accounts of human experience. These studies are based on a fundamentally different approach to the study of social reality from that which underlies the standard quantitative approach to the study of education. One chooses a qualitative design because it is the appropriate method for investigating the problem. Qualitative inquiries demand a set of skills that are not readily learned by examining textbook accounts of methods. Becoming proficient in this approach to inquiry requires fieldwork experience in negotiating access to a site, developing a researcher role, establishing and maintaining trust with participants in the study, conducting and recording interviews and observations, managing data, and performing data analysis. Qualitative research requires a great deal of time and effort.

The major types of qualitative studies covered in this text include ethnography, basic interpretive, case studies, document analysis, phenomenological studies, grounded theory studies, and historical research. The three most widely used qualitative data collection methods are observation, interviews, and documents. The reader who is interested in conducting a qualitative research study or who wants more information is advised to consult textbooks on qualitative methodology, such as Bogdan and Biklen (1998), Marshall and Rossman (1995), Merriam (1998), and Maxwell (1996).

KEY CONCEPTS

case study
chain sampling
collaborative partner
complete observer
complete or covert participant
comprehensive sampling
concern for context and meaning
content or document analysis
convenience sampling
covert participant
critical case sampling
critical research
deviant sampling
discourse analysis
discrepant case sampling
document analysis
emergent design
"emic" perspective
ethnography
"etic" perspective
external criticism
extreme sampling
field notes
focus group
grounded theory
historical research
homogeneous sampling
human as instrument
hypothetico-deductive model
inductive data analysis
intensity sampling
internal criticism
interpretive studies
maximum variation sampling
narrative study
naturalistic observation
natural setting
negative case sampling
network sampling
nonobserver
nonparticipant observation
observation
observer bias
observer effect
observer expectation
observer as participant
participant as observer
phenomenological study
phenomenology
portraiture
primary source
purposive sampling
qualitative inquiry
quantitative research
reciprocity
researcher bias
researcher's relationship to participant
secondary source
semiotics
snowball sampling
stratified sampling
theoretical sampling
typical case sampling
unique case sampling

EXERCISES

1. List four characteristics of qualitative research that distinguish it from quantitative research.
2. How do case studies differ from single-subject experiments?
3. How does the role of the researcher differ in qualitative and quantitative research?
4. Explain the use of theory in qualitative and quantitative studies.
5. An investigator has a letter describing education in Britain in 1985. It is supposed to have been written by Prime Minister Margaret Thatcher.
   a. What question would be asked in external criticism?
   b. What question would be asked in internal criticism?
6. How are participants selected for a qualitative study?
7. What are the advantages and disadvantages of historical research as compared with other types of research?
8. Distinguish between participant and nonparticipant observation; give an example of each.
9. Compare the role of the hypothesis in qualitative and quantitative research.
10. Give an example of disguised participant observation.
11. What are field notes? What should they contain?
12. Suppose you want to determine the extent to which elementary school social studies textbooks are discussing the achievements of black Americans. How would you proceed to obtain data on this question?
13. What roles can a qualitative observer assume in a study?
14. Suggest a research question that could be answered best by using each of the following methods:
   a. Case study
   b. Ethnography

c. Document analysis
d. Phenomenological study

15. School systems in the United States are hiring an increasing number of social workers. You have been asked to gather data on what these social workers do and whether their presence in schools makes any difference for student achievement, student self-concept, discipline, and relations with parents. How would you design a qualitative study to answer this question? Indicate the method and the data-gathering procedure that you think would be most effective.
16. Assume you are going to prepare a qualitative research proposal for your research methods class or for a dissertation. List a question that you would like to investigate and then the qualitative method that would be most appropriate to use.
17. List some ethical concerns that may arise in qualitative research.
18. What is the main difference between the interpretation of qualitative data and quantitative data?
19. What are two main threats to the accuracy of qualitative observations?
20. Give two examples of probes that can be used in an interview.
21. Determine whether each of the following questions would best be answered using quantitative or qualitative research methods.
    a. What goes on in an elementary school classroom during an average week and how do observed practices relate to the teacher's espoused teaching beliefs?
    b. What is the relationship between education level and volume of reading done in various content areas?
    c. How does team teaching influence classroom interactions?
    d. How can a principal improve faculty morale?
    e. What is the impact of AIDS on the U.S. economy?
    f. What is the emotional impact of AIDS on at-risk health care workers?
    g. Are the descriptions of people in the social studies textbooks multiculturally inclusive?
    h. What is the relationship between years of teaching experience and job satisfaction?

ANSWERS

1. a. The nature of the data used; qualitative research uses nonnumeric data.
   b. Qualitative research design evolves as research gets under way; no a priori hypotheses are used.
   c. Type of data analysis used.
   d. Human instrument; the researcher is a participant in the study.
2. Single-subject experiments focus on a single behavior or a very limited number of behaviors. The investigator introduces a specific treatment for the purpose of studying the effect of this treatment on the subject. A case study attempts to describe the subject's entire range of behavior as it occurs in a natural setting. The researcher observes the subject's behavior in relation to the influence of the physical, social, and psychological environment.
3. In quantitative studies, the researcher is expected to be detached and impartial and provide an objective portrayal. In qualitative studies, the researcher is often personally involved, and it is understood that subjectivity may influence the research.
4. Quantitative research is conducted to test theory, whereas qualitative research is more likely to be focused on developing theory.
5. a. Was the letter really written by Margaret Thatcher?
   b. Does it accurately describe education in Britain in 1985?
6. Qualitative research uses purposive samples; subjects are selected because they can provide relevant information about the topic and setting investigated. A number of different strategies are used to get the sample of participants.
7. One advantage of historical research is the unlikelihood of researcher or experimental interaction effects confounding interpretation of findings. A historical perspective can deal with issues and past situations that

cannot be handled experimentally. The main disadvantage is the lack of experimental control, which makes unequivocal interpretation of data and generalization difficult. There is also the possibility of gathering inadequate or inaccurate information that is not verifiable.

8. In participant observation, the researcher actively participates in the group being studied. In nonparticipant observation, the researcher does not participate in any activity but acts only as an observer. Examples will vary.
9. Qualitative researchers do not, typically, formulate hypotheses before the research and then proceed to test them. Hypotheses are formulated inductively as the research proceeds. Quantitative researchers, in contrast, formulate a hypothesis at the beginning of the research then proceed deductively to identify what should be observed if the hypothesis is correct, and then make the observations needed to test the hypothesis.
10. A researcher might take a job as a waitress or waiter in a neighborhood bar in order to study this particular social unit.
11. Field notes are the notes recorded in the field by a researcher doing a qualitative study. They consist of what the researcher sees or hears and interpretations of observations. They have two components: descriptive (what the researcher sees and hears) and reflective (what the researcher thinks or feels).
12. A content analysis would be the appropriate research design. One would obtain a sample of widely used social studies textbooks and then set up categories and proceed to go through the books making counts of the number of times the achievements of black Americans are mentioned within each of the categories. The categories might be males, females, or they might involve the fields in which the achievements were made, such as music, science, literature, and so on.
13. The observer can be a participant observer who engages fully in the activities being studied but is known to the group as a researcher. The researcher can be a nonparticipant observer, who observes but does not participate. In between these roles are combinations of the two extremes. The observer can also be a covert observer in which his or her identity is hidden from the group.
14. Answers will vary.
15. Answers will vary.
16. Answers will vary.
17. The researcher may face ethical dilemmas involving anonymity, confidentiality, what to do with "guilty knowledge," deception, and so on.
18. Quantitative researchers use statistical tests as a basis for interpreting the data. Qualitative researchers analyze data inductively by organizing data into categories, identifying patterns and themes, and writing descriptive narratives.
19. Observer bias, observer effect, observer expectation
20. Answers will vary. Examples include: Can you tell me more? Could you give me an example?
21. a. qualitative, b. quantitative, c. either, d. qualitative, e. quantitative, f. qualitative, g. qualitative, h. quantitative

INFOTRAC COLLEGE EDITION

Using the keyword *grounded theory*, search for an article that used this approach in qualitative research (educational research, if possible). Why do you think grounded theory was the appropriate method to investigate this problem?

Chapter 16

Qualitative Research: Data Analysis, Rigor, and Reporting

COMPLICATING THE STORY IS ONE OF THE KEY FEATURES OF QUALITATIVE DATA.
WEITZMANN (2004)

INSTRUCTIONAL OBJECTIVES

After studying this chapter, the student will be able to:

1 Describe the general procedures followed in the analysis of qualitative data.
2 State the role of categories in qualitative data analysis.
3 Identify the most commonly used approaches to data analysis in qualitative research.
4 Specify the difference between data analysis and data interpretation.
5 Explain the role of technology in qualitative analysis.
6 Describe the major approaches to asserting validity in qualitative studies.
7 Describe the major strategies for enhancing reliability in qualitative studies.
8 Identify the components of a qualitative report.
9 State some of the criteria to use in evaluating a qualitative study.

The final activities in qualitative inquiry are analyzing and interpreting the data collected and presenting the results. Maykut and Morehouse (1994) state that data analysis is the heart of qualitative research and the process that most distinguishes qualitative from quantitative research. The challenge facing the researcher at this stage is to make sense of copious amounts of data and to construct a framework for communicating the essence of what the data reveal. Data analysis is a process whereby researchers systematically search and arrange their data in order to increase their understanding of the data and to enable them to present what they learned to others. As you will see, it is a process of making successive approximations toward the goal of describing and explaining the phenomenon under investigation.

ANALYZING QUALITATIVE DATA

Data analysis is the most complex and mysterious phase of qualitative research. Data analysis in qualitative research is a time-consuming and difficult process because typically the researcher faces massive amounts of field notes, interview transcripts, audio recordings, video data, reflections, or information from documents, all of which must be examined and interpreted. Analysis involves reducing and organizing the data, synthesizing, searching for significant patterns, and discovering what is important. The researcher must organize what he or she has seen, heard, and read and try to make sense of it in order to create explanations, develop theories, or pose new questions.

Data analysis in qualitative research is often done concurrently or simultaneously with data collection through an iterative, recursive, and dynamic process. All qualitative analysis involves attempts to comprehend the phenomenon under study, synthesize information and explain relationships, theorize about how and why the relationships appear as they do, and reconnect the new knowledge with what is already known. Qualitative analysis is partly mechanical but mostly interpretive. The task of analyzing qualitative data can appear overwhelming but becomes manageable when broken down into three key stages: (1) familiarization and organization, (2) coding and recoding, and (3) summarizing and interpreting.

FAMILIARIZATION AND ORGANIZATION

The first stage in analyzing qualitative data involves **familiarization** and **organization** so that the data can be easily retrieved. Initially, the researcher should become familiar with the data through reading and rereading notes and transcripts, viewing and reviewing videotapes, and listening repeatedly to audiotapes. Next, make sure that field notes, audiotapes, videotapes, observer comments, and other data are put into a form ready for analysis. We recommend that the data be typed. Preferably, transcriptions should be made of all data, including tape-recorded interviews, focus groups, video recordings, and handwritten field notes. Words should be transcribed directly to avoid potential bias in selection or interpretation that may come with summarizing. As transcriptions are made, you should include notes that provide nonverbal information (e.g., gestures and laughter) that can give added meaning. While transcribing, do not change words or phrases to make them grammatically correct as it may inadvertently change the sense or meaning of what was said. Typically, during transcription, identifiable information is stripped to ensure confidentiality. Pseudonyms may be given. Analysis without making transcripts is possible but not recommended. The researcher can take notes while playing a recording, for example. Although this may be less time consuming than transcription, you are more likely to miss important information, and your analysis may have less depth and comprehensiveness.

Once transcriptions have been completed, continue to read and reread the data. As you are thus familiarizing yourself with the data, write notes or memos (also called a *reflective log*) to capture your thoughts as they occur. Notes may be taken in the margins of the transcripts indicating key ideas. Once you have made notes in the margins, review them and make a complete list of the different types

PICTURE THIS

Joe Rocco

of information you see. This is an essential preliminary step to developing a coding scheme.

The major task of organizing the large body of information begins after familiarization. Start with creating a complete list of data sources. For organization, Maykut and Morehouse (1994) suggest that each page of data be marked to indicate the kind and source of the data and the page number of the particular data set. For example, the first page (1) of field notes from observing (O) at Central Middle School (CMS) is coded O/CMS-1. You may wish to index each paragraph or phrase or number the lines or paragraphs to enable better tracking later. Files can be organized in a variety of ways, for example, by interview, by questions, by

THINK ABOUT IT 16.1

Find a volunteer and tape record an informal interview (5 to 10 minutes) on the topic of his or her favorite learning experience. Transcribe the interview, including as much nonverbal material as possible. Then answer the following questions: (1) How long did it take to transcribe the tape? (2) What nonverbal communications were you able to include and how did it inform your understanding of the words? (3) Did you ask any leading questions or miss important cues? (4) As you listen to the tape while reading the transcript, did you change any of the words (is the transcription accurate)? (5) What key ideas did you write in the margins?

Answers
Answers will vary.

people, or by places. Photocopy all data pages and work from the copies. Always keep backup copies of the original data.

CODING AND RECODING

After familiarizing yourself with the data and organizing it for easy retrieval, you can begin the **coding** and **recoding** process. This is the core of qualitative analysis and includes the identification of categories and themes and their refinement. Wiersma (2000, p. 203) suggests that coding is analogous to getting ready for a rummage sale: You sort the stuff for the sale into categories—housewares, clothing, furniture, books, and so on. You might further subdivide the categories: The clothing category would include children's clothing, teenagers' clothing, adults' clothing. Then each of these clothing categories could be further subdivided; for example, the children's clothing could be categorized as infants', toddlers', and school-age children's clothes; each of these categories could be further subdivided into boys' and girls' clothes.

The first step in coding is referred to as open coding, preliminary coding, or provisional coding. The most common approach is to read and reread all the data and sort them by looking for units of meaning—words, phrases, sentences, subjects' ways of thinking, behavior patterns, and events that seem to appear regularly and that seem important. Each unit of meaning label should be understandable without any additional information. These initial codes are likely to be modified later. These codes may be named from actual words of respondents or may be names created by the researcher to include a variety of ways an underlying concept is expressed. Or the researcher may begin with a framework for analysis, a set of a priori concepts derived from the literature that are used as codes.

When coding initially, use as many codes as needed. These will be reduced later. Labeling or coding of items is done in order to begin to recognize differences and similarities in the data. The initial coding leads to the development of tentative **categories**. These may be refined and reconceptualized as the analysis process continues. Understand that in qualitative analysis, the boundaries of the categories and themes involve interpretive judgment. As the "big picture" begins to emerge, you may rethink the categories and reestablish boundaries.

The researcher initially goes through all the data and marks each unit (paragraph or sentence, etc.) with the appropriate code. As the codes are developed, qualitative researchers can count the frequency with which these codes appear, which gives some insight into the importance of that category of meaning. However, recall that the goal of qualitative coding is not to count but to break apart the data and rearrange it into categories that facilitate comparisons within and between and to develop theoretical concepts.

After all the data are coded, the researcher should place all units having the same coding together. You can do this manually by cutting with scissors according to the codes and putting material with like codes together in a marked folder. You can code using highlighters with a master sheet indicating which colors are connected with which categories. Or you can do it using one of several computer programs (discussed later in this chapter). Once coding of a transcript is completed and all items with a particular code are placed together, review the sets of items to be sure they belong together. Then begin considering whether codes can be put together into larger categories. Some items may belong in more than one category. Once categories have been established, consider whether some categories may be linked to create major categories or themes. This process of coding, categorizing, and developing themes will be repeated for each transcript or set of data. Then merge these sets together, reviewing categories and themes. Once all coding and categorization is complete, go back and look at the original transcripts and review any areas not coded and consider whether these now fit into categories.

Developing coding enables the researcher to physically separate material bearing on a given topic from other material and is a crucial step in organizing the data. The goal is to come up with a set of codes that provide a reasonable reconstruction of the data that have been collected (Lincoln & Guba, 1985, p. 347). The categories developed from the coded data should be internally consistent and distinct from one another. The categories one investigator uses to organize qualitative data may not be the same categories another researcher would use to organize the same data. The researcher's interests and style and the research question influence to a great extent the categories chosen. Bogdan and Biklen (1998) suggest some *categories* that might be used, although these categories should not be considered exhaustive:

1. *Setting/context*. These categories contain general information—on the setting, topic, subjects, and other materials—that places the study in a larger context. A study of an elementary school, for example, would place descriptive data about the school in this category.
2. *Definition of the situation*. These categories include data on how the subjects view the setting and their role in it. Data on how teachers really view their work ("love it" or "just surviving") would be put in this category.
3. *Perspectives held by subjects*. This category includes more specific ways of thinking that subjects may share, as well as their orientation toward particular aspects of a setting. Particular phrases that subjects use often reflect their perspectives.

4. *Subjects' ways of thinking about people and objects.* Subjects' understandings of each other, of outsiders, and of the objects in their world would be placed in this category. For example, teachers may have labels they apply to students, such as "achievers," "underachievers," or "troublemakers."
5. *Process.* These are words and phrases that enable you to categorize sequences of events, changes over time, or moving from one kind of status to another. For example, a teacher's description of the stages in his or her career would be put in this category.
6. *Activity.* An activity category refers to regularly occurring kinds of behavior within a setting, such as assemblies, lunch, parent conferences, as well as informal behaviors such as students' "horsing around" or "rough housing."
7. *Event.* An event category refers to particular activities in the subjects' lives that happen infrequently or only one time. The events may have happened prior to the research study. For example, a "student protest" or a "teacher strike" would be coded in this category.
8. *Strategy.* Strategy refers to the methods, techniques, ploys, and other ways that subjects accomplish what they want and avoid what they do not want. Teachers, for example, employ strategies in teaching to control students' behavior or to get class assignments they want. Any comments teachers might make relevant to strategies would be placed in this category.
9. *Relationship and social structure.* This category includes regular patterns of behavior in a setting that describe the social structure. Any data about cliques, romances, friendships, enemies, and so on would be coded in this category.
10. *Methods.* This category includes the research procedures, methods, problems, and reflections to which the researcher refers during the inquiry.

See the Bodgan and Biklen text (1998) for a discussion and examples of data to include in each of the preceding coding categories.

The number of categories developed will depend on the type of data collected, the focus of inquiry, and the researcher's analytic skills. If the number of categories is very large, they should be collapsed into a manageable number. In qualitative data analysis, the researcher conducts inductive coding of the individual data pieces and simultaneous comparing of units of meaning. Once the data pieces have been coded, they are merged into categories that are refined through several iterations. After the categories have been refined, the researcher explores the relationships or patterns across categories, identifying major themes. The integration of data into themes yields an understanding of the context and people being studied. Figure 16.1 shows the levels of data analysis in a data pyramid.

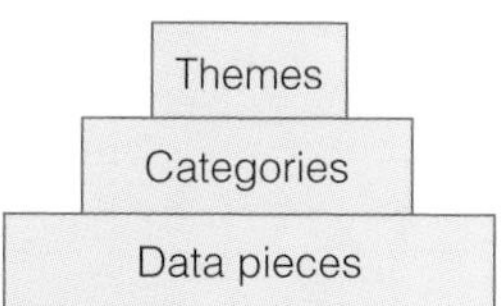

Figure 16.1 Data Pyramid

THINK ABOUT IT 16.2

Following are comments from a series of focus groups with Hispanic/Latino parents for a study that examined parent involvement in urban elementary schools. The researcher held focus groups in four different schools. The study identified points of conflict between parents and the schools, obstacles to resolution, and strategies to resolution. The comments included below identify the category with which each comment was coded when identifying points of conflict. The letter and number combinations identify which parent (1, 2, 3, 4, etc.) in which focus group (A, B, C, D, etc.) made the comment.

Category: Reporting Student Progress
(Parents indicated they were not informed when their child was not being successful in school.)

J7: He's right about whenever, the teachers you know, if you want to get feedback from them as to the progress of your child. Whenever I do want to get feedback as to how my child is doing, where is it that he or she is lacking, I always call and schedule an appointment with the teachers, and that has worked for me. But it is true, I'll agree with him, if you don't ask, they don't say anything. And I do think that maybe that shouldn't be the case because by the time we dig, we find out as to how our child is doing, maybe that will be too late.

J8: I asked from since the beginning of the year that I wanted to know if my kid was going to need help in any class or subject, whatever. I kept asking the teachers, you now, how he is doing. The answer that I was getting—he's doing OK, he's doing OK. But when every day that he was going home, I noticed that he is having a hard time, especially with math.

B3: I have recently been told that my child will be retained this year. You're telling me that my child will be retained this year, yet you had all year long. But you waited until the very last minute. You did not inform me. I had to find out for myself from you when it is too late to do anything about it. And the teacher kept saying, "I was going to send a note." And then the note never got written because she kept forgetting.

Category: Communicating about Incidents
(Parents described a variety of incidents that involved their children and about which they were concerned.)

G4: My daughter had gotten a detention. I don't know whether she was talking or disrupting class. For some reason she was told that she had to mop the floor and do things like this and I kind of flew off the handle. I go, "Mop?" That's not anything you do after school. I mean they have maintenance or you know to do things like that. But they don't talk to me about that.

B9: My kindergartner went to school one day and he was playing with a red marker. He had it all over him and he had it all over his hand, so I told him it's time for you to go wash your hands and I put him to bed. In the morning, I got up early. I go to work and his dad stays home, so he helps them get ready for school. And as soon as I got home from work about three they called me. What was wrong with Abraham because his hand is so red, if I hit him on his hand? So the nurse verifies that I spank him on hand and his hand is all red. I go, "No, I did not hit him." So they send a note to me, I don't really recall what was the name, but I'm abusing kids! I was so upset because I said, she is the nurse, can't she verify red marker on a kid's hand?

G2: Now they're dropped off to school at the same time, but one had five tardies on their report card and the other one had eleven. They're the same grade, dropped off at the same time, and I wrote a letter to each of their teachers asking for an explanation. I got an explanation that, well, that's what we recorded, and that's what it is. I'm like, you know, how can this be? And my daughter was at the school at that time and had zero tardies, so they could not tell me how they came up with these numbers and I never got resolution to that.

J6: In my girls classroom, all those kids were playing with a used condom. They were throwing it to each other. You cannot call that a good school if that is going to happen. And when I tried to talk about it, they [the school] ignored us. They didn't want to talk about it because that was a very delicate subject.

Category: Policies, Programs and Procedures
(Parents indicated they did not have adequate information or understanding about policies, programs and procedures.)

A2: That's one thing I would like to know — why they don't open the door before. They open it right at the time, right at nine o'clock. If they could maybe have another room, an extra room, so they can let them in until, hey, it's time to go to the classroom, that would be all right too. But that's the one thing that I would like to know why they are doing that.

B4: This was last year, but my daughter, she used to tell me how she used to go to the homework club instead of going out to recess, and I thought this is for kids who wanted to just stay inside and work on their homework and then it was this year that I found out that it was for kids who didn't do their homework and weren't allowed to go outside and all year I didn't know that. I think I should have been warned or told maybe.

J8: I asked the teacher, "Does he need help and do you notice that he needs help in reading, math or another class, science?" And she says he was fine, he was okay. But I don't think he was okay because when I was trying to ask questions about how to do the homework, he wasn't too sure. So that's when we found out about the program, through the parents, through the other parents. That's the only way we find information rather than the teacher giving us information or even the principal. They should send information home to the parents about what kind of programs they have.

B11: The only thing is that my son and my daughter they have been here, but I'm from another country. I speak another language at home and for some reason, they put them in the ESL program, which they don't speak another language. I speak the language, but they don't. My husband is born here. He speaks good English. But when I call the school, they say yes, once you speak another language in the house, they should be in ESL class, which I didn't understand because they are good in writing and reading. I don't know why they have to go to ESL. I call them many times and I say I want to take them out of the ESL program, but they say no, once I speak another language in the house, they have to be in ESL.

J3: If this teacher knew that my son, or felt my son, was doing that bad, why did she not recommend these classes that I was not aware of, being early morning, one-hour classes on Tuesdays and Thursdays at the school. I never found out about them. Even though the teacher was complaining about my child, she did not inform me about these classes. I found out through networking with other parents and I started taking my child on my own.

Source: Adapted from S. Hughes, A study of teachers and their relationships with at-risk students, in T. S. Poetter, *Voices of inquiry in teacher education*, pp. 87–91, 1997. Reprinted by permission of Lawrence Erlbaum Associates, Inc.

The researcher later combined these three categories [(1) reporting student progress, (2) communicating about incidents, and (3) policies, programs, and procedures] into a single theme: We are not being told what we need to know. A focus group also was held with principals and comparisons made between parent and principal identification of points of conflict. The researcher later represented her themes from the comparisons of principal and parent comments regarding conflict in the graphic shown in Figure 16.2.

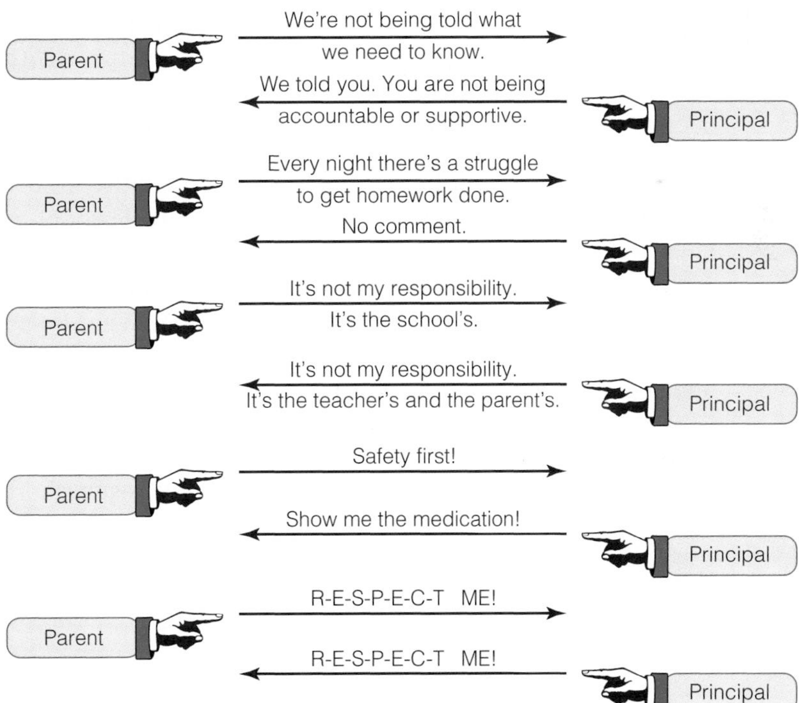

Figure 16.2 Perceptions of Conflict Reported by Elementary School Principals and Parents in an Urban Setting

Source: From *School–community conflict: Perceptions of elementary-school principals and parents in an urban setting*, Dissertation by Sharon A. LaViolette, 2001. Reprinted by permission.

THINK ABOUT IT 16.3

A pilot professional development program was presented by a university to a group of urban teachers. At the conclusion of the program a focus group was held with the teachers to determine their perceptions of the impact of the program. A brief portion of the lengthy transcript is provided below. Review the transcript and code all the items of interest. (*Fac* indicates a facilitator comment. Other labels such as A3, B11, etc. identify respondents.)

Responses

Fac: What aspects of the program have been most useful in your professional practice?

B2: There was theory with practical applications, which is extremely useful in my classroom. The program gave me a spark, made me more innovative. The different modeling of instruction was wonderful.

A2: The team working activities were most beneficial, especially when there is a class with lots of bickering. You can help kids see they can help each other. We were provided with cooperative frames rather than competitive games and it has made a difference in my classes.

B11: We learned how to be resourceful in using our schools and communities. It gave us a boost and a confidence to go out and do that.

A1: I liked the principles of brain-based learning and found ways to teach things from that perspective. Because we were taught that way and the instructor modeled it through a variety of ways, I could then connect things to my own experiences and that helped me have more ideas.

B13: Yeah, the brain-based learning and cognitive systems really caught my attention. It meant something to me personally. Through my reflective journal I learned a lot about myself. It occurred to me if I felt this way, perhaps my students felt the same way. It altered the way I might respond to a child, especially in terms of following through on work and behavior. I also learned from talking to parents. You know things theoretically, but then it's real. Now I have to figure out how to bring all this back to the classroom.

Answers:

The codes are intended as examples. Different researchers may come up with different names for concepts contained in the transcripts.

Comment	Code
B2	Practical application, modeling
A2	Teamwork/cooperation
B11	Connection to community
A1	Brain-based learning, modeling, self-reflection
B13	Brain-based learning, self-reflection

SUMMARIZING

Once all data are sorted into major and minor categories, look at the range of categories and see whether some fit together into themes. For example, in the partial transcript above, there are a number of categories that might be combined into a theme called "connecting." The next step is to summarize; here you begin to see what is in the data. Examine all entries with the same code and then merge these categories into patterns by finding links and connections among categories. This process further integrates the data, and you can begin to make some statements about relationships and themes in the data. For example, when investigating classroom management in a large high school, you might first code the data into categories dealing with teachers' attitudes, students' attitudes, effects of certain techniques, descriptions of behavior, the setting, and so on. Then summarize by trying to find relationships among the categories. Summarizing is beginning to tell the stories and to make connections among stories. The researcher begins to make meaning of the categories and themes, to connect them. At this stage, connections may be displayed using graphs, charts, concept maps, or other visual representations of the patterns observed. There are two widely used strategies in qualitative analysis that we will discuss as part of summarizing and interpreting qualitative data: constant comparison and negative case analysis.

Perhaps the best known qualitative analysis strategy is the **constant comparative method**, which combines inductive category coding with simultaneous comparison of all units of meaning obtained (Glaser & Strauss, 1967). The researcher examines each new unit of meaning (topics or concepts) to determine its distinctive characteristics. Then he or she compares categories and groups them with similar categories. If there are no similar units of meaning, form a new category. Thus, there is a process of continuous refinement; initial categories may be changed, merged, or omitted; new categories are generated; and new relationships can be discovered (Goertz & LeCompte, 1993). Figure 16.3 illustrates the constant comparative method of data analysis. See Chapter 9 of Maykut and Morehouse (1994) for an excellent discussion of how to apply the constant comparative method of data analysis. The book by Miles and Huberman (1994) is also a useful reference for qualitative data analysis.

Another approach used in analysis is the **negative case analysis** or **discrepant data analysis**. Look for data that are negative or discrepant from the main body of data collected. Negative cases contradict the main category or pattern, and discrepant cases provide a different perspective on a category or pattern. This approach provides a counterbalance to a researcher's tendency to hold on to first impressions or hunches. Some researchers revise based on these instances; others go with the substantial accumulation of positive instances.

Once data have been completely analyzed and themes developed, the next step is **interpretation**, going beyond the descriptive data to extract meaning and insights from the data. You state what you found that was important, why it is important, and what can be learned from it.

INTERPRETING DATA

Interpreting involves reflecting about the words and acts of the study's participants and abstracting important understandings from them. It is an inductive

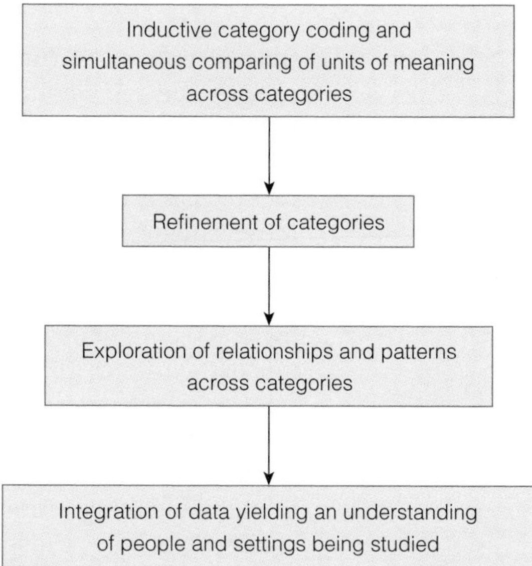

Figure 16.3 Constant Comparative Method of Data Analysis

Source: Maykut and Morehouse (1994, p. 135).

process in which you make generalizations based on the connections and common aspects among the categories and patterns. You evaluate the plausibility of some of the hypotheses that have evolved during the analysis. Hypotheses are tested by going through the data again and searching for supporting data as well as negative or deviant cases.

Interpreting qualitative data is difficult because there are no set rules to follow. The quality of the interpretation depends on the background, perspective, knowledge, and theoretical orientation of the researcher and the intellectual skills he or she brings to the task. Unlike quantitative research, there are no statistical tests of significance to facilitate interpretation of qualitative data. In interpreting qualitative data you confirm what you already know is supported by the data, you question what you think you know and eliminate misconceptions, and you illuminate new insights and important things that you did not know but should have known.

Although interpretation is personal and proceeds without set rules, this does not mean that the qualitative researcher can rely strictly on personal feelings when interpreting the data. The interpretation cannot be just a figment of your imagination but must be supported by the data. The following excerpt from a qualitative study of teacher relationships with at-risk students (Hughes, 1997, pp. 83–97) demonstrates how qualitative data are interpreted.

> The research design began with the selection of four teachers to be primary subjects. Two of the teachers chosen are highly successful in working with at-risk students and the other two teachers have not been successful with at-risk students.
>
> My first less successful (LS) teacher, Paul S., is a veteran teacher. Paul teaches eighth-grade social studies in a traditional style. A daily lesson begins with a 10-

to 15-minute lecture and then the students are to complete a worksheet. Paul considers the book supplied by the school to be "too hard" for the students, so his curriculum is based on a series of worksheets that he writes or copies from printed curriculum. He describes his teaching style as "aided practice with minimal evaluations." He believes that students should be homogeneously grouped. This belief contradicts the district and school policy of heterogeneously grouped students in academic teams. He feels that because students are not grouped by levels, he is unable to teach effectively. Therefore, Paul gears his curriculum toward the low-performing students.

> SHERRY (researcher): How would you describe the effectiveness of your teaching style?
>
> PAUL: For what I have to work with, the attitudes and work habits, I think my teaching style is about the best we can do.

The class sits in rows and the room has a very clean, neat appearance. The bulletin boards are covered with class schedules and administrative bulletins. On the front board hang discipline charts for each class period. The only posters that hang in the room are two computer-printed banners stating the district's theme for the academic year, "Let's Make It Happen!" These banners became somewhat ironic as I learned about Paul's methodology. Paul believes that "There isn't a way to have a successful class with these types of students." He also believes that if a student does not come to school with their "head on right," well-fed, well-rested, prepared for class, and open to learning, then that student should be removed from the classroom.

> SHERRY: What disciplinary procedures achieve appropriate behavior in your classroom?
>
> PAUL: Not that much works. Good teachers aren't in inner-city schools. . . .
>
> PAUL: I have gone to a survival mode, what can I do to get through the day and eliminate damage control? Just survive.

The students interviewed showed little or no respect for either L.S. teacher. Students claimed that they and other students intentionally made fun of and acted defiant in the classroom of the two L.S. subjects.

> SHERRY: What kinds of things did you do in his (Paul's) class?
>
> STUDENT: Throw paper airplanes.

As this example illustrates, reports of qualitative studies present the natural language of the study's participants as drawn from interview data and observation, along with rich descriptions of the setting. The example continues with the researcher providing the reader with an account of a successful teacher of at-risk students:

Jane currently teaches eighth-grade social studies. Jane claims that there are "no typical days in her classroom." She does a variety of assignments including book work, reading maps, class discussions, and making three-dimensional models.

> SHERRY: What do you consider your students' role to be in your classroom?
>
> JANE: They are the workers and the learners; they need to be actively involved.

She is always very eager to try new and different ideas. Jane's room was very organized and the place seemed almost like "home." Scattered throughout the room were big round tables that sat four students comfortably. In the front right corner of the room was the "living room." There was a couch, rocking chair, and a bookshelf filled with a variety of books. The walls were very decorative, and the room was covered with affirmative anecdotes or quotes, such as "We can work it out," and the positive consequences of her discipline management plan. During both observations, the agenda for the day and the instructions for the lesson were written in detail on the front board.

Jane is a very positive, upbeat person, and she emphasizes courtesy and respect in her classroom. She rewards students verbally, and also with personal attention. She gives a variety of rewards for perfect attendance, most improved, and good behavior. Jane enjoys being very involved and "hands-on" with students.

SHERRY: Why do you like Ms. Peterson's class?
STUDENT: Because she is nice to me.
SHERRY: Do you like social studies?
STUDENT: No, I just like Ms. Peterson.

TECHNOLOGY IN QUALITATIVE ANALYSIS

Analysis of qualitative data can seem overwhelming. Analysis by hand generally relies on literally cutting and pasting from printed text and the use of color-coded highlighters. Technologies can assist in qualitative research, although they can never replace the human researcher. The computer is a tool that can be used for executing specific mechanical aspects of the research process and to make your work faster, more accurate, and less tedious. But the computer does not think for the researcher. The researcher must decide what to enter into the computer and what to ask the computer to do. The computer cannot reflect or analyze or transform data into meaningful findings. There are no shortcuts to reading, categorizing, and analyzing the data (Kelle, 1995; Weitzman & Miles, 1995).

Using a computer can save an enormous amount of time in compiling and sorting data. For example, you can take a laptop computer into the field to write notes during observations. You can use word processors to transcribe and enter data. Databases and spreadsheets can help sort and organize data. Graphics software can help show visual representations of how data connect. Qualitative analysis software has evolved since the mid-1980s and can assist in five ways:

1. *Data storage and management.* Technology can help with the storage and management of the data. There are software packages where the researcher can enter raw data directly or import data from word-processed documents. Some software will handle visual materials (photographs, diagrams, video, web page links). Most will let you annotate and edit text after it has been entered. Some have indexing capability and allow you to add your own identification information (name, date, etc.) to better organize the data.
2. *Data searching and retrieval.* Searching for and retrieving data can be simplified using technology. Most qualitative analysis software allows you to search text data for particular words or phrases. The programs can count specific words or phrases to assist in analysis. Most use Boolean operators

(and, or, not, etc.) to refine searches, and typically these programs retrieve data in context (e.g., showing you the word within a phrase or paragraph) and include identification codes.

3. *Coding*. Although the human researcher must identify the codes, technology can assist in the mechanics of **coding**. Sections of data can be highlighted in the text and assigned codes. In many widely used qualitative analysis software, coded items are stored as nodes that can be searched like documents and can be given titles and descriptions by the researcher.
4. *Developing and testing theories*. Qualitative software can help in developing theories by helping to show relationships between nodes. Relationships can be displayed through graphical representations. Some use trees that can help provide overviews of how the data are connected.
5. *Writing reports*. Software programs also can be used to produce reports or to create printouts of an entire data set in one node or code, which can then be included verbatim or quotes pulled out to use in the text. Many of the programs include fields for memos as the researcher documents his or her thinking process, and these memos can be printed out and analyzed as well. Forms can also be created in many of the products.

NUD*IST is a well-known qualitative analysis product. Other software packages to help manage and analyze qualitative data include Ethnograph, NVivo, AtlasTi, and HyperQual. However, because technology changes so rapidly, it is not worthwhile to make a recommendation about a particular program here.

Computers have revolutionized the handling and manipulation of qualitative data. But beware of letting the computer guide the analysis rather than the researcher thinking about the data. Some writers in the field believe that computers are most beneficial to the experienced researcher. They believe that to really understand the data, beginning researchers need to "eyeball" and frequently reexamine the data, rather than depend on what the computer provides. An example of using the computer software called NUD*IST (Non-numerical Unstructured Data Indexing Searching and Theory-Building) in a qualitative study can be found in Buston's article in Bryman and Burgess (1999).

RIGOR IN QUALITATIVE RESEARCH

Dey (1993) lists six questions you should ask to check on the quality of your data:

1. Are the data based on your own observation or is it hearsay?
2. Is there corroboration by others of your observations?
3. In what circumstances was an observation made or reported?
4. How reliable are the people providing the data?
5. What motivations might have influenced a participant's report?
6. What biases might have influenced how an observation was made or reported?

These questions seem to refer to whether the data are valid and reliable, or, in other words, is the quality of your data deemed rigorous? Although the terms

Table 16.1 Standards of Rigor for Research

Quantitative	Qualitative	Issue Addressed
Internal validity	Credibility	Truth value
External validity	Transferability	Generalizability
Reliability	Dependability or trustworthiness	Consistency
Objectivity	Confirmability	Neutrality

validity and *reliability* have most commonly been associated with rigor in quantitative research, the concepts of making valid inferences from data and the consistency of the data are also important issues in qualitative research. As you will see, qualitative researchers use different terms to apply to these criteria. Although the underlying concepts related to rigor are similar, there are differences in the nature of the data and the philosophical assumptions upon which quantitative and qualitative research are based that have led to different terminologies. We will discuss the qualitative terms most commonly used to address these issues of rigor and then discuss strategies used in qualitative research to address concerns. Sometimes a single strategy may address more than one issue of rigor. Table 16.1 summarizes the standards of rigor used in quantitative and qualitative research and the issues of rigor addressed.

CREDIBILITY

Validity cannot be taken for granted. It is relative—related to the purpose and circumstances of the research.

The integrity of qualitative research depends on attending to the issue of validity. Validity concerns the accuracy or truthfulness of the findings. The term most frequently used by qualitative researchers to refer to this characteristic is **credibility**. How confident can you be in the researcher's observations, interpretations, and conclusions? Are they believable (credible)?

Credibility in qualitative research concerns the truthfulness of the inquiry's findings. Credibility or truth value involves how well the researcher has established confidence in the findings based on the research design, participants, and context. The researcher has an obligation to represent the realities of the research participants as accurately as possible and must provide assurances in the report that this obligation was met.

Hammersley (1992) noted that "an account is valid or true if it represents accurately those features of the phenomena that it is intended to describe, explain, or theorize" (p. 69). Krefting (1991) suggests that a qualitative study is considered credible when it "presents such accurate descriptions or interpretations of human experience that people who also share that experience would immediately recognize the description" (p. 215). The term *credibility* in qualitative research is analogous to internal validity in quantitative research.

A number of methods have been identified in the literature for enhancing the credibility (internal validity) of qualitative studies. These methods may be categorized according to five types of evidence: structural corroboration, consensus, referential or interpretive adequacy, theoretical adequacy, and control of bias.

Evidence Based on Structural Corroboration

Eisner (1998) defines **structural corroboration** as a "means through which multiple types of data are related to each other to support or contradict the interpretation and evaluation of a state of affairs" (p. 110). The use of multiple sources of data, multiple observers, and/or multiple methods is referred to as **triangulation**. Structural corroboration uses different sources of data (**data triangulation**) and different methods (**methods triangulation**). A combination of data sources such as interviews, observations, and relevant documents and the use of different methods increase the likelihood that the phenomenon under study is being understood from various points of view. In *data triangulation*, the researcher investigates whether the data collected with one procedure or instrument confirm data collected using a different procedure or instrument. The researcher wants to find support for the observations and conclusions in more than one data source. Convergence of a major theme or pattern in the data from these various sources lends credibility to the findings. *Methods triangulation* uses more than one method (e.g., ethnography and document analysis) in the study. The assumption is that the combination of methods results in better evidence. When these different procedures or different data sources are in agreement, there is corroboration. For example, when interviews, related documents, and recollections of other participants produce the same description of an event or when a participant responds similarly to a question asked on three different occasions, one has evidence of credibility.

Evidence Based on Consensus

Validity based on **consensus** is defined as "agreement among competent others that the description, interpretation, evaluation, and thematics" are right (Eisner, 1998, p. 112). This type of validity is primarily demonstrated through two methods: **peer review** and **investigator triangulation**. In peer review, also called **peer debriefing**, the question is asked, "Given the evidence presented, is there consensus in the interpretation?" Colleagues or peers are provided with the raw data along with the researcher's interpretation or explanation. Discussions then determine whether the reviewer(s) considers the interpretation to be reasonable, given the evidence. Reviewers may identify problems in the interpretation and stress the need for additional data. Investigator triangulation involves having multiple researchers collect data independently and compare the collected data (Johnson & Christensen, 2000). The key questions here are "Did what was reported as taking place actually happen? Did the researcher accurately report what was seen and heard?"

If multiple investigators agree in their description of the context, in their description of events, and in their reporting of what was said, internal validity is enhanced. Using investigator triangulation makes it less likely that outside reviewers of the research will question the data. Several human instruments working together are usually better than one; furthermore, team members act as peer reviewers or "peer debriefers," keeping one another honest (Lincoln & Guba, 1985). A beginning researcher who must work alone on a dissertation can ask an outside person to be a debriefer; that is, the outsider can go through the researcher's data periodically and point out bias when necessary.

Evidence Based on Referential or Interpretive Adequacy

Referential or **interpretive evidence** of validity refers to "accurately portraying the meaning attached by participants to what is being studied by the researcher" and "the degree to which the participants' viewpoints, thoughts, feelings, intentions, and experiences are accurately understood . . . and portrayed" (Johnson & Christensen, 2000, p. 209). Two primary strategies are used to enhance **referential adequacy**: member checks and low-inference descriptors.

Member checks (participant feedback) ask the question "Do the people that were studied agree with what you have said about them?" At the end of the data collection period, the researcher may ask participants to review and critique field notes or tape recordings for accuracy and meaning. Or the researcher's sharing his or her interpretations of the data with the participants can help clear up miscommunication, identify inaccuracies, and help obtain additional useful data. In member checks, the researcher solicits feedback from the participants themselves about the study's findings. Has the researcher accurately described and interpreted their experience? Feedback from the participants may help the researcher gain further insight and/or call attention to something that he or she missed. Furthermore, through member checking, the researcher demonstrates courtesy to the participants by letting them see what has been written about them.

Using many **low-inference descriptors** such as verbatim or direct quotations helps the reader experience the participants' world. Using tape recorders or video cameras enables the researcher to use these descriptors. **Thick, rich description** also helps the research convey an understanding of the study's context. These descriptions are very detailed, helping the reader "see" the setting, or if reporting themes from interviews, using the actual words of the respondents.

Evidence Based on Theoretical Adequacy

Theoretical adequacy or **plausibility** concerns the degree to which a theoretical explanation developed from the study fits the data (Johnson & Christensen, 2000, p. 210) and is defensible. There are three key strategies for promoting theoretical adequacy: extended fieldwork, theory triangulation, and pattern matching.

Extended fieldwork provides time for the researcher to observe a full range of activities in order to identify patterns and relationships and their typicality, which will contribute to valid interpretations. An extended time in the research setting enables the researcher to gain the participants' trust and thus to obtain more detailed and honest responses. Credibility is threatened by errors in data collection caused by participants providing socially acceptable responses or acting differently because of the researcher's presence. Use of extended fieldwork can reduce this possibility because it provides the researcher more opportunities to check perspectives and allows informants to become accustomed to the researcher's presence.

Theory triangulation involves consideration of how the phenomenon under study might be explained by multiple theories. Considering different theories, the researcher may gain better insights. **Interdisciplinary triangulation** uses other disciplines to infer processes and understandings of the findings.

Pattern matching involves making predictions based on theory and testing those predictions. Based on theory, the researcher predicts a certain pattern of results. Then the researcher determines the degree to which the patterns found in the data match the predicted pattern. If the predictions occur, the researcher has strong evidence to support his or her explanations.

Evidence Based on Control of Bias

Researcher bias is a source of invalidity in qualitative studies. Bias may result from selective observations, hearing only what one wants to hear, or allowing personal attitudes, preferences, and feelings to affect interpretation of data. Krefting (1991) writes, "Paradoxically, a major threat to the truth value of a qualitative study lies in the closeness of the relationship between the investigator and the informants that can develop during the prolonged contact required to establish credibility" (p. 219). The most common strategy to control for bias in qualitative studies is reflexivity. **Reflexivity** is the use of self-reflection to recognize one's own biases and to actively seek them out. Krefting (1991) suggests that the researcher keep a reflective journal that includes three types of information: a daily schedule with logistics of the study, a methods log where the researcher describes decisions and the rationale for them, and reflections of the researcher's thoughts, feelings, ideas, questions, concerns, problems, and frustrations. Denzin and Lincoln (1998) refer to a reflective account of the research process and the researcher's perspective as "an explicit statement about where the author is coming from" and "the ethnographic version of truth in advertising" (p. 294). The researcher should refer to his or her journal reflections during the process of data analysis.

Another strategy used to control for bias is **negative case sampling**, where researchers intentionally seek examples that "disconfirm their expectations and explanations" (Johnson & Christensen, 2000, p. 207). Actively seeking information that is the opposite of what you expect makes it more difficult to ignore certain information. To avoid the appearance of bias, researchers should show that they have looked for and explained any discrepant or contradictory data. Johnson and Christensen (2000, p. 212) describe the role of the researcher as a detective, examining each clue and attempting to rule out alternative explanations until the case is made "beyond a reasonable doubt." Table 16.2 summarizes the strategies used for enhancing credibility in qualitative studies.

TRANSFERABILITY

Transferability is the degree to which the findings of a qualitative study can be applied or generalized to other contexts or to other groups. In quantitative research, the term *external validity* is used to refer to the generalizability of the findings. Although the qualitative researcher typically does not have generalizability as a goal, it is his or her responsibility to provide sufficiently rich, detailed, thick descriptions of the context so that potential users can make the necessary comparisons and judgments about similarity and hence transferability. This is referred to as **descriptive adequacy**. The researcher must strive to provide accu-

Table 16.2 Approaches to Enhancing Credibility in Qualitative Studies

Criterion	Strategies
Structural corroboration	Methods triangulation Data triangulation
Consensus	Peer review/peer debriefing Investigator triangulation
Referential or interpretive adequacy	Member checks/participant feedback Low-inference descriptors/thick rich description
Theoretical adequacy	Extended fieldwork Theory triangulation Interdisciplinary triangulation Pattern matching
Control of bias	Reflexivity Negative case sampling

rate, detailed, and complete descriptions of the context and participants to assist the reader in determining transferability.

Qualitative inquirers argue that it is possible to apply qualitative findings to other people, settings, and times to the extent that they are *similar* to the people, settings, and times in the original study. Transferability of a set of findings to another context depends on the **similarity** or "goodness of fit" between the context of the study and other contexts. The transfer is made by the potential user of the findings, who must compare and decide on the similarity of the two contexts. This contrasts with quantitative research, where the original researcher makes generalizations. One strategy to enhance transferability is to include **cross-case comparisons**. The researcher may investigate more than one case. If findings are similar, this would increase the possibility of transferability of findings to other settings or contexts. In some cases, even a single case can be compared with other cases in the published literature that might demonstrate transferability.

Be aware that there are threats to transferability, such as *selection effects* (the fact that the constructs being investigated are unique to a single group), *setting effects* (the fact that results may be a function of the specific context under investigation), and *history effects* (the fact that unique historical experiences of the participants may militate against comparisons) (Goetz & LeCompte 1993). The researcher should recognize limitations of the study in the description. Detailing of circumstances helps the reader to understand the nature of the data and what might be peculiar to your particular study.

Reactivity (the effect of the research itself) might also limit transferability. While eliminating the influence of the researcher may be impossible in a qualitative study as the researcher is the key data collection instrument, the researcher can help the reader understand the potential influence by describing his or her own biases through a reflective statement and providing detailed descriptions of such things as observation strategies and interview questions. Reactivity is a more serious threat in studies using interview techniques. Table 16.3 summarizes the strategies used to enhance transferability.

Table 16.3 Approaches to Enhancing Transferability in Qualitative Studies

Criterion	Strategies
Descriptive adequacy	Thick, rich description
Similarity	Cross-case comparisons Literature comparisons Describing limitations
Limiting reactivity	Reflective statement Detailed description of methods

DEPENDABILITY

Qualitative researchers speak of **dependability** rather than *reliability*. Recall that reliability in quantitative research has to do with consistency of behavior, or the extent to which data and findings would be similar if the study were replicated. However, unlike quantitative research, where tight controls enhance replicability, qualitative studies expect variability because the context of studies changes. Thus, consistency is looked at as the extent to which variation can be tracked or explained. This is referred to as *dependability or* **trustworthiness**. Some strategies to investigate dependability are using an audit trail, replication logic, stepwise replication, code–recoding, interrater comparisons, and triangulation. To enhance reliability, the researcher wants to demonstrate that the methods used are reproducible and consistent, that the approach and procedures used were appropriate for the context and can be documented, and that external evidence can be used to test conclusions.

Documentation

One of the best ways to establish dependability is to use an **audit trail**. Audit trails provide a mechanism by which others can determine how decisions were made and the uniqueness of the situation. It documents how the study was conducted, including what was done, when, and why. The audit trail contains the raw data gathered in interviews and observations, records of the inquirer's decisions about whom to interview or what to observe and why, files documenting how working hypotheses were developed from the raw data and subsequently refined and tested, the findings of the study, and so forth. The researcher must keep thorough notes and records of activities and should keep data well organized and in a retrievable form. He or she should provide information on the sample of people studied, the selection process, contextual descriptions, methods of data collection, detailed field notes, tape-recordings, videotapes, and other descriptive material that can be reviewed by other people. Using the audit trail as a guide, an independent, third-party auditor can examine the inquirer's study in order to attest to the dependability of procedures employed and to examine whether findings are confirmable, that is, whether they are logically derived from and grounded in the data that were collected (Schwandt & Halpern, 1988). A complete presentation of procedures and results enables the reader to make a judgment about the replicability of the research within the limits of the natural context.

Table 16.4 Approaches to Enhancing Dependability in Qualitative Studies

Criterion	Strategies
Documentation	Audit trail
Consistent findings	Replication logic
	Stepwise replication
Coding agreement	Code–recode/intrarater agreement
	Interrater/interobserver agreement
Corroboration	Data triangulation
	Methods triangulation

Consistent Findings

Dependability can be demonstrated by showing consistent findings across multiple settings or multiple investigators. **Replication logic**, which involves conducting the study in multiple locations or with multiple groups, is suggested for determining dependability of a study (Johnson & Christensen, 2000). According to this logic, the more times a finding is found true with different sets of people or in different settings and time periods, the more confident the researcher can be in the conclusions. **Stepwise replication** is another technique suggested for enhancing dependability. In this strategy, two investigators divide the data, analyze it independently, and then compare results. Consistency of results provides evidence of dependability.

Coding Agreement

Intrarater and interrater agreement are strategies for assessing dependability (reliability). An intrarater method is the *code–recode* strategy: A researcher codes the data, leaves the analysis for a period of time, then comes back and recodes the data and compares the two sets of coded materials.

Because much qualitative research involves observation by multiple observers, some researchers suggest **interrater** or **interobserver agreement** methods for assessing dependability. For example, a researcher might randomly select a transcript and ask a peer to code the transcript using the coding labels identified by the researcher. The second coder would be free to add other codes he or she might identify. After the peer completes coding of the transcripts, the results are compared to the original coded transcript to see whether both coders labeled components of the transcript the same.

Corroboration

Triangulation, which we have previously discussed, is also used to establish the dependability of qualitative studies. If multiple data sources or multiple methods result in similar findings, it enhances the reliability of the study. Table 16.4 summarizes strategies to enhance dependability in qualitative studies.

Table 16.5 Approaches to Enhancing Confirmability in Qualitative Research

Criterion	Strategy
Documentation	Audit trail
Corroboration	Triangulation
	Peer review
Control of bias	Reflexivity

CONFIRMABILITY

Confirmability in qualitative research is the same as the quantitative researcher's concept of objectivity. Both deal with the idea of **neutrality** or the extent to which the research is free of bias in the procedures and the interpretation of results. Because it may be impossible to achieve the levels of objectivity that quantitative studies strive for, qualitative researchers are concerned with whether the data they collect and the conclusions they draw would be confirmed by others investigating the same situation. Thus, in qualitative studies, the focus shifts from the neutrality of the researcher to the confirmability of the data and interpretations.

The *audit trail* is the main strategy for demonstrating confirmability. By providing a complete audit trail, the researcher enables another researcher to arrive or not arrive at the same conclusions given the same data and context. Other strategies used to enhance confirmability include triangulation of methods, peer review, and reflexivity—all discussed earlier in this chapter. Table 16.5 summarizes the strategies used to enhance confirmability.

In summary, support for validity and reliability of qualitative studies requires well-documented research and rich description. Mischler (1990) makes an interesting point when he suggests that the ultimate test of the worth of a qualitative study is whether people believe the findings strongly enough to act on them. That is, do other researchers rely on the findings for their own work or do people outside of the research endeavor make decisions based on the findings? Two notable examples of studies that satisfy this criterion are William Perry's (1970) Harvard investigation of intellectual and ethical development during the college years. This study resulted in the formation of a useful (and well known) epistemological theory and paved the way for many additional studies of adult thought and development. Belenky and associates' (1986) investigation of the intellectual development of women has stimulated a great deal of research. Their findings on gender differences in how knowledge is received and integrated influenced some colleges to reconstruct their curriculum.

Finally, as you consider rigor in qualitative research, Daniel and Onwuegbuzie (2002) suggest that you ask these questions:

1. Have you shown the cohesiveness of the evidence? Are related pieces of data used to form a narrative argument and examined collectively to form evidence of cohesiveness?

THINK ABOUT IT 16.4

For each strategy listed, indicate which concern related to rigor it will help address. Note that some strategies address more than one concern.

1. Audit trail
2. Cross case comparisons
3. Data triangulation
4. Extended fieldwork
5. Interrater agreement
6. Investigator triangulation
7. Member checks
8. Methods triangulation
9. Negative case sampling
10. Peer debriefing
11. Reactivity
12. Thick, rich description

Answers

Answers are contained in the tables in this chapter.

2. Have data inconsistencies been examined? Have you looked consciously for negative cases and inconsistencies in findings?
3. Have you considered alternate explanations? Are there contradictions in the broader patterns within the data in which data from one source do not line up with data from another? Might such contradictions indicate systematic misunderstandings of the data or suggest a need to develop a new theory?
4. Do you have confidence (surety) in the results? Have your data been recorded accurately and have codes been applied uniformly and consistently?
5. Have you achieved the elusive goal of data collection? In positivist research this refers to obtaining an accurate understanding of the true score. In qualitative research, the question is whether you have accurately captured the social understanding or social reality underlying events, activities, and behaviors.
6. Is there adequacy of evidence? Similar to the positivist concept of domain sampling, what is the degree to which narrative descriptions provide an adequate view of the social phenomena of interest. Is there adequate thickness of description?

QUALITATIVE REPORTING

Remember that the purpose of the report is to make clear to others what you studied, how you studied it, what you observed, and how you interpreted it. The last step for the qualitative researcher is to write about what he or she saw, heard, and now understands about the phenomenon that was investigated.

TYPICAL REPORT COMPONENTS

The procedure used most frequently by qualitative researchers is reporting by themes, topics, or cases and demonstrating these through descriptive detail. If you have written a good proposal prior to beginning the research, you already have information that can be used in the final report. For example, the proposal contains the problem statement and the methods section, which you can expand to include any further sampling and data collection procedures that were used. Qualitative reports generally include the following elements (or some variation of them):

1. Abstract
2. Introduction
3. Research design, steps to ensure credibility (validity) and dependability (reliability)
4. Methods, site and sample selection, data collection methods, data analysis procedures
5. Findings
6. Interpretations and implications
7. References
8. Appendix

Abstract

An abstract is a very brief summary of the major aspects of the qualitative inquiry: problem, design, methods, and outcomes. Complete and concise abstracts are very helpful to readers who are conducting literature reviews.

Introduction

In the introduction, the writer states the purpose of the research study and provides the reader with some background of the problem and the need for the study. State the focus of inquiry as a question or a statement. Indicate how you became interested in the topic and how the question evolved. Present and discuss any relevant research in this section because, typically, there is not a separate section for review of the literature. The introduction in a qualitative report may also contain an interesting story or quote to capture the reader's interest. In addition, the researcher's preliminary biases or suppositions should be revealed.

Research Design

In the section on research design, explain the qualitative approach used and why you chose it to investigate the problem. Also discuss the steps taken to ensure credibility, dependability, transferability, and confirmability of the study, such as triangulation, audit trail, member checks, and so forth. It is important to describe how bias was controlled and what the limitations are of the study.

Methods

In the methods section, describe the research method that was followed to arrive at the findings. The reader should not have to wonder about what was done, to whom, or how it was done. Some aspects to cover in separate parts of the methods section are as follows.

Site and Sample Selection The researcher describes the site of the study and the participants involved. The investigator describes the participants demographically, how they were selected, and how entry was gained into the site; gives a detailed description of the site; and so on. Researchers generally use fictitious names of people and places to protect the privacy of the participants and the site.

Data Collection Methods The section on data collection methods describes the methods used to gather the data (interviews, observation, document analysis, and so on) and explains why these methods were chosen. Because the *main* instrument in qualitative research is the human instrument, it is important that the writer give some personal or professional information about him- or herself that might be relevant to the inquiry. A complete discussion of the methodology is essential so that readers of the report can understand how the researcher reached conclusions and can agree or disagree with those conclusions.

Data Analysis Procedures The researcher should describe the approach taken in the analysis of the data. If you used the constant comparative procedure, for example, make this explicit.

Findings

This section contains the major findings or propositions relevant to the original focus of inquiry that are revealed in the data. Findings may be reported by data collection method (survey, interviews, documents, etc.), by cases (School 1, School 2, etc.) or by theme or topics (real-world connections, active learning, extrinsic rewards, etc.). Because of the massive amount of data in a qualitative inquiry, you cannot report everything you found. In fact, Wolcott (1990) has said that the real challenge for qualitative researchers is deciding what *not* to include in their reports. The researcher must rank the outcomes primarily on the basis of their relevance and significance. Use direct quotes and field note excerpts to illustrate the outcomes of the study and to help the reader to vicariously experience the research setting and to better understand how the conclusions were reached. Unlike quantitative research, this section also includes your interpretations of the data. You may also relate findings to the literature.

Interpretations and Implications

In the final section, you respond to the implicit question, So what? Here the researcher tries to make sense of the findings. You interpret what you have found. You discuss the meaning of the outcomes reported in the previous section and state major conclusions and implications of the study. You should relate the study to previous research and suggest directions for future research efforts. This is also the section where new or integrating theories may be proposed.

References

A complete alphabetical listing of all works cited in the report is presented in the reference section of the report.

Appendix

The appendix includes interview schedules and other documentation that will help the reader understand the report.

Reports of qualitative inquiry will, of course, vary in form depending on the nature of the publication in which they appear (e.g. an article prepared for the *American Educational Research Journal* will differ from a monograph or book-length study). It will be helpful to the student who is writing a qualitative report to look at journal articles to see how the reports are organized. Some suggested journals that publish qualitative research include: *The International Journal of Qualitative Studies in Education, Qualitative Inquiry*, and *The Qualitative Report* (an online journal).

WRITING STYLE IN QUALITATIVE REPORTS

Writing is extremely important in qualitative research. Qualitative reports are generally heavily narrative in form and contain rich descriptions of setting and context. This "thick description" is intended to place the reader vividly in the research setting so that the reader can follow the logical processes that the researcher went through in collecting the data. The role of the writer is to "tell the story the data tell." In contrast to the more technical and structured style of quantitative reports, a qualitative report is more like a story, with very little, if any, technical language. A qualitative report may not follow a conventional organizational format. Literature may not be found in a separate section of the report but may be woven into the findings with the themes identified from the current study connected to the work of others.

The approaches to writing a qualitative report vary. Some are more journalistic in style, interpreting the connections among events and people. Some approach it as a translator would, interpreting others' worlds. Some appear as realist tales presenting observations and descriptions in great detail. Some may appear as a historical report, following a chronology. Some may read as confessional tales from the author's viewpoint. Some use techniques found in drama and other artistic modes.

Qualitative reports convey the participants' thoughts, feelings, and experiences in their own words as much as possible. Note that it is acceptable in qualitative reports for writers to refer to themselves in the first person, to distinguish their opinions from those of the participants. More recently, qualitative reports are incorporating visual representations (computer-generated graphics, pictures, videos, audio, etc.) as well as relying extensively on quotes to help the reader "see" and "experience" the participants' world.

Dey (1993) says that writing a qualitative report is like telling a story with a setting, characters, and a plot that unfolds toward some resolution. Dey provides six guidelines for writing the report:

1. Engage interest through description and dramatization.
2. Trace the evolution of the account.
3. Develop overall coherence.

4. Select key themes.
5. Use simple language.
6. Make concepts and connections explicit.

EVALUATING QUALITATIVE REPORTS

The following are some of the criteria used to evaluate qualitative reports:

1. Is the research question stated, and does the researcher make clear the conceptual and theoretical framework for the study?
2. Does the researcher show the relationship between the study and previous studies? Are there links to what is known in the literature?
3. Does the researcher indicate how and why the site and or participants were selected for the study? Does the researcher explain the extent to which participants are representative?
4. Are the data collection methods explained so that the reader can judge if they were adequate and appropriate to the question? Does the researcher explain his or her role as participant observer or nonparticipant observer, interviewer, and so on?
5. Does the researcher explain the data analysis procedures used?
6. Are the strategies used to enhance the credibility, transferability, dependability, and confirmability of the data (i.e., triangulation, audit trail, etc.) described? Are competing hypotheses presented and discussed?
7. Are the descriptive data separate from the interpretations? Is there abundant raw data presented (quotes, etc.) to demonstrate the findings?
8. Is there evidence that the researcher maintained ethical standards? Are personal biases and assumptions expressed? Have steps been taken to guard against value judgments in data collection and analysis?
9. Does the study answer the research question and suggest further questions for investigation?
10. Does the researcher make explicit the theoretical significance of the study?
11. Does the report qualify any generalizations that were made, and does it help the reader see how what was learned might be transferred to another similar situation?
12. Is the study reported in a way that is accessible to others?

Reviewing these questions as you write your own report will help you do a better job.

In 2004, the National Science Foundation produced a report, *Workshop on Scientific Foundations of Qualitative Research* (Ragin, Nagel, & White, 2004), that investigated the characteristics of strong qualitative research and provided recommendations on how to strengthen qualitative methods. Their recommendations (on page 17 of the report) are worth noting here as we conclude this chapter. They indicate that these recommendations should be used both to improve the quality of qualitative proposals and reports and also to evaluate the quality of the research conducted. In strong qualitative research, the researcher should:

- Write clearly and engagingly for a broad audience.
- Situate the research in relationship to existing theory.
- Locate the research in the literature specifying comparable cases and building on others' findings.
- Articulate the potential theoretical contribution by indicating what gaps in theory might be filled.
- Clearly outline the research procedures including details about where, when, who, what, and how the research will be conducted.
- Provide evidence of the project's feasibility, including permission to access the site and human subjects approval.
- Provide a description of the data to be collected including kinds of evidence to be gathered, different modes of data collection, and different places data will be obtained.
- Explain the plan for data analysis, including management of the data and procedures for making sense of the information obtained.
- Describe the strategy to refine concepts and construct theory as the investigation continues.
- Include plans to look for and interpret disconfirming evidence, alternative explanations, and unexpected findings.
- Provide an assessment of the possible impact of the researcher's presence and biography on the research from the point of problem selection through data analysis to address potential bias of results.
- Provide information about replicability and suggest ways others might reproduce the research.
- Describe the data archive (audit trail) that will be left for others to use and how you will maintain confidentiality.

SUMMARY

Qualitative studies typically result in a massive amount of data. Analyzing the data is thus a tedious and time-consuming process. The first step in analysis is to organize the data by looking for words, phrases, and events that appear regularly and putting those with similar units of meaning into a category. This continues until one has a set of categories that provide a reasonable reconstruction of the data collected. Next the researcher compares and tries to find connections and common themes among the categories. Interpretation is a highly personal activity in which the researcher explains the meaning of the data and why it is important.

Using thick, rich description, the qualitative researcher writes a narrative report of what was learned in the study. The exact format of the report depends on the nature of the report—whether it is a dissertation, journal article, or perhaps a presentation.

Validity and reliability are important in qualitative as well as quantitative research. Qualitative researchers use the terms credibility, transferability, dependability, and confirmability instead of internal validity, external validity, reliability, and objectivity, respectively. A variety of methods are used to support the validity and reliability of qualitative data and its interpretation. These include peer review, member checks, triangulation, maintaining an audit trail, seeking negative case evidence, and keeping a research journal.

Qualitative reports are written differently in style than quantitative reports, but many of the components covered are similar. Both pose research questions, connect the research to the literature, describe methods of collecting and analyzing data, present findings, and discuss the implications of the study. Many of the criteria for evaluating the quality of qualitative research are also appropriate in quantitative research.

KEY CONCEPTS

audit trail
category
coding
confirmability
consensus
constant comparative method
credibility
cross-case comparison
data triangulation
dependability
descriptive adequacy
discrepant data analysis
extended fieldwork
familiarization
interdisciplinary triangulation
interpretation
interrater agreement
intrarater agreement
investigator triangulation
low-inference descriptors
member checks
methods triangulation
negative case analysis
negative case sampling
neutrality
pattern matching
peer debriefing
peer review
plausibility
reactivity
referential adequacy
reflexivity
replication logic
researcher bias
similarity
stepwise replication
structural corroboration
theoretical adequacy
theory triangulation
thick description
transferability
triangulation
trustworthiness

EXERCISES

1. Explain how data analysis in qualitative and quantitative studies differs.
2. Briefly describe the constant comparative method for analyzing qualitative data.
3. One of the criticisms of qualitative research is that it is subject to bias. Do you agree? What does the qualitative researcher do to rebut this kind of criticism?
4. Would you agree with a friend who believes a qualitative study would be easier for a dissertation than a quantitative study? What are some differences you might point out?
5. How does a qualitative report differ from a report of quantitative research?
6. What is the first step the researcher should take in analyzing qualitative data?
7. What are the three levels of qualitative data analysis?
8. What are the different types of triangulation that can be used to enhance the rigor of a qualitative study?
9. What terms are used in qualitative inquiry to refer to issues of internal and external validity?
10. Name and describe at least two strategies that can be used to enhance the dependability (reliability) of a qualitative study?
11. Describe one strategy for controlling researcher bias in a qualitative study?
12. What is the difference between a member check and a peer debriefing?

ANSWERS

1. Data analysis in qualitative research is inductive; it is a process of categorizing data that are in the form of words, synthesis, and finding meaning. Data analysis in quantitative research is deductive; it involves testing hypotheses using numerical data and statistical tests.
2. It is a process in which the researcher takes each new unit of meaning and compares it to other units of meaning (categories) and then groups it with categories that are similar. It is a way to reduce the data and make it more manageable and conducive to interpretation.
3. A number of procedures are used to contribute to a credible study. Among them are triangulation, audit trails, member checks, and working with a team (using more than one human instrument is better than one).
4. Answers will vary. In some ways, qualitative research may be more difficult than quantitative research: The design is much less prescriptive and structured, data collection is time consuming, and data analysis is more tedious and involved. Writing a qualitative report is likely to take much more time than writing a quantitative report. One aspect that may make qualitative research easier for some is the lack of statistics.
5. A qualitative report is narrative in form, rich with descriptions, quotations, and so forth. One can use the first person, which is never used in quantitative reporting.
6. The researcher should begin by familiarizing him or herself with the data by reading and rereading transcripts, listening to audiotapes, or watching videos.
7. Data pieces, categories (minor), and themes (major).
8. Data triangulation, methods triangulation, investigator triangulation.
9. Credibility and transferability.
10. Answers may vary. Examples include audit trail, replication logic, and intra- and interrater agreement.
11. Answers may include reflexivity or negative case sampling.
12. In a member check, the researcher goes back to the participants in the study and asks them to review the findings and conclusions in order to provide a check on whether the researcher "got the story right." In a peer debriefing, the researcher provides the raw data along with interpretations to a second researcher (peer) in order to check whether others would make the same interpretations given the data.

INFOTRAC COLLEGE EDITION

Using the keywords *data analysis* and *qualitative*, locate a qualitative inquiry and read the section describing data analysis. Did the researcher use the steps described in this chapter for organizing and interpreting the data? Did the data support the interpretations?

EXAMPLE OF A QUALITATIVE RESEARCH STUDY

The following article illustrates many aspects of qualitative research. The dissertation on which this article was based won the American Association of College of Teacher Education (AACTE) 2001 Outstanding Dissertation Award.

Toward a prototype of expertise in teaching: A descriptive case study.

Tracy W. Smith and David Strahan

This study used a prototype view of teaching as a theoretical framework to interpret, analyze, and describe the behaviors and verbal responses of three expert teachers and to determine the degree to which these three teachers share a "family resemblance" to one another. A case study that provides descriptions of what expert teachers do and say contributes to our understanding of the complexity of expertise in teaching. Analysis of data collected for this study reveals six central tendencies of the three participants. The rich descriptions and summary representations provide specific and complex profiles to inform teacher educators and professional development providers in their efforts to improve professional practice among teachers.

> The question of what it means to be an expert teacher has taken on some urgency in the nationwide effort to reform public education. If American public schools are to become centers of excellence, then their most important human resource (i.e., teachers) must be effectively developed. To know what we are developing teachers toward, we need a model of teaching expertise.
>
> Sternberg and Horvath (1995)

For centuries, people in all societies and cultures have had an interest in exceptional performance. We have lauded the finest painters, the most outstanding musicians, the strongest athletes, and the greatest scientists. We have marveled at the "gifts" of such outstanding individuals, accepting their talents as anomalous, innate phenomena. In the last 25 years, however, psychologists have begun to study expertise as a cognitive phenomenon.

The study of expertise seems to fascinate us because it speaks to the possibilities of human endeavor. Maslow (1971) expressed it this way:

> If we want to know how fast a human being can run, then it is no use to average out the speed of a "good sample" of the population; it is far better to collect Olympic gold medal winners and see how well they can do. If we want to know the possibilities for spiritual growth, value growth, or moral development in a human being, then I maintain that we can learn most by studying our moral, ethical, or saintly people. . . . Even when "good specimens," the saints and sages and great leaders of history, have been available for study, the temptation too often has been to consider them not human but supernaturally endowed. (p. 7)

Maslow's statement helps to justify an examination of expertise. His statement implies that the lens of supernatural endowment limits our consideration of human potential.

Most studies of expertise in teaching (as well as other domains) have compared the behaviors and performances of novices to those of experts (Berliner, 1988; Carter, Sabers, Cushing, Pinnegar, & Berliner, 1987; Chi, Glaser, & Farr, 1988; Cushing, Sabers, & Berliner, 1992; Glaser, 1984; Gonzalez & Carter, 1996; Livingston & Borko, 1990; Noice & Noice, 1997; Swanson, O'Connor, & Cooney, 1990; van der Mars, Vogler, Darst, & Cusimano, 1991). In addition, many studies rely on experimental or simulated tasks to examine the complexity of expertise (Berliner, 1988; Carter et al., 1987; Chase & Simon, 1973; Cushing et al., 1992; de Groot, 1946/1965; Feltovich, Ford, & Hoffman, 1997; Noice & Noice, 1997). Rather than contrasting two diverse experienced groups, the present study utilized the similarity-based category of experienced experts and a more naturalistic approach to the study of expertise in teaching. Although the participant focus was narrower, the scope of discovery was wider, yielding richer information about a more particular set of participants.

Other studies that have examined the issue of expertise have operationalized expertise as a function of experience (e.g., Gonzalez & Carter, 1996). Since the mid-1980s, expertise has frequently been identified with a certain disposition, particularly that of the reflective practitioner (Schon, 1983, 1987). Still others have developed "checklists" of expert behaviors or dichotomous tables to be used as determinants of expertise or nonexpertise. Sternberg and Horvath (1995) reject these models and suggest that such simple methods cannot measure the complex phenomenon of teaching expertise. They maintain that there is no well-defined standard that all experts meet and that no nonexperts meet Instead, they assert, "Experts bear a *family resemblance* [emphasis added] to one another, and it is their resemblance to one another that structures the category 'expert'" (p. 9). The present study used case study methodology to explore this notion of family resemblance among expert teachers. The researcher's hope is that this study of expertise in teaching will provide a rich description of what it means to be an expert teacher and that such a description will provide direction for teacher educators and those who provide professional development to practicing classroom teachers.

THEORETICAL PERSPECTIVE

Three models of expertise influenced the framework of this study. The first was the standards-based model of the National Board for Professional Teaching Standards (NBPTS). Experts, or accomplished teachers, as they are called by NBPTS, are those who demonstrate accomplished practice in portfolio and assessment center exercises. The standards used to judge teacher practice are content specific and emerged from consensus among practitioners rather than from empirical research. Teachers determined by NBPTS to be accomplished are awarded national certification that is renewable every 10 years. The NBPTS model of expertise was used to select the cases for this study. All three teachers in this study have been certified by NBPTS.

A second model of expertise that influenced this study was the model developed by Hattie, Jaeger, Strahan, and Baker (1998). This model was designed for the purpose of conducting a validation study of certification decisions made by NBPTS. The goal of this study was to determine if teachers certified by NBPTS are different and more expert than those not certified. Based on a synthesis of 134 meta-analyses related to student outcomes and effects of schooling and an extensive review of the literature related to domain-specific expertise, Hattie et al. propose four major attributes of expertise in teaching: content knowledge, pedagogical knowledge, affective attributes, and comparative teaching outcomes. These attributes have been further separated into 13 specific dimensions. Definitions and rubrics were developed for scoring each of these dimensions. The study was conducted by researchers at the Center for Educational Research and Evaluation (CERE) at the University of North Carolina at Greensboro.

In their validity study of the National Board for Professional Teaching Standards' assessments, Hattie et al. (1998) drew heavily from the third model of expertise that influenced this study. This model, the prototype view of teaching expertise, was developed by Sternberg and Horvath (1995). They suggest that one way to talk about the expert category of teaching is in terms of a "*prototype* that represents the central tendency of all the exemplars in the category" (p. 9, emphasis in original). This prototype can serve as the summary representation of a similarity-based category of expertise. Sternberg and Horvath examined psychological research on expert performance in a variety of domains to develop their model of expertise in teaching.

Although the thorough standards and assessment development processes of NBPTS were systematic and rigorous and the comparative practices study of Hattie et al. (1998) seems comprehensive in its identification of comparative teaching practices and outcomes, some would still argue that these models of teacher expertise compromise the complex and holistic nature of teaching. Sternberg and Horvath (1995) call for a "reconceptualization of teaching expertise" in which teaching expertise is viewed as a category that is structured by the similarity of expert teachers to one another rather than by a set of necessary and sufficient features. They further argue that a prototype of teacher expertise can be represented by the central tendencies of teachers in this category. This prototype can serve as the summary representation of a similarity-based category.

The notion of prototype is derived from Rosch's (1973, 1978) cognitive psychology research on natural language concepts. This work postulates that similarity-based categories exhibit a graded structure wherein some category members are better exemplars of the category than are others. The prototype may be thought of as "the central tendency of feature values across all valid members of the category" (Sternberg & Horvath, 1995, p. 10). The greater the similarity between the subject and the prototype, the greater the probability that it belongs to the category.

Sternberg and Horvath have deduced from Rosch's investigations three properties of prototype-centered categories. First, they suggest that different members of a category may resemble the category prototype on different features. Second, they explain that an important property of a prototype model is the differential weighting of features in the computation of the overall similarity to the prototype. Finally, the features that make up a category prototype may be correlated. Whereas most studies using the similarity-based categorization have required subjects to categorize objects such as musical instruments, birds, fruit, or chairs (see Fehr, 1993; Lakoff, 1987), the present study and Sternberg and Horvath (1995) attempt to apply the properties of a prototype-centered system of categorization to the complex notion of expertise in teaching.

Sternberg and Horvath (1995) call their theoretical orientation a synthetic framework meant to stimulate research and debate. The present study is, therefore, an exploration of their framework and the prototype view of expertise in teaching. The rationale for including only National Board Certified Teachers (NBCTs) in this study is to select teachers who have been identified as experts based on a set of established and well-respected professional standards to generate a descriptive prototype of teaching expertise.

The benefits of the prototype model of expertise include the following:

* A prototype view allows a richer, more descriptive, and inclusive understanding of teacher expertise without making everyone a presumptive expert;
* a prototype view provides a basis for understanding of "general factors" in teaching expertise; and
* a prototype view provides a basis for understanding and anticipating social judgments about teaching expertise.

In this study, a prototype view of teaching was used as a theoretical framework with which to interpret, analyze, and describe the classroom behaviors/practices and verbal responses to structured interviews of three expert teachers and to determine the degree to which these three teachers share a family resemblance to one another. The prototype framework was appropriate for this research because it does not segment teaching into distinct or isolated behaviors; rather, it provides a more holistic way to examine the complex nature of expertise in teaching. The bounded system for this collective case study was a group of three North Carolina teachers who have achieved NBPTS certification and who participated in the validity study conducted by the Center for Educational Research and Evaluation.

A case study that provides descriptions of what expert teachers do and say will contribute to our understanding of the complexity of expertise in teaching. In addition, this case study analyzes the notion of a similarity-based, family resemblance view of teaching expertise and will help us consider the applicability (not generalizability) of a prototype model of teaching expertise. The rich descriptions and summary representations provide specific and complex profiles to inform teacher educators and professional development providers in their efforts to improve professional practice among teachers.

RESEARCH QUESTIONS

The following grand tour question guided this study: How are these three teachers similar in terms of their teaching behaviors, practices, and attitudes? Additional research questions evolved during the study. Because the prototype of expertise that would emerge from this research would be communicated verbally with data collected from the participants' school and classroom contexts as well as other self-reported data, their language became very important to the understanding of the nature of expertise. The following questions guided collection and analysis of data:

1. What words and phrases do these teachers use to describe their practice?
2. What meanings do these teachers attach to these descriptions?
3. What concepts related to teaching practice appear for each individual participant?
4. What concepts related to teaching practice appear across participants?
5. How can these concepts be categorized and integrated into a prototype that represents the central tendency of these teachers?

METHODOLOGY

Case study research was chosen as the method of inquiry because it allows the researcher to capture and describe the complexity of real-life events (Stake, 1995; Yin, 1994). Case study represents a disciplined mode of inquiry that can be organized around issues. The case study researcher is charged with the responsibility of conducting an in-depth analysis of a case and may emphasize "episodes of nuance, the sequentiality of happenings in context, [and] the wholeness of the individual" (Stake, 1995, p. xii). This study provides holistic and meaningful descriptions of the pedagogical and affective attributes of the expert teachers who participated in this study as well as a summary representation of the expert prototype that emerged as a result of the data analysis. Case study research is also an appropriate mode of inquiry because a prototype can best be generated from a cross-case analysis. That is, a holistic case approach provides the best path to a descriptive prototype of expertise in teaching.

Participants

The participants are three North Carolina teachers who have achieved National Board certification. One participant is certified in the Early Adolescence/English Language Arts area, and two are certified in the Middle Childhood/Generalist area. All three were classroom teachers in different schools during the 1998–1999 school year.

Data Sources

Data for this study were collected from a variety of sources: preobservation questions, audiotapes of lessons, lesson transcripts, structured interviews, participant surveys, narrative records of classroom observations, live action coding, documented accomplishments artifacts, researcher notes, and e-mail correspondence between the researcher and each participant. These multiple data sources were used to provide a holistic view of each teacher's classroom and behaviors.

Preobservation questions. Preobservation questions were transmitted by facsimile to teachers approximately 2 days prior to the classroom observation. Teachers were asked to respond to general questions related to the lesson to be observed and the context of the unit in which the lesson was being taught (e.g., What are your goals for the lesson we will observe? How do these goals relate to previous lessons? How will you know what to teach next?). Observers reviewed the questions just before the observations began to get a sense of the subject matter being taught.

Audiotapes of lessons. Each lesson was audiotaped to preserve the exact language of the teachers and students. Whereas transcripts provided the more primary medium for analysis of the lessons, audiotapes were also reviewed to examine teacher tone, wait time, and responsiveness to students.

Transcripts of lessons. Lessons were transcribed verbatim from audiotapes. A sophisticated tape recorder and microphone were used to capture the words of students and teachers during the lesson observation.

Structured interviews. An interview protocol (from the Hattie et al., 1998, study) that included questions related to the dimensions of pedagogical content knowledge and affective attributes was used to provide structure and consistency to teacher interviews. The protocol includes items to stimulate think-aloud responses as well as responses to hypothetical and context specific situations. Additional questions ask teachers to talk about their students as a group and as individuals. Three randomly selected students served as subjects of several questions and probes.

Participant (teacher) surveys. A survey consisting of items derived from the Patterns for Adaptive Learning Survey (PALS) and the National Writing Project Survey were administered to candidates. The items on these surveys are related to teacher goal orientation and feedback to students.

Narrative records of classroom observations. During the on-site observations, one observer kept a "running record" of events in the classroom. This observer noted the body language, classroom and teacher movement, facial expressions, and other important information that could not be captured via audiotape.

Observer-participant live-action coding. A second observer used a form to capture specific aspects of the classroom action, including activity, feedback, student behavior, and teacher response. The information that was analyzed in this study included the records related to "type of activity," "feedback," and "teacher response."

Documented accomplishments artifacts. The documented accomplishments responses were prepared by the teachers as they developed their portfolios for National Board certification. One of these artifacts was related to professional service, commitment, and leadership; the other was related to the teachers' efforts to create partnerships with families. The researcher reviewed these documents during open coding as categories were generated for each teacher.

Researcher notes. The researcher kept written records of analysis records and information from telephone conversations with members of the audit panel. Often, the information provided clarity or insight related to data that had already been collected.

E-mail correspondence. As a courtesy, the researcher e-mailed participants about once every 2 weeks to keep them apprised of the progress of the research. Sometimes, the researcher would ask a question or two for clarification or to test alternative explanations for patterns that were emerging in the data.

Analysis of Data

The analytic tools and coding procedures of Strauss and Corbin (1998) seemed appropriate for analyzing the data for this study. Their procedures provide an open analysis approach appropriate to exploratory research such as this case study. They state that they "have something to offer in the way of techniques and procedures to those researchers who want to do qualitative analysis but who do not wish to build theory" (p. x). They suggest that building theory is not the only reason for doing research and that high-level description and what they call "conceptual ordering" are also important to the generation of knowledge.

Tools of analysis. Analysis of data began with the use of questioning. Questions were used to generate ideas or ways of looking at the data. These questions aided in triangulation of data because the stimulus for a question sometimes occurred in one data source while the answer to that question appeared in a different data source. Questions became stimuli for thinking, and they helped the analyst decide what further questions needed to be asked of participants. Additional tools of analysis included analysis of a word, phrase, or sentence and analysis through comparisons (Strauss & Corbin, 1998).

Microanalysis: Coding procedures. Coding of the data for this study began with open coding, which requires that data be broken into discrete parts before being closely examined and compared. The plan was to follow with axial coding and then selective coding. However, as Strauss and Corbin (1998) suggest, the coding process is "dynamic and fluid." The researcher discovered that analysis was recursive rather than linear.

Within-case analysis. For this research, open coding was performed on each individual participant's data set. All relevant data were broken into data "bits" and were grouped by emerging themes. Eventually, these themes led to concepts and categories that were not necessarily conceptually congruent. After concepts and categories were developed, the process began again. The raw data were examined afresh, and each relevant data bit was field under an appropriate concept. Teachers' exact words and observer descriptions of teacher behaviors were filed within each category. Open coding was completed for each participant before any comparisons were attempted across participants.

A validity panel consisting of two university professors (one at the sponsoring institution; one in another state at another university), one National Board Certified teacher, and one school principal periodically reviewed the researcher's data analysis and theme and category generation to assess whether analyses were consistent with the data.

Once the data had been filed for each participant and categories had been developed, the researcher began to draft descriptions of each individual case. The descriptions, although grounded in the data, seemed flat—unlike the classroom instruction and interactions the researcher had observed. The researcher needed a way to synthesize the data again, to pull together all the data that had been broken apart during open coding. Metaphor was suggested as a way to capture the essence of the individual participants (Merriam, 1998; Stake 1995). The categories generated during open coding, once approved by the researcher's validity panel members, were used to brainstorm professions or avocations in contexts outside education. Once a metaphor topic was determined, the researcher used electronic resources, dictionaries, the preponderance of data, and expert interviews to develop metaphors.

Cross-case analysis. During the cross-case analysis, open coding began again. Categories were generated for the collective data set. Again, each data bit was filed appropriately. After all data were filed, the researcher looked for patterns or ways to group the categories.

For the cross-case analysis, the categories for individual participants seemed to cluster naturally into the themes, which were analyzed further after re-examining the raw data. The researcher changed the label to domains, and the final six cross-case synthesis domains were as follows: self, classroom, teacher/student relationships, instructional approach, professional service and leadership, and content.

The researcher reviewed the data again to derive conceptually congruent synthesis statements for each domain. Subtopics (or properties) derived from the summary ideas for each synthesis statement were also determined in this stage of the analysis. From these themes and categories, the researcher developed summary ideas representing syntheses across candidates in each of the themes.

Table 1 provides a summary (crosswalk) of the research questions, data sources, methods of analysis, and timeline for the study.

RESULTS/FINDINGS

The first time I observed Betty Roberts, Jay Burns, and Rebekah Hertz (1) in their classrooms and spoke to them about their teaching practice and their students, I knew that they were excellent teachers. At the time of my first contact with them, they were not yet participants in my study, but I could not help but notice some similarities among them. When I met Betty, it was in the context of the larger study. As I drove away from her school, I wondered if we would even be able to use her data because the audiotape of her lesson was worthless for transcription. She had only a brief whole-class time, and then she worked among her students as they worked in groups. The transcriptionist confirmed my worries—a few typed pages of transcript followed by a note in all caps: "LONG PERIOD OF BACKGROUND NOISE OF CLASSROOM—NOT ABLE TO UNDERSTAND AND TRANSCRIBE ANY ONE VOICE." As a researcher for the larger study, I knew that the lesson transcript was an important data source and that the research design depended on a rich transcript to answer important questions about the teacher's practice. I feared that her case might be dismissed, and I thought that losing this case would be a shame because she was a great teacher. Then, when I visited Jay and Rebekah, a similar thing happened. Each of

Table 1 Relationship between Research Questions, Data Collection, Analysis, and Time Line

Research Question	Data Sources
What words and phrases do these teachers use to describe their practice?	Lesson transcripts Structured interviews Narrative records Preobservation questions Documented accomplishments artifacts Researcher notes
What meanings do these teachers attach to these descriptions?	Structured interviews Lesson transcripts Preobservation questions Researcher notes E-mail responses
What concepts related to teaching practice appear for each individual participant?	Structured interviews Lesson transcripts Preobservation questions Documented accomplishments artifacts
What concepts related to teaching practice appear across participant cases?	Structured interviews Lesson transcripts Preobservation questions Researcher notes
How can these concepts be categorized and integrated into a "prototype that represents the central tendency" of these teachers?	Structured interviews Lesson transcripts Preobservation questions Participant response to prototype

Research Question	Analysis	Time Line
What words and phrases do these teachers use to describe their practice?	Use of questioning Analysis of words and phrases Open coding	July 1999–August 1999
What meanings do these teachers attach to these descriptions?	Analysis of words and phrases Axial coding	July 1999–August 1999
What concepts related to teaching practice appear for each individual participant?	Use of questioning Analysis of words and phrases Open coding Metaphor development	September 1999
What concepts related to teaching practice appear across participant cases?	Systematic comparison Selective coding	September 1999
How can these concepts be categorized and integrated into a "prototype that represents the central tendency" of these teachers?	Writing the story line Integration Selective coding	October 1999

these teachers had only a short whole-class lesson followed by a period of time in which they interacted with students. Then I thought (and panicked), "Didn't they remember we were coming? We told them we would be recording the lesson." But their instructional design seemed natural to them and to their students and did not seem contrived in any way. The students seemed very comfortable working independently and in small groups, frequently receiving feedback from the teacher. During their lessons, I could hardly worry about the audiotapes; I was too busy trying to keep an accurate record of their movement and interaction with students. They moved often and had individual contact with every student in the classroom at least once. When I left Rebekah's school, I began to reflect on the similarities among these three teachers, not just from a data collector's point of view but also from that of a researcher and a former teacher. I wondered what (besides poor transcripts) these teachers had in common and what the poor transcripts might indicate.

During the majority of their class time, all three teachers spent time working directly with students—not making lesson plans or grading papers. The narrative record and coding demonstrate how they spent their time. All three moved among students—bending, leaning, crouching, smiling, and nodding, both enjoying their students and building relationships with them. The interactions between the teachers and their students were driven by the learning activities. They were not asking about their families or their ball games or their homework habits (I found out later that they knew about these things as well); they were asking about their learning and their thinking. They asked different questions of each student and probed each student's responses differently. It was clear that they knew these students well as individuals.

The transcriptionist's note continued to ring in my mind: "NOT ABLE TO UNDERSTAND AND TRANSCRIBE ANY ONE VOICE" (emphasis added.) This note indicated that there were voices in the classroom but that no single voice could be heard over the others. Often, the teacher's voice is central in classrooms, but in these classrooms, students had a shared voice. Perhaps the lack of a "good" audiotape recording was revealing more about these teachers and their classrooms than an hour-long, crystal clear recording ever could. Another similarity I detected among these teachers was that they were "miners." They seemed to believe that students had all they needed to learn with them. The teacher's job was to "mine" it, to discover it, to draw it out for students to see it themselves—to hold it up to the light and examine it. In her preobservation questions, Betty asserted, "I must discover where each child is on his/her educational journey" and "to discover with the children is what I like best." She explained that she was not a stand-up-and-lecture kind of person and that she does not know it all. Instruction in these classrooms was not teacher centered; the focus was on students. The brief, whole-class time and the mining disposition provided initial evidence that Betty, Jay, and Rebekah had a student-centered teaching practice.

Initially, the most impressive similarity was the volume of knowledge the teachers had about their students. When asked about one student's approach to learning and how it varied, Jay responded by describing the student's family situation, social tendencies and acceptance, academic effort and motivation, physical development, and cognitive processing. He described each student we discussed with the same kind of detail. Betty and Rebekah also described students elaborately, often focusing on their affective attributes and family situations—always linking the students' characteristics and situations to their learning.

My initial observations made me anxious to examine with a critical and careful eye the data collected from these teachers. The analysis was laborious but exciting. I examined each participant individually and found themes that reflected their individual teaching practices. To examine their central tendencies in a different context, I developed metaphors for each teacher. Finally, I used the individual categories to generate categories for the collective case. I was able to group these categories into the domains of self (personal), classroom, instruction, students, profession, and content. After charting the categories in each domain for each participant, I was able to develop synthesizing statements for each domain across all three teachers. These synthesizing statements represent the central tendencies of the collective case and are as follows:

Central Tendency 1: These teachers have a sense of confidence in themselves and in their profession.

Central Tendency 2: These teachers talk about their classroom as communities of learners.

Central Tendency 3: These teachers maximize the importance of developing relationships with students.

Central Tendency 4: These teachers demonstrate a student-centered approach to instruction.

Central Tendency 5: These teachers make contributions to the teaching profession through leadership and service.

Central Tendency 6: These teachers show evidence that they are masters of their content areas.

DISCUSSION

The theoretical foundation for this study began with the premise "that teaching expertise be viewed as a category that is structured by the similarity of expert teachers to one another rather than by a set of necessary and sufficient features" (Sternberg & Horvath, 1995, p. 9). The present study involved an investigation of three individual experts; analysis of the collective case yielded six central tendencies across participants. These central tendencies provide a summary representation of the behaviors, practices, and attitudes of three expert teachers. The central tendencies derived from the present investigation are supported by previous studies of expertise in teaching.

Central Tendency 1

These teachers have a sense of confidence in themselves and in their profession. One of the insights I gained in this study was related to the participants' confidence in themselves and their profession. When I interviewed Betty, she told me about being an assistant to several teachers before she became a teacher herself. She recalled looking at the teachers and thinking, "I can do better than that." Prior to becoming a teacher, Rebekah remembered sitting in a property management office collecting rent and taking complaints. She realized that this was not what she wanted to do, and as she thought about other alternatives, she considered teaching because she felt she had a "gift" for working with children. Betty's and Rebekah's comments illustrate their confidence in themselves. Even before entering the teaching field, they felt confident that they could be effective teachers. None of the studies reported in the review of the literature for this investigation cite confidence as a function of expertise, perhaps because it seems to be an affective quality or personality trait rather than a particular behavior. Two other properties related to the first central tendency are teacher efficacy and altruistic motives. Whereas most studies of efficacy and teaching motives have been tied to teacher retention rather than teacher expertise, Campbell (1990–1991) reported a study of the adaptive strategies of outstanding teachers in professionally inadequate environments. Campbell found eight personal qualities that the teachers in the study seemed to share. Two of the eight personal qualities are related to Central Tendency 1 of the present study. Like the teachers in Campbell's study, Betty, Jay, and Rebekah exhibited a strong sense of mission and a high degree of personal and professional efficacy.

Central Tendency 2

These teachers talk about their classrooms as communities of learners. All three teachers in this study spoke explicitly and often about their classrooms as communities. Their practices also support their emphasis on community. The classrooms were characterized by clear procedures, student ownership, student responsibility, and classroom community. Berliner (1988) supports the notion of clear procedures as a function of expertise. Jay Burns's classroom procedures were evident from the moment students entered the classroom. As students entered, they took their seats and began without direction writing responses to the prompt that was on the board in their notebooks. One student distributed writing folders. When Jay took the "status of the class," students responded quickly and provided information related to the mode that they were writing and their place in the writing process. When Jay gave the direction to begin working, students moved orderly to the editing areas, the filing cabinet, and the computer stations. Although Jay did not give explicit instructions to each student, it was evident that students not only knew the procedures but also seemed to move about the room as if it belonged to them. In many classrooms, students might be reprimanded for shuffling through teachers' filing cabinets or opening computer files. In Jay's classroom, students shared ownership of the items in the room, including certain paper and electronic files with the teacher and with each other. Core Proposition 3 of the NBPTS policy statement suggests that accomplished teachers "are responsible for managing and monitoring student learning." The systems Betty, Jay, and Rebekah have established for managing and monitoring student learning include clear procedures rather than reactive measures. These systems also allow for student ownership in decisions, including decisions about their own learning and assignments. Jay and Rebekah share ownership with students in their lesson and curriculum planning. In response to the question, "What do you think makes you a successful writing teacher?" Jay wrote, "Kids largely have control over topics and content while aiming at a rubric or criterion for the end result." Jay seems to indicate that not only is he willing to share control of the curriculum decision making with his students but also that his success is derived from sharing ownership and control. The properties of Central Tendency 2 (clear procedures, student ownership, student responsibility, and classroom community) are related to what Shulman (1987) calls general pedagogical knowledge. This category of knowledge is related to the "broad principles and strategies of classroom management and organization that appear to transcend subject matter" (p. 8). The teachers in this study exhibit pedagogical knowledge in their student-centered classroom structures.

Central Tendency 3

These teachers maximize the importance of developing relationships with students. This investigation revealed that Betty, Jay, and Rebekah spend the majority of their energies building relationships with students. These teachers develop relationships with their students by gaining knowledge about them, working side-by-side with them, and initiating contact with their families. The data from the structured interview transcripts reveal that each teacher demonstrated extensive knowledge of their individual students. An important difference among the participants was that Jay's descriptions of his students included details and diagnoses of covert processes, whereas Rebekah's and Betty's descriptions seemed more limited to observable behaviors. Another important detail related to the participants' efforts to build relationships with students is related to their proximity to them. In all three classrooms, the teacher's desk was integrated into a student area. None of the teachers had "office areas" away from the students. In addition, while students were working in these classrooms, all three teachers worked side-by-side with students. Rebekah had students sit around her on the floor for part of the lesson. In her interview, she explained that she preferred having students sit in a clump rather than a circle because they could be closer to her in a clump. Betty also moved from group to group during her lesson, bending down and working among groups at tables, on the floor, and at desks circled together. Jay was also moving about the room conferencing with students. He worked closely with them, kneeling, bending, leaning, or crouching to their seated height. In his proposal calling for a new reform in teaching, Shulman (1987) criticized studies of teacher expertise and systems of teacher evaluation because they often focus on student outcomes, particular teacher behaviors, or classroom management. My review of the literature corroborates his position. Although some studies have examined the relationships between students and their teachers, these studies are often focused on the effects of the relationships on students motivation. No studies were found that examined teacher relationships with students as a function of expertise.

Central Tendency 4

These teachers demonstrate a student-centered approach to instruction. Whereas many of the categories reflect the participants' focus on students, the properties of this central tendency suggest that teachers take responsibility for student learning, are responsive to students' needs, assess students often and in a variety of ways, and exhibit a mastery goal orientation. The data from this study provide support to previous findings (Cushing, Sabers, & Berliner, 1992; Gonzalez & Carter, 1996) that suggest when they talk about their instruction, expert teachers talk more about their own behavior than the behavior of their students. Whereas this may seem to contradict the student-centered concept, evidence from the present study indicates that teachers take responsibility for student learning rather than exhibiting "blaming" behavior or attitudes. Betty wrote, "My challenge as a teacher is to find the giftedness and whenever possible use it to enhance learning." Not only does Betty suggest that all of her students possess gifts, but also that it is her "challenge" and responsibility to find and use them. In the same response, Betty elaborates, "I must discover where each child is on his/her educational journey and make adequate connections with his/her body of understanding in order to allow learning to be meaningful for that child." Again, Betty assumes responsibility for student learning and suggests that the "journey" may be different for every child. Her insinuation is that the teacher's approach must be specific to the individual child.

One of the ways that these teachers take responsibility for student learning is by making connections for students. Although each teacher has a different approach for making connections, all of them emphasize this as an important component of student-centered instruction. Betty helps students make connections by integrating her curriculum. She explains,

> A lot of times if you walk into my classroom, you're maybe not real sure what [subject] I'm teaching, because I try to tie things together so that they have lots of connections to

> make so that it does make more sense in more places. . . . So I try to find as many connections as I can and then bring those things in.

Her integration strategy is to base her instruction on science and social studies and then to add reading and writing:

> My reading is almost always a trade book that has something to do with either science or social studies. Right now, it's Island of the Blue Dolphins, which is other cultures, some of the animals that we would find [on our coastal trip].

Betty also suggests that she can "interlace the arts all through the curriculum." She explains that being self-contained allows her to integrate more effectively.

Although research studies on student assessment have become more numerous in recent years, most of these studies are related to student achievement rather than the types or frequency of assessment characteristics of exceptional teaching. In the design of the validity study of NBPTS certification decisions, Hattie et al. (1998) proposed that several teaching practices related to student-centered instruction are critical to expertise in teaching. Those that are supported by data from the present study include that experienced teachers (a) can anticipate, plan, and improvise; (b) are better decision makers and can identify important decisions; and (c) are more adept at monitoring and providing much feedback.

One interesting observation for me was that in all my observations, discussions, e-mails, and interviews with Betty, Jay, and Rebekah, none of them mentioned students' grades. Although this is an absence rather than a presence of evidence, it provided one indicator that their emphasis was on student learning rather than student performance. Their classes were structured around learning objectives rather than performance goals. In Jay's writing workshop, for example, the students were organizing a portfolio that would represent their growth over the course of the school year. It was not a collection of all they had done.

Central Tendency 5

These teachers make contributions to the teaching profession through leadership and service. The teachers in this study were very involved in leadership and service for their profession. Jay and Rebekah were chairpersons for their school professional development committees. Betty has been an advocate for students at the local government level. Rebekah has traveled extensively, receiving and providing training to teachers in a literacy program. What is generally accepted as best practice suggests that expert teachers are involved in making their profession better (Barth, 1990). However, no research studies examining teacher expertise concentrated on teachers' involvement in the professional community. Jay and Rebekah have also been involved in working with new and aspiring teachers. Rebekah began work with a university near her school when the school of education began implementing a year-long practicum for their undergraduates. Rebekah has had three student teachers. She felt that it was her responsibility as cooperating teacher to help her student teachers "bridge the philosophy of university into practice." She wrote dialogue journals with her student teachers. She said the dialogue journals were an excellent tool for opening communication. Student teachers felt they could ask questions and express concerns openly. While Rebekah provided an important service to the university and the student teachers who worked in her classroom, she also benefited from the experience: "Having another adult in my room provided opportunities for me to evaluate my own practice. . . . I was forced to evaluate my own practice and make judgments about my curriculum ideas."

For several years now, Jay has been working with the University Fellows program, "which places undergraduate college students studying education into classrooms to work with experienced teachers for a year." Jay usually has about two of these student interns each year. Jay describes their involvement in his classroom:

> They come once a week to observe, help out where they can, and to try their hands at brief instructional experiences. The activities include simple observation at first, checking papers, responding to student writing about literature, editing essays, conferencing with student authors about what they have written, and occasionally doing a short lesson or leading a discussion. Often, the Fellows have a range of questions they want to talk about. Often, they learn by being involved in the actual process of learning with one of my students. And often they learn by planning and presenting something and then discussing it with me later.

Jay says the Fellows sometimes seem as if they have stored up a thousand questions, waiting for an opportunity to speak to a "real teacher." He says that working with the Fellows "represents an accomplishment because it is a contribution to the wider world of education, to the professional life of a future teacher, and to the lives of the students that teacher will touch."

Central Tendency 6

These teachers show evidence that they are masters of their content areas. Although mastery of content is beyond the scope of this study, data collected from the teachers did provide evidence that they are masters of their content. One of the indicators (although insufficient by itself) of their content mastery was that these teachers were continually seeking to improve their practice by participating in professional development activities and by collaborating with other professionals. This characteristic is supported by Campbell (1990–1991), who found that outstanding teachers adapted to professionally inadequate environments by continually seeking avenues to improve their teaching performance and by seeking and maintaining peer support systems that reinforced their sense of mission. Early in her teaching career, Rebekah began surrounding herself with other teachers who believed in student-centered approaches to literacy. Her collaboration with Lisa and her involvement in the voluntary literacy group are two examples of her professional collaboration. Jay Burns completed a second master's degree, knowing he would receive no financial compensation for it. He did believe, however, that a degree in critical and creative thinking would improve his teaching practice, and that seemed sufficient compensation for him.

Another indicator that these teachers are masters of their content is related to the number of professional presentations they make. All three participants have presented workshops related to curriculum and instructional methods to their peers and colleagues. That they were asked to make these presentations is an indicator that they are considered masters in their field.

The ability of these teachers to diagnose students' learning difficulties and to propose solutions to them is another indicator of their content knowledge. Livingston and Borko (1990) report that expert teachers know their content so well that they can manipulate it and present it in a variety of ways. Shulman (1987) calls this process transformation. Transformation, according to Shulman, is related to the teacher's ability to (a) prepare for instruction by engaging in critical interpretation and analysis; (b) represent the most critical elements using analogies, metaphors, examples, demonstrations, and explanations; (c) select from an elaborate instructional repertoire an appropriate mode of teaching, organizing, managing, and arranging; and (d) adapt and tailor to students' characteristics the critical content and appropriate instructional methods, taking into consideration conceptions, preconceptions, misconceptions, difficulties, language, culture, motivations, social class, gender, age, ability, aptitude, interests, self-concepts, and attention.

Although Shulman's notion of transformation seems almost unattainable, Betty, Jay, and Rebekah, at various times, came close to this ideal. The ability to personalize instruction in such a way requires a teacher to possess tremendous content knowledge, curriculum knowledge, pedagogical content knowledge, and knowledge of learners. Such a combination approaches what Shulman calls the "intersection of content and pedagogy, . . . the capacity of a teacher to transform the content knowledge he or she possesses into forms that are pedagogically powerful and yet adaptive to the variations in ability and background presented by the students" (p. 15).

The final indicator that these teachers are masters of their content lies in the fact that they have been certified by the NBPTS. Content knowledge expertise is difficult to measure because experts cannot agree on the most important concepts in any particular area; however, NBPTS represents the most comprehensive effort to date to involve teachers and other content area specialists in developing standards and measures appropriate for examining content area knowledge and expertise (Hattie et al., 1998).

COMPARISON OF PROTOTYPE PERSPECTIVES

This research represents an earnest acceptance of the invitation by Sternberg and Horvath (1995) to examine expertise in teaching as a similarity-based category. Based on their theoretical concepts of family resemblance, central exemplars, and the prototype view, this researcher set out to explore the similarities among three accomplished teachers with diverse profiles. The results of this inquiry are in-depth cases of three unique teachers who have some similar teaching behaviors, practices, and attitudes.

Thus far, the central tendencies generated from this study have been reported individually. Although individual attention to each of the central tendencies is necessary to deepen our understanding of the collective case, the nature of the prototype view argued for in this investigation would be compromised if the central tendencies were not also considered as critical members of a holistic framework.

One way to think about the central tendencies as a whole is to consider their interrelationships. For example, it is doubtful that a teacher who lacks confidence could relinquish or share ownership of the classroom with students. Also, teachers continually seeking to improve their practice are likely to be teachers involved in school leadership and service. Just as Sternberg and Horvath (1995) acknowledge correlation of the features of their model, this researcher proposes that the central tendencies derived from this research may also be correlated so that fewer critical features might be sufficient to describe expertise in teaching.

Although the prototype view of expertise in teaching provided an initial framework for this investigation, this research did not test the constellation of features proposed by Sternberg and Horvath (1995). Rather, it was exploratory and generative in its approach. Whereas Sternberg and Horvath use psychological research to derive the features of expert performance (knowledge, efficiency, and insight), this research used data collected from teachers in the contexts of their classrooms and profession to derive central tendencies of the collective case. Whereas Sternberg and Horvath examined mainly cognitive mechanisms and/or abilities, this study provides insight related to the practical (or tacit) knowledge of teaching practice that Shulman (1987) and Polanyi (1967) describe. Central Tendencies 5 and 6 include properties related to school and district leadership and service, professional development, collaboration with other professionals, professional presentations, and National Board Certification. These properties seem to suggest that the participants in this study have a well-developed knowledge of the social and political contexts of teaching.

Sternberg and Horvath (1995) maintain that the prototype view of teaching can "accommodate a multitude of prototypes, each based on a different sampling from the population of expert teachers" (p. 15). They propose one way to examine the expert prototype, and this research offers a second. As more studies of expertise assume a prototype approach, our understanding of expertise will increase until, eventually, we will be able to formulate a prototype of the multitude of prototypes.

NOTE

1. These pseudonyms were chosen by the participants.

REFERENCES

Barth, R. S. (1990). *Improving schools from within: Teachers, parents, and principals can make the difference.* San Francisco: Jossey-Bass.

Berliner, D. C. (1988, February). The development of expertise in pedagogy. Charles W. Hunt Memorial Lecture presented at the Annual Meeting of the American Association of Colleges for Teacher Education, New Orleans, LA, February 17–20, 1988. (ERIC Document Reproduction Service No ED 298122)

Campbell, K. P. (1990–1991, Winter). Personal norms of experienced expert suburban high school teachers: Implications for selecting and retaining outstanding individuals. *Action in Teacher Education, 12*, 35–40.

Carter, K., Sabers, D., Cushing, K., Pinnegar, P., & Berliner, D. C. (1987). Processing and using information about students: A study of expert, novice, and postulant teachers. *Teaching and Teacher Education, 3*, 147–157.

Chase, W. G., & Simon, H. A. (1973). The mind's eye in chess. In W. G. Chase (Ed.), *Visual information processing* (pp. 215–281). New York: Academic Press.

Chi, M. T. H., Glaser, R., & Farr, M. J. (Eds.). (1988). *The nature of expertise.* Hillsdale, NJ: Lawrence Erlbaum Associates.

Cushing, K. S., Sabers, D. S., & Berliner, D. C. (1992, Spring). Olympic goals: Investigations of expertise in teaching. *Educational Horizons*, 108–114.

de Groot, A. (1965). *Thought and choice and chess.* The Hague, the Netherlands: Mouton. (Original work published 1946)

Fehr, B. (1993). How do I love thee? Let me consult my prototype. In S. Duck (Ed.), *Individuals in relationships* (pp. 87–120). Newbury Park, CA: Sage.

Feltovich, P. J., Ford, K. M., & Hoffman, R. R. (1997). *Expertise in context.* Menlo Park, CA: AAAI Press.

Glaser, R. (1984). Education and thinking: The role of knowledge. *American Psychologist, 39*(2), 93–104.

Gonzalez, L. E., & Carter, K., (1996). Correspondence in cooperating teachers' and student teachers' interpretations of classroom events. *Teacher & Teacher Education, 12*, 39–47.

Hattie, J., Jaeger, R., Strahan, D., & Baker, W. (1998). Report on the development of the assessment/data collection instruments and protocols. Unpublished manuscript, Center for Educational Research at Evaluation, University of North Carolina at Greensboro.

Lakoff, G. (1987). Cognitive models and prototype theory. In U. Neisser (Ed.), *Concepts and conceptual development: Ecological and intellectual factors in categorization* (pp. 63–100). New York: Cambridge University Press.

Livingston, C., & Borko, H. (1990). High school mathematics review lessons: Expert-novice distinctions. *Journal for Research in Mathematics Education, 21*, 372–387.

Maslow, A. H. (1971). *The farther reaches of human nature*. New York: Viking.

Merriam, S. B. (1998). *Qualitative research and case study applications in education*. San Francisco: Jossey-Bass.

Noice, T., & Noice, H. (1997). *The nature of expertise in professional acting: A cognitive view*. Mahwah, NJ: Lawrence Erlbaum.

Polanyi, M. (1967). *The tacit dimension*. Garden City, NJ: Doubleday.

Rosch, E. (1973). On the internal structure of perceptual semantic categories. In T. E. Moore (Ed.), *Cognitive development and the acquisition of language* (pp. 112–144). New York: Academic Press.

Rosch, E. (1978). Principles of categorization. In E. Rosch & B. Lloyd (Eds.), *Cognition and categorization*. Hillsdale, NJ: Lawrence Erlbaum.

Schon, D. A. (1983). *The reflective practitioner: How professionals think in action*. New York: Basic Books.

Schon, D. A. (1987). *Educating the reflective practitioner: Toward a new design for teaching and learning in the professions*. San Francisco: Jossey-Bass.

Shulman, L. (1987). Knowledge and teaching: Foundations of the new reform. *Harvard Educational Review, 57*, 1–22.

Stake, R. E. (1995). *The art of case study research*. Thousand Oaks, CA: Sage.

Sternberg, R. J., & Horvath, J. A. (1995). A prototype view of expert teaching. *Educational Researcher, 24*(6), 9–17.

Strauss, A., & Corbin, J. (1998). *Basics of qualitative research: Techniques and procedures for developing grounded theory*. Thousand Oaks, CA: Sage.

Swanson, H. L., O'Connor, J. E., & Cooney, J. B. (1990, Fall). An information processing analysis of expert and novice teachers' problem solving. *American Educational Research Journal, 27*, 533–556.

van der Mars, H., Vogler, E. W., Darst, P. W., & Cusimano, B. (1991). Novice and expert physical education teachers: They may think and decide differently . . . but do they behave differently? Paper presented at the American Educational Researcher Association National Conference, Chicago. (ERIC Document Reproduction Service No ED 336 354)

Yin, R. K. (1994). *Case study research: Design and methods* (2nd ed.). Thousand Oaks, CA: Sage.

AUTHOR

Tracy W. Smith is an assistant professor in the Department of Curriculum and Instruction at Appalachian State University in Boone, North Carolina, where she teaches and advises in the undergraduate and graduate middle-level teacher preparation programs. She is a former middle school language arts and social studies teacher. Her publications and research focus on middle-level teacher preparation, teacher expertise, depth of student learning, and writing instruction.

Source: Tracy Smith and David Strahan, Toward a prototype of expertise in teaching: A descriptive case study, *Journal of Teacher Education 55*(4), 357–372, 2004. Reprinted by permission of Corwin Press, Inc.

Chapter 17

Action Research

ACTION RESEARCH STARTS WITH EVERYDAY EXPERIENCE AND IS CONCERNED WITH THE DEVELOPMENT OF LIVING KNOWLEDGE.
REASON AND BRADBURY (2001)

INSTRUCTIONAL OBJECTIVES

After studying this chapter, the student will be able to:

1. Define action research and its underlying assumptions.
2. Give examples of areas where action research can be used in schools.
3. Compare and contrast action research with other types of research.
4. Explain the action research process.
5. Define a problem that could be examined through action research and identify appropriate data sources to be used in investigating the problem.
6. Give examples of approaches to data analysis and interpretation used in action research.
7. Describe what should be included in an action plan.
8. Explain why action research is useful to the field of education.
9. Apply criteria for assessing the quality of an action research report.

PICTURE THIS

Joe Rocco

DEFINING ACTION RESEARCH

In recent years, we have seen an increased interest in action research. The two words themselves, *action* and *research*, indicate the two important components necessary for action research. **Action research** is about taking action based on research and researching the action taken.

Action research has been used in a variety of settings, including schools, hospitals, health clinics, community agencies, government units, and other environments. It can be used to enhance everyday work practices, to resolve specific problems, and to develop special projects and programs. Action research is based on the premise that local conditions vary widely and that the solutions to many problems cannot be found in generalized truths that take no account of local conditions.

In education, action research can be applied to such areas as curriculum development, teaching strategies, school reform, and more. Action research in schools is also called practitioner research, teacher inquiry, or teacher research. The goal of action research in education is to create an inquiry stance toward teaching where questioning one's own practice becomes part of the work and of the teaching culture. Good teachers have always been engaged in a form of action research, although they may not have called it that. Good teachers engage in reflection, a key component of action research. But action research is more than reflection. It emphasizes a systematic research approach that is cyclical in nature, alternating between action and reflection, continuously refining methods and interpretations based on understandings developed in earlier cycles.

There are three main characteristics of action research:

1. The research is situated in a local context and focused on a local issue.
2. The research is conducted by and for the practitioner.
3. The research results in an action or a change implemented by the practitioner in the context.

Here is an example of action research by a teacher. Mr. Rodriguez teaches middle school social studies in an alternative school attended by students who have been unsuccessful in the regular school. He has noticed in his classes that the students seem bored and unmotivated and that their grades in social studies are generally poor. He believes that social studies will help students become more productive citizens and is concerned that they are not learning. Mr. Rodriguez decides to study the problem to see whether he can find ways to better engage the students in the learning process and thus improve their learning. (*Characteristic 1*: Mr. Rodriguez has engaged in a process of reflection and has identified a problem in his own context of practice, his classroom.) Mr. Rodriguez decides to keep a journal for 2 weeks to note his observations about student behavior. He also develops an interview protocol and conducts a series of interviews with the students, asking them to talk about times when they liked learning and times when they did not. He asks them about their school experiences, particularly in social studies. By doing these things, Mr. Rodriguez has engaged in a qualitative research process. (*Characteristic 2*: He is conducting his own research for his own purposes, to improve his teaching.) Mr. Rodriguez reviews his findings in light of the literature and concludes that some specific changes in his teaching strategies, such as using more project-based group work, might make a difference. He implements those teaching strategies and gathers additional evidence, including a review of student performance, to determine whether the strategy worked. He continues his journaling to see whether he observes differences in student behavior. Based on these findings, he will continue to make decisions about his practice. (*Characteristic 3*: He implements changes in his classroom based on his findings.) Mr. Rodriguez is doing action research. There is more about Mr. Rodriguez' research later in this chapter.

ROOTS OF ACTION RESEARCH

While action research has recently gained more attention in the field of education, the concepts are not new. Kurt Lewin, considered the father of action research, is credited with coining the term in the 1940s, primarily associated with social change efforts. In education, some trace the conceptual roots to the progressive views of John Dewey. More recently, this form of inquiry has been given increased attention in response to pragmatic and philosophical pressures associated with federal legislation such as the No Child Left Behind Act and an emphasis on evidence-based practices.

Practical action research emphasizes how to do action research rather than its philosophical orientation. Practical action research focuses on practical problems and is often focused on current educational practice. Mr. Rodriguez' study at the alternative school is an example of practical action research.

ACTION RESEARCH COMPARED TO OTHER TYPES OF RESEARCH

Some have suggested that action research is a new genre of research, different from the quantitative and qualitative approaches with which we are already familiar. Action research may have different purposes, different incentives, and different audiences compared to other forms of research, but it uses the same methodologies we have already discussed. Action research starts, as does all research, with a problem to be solved. However, the problem may not be well defined and is often referred to as a "focus" rather than as a problem.

The key difference is in the primary purpose of action research, which is to take action to solve a local problem or to improve a practice. It is not intended to create theories or to be generalizable. Action research is a practical tool for solving problems experienced by people in their professional lives. It is empirical insofar as it requires people to define and observe the phenomena under investigation. Although action research may use many of the methods, procedures, and concepts associated with quantitative research, it is usually more closely aligned with qualitative methods. While action research involves systematic inquiry, it has some distinctive characteristics that bear consideration. Table 17.1 compares typical action research with the more formal quantitative approaches to research you have studied in this textbook and summarizes differences noted in the literature.

THINK ABOUT IT 17.1

For each of the following statements, indicate "A" for action research or "Q" for formal quantitative research.

1. Occurs within a natural environment.
2. Values collaborative construction of interpretation.
3. Tests theories.
4. Values stakeholders' and practitioners' perspectives.
5. Randomly assigns subjects to experimental and control groups.
6. Seeks solutions to local problems.
7. Seeks objective knowledge that can be generalized.
8. Maintains a clear distinction between researchers and subjects.
9. Uses purposeful samples.
10. Emphasizes the use of professionally developed instruments.

Answers:

1, A; 2, A; 3, Q; 4, A; 5, Q; 6, A; 7, Q; 8, Q; 9, A; 10, Q.

Table 17.1 Comparison of Quantitative Research and Action Research

Formal Quantitative Research	Action Research
Purpose/Goals	
Produces objective knowledge that can be generalized to larger populations in order to predict future events based on a preexisting set of conditions.	Interprets events and enables individuals or groups of people to formulate acceptable solutions to local problems.
Tests theories in order to explain the nature of the world or the nature of reality.	Attains viable, sustainable, effective solutions to common problems.
Investigates larger issues and generalizes.	Identifies and corrects local problems with little regard for generalizability.
Approach	
Generates generalizable truths through studies that are replicable.	Looks at the local context with a focus on a specific issue or problem in a particular context.
Develops a study based on what is known in the professional literature.	Develops a study based on experience and valuing practitioner perspectives.
Uses extensive literature review and relies on primary sources.	Uses cursory literature review and relies on secondary sources.
Dispassionate objectivity and value neutrality are the ideals.	Subjective or authoritative judgments of individuals are respected.
Uses more rigorous procedures and typically has a longer time frame.	Uses less rigorous, looser procedures and more typically has a quick time frame.
Studies smaller units of a phenomenon.	Complexity is embraced.
The ideal is a controlled environment.	Occurs in the natural context.
Methods	
Uses primarily quantitative approaches to measure and predict variables and tests of statistical significance to study cause-and-effect relationships.	Uses description and interpretation from the inside of a situation and primarily implements qualitative approaches to help understand context or the effect of interventions.
Follows carefully prescribed procedures known as the scientific method.	Does not necessarily follow carefully prescribed procedures.
Focuses on conventional research rules and concepts of measurement.	Focuses on the experienced reality of the day to day.
Tests hypotheses, attempts to create and/or validate theories.	Attempts to make a difference in a very specific way for the practitioner or clients.
Assumes that if researchers study two identical groups, differing only in a single variable (the one being tested) then any changes observed must have been caused by the independent variable.	Assumes no one could control for all relevant variables when dealing with human beings in a social situation.
Experimental design is considered the "gold standard" for research.	Asserts that the act of assigning a student to a control group when the researcher believes that the treatment is superior is to deny students the best possible instruction.
Uses random sampling when possible.	Uses purposeful samples.
Uses primarily professionally developed instruments.	Uses primarily teacher-developed or convenient instruments.
Data analysis relies on hypothesis testing, statistical tests, and meta-analysis.	Data analysis focuses on practical, not statistical, significance and reports raw data.
Emphasizes theoretical significance and increased general knowledge.	Emphasizes practical significance and increased knowledge about a particular context.

(continues)

Table 17.1 *Continued*

Formal Quantitative Research	Action Research
Role of Researcher	
Research is often conducted by outsiders—scholars, researchers, professors.	Research is conducted by insiders—the practitioner or teacher.
There is a clear distinction between researcher and subjects.	There is little distinction between the researcher and the subjects, and participants engage in the process.
Subjective opinions of the researcher are never considered as data.	Subjective opinions of the researcher are often considered as data.
Formal training is required to conduct studies.	Little formal training is required to conduct studies.
The researcher reports findings to professional audiences.	The researcher shares informal findings with peers or sometimes in articles, such as the one at the end of this chapter.

ACTION RESEARCH PROCESS

The action research process can be represented as a spiral (Kemmis & McTaggart, 1988) where the researcher reflects, plans, acts, and observes. Some have simplified it: Look, think, act (Stringer, 2004). Figure 17.1 provides a representation of the action research process.

While the action research models described in the literature differ in some ways, they appear to have the common elements shown in the figure. We will describe those elements more fully.

1. ***Reflect.*** Experience and perceptions are used to *identify an area of focus* based on a problem. Time is taken to *review what is already known* about the problem or focus area and to learn more about the problem.
2. ***Plan.*** A *plan is developed* for taking action and/or for gathering data in order to observe or capture the experience or monitor the practice.
3. ***Act.*** The researcher implements the plan or changes a practice and *collects data.*
4. ***Observe.*** The researcher synthesizes and *analyzes the data.* This leads back into the spiral once more.
5. *Reflect.* The researcher reflects on and *interprets the information* and *reports it* to others. A new understanding of the nature of the problem is developed. A new area of focus is identified.
6. *Plan.* A new plan of action is developed to resolve the problem.
7. *Act.* A new action is taken and data are collected (perhaps the same types of data or perhaps something different).
8. *Observe.* The new data are analyzed, synthesized, and interpreted. The researcher then spirals back into the process.

An example of this systematic process is the case of Professor Wang who teaches an online course in curriculum and instruction.

1. *Reflect.* Professor Wang is not satisfied with the level of reflection evident in her online students' postings in the discussion area (*identifying an area of*

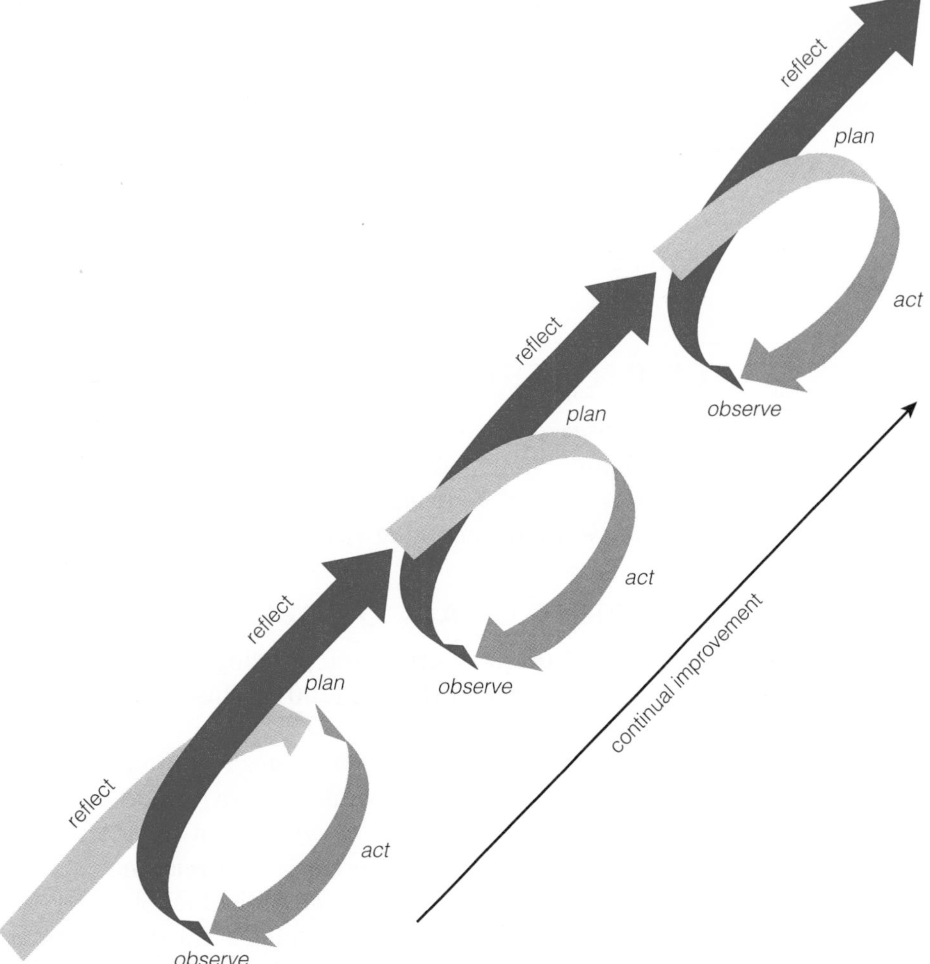

Figure 17.1 Action Research Spiral

Source: http://education.qld.gov.au/ ... /action-cycle.html

focus). She briefly reviews the literature to see what others have learned about improving student communication online (*reviewing what is already known*).

2. *Plan*. Using a categorization framework she found in a journal article, she *develops a plan* to look at the class data.
3. *Act*. She saves the students' online responses over a 2-week period and also interviews two of the students (*data collection*).
4. *Observe*. The data indicate that, in general, low levels of reflection are the norm (*data analysis*).
5. *Reflect*. She decides that students must not understand what is expected (*interpretation*). She *discusses her findings* with her departmental colleagues. Based on the data and what she read in the literature, the professor believes that the students need a rubric to explain the levels of communication and that some modeling might be useful.

6. *Plan*. Together with her colleagues, Professor Wang develops a rubric to use in online discussions and includes samples of the appropriate responses for the different levels.
7. *Act*. Professor Wang uses this rubric in her next class and again collects data.
8. *Observe*. Professor Wang analyzes students' online responses. That will spiral her back into the process as she observes the students' pattern of behavior to determine whether the level of communication has improved. She will again reflect on what she learns in order to make new plans and take new actions.

ACTION RESEARCH PROBLEMS

In action research, as with all research, the first step is to determine what is to be investigated. Your focus should be on your own practice, involve something within your locus of control, be about something you feel passionate about, and provide answers to something you would like to change or improve.

CATEGORIES OF ACTION RESEARCH PROBLEMS

We will look at problem areas in four categories aligned with those identified by Burnaford, Fischer, and Hobson (2001). These categories are applicable in educational contexts.

First are problems arising from a desire to *improve student learning*. Questions asked by the researcher could revolve around perceived needs, such as improving the physical classroom environment for learning, improving the interpersonal interactions among students, or developing students' capacity to reflect. Questions might focus on helping an individual child or group of children or on understanding the teaching and learning context. For example, how might I best organize my first-grade classroom to promote the use of reading materials?

Second are problems arising from a desire to *improve curriculum*. Questions asked by the researcher could arise from such things as how to integrate subjects, how to best construct the curriculum, or how to embed technology use in the curriculum. Questions might focus on enriching the curricula or on developing content knowledge. For example, how can Excel (a popular computer program) be used to teach mathematics concepts?

Third, problems might arise from a desire to *adapt instructional strategies*. Questions might deal with fostering active learning, guiding student self-evaluation, or implementing a specific instructional approach. The researcher might want to experiment with new teaching strategies or techniques. For example, if I use the triarchic model of teaching, will students' problem-solving abilities improve?

Fourth are problems arising out of a desire for one's own *professional development* or to search for connections and meaning in one's work. Questions might deal with analyzing one's own beliefs or personal style of teaching or gaining understanding about who or what influenced you in the development of your practice. The researcher may feel a desire to explore the relationship between beliefs and classroom practices or to look at the intersection of personal and profes-

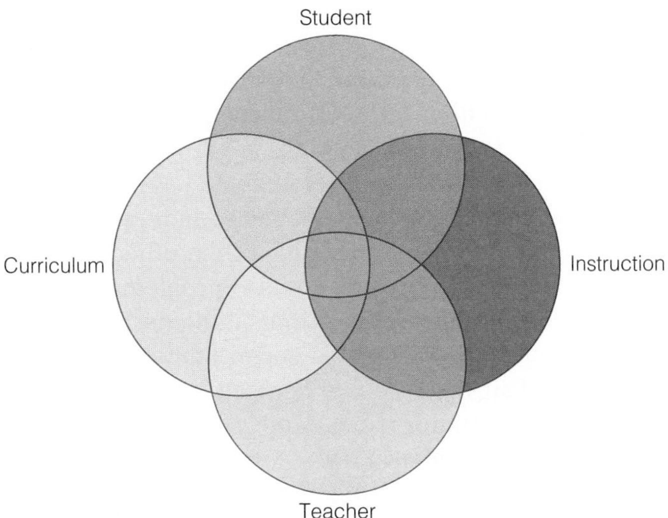

Figure 17.2 Areas of Action Research Focus in the Educational Setting

sional identities. For example, what is my primary curriculum ideology and how is my instructional practice informed by it?

These four areas in which problems or focus areas may be identified in education are not necessarily discrete. They may intersect and overlap in many ways. In the classroom context, action research may be focused on the student, the teacher, the curriculum, the instructional practices, or the intersections of these areas (Figure 17.2).

STRATEGIES FOR IDENTIFYING THE PROBLEM

So how do you identify the specific problem in your context? Several strategies have been recommended.

1. **Reflection** is one strategy. Researchers are advised from an action research viewpoint to think about their own setting and consider what is working well and what might need improvement. Think about what intrigues you about your teaching? What would you like to know more about? What values do you hold? What are your understandings of theories that impact practice? How did you arrive at your beliefs about teaching? Some recommend keeping a daily reflective journal to see if trends emerge. Others recommend conducting a reflective interview where teachers talk through their concerns with one another. These reflective dialogues can be conducted face to face or by telephone or via the Internet. "What if" questions may be asked as part of the reflection process and may help elicit images of what could be. For example, what if I begin teaching the English-speaking children in my first-grade class some basic Spanish words? Would that reduce the anxiety I sense in my English language learners?
2. **Description** is another strategy for determining the problem to be investigated. Insights can be gained by describing the who, what, when, where,

THINK ABOUT IT 17.2

Listed below are some actual action research problems that have been investigated and written about. How do these problems fit into the four categories above using "S" for student learning, "C" for curriculum, "I" for instruction, or "T" for teacher professional development.

1. Mrs. Watson has noticed that some students have more difficulty memorizing their multiplication tables than others and wants to find a better way to identify those likely to have problems.
2. Mr. Rodriguez has noticed that students he teaches in the alternative school appear bored in his social studies class and wonders what instructional strategies could be used to engage them.
3. Ms. Thomas wonders how inquiry science materials could be integrated into her biology laboratory.
4. Mr. Baker is interested in knowing more about how other algebra teachers in the district teach algebra.
5. Mrs. Abbot wants to know how to create a more supportive classroom environment for one of her English language learners after noticing the child seems to have a high level of anxiety.
6. Ms. Carpenter is wondering which computer software package might be easier for students to use in developing creative projects in her art class.

Answers:
1, S; 2, I; 3, C; 4, T; 5, S; 6, C.

and why of a situation. These descriptions come from observations. Begin by describing the situation you wish to change or improve, describing the evidence you have that there is a problem, and describing critical factors you believe affect the situation. Other options include listing incidents or intriguing observations you have had, describing experiences, examining textbooks, curriculum documents, and lesson plans, looking at demographics of students and perhaps recording observations about one subset of students, and comparing your own instructional delivery with best teaching practices advocated by leading national organizations. For example, you might keep a journal for one week about the interactions you observe between English-speaking children and English language learners in your class, describing the type of interactions that occur such as asking for assistance, who is engaged in the interactions (Joe and Danilo), when and where the interactions occur (during free reading time in the language center at the computer station), and your interpretation of the situation. (Danilo appears frustrated as Joe does not understand his questions about how to start the computer program.)

3. **Explanation** is a third strategy for trying to determine a specific problem for investigation. This strategy involves hypothesizing about how and why critical factors affect a situation. Sagor (2000) suggests using a technique called the "priority pie" as a mechanism to help identify variables you believe are most relevant to an issue and to help clarify personal beliefs about the rela-

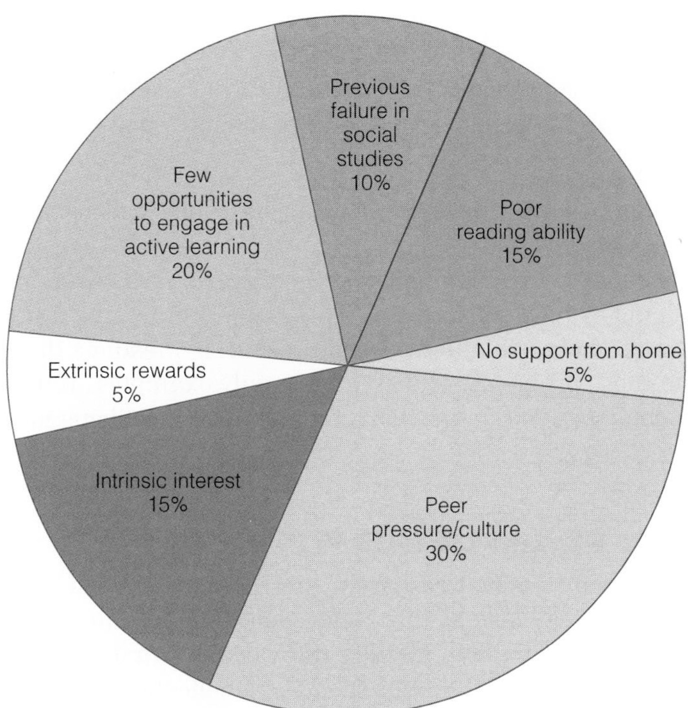

Figure 17.3 Variables Believed Relevant to Failure in Social Studies

tive importance of those variables. Drawing a pictorial representation or graphic representation helps to illustrate the relationships between the variables. Once a pictorial representation is developed, ask two questions: Is this relationship meaningful and are you uncertain about it? If the relationship is not meaningful or you are already certain, do not waste your time investigating it. For example, Mr. Rodriguez might think that several things contribute to poor student engagement in his social studies class. He may believe that some of these factors are a greater problem than others, and he could assign percentages to determine the ones on which he really wants to focus. He might identify the following: previous failure in social studies (10 percent), no support from home (5 percent), poor reading ability (15 percent), peer pressure/culture (30 percent), instrinsic interest (15 percent), extrinsic rewards (5 percent), and few opportunities to engage in active learning (20 percent). These could be represented in an illustration (Figure 17.3).

4. Conducting a limited **literature review** also can help in developing your explanation and clarifying the research question. Reviewing the literature helps in assessing what if anything other researchers have found out about the topic and what theoretical perspectives relate to the topic, as well as providing promising practices. Most people gather information from relevant sources, for example, before making a major family purchase, such as a home. The literature review is covered in depth in Chapter 4. However, in action research, this review is generally more limited than that considered appropriate for more formal studies.

THINK ABOUT IT 17.3

Return to the problems in Think About It 17.2. See whether you can create action research questions related to problems 5 and 6.

Answers

Problem 5. What incidents in the classroom lead to behaviors that indicate anxiety in child X?

Problem 6. Do students using X software have lower frustration levels than students using Y software?

Note: There are other possible research questions that could be developed from these problems. The above are only examples. You may wish to consider developing research questions for the other problems in Think About It 17.2.

ACTION RESEARCH QUESTIONS

As a first step in action research, the researcher must determine the focus or problem and may also at this stage identify a specific research question. A research question can help identify the variables under consideration and determine the type of data that will need to be collected. Often, the problem or focus the researcher identifies can lead to several different research questions. For example, Principal Talbot was concerned that so few Hispanic/Latino parents attended school functions. One research question might be "What are the factors that Hispanic/Latino parents indicate prevent them from attending school functions?" A different research question related to the same problem might be "Does sending Spanish-translated invitations directly to the home (rather than the typically English notes sent home with the students) result in an increase in Hispanic/Latino parent attendance at school functions?" In action research, the "questions" are not always worded as an actual question.

DATA COLLECTION FOR ACTION RESEARCH

In action research, as with other types of research, different research questions require different research approaches. Both quantitative and qualitative approaches may be used in action research, and one approach is not better than the other. However, when you review action research studies, you will find that qualitative strategies are more often used. The focus is on data that is readily accessible to the practitioner.

USING MULTIPLE SOURCES OF DATA

Triangulation is important in action research. Using multiple sources of data and avoiding reliance on a single source enhances corroboration of the findings. Triangulation may incorporate two or more sources of information. If multiple sources lead to the same conclusion, a stronger case is made. Discrepancies in the findings derived from the various sources lead to learning as the researcher tries to provide explanations for the discrepancies and pose new questions. Table 17.2 provides a sample triangulation matrix showing how multiple data sources can be used to look at a single problem.

Table 17.2 Triangulation Matrix for Project Research Questions

Research Question	Data Source 1	Data Source 2	Data Source 3
Can I motivate my distance education students to participate in online discussions?	My own reflections	Student surveys	Logs showing student time online
What is the quality of the discussion online?	Instructor assessment using a rubric	Student self-assessment using the same rubric	Identification of levels of communication based on coding of the printed discussions
Do students feel comfortable expressing their thoughts online?	Student surveys	Interviews with a random sample of students	Online focused discussion in a chat room

DATA COLLECTION STRATEGIES

Before collecting data, you should know why you are collecting the data, what exactly you are collecting, where and when you will collect it and for how long, who will collect it, and how the data will be analyzed and the findings shared. Types of data that can be collected and used in action research projects have been categorized in various ways by different authors. We will use the categories described by Mills (2003) as the *three Es:* **experiencing, enquiring, and examining**.

Experiencing

First, data may be gathered through the researcher's own experience. This category focuses on observational data that may be recorded in various ways (see also Chapter 8). Field notes are the most common data collection strategy used in action research to provide a record of what is going on during an observation. Field notes can include descriptions of places (locations, physical layouts, etc.), people (individuals, types, positions, etc.), objects (buildings, furniture, equipment, materials, etc.), acts (single actions that people take), activities (sets of related acts), events (sets of related activities), purposes (what people are trying to accomplish), time (times, frequency, duration, sequencing, etc.), and feelings (emotional orientations and responses). Other observational data recording strategies are listed in Table 17.3. [For further information on observation strategies see Chapter 15 or Stringer (2004).]

Enquiring

Second, data may be collected by asking participants themselves to respond in some manner, that is, enquiring of them. The most common action research strategy for collecting enquiring data is through interviews. While strategies for interviewing are described in Chapter 14, it is useful to review Stringer's (2004) list of types of interview questions used in action research. Grand tour questions are global and allow participants to describe something in their own terms. (Tell me about your school?) Typical questions ask participants to describe how something typically happens. (Describe a typical science class.) Specific questions ask about specific events or activities. (Tell me about what happened in science class

Table 17.3 Data Collection Strategies.

Experiencing	Enquiring	Examining
Field Notes Places People Objects Acts Activities Events Purposes Time Feelings **Observations** Active observation Participant observation Passive observation Observation logs Mapping or diagramming Audio or videotaping Observation checklists Dialogue scripting Shadow studies **Other Collection Strategies** Diaries Journaling Photographing Rating scales	**Interviews** Focus groups Informal face to face Structured face to face Telephone interviews Internet-based interviews; list serves, chatrooms, email, discussion boards Oral histories or stories **Written Responses** Attitude scales Questionnaires Rating scales Participant journaling Participant logs **Performance Measures** Portfolio development Standardized tests Work samples Conduct activity **Other Collection Strategies** Community meetings	**Student Information** Basic student records Attendance data Existing work samples Portfolios Test scores Individual Education Plans (IEPs) Progress reports Reading records **Teacher Records** Teacher plan books Written lesson plans Teacher correspondence Grade books **Teaching Materials** Curriculum guides Textbooks Teacher manuals Children's literature **District/School Artifacts** Memos Parent newsletters Minutes and official reports Policies and procedures Evaluation reports Press accounts Public relations materials **Other Archival Sources** Films Photographs Maps

yesterday.) Task questions aid in description. (Can you draw me a map or picture of that?) Extension questions ask for more detail. (Can you tell me more about that?) Encouragement questions or statements push the respondent to continue. (Please go on.) Example questions do just what the name implies, ask for a specific example. (Can you give me an example?) Other ideas for collecting enquiring data are listed in Table 17.3.

Examining

Third, data may be collected through examining artifacts and other materials that already exist or that are routinely collected in the setting. Student records and teacher records are useful sources of information. Refer to Table 17.3 for more ideas.

Recall that Mr. Rodriguez has noticed that students he teaches in the alternative school appear bored in his social studies class and wonders what instructional strategies could be used to engage them. Mr. Rodriguez could briefly examine the literature on student engagement (find one or two sources). He could make written observations of student behavior in his social studies class to de-

THINK ABOUT IT 17.4

See if you can identify at least two data collection strategies for the two action research questions identified in Think About It 17.3.

Answers
Problem 5. Observation logs, interviews, anxiety measures.
Problem 6. Videotaping, student surveys, interviews.
Note: These are examples. Other strategies could be used.

termine if there is a pattern. He could individually interview students and ask them to describe their experiences in social studies. He could videotape the class to observe his own teaching practices and students' responses. He could conduct focus groups with the students to ask about their interests and their experiences in school. Based on the data collected, Mr. Rodriguez might then try some different instructional strategies and determine if students demonstrate more engagement.

RIGOR AND ETHICAL TREATMENT IN ACTION RESEARCH

Regardless of the data collection method used, the researcher must strive to assure the rigor of the process and assure that the participants are treated ethically. No research, including action research, is worth doing unless it is done well. Action research in schools should be held to high standards.

First, as educators, we have an obligation to students. Actions based on poorly done research can place students at risk. Second, educators need personal and collective efficacy. Third, there is a need to add to the professional knowledge base in education, whether that knowledge is added informally through sharing with colleagues or more formally through publishing.

RIGOR IN ACTION RESEARCH

Action researchers should be concerned about the issues of rigor or quality addressed by other researchers: validity, credibility, reliability, dependability, neutrality, confirmability, and transferability. These concepts are covered in other sections of this text (see Chapters 9 and 16). There are a few comments about rigor in action research, however, worth noting here.

Action research in schools often relies on authentic student work, which Sagor (2000) compares to primary source materials and claims enhances credibility. Credibility is described as the researcher's ability to take into account the complexities that present themselves in a particular setting and to deal with patterns not easily explained (see Chapter 16 for detailed discussion of credibility). Mills (2003) asserts that if action research is to be viewed as credible, the solution to the problem (the planned intervention) must actually solve the problem.

Being able to generalize is not a primary goal of action research, rather the primary goal is to understand what is happening in a specific context and to determine what might improve things in that context. Action researchers believe that everything is context bound and that the goal is not to develop a generalizable statement but to provide rich and detailed descriptions of the context so that others can make comparisons with their contexts and judge for themselves whether the findings might apply (be transferable).

Action researchers need to understand and reveal their biases, as do qualitative researchers. Like all other researchers, action researchers do not collect data to simply validate existing practices, do not ignore discrepant data, and do not review only literature that supports a particular view. They are open to reflection.

ETHICS IN ACTION RESEARCH

Ethics in action research is based on the same principles as ethics in other research. The first principle is that participants should not be wronged in the name of research. It is just as important to abide by ethical guidelines in action research as it is in other forms of research. However, action researchers may have some unique challenges to overcome in ensuring ethical principles are upheld. Action research is often more open ended and may change as the researcher focuses differently on the problems in the context. In action research, there is little distance between the researcher (e.g., the teacher in the school setting) and the subjects (the students in the teacher's classroom). Action researchers should be aware of the legislation concerning research with human subjects (see Chapter 18).

There is some argument in the field of action research about the need for informed consent. The case made is that the subjects are actually the researchers themselves (the teacher), as the purpose of action research is to improve one's own performance. Proponents argue that students in classes, for example, are simply and naturally living through the teacher researcher's instruction, the same instruction they would have been receiving without action research. However, most experts in the area believe it is wise to obtain permission, particularly if the researcher wishes to present or even publish the findings to others outside of the local context.

Given the scrutiny education is under at the current time, action researchers in schools would be prudent to obtain parental consent. Sagor (2000) recommends a generic letter to parents that conveys four key points: (1) The teacher is conducting research for him or herself that is intended to benefit the children in the class. (2) The research will not mean different things will happen to some of the children and nothing will be granted or denied due to the research. (3) The teacher might use the child's work, words, or ideas in reporting on the research. (4) There will be no negative consequences if permission is denied. Data about that child will then not be used in the study.

DATA ANALYSIS IN ACTION RESEARCH

What do you do with the data you have worked hard to collect in a dependable, accurate, reliable, and correct manner? Data analysis involves reviewing the data as it is being collected and attempting to synthesize and make sense out of what is observed.

Much of what has been written about analysis in action research mirrors strategies used in qualitative research (described further in Chapter 16), although the researcher should always remember that appropriate analysis will depend on the question asked and the method of data collection used. Action research data analysis has been described as a search for patterns or trends in the data to answer two questions: What is the story told by the data? What might explain this story or what factors influenced the story? The action research analysis process has been compared to trying to put together a jigsaw puzzle without the box that shows the completed picture and with some pieces missing.

CODING

One key analysis strategy often described in action research is coding as typically described in qualitative research (see Chapter 16). First, the researcher breaks down and categorizes the data into manageable segments **(open coding)**. Then, the researcher puts the data back together again, making connections between and across categories **(axial coding)**. Sometimes, the researcher has a clear and selective focus and is systematically reviewing the data for that specific category **(selective coding)**.

For example, in the case of Mr. Rodriguez trying to teach social studies to the students in his alternative school, Mr. Rodriguez interviewed the students and coded their comments. Mr. Rodriguez tried to make sense of the comments and coded them as noted in Table 17.4. He has tried to summarize what the students were saying in terms of a category (*open coding*).

Next, Mr. Rodriguez tries to collapse the many categories into fewer categories by trying to identify commonalities (*axial coding*). He recalls reading an article on student engagement in the journal *Educational Leadership* (Newmann & Wehlage, 1993) where the authors described a concept known as authentic work (e.g., meaningful versus nonsensical). Authentic work is identified by its connection to the real world, its ability to provide a sense of ownership for students, and its use of extrinsic rewards and intrinsic interests. Mr. Rodriguez notes several of the comments he coded in the open-coding phase (real-world connections, intrinsic interest, extrinsic rewards) seemed to fit with the description in the literature of authentic work. He combines the coded comments into a broader category called *authentic work*.

Mr. Rodriguez then has several statements left coded as *active learning strategies*. He believes this is an important concept and is different from authentic work. So, he begins looking for other examples in his interview data that describes active learning (*selective coding*).

STAGES OF ANALYSIS

There are two stages of action research analysis, **description** and **sense making**. During the description stage, you review the data and ask yourself what did you see and what was happening (e.g., when Mr. Rodriguez was conducting the initial coding). During the sense-making stage, you try to consider how the pieces fit together and what stands out (e.g., when Mr. Rodriguez interpreted how the pieces fit together). During the sense-making stage, data may be organized in different ways based on such things as chronology, people, key events, key issues (as

Table 17.4 Coding of Student Comments

Student Comments	Coded Category
"Usually, we like did chapters and assignments in the book, but one time I remember to this day, we had an assignment like we had a certain amount of money, like $2,000, and we had to get an apartment and a uniform for the job, and pay the electric bill and get food for the month and all this stuff. And we had to actually go to a grocery store and find out what stuff costs instead of just reading about it in class."	Real-world connections
"He'd give us Snickers or candy or take us to lunch or something if we did really good."	Extrinsic reward
"Sometimes he would bring in a movie or let us bring in a movie and bring pop and chips for everyone if the whole class did well."	Extrinsic reward
"I think you should teach about other people instead of about the stuff you always see in books like Ancient Rome and Greece and all that, like teach about stuff from another country that people never heard of and never thought of before and I think they'd be more interested because it's something new."	Intrinsic interest
"The teachers just sit there and talk and make you take notes. I would rather like them to explain it in more detail and like tell stories."	Active learning strategies
"Teachers should have us participate and like give us rewards and stuff."	Extrinsic rewards
"In the history books, I really didn't like the stuff about Columbus and slavery and stuff, but we never really talked about anything about Latinos and Hispanics and stuff and that would be more interesting for a lot of Hispanics."	Intrinsic interest
"I think the problem is that sometimes its stuff, material that isn't relative to our lives, personally. On areas that really do pertain to our lives, you know, are relevant to what we're doing today, that's what you should emphasize."	Real-world connections
"The first thing he'd do was to talk about what was in the newspaper and we'd talk about what was in the newspaper. Then he'd ask us what was going on in school and at home and how that connected. Then after we got done reading and discussing he'd like everybody loosen up and move to a group and help each other out and we'd be like laughing. Most teachers won't do that, they want you to do your own stuff and get your own work finished, but he would say "you can all work together" like he knew you was all thinking and really helping each other."	Active learning strategies

in Mr. Rodriguez' case), episodes, and the like. Organizing units emerge from the data as they are grouped and sorted into themes.

DATA INTERPRETATION IN ACTION RESEARCH

Data interpretation focuses on the implications or meanings that emerge from the analysis. Interpretation is used to help make the experiences being studied understandable, using description and conceptual frameworks or theories. In the interpretive step, you ask how the patterns in the data inform your thinking and what the patterns might mean. Themes, metaphors, similes, typologies, and vignettes may emerge in the interpretation stage. Claims that you make based on your interpretations must be supported by the data. Asking interpretive questions (why?) may help visualize the situation.

USING VISUALS

Concept mapping can be used to plot elements diagrammatically so you can visualize what different components of the situation relate to the problem under investigation. **Problem analysis** using visuals of antecedents and consequences

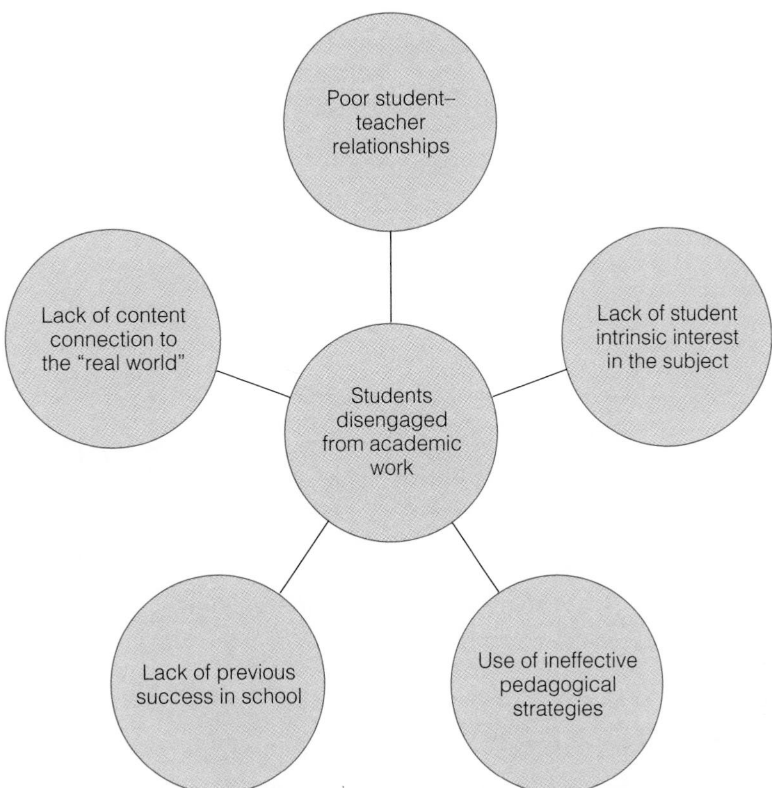

Figure 17.4 Concept Map Showing Potential Factors Leading to Student Disengagement from Social Studies

also can be helpful in interpretation. Similar to concept mapping, problem analysis identifies antecedents to the existing problem (what led up to it) and consequences that derive from the problem. Concept mapping does not try to identify what came first and what came later.

For example, let us look at the problem posed by Mr. Rodriguez in his social studies class: lack of student engagement in academic work. He might create a concept map as pictured in Figure 17.4. Or Mr. Rodriguez might develop a problem analysis to look at the antecedents and consequences related to the problem of academic disengagement as pictured in Figure 17.5.

REFLECTING

The interpretation phase of action research is a process of ongoing reflection and is the most challenging aspect of action research. The researcher continuously reviews the data as the action research process unfolds, remembering that any interpretations reached and conclusions arrived at are not for all time, are not generalizable, and are certainly not conclusive.

Data interpretation in action research is about making educated guesses or reasonable inferences. Once drawn, the interpretation can be connected with personal experience and contextualized. The interpretation provides a rationale for action planning. After interpretation, the researcher must decide what the implications are for practice.

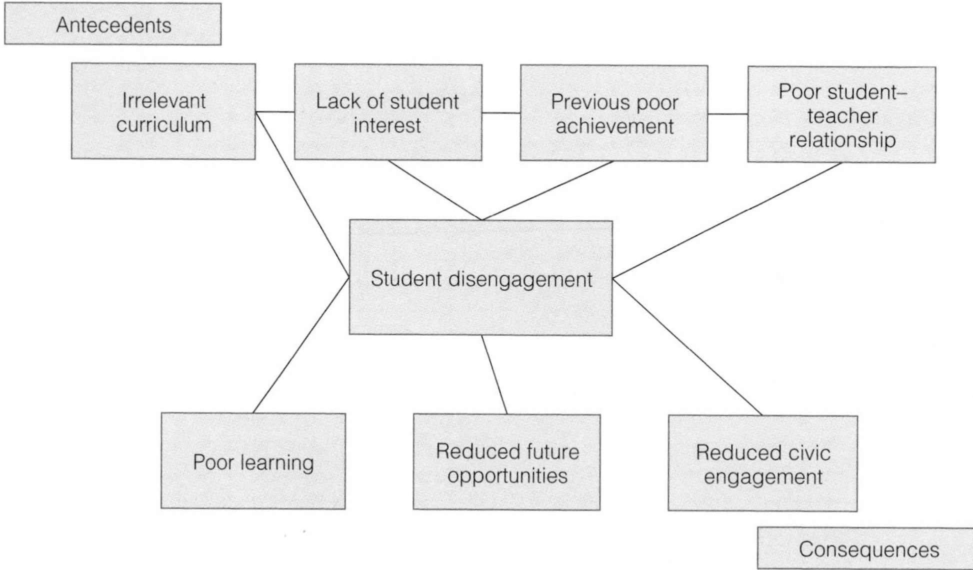

Figure 17.5 Antecedents and Consequences of Student Disengagement from Social Studies Work

ACTION PLAN

The most important step in action research follows analysis and interpretation. That step is acting on the knowledge you have gained. But before you act, you must develop an action plan.

The goal of action research is to take action based on the findings of the study. The findings provide insights for changing practice. The purpose is to formulate practical solutions to the problems that have been the focus of research. The action plan sets priorities for projected actions in order of importance, sets goals for the actions required, lists objectives required to accomplish the goals, stipulates the sequence of tasks, specifies who will carry out tasks, determines the time frame for task completion, and calculates materials, equipment, and funds required to complete the task. While this might sound daunting, in action research this process is generally less formal. For Mr. Rodriguez, the action plan might focus on identifying different teaching strategies (addressing active learning) to incorporate into his teaching repertoire and/or on reviewing the curriculum to determine how historical perspectives from other cultures (addressing intrinsic interest) might be included.

Given what is known from the research, the researcher must determine what precisely to do, what is the course of action. This step also returns the researcher

THINK ABOUT IT 17.5

Review Mr. Rodriguez' data interpretation and develop an action plan matrix (as in Table 17.5) for him to implement in his class.

Table 17.5 Sample Action Plan Matrix

Key Finding	Action	Specific Tasks	Whose Respon- sibility	When (Time)	Where	Resources Needed
Students in the online class exhibited lower levels of communica- tion patterns (initiat- ing and supporting) rather than higher level communication (challenging, summa- rizing, monitoring).	Explicitly, teach the five levels of communication to the students.	Develop a handout for the students.	Teacher	August 2004	Office	Paper
		Model the different levels.	Teacher	First week of fall classes	During class time	None
		Students have practice session.	Students	Second week of fall classes	In lab	Access to website Lab fee Graduate assistant to help monitor

to the problem formulation step (remember the cycle discussed earlier in this chapter?). Action researchers often use a matrix or guide to complete the action plan. Recall the problem in the distance education class mentioned earlier in this chapter. Table 17.5 is an action plan for addressing this problem.

ACTION RESEARCH REPORT

Besides developing and implementing an action plan, it is also important for action researchers to share their findings with others. In school settings, it is important to invite collegial dialogue about the implications of the research. You want other educators to hear what you have learned and you want to hear their reactions to the action plans you have developed. Informal strategies for sharing findings might include simple conversations with peers. More formal report writing might be shared with the school board or presented at a conference.

COMPONENTS OF THE REPORT

An outline for an action research report should include an area of focus statement or purpose statement, a summary of the related literature (usually very limited), the research questions, a description of any intervention or innovation, a description of data collection strategies used, data analysis and interpretation, and the action plan, as well as reporting the results obtained after implementing the action plan. Those familiar with the sections included in other types of research reports will find this outline very familiar.

PUBLISHING AND JUDGING REPORTS

Some action researchers may be interested in publishing their results, although this is not typically the goal in action research. There are several action research journals where researchers may wish to submit such a report: *Action Research*

International, Educational Action Research, The Qualitative Report, The Ontario Action Researcher, and the *Action Research Electronic Reader*.

If action research is to be shared, there should be criteria for judging the quality of those reports. Some argue that the criteria for action research should be based simply on whether the study produced change that resulted in a solution to the problem. Mills (2003) provides a checklist for the practitioner to judge the effectiveness of the educational action research effort (see Table 17.6).

Mr. Rodriguez might answer these questions in the following manner. His research led to action. To address intrinsic interest, he reviewed his curriculum and added historical perspectives from other cultures, particularly the African-American and Latino cultures, representing the backgrounds of the majority of his students. He shared his findings with the other teachers in the alternative school, both in a verbal report at the next teacher inservice day and via a five-page summary report. He discussed with his colleagues his biases when he began the study, thinking that the major reasons for lack of engagement in the class were problems with the students, not with his teaching. He shares that the research experience and the findings have changed his dispositions and his approach to classroom teaching. Participating in the study also has made him more reflective about his practice. Mr. Rodriguez took action to change his curriculum and hopes that by creating a more inclusive curriculum, students will be more engaged and be more successful in their academic careers. The action Mr. Rodriguez took was connected to the data that indicated a need for more authentic work in the classroom, an element of which was work that held intrinsic interest for the students. His interpretation of student data was enhanced by his connecting it to a framework he read about in the literature. He plans to continue monitoring what is happening in the classroom through ongoing observations and a focus group with students next semester, as well as reviewing student progress reports. He will probably not repeat the individual interviews as they were so time consuming. Mr. Rodriguez' colleagues are impressed with his find-

Table 17.6 Mills Criteria for Judging Action Research

Interactability of reform	Does your action research lead to action?
Audience	Who is the intended audience for the report?
Format	Have you presented the report in an acceptable format?
Prejudices	Have you shared prejudices that may affect your findings?
Professional disposition	Has the research contributed to your professional disposition?
Reflective stance	In what ways has it contributed to your reflective stance?
Life-enhancing	How have your efforts enhanced the lives of students?
Action	What action have you taken?
Action–data connection	How is the action connected to data analysis and interpretation?
Impact	How will you monitor the effects of your practice?
Changes	What would you do differently next time?
Colleague response	How did your colleagues respond to your findings and the actions recommended?

Source: Adapted from Geoffrey Mills, *Action research: A guide for the teacher researcher*, 2nd ed., 2003, p. 157. Reprinted by permission of Pearson Education, Upper Saddle River, NJ.

ings, and together they begin a study group to examine practices in the school, focusing on ways to create more authentic work for students. They encouraged Mr. Rodriguez to publish his findings in an action research forum.

INCREASING USE OF ACTION RESEARCH IN EDUCATION

Advocates for action research in education and cases of teachers doing research go back more than 50 years, but there has been a recent surge of activity in this area. Professional organizations, graduate programs, and state and federal government are increasing their focus on action research and support for teacher researchers. Why action research now?

Sagor (2000) makes the case that the focus on action research can help to professionalize teaching, enhance teacher motivation and efficacy, better meet the needs of diverse learners by looking for solutions to ever changing problems, and help schools achieve success in a standards-based environment. The standards movement and its demands for high accountability, high standards, and quality assessments, often with expectations set in legislation, presents a challenge to educators. One reason for action research gaining priority in the United States is the passage of what is referred to as the No Child Left Behind legislation that pushes educators to study the effects of teaching on student learning. Demands are being placed on educators to be more deliberate in documenting and evaluating their efforts.

Action research has been held out as a mechanism both for individual teachers to improve their practice and for entire schools to implement reform (Thomas, 2005). It has been closely tied to what has been called teacher research and has increasingly been incorporated into degree work, certification programs, professional development, and school reform. For example, in several master's degree programs in the College of Education at Northern Illinois University, action research projects are now an option for a culminating experience in place of more traditional requirements such as comprehensive examinations or theses. In one professional development program designed to assist teachers in becoming certified by the National Board of Professional Standards, action research is a key component and is tied to teachers' reflections on their practice. Proponents of action research in education assert that one key purpose of action research is to improve the practice of the individual teacher by building reflective practitioners. Teacher action research is a vehicle that can be used by teachers to untangle some of the complexity that occurs in the profession, raise teachers' voices in discussion of educational reform, and transform assumptions about the teaching profession. Action research honors the skills of educators and their inclination to influence their environment with an aim toward improving it.

ACTION RESEARCH IN PROFESSIONAL DEVELOPMENT AND SCHOOL IMPROVEMENT

Tying action research to staff development and professional growth evaluation is recommended in the literature as a part of changing the school culture and is already in practice in some schools. Action research is increasingly being used for district, state, and national school reform initiatives. For example, grant funding through the U.S. Department of Education is available for initiating field studies of reform initiatives that show promise. In one school district in Illinois, part of the school improvement plan calls for teachers working in teams to gather data as the school implements several new strategies in order to examine the impact on students and to make recommendations for changes in implementation. Using action research in schools can help teachers develop a common focus, build a professional culture and eventually a community of learners, and promote organizational learning.

STUDY GROUPS

Incorporating action research through school-based study groups can provide a means for collaboration as well as a source for energy and support. Dana and Yendol-Silva (2003) describe the following ways to collaborate: (1) In *shared inquiry*, teachers define and conduct a single research project together. (2) In *parallel inquiry*, teachers conduct two parallel but individual studies, working to support each others' individual endeavors, at times collecting data for each other, and discussing findings together. (3) In *intersecting inquiry*, teachers explore different questions but about the same topic. (4) Finally, *inquiry support* is a method of inviting others to serve as critical friends to help formulate meaningful questions, design the project, and aid in collection and analysis of data.

ACTION RESEARCH AND PROFESSIONAL DEVELOPMENT SCHOOLS

In the past decade, the field of education has seen growth in the creation of professional development schools (PDS). The National Council for the Accreditation of Teacher Education (NCATE) describes professional development schools as innovative institutions formed through partnerships between professional education programs and P to 12 schools with a fourfold mission: (1) enhanced student achievement, (2) teacher development, (3) inquiry directed at the improvement of practice, and (4) the preparation of new teachers. A PDS is often compared to teaching hospitals, hybrid institutions created in the early twentieth century. As practicing professions, both teaching and medicine require a sound academic program and intense clinical preparation. The teaching hospital was designed to provide such clinical preparation for medical students and interns; a PDS serves the same function for teacher candidates and inservice faculty. Both settings provide support for professional learning in a real-world setting in which practice takes place. NCATE recently published standards for evaluating the effectiveness of PDSs. Reflection and collaborative approaches to solving problems in the school are part of what should happen in a PDS. Collaborative action research, where researchers from both the university and school mutually define problems in the school and work to mutually solve them, is recommended in PDSs and is occurring in PDS sites across the country. In the action research process in PDS schools, teachers develop research skills, university faculty develop field-based methods, and both cultures are professionally renewed.

CHALLENGES

Of course, there are challenges to implementing action research in schools. These challenges can include lack of resources, the amount of support received, resistance to change, the nature of colleagueship in the school, reluctance to interfere with others' professional practice, reluctance to admit difficult truths, the amount of encouragement received from school leaders, the climate for risk taking in the school, and the commitment for making time for action research endeavors. In the end, however, most in the education research field would agree that using research methods to inform practice is a positive trend in schools and is worthy of support.

RESOURCES FOR MORE INFORMATION

The following are some online resources available for those interested in action research:

Access Excellence	Teacher Research in Classrooms of the 21st Century	http://www.accessexcellence.org/21st/TL/AR
ALARPM	Action Learning Action Research & Process Management Incorporated	http://www.alarpm.org.au
ARN	Action Research Network	http://actionresearch.altec.org
AROW	Action Research Open Web	http://www2.fhs.usyd.edu.au/arow/
ARR	Action Research Resources	http://www.scu.edu.au/schools/gcm/ar
CARE	Center for Applied Research in Education	http://www.uea.ac.uk/care/
CARPP	Center for Action Research in Professional Practice	http://www.bath.ac.uk/carpp
EAR	Educational Action Research	http://www.triangle.co.uk/ear
PARnet	Participatory Action Research Network	http://www.parnet.org
Queen's University	Action Research at Queen's University	http://educ.queensu.ca/~ar/
TAR	Teacher Action Research	http://www.edchange.org/multicultural/tar.html
Web Links	Goshen College	http://www.goshen.edu/soan/soan96p.htm

ACTION RESEARCH EXAMPLE

The following example of an action research report is taken from the *Ontario Action Researcher*, Vol. 2.11, Papers (1999).

Building Confidence through Math Problem-Solving

Linda Miller

My class of grade four students was not empowered. Their lack of confidence, when approaching assignments in any academic area, was very evident. They constantly asked for clarification as to the accuracy of their work or for assistance. They needed me by their side all the time. I wanted my students to become confident, capable, independent learners. I particularly wanted them to enjoy mathematics, to discuss mathematics using mathematical language, and to be able to explain what they were doing. This became the focus of my investigation.

I was taking my Mathematics Specialist Part III qualification at Brock University and became interested in a problem solving approach to Mathematics. The Ontario Curriculum Grades 1–8: Mathematics (1997) recognized that: students' attitudes have a significant effect on how they approach problem solving and how well they succeed in mathematics. Students need to understand that for some mathematics problems there may be several ways to get the correct answer. . . . Teachers can help students develop the confidence they need by modeling positive attitudes in their approach to problems. . . . By helping students to understand this, teachers can encourage them to develop the willingness to persist, to explore, and to take risks that they need to become successful problem solvers. (p. 73)

I found two articles particularly helpful in clarifying my thinking about problem solving and the development of self confidence. The first was "Promoting a problem-posing classroom," (1997), by Lyn English. English wrote that one of the main strengths of a problem-posing learning environment is ". . . that it can empower children to explore problem situations. This atmosphere creates a context for learning that is more productive and enjoyable for mathematics learning." English went on the write that, ". . . problem-posing can encourage children to take greater responsibility for their learning and dissipate common fears and anxieties about mathematics learning." (p. 173)

The second article that helped me was "Enriching mathematical creativity in the elementary classroom," by McDougall and Kajander (1997). They stated ". . . that the exploratory process is important to learning to develop concrete levels of understanding." (p. 5) Teachers need to give students appropriate time, tasks, and encouragement to think deeply and to talk about mathematical ideas. Children need manipulatives. They need time to explore and develop their problem solving abilities. Games are a motivating resource. Journal writing allows children to express the process they have used as they explored and to share their thinking processes.

Based on my reading, my question became, "If I teach a series of problem solving strategies to the students and allow time to practice each strategy, and if I provide lots of problem solving activities using manipulatives, real-life contexts and patterned activities, would I increase my students' confidence, capabilities, and independence in mathematics and as overall learners?"

CONDUCTING THE STUDY

Over the next four months, I introduced the problem solving strategies one at a time. Every day I gave students a problem of the day. They had little booklets, which were novel to them, where they did some of their problems. They started using a math journal but writing and recording their thinking processes were difficult. After a colleague's workshop, I gave them a sheet divided in half where they completed calculations on one side and explanations on the other and I believe that this helped them organize their thinking. However, this format has not been used enough yet to determine its success. Many of the activities they did for their numeration studies were game-oriented or presented in the form of patterning and algebraic format. I also gave the children lots of praise when they were successful. I encouraged them to share the work that they were doing with the principal. Samples of students' work were shared and used as models to encourage and motivate the others.

As I conducted the study, I collected data about student achievement in mathematics in a number of ways. I kept the usual records of achievement on tests and assignments. I collected and compared samples of students' work at the beginning, in the middle, and at the end of the project, and I observed how the level of support they required from me to complete work changed over time. In addition, I conducted a survey of student attitudes toward mathematics. I continued to meet weekly with my critical friends in the Mathematics Specialist course and talked through my experiences and data with them.

FINDINGS

When I first started focusing on problem solving activities, I had to walk the children through every step of the process, even after I had taught them the introductory lesson on the particular problem solving teaching method. They definitely needed my constant input. Gradually, the class became split between those who could work on their own and those who still needed my constant, "Yes, you are doing it right," statements. I had to keep reminding them that they were capable and that they could do this. One day in December, though, I realized that I had just given them an assignment and no one had whined that they could not do it, nor did it appear that I was needed while they worked. It was as if we "had arrived." I remember that day vividly. It felt so good. When the period was over, I told them what had just happened. They were very proud of themselves. Then came the day when Philip came to me after math period and said, "You know, Mrs. Miller, I didn't use to like math, but I like math now." I knew I was getting somewhere with them.

Early in January, another change was noted when I gave the students the following problem to solve:

> *An owner of a store wanted to decorate the front window with pictures of snowmen. Her design was finished when she decided to add colour to the snowmen. She wanted to use four colours: one colour each for the hat, head, middle section and bottom section of the snowmen. In how many different ways can the snowmen be coloured for the window display?*

When I asked students to complete the activity, I was happy to see that the majority of them buckled down to work with great confidence that they could do it. Most, however, were not attacking the problem in a way that would bring about a solution. On the other hand, one very quiet student, named Jill, had made an organized chart and was working on the problem in such a way that she would actually find the answer. It was so exciting and rewarding to see her do this. I shared her strategy with the other students and they also ordered their thinking and come up with solutions. Jill's confidence in her ability in Mathematics certainly rose as a result of this experience and that new-found confidence is now evident in all aspects of her work.

One week, I challenged students to design an Olympic Village. It was really an introductory lesson to pentominoes. Students were told that they had been hired to design a building for all of the Canadian athletes to live in while they were competing in the Winter Olympics. The building had to be made of 5 modules. A module was a cube. The modules had to be all the same size and had to be all on one level (no two-story buildings). Every edge of the modules was to line up with another edge. I was happy to see that everyone was able to do this task, after the initial introductory lesson using centicubes and centimetre graph paper.

Two days later, as students were completing their work on the Olympic Village, I told them that this question was from one of last year's province wide tests. One of the students spoke out and said, "Yeah, but this was a lot easier than those questions." I said, "Really? Well then, you'll be surprised to hear that this was a question from the grade 6 province wide test."

Another student then said, "Wow, grade fours doing grade six work!" They all felt ten feet tall.

Then the first student blurted out, "But it was easier because you made us believe in ourselves and believe that math is easy."

QUESTIONNAIRE RESULTS

Near the end of the project, I gave the children a questionnaire on their feelings about mathematics. I asked them to tell me what math is to them. All but one of the students said that they had changed as math learners because now they liked math whereas they did not at the beginning of the year. Of the eighteen students who responded, ten said, "Math is fun." Seven said that it was numbers and all that came with number work. Other responses included, "Math is cool because it helps you to learn a lot of things," and, "Math is a subject that teaches you neat things to do with numbers." Perhaps the most thoughtful response came from one young lady who wrote, "Math is a learning experience that helps us learn or become learners. It helps us understand better and to have knowledge. I feel math is something you need in life, and it makes you smart and intelligent."

I also asked students to rank from one to five, with one being their favourite, the strands of mathematics identified in the Ontario Curriculum, Grades 1–8: Mathematics (1997). Here are the results:

	1st	2nd	3rd	4th	5th
Numeration	*4*	*3*	*3*	*6*	*2*
Geometry	*9*	*2*	*4*	*2*	*1*
Measurement	*0*	*0*	*2*	*5*	*9*
Pattern/Algebra	*0*	*4*	*8*	*3*	*3*
Data Management	*4*	***10***	*1*	*2*	*1*

I found the results interesting. Geometry was the favourite of all the strands and measurement the least favourite although it was almost tied for fourth. I wonder if this was because we were doing geometry the week of this survey and the children were having great success in the work. I also wonder if it was because we had not done enough measurement to make students feel confident in their abilities. We had done a great deal of data management work and they had really enjoyed the work they did on the computer.

CONCLUSIONS

If I had to evaluate the success of my research, I would say that it has been successful. The children are more confident and independent as learners. However, I wish to qualify that success. It has been at the expense of other subjects. I gave extra time to problem solving activities and mathematics and took time away from other subjects, especially from Environmental Studies. Sometimes, I carried on too long with an activity. The children do not understand the concept of a deadline and do not seem to care that they take too long at an activity. Next year I will survey the students at the beginning of the year, during the middle and at the end to evaluate their feelings about math. I should have done one right at the beginning. The children are still not proficient at recording their thoughts in their math journals but I no longer hear, "I did it in my head," and I no longer have to reply, "Tell me what you did in your head."

I have changed as a teacher of math this year. I finally feel capable and confident introducing and teaching problem solving strategies. I am still reworking my teaching strategies, but that is what teaching is all about, making connections and refining ideas. I believe even more strongly in the value of games and activities as learning tools. As the Ontario Curriculum Grades 1–8: Mathematics puts it, "The freedom to explore and the process of exploration itself are essential elements in the maturation of students' capacity for mathematical reasoning." (p.76) I want my students to have the freedom to explore, but I need that freedom too. We will explore together.

REFERENCE LIST

Clements, Douglas. (1997). "(Mis?)constructing constructivism." Teaching Children Mathematics, December. p. 198–200.

English, Lyn D. (1997). "Promoting a problem-posing classroom." Teaching Children Mathematics. November. p. 172–179.

McDougall, Douglas & Kajander, Ann. (1997). "Enriching mathematical creativity in the elementary classroom." OAME/AOEM Gazette, December. p. 5–9.

Ontario Ministry of Education and Training. (1997). The Ontario curriculum, grades 1–8, Mathematics. Toronto: Ontario Ministry of Education and Training. 1997.

THINK ABOUT IT 17.6

After reading the sample action research article, answer the following questions:

1. What was the problem or focus of research for the teacher?
2. What did she learn from reviewing the literature?
3. How did she frame her research question?
4. What did she do differently in her class?
5. What types of data did she collect?
6. How did she analyze her data?
7. What interpretations did she make?
8. Based on her concluding statements, what action do you think the teacher proposes next?

Answers:

1. Helping her students enjoy mathematics and develop confidence.
2. That a problem-posing atmosphere empowers children to develop their problem-solving abilities and enhances their self-esteem.
3. "If I teach a series of problem solving strategies to the students and allow time to practice each strategy, and if I provide lots of problem solving activities using manipulatives, real-life contexts and patterned activities, would I increase my students' confidence, capabilities, and independence in mathematics and as overall learners?"
4. Gradually introduced problem-solving strategies and game-oriented activities. Encouraged sharing and praised success.
5. Data about student achievement over time, tests and samples of students' work, students' attitudes toward mathematics.
6. Discussion of observations with peers and qualitative analysis of observations, attitude questionnaires analyzed quantitatively and qualitatively.
7. The strategies she employed did lead to student empowerment, greater problem-solving performance, and more positive attitudes toward mathematics.
8. She will assess the children's attitude toward mathematics and problem-solving skills early in the year, as well as during and at the end of the year, and will strive to improve her own and her students' time management skills.

SUMMARY

Action research in the field of education has recently experienced a resurgence. Focused on solving practical problems in everyday settings, action research does not aim to generalize. The three main characteristics of action research are that it is locally focused, conducted by the practitioner, and results in changes in practice. It most commonly uses qualitative research approaches.

The action research process is cyclical, involving reflection, planning, acting, and observing. In education, problems investigated using action research typically focus on student learning, curriculum, instructional strategies, and professional development. Triangulation of data is important in action research. The types of data collected can be categorized as experiencing, enquiring, or examining. Rigor and ethical treatment are important in action research as in other research.

Data analysis typically relies on qualitative coding processes and focuses on description and sense making. Interpretation can be enhanced through the use of visuals, such as concept maps. Once interpretation is completed, the most important step is developing an action plan and then taking action based on the findings.

KEY CONCEPTS

act
action research
axial coding
concept mapping
description
enquiring
examining
experiencing
explanation
literature review
observe
open coding
plan
practical action research
problem analysis
reflect
reflection
selective coding
sense making
triangulation

EXERCISES

1. What are the three key components in the definition of action research?
2. List at least five ways that action research may differ from other approaches to research.
3. Describe a problem or area of focus in education from your own experience that might be investigated using action research.
4. Draw a pictorial representation of the variables or elements you think contribute to the problem.
5. What are the three categories of data described. Provide at least two examples of data sources that would be in each category.
6. Name three different types of coding that might be used in action research.
7. Some authors in the field claim that only one criterion of validity is necessary in action research. What is that criterion?
8. How important is generalizability in action research?
9. Why is action research seeing a resurgence in the field?
10. Listed below are some actual action research problems that have been investigated and written about. How do these problems fit into the four categories discussed, using "S" for student learning, "C" for curriculum, "I" for instruction, or "T" for teacher professional development.
   a. Mr. Daniels was worried about taking over a class midyear from a teacher whose style was much more laid back, while his style was much more structured.
   b. Ms. Grace wondered what strategies she could use to make smoother transitions between classroom activities so as to reduce wasted time.
   c. Mrs. Hall was concerned about the lack of reinforcement opportunities students in her French class had available once they went home at the end of the day.
   d. Mr. Robbins wondered whether WebCT (an online course development tool) could provide an improved alternative for students to share their reflections on student teaching.
   e. Ms. Stevens wonders whether the new district-adopted character education curriculum is biased.
   f. Principal Talbot is concerned that so few Hispanic/Latino parents attend school functions.

ANSWERS

1. The research is situated in a local context and focused on a local issue. The research is conducted by and for the practitioner. The research results in an action or a change implemented by the practitioner in the context.
2. Responses may vary. Based on Table 17.3.
3. Responses will vary.
4. Responses will vary.
5. Experiencing, enquiring, and examining. Examples in each may vary. For experiencing, typical responses might be observation logs or field notes, journaling, and shadow studies. For enquiring, typical responses might be interviews, focus groups, and surveys. For examining, typical responses might be student work samples, records, and test scores.
6. Open, axial, and selective coding.
7. Whether or not the solution developed from the study actually solves the problem.
8. Generalizability is not the goal in action research. The primary goal is to solve a real problem in the practitioner's context and to do something to improve it.
9. Movements to professionalize teaching and calls for accountability and data-driven decision making at both the state and national levels.
10. a, T; b, T; c, S; d, I; e, C; f, S

INFOTRAC COLLEGE EDITION

Use the keyword **action research** to locate a study that used this research strategy. What type of data did the researcher collect?

Chapter 18

Guidelines for Writing Research Proposals

IT IS VERY IMPORTANT TO PLAN AHEAD.

INSTRUCTIONAL OBJECTIVES

After studying this chapter, the student will be able to:

1. Describe the components of a quantitative research proposal.
2. Describe the components of a qualitative research proposal.
3. Identify common weaknesses in quantitative research proposals.
4. Critique quantitative research proposals.
5. Critique qualitative research proposals.
6. Select statistics appropriate for the questions being asked and the data involved.
7. Describe ethical and legal considerations in research.
8. Describe the role of an institutional review board.
9. Write a research proposal that meets the guidelines.

In most cases researchers will need to present their projects in organized written form at two stages: (1) the initial stage, which requires preparation of a research proposal to be presented to a professor or to a dissertation committee and (2) the final stage, a finished report of the results of the research. This chapter deals with the initial stage; Chapter 19 discusses the final stage.

In research, as in sampler making, planning ahead is essential.

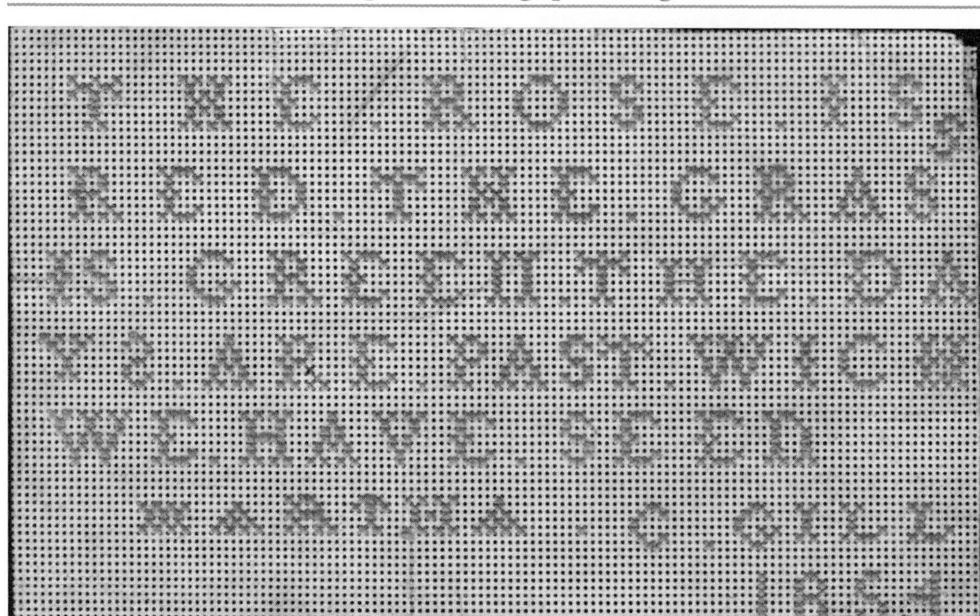

Figure 18.1 Nineteenth-Century Sampler Discovered by One of the Authors in a Box of Books Purchased at a Farm Auction

WRITING A RESEARCH PROPOSAL

A research proposal is a written plan for a project that will be submitted to others for evaluation. Writing the research proposal can be the most crucial and exciting step in the research process. At this stage the whole project crystallizes into concrete form. The researcher's inspirations and insights are translated into step-by-step plans for discovering new knowledge. In a well-organized and well-written proposal, researchers demonstrate that they know what they are seeking and that they will know how to successfully complete the planned project. The readers will evaluate the worth of the proposed study and may make suggestions for improving it. The format of a proposal may be the relatively informal outline offered by a student to satisfy the requirements of a research course, a formal thesis, or dissertation proposal presented to a committee or a funding request to a foundation or governmental agency.

QUANTITATIVE RESEARCH PROPOSAL

The following suggested outline for writing a quantitative research proposal contains the steps essential to formulate and propose a research study:

1. Introduction
   a. Statement of the problem
   b. Review of the literature
   c. Statement of the hypothesis(es)

2. Methodology
   a. Subjects
   b. Instruments
   c. Procedures
3. Analysis of data
   a. Data organization
   b. Statistical procedures
4. Significance of the study
   a. Implications
   b. Applications
5. Time schedule and budget
   a. Time schedule
   b. Budget
6. References

Although you need not follow this outline rigidly, it should provide a useful guide for writing any proposal because all aspects listed here must be considered.

INTRODUCTION

A crucial part of a research proposal for quantitative research is the introduction to the proposed study. In the very first paragraph, state the research problem clearly and unambiguously, avoiding emotionally charged words or phrases. Then link the problem to the body of information available in the field and establish the importance of and the need for carrying out the proposed research. The introduction should convince the readers that you have reviewed the related research and have a thorough understanding of the problem. Regardless of how tightly you formulate the design of the study and how well you select the statistical procedures, unless the introduction is written carefully and intelligently, other parts of the proposal will probably not receive serious consideration. It is not unusual for proposals to be turned down solely on the basis of a poor introduction, without much consideration being given to the proposed methodology and statistical design. The introduction provides the framework for the rest of the proposal. So prepare this section with care, caution, and the aim of promoting the reader's interest in the problem.

The introduction to a research proposal should include (1) a statement of the problem, (2) a review of the literature, and (3) a statement of the hypothesis(es).

Statement of the Problem

State the problem clearly and directly very early in the introduction, ideally at the beginning of the first paragraph. The problem statement should imply a question about the relationship between specified variables. The statement can take interrogative form or can simply say, "The purpose of the study is to explore the relationship between . . . and . . ." You need not operationalize the variables at this point, only mention them in conceptual form. This section of the introduction should also include a brief description of the background of the problem and the potential significance of the study, although it is imperative to avoid the temptation to sell the importance of the topic before stating it. Two common errors to watch for are (1) beginning the introduction with an elaborate presentation of the background of a problem before you have clearly stated the problem itself and (2) concentrating on a justification for the study at this point, burying the problem statement in the discussion or bringing it in only vaguely near the end. Another common error is to assume that the reader knows as much about the content of the question as you do. State the problem so that it can be understood by someone who is generally sophisticated but who is relatively uninformed concerning your specific problem.

At an appropriate point in this section, define, in the way they will be used in the study, any terms that may not be familiar to the reader or to which you are ascribing special meanings. The specific limitations of the scope of the study and a foreshadowing of the hypothesis should close the section.

Review of the Literature

The literature review presents what is currently known about the problem under consideration and thus sets the scholarly context for the question or hypotheses of the proposed study. The review shows how the proposed research fits in with the existing body of knowledge. Include some of the landmark studies in the field as well as the most recent research. Readers can see that your question has been investigated by others over a period of years and may be convinced that it is a problem worthy of further investigation. You should include not only literature dealing with research on the variables of the proposed study but also discussions of the theoretical background of the problem. The literature review allows you to show your committee or other readers that you really know the scholarship that has been done on the question. The literature cited need not be exhaustive but should contain the most important research relating to the hypothesis of the study.

Organize the literature by topic. Topical organization points out to the reader what is known about various aspects of the study. Thus, a complete picture of the background of the study is put together step by step. Including a critique of some of the most pertinent research further convinces the reader that you have a good grasp of the problem. A pitfall to avoid in discussing related literature is to present a series of abstracts, one per paragraph. This offers the audience tedious reading and misses the opportunity for laying meaningful groundwork for the study. It is much better to organize by topic and to point out how the studies presented relate to the planned research.

Not all related studies need be discussed in detail. In reviewing several similar studies, you can describe the most important one and then simply state that the results were confirmed in similar studies that are mentioned but not described in detail. Enthusiastic beginning researchers often imagine their proposed study is unique and that no related research is available. This is very rarely the case. A thorough search almost always turns up several research studies related to at least some aspects of a proposed study. Even if there is no research in the field, there is usually literature of a theoretical or speculative nature that should be included as part of the background of a study. Of course, you should include theories and research results contrary to your stated hypothesis as well as those in agreement with it.

The related literature section should conclude with a discussion of the findings and their implications. Here you share the insights gained from your review of the literature and can point out gaps in what is known about the topic, thus leading directly to the question you propose to investigate.

Statement of the Hypothesis(es)

The hypothesis should state concisely the expected relationship between the variables in the study. The research hypothesis is typically determined by the implications of the related research findings and the deductive logic of the underlying theory. Explain the link between theory and hypothesis so that the reader will be able to see the rationale for the hypothesis.

Some research, such as surveys, may simply state the problem in question form. For example: How do the parents in the Monroe County School District feel about a longer school day? But most quantitative research states a hypothesis. It should probably be stated in operational form; however, if this is not possible, it can be stated in conceptual terms followed by any operational definitions of the variables. Operational definitions of all variables are essential in any research proposal.

METHODOLOGY

In the methodology part of the proposal, the author shows *how* the study will be carried out so that the research question will be answered or the hypothesized relationships will be observed, if in fact these relationships exist. This section should also convince the reader that what you plan to do is the best procedure for investigating the problem. Note that this section is written using future tense because nothing has yet been done. If the methodology you describe in the proposal is actually the same as the method you eventually use in conducting the study, then you have a big section of the final report already written. It is only necessary to change the future tense of the proposal to the past tense used in the final report.

In previous chapters, we introduced appropriate research designs for different types of research. Select from among these research designs, experimental or otherwise, the one that best suits the question and/or hypothesis under consideration. For example, if you are to compare two methods of teaching chemistry, you are in fact raising an experimental question. This research problem requires at least two groups of subjects: experimental and control. If you also wish to investigate the interaction effect between methods of teaching chemistry and another variable—aptitude, for instance—the question, although still experimental, asks for a more sophisticated design than that of a two-group design. In this case you need to set up a factorial design with at least four groups for such a study.

In the methodology part of the proposal, the author includes a description of the population of interest, proposed sampling procedures, methods of data collection, and instruments to be used. A convenient way of presenting the research methodology is to categorize all information regarding the design as (1) subjects, (2) instruments, or (3) procedures, as appropriate.

Subjects

The first step in identifying the subjects in a study is to describe the population of interest: Is the study concerned with college freshmen, dyslexic 6-year-olds, principals of elementary schools, and so forth? Then the author/researcher describes the procedure for drawing the sample from the population. If random selection is not possible, explain why you have chosen a particular procedure for sample selection and how well the sample to be used will resemble the population of interest. You need to include the number of subjects and a description of their most important characteristics such as age, gender, academic level, ethnicity, ability level (if relevant) and so on. A careful description of the subjects can help the reader of the proposal to determine if, in the reader's view, the results of the study can be generalized from your sample to the appropriate population.

The following example describes the subjects in a proposal: "The children in this experiment all attend a public elementary school in the southeastern United States. Three intact classrooms will participate. There will be 17 children (11 boys and 6 girls) in kindergarten; 24 in second grade (13 boys and 11 girls); and 21 in fourth grade (10 boys and 11 girls). The children represent a variety of social, economic, and cultural backgrounds: Approximately one-third are African Americans, a few are Asian Americans, and the majority are European Americans."

Instruments

The goal of a research project is to investigate relationships between constructs. However, because constructs are usually impossible to measure directly, you must select or develop indicators that will approximate them as well as possible. If an instrument is already established, the proposal should include reported evidence of its reliability and validity for the purpose of the study. In cases where the instruments are to be developed by the researcher, it is necessary to outline the procedure to be followed in developing them. This outline should include the steps that will be taken to obtain validity and reliability data on these instruments. If describing the reliability and validity procedures results in so much detail that it interrupts the continuity of the proposal, it is preferable to include this material in an appendix rather than in the text.

A description of the instrument might include, for example, "Students' prerecess and postrecess classroom behavior and their outdoor recess behavior will be observed daily for two months. A total of four observers, blind to the purpose of the study will be used: Three will be regular observers and one will be a rotating observer whose primary job is to be a reliability judge. Reliability will be measured with a κ coefficient."

Procedures

A careful description of the procedures of a study is a basic requirement of a quantitative research proposal. In this section the author describes the way in which the study will be carried out so the hypothesized relationships can be observed, if these relationships in fact exist. By designing the study explicitly as an operation to permit the observation of the hypothesized relationships, you lay the foundation for the study.

In this section, one includes all the information necessary for replication of the study. In an experimental research proposal, for example, the author should list the groups and how subjects will be assigned to groups and give a step-by-step description of the manipulations planned for each. These steps should be completely designated in operational form. You should also mention the possibility of confounding variables and specify how you propose to control for these variables. For instance, you might control for student and teacher differences by randomly assigning students and teachers to the control and experimental groups and making the time spent, physical setting, and facilities equivalent. If the proposal involves a survey, you need to describe all the steps involved in the development of the instrument, its distribution, follow-up procedures, training of the interviewers, and so on.

You should also mention any known limitations of the proposed methodology. The limitations are any factors that may negatively impact the results of the study or the generalizability of the results. Limitations may include size of the sample, selection of the subjects, the setting for the study, use of a pretest, length of the study, and so on. But you should be careful about pointing out too many weaknesses. Bryant (2004) writes: "Don't downplay the potential importance of your study. One wants to be cognizant of weaknesses in design and method, but I think it is a strategic mistake to speak too loudly of weaknesses in concept or method until after the dissertation proposal has been approved" (p. 59). Assuming the study goes forward, one can always discuss limitations in the final report.

Documents such as teaching or reading materials planned for an experiment need not be included in the main text of the proposal because discussion of such details usually interrupts continuity of the proposal. We recommend that the author place these documents in an appendix, describing them briefly but clearly in the procedures section. It is, however, essential to explain in this section any differences in the presentation of these materials to the different groups involved in the experiment.

After the section on procedures has been drafted, read it to verify that you have described all steps necessary to answer every question and test every hypothesis. You can check the completeness of this section with the question: Given the time and resources needed, could the reader carry out this research by following the steps as described? If you can answer this question in the affirmative, this section is complete.

ANALYSIS OF DATA

The next part of the research proposal describes the methods of handling and presenting data and outlines the statistical procedures to be used. Group this information in sections covering (1) data organization and (2) statistical procedures.

Data Organization

The presentation of the results of a research study can take different forms depending on the way the findings are organized. You must plan in advance for the arrangement of research results into an organized form. This is best done by reference to questions or hypotheses of the study. Planning in advance for the organization and presentation of data enables a researcher to determine whether the information being collected is relevant to the research questions. Those who bypass this step often find they have wasted considerable time and money in collecting irrelevant pieces of information.

Tables, figures, and charts are essential means for organizing and summarizing a whole set of data. While the research is in the planning stage, you should be able to picture how the data will be organized and presented in tabular form. At this stage you should list the bits of information that will be available for each subject, decide how you will present and summarize the information, and decide what statistical procedures to employ.

Statistical Procedures

The design of the study determines what statistical techniques should be employed, not vice versa. In other words, the researcher decides what design will permit observation of the hypothesized relationships, then selects the statistical procedure that fits the questions asked and the nature of the data involved. In this section, one should explain what data will be considered, what statistical procedures will be used and why, and what results will be important in confirming the hypothesis.

The most commonly used statistical procedures have been described in earlier chapters. They are summarized for convenience in Tables 18.1 and 18.2. Table 18.1 is designed to help identify the indexes that may be used to describe in summary form the data of a study. The reader is also referred to Rowntree (2004) for a discussion of statistical procedures.

The appropriate statistical procedure is determined partly by the type of measurement scale characterizing the dependent variable. Therefore, the rows in the table are identified as interval, ordinal, and nominal. Columns (1), (2), and (3) list the various purposes descriptive statistics may serve. The most common uses of these statistics are the following:

1. To provide an index to describe a group or the difference between groups (measures of central location)
2. To provide an index to describe the variability of a group or differences in the variability of groups (measures of variability)
3. To locate an individual in a group (indexes of individual location)
4. To provide an index to describe the relationship of variables within a population (measures of correlation)
5. To describe how a set is divided into subsets
6. To describe the interaction among two or more variables in relation to a criterion (measures of interaction)

The required cell can be located by identifying the row and column heading appropriate to your study. Each cell is divided, and the section to use is determined by whether the study is concerned with one group or with more than one group. (Recall that you *may* choose a procedure for a lower scale of measurement but not the reverse; for example, you may use a median or a mode to describe inter-

Table 18.1 Descriptive Statistics

Type of Scale of Dependent Variable	Purpose of the Statistic: (1) Central Tendency		(2) Variability		(3) Location	
	One Group	More Than One Group	One Group	More Than One Group	One Group	More Than One Group
Interval	Mean	Difference between means	Standard deviation or variance	Difference between standard deviations or variances	z Score, or other standard score	Difference between an individual's score in more than one distribution
Ordinal	Median	Difference between medians	Quartile deviation[a]	Difference between quartile deviations[a]	Percentile rank	Difference between an individual's percentile rank in more than one distribution
Nominal	Mode	Difference between modes	Range	Difference between ranges	Label or categorization	Label or categorization

Type of Scale of Dependent Variable	Purpose of the Statistic: (4) Correlation		(5) Subsets		(6) Interaction	
	One Group	More Than One Group	One Group	More Than One Group	One Group	More Than One Group
Interval	Pearson r	Difference in Pearson r for same variables in two groups			Difference between observed cell means and expected cell means in factorial ANOVA (observed interaction)	Differences in observed interaction among groups
Ordinal	Spearman's rho or Kendall's tau[a] or W[a]	Difference in Spearman rho, Kendall's tau, or W				
Nominal	point biserial correlation,[a] biserial correlation,[a] or phi coefficient	Difference in correlations for same variables in two groups	Proportion or percentage	Differences in proportions or percentages	Differences between observed cell frequencies and expected cell frequencies	Differences in observed interaction among groups

[a]This statistic is not described in this text but may be found in any number of statistics texts.

val data but may not use a mean to describe ordinal or nominal data.) In determining what type of scale to use in expressing the data, consider the advantages of each of three scales. Interval data provide more information than ordinal data, and ordinal data provide more information than nominal data. In making inferences, statistical tests of interval data are more "powerful" than tests of ordinal data; that is, you have a greater chance of rejecting a null hypothesis when you use interval measures than when you use ordinal measures. In the same man-

Table 18.2 Inferential Statistics

Type of Scale of Dependent Variable	Purpose of the Statistic: (1) Central Location		(2) Variability		(3) Individual Location	
	One Group	More Than One Group	One Group	More Than One Group	One Group	More Than One Group
Interval	Standard error of the mean	*t* Test or one-way ANOVA		Bartlett's test[a] or *t* test for homogeneity of variance;[a] *F*-max[a] statistics	Standard error of measurement[a]	Standard error of difference scores[a]
Ordinal	Standard error of median[a]	Wilcoxon and Mann–Whitney tests,[a] Kruskal–Wallis one-way ANOVA,[a] or Friedman's test[a]				
Nominal						

Type of Scale of Dependent Variable	Purpose of the Statistic: (4) Correlation		(5) Subsets		(6) Interaction	
	One Group	More Than One Group	One Group	More Than One Group	One Group	More Than One Group
Interval	*t* Test for Fisher's *z* transformation or *F* test for linearity[a]	*t* Test for Fisher's *z* transformation[a]			*F* test for multifactor ANOVA	*F* test for multifactor ANOVA
Ordinal	Test for Spearman's rho or Kendall's tau[a]	Test for Kendall's *W*				
Nominal	Chi-square test for goodness of fit	Cochran's *Q*[a]	Chi-square or binomial test[a]	Chi-square test of independence	Log linear analysis[a]	Chi-square test for log linear analysis[a]

[a]This statistic is not described in this text but may be found in any number of statistics texts.

ner, ordinal tests are more powerful than nominal measures. Therefore, when a choice is possible, prefer interval data to ordinal and ordinal data to nominal. For example, if you have interval data for the dependent variable and want an index to describe the difference between groups, Table 18.1 identifies the difference between two means as an appropriate statistic. (You could, if you chose, use the difference between medians, but this would be less powerful than the difference between means.)

If the study is inferential in nature, the researcher will proceed to test the statistical significance of the index selected. Table 18.2 lists appropriate statistics for this purpose.

Remember that a statistical procedure is selected on the basis of its appropriateness for answering the question involved in the study. Nothing is gained by using a complicated procedure when a simple one will do just as well. Statistics are to serve research, not to dominate it. We often tell our students, "Imagine you have gotten a fantastic grant for doing your study, but you are run over by a truck the very next day. Could a colleague pick up your proposal, actually conduct the study and analyze the data?" If you can honestly answer this question in the affirmative, the data analysis part of the proposal is complete.

SIGNIFICANCE OF THE STUDY

In this section you need to explain why the problem is an important one to study. Try to answer the question: What difference will this study make to anyone? Some researchers prefer to discuss the significance of the problem in the introduction to the proposal. The literature review also helps to establish the significance of the study. But having a separate section on significance provides the opportunity to relate the problem to both the background and the design of the study. This section is best handled in two stages: (1) implications and (2) applications.

Implications

Because the aim of research is to increase knowledge, the author of the proposal should show how his or her particular study will do this, by discussing how the results will contribute to theory and knowledge in the specific area to which the research question is related, and to what extent these results will be useful in solving problems and answering questions in the general field. Finally, you show how the results of the study will provide grounds for further research in the area. In addition, you may explain how your own experience and expertise, coupled with the facilities and goals of the institution where the study is being carried out, place you in a favorable position to solve the problem in question.

Applications

The author should be able to convince readers of the potential application of the findings to educational practice. This discussion should show how and to what extent educational practitioners could use the results to improve their work. To find the extent to which the study has application to educational practice, you may ask the following questions: Will the results of my study change anything in my field? Would my results help teachers, school counselors, principals, or other educators to improve their work? This aspect carries considerable weight in attracting research funds for carrying out the study. Many foundations evaluate research proposals on the basis of potential application to practice.

TIME SCHEDULE AND BUDGET

All research should be planned with regard to the feasibility of carrying out the work. A proposal should conclude with a presentation of (1) schedule and (2) budget.

Time Schedule

The researcher needs to identify the sequence of stages necessary to complete the proposed research and to estimate the time needed to complete each stage. Dividing the project into manageable stages, then assigning a date to complete each stage helps systematize the project, enables you to estimate the effort that will be required to complete the entire project, and provides opportunities for periodically evaluating the development of the project.

Budget

Reviewing the previous sections of the proposal, the researcher now needs to determine the resources necessary to carry out the proposed research and make careful estimates of the costs of such things as supplies, travel expenses, duplicating, personnel, and consultant fees. If you are requesting external funding, most institutions have someone, such as a contract officer, to help plan the budget and fit it into the requirements of the anticipated funding agency.

REFERENCES

In this section, the researcher must list the references that were cited in the literature review as well as any other sources cited in the development of the proposal. The reference list includes the full publication information for each entry, arranged in alphabetical order according to the senior author's last name. In the field of education, the APA format is the most popular for listing references in journals, dissertations, and other research publications (APA, 2001, pp. 215–281). Beginning researchers should become familiar with APA style.

CRITIQUING THE PROPOSAL

After completing the draft of a proposal, the author/researcher should go through it again carefully with a critical eye. It is also profitable to have colleagues read the proposal. Often someone else can identify weaknesses or omissions that are not evident to the author. Some of the common weaknesses found in proposals are as follows:

Introduction

1. The problem is not clearly and unambiguously stated. The reader cannot be certain what the researcher plans to do.
2. The problem is too broad for a single study.
3. The problem lacks practical or theoretical significance.
4. The study has not been linked to the existing body of knowledge in the field.

Methodology

5. The proposed design is not appropriate for answering the research question.
6. There is no discussion of extraneous variables and how they might be controlled.
7. The proposal does not provide operational definitions of the variables.
8. The proposal does not adequately discuss the validity and reliability of measuring instruments.
9. The proposal is not sufficiently detailed to allow for replication.

Analysis of Data

10. The statistical procedures are not appropriate for analyzing the data.

QUALITATIVE RESEARCH PROPOSAL

The qualitative research proposal starts with a broad picture of the intended study and ends with details on how the inquiry will be conducted. Some authors recommend using the standard outline for a quantitative proposal in writing a proposal for a qualitative study (Fitzpatrick, Secrist, & Wright, 1998; Glatthorn, 1998). Maxwell (1996) states, "The purpose of a proposal is to explain and justify your proposed study to an audience of nonexperts on your topic" (p. 100). Many of the key concerns that must be addressed in designing a qualitative proposal are similar to those that are addressed in quantitative proposals. There also are some significant differences.

Qualitative research is an iterative process (Piantanida & Garman, 1999), hence the initial proposal is the best guess of the researcher as to what will happen. The contours and details of the study, including the guiding questions and procedures, may change during the research process. Since qualitative studies may evolve, the proposal may not in the end be entirely aligned with what actually happens, but that is no excuse for not developing a detailed plan. You must simply explain the flexibility required and indicate how you will go about making future decisions as the research process unfolds.

The qualitative research proposal helps others understand what is under study, why the study is needed and important, how the inquiry will be conducted, and how the results will contribute to body of knowledge. As in the quantitative proposal, the qualitative proposal describes the focus and research questions, reviews the literature, and provides a description of the research procedures (methodology). A brief outline of recommended components in a qualitative proposal follows.

1. Introduction
   - a. Intent of the study/focus/purpose
   - b. Situating the self
   - c. Guiding questions
   - d. Review of relevant literature/discourse
2. Research process/methodology
   - a. Relationship to research genre
   - b. Selection of site/case/subjects/participants
   - c. Description of setting
   - d. Data collection process
3. Data analysis/presentation
   - a. Data analysis procedures
   - b. Validity issues
   - c. Ethical issues
4. Importance/significance of the study
5. Time schedule and budget
6. References

FOCUS AND RESEARCH QUESTIONS

The introduction section of a proposal describes the purpose of the study and its significance. It provides background information to place the study in context. In identifying the research focus or purpose, you should take care to assess your own emotional involvement in the topic. While you should be interested, perhaps even passionate, about your topic, you must not be so emotionally involved that your own biases prevent you from adequate interpretation of the findings. One way to ensure that you consider this aspect is to include a section in the introduction that situates yourself in the study. Why are you interested in this topic? What personal background and knowledge do you bring to the study? Some authors recommend an autobiographical section that addresses the potential for bias.

The research focus or purpose may be written as a central overarching question. It describes something that "perplexes or challenges the mind" (Merriam, 1998, p. 56). The research focus must be realistic, not too vast and not too narrow. The focus may be identified from everyday practice or experience, from literature, or from current political or social issues. Although not as common as in quantitative research, the focus may also be derived from theory with an intent to elaborate or modify the theory. Once the focus is defined, you can identify the guiding questions or subquestions for the study. The guiding questions lay out the conceptual structure of the inquiry. Qualitative research questions are typically about process or understanding (why or how something happened, what happened, how do those involved understand the experience, what does it mean to them). These questions help identify what to observe or what to ask in interviews and direct the analysis approach, similar to how hypotheses in quantitative research direct the methodology. Hypotheses in quantitative research, however, are more precise.

RELATED LITERATURE AND DISCOURSE

Some qualitative researchers say not to review the literature until data collection is underway to avoid creating bias. We do not subscribe to this view. No problem exists in isolation and the literature should not be ignored. Reviewing the literature provides a context for the study. It connects aspects of the inquiry to broader bodies of knowledge. If nothing else, reviewing the literature helps prevent duplicating research and helps avoid making mistakes in research design that others have made. The literature can provide a foundation for your study, and no matter the topic there is always related literature. The literature helps you identify what is already known, how it relates to your question, how your study might contribute to understanding of this topic, and what are potential theoretical frameworks that might inform the study.

There are two key differences in the literature review in quantitative and qualitative studies. First, in a qualitative proposal, it is not assumed that the literature review is complete in the proposal. Reviewing literature in a qualitative study is an ongoing process and involves an interactive process throughout the study. As the study evolves, new literature may need to be explored. Also, literature may be embedded throughout the final document to support findings and is not restricted to a particular section of the report. Second, different kinds of information are considered appropriate to be included in the qualitative proposal, hence the call by some authors to call this section a "review of discourse" rather than a review of literature. For example, it may be appropriate to trace the historical evolution of the study topic, to trace the conceptual threads or themes within discourse on the topic, to map various schools of thought or ideological positions or disciplinary perspectives related to the topic, or to describe the positions of various stakeholder groups. You may also review personal experience and knowledge that are relevant to the inquiry.

RESEARCH PROCEDURES/METHODS

The procedures section of a qualitative proposal explains how each guiding question will be addressed—what information will be used to address each question, how that information will be gathered, from what sources, and so forth. Qualitative proposals often include a rationale for the selection of the specific research genre. In addition, the procedures section often includes a description of the research context (e.g., the description of the case).

As with quantitative proposals, qualitative proposals should address the topics of sampling and data collection methods. If you use purposive sampling, you should describe the selection critiera, the essential attributes participants must have, and explain why these criteria are important to the study. In case studies, you should describe the parameters of the study or how the case is "bounded." Although you may not know the exact number of individuals or cases or documents you will eventually include in the study, you should approximate and explain how adjustments may be made as the study is underway. It is advisable to specify a minimum number based on reasonable expectations.

Also as in quantitative proposals, data collection methods should be described. What kind of observations will be conducted? Where will they be conducted? Will semistructured or open interview processes be used? What are examples of questions that might be asked? How will documents be collected? You should provide some detail about the research techniques proposed.

DATA ANALYSIS

Although it may not be as simple to describe the analysis techniques to be used in a qualitative study as in a quantitative study, the researcher must still provide the proposal reader with enough information to be able to understand the analysis process. How data will be managed and processed is important. Specific analysis procedures are described in Chapter 16. This section of the proposal should foreshadow how information will be presented in the final study. What form of representation do you envision for capturing the phenomenon under study?

The data analysis portion of the proposal should address issues related to the validity of the study as well. What strategies will you use to enhance credibility? (See Chapter 16 for a discussion of potential strategies.) And how will you ensure that the rights of human subjects are protected. Issues of ethical treatment of human subjects are discussed more fully later in this chapter.

OTHER SIMILARITIES AND DIFFERENCES

As in quantitative proposals, it is also important to explain in the proposal why your study is significant. What will you learn as a result of the study and why is it worth knowing? And you should also estimate costs and time involved in conducting the study. These aspects are similar to information needed in quantitative proposals.

There is one final aspect of the qualitative proposal, however, that is often quite different from a quantitative proposal. The style or form of the writing may vary from the quantitative style. Quantitative proposals tend to read more as a science report, while qualitative proposals may read more like a book or story and have a more narrative style. The proposal should reflect the format and style anticipated for the final product. A more personalized style, including the use of the first person "I," is considered acceptable in a qualitative proposal.

IMPORTANCE OF COMPLETING THE PROPOSAL BEFORE COLLECTING DATA

In research a clear, well-stated, complete proposal indicates that the prospective researcher is actually ready to set the study in motion. It shows that the researcher knows what to do, why to do it, and how to do it. A prospective researcher who cannot produce a complete and coherent proposal is clearly not yet ready to proceed to the data-collecting stage of the project. Novice researchers are often inclined to say, "Let me collect my data now and decide what to do with it later."

Simultaneously collecting data and writing the proposal may seem to be a time-saving procedure, but that is seldom the case. Countless work-hours and thousands of dollars have been wasted in just that way. Until the proposal is formulated, you cannot be sure exactly what data you will need nor what will be the best way to handle this information in the light of the study's purpose. Researchers working under deadlines should set for themselves a date for completing the proposal well in advance of the target date for completing the entire project.

ETHICAL AND LEGAL CONSIDERATIONS

Strict adherence to ethical standards in planning and conducting both qualitative and quantitative research is most important. Researchers have obligations both to their subjects and to their profession. The proposal should state how informed consent, confidentiality, and other ethical issues will be handled. The American Educational Research Association's (AERA) code of ethics incorporates a set of standards designed specifically to guide the work of researchers in education. The ethical standards for the AERA, adopted in 1992, state that as educational researchers we should strive to maintain the integrity of our research, of our research community, and of all those with whom we have professional relations. We should pledge ourselves to do this by maintaining our own competence and that of people we induct into the field, by continually evaluating our research for its ethical and scientific adequacy, and by conducting our internal and external relations according to the highest ethical standards. (American Educational Research Association, 2004).

OBLIGATION TO SUBJECTS

When employing human subjects in research, you must respect their rights, dignity, privacy, and sensitivities. Eleven aspects of researchers' obligations to subjects are identified in the AERA standards (American Educational Research Association, 2004):

1. Participants, or their guardians, in a research study have the right to be informed about the likely risks involved in the research and of potential consequences for participants and to give their **informed consent** before participating in research. Educational researchers should communicate the aims of the investigation as well as possible to informants and participants (and their guardians), and appropriate representatives of institutions, and keep them updated about any significant changes in the research program.
2. Informants and participants normally have a right to **confidentiality**, which ensures that the source of information will not be disclosed without the express permission of the informant. This right should be respected when no clear understanding to the contrary has been reached. Researchers are responsible for taking appropriate precautions to protect the confidentiality of both participants and data to the full extent provided by law.
3. **Honesty** should characterize the relationship between researchers and participants and appropriate institutional representatives. Deception is discouraged; it should be used only when clearly necessary for scientific studies and should then be minimized. After the study the researchers must explain to the participants and institutional representatives the reasons for the deception.
4. Educational researchers should be sensitive to any locally established institutional policies or guidelines for conducting research.
5. Participants have the right to withdraw from the study at any time.
6. Educational researchers should exercise caution to ensure that there is no exploitation for personal gain of research populations or of institutional settings of research. Educational researchers should not use their influence over subordinates, students, or others to compel them to participate in research.
7. Researchers have a responsibility to be mindful of cultural, religious, gender, and other significant differences within the research population in the planning, conduct, and reporting of their research.
8. Researchers should carefully consider and minimize the use of research techniques that might have negative social consequences, for example, experimental interventions that might deprive students of important parts of the standard curriculum.
9. Educational researchers should be sensitive to the integrity of ongoing institutional activities and should alert appropriate institutional representatives of possible disturbances in such activities that may result from the conduct of the research.
10. Educational researchers should communicate their findings and the practical significance of their research in clear, straightforward, and appropriate language to relevant research populations, institutional representatives, and other stakeholders.

11. Informants and participants have a right to remain anonymous. This right should be respected when no clear understanding to the contrary has been reached. Researchers are responsible for taking appropriate precautions to protect the confidentiality of both participants and data. Those being studied should be made aware of the capacities of the various data-gathering technologies to be used in the investigation so that they can make an informed decision about their participation. It should also be made clear to informants and participants that despite every effort made to preserve it, anonymity may be compromised. Secondary researchers should respect and maintain the **anonymity** established by primary researchers.

OBLIGATION TO THE PROFESSION

The researcher is also responsible to the consumers of research. Many research studies, in education as well as in other fields, are published in journals, monographs, books, and other media and are referred to and used by professionals in the field. You are morally obligated to plan a study in such a way that the findings obtained would not result in offering misleading information. Even more, you are obligated to report exactly and honestly what the findings were. Reporting research in a misleading way is a serious abuse of a researcher's responsibility to the profession. It is dismayingly easy to conduct research that becomes unintentionally deceptive.

In a survey a researcher may inadvertently phrase questions in such a way as to elicit the answers sought. In conducting research someone may, without noticing, arrange things so that the experimental group has advantages the control group does not have that are not part of the independent variable. Before beginning the research, it is recommended that a trusted colleague go through the research plan to look for potential sources of misleading outcomes.

If the statistical analyses fail to support, or contradict, one's hypothesis, it is very tempting to suppose that a different statistical analysis would have "come out right." It is important to select the most appropriate statistical analysis before conducting a study and then derive conclusions from those statistics. It is also important to report the results of *all* statistical analyses, not just those that are statistically significant. For example, if you test 50 hypotheses, and find that 2 are statistically significant, reporting only those 2 implies that they were unlikely to be a function of chance—when actually 2 statistically significant results in 50 are very likely to be a function of chance.

With computers it is very easy to search through the data for subsets of the sample in which one's hypotheses are confirmed despite retained null hypotheses for the total sample. You may, for example, discover what you seek among sixth-grade girls with Spanish surnames. It is appropriate to plan statistical contrasts between treatments, between sexes, between grade levels, and between ethnic groups before conducting a study. However, the results of unplanned post hoc analyses of subgroups can lead to misleading conclusions.

LEGAL OBLIGATIONS

Researchers' obligations to human subjects are not only incorporated into the professional ethics statements of professional organizations such as AERA and the American Psychological Association, but they have also been incorporated into federal regulations. Prior to 1974, there were several infamous studies in which researchers placed subjects at definite risk in order to conduct their study. One of the most heinous (critiqued by Jones, 1982) was the Tuskegee syphilis experiment, begun in 1932 in Tuskegee, Alabama, to study the progression of the disease without treatment. Later, when penicillin was discovered, subjects were not treated because they were part of the control group in a comparative study of the treatment. Stanley Milgram's research (1963) on reaction to authority deceived participants into administering "electric shocks" of up to 450 volts to accomplices who acted as though they were in pain. The participants later experienced stress and anxiety because they thought they had deliberately caused pain to others. Laud Humphrey's (1970) study of homosexuality was another controversial study because of its deception and gross invasion of privacy.

Studies such as these prompted the government to set down a unified set of regulations for research. In 1974, the federal government passed legislation that applies to all research performed by or under the general supervision of institutions receiving federal research funds. The National Research Act of 1974 requires that, to ensure protection of participants, all proposed research involving human subjects be reviewed and approved by an authorized board before the study begins. The Act resulted in the establishment of the National Commission for the Protection of Human Subjects of Biomedical and Behavioral Research to develop a basic set of ethical guidelines for conducting research.

This commission produced the **Belmont Report** (1979), which identified three essential ethical principles that must be followed in all research with human subjects: (1) protection of the human subjects from harm (physical or mental), (2) respect for subjects' right to know the nature and purpose of the study and their right to give or withhold consent to participate (the right of informed consent), and (3) respect for subjects' privacy. One stipulation of the law is that colleges and universities engaging in research with human subjects have an **Institutional Review Board (IRB)** that must approve each proposal and certify that the research will be conducted in accordance with the law. These boards, usually referred to as human subjects review boards, require researchers to complete a lengthy form that provides a summary of the purpose and procedures of the proposed project and specific information about possible risks to subjects. Exhibit 18.1 lists the questions that the researcher must answer in a Summary Safeguard Statement.

If the members of the review board are satisfied that the research will not place subjects at risk, they sign the approval form. Failure to follow all the procedures almost guarantees that the research will not be approved. Exhibit 18.2 shows an example of the form used by the Human Subjects Review Committee at Indiana University, Bloomington, to indicate *approval* of the project.

Protecting Subjects from Harm

For research that is funded by the Department of Health and Human Services and that involves human subjects outside the exempted categories (see discussion under Right to Privacy later in this chapter), the federal regulations require a determination of whether the subjects will be placed "at risk" by the research procedures. If the researcher can demonstrate that the physical, mental, and social risks involved in the proposed project are no greater than those encountered "in daily life or during the performance of routine physical or psychological exami-

Bloomington Campus Committee for the Protection of Human Subjects
Summary Safeguard Statement

Project Title (if you wish to use a different title in the consent statement than is listed on page 3, explain here).

____

____

A. Briefly describe, in lay terms, the general nature and purpose of the proposed research, and where the study will take place. If student research, indicate whether for a course, thesis, dissertation, or independent research. If the study is only for a course, please review the Student Research Policy to ascertain if this project requires HSC review.

B. Describe how subjects will be recruited, how many (or estimate) subjects will be involved in the research, and how much time will be required of them. List specific eligibility requirements for subjects (or describe screening procedures), including those criteria that would exclude otherwise acceptable subjects. If your study uses only male or female subjects, explain why. For NIH-funded research only, address the inclusion of women, minorities, and children in the research. Disclose any relationship between researcher and subjects—such as, teacher/student. superintendent/principal/teacher; employer/employee.

C. Check appropriate box for type of vulnerable subject population involved when investigation specifically studies:
☐ minors (under age 18), ☐ fetuses, ☐ pregnant women, ☐ persons with mental disabilities, ☐ prisoners, ☐ persons with physical disabilities, ☐ economically or educational disadvantaged, ☐ other vulnerable population.
If any of the above are used, state the necessity for doing so. Please indicate the approximate age range of the minors to be involved.

D. List all procedures to be used on human subjects or describe what subjects will do. If done during regular class time, explain what non-participants will do. If you are taping, explain that here. *Asterisk* those you consider experimental. For those as-

Exhibit 18.1 Indiana University, Bloomington Campus Committee for the Protection of Human Subjects Summary Safeguard Statement, 2004

nations or tests," the subjects are not considered "at risk." If the subjects are "at risk," then the researcher must be able to argue that (1) the value of the knowledge that is likely to be gained exceeds the potential harm; (2) all subjects will be fully informed of the risks in the procedures, and the voluntary and written consent of each subject will be obtained; and (3) appropriate medical or other support services will be available to subjects who participate in the research. If these conditions are met, the IRB will usually approve the proposed work. Typically, there is no appeal procedure from an IRB.

Obtaining Informed Consent

Another stipulation of the National Research Act is that the researcher must obtain **informed consent** from research participants. Consent should be (1) voluntary, (2) informed, and (3) given by a competent individual. Obtaining consent terisked procedures, describe the usual method(s), if any, that were considered and why they were not used.

E. State the potential risks—for example, physical, psychological, financial, social, legal or other—connected with the proposed procedures. Briefly describe how risks to subjects are reasonable in relation to anticipated benefits. Describe procedures for protecting against, or minimizing, potential risks. Assess their likely effectiveness. If you are using an electrical device that is attached directly to subjects, explain how the subjects will be protected from shock.

F. Describe methods for preserving confidentiality. How will data be recorded and stored, with or without identifiers? If identifiers are used, describe the type: names, job titles, number code, etc. How long are identifiers kept? If coding system is used, is there a link back to the subject's ID? If yes, where is the code list stored in relation to data and when is the code list destroyed? How will reports be written, in aggregate terms or will individual responses be described? Will subjects be identified in reports? Describe disposition of tapes/films at the end of the study. If tapes are to be kept, indicate for how long and describe future uses of tapes.

G. What, if any, benefit is to be gained by the subject? In the event of monetary gain, include all payment arrangements (amount of payment and the proposed method of disbursement), including reimbursement of expenses. If class credit will be given, list the amount and the value as it relates to the total points needed for an A. List alternative ways to earn the same amount of credit. If merchandise or a service is given, indicate the value. Explain the amount of partial payment/class credit if the subject withdraws prior to completion of the study.

H. What information may accrue to science or society in general as a result of this work?

I. Coinvestigators, . . . , Cooperating Institutions. If there are multiple investigators, please indicate only one person on the Documentation of Review and Approval . . . as the principal investigator; others should be designated as coinvestigators here. Coinvestigators . . . should sign here. . . . If you are working with another institution, please include a letter of cooperation from that institution.

Exhibit 18.1 *Continued*

is more than simply having a potential research participant sign a form. An informed consent statement has two purposes: (1) to enable potential research subjects to make an informed choice as to their participation in the study, and (2) to document their decision to participate. To make an informed choice, potential subjects must understand the purpose of the study, the procedures, the risks, and benefits of the project, as well as the obligations of both the participants and the researcher. Informed consent is documented by the use of a written consent form approved by the institution's IRB and signed by the subject or the subject's legally authorized representative.

In some cases, it may be argued that prior knowledge of the purposes of the study would bias the results. Participants may change their normal behavior or they may respond in the way they think the researchers expect. Thus, researchers sometimes do not tell participants the *true* purpose of the study but

Indiana University
Bloomington Campus Committee for the Protection of Human Subjects

Documentation of Review and Approval
of
Research Project Utilizing Human Subjects

Protocol # ________

TITLE OF PROJECT ______________________________

PROJECT DURATION – START DATE ____________ END DATE ____________

PRIN. INVESTIGATOR ____________ SCHOOL/DEPARTMENT ____________

ADDRESS ____________ E-MAIL ____________ PHONE ____________

RANK: Faculty __ Res. Scientist __ Post-Doc __ Staff __ Student: undergrad __ masters __ PhD/EdD __

If PI's rank is *OTHER* than faculty, name of faculty overseeing the research
(SPONSOR) ______________________________

____

SPONSOR'S E-MAIL & CAMPUS ADDRESS ____________ PHONE ____________

FUNDING AGENCY ____________ APPL. DEADLINE ____________

AGENCY PROJECT # ____________ New ___ Continuation ___

As the principal investigator, my signature testifies that I pledge to conform to the following:

As one engaged in investigation utilizing human subjects, I acknowledge the rights and welfare of the human subjects involved.

I acknowledge my responsibility as an investigator to secure the informed consent of the subject by explaining the procedures, insofar as possible, and by describing the risks as weighed against the potential benefits of the investigation.

Exhibit 18.2 Indiana University Bloomington Campus Committee for the Protection of Human Subjects Documentation of Review and Approval of Research Project Utilizing Human Subjects, 2004

instead use **deception**. There are two types of deception: (1) passive deception in which subjects are not told untruths but are simply not given sufficient information about the purpose of the study and (2) active deception in which subjects are deliberately given misinformation about the true purpose of the study. The true purpose is completely different from what the researcher tells the subjects. Ethical guidelines state that the deception must be justified in terms of benefits that outweigh the risks. It is still important to maintain the voluntary nature of participation even if the purposes are not fully or accurately presented prior to the procedures. In cases where it is important to use deception, the researcher must debrief the participants by giving a full explanation

I assure the Committee that all procedures performed under the project will be conducted in accordance with those Federal regulations and University policies which govern research involving human subjects. **Any deviation from the project (e.g., change in principal investigator, research methodology, subject recruitment procedures, etc.) will be submitted to the Committee in the form of an amendment for its approval prior to implementation.**

PRINCIPAL INVESTIGATOR

______________________	______________________	______________________
(typed/printed name)	(signature)	(date)

As the faculty sponsor, my signature testifies that I have reviewed this application and that I will oversee the research in its entirety.

FACULTY SPONSOR

______________________	______________________	______________________
(typed/printed name)	(signature)	(date)

* *

CAMPUS LEVEL REVIEW

This protocol for the use of human subjects has been reviewed and approved by the Indiana University/Bloomington Campus Committee for the Protection of Human Subjects.

____ Exempt Review¶# ____, ____ Exempt ¶# ____ with signed/documentation of consent,

____ Expedited Review, ____ Full Review, ____ Not Approved, ____ Withdrawn

______________________________________	______________________
Chairperson/Agent IUB Committee	Date

logged in ts ______ approval logged ______ copy to PI ______ notice to agency ______

Exhibit 18.2 *Continued*

after the completion of the study. Coercion of subjects and fraudulent explanations of purpose are prohibited by virtually every professional code of ethical standards.

The obtaining of informed consent from people who are not considered capable of representing themselves is problematic. If their competence limits their ability to give consent, researchers should obtain these individuals' *assent* to participate and the *consent* for their participation from their guardians. Researchers facing this problem are advised to consult with the chair of their IRB or with the legal counsel of their institution or organization. The Office for Protection from Research Risks in the Department of Health and Human Services is usually willing to consult on these matters and may be able to provide current information on legal rulings relevant to various groups.

Right to Privacy

Respect for **privacy** is at the heart of the conduct of ethical research with human participants. Participants must be protected from the risk that information they give during a study could be released to outsiders where it might have damaging consequences. Two aspects of the privacy issue are: *anonymity* and *confidentiality*. *Anonymity* refers to the process of protecting the identity of specific individuals. No identification is attached to the data obtained; not even the researcher knows who contributed the data. *Confidentiality* refers to the process of keeping the information obtained from an individual during a study secret and private. There is broad professional agreement that all subjects have an inherent right to privacy. If the researcher does not need to collect the individual's name and other identifying information, it is recommended that the information not be collected. If it is necessary to collect the data for follow-up or other purposes, then it is the researcher's responsibility to provide secure storage for that information and to control access to it. In general, it is recommended that only the principal researcher and those staff members who must know individual data for work-related purposes have access to them. If students or colleagues are to be given access to the data or if it is to be placed in an archive, then it is the responsibility of the principal researcher to remove all personal identifying information from those files.

For research funded by the Department of Education, the investigator must provide assurance for the secure storage and maintenance of all names and other identifying information. If the research project collects any personally incriminating or socially damaging information, this obligation is even more important. Failure to keep information of this type secure could lead to sanctions under the federal regulations (disqualification from further grant support) or to civil suits for personal damages.

Present regulations limit the federal regulations to those projects funded by grants from the Department of Health and Human Services and provide several broad **categorical exemptions** from the regulations. The five major categorical exemptions as set forth in the federal document, *Protection of Human Subjects* (Public Welfare, 1993) are as follows:

> (1) Research conducted in established or commonly accepted educational settings, involving normal educational practices, such as (i) research on regular and special education instructional strategies or (ii) research on the effectiveness of or the comparison among instructional techniques, curricula, or classroom management methods.
>
> (2) Research involving the use of educational tests (cognitive, diagnostic, aptitude, achievement), survey procedures, interview procedures or observation of public behavior, unless: (i) Information obtained is recorded in such a manner that human subjects can be identified, directly or through identifiers linked to the subjects; and (ii) any disclosure of the human subjects' responses outside the research could reasonably place the subjects at risk of criminal or civil liability or be damaging to the subjects' financial standing, employability, or reputation.
>
> (3) Research involving the use of educational tests (cognitive, diagnostic, aptitude, achievement), survey procedures, interview procedures, or observation of public

behavior that is not exempt under paragraph (b)(2) of this section, if: (i) The human subjects are elected or appointed public officials or candidates for public office; or (ii) federal statute(s) require(s) without exception that the confidentiality of the personally identifiable information will be maintained throughout the research and thereafter.

(4) Research, involving the collection or study of existing data, documents, records, pathological specimens, or diagnostic specimens, if these sources are publicly available or if the information is recorded by the investigator in such a manner that subjects cannot be identified, directly or through identifiers linked to the subjects.

(5) Research and demonstration projects which are conducted by or subject to the approval of department or agency heads, and which are designed to study, evaluate, or otherwise examine:

(i) Public benefit or service programs; (ii) procedures for obtaining benefits or services under those programs; (iii) possible changes in or alternatives to those programs or procedures; or (iv) possible changes in methods or levels of payment for benefits or services under those programs. (pp. 293–294)

While these regulations exempt much of educational research from direct federal regulations, the IRBs remain in place, and institutions may elect to continue regulations that are more restrictive in character or broader in scope than the federal regulations. There has been some informal pressure for institutions to continue the broader regulations. The researcher should plan to consult his or her IRB to determine institutional rules and policies.

SUMMARY

A research proposal presents the exact nature of the problem to be investigated and a detailed description of the methods to be used. It is the researcher's step-by-step plan for discovering new knowledge. It is at this stage that the researcher's inspiration and insights crystallize into concrete form. The following categories of information should be included in a quantitative research proposal.

First, a clear statement of the problem, accompanied by unambiguous definitions of terms, should be made early in the proposal.

Second, a review of pertinent literature should follow. A good review of literature shows what is so far known about the problem and lays the foundation for stating hypotheses regarding relationships between variables under consideration. In addition, this part should be written with the aim of providing a foundation for interpreting results.

Third, in the discussion of methodology that follows the introductory section, methods for subject selection, methods of data collection, observational procedures, and measurement techniques should all be described with sufficient detail so that a reader could carry out the research by following the proposed steps exactly as the original writer of the proposal would.

Fourth, the next part of the research proposal describes the procedures to be used for data presentation, such as tables, figures, and charts, and introduces the statistical techniques that will be used for data analysis.

Fifth, a discussion of the potential importance of the study should follow. Here the researcher should attempt to show how the findings will increase knowledge and what the results will mean to theory and research in the field of interest. A discussion of the applications of the findings to practice is helpful to readers who wish to assess the importance of the proposed research.

Sixth, the final section of the proposal contains the time schedule and estimated budget of the study. This information is useful to readers in making an overall evaluation of the proposal.

Proposals for qualitative research do not follow a fixed format, but they should provide general information about the purpose of the study, a rationale, a description of subjects and setting, the methodology and data collection procedures, and importance.

A matter of considerable weight in planning research is the observation of ethical standards. Subjects must have the right of informed consent, they must be protected from harm, and their privacy must be respected.

KEY CONCEPTS

anonymity
Belmont Report
categorical exemptions
confidentiality
deception
honesty
informed consent
institutional review board (IRB)
privacy

EXERCISES

1. What are the basic components of a quantitative research proposal?
2. How does a qualitative research proposal differ from a quantitative one?
3. At what point in the proposal should a clear statement of the problem be made?
4. Rewrite the following hypotheses, operationalizing all variables:
   a. Children who learn reading by the whole-language approach read better than those taught by a traditional approach.
   b. High school students who score above the top quartile of the XYZ Mechanical Aptitude Test make better mechanics.
   c. Scores on the math subtest of the SRA Achievement Test for smart seventh-grade students who have been instructed with the inductive math approach for one year will exceed scores of smart seventh-grade students who have been instructed with a textbook-centered approach.
5. What are some confounding variables that may affect differences of mean achievement scores between classes of the same grade level? How could you control for these variables in your proposed procedures?
6. What is the appropriate statistic for measuring correlation if the scales of the variables are nominal?
7. What measure of central tendency is appropriate for interval data?
8. For what types of data is ANOVA appropriate?
9. What is the function of an institutional review board?
10. How might some research results be affected by subjects' knowledge of the purpose of the research? How is the requirement of informed consent met in these circumstances?
11. What precautions should be taken to ensure confidentiality of responses and subjects' privacy in research projects?
12. List some common faults to avoid in preparing a quantitative research proposal.
13. Read about one of the infamous studies mentioned in this chapter (Milgram, Humphrey, Tuskegee, etc.) and list the ethical principles that were violated.
14. Which of the following proposed studies would *not* be exempt from federal regulations for research with human subjects?
    a. A study comparing two methods of teaching reading in the elementary schools of a district.
    b. A survey of the attitudes of college freshmen toward the advising procedures at a university.
    c. A history of the School of Education at Indiana State University.

d. A study of the effectiveness of Ritalin in the treatment of hyperactivity among elementary school children.

15. Which of the following is *not* an ethical principle in research with humans?
    a. Keep the identity of individual participants and the results of their participation private.
    b. Obtain informed consent on part of all participants.
    c. Deceive participants about the nature and purpose of the research.
    d. Allow participants to withdraw from the study at any time.
    e. Explain the nature and value of the research to the participants.
16. In the middle of your research project, some participants decide they do not want to continue in the study. What should you do?
    a. Try to convince them to continue because of the importance of the study.
    b. Have them explain to you exactly why they do not want to continue.
    c. Agree to let them drop out of the study.
    d. Use what data you have already obtained from them.
17. Informed consent implies that researchers must inform participants about which of the following?
    a. The procedures to be followed in the study and any associated risks
    b. A detailed description of the purpose of the study
    c. The hypothesis(es) of the study
    d. The independent and dependent variables of the study
18. Distinguish between anonymity and confidentiality.

ANSWERS

1. Introduction, methodology, analysis of data, significance of the study, and time schedule and budget
2. A qualitative proposal is not as specific as a quantitative one because qualitative research evolves as the study gets underway.
3. In the first paragraph of the introduction
4. a. Third-graders who learned reading in first and second grade by the whole-language approach will score higher on the California Reading Test than third-graders who learned to read using a basal reading approach.
   b. Juniors and seniors who scored above the top quartile of the XYZ Mechanical Aptitude Test before becoming apprentices will be rated more highly by supervisors after one year in a mechanic's apprenticeship program than those scoring below the top quartile.
   c. Scores on the math subtest of the SRA Achievement Test of seventh-graders with IQs above 115 on the WISC who have been instructed with the inductive math approach for one year will exceed scores of similar students who have been instructed with the textbook-centered approach.
5. Different average ability levels, physical class environments, teachers, and types and amount of materials are some factors. One can control for some of these variables by pretesting for ability level, selecting classes with similar environments, and training teachers to certain levels of competence. Using large numbers of classes randomly assigned to conditions offers a different type of control.
6. Phi coefficient
7. The mean
8. Nominal-independent variables and interval-dependent variables
9. The institutional review board determines if the subjects in a proposed experiment are at risk under federal and institutional guidelines, determines if benefits outweigh the risks, then grants or does not grant approval for the research to proceed.
10. Knowing that an unusual or experimental treatment is being used can influence subjects' psychological state and/or expectancy, which may detract from or otherwise influence the actual treatment effects. The subjects in such circumstances should be told that they will be informed of the purpose of the study when it is completed.

11. Subjects should not have to identify themselves unless necessary and should not be identified as individuals in the public report of the study unless they have given their consent.

12. Some possibilities include the following: The problem is trivial. The problem is not delimited. The objectives, hypotheses, or questions are too broadly stated. The procedures are lacking in detail. A simple design is proposed for a complex problem. Relevant variables are not considered.

13. Answers will vary.

14. d

15. c

16. c

17. a

18. Anonymity ensures that an individual's name is not associated with the data obtained in a study; confidentiality refers to the practice of keeping information obtained from an individual private.

INFOTRAC COLLEGE EDITION

Using the keywords, *ethics* and *research*, locate a quantitative or qualitative research article in which there were ethical concerns. Identify the ethical issue and explain how the researcher dealt with this issue.

Chapter 19

Interpreting and Reporting Results of Quantitative Research

WHAT YOU LEARN THROUGH RESEARCH DOESN'T DO THE WORLD ANY GOOD UNLESS YOU COMMUNICATE IT.

INSTRUCTIONAL OBJECTIVES

After studying this chapter, the student will be able to:

1. Explain the framework for writing the final report and why conciseness is important.
2. Prepare tables and figures needed in presenting the results of the report.
3. List the principles for interpreting both anticipated and unanticipated results.
4. Distinguish between statistical and practical significance.
5. Explain the various circumstances that might result in the retention of the null hypothesis and discuss the implications of a retained null hypothesis.
6. Explain what the research findings mean in conceptual terms.
7. Write an appropriate title for a dissertation or research report.
8. Describe the nature of the content to be included in each section of a thesis or dissertation.
9. State the procedure to follow when preparing a research article for a professional journal.
10. State the procedure to follow when preparing a paper to be presented at a professional conference.
11. List points that should be included in a checklist for evaluating a quantitative research report.

Once the proposal has been accepted, the researcher can begin to collect and analyze the data. When hypothesis-testing research is set in motion, it is important that the study be carried out exactly as planned. This rule has ethical as well as practical implications.

To illustrate the ethical implications, suppose that Mr. Williams, a language teacher, has developed, with a great expenditure of time and effort, a system of teaching French that he believes greatly superior to existing methods. To test the efficacy of this method, he establishes an experimental group taught by his method and a control group taught by another method. He devises a series of weekly French achievement tests to serve as the dependent variable. Suppose he discovers in the first few weeks that the mean test scores for the two groups are almost identical. Having a big investment in his own method, he finds it hard to believe that it is no better than the other, so he decides to sit in on the two classes to see what has "gone wrong." He discovers that the experimental group seems to show much greater knowledge and appreciation of French life and culture. Because he is determined to find a difference between scores, he decides to change his dependent variable to scores on tests on French life and culture.

Such a change would be unethical. Given two random groups, one can always find through chance alone a superiority in either group if one looks long enough. If the experimental group had not appeared superior on French life and culture, it might have been superior in verbal fluency, listening skills, on-task behavior, or some other variable. The language teacher *must* carry out the experiment as planned and not change the dependent variable. The investigator should report the evidence, suggesting a relationship between method and appreciation of French life and culture, but should make it clear to readers that this relationship was not hypothesized and therefore could easily have been a function of chance. It is unethical to abandon independent or dependent variables that do not seem to be "working out" or to add promising new ones.

Adding new variables is also unwise from a practical standpoint. Such a tactic can confuse the results of a hypothesis-testing study and obscure the meaning of the results. Researchers are often tempted to add interesting new variables that crop up in their study. However, the theoretical base for interpreting these variables has not been laid, and again the best advice to researchers is to leave them for later studies.

Of course, this caveat only applies to research in which predetermined hypotheses are being tested. In qualitative research the hypotheses emerge as the study proceeds and are redefined when appropriate. Also, in descriptive research—such as developmental studies and trend analyses that do not begin with a hypothesis—there is no reason why a researcher should not add variables when appropriate.

WRITING THE FINAL REPORT

Following data analysis, the researcher is ready to write the final report. A research project is of little value unless the findings can be communicated to others. The final report will tell what you did, what you found, and how your study is related to the body of knowledge in your area. Writing the final report is not as difficult a task as a beginning researcher might think. Much of the writing, such as the introduction, review of literature, and methodology has already been done in the initial proposal. Only minor revisions and a switch to the past tense should be needed on these preliminary sections. At this point, the researcher's major task is to present the findings, discuss the findings, and draw conclusions. We now briefly discuss each of these tasks.

RESULTS

The results section follows the section on methodology and presents the outcomes of the statistical analyses of the data. A recommended technique for presenting the results is to organize findings around the hypotheses; that is, the researcher restates the first hypothesis and presents findings concerning it, then repeats this procedure for each hypothesis in turn. Note that he or she does *not* interpret or discuss the results at this point, but merely presents the findings. This section of the final report is thus relatively brief.

To facilitate comprehension, tables and figures are typically used to present the findings. Tables and figures present the numbers and statistics more clearly and more concisely than is possible if the same information is presented in text form. A *table* shows the quantitative data organized in rows and columns. A *figure* shows the data in diagram or graphical form. Well-constructed tables and figures should "stand alone"; readers should be able to understand them without having to refer to the text.

The first table in the report usually summarizes the descriptive statistics, such as means, standard deviations, correlations, percentages, and so on. Later tables present the results of applying inferential statistics and tests of significance to the data. Name the calculated statistic, give the degrees of freedom, and give the probability level at which the statistic was significant (or not significant). Use a summary table, for example, to present the results of an analysis of variance. Most style manuals such as the *Publication Manual* (American Psychological Association, 2001) provide examples of commonly used types of tables and figures and instructions for their construction. Nicol (1999) also provides suggestions for creating tables. Computer software has greatly simplified the task of preparing tables and figures for research papers.

When writing the results section, the researcher refers to each table and each figure by number and comments on the most important and interesting finding in each. Use present tense when pointing out the significant aspects of a table or figure. The following example was taken from Baumann, Edwards, Boland, Olejnik, and Kame'enui (2003):

> Table 4 presents inferential statistics for the seven MC versus the TV ANCOVAs. The eta squared (η^2) values present the proportion of variation in the outcome measure that is explained by the intervention treatment without adjusting for the covariate. We used the unadjusted, and hence more conservative, effect size measure, so that our effects could be compared with Cohen's (1988) suggested guidelines. For the Textbook Vocabulary (TV) Test, there was a statistically significant effect for classroom, $F(6, 148) = 2.52$, $p = .024$; therefore, to test the difference between the Morphemic Contextual (MC) interventions, we used the classroom as the unit of analysis. As predicted, the TV treatment scored significantly higher than the MC treatment both statistically, $F(1, 6) = 23.678$, $p = .002$ (directional test), and practically, $\eta^2 = .179$ (a large effect). Classrooms receiving the TV instruction scored an average of 7.68 points higher on the Textbook Vocabulary Test than classrooms using the MC instructional method. (pp. 475–476)

DISCUSSION

Following the results section, you are ready for the discussion in which you provide an interpretation and discussion of the implications of the findings. The following presents a summary of Baumann's et al. (2003) discussion of their overall results:

> The results indicated that (a) TV students were more successful at learning textbook vocabulary; (b) MC students were more successful at inferring the meanings of novel affixed words; (c) MC students were more successful at inferring the meanings of morphologically and contextually decipherable words on a delayed test but not on an immediate test; and (d) the groups did not differ on a comprehension measure or a social studies learning measure. (p. 480)

A beginning researcher will probably find the discussion section the most difficult but also the most rewarding to write. This section is more difficult because there is no standard format for the content; you must use insight and original thinking to provide an explanation and interpretation of the results that you presented in the previous section. Be ready to provide the answer to the original research question. First, discuss how the results support or fail to support the hypotheses of the study. In this *interpretation*, you must deal not only with expected results but also occasionally with unexpected or negative results. We now provide some guidelines for interpreting various results.

Interpreting Expected Results

Researchers are understandably pleased when the results of a study fit into the previously constructed framework and interpretation can proceed as expected. The study has "worked," and there is agreement between rationale and results. Only a few words of caution need apply in **interpreting expected results**:

1. *Do not make interpretations that go beyond the information.* This injunction may seem patently obvious, but researchers often get so excited when results are as expected that they draw conclusions that do not have a valid basis in the data. Even published research sometimes offers more interpretations than the data warrant.
2. *Do not forget the limitations of the study.* These limitations, of course, should have been previously identified in the study—limitations inherent in the less-than-perfect reliability and validity of the instruments, limitations caused by the restriction in sampling, the internal validity problems, and so forth.
3. *Ethics require that the researcher report internal validity problems that could account for the results.* If, despite the researcher's best efforts, the nonexperimental variables were particularly benign for the experimental group and those for the control group were particularly malign, these conditions must be reported and taken into account in interpreting results. (For example, despite random assignment of teachers to groups, the experimental group may have mostly experienced teachers and the control group may have mostly inexperienced teachers.)
4. *Remember that statistical significance means only that for the appropriate degrees of freedom, the results are unlikely to be a function of chance.* **Practical and statistical significance** have very different meanings. Statistical significance does not mean that the results are significant in the generally accepted meaning of the word—that is, important, meaningful, or momentous. Do not assume that statistical significance guarantees momentous import to your findings.

Suppose that two equivalent groups have been subjected to two different systems of learning spelling over a 2-year period. Those using system A show a mean gain equivalent of 2.15 years of growth on standardized tests during the experiment, whereas those using system B show a gain of 2.20 in the same period. If the groups are large and/or if the differences within groups are small, the differences between the means would be statistically significant. But a difference of half a month over a 2-year period is relatively meaningless in practical terms. If system B is more expensive in terms of student time, teacher time, or materials, teachers would be unwise to adopt it simply because it produced statistically significantly greater gains than system A. If, in contrast, system B is less expensive, teachers would be inclined to favor it because its results are so similar to those of system A in practical terms.

The potential importance or meaningfulness of results must be established in the proposal before the study begins. A study is not important if it does not add meaningful information to the existing body of knowledge, no matter how statistically significant the results may be.

Interpreting Negative Results

Researchers who find **negative results**, results opposite to those hypothesized, often develop sudden revelations concerning the shortcomings of their study. Their interpretation of results reads like a confession. The instruments were inadequate for measuring the variables involved, the sample was too small and was so unrepresentative that results cannot be validly generalized to a meaningful target population, and so on. Hindsight reveals internal validity problems that explain why the study did not come out as it "should have." Of course, any or all of these things could be true, and the shortcomings of any study should be reported no matter what the results. However, research is always a venture into the unknown, so there is no ultimate "should be." An investigator predicts the expected results of a study on the basis of theory, deduction, experiences, and the results of previous research. If these are so conclusive that there can be absolutely no doubt as to the results of this study, then the study is pointless in the first place.

When you undertake a study, you implicitly state that the outcome is a matter of conjecture, not a matter of certainty. When you complete your proposal, it is understood that you declare you will impartially seek to determine the true state of affairs with the best instruments and procedures available to use for that purpose. Therefore, you are obliged to accept and interpret your data no matter how the data stand. When the results contradict the theoretical rationale of the study, the discussion section of your report should include a reconsideration of the original theory in light of the findings. Researchers are often reluctant to present and interpret data that conflict with previous research or with well-established theory. However, it may be that their results are right and previous results wrong. The progress of the science of education will be retarded if investigators are reluctant to report findings that disagree with those reported in earlier studies. Contradictory results indicate that a question is not settled and may stimulate further research. Additional research or theory formation may eventually reconcile seemingly contradictory results. Theory is tentative and should not deter investigators from giving a straightforward interpretation of what was found.

Reconsideration of the theoretical base of a study belongs in the discussion section. One must *not* go back and rewrite the related literature and hypothesis sections of the report.

Interpreting Results When the Null Hypothesis Is Retained

Because a null hypothesis may be retained for a variety of reasons, **interpreting a retained null hypotheses** can be particularly difficult. A retained null hypothesis may occur for the following reasons:

1. The null hypothesis is, in fact, true. There may be no relationship between variables. The experimental treatment may be no more effective than the control treatment.
2. The null hypothesis is false, but internal validity problems contaminated the investigation so badly that the actual relationship between variables could not be observed.
3. The null hypothesis is false, but the research design lacked the power to reject it.

Any of these states of affairs may be the case, but the investigator does not know which is true and therefore should not claim any one of them as the explanation for the results.

It is incorrect to present a retained null hypothesis as evidence of no relationship between variables. A retained null hypothesis must be interpreted as lack of evidence for either the truth or falsity of the hypothesis. A widely used toothpaste commercial stated that tests showed a particular toothpaste was unsurpassed in reducing tooth decay. Interpreting the term *unsurpassed* to mean "no significant difference," we can imagine a test in which a very small number of subjects were used and/or numerous internal validity problems were present. If a retained null hypothesis is the desired result of an experiment, it is remarkably easy to arrange for such an outcome.

There is a danger that investigators who become too enamored of their experimental hypothesis may be tempted to explain away a retained null hypothesis. They cite internal validity problems and declare that the results would certainly have been significant if only those unanticipated problems had not ruined the experiment. As previously noted, one should report all internal validity problems that arise in a study, but one should not use them to explain away disappointing results. One may suggest additional research, planned in such a way as to avoid the internal validity problems encountered, but still one must report a retained null hypothesis as lack of evidence and no more.

Recall from Chapter 7 that the *power* of an experiment refers to the statistical ability to reject a null hypothesis when it is, in fact, false. This power is a function of the size of the sample, the heterogeneity of subjects with reference to the dependent variable, the reliability of the measuring instruments used, and the nature of the statistical procedure used to test the hypothesis, as well as effect size. Researchers should take these factors into account when planning an experiment. The power of an experiment should be considered in planning the study. It must not be brought in at the end of a study to explain away lack of statistical significance. For example, one should not say, "The results would have been statistically significant if the sample had been larger."

With rare exceptions, the only legitimate interpretation of a retained null hypothesis is that "sufficient evidence for a conclusion has not been observed." Of course, if you are studying a small population and can do a complete census of that population, a retained null hypothesis can legitimately be interpreted as a lack of relationship between variables within that particular population. A retained null hypothesis also acquires credibility if you can show that the study was free of internal validity problems and had sufficient power to reject the null hypothesis with a relatively trivial effect size.

Interpreting *Unhypothesized (Serendipitous) Relationships*

We emphasized earlier that a researcher should not abandon a hypothesis during the conduct of a study in order to pursue more promising avenues that present themselves during the course of the study. This does not mean that you should ignore any **unhypothesized relationships** that you may observe in conducting a study. On the contrary, you should record and analyze them with the same rigor you employ in pursuing hypothesized relationships. Throughout the history of science, such **serendipitous discoveries** have often proved important. However, such findings should always be viewed with more suspicion than findings directly related to the hypothesis because there is a relatively great possibility that a spurious unhypothesized relationship will appear in a study. Such relationships should be reported, but they should be considered incidental to the main thrust of the investigation. Before they can be employed as the basis for conclusions, they should be made the subject of a later study specifically designed to investigate them.

In the discussion section, it is very important that the researcher point out the specific *implications* of the research. The results may support or not support relevant theoretical positions. You may explain how the theory should be modified and may suggest further studies that would logically follow. Also, discuss how the results fit in with previous research findings. Lastly, give some attention to stating the possible *application* of the findings to educational practice. The sections on implications and applications of the results are often not sufficiently developed because the writer assumes these will be as obvious to the reader as they are to the investigators. In fact, in the conduct of the study the investigators probably gained insights into the problem that are deeper than those most of their readers can be assumed to have. Therefore, researchers' interpretations should be more meaningful than those that readers might make for themselves.

CONCLUSIONS AND SUMMARY

The conclusions and summary sections together form the capstone of the report.

Conclusions

In the conclusions section, the researcher tells what the research findings really mean in conceptual terms. The conclusions indicated by the research findings should be limited to those that have direct support in the research findings. Researchers are often tempted to conclude too much. The hypotheses provide a convenient framework for stating conclusions; that is, indicate in this section whether the findings support the hypotheses. It is important to distinguish between *results* and *conclusions*. Results are direct observations summarized and integrated by the statistical analysis, such as a comparison of two group means. A conclusion is an inference based on the results, expressed in terms of the study's hypothesis, such as one group's treatment being more effective than the other group's. For example, a study might result in the observation that the mean spelling test scores of students taught spelling by method A are significantly higher than the mean of students taught by method B. The conclusion that method A is more effective than method B is not a direct result of the study but rather is an inference based on the results of the study.

In the Baumann et al. (2003) study mentioned above, the researchers concluded: "The results were interpreted as support for teaching specific vocabulary and morphemic analysis, with some evidence for the efficacy of teaching contextual analysis" (p. 487).

Summary

Because the summary will be more widely read than other sections of the report, its wording must be particularly clear and concise. The summary usually includes a brief restatement of the problem(s), the main features of the methods,

THINK ABOUT IT 19.1

A study was conducted to determine what high school data provided the best predictor of freshman success as measured by GPA. The study looked at total high school GPA, GPA in only "academic" courses, such as English, math, science, history, foreign language, and the like, rank in high school class, and SAT scores. Interpret the following table that was included in the report of this study.

Table 1 Correlation Matrix for Variables in a Prediction Study

	Freshman GPA	Total HS GPA	Academic HS GPA	SAT
HSGPA(total)	.52			
Academic GPA	.57	.85		
SAT	.44	.43	.41	
HS Rank*	−.54	−.68	−.77	−.37

*Highest rank is 1.

Answer

Table 1 shows that the single variable having the highest correlation with freshman college GPA is the high school GPA based on academic courses only (.57). The next highest correlation (−.54) is between rank in high school class and freshman GPA. The correlation between total high school GPA and college freshman grades (.52) is just slightly lower. SAT scores have a lower correlation with college GPA than do the other high school measures.

and the most important findings. On completing a draft of this section, check it carefully to determine whether it gives a concise but reasonably complete description of the study and its findings. Also check to ascertain that no information has been introduced here that was not included in the appropriate preceding sections. It is a good idea to have a colleague read the conclusions section to see if you are communicating as well as you intended.

PUTTING IT ALL TOGETHER

We have looked at the major components of a formal quantitative research project. In this section, we give some general suggestions to follow in the organization and presentation of various types of written reports. For specific rules on style and format, consult a style manual.

Because busy professionals will read the report, it should be as concise and as logically organized as possible. Anecdotes, stories of personal experiences, and argumentative discourses are out of place in a quantitative research report. This does not mean the report must be dull and pedantic. If the researcher has approached the study with enthusiasm, this spirit tends to be conveyed between the lines.

And because the purpose of the report is to present the research rather than the personality of the author, keep the tone impersonal. In keeping with this, first-person pronouns are never used in quantitative reports, although they are acceptable in qualitative reports. Thus, you would *not* write, "I randomly assigned subjects to the two treatment groups," but rather "Subjects were randomly assigned to the two treatment groups." Despite a natural enthusiasm about the importance of the work, the author should not brag about it but should leave its evaluation to readers and to posterity.

A formal and uniform method of presenting research reports has evolved. Although at first glance these formalities may seem inhibiting, in practice they serve a useful purpose. It is important to have research reports arranged in such a way that readers know exactly where to find those specific parts they may be seeking. Otherwise time is lost seeking relevant information. In addition, the use of an established format eliminates the need for devising one's own. As this topic is discussed, it will be seen that the established format follows logically the steps in a research project presented in earlier chapters.

A research report may be presented as (1) a thesis or dissertation, (2) a journal article, or (3) a conference paper. A different reporting approach is required in each of these cases.

THE THESIS OR DISSERTATION

Most universities have a preferred **style manual** that describes in detail the form the university requires. For students who are free to choose, several style manuals are listed at the end of this chapter. Once a manual has been chosen, the entire report should be styled according to its recommendations.

The following outline lists the sequence and general components described in most style manuals:

1. Preliminary pages
    a. Title page
    b. Abstract
    c. Acceptance page
    d. Acknowledgments or preface
    e. Table of contents
    f. List of tables
    g. List of figures
2. Text
    a. Introduction
        (1) Statement of the problem and rationale for the study
        (2) Statement of the hypotheses
        (3) Definitions of terms
        (4) Related literature
    b. Methods
        (1) Subjects
        (2) Procedures
        (3) Instruments
    c. Results
        (1) Presentation of data
        (2) Analysis of data
    d. Discussion
        (1) Interpretation of findings
        (2) Implications
        (3) Applications
    e. Conclusions and summary
        (1) Conclusions
        (2) Summary
3. Supplementary pages
    a. References
    b. Appendixes
    c. Vita (if required)

Preliminary Pages

The preparation of the preliminary pages is largely a matter of following the rules of the style manual. However, one aspect of these pages that needs additional explanation at this point is the title of the study itself.

The title should describe, as briefly as possible, the specific nature of the study. A rule-of-thumb states that a title should have no more than 12 to 15 words. For example, consider (1) a study of culturally disadvantaged children that compares the reading readiness of those who have participated in a Project Head Start program with that of a matched group of children with no formal preschool experience, and (2) the title, "A Comparison of Reading Readiness Test Scores of Disadvantaged Children Who Have Attended Head Start Classes for Six Weeks or More with Similar Children with No Preschool Experience." Although this title does convey what the study is about, it is too long. Such phrases as "a comparison of," "a study of," and "an investigation into" are usually superfluous. Furthermore, most prospective readers will know that Project Head Start is a preschool experience designed for culturally disadvantaged children. However, to go to the other extreme by providing a title that is too brief or too vague to convey the nature of the study is a much more serious mistake. With vague or overly brief titles, a prospective reader must search out the article to determine what it is about. Titles such as "Head Start and Readiness" or "Reading among the Disadvantaged" illustrate this shortcoming. *The title should identify the major variables and the populations of interest.* The operational definitions of the major variables and the description of the samples need not be included in the title. Because correct titling will ensure correct indexing, a useful strategy is for researchers first to decide under what keywords they want their studies to be indexed, working from there to a concise title. In addition, the title should, if possible, begin, not with an article (a, an, the) but with a keyword. Any fanciful part should be relegated to subtitle because bibliographers often cut off the subtitle or alphabetize under the article (the, a), ensuring real confusion or loss to searchers. In our example, the important keywords for indexing would be *reading readiness* and *Project Head Start*. So an appropriate title might be "Reading Readiness of Project Head Start and Non–Head Start Children." This title is reasonably brief, yet it gives the prospective reader a fairly precise indication of what the study is about.

Avoid at all costs emotion-laden titles, such as "We Must Expand the Head Start Program" or "Don't Let the Disadvantaged Become Poor Readers." The prospective reader will not expect research findings under such titles but rather armchair articles attempting to sell a point of view.

Abstract Most institutions require a separate abstract of the dissertation, which should include a definitive statement of the problem and concise descriptions of the research methods, major findings, conclusions, and implications. The abstract must be limited in length (typically 600 words or less). The abstract follows the title page. The main body of the dissertation includes the introduction, sections on methods and results, the discussion of results, and the conclusions and summary. Each of these sections is typically a chapter in the dissertation. We have already familiarized you with the writing of these sections; no further discussion is needed.

Supplementary Pages

References The reference list must include all sources mentioned in the text. Most universities insist that *only* these be listed, but a few ask that pertinent references not specifically mentioned also be listed. The style manual previously selected will give complete details on the method of listing references. It is important to follow these rules rigorously and completely. In fact, it is good strategy to learn them before carrying out the search through the literature for the proposal. By listing each reference in the correct form as it is encountered, you can avoid the extra time involved in finding the references again in order to have them in complete form for the bibliography. List them on cards or enter them in your computer so you can file them in alphabetical order.

Appendixes The appendixes contain pertinent materials that are not important enough to include in the body of the report but may be of value to some readers. Such materials may include complete copies of locally devised tests or questionnaires together with the instructions and scoring keys for such instruments, item analysis data for measurements used, verbatim instructions to subjects, and tables that are very long or of only minor importance to the study.

Vita The authors of research reports are sometimes asked to include brief accounts of their training, experience, professional memberships, and previous contributions.

THINK ABOUT IT 19.2

Critique each of the following titles of quantitative research articles taken from professional journals:

1. "Persuasion as a Dynamic, Multidimensional Process: An Investigation of Individual and Intraindividual Differences."
2. "Are We Creating Separate and Unequal Tracks of Teachers? The Effects of State Policy, Local Conditions, and Teacher Characteristics on New Teacher Socialization."
3. "Can Anything Good Come from Nazareth? Race, Class, and African American Schooling and Community in the Urban South and Midwest."
4. "The Alchemy of the Mathematics Curriculum: Inscription and the Fabrication of the Child."
5. "The Chilly Climate: Fact or Artifact?"

Answers

1. The title is too vague to convey clearly what the study is about. What individual and intraindividual differences are being investigated?
2. The title is a little long; the first part of the title seems loaded and could be eliminated. It would be better to start with "The Effects of . . ."
3. The first part of the title seems irrelevant and could be eliminated without sacrificing clarity.
4. The title is vague and a bit flowery. We may know that the study has to do with mathematics, but we do not know the variables being investigated.
5. The title is entirely too brief! One would have no idea what the study is about or what population was involved.

THE JOURNAL ARTICLE

In preparing a research article for publication in a journal, a good first step is to look through your bibliography to determine which journal has published the greatest amount of work in your area of interest. Information concerning the procedure for submission of manuscripts is usually on the inside of a journal's front cover or can be found on the journal's website. Many journals now accept electronic submissions. Most journals specify which style manual should be used (e.g., the *Publication Manual of the American Psychological Association*, fifth edition, 2001). If a manual is not specified, you can determine the preferred style, method of referencing, and so on from looking at the articles included in a recent issue of the journal. A research article follows the same general outline as a dissertation but must be much shorter. A thesis or dissertation functions to demonstrate a student's competence and requires a full setting forth of the related research, complete description of the procedures, complete tabulation of results, and reflective elaboration. The journal article, in contrast, requires only communication of the author's contribution to knowledge. For the sake of economy of journal space and readers' time, the article must be concise. The section on related literature contains only those results and arguments that provide the basis for the problem. The general statement of the problem is given in one paragraph, or possibly even omitted, in which case the article would begin with the hypothesis. The procedures section is also presented very briefly, although all the information needed to replicate the experiment should be included if at all possible. The results section is of greatest interest to the reader and therefore represents a greater proportion of the article than it would in a dissertation. Only the most important findings should be discussed in any detail.

A brief cover letter should accompany the manuscript. The editor usually sends the author a postcard acknowledging receipt of the manuscript and circulates copies of it among the appropriate members of the editorial board for review. From this point considerable time usually elapses before the author is informed whether the article has been accepted (6 weeks is probably typical). After an article is accepted, it is usually many months before it appears in print. When a manuscript is rejected by a journal, the rejection notice is usually accompanied by a statement of the reasons for this rejection. A rejection by one journal does not necessarily mean that the article is unworthy of publication. A number of factors—such as competition for space, changes in editorial policy, or bias of reviewers—can influence the decision on publication. An article that has been rejected by one journal may be revised and submitted to another. Many articles make the rounds of several journals before finding a home. It is not ethical, however, to submit an article to more than one journal at a time.

THE PROFESSIONAL CONFERENCE PAPER

Many researchers find that hearing papers presented at professional conferences is a good way to keep up to date in their field. The reason for this is that there is a great lapse of time between the completion of a research project and its appearance in print. This time lag is often so long that professional journals have sometimes been described as being archival in nature.

You may want to present your research study at a professional association conference. You will need to find out the requirements for submitting a presentation proposal. This information is usually included in the association's journal well in advance of the conference. You may submit your proposal either in hard copy or online. You will find that some organizations now only accept online proposals.

Papers presented ("read") at professional meetings are prepared in much the same manner as journal articles. They are not necessarily always reports of completed research but may be progress reports of ongoing projects. While at some conferences papers are read, we feel it is much more effective to present the paper from notes rather than to read the content word for word. It is more interesting and the audience generally reacts more positively to a paper that is presented rather than read. If the audience has a copy of the paper in hand, they can read the paper silently more rapidly than the author can read it aloud; thus there may be a gap in attention.

It is fairly common now for presenters to use PowerPoint presentations at conferences. A conference paper is less formal than a journal article and can usually be more precisely geared to its audience. The audience can generally be expected to be familiar with details of related research and methods of measurement.

The paper is frequently organized as follows:

1. Title
2. Abstract
3. Direct statement of the hypothesis
4. Brief description of the procedures
5. Findings, conclusions, and implications

The time allowed for presenting a paper is usually quite brief, frequently less than 30 minutes. Therefore, the paper should focus on the most important aspects of one's study.

Many attendees will want the presented paper for later reference. Rather than taking hard copies of the paper to distribute as was done in the past, presenters now simply provide a web address for the attendees to check and download the paper if they wish. Some presenters even distribute a CD or DVD rather than a paper copy.

POSTER SESSION PRESENTATIONS

Professional conventions often include poster sessions. Poster presenters are assigned a bulletin board (typically 4 ft × 8 ft) in a designated room and a designated time frame, typically 1 to 1½ hours. The author mounts the presentation on the bulletin board and stands by it during the designated time. Those interested in the presentation will inspect it and may ask the presenter about it. Only a brief review of the study can fit onto the bulletin board, so only the abstract and highlights can be presented in this format. The presenter should have available the details needed to answer any questions that may be asked. Presenters often choose to have copies of the complete report available for those who request them. Technology is changing poster presentations as well. Now some have laptop displays and distribute DVDs or CDs with their information or provide cards with URLs to access.

CHECKLIST FOR EVALUATING QUANTITATIVE RESEARCH REPORTS

The following checklist should be useful for evaluating your own quantitative research reports and the reports of others. It brings together many of the topics presented in this text.

Title
Is the title brief but informative?

Does the title make clear the population of interest and the major variables?

Have vague, ambiguous, and emotion-laden terms been avoided?

Statement of the Problem
Have the variables of interest been identified?

Has the theoretical foundation for the study been developed?

Is the problem clearly stated?

Is there a justification or rationale for the study?

Related Literature
Is the related literature relevant and sufficient?

Are the connections between the present study and the previous research and theory made clear?

Hypotheses
Are the hypotheses explicit?

Do the hypotheses follow logically from the statement of the problem?

Subjects
Is the population of interest defined?

Is the method for selecting the sample explicit?

Does the sampling allow for generalization to the population of interest?

Procedures
Are the procedures described well enough to allow replication of the study?

Do the procedures include appropriate operational definitions of the independent and dependent variables?

Do the procedures provide sufficient control for internal validity?

Do the procedures provide sufficient control for external validity?

Instruments
Are the instruments adequately described?

Is information on the validity and reliability of the instruments provided?

Are the instruments appropriate operational definitions of the dependent variables?

Analysis of the Data

Are the descriptive statistics used appropriate for summarizing the data?

Are the inferential statistics used appropriate for testing the hypotheses?

Have the statistics been interpreted appropriately?

Are the statistics appropriate for the level of measurement of the data?

Results

Are the results of all hypothesis tests presented?

Are the statistics interpreted correctly?

Are the results clearly presented?

Are tables and figures used appropriately?

Discussion

Is there a clear interpretation of the results?

Does the author present implications of the study results?

Are the implications presented based on the results of the study, not on what the author hoped or expected to be true?

Are appropriate applications discussed?

Do the applications follow logically from the results of the study?

Are the connections between the results and theory and existing literature shown?

Are there suggestions for future research?

Conclusions

Are the conclusions clearly presented?

Do the conclusions follow logically from the results of the study?

Has the author avoided reaching conclusions that are not directly supported by the outcomes of the study?

Summary

Is the summary clear, concise, and sufficiently complete?

The reader is referred to Mitchell and Jolley (2004) for a helpful format checklist (pp. 461–467) and to Girden (1996) for further discussion on the evaluation of research articles.

STYLE MANUALS

The following are widely used manuals detailing general form and style for theses and dissertations:

Amato, C. J. (2002). *The world's easiest guide to using the APA: A user-friendly manual for formatting research papers according to the APA style guide* (3rd ed.). Corona, CA: Stargazer.

American Psychological Association. (2001). *Publication manual of the American Psychological Association* (5th ed.) Washington, DC: American Psychological Association.

American Psychological Association. (2005). StyleHelper 5.0 software. Compatible with Microsoft Word 2000 or greater. Conforms to the fifth edition of the *Publication Manual.*

American Psychological Association. Free online style tips at http://www.apastyle.org/styletips html

Campbell, W. G., & Ballou, S. V. (1990). *Form and style: Theses, reports, term papers* (8th ed.). Boston: Houghton Mifflin.

Gelfand, H. (2002). *Mastering APA style: Student workbook and training guide*. Washington, DC: APA.

MLA handbook for writers of research papers, theses, and dissertations. (2003, 6th ed.) New York: Modern Language Association.

Nicol, A. (1999). *Presenting your findings: A practical guide for creating tables*. Washington, DC: ARA.

Strunk, W., Jr., & White, E. B. (2000). *The elements of style* (4th ed.). New York: Longman.

Turabian, K. (1996). *A manual for writers of term papers, theses, and dissertations* (6th ed.). Chicago: University of Chicago Press.

University of Chicago Press (2003). *The Chicago manual of style* (15th ed.). Chicago: University of Chicago Press.

SUMMARY

Researchers communicate the results of their investigations in written reports. They communicate what question was investigated, why and how it was investigated, and what was found. The research report may take the form of a thesis or dissertation, journal article, or presentation at a professional meeting.

The main text of a report of quantitative research includes introduction, method, results, discussion, and conclusions/summary. Following the text is a list of references that indicates *all* the sources cited in the report and *only* those sources. The researcher follows standard guidelines for writing each of these sections. Probably the most difficult section to write is the discussion because here the researcher must explain the findings. Interpreting the results of a study is a straightforward task if, in the proposal, the researcher has laid a proper foundation for the research. The following cautions should be kept in mind:

1. Interpretation should be strictly based on the data derived from the study.
2. Internal and external validity problems and other limitations of the study should be considered.
3. Conclusions must be presented as probability statements rather than as facts.

Negative results deserve the same respect and interpretation as do positive results. A retained null hypothesis is interpreted as indication of insufficient evidence and no more. Unhypothesized results deserve attention as sources of future hypotheses.

Formal procedures have been developed for preparing dissertations, journal articles, and papers. Researchers need to familiarize themselves with the style manual required at a university or journal and follow it in the preparation of the final manuscript. The most popular format for educational research reports is the APA *Publication Manual* (5th ed., 2001).

KEY CONCEPTS

interpreting expected results
interpreting retained null hypotheses
negative results
practical and statistical significance
serendipitous discoveries
style manual
unhypothesized relationships

EXERCISES

1. Indicate in which section of a journal article reporting quantitative research (introduction, methods, results, discussion) the following statements would belong:
   a. "Subjects were first-grade students in three schools located in the same rural district of a state in the Far West. Students were predominantly lower- to lower-middle-class Anglo Americans, with a few Hispanics."
   b. "The purpose of this research is to examine the effects of implementing two reading programs in comparable first-grade classes during one school year."
   c. "All first-graders were pretested on the Peabody Picture Vocabulary Test and the Woodcock Reading Mastery Test."
   d. "Students using program A tended to perform least well relative to program B students on Passage Comprehension, while surpassing them on Word Attack. One possible explanation lies in the students' previous experiences with the tasks required by the different reading comprehension testing formats."
   e. "Results of the ANOVA performed on the overall sample ($n = 184$) were significant, $F(4, 176) = 5.89$, $p < .001$."
   f. "There is a need to continue this study over time, replicate it elsewhere, and to experiment with combinations of the two reading programs and other strategies."
2. Indicate whether the format of the following statements written for a quantitative journal article is correct or incorrect. If incorrect, tell why and rewrite the statement using acceptable format.
   a. "I administered a pretest to both groups of subjects."
   b. "The means of the pretest and posttest for the two groups are summarized in the following table and the interaction is shown in the graph below."
   c. "The experimental group will be shown a series of films designed to change attitudes toward smoking."
   d. "Recently, a study at Indiana State evaluated the Reading Recovery Program in comparison to three alternative programs in four Indiana school districts."
   e. "Groups of mothers were randomly assigned to one of four interview discussion groups ($n = 5$) held in a quiet setting within the school."
3. What is the difference between results and conclusions?
4. Explain the difference between statistical significance of the results and the significance of the study.
5. What states of affairs can lead to a retained null hypothesis in a quantitative study?
6. Decide whether each of the following titles is acceptable or unacceptable for quantitative research and give reasons for your choices:
   a. Grade-Point Average and Driver Education
   b. The Effects of Individualized Tutoring by Sixth-Grade Students Three Times a Week on Reading Performance of Below-Average Second-Grade Readers
   c. Children Should Be Taught through Discovery Learning!
   d. Relationship between Personality Characteristics and Attitudes toward Achievement of Good and Poor Readers
7. What are the differences in format for research reported in dissertation form, in journal form, and in a paper to be read at a conference?
8. Should one discuss research results that do not agree with one's hypothesis?

9. For the following situations, indicate whether you would report your research in a journal article or in a paper at a professional meeting.
  a. A progress report of an incomplete but ongoing research project.
  b. Your goal is to communicate to the widest possible audience in the field.
  c. You wish to avoid the time lag in communicating results.

10. A researcher reported the following: "Achievement test scores for 36 subjects working under tangible incentives were mean = 72.0 and standard deviation = 10.9 on test 1 and mean = 76.0 with a SD = 9.7 on test 2. Combined average = 74.0, SD = 10.3. Scores for 34 subjects working under intangible incentives were mean = 68.0 with SD = 8.5 on test 1 and mean = 70.0 with SD = 10.2 on test 2. Combined average for intangible incentive group = 69.0 with SD = 9.3." Show how the researcher could use a table to present these findings so that they could be more readily comprehended by readers.

11. Select a journal to which you might want to submit an article and describe its requirements for submission.

ANSWERS

1. a. Methods
  b. Introduction
  c. Methods
  d. Discussion
  e. Findings
  f. Discussion

2. a. Incorrect, personal pronouns are not used in quantitative research reports: "A pretest was administered to both groups of subjects."
  b. Incorrect, tables and figures are always referred to by number: "The means of the pre- and posttests for the two groups are summarized in Table 1 and the interaction is shown in Figure 1."
  c. Incorrect, use past tense when writing the methods section: "The experimental group was shown a series of films designed to change attitudes toward smoking."
  d. Incorrect, no name or date is given for the reference to the research reported: "Smith and Green (1999) evaluated the Reading Recovery Program in comparison to three alternative programs in four Indiana school districts."
  e. Correct

3. A result is a direct observation. A conclusion is an inference based on results.

4. Statistical significance means only that the results are not likely to be a function of chance; the significance of the study is determined by the importance of the findings in regard to theory testing or practical implications.

5. A retained null hypothesis could result from the null hypothesis's actually being true in nature; or it could result from contamination by internal validity problems that obscure treatment effects, from lack of statistical power of the design used in the study, or from an inability of the instruments to measure accurately the effects of treatment on the dependent variable.

6. a. Unacceptable; no statement of relationship is given.
  b. Unacceptable; too wordy.
  c. Unacceptable; emotion-laden titles are not appropriate for research articles.
  d. Acceptable; meets criteria for title.

7. Dissertation form is the most formal and detailed in presentation; it follows the specifics of a particular style manual. The journal article is a more concise presentation, with a brief statement of the problem, related literature, and methodology; a greater proportion of the article is devoted to major results and a discussion of their significance. A paper that is to be read at a conference is the most informal; geared to its audience, it states the hypothesis, briefly describes the procedure, and emphasizes the most important findings.

8. Yes. Results contrary to one's expectations are as legitimate as any other results and should be interpreted as such.
9. a. Paper at a professional meeting
   b. Journal article
   c. Paper at a professional meeting
10. Answers will vary. The following is simply a suggestion.

	Test		
Incentive	**1**	**2**	**Combined**
Tangible (n = 36)			
M	72.0	76.0	74.0
SD	10.9	9.7	10.3
Intangible (n = 34)			
M	68.0	70.0	69.0
SD	8.5	10.2	9.3

11. Answers will vary.

INFOTRAC COLLEGE EDITION

Search InfoTrac College Edition to find a research article on a topic you are interested in knowing more about. Does it have all the sections we discussed in this chapter? Evaluate the article using the criteria presented.

APPENDIX

Table A.1 Areas of the Normal Curve

(1) z	(2) Area between the Mean and z	(3) Area beyond z	(1) z	(2) Area between the Mean and z	(3) Area beyond z
0.00	.0000	.5000	0.35	.1368	.3632
0.01	.0040	.4960	0.36	.1406	.3594
0.02	.0080	.4920	0.37	.1443	.3557
0.03	.0120	.4880	0.38	.1480	.3520
0.04	.0160	.4840	0.39	.1517	.3483
0.05	.0199	.4801	0.40	.1554	.3446
0.06	.0239	.4761	0.41	.1591	.3409
0.07	.0279	.4721	0.42	.1628	.3372
0.08	.0319	.4681	0.43	.1664	.3336
0.09	.0359	.4641	0.44	.1700	.3300
0.10	.0398	.4602	0.45	.1736	.3264
0.11	.0438	.4562	0.46	.1772	.3228
0.12	.0478	.4522	0.47	.1808	.3192
0.13	.0517	.4483	0.48	.1844	.3156
0.14	.0557	.4443	0.49	.1879	.3121
0.15	.0596	.4404	0.50	.1915	.3085
0.16	.0636	.4364	0.51	.1950	.3050
0.17	.0675	.4325	0.52	.1985	.3015
0.18	.0714	.4286	0.53	.2019	.2981
0.19	.0753	.4247	0.54	.2054	.2946
0.20	.0793	.4207	0.55	.2088	.2912
0.21	.0832	.4168	0.56	.2123	.2877
0.22	.0871	.4129	0.57	.2157	.2843
0.23	.0910	.4090	0.58	.2190	.2810
0.24	.0948	.4052	0.59	.2224	.2776
0.25	.0987	.4013	0.60	.2257	.2743
0.26	.1026	.3974	0.61	.2291	.2709
0.27	.1064	.3936	0.62	.2324	.2676
0.28	.1103	.3897	0.63	.2357	.2643
0.29	.1141	.3859	0.64	.2389	.2611
0.30	.1179	.3821	0.65	.2422	.2578
0.31	.1217	.3783	0.66	.2454	.2546
0.32	.1255	.3745	0.67	.2486	.2514
0.33	.1293	.3707	0.68	.2517	.2483
0.34	.1331	.3669	0.69	.2549	.2451

(continued)

Table A.1 Areas of the Normal Curve (*continued*)

(1) z	(2) Area between the Mean and z	(3) Area beyond z	(1) z	(2) Area between the Mean and z	(3) Area beyond z
0.70	.2580	.2420	1.05	.3531	.1469
0.71	.2611	.2389	1.06	.3554	.1446
0.72	.2642	.2358	1.07	.3577	.1423
0.73	.2673	.2327	1.08	.3599	.1401
0.74	.2704	.2296	1.09	.3621	.1379
0.75	.2734	.2266	1.10	.3643	.1357
0.76	.2764	.2236	1.11	.3665	.1335
0.77	.2794	.2206	1.12	.3686	.1314
0.78	.2823	.2177	1.13	.3708	.1292
0.79	.2852	.2148	1.14	.3729	.1271
0.80	.2881	.2119	1.15	.3749	.1251
0.81	.2910	.2090	1.16	.3770	.1230
0.82	.2939	.2061	1.17	.3790	.1210
0.83	.2967	.2033	1.18	.3810	.1190
0.84	.2995	.2005	1.19	.3830	.1170
0.85	.3023	.1977	1.20	.3849	.1151
0.86	.3051	.1949	1.21	.3869	.1131
0.87	.3078	.1922	1.22	.3888	.1112
0.88	.3106	.1894	1.23	.3907	.1093
0.89	.3133	.1867	1.24	.3925	.1075
0.90	.3159	.1841	1.25	.3944	.1056
0.91	.3186	.1814	1.26	.3962	.1038
0.92	.3212	.1788	1.27	.3980	.1020
0.93	.3238	.1762	1.28	.3997	.1003
0.94	.3264	.1736	1.29	.4015	.0985
0.95	.3289	.1711	1.30	.4032	.0968
0.96	.3315	.1685	1.31	.4049	.0951
0.97	.3340	.1660	1.32	.4066	.0934
0.98	.3365	.1635	1.33	.4082	.0918
0.99	.3389	.1611	1.34	.4099	.0901
1.00	.3413	.1587	1.35	.4115	.0885
1.01	.3438	.1562	1.36	.4131	.0869
1.02	.3461	.1539	1.37	.4147	.0853
1.03	.3485	.1515	1.38	.4162	.0838
1.04	.3508	.1492	1.39	.4177	.0823

Table A.1 Areas of the Normal Curve (*continued*)

(1) z	(2) Area between the Mean and z	(3) Area beyond z	(1) z	(2) Area between the Mean and z	(3) Area beyond z
1.40	.4192	.0808	1.75	.4599	.0401
1.41	.4207	.0793	1.76	.4608	.0392
1.42	.4222	.0778	1.77	.4616	.0384
1.43	.4236	.0764	1.78	.4625	.0375
1.44	.4251	.0749	1.79	.4633	.0367
1.45	.4265	.0735	1.80	.4641	.0359
1.46	.4279	.0721	1.81	.4649	.0351
1.47	.4292	.0708	1.82	.4656	.0344
1.48	.4306	.0694	1.83	.4664	.0336
1.49	.4319	.0681	1.84	.4671	.0329
1.50	.4332	.0668	1.85	.4678	.0322
1.51	.4345	.0655	1.86	.4686	.0314
1.52	.4357	.0643	1.87	.4693	.0307
1.53	.4370	.0630	1.88	.4699	.0301
1.54	.4382	.0618	1.89	.4706	.0294
1.55	.4394	.0606	1.90	.4713	.0287
1.56	.4406	.0594	1.91	.4719	.0281
1.57	.4418	.0582	1.92	.4726	.0274
1.58	.4429	.0571	1.93	.4732	.0268
1.59	.4441	.0559	1.94	.4738	.0262
1.60	.4452	.0548	1.95	.4744	.0256
1.61	.4463	.0537	1.96	.4750	.0250
1.62	.4474	.0526	1.97	.4756	.0244
1.63	.4484	.0516	1.98	.4761	.0239
1.64	.4495	.0505	1.99	.4767	.0233
1.65	.4505	.0495	2.00	.4772	.0228
1.66	.4515	.0485	2.01	.4778	.0222
1.67	.4525	.0475	2.02	.4783	.0217
1.68	.4535	.0465	2.03	.4788	.0212
1.69	.4545	.0455	2.04	.4793	.0207
1.70	.4554	.0446	2.05	.4798	.0202
1.71	.4564	.0436	2.06	.4803	.0197
1.72	.4573	.0427	2.07	.4808	.0192
1.73	.4582	.0418	2.08	.4812	.0188
1.74	.4591	.0409	2.09	.4817	.0183

(*continued*)

Table A.1 Areas of the Normal Curve (*continued*)

(1) z	(2) Area between the Mean and z	(3) Area beyond z	(1) z	(2) Area between the Mean and z	(3) Area beyond z
2.10	.4821	.0179	2.45	.4929	.0071
2.11	.4826	.0174	2.46	.4931	.0069
2.12	.4830	.0170	2.47	.4932	.0068
2.13	.4834	.0166	2.48	.4934	.0066
2.14	.4838	.0162	2.49	.4936	.0064
2.15	.4842	.0158	2.50	.4938	.0062
2.16	.4846	.0154	2.51	.4940	.0060
2.17	.4850	.0150	2.52	.4941	.0059
2.18	.4854	.0146	2.53	.4943	.0057
2.19	.4857	.0143	2.54	.4945	.0055
2.20	.4861	.0139	2.55	.4946	.0054
2.21	.4864	.0136	2.56	.4948	.0052
2.22	.4868	.0132	2.57	.4949	.0051
2.23	.4871	.0129	2.58	.4951	.0049
2.24	.4875	.0125	2.59	.4952	.0048
2.25	.4878	.0122	2.60	.4953	.0047
2.26	.4881	.0119	2.61	.4955	.0045
2.27	.4884	.0116	2.62	.4956	.0044
2.28	.4887	.0113	2.63	.4957	.0043
2.29	.4890	.0110	2.64	.4959	.0041
2.30	.4893	.0107	2.65	.4960	.0040
2.31	.4896	.0104	2.66	.4961	.0039
2.32	.4898	.0102	2.67	.4962	.0038
2.33	.4901	.0099	2.68	.4963	.0037
2.34	.4904	.0096	2.69	.4964	.0036
2.35	.4906	.0094	2.70	.4965	.0035
2.36	.4909	.0091	2.71	.4966	.0034
2.37	.4911	.0089	2.72	.4967	.0033
2.38	.4913	.0087	2.73	.4968	.0032
2.39	.4916	.0084	2.74	.4969	.0031
2.40	.4918	.0082	2.75	.4970	.0030
2.41	.4920	.0080	2.76	.4971	.0029
2.42	.4922	.0078	2.77	.4972	.0028
2.43	.4925	.0075	2.78	.4973	.0027
2.44	.4927	.0073	2.79	.4974	.0026

Table A.1 Areas of the Normal Curve (*continued*)

(1) z	(2) Area between the Mean and z	(3) Area beyond z	(1) z	(2) Area between the Mean and z	(3) Area beyond z
2.80	.4974	.0026	3.10	.4990	.0010
2.81	.4975	.0025	3.11	.4991	.0009
2.82	.4976	.0023	3.12	.4991	.0009
2.83	.4977	.0024	3.13	.4991	.0009
2.84	.4977	.0023	3.14	.4992	.0008
2.85	.4978	.0022	3.15	.4992	.0008
2.86	.4979	.0021	3.16	.4992	.0008
2.87	.4979	.0021	3.17	.4992	.0008
2.88	.4980	.0020	3.18	.4993	.0007
2.89	.4981	.0019	3.19	.4993	.0007
2.90	.4981	.0019	3.20	.4993	.0007
2.91	.4982	.0018	3.21	.4993	.0007
2.92	.4982	.0018	3.22	.4994	.0006
2.93	.4983	.0017	3.23	.4994	.0006
2.94	.4984	.0016	3.24	.4994	.0006
2.95	.4984	.0016	3.30	.4995	.0005
2.96	.4985	.0015	3.40	.4997	.0003
2.97	.4985	.0015	3.50	.4998	.0002
2.98	.4986	.0014	3.60	.4998	.0002
2.99	.4986	.0014	3.70	.4999	.0001
3.00	.4987	.0013	3.90	.49995	.00005
3.01	.4987	.0013	4.00	.49997	.00003
3.20	.4987	.0013	4.50	.4999966	.0000034
3.03	.4988	.0012	5.00	.4999997	.0000003
3.04	.4988	.0012	5.50	.499999981	.000000019
3.05	.4989	.0011	6.00	.499999999	.000000001
3.06	.4989	.0011			
3.07	.4989	.0011			
3.08	.4990	.0010			
3.09	.4990	.0010			

Table A.2 Table of *t*-Values

	Level of Significance for a Directional (One-Tailed) Test					
	.10	.05	.025	.01	.005	.0005
	Level of Significance for a Nondirectional (Two-Tailed) Test					
df	.20	.10	.05	.02	.01	.001
1	3.078	6.314	12.706	31.821	63.657	636.619
2	1.886	2.920	4.303	6.965	9.925	31.598
3	1.638	2.353	3.182	4.541	5.841	12.941
4	1.533	2.132	2.776	3.747	4.604	8.610
5	1.476	2.015	2.571	3.365	4.032	6.859
6	1.440	1.943	2.447	3.143	3.707	5.959
7	1.415	1.895	2.365	2.998	3.499	5.405
8	1.397	1.860	2.306	2.896	3.355	5.041
9	1.383	1.833	2.262	2.821	3.250	4.781
10	1.372	1.812	2.228	2.764	3.169	4.587
11	1.363	1.796	2.201	2.718	3.106	4.437
12	1.356	1.782	2.179	2.681	3.055	4.318
13	1.350	1.771	2.160	2.650	3.012	4.221
14	1.345	1.761	2.145	2.624	2.977	4.140
15	1.341	1.753	2.131	2.602	2.947	4.073
16	1.337	1.746	2.120	2.583	2.921	4.015
17	1.333	1.740	2.110	2.567	2.898	3.965
18	1.330	1.734	2.101	2.552	2.878	3.922
19	1.328	1.729	2.093	2.539	2.861	3.883
20	1.325	1.725	2.086	2.528	2.845	3.850
21	1.323	1.721	2.080	2.518	2.831	3.819
22	1.321	1.717	2.074	2.508	2.819	3.792
23	1.319	1.714	2.069	2.500	2.807	3.767
24	1.318	1.711	2.064	2.492	2.797	3.745
25	1.316	1.708	2.060	2.485	2.787	3.725
26	1.315	1.706	2.056	2.479	2.779	3.707
27	1.314	1.703	2.052	2.473	2.771	3.690
28	1.313	1.701	2.048	2.467	2.763	3.674
29	1.311	1.699	2.045	2.462	2.756	3.659
30	1.310	1.697	2.042	2.457	2.750	3.646
40	1.303	1.684	2.021	2.423	2.704	3.551
60	1.296	1.671	2.000	2.390	2.660	3.460
120	1.289	1.658	1.980	2.358	2.617	3.373
∞	1.282	1.645	1.960	2.326	2.576	3.291

Source: Table A.2 is taken from Table III of Fisher and Yates, *Statistical Tables for Biological, Agricultural, and Medical Research*, published by Pearson Education Ltd., 1974.

Table A.3 Critical Values of the Pearson Product Moment Correlation Coefficient

	Level of Significance for a Directional (One-Tailed) Test				
	.05	.025	.01	.005	.0005
	Level of Significance for a Nondirectional (Two-Tailed) Test				
$df = N - 2$	.10	.05	.02	.01	.001
1	.9877	.9969	.9995	.9999	1.0000
2	.9000	.9500	.9800	.9900	.9990
3	.8054	.8783	.9343	.9587	.9912
4	.7293	.8114	.8822	.9172	.9741
5	.6694	.7545	.8329	.8745	.9507
6	.6215	.7067	.7887	.8343	.9249
7	.5822	.6664	.7498	.7977	.8982
8	.5494	.6319	.7155	.7646	.8721
9	.5214	.6021	.6851	.7348	.8471
10	.4973	.5760	.6581	.7079	.8233
11	.4762	.5529	.6339	.6835	.8010
12	.4575	.5324	.6120	.6614	.7800
13	.4409	.5139	.5923	.6411	.7603
14	.4259	.4973	.5742	.6226	.7420
15	.4124	.4821	.5577	.6055	.7246
16	.4000	.4683	.5425	.5897	.7084
17	.3887	.4555	.5285	.5751	.6932
18	.3783	.4438	.5155	.5614	.6787
19	.3687	.4329	.5034	.5487	.6652
20	.3598	.4227	.4921	.5368	.6524
25	.3233	.3809	.4451	.4869	.5974
30	.2960	.3494	.4093	.4487	.5541
35	.2746	.3246	.3810	.4182	.5189
40	.2573	.3044	.3578	.3932	.4896
45	.2428	.2875	.3384	.3721	.4648
50	.2306	.2732	.3218	.3541	.4433
60	.2108	.2500	.2948	.3248	.4078
70	.1954	.2319	.2737	.3017	.3799
80	.1829	.2172	.2565	.2830	.3568
90	.1726	.2050	.2422	.2673	.3375
100	.1638	.1946	.2301	.2540	.3211

Source: Table A.3 is taken from Table VII of Fisher and Yates, *Statistical Tables for Biological, Agricultural, and Medical Research*, published by Pearson Education Ltd., 1974.

Table A.4 The 5 (Roman Type) and 1 (Boldface Type) Percent Points for the *F* Distribution

Denominator $df = N_1$	N_1 Degrees of Freedom for Numerator 1	2	3	4	5	6	7	8	9	10	11	12	14	16	20	24	30	40	50	75	100	200	500	∞
1	161	200	216	225	230	234	237	239	241	242	243	244	245	246	248	249	250	251	252	253	253	254	254	254
	4,052	**4,999**	**5,403**	**5,625**	**5,764**	**5,859**	**5,928**	**5,981**	**6,022**	**6,056**	**6,082**	**6,106**	**6,142**	**6,169**	**6,208**	**6,234**	**6,258**	**6,286**	**6,302**	**6,323**	**6,334**	**6,352**	**6,361**	**6,366**
2	18.51	19.00	19.16	19.25	19.30	19.33	19.36	19.37	19.38	19.39	19.40	19.41	19.42	19.43	19.44	19.45	19.46	19.47	19.47	19.48	19.49	19.49	19.50	19.50
	98.49	**99.00**	**99.17**	**99.25**	**99.30**	**99.33**	**99.34**	**99.36**	**99.38**	**99.40**	**99.41**	**99.42**	**99.43**	**99.44**	**99.45**	**99.46**	**99.47**	**99.48**	**99.48**	**99.49**	**99.49**	**99.49**	**99.50**	**99.50**
3	10.13	9.55	9.28	9.12	9.01	8.94	8.88	8.84	8.81	8.78	8.76	8.74	8.71	8.69	8.66	8.64	8.62	8.60	8.58	8.57	8.56	8.54	8.54	8.53
	34.12	**30.82**	**29.46**	**28.71**	**28.24**	**27.91**	**27.67**	**27.49**	**27.34**	**27.23**	**27.13**	**27.05**	**26.92**	**26.83**	**26.69**	**26.60**	**26.50**	**26.41**	**26.35**	**26.27**	**26.23**	**26.18**	**26.14**	**26.12**
4	7.71	6.94	6.59	6.39	6.26	6.16	6.09	6.04	6.00	5.96	5.93	5.91	5.87	5.84	5.80	5.77	5.74	5.71	5.70	5.68	5.66	5.65	5.64	5.63
	21.20	**18.00**	**16.69**	**15.98**	**15.52**	**15.21**	**14.98**	**14.80**	**14.66**	**14.54**	**14.45**	**14.37**	**14.24**	**14.15**	**14.02**	**13.93**	**13.83**	**13.74**	**13.69**	**13.61**	**13.57**	**13.52**	**13.48**	**13.46**
5	6.61	5.79	5.41	5.19	5.05	4.95	4.88	4.82	4.78	4.74	4.70	4.68	4.64	4.60	4.56	4.53	4.50	4.46	4.44	4.42	4.40	4.38	4.37	4.36
	16.26	**13.27**	**12.06**	**11.39**	**10.97**	**10.67**	**10.45**	**10.27**	**10.15**	**10.05**	**9.96**	**9.89**	**9.77**	**9.68**	**9.55**	**9.47**	**9.38**	**9.29**	**9.24**	**9.17**	**9.13**	**9.07**	**9.04**	**9.02**
6	5.99	5.14	4.76	4.53	4.39	4.28	4.21	4.15	4.10	4.06	4.03	4.00	3.96	3.92	3.87	3.84	3.81	3.77	3.75	3.72	3.71	3.69	3.68	3.67
	13.74	**10.92**	**9.78**	**9.15**	**8.75**	**8.47**	**8.26**	**8.10**	**7.98**	**7.87**	**7.79**	**7.72**	**7.60**	**7.52**	**7.39**	**7.31**	**7.23**	**7.14**	**7.09**	**7.02**	**6.99**	**6.94**	**6.90**	**6.88**
7	5.59	4.74	4.35	4.12	3.97	3.87	3.79	3.73	3.68	3.63	3.60	3.57	3.52	3.49	3.44	3.41	3.38	3.34	3.32	3.29	3.28	3.25	3.24	3.23
	12.25	**9.55**	**8.45**	**7.85**	**7.46**	**7.19**	**7.00**	**6.84**	**6.71**	**6.62**	**6.54**	**6.47**	**6.35**	**6.27**	**6.15**	**6.07**	**5.98**	**5.90**	**5.85**	**5.78**	**5.75**	**5.70**	**5.67**	**5.65**
8	5.32	4.46	4.07	3.84	3.69	3.58	3.50	3.44	3.39	3.34	3.31	3.28	3.23	3.20	3.15	3.12	3.08	3.05	3.03	3.00	2.98	2.96	2.94	2.93
	11.26	**8.65**	**7.59**	**7.01**	**6.63**	**6.37**	**6.19**	**6.03**	**5.91**	**5.82**	**5.74**	**5.67**	**5.56**	**5.48**	**5.36**	**5.28**	**5.20**	**5.11**	**5.06**	**5.00**	**4.96**	**4.91**	**4.88**	**4.86**
9	5.12	4.26	3.86	3.63	3.48	3.37	3.29	3.23	3.18	3.13	3.10	3.07	3.02	2.98	2.93	2.90	2.86	2.82	2.80	2.77	2.76	2.73	2.72	2.71
	10.56	**8.02**	**6.99**	**6.42**	**6.06**	**5.80**	**5.62**	**5.47**	**5.35**	**5.26**	**5.18**	**5.11**	**5.00**	**4.92**	**4.80**	**4.73**	**4.64**	**4.56**	**4.51**	**4.45**	**4.41**	**4.36**	**4.33**	**4.31**
10	4.96	4.10	3.71	3.48	3.33	3.22	3.14	3.07	3.02	2.97	2.94	2.91	2.86	2.82	2.77	2.74	2.70	2.67	2.64	2.61	2.59	2.56	2.55	2.54
	10.04	**7.56**	**6.55**	**5.99**	**5.64**	**5.39**	**5.21**	**5.06**	**4.95**	**4.85**	**4.78**	**4.71**	**4.60**	**4.52**	**4.41**	**4.33**	**4.25**	**4.17**	**4.12**	**4.05**	**4.01**	**3.96**	**3.93**	**3.91**
11	4.84	3.98	3.59	3.36	3.20	3.09	3.01	2.95	2.90	2.86	2.82	2.79	2.74	2.70	2.65	2.61	2.57	2.53	2.50	2.47	2.45	2.42	2.41	2.40
	9.65	**7.20**	**6.22**	**5.67**	**5.32**	**5.07**	**4.88**	**4.74**	**4.63**	**4.54**	**4.46**	**4.40**	**4.29**	**4.21**	**4.10**	**4.02**	**3.94**	**3.86**	**3.80**	**3.74**	**3.70**	**3.66**	**3.62**	**3.60**
12	4.75	3.88	3.49	3.26	3.11	3.00	2.92	2.85	2.80	2.76	2.72	2.69	2.64	2.60	2.54	2.50	2.46	2.42	2.40	2.36	2.35	2.32	2.31	2.30
	9.33	**6.93**	**5.95**	**5.41**	**5.06**	**4.82**	**4.65**	**4.50**	**4.39**	**4.30**	**4.22**	**4.16**	**4.05**	**3.98**	**3.86**	**3.78**	**3.70**	**3.61**	**3.56**	**3.49**	**3.46**	**3.41**	**3.38**	**3.36**
13	4.67	3.80	3.41	3.18	3.02	2.92	2.84	2.77	2.72	2.67	2.63	2.60	2.55	2.51	2.46	2.42	2.38	2.34	2.32	2.28	2.26	2.24	2.22	2.21
	9.07	**6.70**	**5.74**	**5.20**	**4.86**	**4.62**	**4.44**	**4.30**	**4.19**	**4.10**	**4.02**	**3.96**	**3.85**	**3.78**	**3.67**	**3.59**	**3.51**	**3.42**	**3.37**	**3.30**	**3.27**	**3.21**	**3.18**	**3.16**

Table A.4 The 5 (Roman Type) and 1 (Boldface Type) Percent Points for the *F* Distribution (*continued*)

Denominator	N_1 Degrees of Freedom for Numerator																							
$df = N_1$	1	2	3	4	5	6	7	8	9	10	11	12	14	16	20	24	30	40	50	75	100	200	500	∞
14	4.60	3.74	3.34	3.11	2.96	2.85	2.77	2.70	2.65	2.60	2.56	2.53	2.48	2.44	2.39	2.35	2.31	2.27	2.24	2.21	2.19	2.16	2.14	2.13
	8.86	**6.51**	**5.56**	**5.03**	**4.69**	**4.46**	**4.28**	**4.14**	**4.03**	**3.94**	**3.86**	**3.80**	**3.70**	**3.62**	**3.51**	**3.43**	**3.34**	**3.26**	**3.21**	**3.14**	**3.11**	**3.06**	**3.02**	**3.00**
15	4.54	3.68	3.29	3.06	2.90	2.79	2.70	2.64	2.59	2.55	2.51	2.48	2.43	2.39	2.33	2.29	2.25	2.21	2.18	2.15	2.12	2.10	2.08	2.07
	8.68	**6.36**	**5.42**	**4.89**	**4.56**	**4.32**	**4.14**	**4.00**	**3.89**	**3.80**	**3.73**	**3.67**	**3.56**	**3.48**	**3.36**	**3.29**	**3.20**	**3.12**	**3.07**	**3.00**	**2.97**	**2.92**	**2.89**	**2.87**
16	4.49	3.63	3.24	3.01	2.85	2.74	2.66	2.59	2.54	2.49	2.45	2.42	2.37	2.33	2.28	2.24	2.20	2.16	2.13	2.09	2.07	2.04	2.02	2.01
	8.53	**6.23**	**5.29**	**4.77**	**4.44**	**4.20**	**4.03**	**3.89**	**3.78**	**3.69**	**3.61**	**3.55**	**3.45**	**3.37**	**3.25**	**3.18**	**3.10**	**3.01**	**2.96**	**2.89**	**2.86**	**2.80**	**2.77**	**2.75**
17	4.45	3.59	3.20	2.96	2.81	2.70	2.62	2.55	2.50	2.45	2.41	2.38	2.33	2.29	2.23	2.19	2.15	2.11	2.08	2.04	2.02	1.99	1.97	1.96
	8.40	**6.11**	**5.18**	**4.67**	**4.34**	**4.10**	**3.93**	**3.79**	**3.68**	**3.59**	**3.52**	**3.45**	**3.35**	**3.27**	**3.16**	**3.08**	**3.00**	**2.92**	**2.86**	**2.79**	**2.76**	**2.70**	**2.67**	**2.65**
18	4.41	3.55	3.16	2.93	2.77	2.66	2.58	2.51	2.46	2.41	2.37	2.34	2.29	2.25	2.19	2.15	2.11	2.07	2.04	2.00	1.98	1.95	1.93	1.92
	8.28	**6.01**	**5.09**	**4.58**	**4.25**	**4.01**	**3.85**	**3.71**	**3.60**	**3.51**	**3.44**	**3.37**	**3.27**	**3.19**	**3.07**	**3.00**	**2.91**	**2.83**	**2.78**	**2.71**	**2.68**	**2.62**	**2.59**	**2.57**
19	4.38	3.52	3.13	2.90	2.74	2.63	2.55	2.48	2.43	2.38	2.34	2.31	2.26	2.21	2.15	2.11	2.07	2.02	2.00	1.96	1.94	1.91	1.90	1.88
	8.18	**5.93**	**5.01**	**4.50**	**4.17**	**3.94**	**3.77**	**3.63**	**3.52**	**3.43**	**3.36**	**3.30**	**3.19**	**3.12**	**3.00**	**2.92**	**2.84**	**2.76**	**2.70**	**2.63**	**2.60**	**2.54**	**2.51**	**2.49**
20	4.35	3.49	3.10	2.87	2.71	2.60	2.52	2.45	2.40	2.35	2.31	2.28	2.23	2.18	2.12	2.08	2.04	1.99	1.96	1.92	1.90	1.87	1.85	1.84
	8.10	**5.85**	**4.94**	**4.43**	**4.10**	**3.87**	**3.71**	**3.56**	**3.45**	**3.37**	**3.30**	**3.23**	**3.13**	**3.05**	**2.94**	**2.86**	**2.77**	**2.69**	**2.63**	**2.56**	**2.53**	**2.47**	**2.44**	**2.42**
21	4.32	3.47	3.07	2.84	2.68	2.57	2.49	2.42	2.37	2.32	2.28	2.25	2.20	2.15	2.09	2.05	2.00	1.96	1.93	1.89	1.87	1.84	1.82	1.81
	8.02	**5.78**	**4.87**	**4.37**	**4.04**	**3.81**	**3.65**	**3.51**	**3.40**	**3.31**	**3.24**	**3.17**	**3.07**	**2.99**	**2.88**	**2.80**	**2.72**	**2.63**	**2.58**	**2.51**	**2.47**	**2.42**	**2.38**	**2.36**
22	4.30	3.44	3.05	2.82	2.66	2.55	2.47	2.40	2.35	2.30	2.26	2.23	2.18	2.13	2.07	2.03	1.98	1.93	1.91	1.87	1.84	1.81	1.80	1.78
	7.94	**5.72**	**4.82**	**4.31**	**3.99**	**3.76**	**3.59**	**3.45**	**3.35**	**3.26**	**3.18**	**3.12**	**3.02**	**2.94**	**2.83**	**2.75**	**2.67**	**2.58**	**2.53**	**2.46**	**2.42**	**2.37**	**2.33**	**2.31**
23	4.28	3.42	3.03	2.80	2.64	2.53	2.45	2.38	2.32	2.28	2.24	2.20	2.14	2.10	2.04	2.00	1.96	1.91	1.88	1.84	1.82	1.79	1.77	1.76
	7.88	**5.66**	**4.76**	**4.26**	**3.94**	**3.71**	**3.54**	**3.41**	**3.30**	**3.21**	**3.14**	**3.07**	**2.97**	**2.89**	**2.78**	**2.70**	**2.62**	**2.53**	**2.48**	**2.41**	**2.37**	**2.32**	**2.28**	**2.26**
24	4.26	3.40	3.01	2.78	2.62	2.51	2.43	2.36	2.30	2.26	2.22	2.18	2.13	2.09	2.02	1.98	1.94	1.89	1.86	1.82	1.80	1.76	1.74	1.73
	7.82	**5.61**	**4.72**	**4.22**	**3.90**	**3.67**	**3.50**	**3.36**	**3.25**	**3.17**	**3.09**	**3.03**	**2.93**	**2.85**	**2.74**	**2.66**	**2.58**	**2.49**	**2.44**	**2.36**	**2.33**	**2.27**	**2.23**	**2.21**
25	4.24	3.38	2.99	2.76	2.60	2.49	2.41	2.34	2.28	2.24	2.20	2.16	2.11	2.06	2.00	1.96	1.92	1.87	1.84	1.80	1.77	1.74	1.72	1.71
	7.77	**5.57**	**4.68**	**4.18**	**3.86**	**3.63**	**3.46**	**3.32**	**3.21**	**3.13**	**3.05**	**2.99**	**2.89**	**2.81**	**2.70**	**2.62**	**2.54**	**2.45**	**2.40**	**2.32**	**2.29**	**2.23**	**2.19**	**2.17**
26	4.22	3.37	2.98	2.74	2.59	2.47	2.39	2.32	2.27	2.22	2.18	2.15	2.10	2.05	1.99	1.95	1.90	1.85	1.82	1.78	1.76	1.72	1.70	1.69
	7.72	**5.53**	**4.64**	**4.14**	**3.82**	**3.59**	**3.42**	**3.29**	**3.17**	**3.09**	**3.02**	**2.96**	**2.86**	**2.77**	**2.66**	**2.58**	**2.50**	**2.41**	**2.36**	**2.28**	**2.25**	**2.19**	**2.15**	**2.13**

Table A.4 The 5 (Roman Type) and 1 (Boldface Type) Percent Points for the *F* Distribution (*continued*)

Denominator $df = N_1$	N_1 Degrees of Freedom for Numerator																						
	1	2	3	4	5	6	7	8	9	10	11	12	14	16	20	24	30	40	50	75	100	200	500	∞
27	4.21	3.35	2.96	2.73	2.57	2.46	2.37	2.30	2.25	2.20	2.16	2.13	2.08	2.03	1.97	1.93	1.88	1.84	1.80	1.76	1.74	1.71	1.68	1.67
	7.68	**5.49**	**4.60**	**4.11**	**3.79**	**3.56**	**3.39**	**3.26**	**3.14**	**3.06**	**2.98**	**2.93**	**2.83**	**2.74**	**2.63**	**2.55**	**2.47**	**2.38**	**2.33**	**2.25**	**2.21**	**2.16**	**2.12**	**2.10**
28	4.20	3.34	2.95	2.71	2.56	2.44	2.36	2.29	2.24	2.19	2.15	2.12	2.06	2.02	1.96	1.91	1.87	1.81	1.78	1.75	1.72	1.69	1.67	1.65
	7.64	**5.45**	**4.57**	**4.07**	**3.76**	**3.53**	**3.36**	**3.23**	**3.11**	**3.03**	**2.95**	**2.90**	**2.80**	**2.71**	**2.60**	**2.52**	**2.44**	**2.35**	**2.30**	**2.22**	**2.18**	**2.13**	**2.09**	**2.06**
29	4.18	3.33	2.93	2.70	2.54	2.43	2.35	2.28	2.22	2.18	2.14	2.10	2.05	2.00	1.94	1.90	1.85	1.80	1.77	1.73	1.71	1.68	1.65	1.64
	7.60	**5.42**	**4.54**	**4.04**	**3.73**	**3.50**	**3.33**	**3.20**	**3.08**	**3.00**	**2.92**	**2.87**	**2.77**	**2.68**	**2.57**	**2.49**	**2.41**	**2.32**	**2.27**	**2.19**	**2.15**	**2.10**	**2.06**	**2.03**
30	4.17	3.32	2.92	2.69	2.53	2.42	2.34	2.27	2.21	2.16	2.12	2.09	2.04	1.99	1.93	1.89	1.84	1.79	1.76	1.72	1.69	1.66	1.64	1.62
	7.56	**5.39**	**4.51**	**4.02**	**3.70**	**3.47**	**3.30**	**3.17**	**3.06**	**2.98**	**2.90**	**2.84**	**2.74**	**2.66**	**2.55**	**2.47**	**2.38**	**2.29**	**2.24**	**2.16**	**2.13**	**2.07**	**2.03**	**2.01**
32	4.15	3.30	2.90	2.67	2.51	2.40	2.32	2.25	2.19	2.14	2.10	2.07	2.02	1.97	1.91	1.86	1.82	1.76	1.74	1.69	1.67	1.64	1.61	1.59
	7.50	**5.34**	**4.46**	**3.97**	**3.66**	**3.42**	**3.25**	**3.12**	**3.01**	**2.94**	**2.86**	**2.80**	**2.70**	**2.62**	**2.51**	**2.42**	**2.34**	**2.25**	**2.20**	**2.12**	**2.08**	**2.02**	**1.98**	**1.96**
34	4.13	3.28	2.88	2.65	2.49	2.38	2.30	2.23	2.17	2.12	2.08	2.05	2.00	1.95	1.89	1.84	1.80	1.74	1.71	1.67	1.64	1.61	1.59	1.57
	7.44	**5.29**	**4.42**	**3.93**	**3.61**	**3.38**	**3.21**	**3.08**	**2.97**	**2.89**	**2.82**	**2.76**	**2.66**	**2.58**	**2.47**	**2.38**	**2.30**	**2.21**	**2.15**	**2.08**	**2.04**	**1.98**	**1.94**	**1.91**
36	4.11	3.26	2.86	2.63	2.48	2.36	2.28	2.21	2.15	2.10	2.06	2.03	1.98	1.93	1.87	1.82	1.78	1.72	1.69	1.65	1.62	1.59	1.56	1.55
	7.39	**5.25**	**4.38**	**3.89**	**3.58**	**3.35**	**3.18**	**3.04**	**2.94**	**2.86**	**2.78**	**2.72**	**2.62**	**2.54**	**2.43**	**2.35**	**2.26**	**2.17**	**2.12**	**2.04**	**2.00**	**1.94**	**1.90**	**1.87**
38	4.10	3.25	2.85	2.62	2.46	2.35	2.26	2.19	2.14	2.09	2.05	2.02	1.96	1.92	1.85	1.80	1.76	1.71	1.67	1.63	1.60	1.57	1.54	1.53
	7.35	**5.21**	**4.34**	**3.86**	**3.54**	**3.32**	**3.15**	**3.02**	**2.91**	**2.82**	**2.75**	**2.69**	**2.59**	**2.51**	**2.40**	**2.32**	**2.22**	**2.14**	**2.08**	**2.00**	**1.97**	**1.90**	**1.86**	**1.84**
40	4.08	3.23	2.84	2.61	2.45	2.34	2.25	2.18	2.12	2.07	2.04	2.00	1.95	1.90	1.84	1.79	1.74	1.69	1.66	1.61	1.59	1.55	1.53	1.51
	7.31	**5.18**	**4.31**	**3.83**	**3.51**	**3.29**	**3.12**	**2.99**	**2.88**	**2.80**	**2.73**	**2.66**	**2.56**	**2.49**	**2.37**	**2.29**	**2.20**	**2.11**	**2.05**	**1.97**	**1.94**	**1.88**	**1.84**	**1.81**
42	4.07	3.22	2.83	2.59	2.44	2.32	2.24	2.17	2.11	2.06	2.02	1.99	1.94	1.89	1.82	1.78	1.73	1.68	1.64	1.60	1.57	1.54	1.51	1.49
	7.27	**5.15**	**4.29**	**3.80**	**3.49**	**3.26**	**3.10**	**2.96**	**2.86**	**2.77**	**2.70**	**2.64**	**2.54**	**2.46**	**2.35**	**2.26**	**2.17**	**2.08**	**2.02**	**1.94**	**1.91**	**1.85**	**1.80**	**1.78**
44	4.06	3.21	2.82	2.58	2.43	2.31	2.23	2.16	2.10	2.05	2.01	1.98	1.92	1.88	1.81	1.76	1.72	1.66	1.63	1.58	1.56	1.52	1.50	1.48
	7.24	**5.12**	**4.26**	**3.78**	**3.46**	**3.24**	**3.07**	**2.94**	**2.84**	**2.75**	**2.68**	**2.62**	**2.52**	**2.44**	**2.32**	**2.24**	**2.15**	**2.06**	**2.00**	**1.92**	**1.88**	**1.82**	**1.78**	**1.75**
46	4.05	3.20	2.81	2.57	2.42	2.30	2.22	2.14	2.09	2.04	2.00	1.97	1.91	1.87	1.80	1.75	1.71	1.65	1.62	1.57	1.54	1.51	1.48	1.46
	7.21	**5.10**	**4.24**	**3.76**	**3.44**	**3.22**	**3.05**	**2.92**	**2.82**	**2.73**	**2.66**	**2.60**	**2.50**	**2.42**	**2.30**	**2.22**	**2.13**	**2.04**	**1.98**	**1.90**	**1.86**	**1.80**	**1.76**	**1.72**
48	4.04	3.19	2.80	2.56	2.41	2.30	2.21	2.14	2.08	2.03	1.99	1.96	1.90	1.86	1.79	1.74	1.70	1.64	1.61	1.56	1.53	1.50	1.47	1.45
	7.19	**5.08**	**4.22**	**3.74**	**3.42**	**3.20**	**3.04**	**2.90**	**2.80**	**2.71**	**2.64**	**2.58**	**2.48**	**2.40**	**2.28**	**2.20**	**2.11**	**2.02**	**1.96**	**1.88**	**1.84**	**1.78**	**1.73**	**1.70**

Table A.4 The 5 (Roman Type) and 1 (Boldface Type) Percent Points for the *F* Distribution (*continued*)

Denominator $df = N_1$	N_1 Degrees of Freedom for Numerator																							
	1	2	3	4	5	6	7	8	9	10	11	12	14	16	20	24	30	40	50	75	100	200	500	∞
50	4.03	3.18	2.79	2.56	2.40	2.29	2.20	2.13	2.07	2.02	1.98	1.95	1.90	1.85	1.78	1.74	1.69	1.63	1.60	1.55	1.52	1.48	1.46	1.44
	7.17	**5.06**	**4.20**	**3.72**	**3.41**	**3.18**	**3.02**	**2.88**	**2.78**	**2.70**	**2.62**	**2.56**	**2.46**	**2.39**	**2.26**	**2.18**	**2.10**	**2.00**	**1.94**	**1.86**	**1.82**	**1.76**	**1.71**	**1.68**
55	4.02	3.17	2.78	2.54	2.38	2.27	2.18	2.11	2.05	2.00	1.97	1.93	1.88	1.83	1.76	1.72	1.67	1.61	1.58	1.52	1.50	1.46	1.43	1.41
	7.12	**5.01**	**4.16**	**3.68**	**3.37**	**3.15**	**2.98**	**2.85**	**2.75**	**2.66**	**2.59**	**2.53**	**2.43**	**2.35**	**2.23**	**2.15**	**2.06**	**1.96**	**1.90**	**1.82**	**1.78**	**1.71**	**1.66**	**1.64**
60	4.00	3.15	2.76	2.52	2.37	2.25	2.17	2.10	2.04	1.99	1.95	1.92	1.86	1.81	1.75	1.70	1.65	1.59	1.56	1.50	1.48	1.44	1.41	1.39
	7.08	**4.98**	**4.13**	**3.65**	**3.34**	**3.12**	**2.95**	**2.82**	**2.72**	**2.63**	**2.56**	**2.50**	**2.40**	**2.32**	**2.20**	**2.12**	**2.03**	**1.93**	**1.87**	**1.79**	**1.74**	**1.68**	**1.63**	**1.60**
65	3.99	3.14	2.75	2.51	2.36	2.24	2.15	2.08	2.02	1.98	1.94	1.90	1.85	1.80	1.73	1.68	1.63	1.57	1.54	1.49	1.46	1.42	1.39	1.37
	7.04	**4.95**	**4.10**	**3.62**	**3.31**	**3.09**	**2.93**	**2.79**	**2.70**	**2.61**	**2.54**	**2.47**	**2.37**	**2.30**	**2.18**	**2.09**	**2.00**	**1.90**	**1.84**	**1.76**	**1.71**	**1.64**	**1.60**	**1.56**
70	3.98	3.13	2.74	2.50	2.35	2.23	2.14	2.07	2.01	1.97	1.93	1.89	1.84	1.79	1.72	1.67	1.62	1.56	1.53	1.47	1.45	1.40	1.37	1.35
	7.01	**4.92**	**4.08**	**3.60**	**3.29**	**3.07**	**2.91**	**2.77**	**2.67**	**2.59**	**2.51**	**2.45**	**2.35**	**2.28**	**2.15**	**2.07**	**1.98**	**1.88**	**1.82**	**1.74**	**1.69**	**1.62**	**1.56**	**1.53**
80	3.96	3.11	2.72	2.48	2.33	2.21	2.12	2.05	1.99	1.95	1.91	1.88	1.82	1.77	1.70	1.65	1.60	1.54	1.51	1.45	1.42	1.38	1.35	1.32
	6.96	**4.88**	**4.04**	**3.56**	**3.25**	**3.04**	**2.87**	**2.74**	**2.64**	**2.55**	**2.48**	**2.41**	**2.32**	**2.24**	**2.11**	**2.03**	**1.94**	**1.84**	**1.78**	**1.70**	**1.65**	**1.57**	**1.52**	**1.49**
100	3.94	3.09	2.70	2.46	2.30	2.19	2.10	2.03	1.97	1.92	1.88	1.85	1.79	1.75	1.68	1.63	1.57	1.51	1.48	1.42	1.39	1.34	1.30	1.28
	6.90	**4.82**	**3.98**	**3.51**	**3.20**	**2.99**	**2.82**	**2.69**	**2.59**	**2.51**	**2.43**	**2.36**	**2.26**	**2.19**	**2.06**	**1.98**	**1.89**	**1.79**	**1.73**	**1.64**	**1.59**	**1.51**	**1.46**	**1.43**
125	3.92	3.07	2.68	2.44	2.29	2.17	2.08	2.01	1.95	1.90	1.86	1.83	1.77	1.72	1.65	1.60	1.55	1.49	1.45	1.39	1.36	1.31	1.27	1.25
	6.84	**4.78**	**3.94**	**3.47**	**3.17**	**2.95**	**2.79**	**2.65**	**2.56**	**2.47**	**2.40**	**2.33**	**2.23**	**2.15**	**2.03**	**1.94**	**1.85**	**1.75**	**1.68**	**1.59**	**1.54**	**1.46**	**1.40**	**1.37**
150	3.91	3.06	2.67	2.43	2.27	2.16	2.07	2.00	1.94	1.89	1.85	1.82	1.76	1.71	1.64	1.59	1.54	1.47	1.44	1.37	1.34	1.29	1.25	1.22
	6.81	**4.75**	**3.91**	**3.44**	**3.14**	**2.92**	**2.76**	**2.62**	**2.53**	**2.44**	**2.37**	**2.30**	**2.20**	**2.12**	**2.00**	**1.91**	**1.83**	**1.72**	**1.66**	**1.56**	**1.51**	**1.43**	**1.37**	**1.33**
200	3.89	3.04	2.65	2.41	2.26	2.14	2.05	1.98	1.92	1.87	1.83	1.80	1.74	1.69	1.62	1.57	1.52	1.45	1.42	1.35	1.32	1.26	1.22	1.19
	6.76	**4.71**	**3.88**	**3.41**	**3.11**	**2.90**	**2.73**	**2.60**	**2.50**	**2.41**	**2.34**	**2.28**	**2.17**	**2.09**	**1.97**	**1.88**	**1.79**	**1.69**	**1.62**	**1.53**	**1.48**	**1.39**	**1.33**	**1.28**
400	3.86	3.02	2.62	2.39	2.23	2.12	2.03	1.96	1.90	1.85	1.81	1.78	1.72	1.67	1.60	1.54	1.49	1.42	1.38	1.32	1.28	1.22	1.16	1.13
	6.70	**4.66**	**3.83**	**3.36**	**3.06**	**2.85**	**2.69**	**2.55**	**2.46**	**2.37**	**2.29**	**2.23**	**2.12**	**2.04**	**1.92**	**1.84**	**1.74**	**1.64**	**1.57**	**1.47**	**1.42**	**1.32**	**1.24**	**1.19**
1000	3.85	3.00	2.61	2.38	2.22	2.10	2.02	1.95	1.89	1.84	1.80	1.76	1.70	1.65	1.58	1.53	1.47	1.41	1.36	1.30	1.26	1.19	1.13	1.08
	6.66	**4.62**	**3.80**	**3.34**	**3.04**	**2.82**	**2.66**	**2.53**	**2.43**	**2.34**	**2.26**	**2.20**	**2.09**	**2.01**	**1.89**	**1.81**	**1.71**	**1.61**	**1.54**	**1.44**	**1.38**	**1.28**	**1.19**	**1.11**
∞	3.84	2.99	2.60	2.37	2.21	2.09	2.01	1.94	1.88	1.83	1.79	1.75	1.69	1.64	1.57	1.52	1.46	1.40	1.35	1.28	1.24	1.17	1.11	1.00
	6.64	**4.60**	**3.78**	**3.32**	**3.02**	**2.80**	**2.64**	**2.51**	**2.41**	**2.32**	**2.24**	**2.18**	**2.07**	**1.99**	**1.87**	**1.79**	**1.69**	**1.59**	**1.52**	**1.41**	**1.36**	**1.25**	**1.15**	**1.00**

Source: Reprinted by permission from *Statistical Methods*, 8th ed., by George W. Snedecor and William G. Cochran. Published by Blackwell Publishing, Ames, Iowa 50010.

Table A.5 Table of χ^2

df	.99	.98	.95	.90	.80	.70	.50	.30	.20	.10	.05	.02	.01	.001
1	.000157	.000628	.00393	.0158	.0642	.148	.455	1.074	1.642	2.706	3.841	5.412	6.635	10.827
2	.0201	.0404	.103	.211	.446	.713	1.386	2.408	3.219	4.605	5.991	7.824	9.210	13.815
3	.115	.185	.352	.584	1.005	1.424	2.366	3.665	4.642	6.251	7.815	9.837	11.345	16.266
4	.297	.429	.711	1.064	1.649	2.195	3.357	4.878	5.989	7.779	9.488	11.668	13.277	18.467
5	.554	.752	1.145	1.610	2.343	3.000	4.351	6.064	7.289	9.236	11.070	13.388	15.086	20.515
6	.872	1.134	1.635	2.204	3.070	3.828	5.348	7.231	8.558	10.645	12.592	15.033	16.812	22.457
7	1.239	1.564	2.167	2.833	3.822	4.671	6.346	8.383	9.803	12.017	14.067	16.622	18.475	24.322
8	1.646	2.032	2.733	3.490	4.594	5.527	7.344	9.524	11.030	13.362	15.507	18.168	20.090	26.125
9	2.088	2.532	3.325	4.168	5.380	6.393	8.343	10.656	12.242	14.684	16.919	19.679	21.666	27.877
10	2.558	3.059	3.940	4.865	6.179	7.267	9.342	11.781	13.442	15.987	18.307	21.161	23.209	29.588
11	3.053	3.609	4.575	5.578	6.989	8.148	10.341	12.899	14.631	17.275	19.675	22.618	24.725	31.264
12	3.571	4.178	5.226	6.304	7.807	9.034	11.340	14.011	15.812	18.549	21.026	24.054	26.217	32.909
13	4.107	4.765	5.892	7.042	8.634	9.926	12.340	15.119	16.985	19.812	22.362	25.472	27.688	34.528
14	4.660	5.368	6.571	7.790	9.467	10.821	13.339	16.222	18.151	21.064	23.685	26.873	29.141	36.123
15	5.229	5.985	7.261	8.547	10.307	11.721	14.339	17.322	19.311	22.307	24.996	28.259	30.578	37.697
16	5.812	6.614	7.962	9.312	11.152	12.624	15.338	18.418	20.465	23.542	26.296	29.633	32.000	39.252
17	6.408	7.255	8.672	10.085	12.002	13.531	16.338	19.511	21.615	24.769	27.587	30.995	33.409	40.790
18	7.015	7.906	9.390	10.865	12.857	14.440	17.338	20.601	22.760	25.989	28.869	32.346	34.805	42.312
19	7.633	8.567	10.117	11.651	13.716	15.352	18.338	21.689	23.900	27.204	30.144	33.687	36.191	43.820
20	8.260	9.237	10.851	12.443	14.578	16.266	19.337	22.775	25.038	28.412	31.410	35.020	37.566	45.315
21	8.897	9.915	11.591	13.240	15.445	17.182	20.337	23.858	26.171	29.615	32.671	36.343	38.932	46.797
22	9.542	10.600	12.338	14.041	16.314	18.101	21.337	24.939	27.301	30.813	33.924	37.659	40.289	48.268
23	10.196	11.293	13.091	14.848	17.187	19.021	22.337	26.018	28.429	32.007	35.172	38.968	41.638	49.728
24	10.856	11.992	13.848	15.659	18.062	19.943	23.337	27.096	29.553	33.196	36.415	40.270	42.980	51.179
25	11.524	12.697	14.611	16.473	18.940	20.867	24.337	28.172	30.675	34.382	37.652	41.566	44.314	52.620
26	12.198	13.409	15.379	17.292	19.820	21.792	25.336	29.246	31.795	35.563	38.885	42.856	45.642	54.052
27	12.879	14.125	16.151	18.114	20.703	22.719	26.336	30.319	32.912	36.741	40.113	44.140	46.963	55.476
28	13.565	14.847	16.928	18.939	21.588	23.647	27.336	31.391	34.027	37.916	41.337	45.419	43.278	56.893
29	14.256	15.574	17.708	19.768	22.475	24.577	28.336	32.461	35.139	39.087	42.557	46.693	49.588	58.302
30	14.953	16.306	18.493	20.599	23.364	25.508	29.336	33.530	36.250	40.256	43.773	47.962	50.892	59.703

Source: Taken from Table IV of Fisher and Yates, *Statistical Tables for Biological, Agricultural and Medical Research*, published by Pearson Education Ltd., 1974.

GLOSSARY

ABAB design A single-subject experimental design in which baseline measurements of the target behavior are made (A) followed by a treatment (B) and then a second baseline measurement (A) and a second treatment (B).

abstract A brief summary of the contents of a document.

accessible population The population of subjects that is accessible to the researcher for a study, and the one to which the findings can be generalized.

accidental sampling A nonprobability sampling technique that simply uses conveniently available subjects without regard to how well the sample represents the population of interest.

achievement test A measure of the extent to which a person has acquired certain information or skills, often as a result of specific instruction.

action plan In action research, the step taken after analysis of data in which the researcher determines a course of action that incorporates potential solutions to the problem that was the focus of the research.

action research A form of research conducted by practitioners to study a particular context and use findings to change practice; typically uses qualitative research strategies.

active independent variable An independent variable created through active manipulation in the course of an experiment. Active independent variables are characteristic of experimental research.

agreement coefficient The percentage of persons for whom the same decision (mastery or nonmastery) is made on two administrations of a *criterion-referenced test*. Used as an index of reliability for criterion-referenced tests.

alpha coefficient *See* **Cronbach alpha.**

alternate form (estimate of reliability) *See* **equivalent form.**

analysis of covariance (ANCOVA) A statistical technique that provides partial statistical control for one or more variables, removing their influence from the comparison of groups on the dependent variable.

analysis of variance (ANOVA) An inferential statistical test used for experimental designs with more than one independent variable or more than two levels of an independent variable.

anonymity The practice of not associating individuals' names with the information or measurements obtained from those individuals.

applied research Research that aims to solve an immediate practical problem.

aptitude test A test that measures general abilities or characteristics believed to indicate a person's ability to learn a future task or to achieve in a particular area.

attitude scale A measure of the degree of favorableness or unfavorableness a subject has toward a group, institution, construct, or object.

attribute independent variable An independent variable on which subjects differ before a study begins. Attribute independent variables are characteristics of ex post facto research.

audit trail A qualitative researcher's documentation of how a study was conducted, including what was done, when, and why. It allows an independent auditor to examine the study from beginning to end and judge the trustworthiness of the outcome.

axial coding The process of making connections between and across categories in qualitative data analysis.

baseline Measures of the dependent variable taken prior to the introduction of the treatment in a time-series experimental design and used as the standard of comparison.

basic research Research that aims to obtain empirical data that can be used to formulate, expand, or evaluate a theory rather than to solve a practical problem.

between-groups design An experimental design that uses different groups of subjects for the different treatment conditions being compared.

biased sample A sample in which certain elements in the parent population are systematically under- or over-represented.

Boolean search Named after the 19th-century mathematician George Boole, a search allowing the inclusion or exclusion of documents through the use of Boolean operators such as AND, NOT, and OR in the query.

canonical correlation A statistical procedure for determining the relationship between several independent variables and more than one dependent variable.

case study A qualitative examination of a single individual, group, event, or institution.

categorical variables Variables that differ in kind, not in degree or amount.

causal-comparative research *See* **ex post facto research.**

causal relationship A relationship in which changes in one variable produce changes in another variable.

ceiling effect An effect that occurs when the performance range on a measure is so restricted on the upper end that subjects cannot perform to their maximum ability.

census A survey that includes the entire population of interest.

central tendency (measures of) Averages such as mean, median, and mode, commonly used to summarize the data in a frequency distribution.

chain sampling *See* **snowball sampling.**

change score The difference between subjects' pre- and postexperimental scores on the dependent variable(s).

checklist A type of survey question that presents a number of possible answers, of which respondents are asked to check those that apply.

chi-square (χ^2) An inferential statistic that compares the frequencies of nominal measures actually observed in a study with frequencies expected under a null (chance) hypothesis.

closed-ended question A question followed by a fixed set of alternative responses from which the respondent chooses.

cluster sampling A probability sampling technique that randomly selects intact groups (clusters) such as classrooms or voting precincts and then includes every element in each of the selected clusters in the sample.

coding A process of organizing qualitative data that results in data reduction. It helps the researcher see what is in the data.

coefficient alpha *See* **Cronbach alpha.**

coefficient of correlation *See* **correlation coefficient.**

coefficient of determination The square of the correlation coefficient. It indicates the percentage of variance in one variable in common with another variable.

Cohen's *d* A measure of effect size found by dividing the difference between two sample means by the weighted average of their standard deviations.

cohort study A longitudinal survey study in which a specific population is studied by taking different random samples from the population at various points in time.

collaborative partner A qualitative term, most often used in action or feminist research, that refers to the partnership between the researcher and the participant in the research process.

common cause A variable that accounts for differences in both the assumed independent variable and the dependent variable.

comparison group The group in a study that receives no treatment or a treatment different from the treatment received by the experimental group.

complete observer A researcher who is hidden from the group under study or who observes public behavior in a public setting.

complete participant A member of a group under study who gathers data on the natural activity of the group without informing them that they are under study.

comprehensive sampling A form of qualitative sampling where every unit of interest is included.

computer search Using a computer to locate information in databases.

concept mapping Using a diagram to plot elements in an action research study to determine visually how the elements are related to each other and to the problem under investigation.

concurrent validity *See* **criterion-related validity evidence.**

confidentiality The practice of keeping the information obtained from an individual in a study secret and private.

confirmability A qualitative term related to the degree to which findings in a study can be corroborated by others investigating the same situation.

confirmatory factor analysis An advanced factor analysis that allows for formal tests of hypotheses about the number and nature of factors and a comparison of different models or factor solutions.

confounding variable An uncontrolled extraneous variable whose effects on the dependent variable may incorrectly be attributed to the independent variable.

constant A characteristic that takes on the same value for all individuals in a study; contrasts with *variable.*

constant comparison A method of analyzing qualitative data that combines inductive category coding and simultaneous comparison of such units of meaning. Similar units of meaning are grouped together.

constitutive definition A definition in which a word is defined by using other words.

construct An abstraction at a higher level than a concept used to explain, interpret, and summarize observations and to form part of the conceptual content of a theory.

construct-irrelevant variance The effect on test scores from processes that are extraneous to the construct being measured. It affects the validity of the test. For example, reading ability may affect performance on a math test.

construct underrepresentation A term that is applied to assessment that is too narrow and fails to include important dimensions of the construct. It threatens the validity of the assessment.

construct validity (measurement) The extent to which a test or other instrument measures what the researcher claims it does; the degree to which evidence and theory support the interpretations of test scores entailed by the proposed use of the test.

construct validity (research) The extent to which inferences made from the observed subjects, settings, and operations sampled to the constructs that the samples represent are justified.

content analysis A research method applied to written or visual materials to analyze characteristics of the material.

content evidence (of validity) Evidence based on the degree to which the items of a test representatively sample an intended content domain. Determined mainly by logical analysis.

contingency question A survey question whose answer depends on the answer to a previous question.

continuous variable A variable whose measure can take an infinite number of points within a range.

contrived observation Observation of subjects in a prearranged simulation.

control Steps taken by the researcher to remove the effects of any variable(s) other than the independent variable that might influence the dependent variable.

control group The group in a study that does not receive the experimental treatment; it is compared with the experimental group to determine the effects of the treatment.

convenience sampling Choosing a sample based on availability, time, location, or ease of access; not recommended as a credible strategy for either qualitative or quantitative research.

convergent evidence Evidence for test validity based on the relationship to other measures intended to assess a similar construct. It shows that the intended construct is being measured.

correlation A technique for determining the covariation between sets of scores; paired scores may vary directly (increase or decrease together) or vary inversely (as one increases, the other decreases).

correlational research Research that attempts to determine the extent and the direction of the relationship between two or more variables.

correlation coefficient A statistic that shows the degree of relationship between two variables; its value ranges between -1.00 and $+1.00$.

correlation matrix A table that shows the coefficients of correlation between every measure and every other measure.

counterbalanced design An experimental design in which the effects of order are controlled by having all groups receive all treatments, but in a different order.

covert participant *See* **complete participant.**

credibility In qualitative research, the accuracy or truthfulness of the findings; similar in concept to internal validity in quantitative research.

criterion-referenced test An instrument that measures an individual's level of mastery of a predefined content or skill domain.

criterion-related validity evidence The degree to which scores on an instrument are related to other indicators of the same thing (the criterion). If the criterion scores are collected at the same point in time, the correlation is evidence of *concurrent validity*. If the criterion scores are collected at a later time, the resulting correlation between scores and criterion is evidence of *predictive validity*.

critical case sampling A single unit is selected for qualitative study because it provides a crucial test of a theory or a program.

critical research A form of qualitative research that seeks to analyze underlying assumptions revealed in various forms of communication.

Cronbach alpha An internal-consistency reliability coefficient that measures the extent to which the scores of the individual items agree with one another. It is especially useful for attitude scales or essay tests.

cross case comparison A strategy used in qualitative research to enhance transferability by investigating more than one case to determine whether findings are similar.

cross-sectional survey A survey in which data are collected at one point in time from a specified population.

cross tabulation A table showing how frequently various combinations of two or more categorical variables occur, from which one can "see" the relationship (if any) between the variables.

cross validation The process of validating a prediction equation based on one group by using it with a different group.

cumulative frequency The number of cases in a distribution with scores equal to or less than a given score.

curvilinear relationship A correlational relationship where a scatterplot of the paired scores is better described by a curve than by a straight line. For example, if high scores on Y were paired with average scores on X and low scores on Y were paired with both high and low scores on X, the relationship would be curvilinear.

data saturation In qualitative research, the point at which no new information is forthcoming from additional participants or settings. Also called *redundancy*.

deduction Beginning with general premises or already known facts and deriving specific logical conclusions.

deductive hypothesis A hypothesis derived by deduction from a theory.

degrees of freedom (*df*) The number of observations free to vary around a constant parameter. Each inferential statistic has a defined procedure for calculating its degrees of freedom, which are used to determine the appropriate critical values in statistical tables for determining the probabilities of observed statistics.

delta Smith and Glass's effect size, defined as the experimental group mean minus the control group mean divided by the control group standard deviation.

dependability In qualitative research, the consistency or stability of the results; the extent to which the same general results would occur with different sets of people or in different settings and time periods.

dependent variable A variable that is a consequence of or dependent on an antecedent (independent) variable; also called the *outcome* or *effect variable*.

descriptive adequacy The qualitative researcher's responsibility to provide accurate, detailed, and complete descriptions of the context and participants in a study so the reader can determine transferability.

descriptive research Research that asks questions about the nature, incidence, or distribution of variables; it involves describing but not manipulating variables.

descriptive statistics Techniques for organizing, summarizing, and describing observations.

developmental study Investigation of how children change as they mature and respond to their environment.

deviant case sampling *See* **extreme case sampling.**

dichotomous variable A categorical variable that has only two classes.

differential selection Creating experimental and control groups in such a way that they differ before treatment; an internal-validity problem.

directional hypothesis A hypothesis that specifies the direction of the expected findings—that is, whether a "greater than" or "less than" result is expected.

directional test (one-tailed test) A statistical test of a hypothesis that only states that the population parameter is greater than or less than the value of the parameter specified in the null hypothesis.

direct observation Observation of subjects to record the frequency and duration of behaviors falling within predetermined categories.

discourse analysis *See* **semiotics.**

discrepant data analysis *See* **negative case analysis.**

discriminant analysis A correlational procedure using a number of predictor variables to predict membership in categorical dependent variables.

discriminant evidence Evidence for test validity based on the relationship between the test scores and measures of purportedly different constructs. It shows that the wrong construct is not being measured.

documentary analysis The systematic examination of documents to investigate specific topics or themes.

double-barreled question A single-survey question that actually asks two questions in one.

double-blind experiment An experiment in which neither the observers nor the subjects know which is the experimental group and which is the control group.

double-dipped sample A sample drawn from the nonrespondents to a survey, who are then interviewed to determine if they differ significantly from respondents.

dummy variable A categorical variable that has been recoded as a binary variable for entry into a multiple regression. For example, gender could be coded as 1 or 0.

effect size A measure of the strength of the relationship between two variables shown by the difference between two means calculated by either Cohen's *d* or Smith and Glass's delta.

emergent design A design typical of qualitative research in which an initial problem or sampling strategy is changed or refined as data are collected and analyzed.

equivalent form (estimate of reliability) Reliability assessment procedure correlating the scores of the same subjects on two tests that are as similar as possible in content, difficulty, length, format, and so on.

ERIC system A very extensive database maintained by Computer Sciences Corporation (CSC) available at a website.

error of central tendency A tendency for a rater to avoid extreme scale positions, rating all individuals near the middle of the scale.

error of severity A tendency to rate all subjects too low.

ethnography A form of qualitative research that aims for a holistic picture of a cultural group; it uses in-depth interviewing and prolonged participant observation.

experimental design A plan for an experiment that specifies what independent variables will be applied, the number of levels of each, how subjects are assigned to groups, and the dependent variable.

experimental group The group in a research study that receives the experimental treatment.

experimental mortality Attrition of subjects during a study. An internal-validity problem if attrition is not the same for experimental and control groups.

experimental research Research in which the investigator manipulates one or more independent variables (the treatment) and observes the effect on one or more dependent variables.

experimenter bias The effects of the experimenter's attitudes, behavior, and expectancies on the behavior of the subjects in an experiment.

exploratory factor analysis A factor analysis in which no formal hypotheses are tested about the nature of the factors that might be found.

ex post facto research A type of research that attempts to determine the causes for, or the consequences of, differences that already exist in groups of individuals. Also called *causal-comparative research*.

external criticism Evaluation of the authenticity of a document or other concrete evidence in historical research.

external validity The extent to which the findings of a particular study can be generalized to other subjects, other settings, and/or other operational definitions of the variables.

extraneous variable An uncontrolled variable that may affect the dependent variable of a study; its effect may be mistakenly attributed to the independent variable of the study.

extreme case sampling An atypical or unusual unit is selected for qualitative study.

factor An underlying construct accounting for the covariation among a larger number of variables.

factor analysis A statistical procedure for analyzing the intercorrelations among three or more measures that reduces the set to a smaller number of underlying factors.

factorial design An experimental design that investigates two or more independent variables at the same time, in order to study their effects singly or in interaction with each other.

factor loading In factor analysis, the correlation between a variable and a factor. The higher the loading, the more the variable is seen as contributing to a particular factor.

falsifiable A term applied to a theory or hypothesis that is capable of being proven wrong. It is possible to gather data that contradict the theory or hypothesis.

field experiment An experiment conducted in a naturally occurring environment.

field notes The researcher's reflections and the written records of observations and conversations made during a qualitative research project.

field testing A process of testing a research instrument with a small number of persons, in order to identify ambiguities or other problems before the final form is prepared.

floor effect An effect that occurs when the performance range of a measure is so restricted at the lower end that subjects cannot show their ability to perform. The floor effect occurs when the task is too difficult for the subjects.

focused interview A qualitative research data-gathering technique employing open and flexible questions that respondents are free to answer in their own words.

focus group A data-gathering tool in which a researcher interviews a small group of people to obtain different perspectives on a particular issue.

focus of inquiry In qualitative research, the initial topic (problem) that a researcher pursues. It may be presented in the form of a question or a statement.

follow-up study An investigation of subsequent development of subjects after a specified treatment or program.

frequency distribution A tabular representation of the scores obtained by a group of individuals.

***F* test** A statistical procedure used for testing hypotheses about differences among two or more means, and for other purposes.

generosity error A tendency for a rater to give every subject the benefit of the doubt and, when uncertain, to give high ratings.

grounded theory Theory derived inductively from the data collected in a natural setting rather than from a priori ideas or theorems.

halo effect The tendency for a rater's general impression of a subject to influence the rating given for specific aspects or behaviors of the subject.

Hawthorne effect An effect on the dependent variable resulting from the treatment group's knowledge that the members are participating in an experiment.

histogram A graph in which the frequency distribution of scores is represented by vertical bars.

historical research A systematic attempt to establish facts and arrive at conclusions about the past.

history (an internal validity problem) Events or conditions other than the independent variable that produce changes in the dependent variable.

homogeneous group A set of subjects who are the same or similar on a relevant variable.

homogeneous sampling Subsets of units are selected for qualitative study because they are similar in the phenomenon of interest.

homogeneous selection Employing subjects that are as alike as possible in regard to relevant characteristics, to reduce the influence of extraneous variables.

human instrument The investigator as the means of data gathering in qualitative inquiry.

hypothesis A tentative proposition suggested as a solution to a problem; a statement of the researcher's expectations about the relationship among the variables of a study.

hypothesis test Collection of observations to determine whether these observations confirm or fail to confirm a hypothesized relationship.

imperfect induction The process of inferring from a sample of a group to what is characteristic of the whole group.

implementation threat A threat to the internal validity of a study resulting from possible variations in implementing the treatment.

independent variable A variable that is antecedent to the dependent variable; also called the *experimental* or *treatment variable*.

induction Gaining knowledge through systematic study and observation of specific facts or episodes and then arriving at generalized conclusions.

inductive analysis A process of beginning with observations (data) and then proceeding to hypothesis formation and refinement and finally to theory.

inductive hypothesis A hypothesis derived through generalization from observation.

inferential statistics Procedures that permit one to make tentative generalizations from sample data to the population from which the sample was drawn.

informed consent, right to The right of a subject in a research study to know the nature and purpose of the study and to give or withhold consent to participate.

institutional review board (IRB) A committee that determines whether proposed research meets federal and other legal and ethical standards.

instrument A device for operationally defining a variable.

instrumentation threat The possibility that results of a study are caused by variations in the way instruments are used to operationally define the variables; a threat to internal validity.

intensity sampling Units are selected for qualitative study because they exhibit different levels of a phenomenon of interest.

interaction The outcome of a factorial experiment when the effects of one independent variable on a dependent variable change at different levels of the second independent variable.

internal consistency Reliability assessment procedure measuring the extent to which items of a test (or subtest or scale) are positively intercorrelated and thus all measure the same construct or trait; the extent to which a test measures only one characteristic.

internal criticism Evaluation of the truthfulness of a document in historical research.

internal structure evidence (of validity) Evidence based on an analysis of the internal structure of a test; it looks at the intercorrelations among test items to determine whether the test is measuring a single construct and whether the interrelationships conform to the theory behind the construct being measured.

internal validity The extent to which observed differences on the dependent variable in an experiment are the result of the independent variable, not of some uncontrolled extraneous variable or variables.

Internet An interconnected system of computer networks allowing for information sharing.

interobserver agreement A qualitative strategy for enhancing the dependability of findings by comparing coding of a peer observer with the original coded data.

interpretive study A basic form of qualitative research that provides detailed accounts targeted to understanding a process, a phenomenon, or a particular point of view.

interrater reliability The extent to which two or more observers produce similar quantitative results when observing the same individual during the same time period.

interval scale A scale of measurement that orders objects or events and has points equidistant from one another.

interview Oral questioning of a subject.

interviewer bias A bias that occurs in interviews when the interviewer verbally or nonverbally rewards the subject's correct responses or negatively reinforces wrong responses.

interview schedule A document used by an interviewer that contains the instructions, the questions in a fixed order, and any transition phrases.

inventory A collection of statements to which subjects respond by indicating whether the statement describes them or not; used in assessing personality.

item analysis Analysis of a test determining for each item the number and proportion of correct responses and the correlation of scores on that item with total test scores.

John Henry effect An effect that occurs when the control group performs above its usual average when it perceives itself in competition with an experimental group that is using a new method or procedure.

known-groups technique A method for determining the validity of a measure by seeing whether groups known to differ on the construct also differ on the measure itself.

Kruskal–Wallis test A one-way analysis of variance carried out on ranks.

Kuder–Richardson formulas Formulas for determining the internal-consistency reliability (homogeneity) of an instrument from a single administration and without splitting the test into halves.

laboratory experiment An experiment conducted in a highly controlled environment.

law of the single independent variable Rule stating that to unambiguously determine the effect of an independent variable on a dependent variable, the independent variable must be the only difference between the experimental and control groups before the dependent variable is measured.

level of significance The largest probability of error acceptable for rejection of the null hypothesis. Often $p = .05$ or $p = .01$ in educational research.

Likert scale A measurement scale consisting of a series of statements followed by five response categories, typically ranging from "strongly agree" to "strongly disagree."

Likert-type item A statement similar to those in a Likert scale, where the response options are on a continuum from "strongly agree" to "strongly disagree."

linear relationship A correlational relationship where the plotted points in a scatterplot of the paired scores fit around a straight line.

longitudinal survey A survey in which data are collected several times over an extended period of time.

low-inference descriptor Verbatim or direct quotations from the participants in qualitative research that help a reader experience the participants' world.

main effect The effect that an independent variable has on the dependent variable in a factorial experiment irrespective of the influence of the other independent variables.

manipulated variable The variable that is systematically altered by an experimental researcher in order to observe the effect on a dependent variable.

Mann–Whitney test A statistical test for the difference in the group means for two independent samples when the dependent variable is ranked data.

margin of error An estimate of the extent to which sample results are likely to deviate from the population value.

matching Identifying pairs of subjects who are as alike as possible before a study begins.

maturation A threat to internal validity from factors that occur as a result of the passage of time. In addition to the experimental treatment, factors such as growing older, hungrier, more fatigued, or less motivated may influence performance on the dependent variable and thus threaten internal validity.

maximum variation sampling A sampling technique widely used in qualitative inquiry in which a researcher attempts to understand a phenomenon by seeking out people or settings that represent the greatest difference in that phenomenon.

mean A measure of central tendency for a distribution of interval data; the sum of the scores divided by the number of scores in the distribution; the arithmetic average.

median The point in a distribution below which are 50 percent of the scores (the 50th percentile); used with ordinal or interval data.

member check A process in which a qualitative researcher asks the participants in a study whether they have accurately and realistically described their experience. The participant feedback contributes to the trustworthiness of qualitative inquiry.

Mental Measurements Yearbooks Serial publication listing tests available, with descriptions and critical reviews of these tests.

meta-analysis The systematic combination of quantitative data from a number of studies investigating the relationship between the same variables. A weighted average of effect sizes.

mode The score that occurs most frequently in a distribution of scores; used with nominal, ordinal, interval, or ratio data.

mortality A threat to internal validity that occurs when some participants drop out of a study before it is completed.

multifactor analysis of variance An analysis of variance with more than one independent variable.

multiple-baseline design An experiment in which several dependent variable baseline measures are determined for a single subject and then treatments designed to change dependent variables are instituted at different times for each dependent variable. It is also used to determine the effects of the same treatment instituted at different times for different subjects.

multiple regression The prediction of a criterion using two or more predictor variables in combination. Each predictor is weighted in proportion to its contribution to prediction accuracy. The equation showing the weights assigned to each predictor is the *multiple regression equation*.

narrative study A form of qualitative research, also called *biography*, *life stories*, and *life narratives*, that provides accounts of a person's experiences.

naturalistic inquiry The study of subjects in their normal environment without predetermined hypotheses.

naturalistic observation A qualitative research term that indicates that the researcher is not attempting to alter a situation in any way, but is merely observing and recording events as they naturally occur.

natural setting A research environment in which activities occur in the ordinary course of events as opposed to an environment in which events are contrived or manipulated for the purpose of the research.

negative case analysis A strategy used in qualitative research that involves intentionally looking for data that contradict the emerging category or pattern.

negative correlation A correlation with high scores on one variable associated with low scores on the other variable.

negative evidence Evidence that contradicts a theory and thus leads to its rejection or revision.

negatively skewed curve A polygon showing many scores piled up at the high (right) end and the lower scores spread out toward the low (left) end; the tail of the curve extends to the left.

network sampling *See* **snowball sampling.**

neutrality In qualitative research, the extent to which the research is free of bias in the procedures and interpretation of results.

nominal scale A scale of measurement that classifies objects or individuals into categories that are qualitatively but not quantitatively different.

nondirectional hypothesis A hypothesis that states that a relationship between variables will be observed but does not specify the direction of the expected findings.

nondirectional test (two-tailed test) A statistical test that takes into account differences in either direction (greater or less than) from the value specified in the null hypothesis; the null hypothesis is rejected if the difference is large enough in *either* tail of a sampling distribution of the statistic.

nonparticipant observation A research method in which the observer does not participate in the situation being studied but is only an observer.

nonprobability sampling Sampling through other than random selection.

nonresponse A situation in which people receive a survey but fail to return the completed instrument.

normal curve A hypothetical symmetrical, bell-shaped distribution of scores used as a model for many naturally occurring distributions and for many statistical tests.

norm-referenced test A test that enables one to compare an individual's performance with the performance of others who have taken the test.

null hypothesis A hypothesis that states there is no effect, no difference, or no relationship between variables; it is a negation of the research hypothesis—hence one that the researcher hopes to reject.

observer bias An effect that occurs when the observer's personal attitudes and values affect the observation and/or the interpretation of the observation. Can especially be a problem in qualitative research.

observer effect The impact that an observer has on a study's participants so that they behave differently from the way they normally would. It destroys the naturalness and results in an inaccurate picture of a situation.

observer expectation A tendency for an observer who knows the participants he or she is studying to expect certain behaviors and hence to see or interpret actions or events in a certain way.

observer participant An observer who interacts with subjects enough to establish rapport but does not really become involved in the behavior or activities of the group. The person's status as an observer/researcher is known to the group.

one-tailed test *See* **directional test.**

open coding The process of breaking down and categorizing qualitative data into manageable segments.

open-ended question A question that does not have fixed response alternatives but allows the respondent to respond as he or she chooses.

operational definition A definition that specifies the procedure or operation to be followed in producing or measuring a concept.

ordinal scale A scale of measurement that rank-orders objects and events according to the extent to which they possess the characteristic of interest, but the distance between points cannot be assumed to be equal.

panel study A longitudinal survey study in which data are gathered from the same sample of people at different points in time.

parallel form *See* **equivalent form.**

parameter A characteristic of a population, such as the population mean (μ) or the population standard deviation (σ).

parsimony principle The principle that states that, other things being equal, the simplest explanation of a phenomenon is preferred over a more complicated explanation.

partial control Some but not complete control over relevant extraneous variables.

partial correlation A statistical procedure for describing the relationship between two variables, with the correlation between these variables and a third variable removed.

participant observation A research method in which the researcher becomes a part of and participates in the activities of the group or situation being studied.

path analysis A statistical procedure for investigating the causal relationships among correlated variables.

pattern matching A qualitative analysis strategy involving making predictions based on theory and then determining how well patterns in the data fit the predicted pattern.

Pearson product moment coefficient (Pearson *r*) An index of correlation for interval or ratio data; it is the mean of paired *z*-score products of the two variables.

peer debriefers Members of a qualitative research team who check one another's work and look for evidence of bias. They act to keep one another honest.

performance assessment A type of assessment that requires subjects to show what they know by performing specified tasks rather than by filling out a paper-and-pencil instrument.

phenomenological approach A philosophy of research that focuses on understanding the meaning events have for people in particular situations. It underlies qualitative research.

phenomenology A type of qualitative research designed to gain an understanding of how participants experience and give meaning to an event, concept, or phenomenon.

phi coefficient A correlation coefficient for use when both variables are measured on a nominal scale.

pilot study A trial run with a few subjects to assess the appropriateness and practicability of the procedures and data-collecting instruments.

placebo A chemically inert or neutral material given to subjects in an experiment to make them believe they are receiving a drug or experimental treatment.

plausibility Concerns the theoretical adequacy or the degree to which theory fits the data; used in qualitative research.

polygon A graph showing scores and frequency of scores by connecting the intersections of each of the scores and the frequencies.

population The larger group to which a researcher wishes to generalize; it includes *all* members of a defined class of people, events, or objects.

portraiture A form of qualitative research whose goal is to paint a vivid story that reflects the perspectives of both the researcher and the participants.

positive correlation A correlation with high scores on one variable associated with high scores on the other variable, and low scores associated with low scores.

positively skewed distribution A polygon showing many scores piled up at or near the low (left) end and higher scores spread out toward the high (right) end; the tail extends to the right.

positivism A philosophy of research characterized by objective inquiry based on measurable variables; believes that science should be primarily concerned with the explanation and the prediction of observable events. It underlies quantitative research.

power The ability of a significance test to find significant differences when differences truly exist; the ability to avoid making a Type II error.

power calculation A mathematical procedure for determining the sample size needed to reject the null hypothesis at a given level of significance with a given effect size.

predictive validity *See* **criterion-related validity evidence.**

predictor A variable from which predictions are made in a prediction study.

preexperimental research Experimental designs with little or no control of extraneous variables and therefore little internal validity.

pretest sensitization The effect of a pretest on subjects that causes them to respond differently to the treatment from the way they would without the pretest.

primary source Original documents, relics, remains, or the records of an eyewitness used in historical research.

probability sampling Sampling employing random selection, which means that every element in the population has a nonzero chance of being selected.

probe A follow-up question used during an interview to elicit clearer and more complete responses from the interviewee.

problem analysis Using visual representations to show antecedents to and consequences of the problem under investigation in action research.

Professional Development School A partnership between a college/university and a K–12 school designed to enhance professional development, provide clinical experiences for preservice teachers, conduct inquiry to improve practice, and enhance student achievement; sometimes compared to a teaching hospital.

projective technique A method for assessing personality by analyzing subjects' responses to ambiguous material.

purposive sampling A nonprobability sampling technique in which subjects judged to be representative of the population are included in the sample.

qualitative research A generic term for a variety of research approaches that study phenomena in their natural settings, without predetermined hypotheses.

quantitative research Inquiry employing operational definitions to generate numeric data to answer predetermined hypotheses or questions.

quasi-experimental research Research in which the investigator can control the treatment and the measurement of the dependent variable but cannot control assignment of the subjects to treatment.

questionnaire An instrument in which respondents provide written responses to questions or mark items that indicate their responses.

quota sampling A nonprobability sampling technique that determines the size of each relevant subgroup in the population and then nonrandomly selects subjects to produce a sample in which the proportion of each subgroup is the same in the sample as it is in the population.

random assignment (randomization) Assigning members of a sample to experimental or control groups through a chance procedure.

randomized experiment An experiment in which subjects are randomly assigned to groups.

randomized matching A procedure in which subjects are first paired (matched) on relevant variables, and then a chance procedure is used to assign one member of each pair to the experimental group and the other to the control group.

random sample A sample selected by a chance procedure so that every member of the population has an equal probability of being selected.

random selection The process of selecting a sample by chance means, so that every member of the population has an equal probability of being included.

range A nominal measure of dispersion; the difference between the highest and lowest scores plus one unit of measure.

ranking item A type of survey question that asks respondents to indicate the order of their preference among a number of options.

ratio scale A scale of measurement that provides a true zero point as well as equal intervals.

referential accuracy (or interpretive accuracy) A term used in qualitative research to refer to the degree to which participants' viewpoints, thoughts, feelings, and experiences are accurately understood.

reflexivity Qualitative researchers' use of self-reflection to recognize and actively look for their own biases.

regression (statistical) The statistical tendency for extreme scores on the first measurement to move closer to the mean on a second measurement.

regression threat The internal-validity problem that arises when results in a study are caused by a tendency for groups selected on the basis of extreme scores to move (regress) toward the average on subsequent measures, regardless of the experimental treatment.

reliability The extent to which a measure yields consistent results; the extent to which scores are free of random error.

replication logic A process whereby one conducts a qualitative study in multiple locations or with multiple groups in order to assess the dependability of the findings.

research proposal A step-by-step plan for conducting and completing a research study.

response process evidence (of validity) Evidence about what a test measures obtained by looking at the mental processes and skills that subjects use when responding to the items on a test.

response set A habitual way of responding that is independent of the content of a particular survey or test item, as when a subject always checks "undecided" regardless of the statement.

reverse causality An alternative hypothesis stating that the supposed dependent variable is in actuality the independent variable (Y causes X, not X causes Y).

sample A group selected from a population for observation in a study.

sample survey A survey done on only a portion (a sample) of a population, often using a questionnaire or interview.

sampling error The difference between a sample statistic and a population parameter.

scale A continuum, usually having quantitative units, that measures the extent to which individuals exhibit certain traits or characteristics.

scatterplot A figure using plotted points to represent the intersection of individuals' paired X and Y scores; used to show the relationship between the X and Y variables.

scholastic aptitude test A test that measures abilities that are predictive of success in academic tasks.

scientific approach A way of seeking knowledge that involves both inductive and deductive reasoning to develop hypotheses that are then subjected to rigorous and objective testing.

search engine The software that searches an index of Internet web pages and returns matches.

secondary source Secondhand information, such as a description of a historical event written by someone other than an eyewitness.

selection–maturation interaction An internal-validity problem created when subjects are selected in such a way that the experimental and control groups mature at different rates.

selective coding The process of systematically reviewing qualitative data to look for a specific category or theme.

semiotics A qualitative study of linguistic units to look at the relationship between words and their meanings.

significance fallacy An incorrect assumption that the statistical significance of results also indicates practical significance.

single-subject research An experiment with only one subject or intact group.

snowball sampling A sampling procedure used in qualitative research that occurs when the initially selected subjects suggest the names of others who would be appropriate for the sample, and the latter suggest others and so on. Also called *chain sampling* or *network sampling*.

social desirability bias A bias that occurs in interviews when subjects give responses to enhance their image rather than honest responses.

Social Science Citation Index A periodic journal; its citation index enables users to start with an older article on a topic of interest, then identify more recent works that cite that original work in their bibliographies or footnotes. It enables the researcher to locate updated research and find retractions and corrections. Its corporate index identifies the institutional source of published works. Its permuterm index identifies interconnections in article titles.

Solomon four-group design An experimental design that involves random assignment of subjects to each of four groups; two groups are pretested, two are not; one of the pretested and one of the nonpretested groups receive the treatment; and all four groups are posttested.

Solomon three-group design An experimental design in which subjects are randomly assigned to three groups: (A) pretest plus treatment, (B) pretest plus no treatment, or (C) no pretest plus treatment.

Spearman–Brown formula A statistical procedure employing the correlation between split halves of a test to estimate the reliability of the whole test.

Spearman rho An index of correlation for use with ordinal data.

split-half reliability A type of internal-consistency reliability obtained by artificially splitting a test into two halves and correlating individuals' scores on the two half tests.

spurious result An apparent relationship between variables that is not genuine.

standard deviation A measure of the extent to which individual scores deviate from the mean of the distribution; the square root of the variance; a measure of dispersion used with interval data.

standard error of estimate A measure of the expected difference between predicted scores and actual scores.

standard error of measurement An index of the amount of measurement error in test scores; theoretically, the standard deviation of the distribution of observed scores around an individual's true score.

standard error of the mean The standard deviation of sampling errors of the mean; indicates how much the means of random samples drawn from a single population can be expected to differ through chance alone.

standardized test A test with specified content, prescribed directions for administering and scoring, norms, and reliability and validity information derived from administration to representative samples.

standard score A transformed score expressed in terms of the number of standard deviation units the score is above or below the mean; standard scores have a mean and a standard deviation set to some arbitrary standard. For example, a z score has a mean of 0 and a standard deviation of 1; T scores use a mean of 50 and a standard deviation of 10.

static group comparison A preexperimental design that involves at least two nonequivalent groups; one receives a treatment and both are posttested. Provides little or no control.

statistic A characteristic of a sample.

statistical conclusion validity The validity of the inferences about the covariation between two variables in an experimental study.

statistical equivalence Condition occurring when any difference between groups is a function of chance alone; random assignment of subjects to groups results in statistically equivalent groups.

statistically significant result A result that has less than a previously specified probability of being a function of chance.

stepwise replication A process in which two investigators divide the data from a qualitative inquiry, analyze them independently, and then compare results. A way of checking on the dependability of the research.

stratified sampling A probability sampling technique that first divides a population into subgroups by relevant variables such as age, social status, or education and then randomly selects subjects from each subgroup.

structural corroboration The use of different sources of qualitative data and different methods to see if there is agreement (corroboration) in the description and interpretation of a state of affairs.

structural equation modeling A generic term for a group of advanced techniques used in the analysis of causality. It includes path analysis and confirmatory factor analysis.

style manual A book detailing form and style for theses, dissertations, and other formal written works.

subject A person in a study.

subject descriptors A controlled vocabulary list of terms and phrases. Descriptors, also called *subject headings*, are standardized terms used in indexes and catalogs to describe the content of an indexed document. Controlled vocabularies are often arranged with broader, narrower, and related terms, as in the ERIC thesaurus, which provides the searcher with an idea of the relationships of terms and concepts.

summated rating scale A scale that arrives at a person's total score by finding the sum of the weighted responses made to all the items in the scale. *See* **Likert scale.**

survey Study of a sample to investigate the incidence and distribution of variables.

symmetrical distribution A distribution that can be represented by a polygon whose right side is a mirror image of its left side.

systematic sampling A probability sampling in which every kth element of the population list is selected for the sample.

target population The total group (population) to which the researcher would like to generalize the results of a study.

test A systematic procedure for measuring a sample of behavior presumed to represent an educational or psychological characteristic.

testable A term applied to a theory or hypothesis that can be verified through empirical observation.

test of significance A statistical test used to determine whether the obtained results are likely to be a function of chance. Used to assess the credibility of the null hypothesis.

test–retest reliability A measure of reliability obtained by correlating scores from two administrations of the same measure to the same subjects.

theoretical sampling A qualitative sampling strategy that involves continuing to select new cases as the research unfolds based on any emerging theories developed from the data.

theory A set of interrelated propositions or hypotheses that presents an explanation of some phenomenon.

thick description A term used in qualitative research that refers to descriptions that are written to create vivid images of the setting and behaviors being observed.

time-series design An experiment in which dependent variable measures are made several times before and after treatment.

transferability In qualitative research, the degree to which the findings of a study can be generalized to other contexts or to other groups.

treatment group The group in an experimental study that receives the independent variable of interest.

trend study A longitudinal survey in which data are gathered from different samples of a general population at different points in time to investigate changes over time.

triangulation Confirming data using multiple data-gathering procedures or multiple sources of data; used in qualitative research.

true experimental design An experimental design in which the researcher controls the treatment and uses randomization to assign subjects to treatments.

trustworthiness A qualitative term that refers to how well variations can be tracked or explained; also called *dependability* and is similar to the quantitative concept of reliability.

***T* score** A standard score with a mean of 50 and a standard deviation of 10.

***t* test** A statistical procedure for testing hypotheses concerning the difference between two means; also used for other purposes.

two-tailed test *See* **nondirectional test.**

Type I error The error that occurs when a researcher rejects a null hypothesis that is in fact true.

Type II error The error that occurs when a researcher fails to reject a null hypothesis that is in fact false.

typical case sampling Units are selected for a qualitative study because they are considered average or "typical" of the phenomenon of interest.

unique case sampling *See* **extreme case sampling.**

validity (of measurement) The extent to which a measure actually taps the underlying concept that it purports to measure.

variability The dispersion or spread in a distribution of scores.

variable A representation of a construct that takes on a range of values. For example, height, reading test score, aptitude, and gender are variables.

variance The mean of squared deviation scores; an interval measure of dispersion of scores around the mean.

Wilcoxon test A statistical test for ranked data that serves the same purpose as the dependent *t* test.

within-groups design An experimental design in which the same subjects participate in all of the different treatment conditions. Also called *repeated-measures design*.

World Wide Web The use of graphical user interfaces and hypertext links to access information on the Internet. Also, the complete set of documents residing on the Internet that can be accessed through the web.

***z* score** A standard score that indicates how far a score is above or below the mean score in terms of standard deviation units.

REFERENCES

Adams-Byers, J., Whitsell, S., & Moon, S. (2004). Gifted students' perceptions of the academic and social/emotional effects of homogeneous and heterogeneous grouping. *Gifted Child Quarterly, 48*, 7–20.

AIDSLINE. (1980–). Available: Internet Grateful Med at http://igm.nlm.nih.gov

Alcohol, tobacco, and other drug use by Indiana children and adolescents. Retrieved April 16, 2004, from http://www.drugs.indiana.edu/survey/ATOD/index/ html

Allen, A. M., Allen, D. N., & Sigler, G. (1993). Changes in sex-role stereotyping in Caldecott Medal award picture books 1938–1988. *Journal of Research in Childhood Education, 7*, 67–73.

Altbach, P. G. (Ed.). (1991). *International higher education: An encyclopedia* (2 vols.). Hamden, CT: Garland.

American doctoral dissertations. (1957–). Ann Arbor, MI: University Microfilms.

American Educational Research Association. (2004). *Encyclopedia of educational research* (7th ed., 4 vols.). New York: Macmillan.

American Educational Research Association, American Psychological Association, National Council on Measurement in Education. (1999). *Standards for educational and psychological tests*. Washington, DC: Author.

American Psychological Association. (2001). *Publication manual of the American Psychological Association* (5th ed.). Washington, DC: Author.

American statistics index. (1973–). Bethesda, MD: Congressional Information Service.

Anderson, G. L. (2002). Reflecting on research for doctoral students in education. *Educational Researcher, 31*, 22–25.

Annual review of psychology. (1950–). Stanford, CA: Annual Reviews.

Ary, D., & Jacobs, L. C. (1976). *Introduction to statistics*. New York: Holt, Rinehart & Winston.

Atkinson, J. W., & Birch, D. (1978). An introduction to motivation. New York: Van Nostrand.

Atkinson, R. (1998). *The life story interview*. Thousand Oaks, CA: Sage.

Balay, R., Carrington, V. F., & Martin, M. S. (Eds.). (1996). *Guide to reference books* (11th ed.). Chicago: American Library Association.

Banks, J. A., & McGee-Banks, C. A. (Eds.). (2003). *Handbook of research on multicultural education*. New York: Wiley.

Baumann, J., Edwards, E., Boland, E., Olejnik, S., & Kame'enui, E. (2003). Vocabulary tricks: Effects of instruction in morphology and context on fifth-grade students' ability to derive and infer word meanings. *American Educational Research Journal, 40*, 447–494.

Becker, B. J., & Hedges, L. V. (Eds.). (1992). *Journal of Educational Statistics, 17*(4), 583–587.

Belenky, M. F., Clinchy, B. M., Goldberger, N. R., & Tarule, J. M. (1986). *Women's ways of knowing: The development of self, voice, and mind*. New York: Basic Books.

Bencze, J. L. (2004). Faculty web site at University of Toronto. Available: http://tortoise.oise.utoronto.ca/~lbencze

Bentler, P., & Chou, C. (1988). Practical issues in structural modeling. In J. S. Long (Ed.), *Common problems/proper solutions: Avoiding error in quantitative research*. Newbury Park, CA: Sage.

Berliner, D. C., & Calfee, R. C. (1996). *Handbook of research on educational psychology*. New York: Macmillan.

Berry, D. M. (1990). *A bibliographic guide to educational research* (3rd ed.). Metuchen, NJ: Scarecrow Press.

Bleeker, M. M., & Jacobs, J. E. (2004). Achievement in math and science: Do mothers' beliefs matter 12 years later? *Journal of Educational Psychology, 96*, 97–109.

Bogdan, R. C., & Biklen, S. K. (1998). *Qualitative research for education: An introduction to theory and methods* (3rd ed.). Boston: Allyn & Bacon.

Bogdan, R. C., & Biklen, S. K. (2003). *Qualitative research for education*. Boston: Allyn & Bacon.

Borenstein, M., & Cohen, J. (1989). *Statistical power analysis*. Hillsdale, NJ: Erlbaum.

Brennan, R. L. (2001). Some problems, pitfalls, and paradoxes in educational measurement. *Educational Measurement Issues and Practices, 20*(4), 6–18.

Brott, P. E., & Myers, J. E. (1999). Development of professional school counselor identity: A grounded theory. *Professional School Counseling, 2*(5), 339–348.

Bryant, M. T. (2004). *The portable dissertation advisor*. Thousand Oaks, CA: Corwin Press.

Burnaford, G., Fischer, J., & Hobson, D. (2001). *Teachers doing research: The power of action through inquiry* (2nd ed.). Mahwah, NJ: Erlbaum.

Buston, K. (1999). NUD*IST in action: Its use and usefulness in a study of chronic illness in young people. In A. Bryman & R. G. Burgess (Eds.), *Qualitative research* (Vol. 3, pp. 183–202). Thousand Oaks, CA: Sage.

Butler, R. J. (2001). *The self-image profile for children*. Oxford: Psychological Corporation.

Campbell, D. T., & Stanley, J. C. (1963). *Experimental and quasi-experimental designs for research*. Chicago: Rand McNally.

Campbell, D. T., & Stanley, J. C. (1966). *Experimental and quasi-experimental designs for research*. Boston: Houghton Mifflin.

Carspecken, P. F. (1995). *Critical ethnography in educational research: A theoretical and practical guide*. London: Routledge.

Chandler, D. (2001). *Semiotics: The basics*. London: Routledge.

Chilcott, J. H. (1992). Some contributions of anthropology to professional education. *Educational Researcher, 21*(2), 31–35.

Child development abstracts and bibliography. (1927–). Lafayette, IN: Purdue University, Society for Research in Child Development.

Chronicle survey of public opinion on higher education. (2004, May 7). *Chronicle of Higher Education, 50*, A12–A13.

Cicirelli, V. (1969). *The impact of Head Start: An evaluation of the effects of Head Start on children's cognitive and affective development*. (A report presented to the Office of Economic Opportunity pursuant to contract B89-4536.) Westinghouse Learning Corporation and Ohio University. (Distributed by the Clearinghouse for Federal Scientific and Technical Information, U.S. Department of Commerce, National Bureau of Standards, Institute for Applied Technology. PB 184 328.)

Clark, B. R., & Neave, G. R. (Eds.). (1992). *The encyclopedia of higher education* (4 vols.). Tarrytown, NY: Pergamon Press.

Cleary, T. J., & Zimmerman, B. J. (2004). Self-regulation empowerment program: A school-based program to enhance self-regulated and self-motivated cycles of student learning. *Psychology in the Schools, 41*, 537–550.

Coalition for Evidence-Based Policy. (2003). *Identifying and implementing educational practices supported by rigorous evidence: A user friendly guide*. Washington, DC: U.S. Department of Education.

Cochran, W. C. (1985). *Sampling techniques* (2nd ed.). New York: Wiley.

Cohen, J. (1988). *Statistical power analysis for the behavioral sciences*. Hillsdale, NJ: Erlbaum.

Cohen, J., Cohen, P., West, S., & Aiken, L. (2003). *Applied multiple regression/correlational analysis for the behavioral sciences* (3rd ed.). Mahwah, NJ: Erlbaum.

Committee on Research in Education. (2003). *Implementing randomized field trials in education: Report of a workshop*. Washington, DC: National Academies Press.

Committee on Research in Education. (2004). *Advancing scientific research in education*. Washington, DC: National Academies Press.

Committee on Scientific Principles for Educational Research. (2002). *Scientific research in education*. Washington, DC: National Academies Press.

Compton, C. (1984). *Guide to 75 diagnostic tests for special education*. Belmont, CA: Fearon Education.

Condition of education. (1975–). Washington, DC: National Center for Educational Statistics.

Cook, C., Heath, F., & Thompson, R. (2000). A meta-analysis of response rates in web or Internet-based surveys. *Educational and Psychological Measurement, 60*(6), 821–836.

Cook, T. D., & Campbell, D. T. (1979). *Quasi-experimentation: Design and analysis issues for field settings*. Chicago: Rand McNally.

Corsini, R. J. (2000). *Encyclopedia of psychology* (3rd ed.). New York: Wiley.

Crawford, C. (1928). *The technique of study*. Boston: Houghton Mifflin.

Creswell, J. (2003). *Research design: Qualitative, quantitative, and mixed methods approach*. Thousand Oaks, CA: Sage.

Creswell, J. W. (2005). *Educational research: Planning, conducting, and evaluating quantitative and qualitative research*. Upper Saddle River, NJ: Merrill-Prentice Hall.

Cronbach, L. J. (1951). Coefficient alpha and the internal structure of tests. *Psychometrika, 16*, 297–334.

Crumlish, C. (2004). *The power of many: How the living web is transforming politics, business, and everyday life*. Berkeley, CA: Sybex.

Culver, S. M., Wolfle, L. E., & Cross, L. H. (1990). Testing a model of teacher satisfaction for blacks and whites. *American Educational Research Journal, 27*, 323–349.

Cumulative index to nursing and allied health literature (CINAHL). (1982–). Ann Arbor, MI: Bell & Howell.

Dana, N. F., & Yendol-Silva, D. (2003). *The reflective educator's guide to classroom research: Learning to teach and teaching to learn through practitioner inquiry*. Thousand Oaks, CA: Corwin Press.

Daniel, L. G., & Onwuegbuzie, A. J. (2002). Reliability and quantitative data: Are psychometric concepts relevant within an interpretive research program? Paper presented at Mid-West Education Research Association, Chattanooga, TN. ERIC document reproduction #ED471306.

Darwin, F. (Ed.). (1887). *The life and letters of Charles Darwin* (Vol. 1). New York: Appleton.

Dejnozka, E. L., & Kapel, D. E. (1991). *American educators' encyclopedia*. Westport, CT: Greenwood Press.

Denzin, N. K. (1989). *Interpretive biography*. Newbury Park, CA: Sage.

Denzin, N. K., & Lincoln, Y. S. (1998). *Collecting and interpreting qualitative materials*. Thousand Oaks, CA: Sage.

Denzin, N. K., & Lincoln, Y. S. (Eds.). (2000). *Handbook of qualitative research*. Thousand Oaks, CA: Sage.

DeVaus, D. (2002). *Conducting surveys using the Internet*. Thousand Oaks, CA: Sage.

Dewey, J. (1933). *How we think*. Boston: Heath.

Dey, I. (1993). *Qualitative data analysis*. New York: Routledge.

Dey, I. (1999). *Grounding grounded theory: Guidelines for qualitative inquiry*. San Diego: Academic Press.

Digest of educational statistics. (1962–). Washington, DC: National Center for Educational Statistics.

Dillman, D. A. (2000). *Mail and Internet surveys: The tailored design method* (2nd ed.). New York: Wiley.

Dillman, D. A., & Bowker, D. K. (2001). The web questionnaire challenge to survey methodologists. In U. D. Reips & M. Bosnjak (Eds.), *Dimensions of Internet science*. Lengerich, Germany: Pabst Science.

Dillon, M., & Hysell, S. G. (Eds.). (2004). *American reference books annual*. Littleton, CO: Libraries Unlimited.

Dissertation abstracts international. (1938–). Ann Arbor, MI: University Microfilms.

Doll, E. A. (1935, 1949, 1965). *Vineland social maturity scale*. Circle Pines, MN: American Guidance Service.

Drew, C. J., Hardman, M. L., & Hart, A. W. (1996). *Designing and conducting research*. Boston: Allyn & Bacon.

Education abstracts. (1986–). New York: H. W. Wilson.

Education index. (1929–). New York: H. W. Wilson.

Education Resources Information Center (ERIC). (2000, June). *Directory of ERIC resource collections*.

Education Resources Information Center (ERIC). (2001, February). *All about ERIC*.

Education Resources Information Center (ERIC). (2001, March). *ERIC sites*.

Education: The complete encyclopedia. (1998). [CD-ROM]. Available: New York: Pergamon Press.

Educational administration abstracts. (1966–). Beverly Hills, CA: Sage.

Educational testing service test collection catalog. (1986–1993). Phoenix: Oryx Press.

Eisner, E. W. (1998). *The enlightened eye: Qualitative inquiry and the enhancement of educational practice*. Upper Saddle River, NJ: Merrill-Prentice Hall.

Elliot, A. J., & Church, M. A. (1997). A hierarchical model of approach and avoidance achievement motivation. *Journal of Personality and Social Psychology*, *72*(1), 218–232.

Elliott, J. (1991). *Action research for educational change*. Berkshire, UK: Open University.

Erikson, E. H. (1959). *Identity and the life cycle: Selected papers*. Psychological Issue Monograph Series, 1(1). New York: International Universities Press.

Exceptional child education resources. (1969–). Reston, VA: Council for Exceptional Children.

Experts find link between seasonal change and cholesterol. (2004, April 28). *The Herald-Times* (Bloomington, IN), p. A9.

Feldt, L. S., & Brennan, R. L. (1989). Reliability. In R. Linn (Ed.), *Educational measurement* (pp. 105–146). New York: American Council on Education and Macmillan.

Festinger, L. (1957). *A theory of cognitive dissonance*. Evanston, IL: Row, Peterson.

Fisher, R. A. (1925). *Statistical methods for research workers*. London: Oliver & Boyd.

Fitzpatrick, J., Secrist, J., & Wright, D. J. (1998). *Secrets for a successful dissertation*. Thousand Oaks, CA: Sage.

Flanders, N. A. (1970). *Analyzing teacher behavior*. Boston: Addison-Wesley.

Flatley, J. (2001, May 11–12). The Internet as a mode of data collection in government social surveys:

Issues and investigation. International Conference on Survey Research Methods, Latimer, UK.

Fowler, F. J. (2002). *Survey research methods* (3rd ed.).Thousand Oaks, CA: Sage.

Freeman, D. (1983). *Margaret Mead and Samoa: The making and unmaking of an anthropological myth*. Cambridge, MA: Harvard University Press.

Gage, N. L. (Ed.). (1963). *Handbook of research on teaching*. Chicago: Rand McNally.

Gardner, H. (1993). *Multiple intelligences: The theory in practice*. New York: Basic Books.

Gee, J. P. (1999). *An introduction to discourse analysis: Theory and method*. London: Routledge.

Geertz, C. (1980). Blurred genres: The reconfiguration of social thought. *American Scholar, 49*, 165–179.

Glaser, B. G., & Strauss, A. L. (1967). *The discovery of grounded theory*. Chicago: Aldine.

Glass, G. V., & Hopkins, K. D. (1996). *Statistical methods in education and psychology* (3rd ed.). Englewood Cliffs, NJ: Prentice Hall.

Glatthorn, A. A. (1998). *Writing the winning dissertation: A step-by-step guide*. Thousand Oaks, CA: Corwin Press.

Glesne, C., & Peshkin, A. (1992). *Becoming qualitative researchers*. White Plains, NY: Longman.

Goetz, J. P., & LeCompte, M. D. (1993). *Ethnography and qualitative design in educational research*. New York: Academic Press.

Good, C. V. (Ed.). (1973). *Dictionary of education* (3rd ed.). New York: McGraw-Hill.

Gorn, V. (1997). *Special education dictionary*. Horsham, PA: LRP Publications.

GPO monthly catalog. (1895–). [Online]. Available: OCLC Firstsearch at http://www.oclc.org/firstsearch

Grant, C. A., & Ladson-Billings, G. (1997). *Dictionary of multicultural education*. Phoenix: Oryx Press.

Gribbin, J. (1999). *Almost everyone's guide to science*. New Haven, CT: Yale University Press.

Guba, E. G., & Lincoln, Y. S. (1981). *Effective evaluation*. San Francisco: Jossey-Bass.

Haladyna, T. M. (2004). *Developing and validating multiple-choice test items*. Mahwah, NJ: Erlbaum.

Hammersly, M. (1992). *What's wrong with ethnography? Methodological explorations*. London: Routledge.

Hammill, D. D. (1992). *A consumer's guide to tests in print* (2nd ed.). Austin, TX: Pro-Ed.

Hartshorne, H., & May, M. A. (1928). *Studies in the nature of character: Studies in deceit* (Vol. 1). New York: Macmillan.

Hartshorne, H., May, M. A., & Shuttleworth, F. K. (1928). *Studies in the organization of character*. New York: Macmillan.

Hedges, L. V., & Nowell, A. (1995). Sex differences in mental test scores, variability, and numbers of high scoring individuals. *Science, 269*, 41–45.

Helgeson, J., Voss, K., & Terpening, W. (2002). Determinants of mail survey response: Survey design factors and respondent factors. *Psychology and Marketing, 19*, 303–328.

Heward, W., Dardig, J. C., & Rossett, A. (1979). *Working with parents of handicapped children*. Columbus, OH: Merrill.

Higher education abstracts. (1984–). Claremont, CA: Claremont Institute for Administrative Studies.

Holbrook, A., Green, M., & Krosnick, J. (2003). Telephone versus face-to-face interviewing of national probability samples with long questionnaires. *Public Opinion Quarterly, 67*, 79–125.

Hollingshead, A. B. (1949). *Elmstown's youth*. New York: Wiley.

Honan, W. H. (1999, June 25). College freshmen's Internet use a way of life. *New York Times*, Late Edition, p. A11.

Hotz, R. (2002, April 15). Outgoing toddlers have higher IQs as preteens. *The Indianapolis Star*, p. 1.

Howell, M., & Prevenier, W. (2001). *From reliable sources: An introduction to historical research*. Ithaca, NY: Cornell University Press.

Hoyle, R. H., Harris, M. J., & Judd, C. M. (2002). *Research methods in social relations*. Belmont, CA: Wadsworth.

Huberty, C. (1994). *Applied discriminant analysis*. New York: Wiley.

Huessy, H. R., & Cohen, A. H. (1976). Hyperkinetic behaviors and learning disabilities followed over seven years. *Pediatrics, 57*, 4–10.

Hughes, S. (1997). A study of teachers and their relationships with at-risk students. In T. S. Poetter (Ed.), *Voices of inquiry in teacher education* (pp. 83–97). Mahwah, NJ: Erlbaum.

Humphreys, L. (1970). *The teahouse trade: Impersonal sex in public places*. Chicago: Aldine-Atherton.

Husen, T., & Postlethwaite, T. N. (Eds.). (1985). *The international encyclopedia of education: Research and studies*. New York: Pergamon Press.

Husen, T., & Postlethwaite, T. N. (Eds.). (1994). *The international encyclopedia of education* (2nd ed.). New York: Pergamon Press.

Hycner, R. H. (1999). Some guidelines for the phenomenological analysis of interview data. In

A. Bryman & R. G. Burgess (Eds.), *Qualitative research* (Vol. 3, pp. 143–164). Thousand Oaks, CA: Sage.

Hyde, J. S., Fennema, E., & Lamon, S. J. (1990). Gender differences in mathematics performance: A meta-analysis. *Psychological Bulletin, 107*, 139–155.

Index to international statistics. (1982–). Bethesda, MD: Congressional Information Service.

Information please almanac. (1947–). Boston: Houghton Mifflin.

Itard, J. G. (1962). *The wild boy of Aveyron* (G. Humphrey & M. Humphrey, Trans.). New York: Appleton.

Jackson, P. W., & Lahaderne, H. M. (1967). Scholastic success and attitude toward school in a population of sixth graders. *Journal of Educational Psychology, 58*, 15–18.

Janesick, V. J. (1994). The dance of qualitative research design: Metaphor, methodolatry, and meaning. In N. Denzin & Y. Lincoln (Eds.), *Handbook of qualitative research* (pp. 209–219). Thousand Oaks, CA: Sage.

Jobber, D., Saunders, J., & Mitchell, V. (2004). Prepaid monetary incentive effects on mail survey research. *Journal of Business Research, 57*(4), 347–350.

Johnson, B., & Christensen, L. (2000). *Educational research: Quantitative and qualitative approaches.* Boston: Allyn & Bacon.

Jones, J. H. (1982). *Bad blood: The Tuskegee syphilis experiment.* New York: Free Press.

Kagan, D. M., Dennis, M. B., Igou, M., & Moore, P. (1993). The experience of being a teacher in residence. *American Educational Research Journal, 30*(2), 426–443.

Kelle, E. (Ed.). (1995). *Computer-aided qualitative analysis.* Thousand Oaks, CA: Sage.

Kemmis, S., & McTaggart, R. (1988). *The action research planner.* Geelong, Victoria, Australia: Deakin University Press.

Keogh, B. K. (1980–). *Advances in special education: A research annual.* Greenwich, CT: JAI Press.

Keyser, D. J. (Ed.). (1994). *Test critiques* (4th ed.). Austin, TX: Pro-Ed.

Keyser, D. J., & Sweetland, R. C. (Eds.). (1984–). *Test critiques* (Vol. 1–). Kansas City, MO: Test Corporation of America.

King, L. A. (2004). Measures and meanings: The use of qualitative data in social and personality psychology. In C. Sansone, C. Morf, & A. T. Panter (Eds.), *Handbook of methods in social psychology.* Thousand Oaks, CA: Sage.

Krefting, L. (1991). Rigor in qualitative research: The assessment of trustworthiness. *American Journal of Occupational Therapy, 45*, 214–222.

Kreuger, R. A. (2000). *Focus groups: A practical guide for applied research.* Thousand Oaks, CA: Sage.

Kreuger, R. A., & Casey, M. A. (2000). *Focus groups: A practical guide for applied research* (3rd ed.). Thousand Oaks, CA: Sage.

Krippendorf, K. (2003). *Content analysis: An introduction to its methodology* (2nd ed.). Thousand Oaks, CA: Sage.

Kubiszyn, T., & Borich, G. (2003). *Educational testing and measurement.* New York: Wiley.

Kuder, G. F., & Richardson, M. W. (1937). The theory of estimation of test reliability. *Psychometrika, 2*, 151–160.

Langenbach, M., Vaughn, C., & Aagaard, L. (1994). *An introduction to educational research.* Boston: Allyn & Bacon.

LaViolette, S. A. (2001). *School-community conflict: Perceptions of elementary school principals and parents in an urban setting.* Dissertation, Northern Illinois University, DeKalb, IL.

Lawrence-Lightfoot, S., & Davis, J. H. (1997). *The art and science of portraiture.* San Francisco: Jossey-Bass.

Lee, V. E., & Loeb, S. (2000). School size in Chicago elementary schools: Effects on teachers' attitudes and students' achievement. *American Educational Research Journal, 37*, 1–31.

Likert, R. (1932). A technique for the measurement of attitudes. *Archives of Psychology, 140.*

Lincoln, Y. S., & Guba, E. G. (1985). *Naturalistic inquiry.* Beverly Hills, CA: Sage.

Linn, R. L., & Gronlund, N. E. (2000). *Measurement and assessment in teaching* (8th ed.). Upper Saddle River, NJ: Merrill.

Locke, L. F., Spirduso, W. W., & Silverman, S. J. (2000). *Proposals that work: A guide for planning dissertations and grant proposals.* Thousand Oaks, CA: Sage.

Loehlin, J. (2004). *Latent variable models: An introduction to factor, path, and structural equation analysis.* Mahwah, NJ: Erlbaum.

Lynch, M. J. (1996). *Electronic services in academic libraries: ALA survey report.* Chicago: American Library Association.

Lynd, R. S., & Lynd, H. M. (1929). *Middletown.* New York: Harcourt Brace.

Lynd, R. S., & Lynd, H. M. (1937). *Middletown in transition.* New York: Harcourt, Brace, and World.

Maddox, T. (2003). *Tests: A comprehensive reference for assessments in psychology, education, and business* (5th ed.). Austin, TX: Pro-Ed.

Marsh, H. W. (1988). *Self description questionnaire: A theoretical and empirical basis for the measurement of multiple dimensions of preadolescent self-concept: A test manual and a research monograph.* San Antonio: Psychological Corporation.

Marshall, C., & Rossman, G. B. (1989). *Designing qualitative research.* Thousand Oaks, CA: Sage.

Marshall, C., & Rossman, G. B. (1995). *Designing qualitative research* (2nd ed.). Thousand Oaks, CA: Sage.

Marshall, C., & Rossman, G. B. (1999). *Designing qualitative research* (3rd ed.). Thousand Oaks, CA: Sage.

Marshall, R. M., Schafer, V. A., & O'Donnell, L. (1999). Arithmetic disabilities and ADD subtypes: Implications for DSM-IV. *Journal of Learning Disabilities, 32*, 239–247.

Maslow, A. H. (1954). *Motivation and personality.* New York: Harper & Row.

Masters abstracts international. (1986–). Ann Arbor, MI: University Microfilms.

Maxwell, J. A. (1996). *Qualitative research design: An interpretive approach.* Thousand Oaks, CA: Sage.

Maxwell, J. A. (2004). Causal explanation, qualitative research, and scientific inquiry in education. *Educational Researcher, 33*, 3–11.

Maykut, P., & Morehouse, R. (1994). *Beginning qualitative research: A philosophic and practical guide.* Washington, DC: Falmer.

McBurney, D. H., & White, T. L. (2004). *Research methods.* Belmont, CA: Thomson.

McCarty, C. (2003). Differences in response rates using most recent versus final dispositions in telephone surveys. *Public Opinion Quarterly, 67*, 396–406.

McClelland, D. C. (1953). *The achievement motive.* New York: Appleton-Century-Crofts.

Mead, M. (1928). *Coming of age in Samoa.* New York: William Morrow.

Mees, C. E. K. (1934). Scientific thought and social reconstruction. *General Electric Review, 37*, 113–119.

Meister, D., & Melnick, S. (2003). National new teacher study: Beginning teachers' concerns. *Action in Teacher Education, 24*(4), 87–94.

Menard, S. (1991). *Longitudinal research.* Thousand Oaks, CA: Sage.

Merriam, S. B. (1998). *Qualitative research and case study application in education.* San Francisco: Jossey-Bass.

Merriam, S. B., & Associates (2002). *Qualitative research in practice.* San Francisco: Jossey-Bass.

Messick, S. (1995). Validity of psychological assessment. *American Psychologist, 50*(9), 741–749.

Miles, M. B., & Huberman, A. M. (1994). *Qualitative data analysis* (2nd ed.). Thousand Oaks, CA: Sage.

Milgram, S. (1963). Behavioral study of obedience. *Journal of Abnormal and Social Psychology, 67*, 371–378.

Mill, J. S. (1846). *A system of logic* (2nd ed.). New York: Harper & Brothers.

Miller, A., Gouley, K., & Seifer, R. (2004). Emotions and behaviors in the Head Start classroom: Associations among observed dysregulation, social competence, and preschool adjustment. *Early Education and Development, 15*(2), 147–165.

Mills, G. E. (2003). *Action research: A guide for the teacher researcher* (2nd ed.). Upper Saddle River, NJ: Pearson Education.

Mischler, E. G. (1990). Validation in inquiry-guided research: The role of exemplars in narrative studies. *Harvard Educational Review, 60*, 415–442.

Mitchell, M. L., and Jolley, J. M. (2004). *Research design explained* (5th ed.). Belmont, CA: Wadsworth.

Moustakas, C. (1994). *Phenomenological research.* Thousand Oaks, CA: Sage.

Murphy, J., & Louis, K. S. (Eds.). (1999). *Handbook of research on educational administration: A project of the American Educational Research Association.* New York: Jossey-Bass.

Murphy, L. L., Plake, B. S., Impara, J. C., & Spies, R. A. (Eds.). (2002). *Tests in print VI: An index to tests, test reviews and literature on specific tests.* Lincoln: University of Nebraska, Buros Institute of Mental Measurements.

Naples, N. A. (2003). *Feminism and method: Ethnography, discourse, and activist research.* London: Routledge.

National Center for Educational Statistics. *Encyclopedia of ED Stats* [link]: http://nces.ed.gov

National Commission for the Protection of Human Subjects of Biomedical and Behavioral Research. (1979). *Ethical principles and guidelines for the protection of human subjects of research.* The Belmont Report. Washington, DC: U.S. Government Printing Office.

National Science Foundation. (2000). *Women, minorities, and persons with disabilities in science and engineering.* NSF Report No. 00-327. Arlington, VA: Author.

Neuman, W. L., & Kreuger, L. (2003). *Social work research methods: Qualitative and quantitative approaches.* Boston: Allyn & Bacon.

Newborg, J., Stock, J., Wnek, L., Guidubaldi, J., & Svinicki, J. (1988). *The Battelle Developmental Inventory (BDI)*. Chicago: Riverside Publishing.

Newby, R., Watson, J., & Woodliff, D. (2003). SME survey methodology: Response rates, data quality, and cost effectiveness. *Entrepreneurship Theory and Practice, 28*, 163–172.

Newmann, F. M., & Wehlage, G. G. (1993). Five standards of authentic instruction. *Educational Leadership, 50*, 8–12.

Noldus Information Technology. (1995). *The observer: System for collection and analysis of observational data* (Version 3.0). Sterling, VA: Author.

Nozaki, Y. (2000). Essentializing dilemma and multiculturalist pedagogy: An ethnographic study of Japanese children in a U.S. school. *Anthropology and Education Journal, 31*(3), 355–380.

O'Brien, N. P., & Fabiano, E. (1991). *Core list of books and journals in education*. Phoenix: Oryx Press.

Onwuegbuzie, A. D. (2003). Effect sizes in qualitative research: A prolegomenon. *Quality and Quantity, 37*, 393–409.

Ostrow, A. C. (1996). *Directory of psychological tests in the sport and exercise sciences* (2nd ed.). Morgantown, WV: Fitness Information Technology.

Page, G. T., Thomas, J. B., & Marshall, A. R. (1980). *International dictionary of education*. Cambridge, MA: MIT Press.

Parten, M. B. (1932). Social participation among preschool children. *Journal of Abnormal Social Psychology, 27*, 243–269.

Patton, M. Q. (1990). *Qualitative evaluation and research methods* (2nd ed.). Newbury Park, CA: Sage.

Patton, M. Q. (1995). *Qualitative evaluation methods* (3rd ed.). Thousand Oaks, CA: Sage.

Pedhazur, E. (1997). *Multiple regression in behavioral research: Explanation and prediction* (3rd ed.). Belmont, CA: Wadsworth.

Perry, W. G. (1970). *Forms of intellectual and ethical development in the college years: A scheme*. New York: Holt, Rinehart & Winston.

Peshkin, A. (1982). *The imperfect union: School consolidation and community conflict*. Chicago: University of Chicago Press.

Peshkin, A. (1984). Odd man out: The participant observer in an absolutist setting. *Sociology of Education, 57*, 254–264.

Peshkin, A. (1991). *The color of strangers, the color of friends: The play of ethnicity in school and community*. Chicago: University of Chicago Press.

Piaget, J. (1968). *Six psychological studies*. New York: Vintage Books.

Piaget, J. (1999). *The moral judgement of the child*. New York: Routledge.

Piantanida, M., & Garman, N. (1999). *The qualitative dissertation: A guide for students and faculty*. Thousand Oaks, CA: Corwin Press.

Pirsig, R. M. (1974). *Zen and the art of motorcycle maintenance: An inquiry into values*. New York: Morrow.

Plake, B. S., Impara, J. C., & Spies, R. A. (Eds.). (2003). *The fifteenth mental measurements yearbook*. Lincoln: University of Nebraska, Buros Institute of Mental Measurements.

Popham, W. J. (2000). *Modern educational measurement*. Boston: Allyn & Bacon.

Projections of education statistics. (1975–). Washington, DC: National Center for Educational Statistics.

Psychological abstracts. (1927–). Lancaster, PA: American Psychological Association.

PsycINFO. (1887–). Washington, DC: American Psychological Association. Available through http://www.ovid.com

Public Welfare. (1993). *Protection of human subjects*. 45 C.F.R. 546.101.

Qin, Z., Johnson, D. W., & Johnson, R. T. (1995). Cooperative versus competitive efforts and problem solving. *Review of Educational Research, 65*(2), 129–143.

Ragin, C., Nagel, J., & White, P. (2004). *Workshop on scientific foundations of qualitative research*. Washington, DC: National Science Foundation.

Ramazanoglu, C., & Holland, J. (2002). *Feminist methodology: Challenge and choices*. Thousand Oaks, CA: Sage.

Readers' guide to periodical literature. (1905–). Minneapolis: H. W. Wilson.

Reason, P., & Bradbury, H. (Eds.). (2000). *Handbook of action research: Participative inquiry and practice*. London: Sage.

Reichardt, C. S. (2000). A typology of strategies for ruling out threats to validity. In L. Bickman (Ed.), *Research design: Donald Campbell's legacy* (Vol. 2, pp. 89–115). Thousand Oaks, CA: Sage.

Reichert, M. C., & Kuriloff, P. (2004). Boys' selves: Identity and anxiety in the looking glass of school life. *Teachers College Record, 106*, 544–573.

Review of educational research. (1931–). Washington, DC: American Educational Research Association.

Review of research in education. (1973–). Washington, DC: American Educational Research Association.

Reynolds, C. R., & Fletcher-Janzen, E. (2000). *Encyclopedia of special education: A reference for the education of the handicapped and other excep-*

tional children and adults (2nd ed.). New York: Wiley.

Rice, J. M. (1897). The futility of the spelling grind. *Forum, 23*, 163–172, 409–419.

Rice, J. M. (1912). *Scientific management in education*. New York: Hinds, Noble & Eldredge.

Richardson, V. (Ed.). (2001). *Handbook of research on teaching* (4th ed.). New York: Macmillan.

Rose, L., & Gallup, A. (2003). The 35th annual Phi Delta Kappa/Gallup poll of the public's attitudes toward the public schools. *Phi Delta Kappan, 85*(1), 41–56.

Rosenthal, R. (1966). *Experimenter effects in behavioral research*. New York: Appleton-Century-Crofts.

Rosenthal, R. (1973). The mediation of Pygmalion effects: A four-factor theory. *Papua New Guinea Journal of Education, 9*, 1–12.

Rosenthal, R., & Rosnow, R. L. (1991). *Essentials of behavioral research: Methods and data analysis*. New York: McGraw-Hill.

Rowntree, D. (2004). *Statistics without tears: A primer for non-mathematicians*. Boston: Pearson.

Royer, J. M., Tronsky, L. N., Chan, Y., Jackson, S., & Marchant, H. (1999). Math-fact retrieval as the cognitive mechanism underlying gender differences in math test performance. *Contemporary Educational Psychology, 24*, 181–266

Sagor, R. (2000). *Guiding school improvement with action research*. Alexandria, VA: Association for Supervision and Curriculum Development.

Sales, B. D., & Folkman, S. (Eds.). (2000). *Ethics in research with human participants*. Washington, DC: American Psychological Association.

Saslow, C. (1982). *Basic research methods*. Reading, MA: Addison-Wesley.

Saxon, D., Garratt, D., Gilroy, P., & Cairns, C. (2003). Collecting data in the information age: Exploring web-based survey methods in educational research. *Research in Education, 69*, 51–66.

Schostak, J. F. (2002). *Understanding, designing, and conducting qualitative research in education: Framing the project*. Philadelphia: Open University Press.

Schwandt, T. A., & Halpern, E. S. (1988). *Linking auditing and metaevaluation*. Beverly Hills, CA: Sage.

Shadish, W. R., Cook, T. D., & Campbell, D. T. (2002). *Experimental and quasi-experimental designs for generalized causal inference*. Boston: Houghton Mifflin.

Shavelson, R. J., Hubner, J. J., & Stanton, G. C. (1976). Self-concept: Validation of construct interpretations. *Review of Educational Research, 46*, 407–441.

Siegel, S., & Castellan, N. J., Jr. (1988). *Nonparametric statistics for the behavioral sciences* (2nd ed.). New York: McGraw-Hill.

Silvey, H. M. (1951–). *Master's theses directories*. Cedar Falls, IA: Research Publications.

Singer, E., Van Hoewyk, J., & Maher, M. (2000). Experiments with incentives in telephone surveys. *Public Opinion Quarterly, 64*, 171–188.

Skinner, B. F. (1953). *Science and human behavior*. New York: Macmillan.

Skinner, M., Buysse, V., & Bailey, D. (2004). Effects of age and developmental status of partners on play of preschoolers with disabilities. *Journal of Early Intervention, 26*(3), 194–203.

Slavin, R. E. (2004). Education research can and must address "What works" questions. *Educational Researcher, 33*, 27–28.

Smith, M. L., & Glass, G. V. (1977). Meta-analysis of psychotherapy outcome studies. *American Psychologist, 32*, 752–760.

Smith, T. W., & Strahan, D. (2004). Toward a prototype of expertise in teaching: A descriptive study. *Journal of Teacher Education, 54*(4), 357–371.

Social sciences citation index. (1973–). Philadelphia: Institute for Scientific Information.

Sociological abstracts. (1953–). San Diego: Sociological Abstracts.

Solomon, R. L. (1949). On extension of control group design. *Psychological Bulletin, 46*, 137–150.

Spafford, C. S., Pesce, A. J., & Grosser, G. S. (1998). *The cyclopedic education dictionary*. Albany, NY: Delmar.

Spicer, J. (2005). *Making sense of multivariate data analysis*. Thousand Oaks, CA: Sage.

Spindler, G. D., & Hammond, L. (2000). The use of anthropological methods in educational research: Two perspectives. *Harvard Educational Review, 70*(1), 39–48.

Spradley, J. P. (1980). *Participant observation*. New York: Holt, Rinehart & Winston.

Stake, R. E. (1995). *The art of case study research*. Thousand Oaks, CA: Sage.

Starkey, P., Klein, A., & Wakeley, A. (2004). Enhancing young children's mathematical knowledge through a pre-kindergarten mathematics intervention. *Early Childhood Research Quarterly, 19*, 99–120.

Statistical abstract of the United States. (1878–). Washington, DC: U.S. Census Bureau.

Statistical reference index. (1980–). Bethesda, MD: Congressional Information Service.

Stevens, S. S. (1951). Mathematics, measurement, and psychophysics. In S. S. Stevens (Ed.), *Hand-*

book of experimental psychology (p. 1). New York: Wiley.

Stiggins, R. J. (2001). *Student-involved classroom assessment* (3rd ed.). Upper Saddle River, NJ: Merrill-Prentice Hall.

Strauss, A. L., & Corbin, J. (1998). *Basics of qualitative research: Techniques and procedures for developing grounded theory* (2nd ed.). Thousand Oaks, CA: Sage.

Stringer, E. T. (2004). *Action research in education.* Upper Saddle River, NJ: Pearson Education.

Students' political awareness hits highest level in a decade. (2004). *Chronicle of Higher Education, 50*, A30–A32.

Subkoviak, M. J. (1988). A practitioner's guide to computation and interpretation of reliability indices for mastery tests. *Journal of Educational Measurement, 25*, 47–55.

Sudman, S. (1976). *Applied sampling.* New York: Academic Press.

Suen, H. K., & Ary, D. (1989). *Analyzing quantitative behavioral observation data.* Hillsdale, NJ: Erlbaum.

Sullivan, D. (2001). *Search Engine Watch* [online]. Available: http://www.searchenginewatch.com

Survey growth in distance education in the 1990's. (2003). *Chronicle of Higher Education, 49*(48), A28.

Tashhakkori, A., & Teddlie, C. (2003). *Handbook on mixed methods in the behavioral and social sciences.* Thousand Oaks, CA: Sage.

Teitler, J., Reichman, N., & Sprachman, S. (2003). Costs and benefits of improving response rates for a hard-to-reach population. *Public Opinion Quarterly, 67*, 126–138.

Terman, L. M. (1926). The mental and physical traits of a thousand gifted children. In *Genetic studies of genius* (Vol. 1). Stanford, CA: Stanford University Press.

Terman, L. M. (1959). The gifted group in mid-life. In *Genetic studies of genius* (Vol. 5). Stanford, CA: Stanford University Press.

Tests in microfiche. (1975–1994). Princeton, NJ: Educational Testing Service.

Thomas, R. M. (2003). *Blending qualitative and quantitative research methods.* Thousand Oaks, CA: Corwin Press.

Thomas, R. M. (2005). *Teachers doing research: An introductory guidebook.* Boston: Pearson Education.

Thompson, B. (1984). *Canonical correlation analysis: Uses and interpretation.* Beverly Hills, CA: Sage.

Thompson, B. (2004). *Exploratory and confirmatory factor analysis: Understanding concepts and applications.* Washington, DC: American Psychological Association.

Thorndike, E. L. (1924). Mental discipline in high school subjects. *Journal of Educational Psychology, 15*, 1–22, 83–98.

Tierney, P. (2000). *Darkness in El Dorado: How scientists and journalists devastated the Amazon.* New York: Norton.

Travers, R. (Ed.). (1973). *Second handbook of research on teaching* (2nd ed.). Chicago: Rand McNally.

U.S. Census Bureau. (2003). *Statistical abstract of the United States.* Washington, DC: Author.

U.S. Library of Congress, Exchange and Gift Division. (1910–1994). *Monthly checklist of state publications.* Washington, DC: U.S. Government Printing Office.

U.S. Superintendent of Documents. (1895–). *Monthly catalog of U.S. government publications.* Washington, DC: U.S. Government Printing Office.

Villaume, S. K. (2000). The necessity of uncertainty: A case study of language arts reform. *Journal of Teacher Education, 51*, 18–25.

Vygotsky, L. S. (1978). In M. Cole, V. John-Steiner, S. Scribner, & E. Souberman (Eds.), *Mind in society.* Cambridge, MA: Harvard University Press.

Waddell, D. L., & Blankenship, J. C. (1994). Answer changing: A meta-analysis of the prevalence and patterns. *Journal of Continuing Education in Nursing, 25*, 155–158.

Walberg, H. J., & Haertel, G. D. (Eds.). (1990). *The international encyclopedia of educational evaluation.* Elmsford, NY: Pergamon Press.

Wasserman-O'Brien, S. R. (Ed.). (2001). *Statistics sources* (24th ed.). Detroit: Gale Research.

Weiner, B. (1994). Integrating social and personal theories of achievement striving. *Review of Educational Research, 64*, 557–573.

Weitzman, E. A. (2004). Advancing the scientific basis of qualitative research. In C. Ragin, J. Nagel, & P. White (Eds.), *Workshop on the scientific foundations of qualitative research.* Washington, DC: National Science Foundation.

Weitzman, E. A., & Miles, M. B. (1995). *Computer programs for qualitative data analysis.* Thousand Oaks, CA: Sage.

Whitcomb, M. E. (2003). The impact of contact type on web survey response rates. *Public Opinion Quarterly, 67*, 579–588.

Wiersma, W. (2000). *Research methods in education: An introduction* (7th ed.). Boston: Allyn & Bacon.

Wittrock, M. C. (Ed.). (1985). *Handbook of research on teaching* (3rd ed.). New York: Macmillan.

Wolcott, H. F. (1990). *Writing up qualitative research.* Newbury Park, CA: Sage.

World almanac and book of facts. (1868–). New York: Newspaper Enterprise Association.

WorldCat. (1991–). [Online]. Available: OCLC First-search at http://firstsearch.oclc.org/

Yin, R. K. (1991). *Applications of case study research*. Washington, DC: Cosmos Corporation.

Young, J. R. (2004). Students' political awareness hits highest level in a decade. *Chronicle of Higher Education, 50*(21), A30–A32.

Young, L. J. (2001). Border crossings and other journeys: Re-visioning the doctoral preparation of education researchers. *Educational Researcher, 30*(5), 3–5.

LEEDS COL OF ART & DESIGN
R03377Y 0084